MILITARY MARKINGS 2012

REVISED 33RD EDITION

Howard J. Curtis

MIDLAND

An imprint of Ian Allan Publishing
www.ianallanpublishing.co.uk

Contents

Photographs by Howard J Curtis (HJC) unless
otherwise credited

This 33rd edition published 2012

ISBN 978 1 85780 358 2

Published by Ian Allan Publishing
an imprint of Ian Allan Publishing Ltd,
Hersham, Surrey KT12 4RG.

Printed in England by Ian Allan Printing Ltd,
Hersham, Surrey, KT12 4RG

Front cover: A Tornado GR4 of No 31 Squadron 'Goldstars'
tips in on a target. *Jamie Hunter*

Introduction

This 33rd annual edition of *abc Military Aircraft Markings*, follows the pattern of previous years and lists in alphabetical and numerical order the aircraft that carry a United Kingdom military serial and which are normally based, or might be seen, in the UK. It also includes airworthy and current RAF/RN/Army aircraft that are based permanently or temporarily overseas. The term 'aircraft' used here covers powered, manned aeroplanes, helicopters, airships and gliders as well as target drones. Included are all the current Royal Air Force, Royal Navy, Army Air Corps, Ministry of Defence, QinetiQ - operated, manufacturers' test aircraft and civilian-owned aircraft with military markings or operated for the Ministry of Defence.

Aircraft withdrawn from operational use but which are retained in the UK for ground training purposes or otherwise preserved by the Services and in the numerous museums or collections are listed. The serials of some incomplete aircraft have been included, such as the cockpit sections of machines displayed by the RAF, aircraft used by airfield fire sections and for service battle damage repair training (BDRT), together with significant parts of aircraft held by preservation groups and societies. Where only part of the aircraft fuselage remains, the abbreviation <ff> for front fuselage/cockpit section or <rf> for rear fuselage, is shown after the type. Many of these aircraft are allocated, and sometimes wear, a secondary identity, such as an RAF 'M' maintenance number; these numbers are listed against those aircraft to which they have been allocated.

A serial 'missing' from a sequence is either because it was never issued as it formed part of a 'black-out block' or because the aircraft has been written off, scrapped, sold abroad or allocated an alternative marking. Aircraft used as targets on MoD ranges to which access is restricted, and UK military aircraft that have been permanently grounded overseas and unlikely to return to Britain have generally been omitted. With the appearance of some military-registered UAVs, drones and small target aircraft at public events, these have now been included if they are likely to be seen.

In the main, the serials listed are those markings presently displayed on the aircraft. Where an aircraft carries a false serial it is quoted in italic type. Very often these serials are carried by replicas, that are denoted by <R> after the type. The manufacturer and aircraft type are given, together with recent alternative, previous, secondary or civil identity shown in round brackets. Complete records of multiple previous identities are only included where space permits. The operating unit and its based location, along with any known unit and code markings, in square brackets, are given as accurately as possible. Where aircraft carry special or commemorative markings, a $ indicates this. Unit markings are normally carried boldly on the sides of the fuselage or on the aircraft's tail. In the case of RAF and AAC machines currently in service, they are usually one or two letters or numbers, while the RN continues to use a well-established system of three-figure codes between 000 and 999 often with a two-letter code on the tail, denoting the aircraft's operational base. RN squadrons, units and bases are allocated blocks of numbers from which individual aircraft codes are issued. To help identification of RN bases and landing platforms on ships, a list of tail-letter codes with their appropriate name, helicopter code number, ship pennant number and type of vessel, is included; as is a helicopter code number/ships' tail-letter code grid cross-reference.

Code changes, for example when aircraft move between units and therefore the markings currently painted on a particular aircraft, might not be those shown in this edition because of subsequent events. Aircraft still under manufacture or not yet delivered to the Service, such as Eurofighter Typhoons and Airbus A400Ms are listed under their allocated serial numbers. Likewise there are a number of newly built aircraft for overseas air arms that carry British serials for their UK test and delivery flights. The airframes which will not appear in the next edition because of sale, accident, etc., have their fates, where known, shown in italic type in the locations column.

The Irish Army Air Corps fleet is listed, together with the serials of other overseas air arms whose aircraft might be seen visiting the UK from time to time. The serial numbers are as usually presented on the individual machine or as they are normally identified. Where possible, the aircraft's base and operating unit have been shown.

USAF, US Army and US Navy aircraft based in the UK and in Western Europe, and types that regularly visit the UK from the USA, are each listed in separate sections by aircraft type. The serial number actually displayed on the aircraft is shown in full, with additional Fiscal Year (FY) or full serial information also provided. Where appropriate, details of the operating wing, squadron allocation and base are added. The USAF is, like the RAF, in a continuing period of change, resulting in the adoption of new unit titles, squadron and equipment changes and the closure of bases. Only details that concern changes effected by January 2011 are shown.

Veteran and vintage aircraft which carry overseas military markings but which are based in the UK or regularly visit from mainland Europe, have been separately listed, showing their principal means of identification. The growing list of aircraft in government or military service, often under contract to private operating companies, which carry civil registrations has again been included at the end of the respective country.

With the use of the Internet now very well established as a rich source of information, the section listing a selection of military aviation 'world wide web' sites, has again been updated this year. Although only a few of these provide details of aircraft serials and markings, they do give interesting insights into air arms and their operating units, aircraft, museums and a broad range of associated topics.

Information shown is believed to be correct at 31 January 2012.

Acknowledgements

The compiler wishes to thank the many people who have taken the trouble to send comments, additions, deletions and other useful information since the publication of the previous edition of Military Aircraft Markings. In particular the following individuals: Chris Barkby, Allan Barley, Lee Barton, Peter Budden, Rod Burden, Mike Bursell, Glyn Coney, Patrick Dirksen, Matt Ellis, Gilmar Green, Willy Henderickx, Andrew Horrex, Lakes Lightnings, Alan Macey, Peter R. March, Doug McDonald, Richard Peckham, Norman Roberson, Mike Screech, Kev Slade, Warren Smith, John Spencer, Dave Taylor, David Thompson, Mike Tighe, Simon Titchmarsh, Stuart Wallis, Keith Whitaker & Jack Wingrove.

The 2011 edition has also relied upon the printed publications and/or associated internet web-sites as follows: Aerodata Quantum+, 'Aircraft' magazine, Airfields Yahoo! Group, 'Air Forces Monthly' magazine, BAEG Yahoo! Group, Breizh Spotting Team, Andy Carney/ British Military Aviation Lists, CAA G-INFO Web Site, 'Combat Aircraft' magazine, Delta Reflex, Graham Gaff/East London Aviation Society, Fighter Control, 'FlyPast' magazine, 'Jets Monthly' magazine, Joe Baugher's Home Page, Roger Smith/Lowestoft Aviation Society, Brian Pickering/'Military Aviation Review', Mil Spotters' Forum, NAMAR Yahoo! Group, Howard Heeley/Newark Air Museum, P-3 Orion Research Group, RAF Leeming Yahoo! Group, RAF Shawbury Yahoo! Group, 'Scramble' magazine, 'Sitting Ducks & Peeping Toms' (M. I. Draper, Air-Britain Publicatrions), Souairport e-mail group, Tom McGhee/UK Serials Resource Centre, Vintage British Military Jets Yahoo! Group, Mark Ray/Wolverhampton Aviation Group and 'Wrecks & Relics'.

HJC
January 2012

Abbreviations

$	Aircraft in special markings
AAC	Army Air Corps
ACC	Air Combat Command
ACCGS	Air Cadets Central Gliding School
ACS	Air Control Squadron
ACTS	Air Control Training Squadron
ACW	Air Control Wing
AD&StA	Aberdeen, Dundee & St Andrews
AEF	Air Experience Flight
AESS	Air Engineering & Survival School
AEW	Airborne Early Warning
AF	Arméflyget (Army Air Battalion)
AFB	Air Force Base
AFD	Air Fleet Department
AFRC	Air Force Reserve Command
AFSC	Air Force Systems Command
AFSK	Armeflygskolan (Army Flying School)
AFWF	Advanced Fixed Wing Flight
AG	Airlift Group
AGA	Academia General del Aire (General Air Academy)
AkG	Aufklärungsgeschwader (Reconnaissance Wing)
AMC	Air Mobility Command
AMD-BA	Avions Marcel Dassault-Breguet Aviation
AMF	Aircraft Maintenance Flight
AMG	Aircraft Maintenance Group
AMIF	Aircraft Maintenance Instruction Flight
AMW	Air Mobility Wing
ANG	Air National Guard
APS	Aircraft Preservation Society
ARF	Aircraft Repair Flight
ARS	Air Refueling Squadron
ARW	Air Refueling Wing
ARWS	Advanced Rotary Wing Squadron
AS	Airlift Squadron/Air Squadron
ASF	Aircraft Servicing Flight
AS&RU	Aircraft Salvage and Repair Unit
ATC	Air Training Corps
ATCC	Air Traffic Control Centre
AVDEF	Aviation Defence Service
Avn	Aviation
AW	AgustaWestland/Airlift Wing/Armstrong Whitworth Aircraft
AWC	Air Warfare Centre
BAC	British Aircraft Corporation
BAe	British Aerospace PLC
BAPC	British Aviation Preservation Council
BATSUB	British Army Training Support Unit Belize
BATUS	British Army Training Unit Suffield
BBMF	Battle of Britain Memorial Flight
BDRF	Battle Damage Repair Flight
BDRT	Battle Damage Repair Training
Be	Beech
Bf	Bayerische Flugzeugwerke
BG	Bomber Group
BGA	British Gliding & Soaring Association
bk	black (squadron colours and markings)
bl	blue (squadron colours and markings)
BNFL	British Nuclear Fuels Ltd
BP	Boulton & Paul
br	brown (squadron colours and markings)
BS	Bomber Squadron
B-V	Boeing-Vertol
BW	Bomber Wing
CAARP	Co-operative des Ateliers Air de la Région Parisienne
CAC	Commonwealth Aircraft Corporation
CARG	Cotswold Aircraft Restoration Group
CASA	Construcciones Aeronautics SA
Cav	Cavalry
CC	County Council
CCF	Combined Cadet Force/Canadian Car & Foundry Company
CDE	Chemical Defence Establishment
CEAM	Centre d'Expérimentation Aériennes Militaires (Military Air Experimental Centre)
CEPA	Centre d'Expérimentation Pratique de l'Aéronautique Navale
CEV	Centre d'Essais en Vol (Flight Test Centre)
CFS	Central Flying School
CGMF	Central Glider Maintenance Flight
CHFMU	Commando Helicopter Force Maintenance Unit
CinC	Commander in Chief
CinCLANT	Commander in Chief Atlantic
CLV	Centrum Leteckeho Vycviku (Air Training Centre)
CMU	Central Maintenance Unit
Co	Company
COMALAT	Commandement de l'Aviation Légère de l'Armée de Terre
Comp	Composite with
CT	College of Technology
CTE	Central Training Establishment
CV	Chance-Vought
D-BA	Daimler-Benz Aerospace
D-BD	Dassault-Breguet Dornier
D&G	Dumfries and Galloway
DCAE	Defence College of Aeronautical Engineering
DE&S	Defence Equipment & Support
DEFTS	Defence Elementary Flying Training School
DEODS	Defence Explosives Ordnance Disposal School
Det	Detachment
DFTDC	Defence Fire Training and Development Centre
DGA	Délégation Générale de l'Armement
DH	de Havilland
DHC	de Havilland Canada
DHFS	Defence Helicopter Flying School
DLMW	Dywizjon Lotniczy Marynarki Wojennej
DMS	Defence Movements School
DSDA	Defence Storage & Distribution Agency
DS&TL	Defence Science & Technology Laboratory
DSG	Defence Support Group
DTI	Department of Trade and Industry
EA	Escadron Aérien (Air Squadron)
EAAT	Escadrille Avions de l'Armée de Terre
EAC	Ecole de l'Aviation de Chasse (Fighter Aviation School)
EALAT	Ecole de l'Aviation Légère de l'Armée de Terre
EAP	European Aircraft Project
EAT	Ecole de l'Aviation de Transport (Transport Aviation School)
EC	Escadre de Chasse (Fighter Wing)
ECG	Electronic Combat Group
ECM	Electronic Counter Measures
ECS	Electronic Countermeasures Squadron
EDA	Escadre de Detection Aéroportée (Air Detection Wing)
EdC	Escadron de Convoyage
EDCA	Escadron de Détection et de Control Aéroportée (Airborne Detection & Control Sqn)
EE	English Electric/Escadrille Electronique
EEA	Escadron Electronique Aéroporté
EFA	Ecole Franco Allemande
EFTS	Elementary Flying Training School
EH	Escadron d'Helicoptères (Helicopter Flight)

7

EHADT	Escadrille Helicoptères de l'Armée de Terre
EHI	European Helicopter Industries
EKW	Eidgenössiches Konstruktionswerk stätte
EL	Escadre de Liaison (Liaison Wing)
EL	Eskadra Lotnicza (Air Sqn)
ELT	Eskadra Lotnictwa Taktycznego (Tactical Air Squadron)
ELTR	Eskadra Lotnictwa Transportowego (Air Transport Squadron)
EMA	East Midlands Airport
EMVO	Elementaire Militaire Vlieg Opleiding (Elementary Flying Training)
ENOSA	Ecole des Navigateurs Operatioales Systemes d'Armees (Navigatio School)
EoN	Elliot's of Newbury
EPAA	Ecole de Pilotage Elementaire de lʌArmée de lʌAir (Air Force Elementary Flying School)
EPE	Ecole de Pilotage Elementaire (Elementary Flying School)
EPNER	Ecole du Personnel Navigant d'Essais et de Reception
ER	Escadre de Reconnaissance (Reconnaissance Wing)
ERS	Escadron de Reconnaissance Stratégique (Strategic Reconnaissance Squadron)
ES	Escadrille de Servitude
ESAM	Ecole Supérieur d'Application du Matériel
Esc	Escuadron (Squadron)
Esk	Eskadrille (Squadron)
Eslla	Escuadrilla (Squadron)
Esq	Esquadra (Squadron)
ET	Escadre de Transport (Transport Squadron)
ETE	Escadron de Transport et Entrainment (Transport Training Squadron)
ETEC	Escadron de Transport d'Entrainement et de Calibration (Transport Training & CalibrationSqn)
ETED	Escadron de Transformation des Equipages Mirage 2000D
ETL	Escadron de Transport Légère (Light Transport Squadron)
ETO	Escadron de Transition Operationnelle
ETOM	Escadron de Transport Outre Mer (Overseas Transport Squadron)
ETPS	Empire Test Pilots' School
ETR	Escadron de Tranformation Rafale
ETS	Engineering Training School
EVAA	Ecole de Voltige de l'Armée de l'Air (French Air Force Aerobatics School)
FAA	Fleet Air Arm/Federal Aviation Administration
FBS	Flugbereitschaftsstaffel
FBW	Fly-by-wire
FC	Forskokcentralen (Flight Centre)
FE	Further Education
FETC	Fire and Emergency Training Centre
ff	Front fuselage
FG	Fighter Group
FH	Fairchild-Hiller
FI	Falkland Islands
FJWOEU	Fast Jet & Guided Weapon Operational Evaluation Unit
FLO	Forsvarets Logistikk Organisasjon (Defence Logistics Organisation)
FlSt	Flieger Staffel (Flight Squadron)
Flt	Flight
FMA	Fabrica Militar de Aviones
FMT	Flotila Militara de Transport (Transport Regiment)
FMV	Forsvarets Materielwerk
FONA	Flag Officer Naval Aviation
FRADU	Fleet Requirements and Air Direction Unit
FRA	FR Aviation
FS	Fighter Squadron
FSAIU	Flight Safety & Accident Investigation Unit
FSCTE	Fire Services Central Training Establishment
FTS	Flying Training School
FTW	Flying Training Wing
Fw	Focke Wulf
FW	Fighter Wing/Foster Wickner
FWTS	Fixed Wing Test Squadron
FY	Fiscal Year
F3 OCU	Tornado F3 Operational Conversion Unit
GAF	Government Aircraft Factory
GAFFTC	German Air Force Flight Training Centre
GAL	General Aircraft Ltd
GAM	Groupe Aerien Mixte (Composite Air Group)
GAM/STAT	Groupement Aéromobile/Section Technique de l'Armée de Terre
gd	gold (squadron colours and markings)
GD	General Dynamics
GDSH	Gazelle Depth Support Hub
GHL	Groupe d'Helicopteres Legeres (Light Helicopter Group)
GI	Ground Instruction/Groupement d'Instruction (Instructional Group)
gn	green (squadron colours and markings)
GRD	Gruppe fur Rustunggdienste (Group for Service Preparation)
GRV	Groupe de Ravitaillement en Vol (Air Refuelling Group)
GT	Grupo de Transporte (Transport Wing)
GTT	Grupo de Transporte de Tropos (Troop Carrier Wing)
gy	grey (squadron colours and markings
H&W	Hereford and Worcester
HAF	Historic Aircraft Flight
HAT&ES	Heavy Aircraft Test & Evaluation Squadron
HC	Helicopter Combat Support Squadron
HCS	Hunting Contract Services
HF	Historic Flying Ltd
HFUS	Heeresfliegerunterstützungsstaffel
HFVAS	Heeresfliegerverbindungs/ Aufklärungsstaffel
HFVS	Heeresfliegerversuchstaffel
HFWS	Heeresflieger Waffenschule (Army Air Weapons School)
HGS	Hubschraubergeschwader
Hkp.Bat	Helikopter Bataljon (Helicopter Battalion)
HMA	Helicopter Maritime Attack
HMF	Harrier Maintenance Flight/ Helicopter Maintenance Flight
HMS	Her Majesty's Ship
HM&SF	Harrier Maintenance & Storage Flight
HOCU	Harrier OCU
HP	Handley-Page
HPAC SAM	Harrier Platform Availability Contract and Service and Aircraft Maintenance
HQ	Headquarters
HS	Hawker Siddeley
IAF	Israeli Air Force
IAP	International Airport
INTA	Instituto Nacional de Tecnica Aeroespacial
IOW	Isle Of Wight
IWM	Imperial War Museum
JARTS	Joint Aircraft Recovery & Transportation Sqn
JATE	Joint Air Transport Establishment
JbG	Jagdbombergeschwader (Fighter Bomber Wing)
JFACTSU	Joint Forward Air Control Training & Standards Unit
JG	Jagdgeschwader (Fighter Wing)

JHC	Joint Helicopter Command	MTHR	Mittlerer Transporthubschrauber
JHF	Joint Helicopter Force		Regiment (Medium Transport
KHR	Kampfhubschrauberregiment		Helicopter Regiment)
Kridlo	Wing	MTM	Mira Taktikis Metaforon
lbvr	letka Bitevnich Vrtulník		(Tactical Transport Sqn)
	(Attack Helicopter Squadron)	MTSF	Medium Term Storage Flight
Letka	Squadron	NA	North American
LTG	Lufttransportgeschwader	NACDS	Naval Air Command Driving School
	(Air Transport Wing)	NAEW&CF	NATO Airborne Early Warning &
LTO	Transportna en Letalska		Control Force
	Transportni Oddelek	NAF	Naval Air Facility
LTSF	Long Term Storage Flight	NAS	Naval Air Squadron
LTV	Ling-Temco-Vought		(UK)/Naval Air Station (US)
LVG	Luftwaffen Versorgungs	NASU	Naval Air Support Unit
	Geschwader (Air Force Maintnance	NATO	North Atlantic Treaty Organisation
	Wing)/Luft Verkehrs Gsellschaft	NAWC	Naval Air Warfare Center
LZO	Letecky Zku ební Odbor (Aviation	NAWC-AD	Naval Air Warfare Center Aircraft Division
	Test Department)	NBC	Nuclear, Biological and Chemical
m	multi-coloured (squadron colours	NE	North-East
	and markings)	NFATS	Naval Force Aircraft Test Squadron
MAPK	Mira Anachestisis Pantos Kerou	NI	Northern Ireland
	(All Weather Interception Sqn)	NMSU	Nimrod Major Servicing Unit
MASD	Marine Air Support Detachment	NOCU	Nimrod Operational Conversion Unit
MASU	Mobile Aircraft Support Unit	NSW	Naval Strike Wing
MBB	Messerschmitt Bolkow-Blohm	NTOCU	National Tornado Operational
MCAS	Marine Corps Air Station		Conversion Unit
McD	McDonnell Douglas	NYARC	North Yorks Aircraft Restoration Centre
MDMF	Merlin Depth Maintenance Facilities	OCU	Operational Conversion Unit
Med	Medical	OEU	Operation Evaluation Unit
MFG	Marine Flieger Geschwader (Naval Air Wing)	OFMC	Old Flying Machine Company
MH	Max Holste	OGMA	Oficinas Gerais de Material Aeronautico
MIB	Military Intelligence Battalion	or	orange (squadron colours and markings)
MiG	Mikoyan — Gurevich	OSAC	Operational Support Airlift Command
Mod	Modified	OSBL	Oddelek Sholskih Bojni Letal
MoD	Ministry of Defence		(Training & Combat School)
MR	Maritime Reconnaissance	OVH Kmp	Observations-Helicopter Kompagni
MRH	Multi-role Helikopters	PAT	Priority Air Transport Detachment
M&RU	Marketing & Recruitment Unit	PBN	Pilatus Britten-Norman
MS	Morane-Saulnier	PDSH	Puma Depth Support Hub

PLM	Pulk Lotnictwa Mysliwskiego (Fighter Regiment)	**Sz.D.REB**	'Szentgyörgyi Deszö' Harcászati Repülö Bázis
pr	purple (squadron colours and markings)	**TA**	Territorial Army
PRU	Photographic Reconnaissance Unit	**TAP**	Transporten Avio Polk (Air Transport Regiment)
PVH Kmp	Panservaerns-Helicopter Kompagni	**TCF**	Training Consolidation Flight
r	red (squadron colours and markings)	**TEF**	Tornado Engineering Flight
R	Replica	**TFC**	The Fighter Collection
RAeS	Royal Aeronautical Society	**TGp**	Test Groep
RAF	Royal Aircraft Factory/Royal Air Force	**TIARA**	Tornado Integrated Avionics Research Aircraft
RAFC	Royal Air Force College	**TL**	Taktická Letka (Tactical Squadron)
RAFM	Royal Air Force Museum	**TMF**	Tornado Maintenance Flight
RAFGSA	Royal Air Force Gliding and Soaring Association	**TMTS**	Trade Management Training School
RE	Royal Engineers	**TOCU**	Typhoon Operational Conversion Unit
Regt	Regiment	**tpzlt**	taktická a pruzkumná letka (Tactical & Reconnaissance Squadron)
REME	Royal Electrical & Mechanical Engineers	**TS**	Test Squadron
rf	Rear fuselage	**TsAGI**	Tsentral'ny Aerogidrodinamicheski Instut (Central Aero & Hydrodynamics Institute)
RFA	Royal Fleet Auxiliary		
RHC	Régiment d'Helicoptères de Combat	**TsLw**	Technische Schule der Luftwaffe (Luftwaffe Technical School)
RHFS	Régiment d'Helicoptères des Forces Spéciales		
RJAF	Royal Jordanian Air Force	**TW**	Test Wing
RM	Royal Marines	**UAS**	University Air Squadron
RMB	Royal Marines Base	**UAV**	Unmanned Air Vehicle
RMC of S	Royal Military College of Science	**Uberwg**	Uberwachunggeschwader (Surveillance Wing)
RN	Royal Navy	**UK**	United Kingdom
RNAS	Royal Naval Air Station	**UKAEA**	United Kingdom Atomic Energy Authority
RNGSA	Royal Navy Gliding and Soaring Association	**UNFICYP**	United Nations' Forces in Cyprus
ROF	Royal Ordnance Factory	**US**	United States
RQS	Rescue Squadron	**USAF**	United States Air Force
R-R	Rolls-Royce	**USAFE**	United States Air Forces in Europe
RS	Reid & Sigrist/Reconnaissance Squadron	**USAREUR**	US Army Europe
RSV	Reparto Sperimentale Volo (Experimental Flight School)	**USCGS**	US Coast Guard Station
		USEUCOM	United States European Command
RTP	Reduction To Produce	**USMC**	United States Marine Corps
RW	Reconnaissance Wing	**USN**	United States Navy
SA	Scottish Aviation	**NWTSPM**	United States Navy Test Pilots School
SAAB	Svenska Aeroplan Aktieboleg	**VAAC**	Vectored thrust Advanced Aircraft flight Control
SAH	School of Air Handling		
SAL	Scottish Aviation Limited	**VFW**	Vereinigte Flugtechnische Werke
SAR	Search and Rescue	**VGS**	Volunteer Gliding Squadron
Saro	Saunders-Roe	**VISSAGE**	VC10 Integrated Systems & Structures Ageing Exploration
SARTU	Search and Rescue Training Unit		
SCW	Strategic Communications Wing	**VLA**	Vojenska Letecka Akademia
SEAE	School of Electrical & Aeronautical Engineering	**vlt**	vycviková letka (Training Squadron)
		VMGR	Marine Aerial Refuelling/Transport Squadron
SEPECAT	Société Européenne de Production de l'avion Ecole de Combat et d'Appui Tactique	**VMGRT**	Marine Aerial Refuelling/Transport Training Squadron
		VQ	Fleet Air Reconnaissance Squadron
SFDO	School of Flight Deck Operations	**VR**	Fleet Logistic Support Squadron
SHAPE	Supreme Headquarters Allied Forces Europe	**VrK**	Vrtulnikové Letecké Kridlo
		VS	Vickers-Supermarine
SHOPS	Sea Harrier Operational Support Unit	**VSD**	Vegyes Szàllitorepülö Dandàr (Aircraft Transport Brigade)
si	silver (squadron colours and markings)		
SIET	Section d'Instruction et d'Etude du Tir	**w**	white (squadron colours and markings)
SKAMG	Sea King Aircraft Maintenance Group	**Wg**	Wing
SKTU	Sea King Training Unit	**WHL**	Westland Helicopters Ltd
Skv	Skvadron (Squadron)	**WLT**	Weapons Loading Training
SLK	Stíhacie Letecké Krídlo (Fighter Air Wing)	**WRS**	Weather Reconnaissance Squadron
slt	stíhací letka (Fighter Squadron)	**WS**	Westland
SLV	School Licht Vliegwezen (Flying School)	**WSK**	Wytwornia Sprzetu Kominikacyjnego
Sm	Smaldeel (Squadron)	**WTD**	Wehrtechnische Dienstelle (Technical Support Unit)
smdl	Smisena Dopravní Letka		
SNCAN	Société Nationale de Constructions Aéronautiques du Nord	**WW2**	World War II
		y	yellow (squadron colours and markings)
SOF	Special Operations Flight	**zDL**	základna Dopravního Letectva (Air Transport Base)
SOG	Special Operations Group		
SOS	Special Operations Squadron	**zL**	základna Letectva
SoTT	School of Technical Training	**zSL**	základna Speciálního Letectva (Training Air Base)
SOW	Special Operations Wing		
SPAD	Société Pour les Appareils Deperdussin	**zTL**	základna Taktického Letectva (Tactical Air Base)
SPP	Strojirny Prvni Petilesky	**zVrL**	základna Vrtulníkového Letectva (Helicopter Air Base)
Sqn	Squadron		

This section is to assist the reader to locate the places in the United Kingdom where operational military aircraft (including helicopters and gliders) are based.

The alphabetical order listing gives each location in relation to its county and to its nearest classified road(s) (by means adjoining; of means proximate to), together with its approximate direction and mileage from the centre of a nearby major town or city. Some civil airports are included where active military units are also based, but **excluded** are MoD sites with non-operational aircraft (eg gate guardians), the bases of privately-owned civil aircraft that wear military markings and museums.

User	Base Name	County/Region	Locationn	Distance/direction from (town)
Army	Abingdon	Oxfordshire	W by B4017, W of A34	5m SSW of Oxford
Army	Aldergrove/Belfast	Co Antrim	W by A26	13m W of Belfast Airport
RM	Arbroath	Angus	E of A933	2m NW of Arbroath
RAF	Barkston Heath	Lincolnshire	W by B6404, S of A153	5m NNE of Grantham
RAF	Benson	Oxfordshire	E by A423	1m NE of Wallingford
QinetiQ/RAF	Boscombe Down	Wiltshire	S by A303, W of A338	6m N of Salisbury
AF	Boulmer	Northumberland	E of B1339	4m E of Alnwick
RAF	Brize Norton	Oxfordshire	W of A4095	5m SW of Witney
Marshall	Cambridge Airport/Teversham	Cambridgeshire	S by A1303	2m E of Cambridge
RM/RAF	Chivenor	Devon	S of A361	4m WNW of Barnstaple
RAF	Church Fenton	Yorkshire North	S of B1223	7m WNW of Selby
Army	Colerne	Wiltshire	S of A420, E of Fosse Way	5m NE of Bath
RAF	Coningsby	Lincolnshire	S of A153, W by B1192	10m NW of Boston
DCAE	Cosford	Shropshire	W of A41, N of A464	9m WNW of Wolverhampton
RAF	Cranwell	Lincolnshire	N by A17, S by B1429	5m WNW of Sleaford
RN	Culdrose	Cornwall	E by A3083	1m SE of Helston
Army	Dishforth	Yorkshire North	E by A1	4m E of Ripon
USAF	Fairford	Gloucestershire	S of A417	9m ESE of Cirencester
RN	Fleetlands	Hampshire	E by A32	2m SE of Fareham
RAF	Halton	Buckinghamshire	N of A4011, S of B4544	4m ESE of Aylesbury
RAF	Henlow	Bedfordshire	E of A600, W of A6001	1m SW of Henlow
Army	Hullavington	Wiltshire	W of A429	1m N of M4 jn 17
RAF	Kenley	Greater London	W of A22	1m W of Warlingham
RAF	Kirknewton	Lothian	E by B7031, N by A70	8m SW of Edinburgh
USAF	Lakenheath	Suffolk	W by A1065	8m W of Thetford
RAF	Leeming	Yorkshire North	E by A1	5m SW of Northallerton
RAF	Leuchars	Fife	E of A919	7m SE of Dundee
RAF	Linton-on-Ouse	Yorkshire North	E of B6265	10m NW of York
RAF	Lossiemouth	Grampian	W of B9135, S of B9040	4m N of Elgin
RAF	Marham	Norfolk	N by A1122	6m W of Swaffham
Army	Middle Wallop	Hampshire	S by A343	6m SW of Andover
USAF	Mildenhall	Suffolk	S by A1101	9m NNE of Newmarket
RAF	Northolt	Greater London	N by A40	3m E of M40 jn 1
RAF	Odiham	Hampshire	E of A32	2m S of M3 jn 5
RN	Predannack	Cornwall	W by A3083	7m S of Helston
MoD	St Athan	South Glamorgan	N of B4265	13m WSW of Cardiff
RAF	Scampton	Lincolnshire	W by A15	6m N of Lincoln
RAF	Shawbury	Shropshire	W of B5063	7m NNE of Shrewsbury
RAF	Syerston	Nottinghamshire	W by A46	5m SW of Newark
RAF	Ternhill	Shropshire	SW by A41	3m SW of Market Drayton
RAF/Army	Topcliffe	Yorkshire North	E of A167, W of A168	3m SW of Thirsk
RAF	Valley	Gwynedd	S of A5 on Anglesey	5m SE of Holyhead
RAF	Waddington	Lincolnshire	E by A607, W by A15	5m S of Lincoln
Army/RAF	Wattisham	Suffolk	N of B1078	5m SSW of Stowmarket
RAF	Woodvale	Merseyside	W by A565	5m SSW of Southport
RAF	Wyton	Cambridgeshire	E of A141, N of B1090	3m NE of Huntingdon
RN	Yeovilton	Somerset	S by B3151, S of A303	5m N of Yeovil

The Committee of Imperial Defence through its Air Committee introduced a standardised system of numbering aircraft in November 1912. The Air Department of the Admiralty was allocated the first batch 1-200 and used these to cover aircraft already in use and those on order. The Army was issued with the next block from 201-800, which included the number 304 which was given to the Cody Biplane now preserved in the Science Museum. By the outbreak of World War I, the Royal Navy was on its second batch of serials 801-1600 and this system continued with alternating allocations between the Army and Navy until 1916 when number 10000, a Royal Flying Corps BE2C, was reached.

It was decided not to continue with five digit numbers but instead to start again from 1, prefixing RFC aircraft with the letter A and RNAS aircraft with the prefix N. The RFC allocations commenced with A1 an FE2D and before the end of the year had reached A9999 an Armstrong Whitworth FK8. The next group commenced with B1 and continued in logical sequence through the C, D, E and F prefixes. G was used on a limited basis to identify captured German aircraft, while H was the last block of wartime-ordered aircraft. To avoid confusion I was not used, so the new post-war machines were allocated serials in the J range. A further minor change was made in the serial numbering system in August 1929 when it was decided to maintain four numerals after the prefix letter, thus omitting numbers 1 to 999. The new K series therefore commenced at K1000, which was allocated to an AW Atlas.

The Naval N prefix was not used in such a logical way. Blocks of numbers were allocated for specific types of aircraft such as seaplanes or flying-boats. By the late 1920s the sequence had largely been used up and a new series using the prefix S was commenced. In 1930 separate naval allocations were stopped and subsequent serials were issued in the 'military' range which had by this time reached the K series. A further change in the pattern of allocations came in the L range. Commencing with L7272 numbers were issued in blocks with smaller blocks of serials between not used. These were known as 'black-out blocks'. As M had already been used as a suffix for Maintenance Command instructional airframes it was not used as a prefix. Although N had previously been used for naval aircraft it was used again for serials allocated from 1937.

With the build-up to World War II, the rate of allocations quickly accelerated and the prefix R was being used when war was declared. The letters O and Q were not allotted, nor was S, which had been used up to S1865 for naval aircraft before integration into the RAF series. By 1940 the serial Z9999 had been reached, as part of a black-out block, with the letters U and Y not used to avoid confusion.

The option to recommence serial allocation at A1000 was not taken up; instead it was decided to use an alphabetical two-letter prefix with three numerals running from 100 to 999. Thus, AA100 was allocated to a Blenheim IV and this two-letter, three-numeral serial system which started in 1940 continues today. The letters C, I, O, Q, U and Y were, with the exception of NC, not used. For various reasons the following letter combinations were not issued: DA, DB, DH, EA, GA to GZ, HA, HT, JE, JH, JJ, KR to KT, MR, NW, NZ, SA to SK, SV, TN, TR and VE. The first post-war serials issued were in the VP range while the end of the WZs had been reached by the Korean War.

In January 1952 a civil servant at the then Air Ministry penned a memo to his superiors alerting them to the fact that a new military aircraft serial system would soon have to be devised. With allocations accelerating to accommodate a NATO response to the Korean War and a perceived Soviet threat building, he estimated that the end of the ZZs would quickly be reached. However, over five decades later the allocations are only at the start of the ZKs and at the present rate are unlikely to reach ZZ999 until the end of this century!

Military aircraft serials are allocated by Defence Equipment & Support, where the Military Aircraft Register is maintained. A change in policy in 2003 resulted in the use of the first 99 digits in the ZK sequence (ZK001 to ZK099), following on from ZJ999. The first of these, ZK001 to ZK004, were allocated to AgustaWestland Merlins. There is also a growing trend for 'out-of-sequence' serial numbers to be issued. At first this was to a manufacturer's prototype or development aircraft. However, following the Boeing C-17 Globemasters leased and subsequently purchased from Boeing (ZZ171-ZZ177), more allocations have been noted, including ZM400 to ZM424 for the RAF's prospective Airbus A400Ms and ZR321 to ZR323 for a trio of Agusta A.109Es for No 32 (The Royal) Squadron. In a strange twist, serials ZZ190 and ZZ191 were allocated to a pair of former Swiss Air Force Hawker Hunter F58s operated under a military contract.

Since 2002 there has also been a new official policy concerning the use of military serial numbers on some types of UAV. 'Where a UAV is of modular construction the nationality and registration mark shall be applied to the fuselage of the vehicle or on the assembly forming the main part of the fuselage. To prevent the high usage of numbers for target drones which are eventually destroyed, a single registration mark (prefix) should be issued relating to the UAV type. The agency or service operating the target drone will be responsible for the identification of each individual UAV covered by that registration mark by adding a suffix.' This has resulted in the use of the same serial on a number of UAVs with a letter following it. Hence the appearance of ZK201A, ZK201B, ZK201C et seq on Army Meggitt Banshee drones. UAVs using this system are denoted in the text by an asterisk (*).

Note: The compiler will be pleased to receive comments, corrections and further information for inclusion in subsequent editions of *Military Aircraft Markings* and the monthly up-date of additions and amendments. Please send your information to Military Aircraft Markings, Ian Allan Publishing Ltd, Riverdene Business Park, Molesey Road, Hersham, Surrey, KT12 4RG or e-mail to HJCurtis@aol.com.

A serial in *italics* denotes that it is not the genuine marking for that airframe.

Serial	Type (code/other identity)	Owner/operator location or fate	Notes
46	VS361 Spitfire LF IX <R> (*MH486*/BAPC 206) [FT-E]	RAF Museum, Hendon	
168	Sopwith Tabloid Scout <R> (G-BFDE)	RAF Museum, Hendon	
304	Cody Biplane (BAPC 62)	Science Museum, South Kensington	
347	RAF BE2c <R> (G-AWYI)	Privately owned, Sywell	
687	RAF BE2b <R> (BAPC 181)	RAF Museum, Hendon	
2345	Vickers FB5 Gunbus <R> (G-ATVP)	RAF Museum, Hendon	
2699	RAF BE2c	Imperial War Museum, Lambeth	
2783	RAF BE2b <R>	Privately owned, stored Old Sarum	
3066	Caudron GIII (G-AETA/9203M)	RAF Museum, Hendon	
5964	DH2 <R> (BAPC 112)	Privately owned, Stretton on Dunsmore	
5964	DH2 <R> (G-BFVH)	Privately owned, Wickenby	
6232	RAF BE2c <R> (BAPC 41)	Yorkshire Air Museum, stored Elvington	
8359	Short 184 <ff>	FAA Museum, RNAS Yeovilton	
9917	Sopwith Pup (G-EBKY/N5180)	The Shuttleworth Collection, Old Warden	
A301	Morane BB (frame)	RAF Museum Reserve Collection, Stafford	
A1452	Vickers FB5 Gunbus <R>	Privately owned, Sywell	
A1742	Bristol Scout D <R> (BAPC 38)	Privately owned, Old Warden	
A6526	RAF FE2b <R>	RAF Museum, Hendon	
A7288	Bristol F2b Fighter <R>	Bristol Aero Collection, Filton	
A7317	Sopwith Pup <R> (BAPC 179)	Privately owned, Sywell	
A8226	Sopwith 1½ Strutter <R> (G-BIDW)	RAF Museum, Hendon	
B595	RAF SE5a <R> (G-BUOD) [W]	Privately owned, Defford	
B2458	Sopwith 1F.1 Camel <R> (G-BPOB/F542) [R]	Privately owned, Booker	
B5539	Sopwith 1F.1 Camel <R>	Privately owned, Booker	
B5577	Sopwith 1F.1 Camel <R> (D3419/BAPC 59) [W]	Montrose Air Station Heritage Centre	
B6401	Sopwith 1F.1 Camel <R> (G-AWYY/C1701)	FAA Museum, stored RNAS Yeovilton	
B7270	Sopwith 1F.1 Camel <R> (G-BFCZ)	Brooklands Museum, Weybridge	
C1904	RAF SE5a <R> (G-PFAP) [Z]	Privately owned, Castle Bytham, Lincs	
C3009	Currie Wot (G-BFWD)	Privately owned, Dunkeswell	
C3011	Phoenix Currie Super Wot (G-SWOT) [S]	Privately owned,	
C3988	Sopwith 5F.1 Dolphin (comp D5329)	RAF Museum Restoration Centre, Cosford	
C4451	Avro 504J <R> (BAPC 210)	Solent Sky, Southampton	
C4918	Bristol M1C <R> (G-BWJM)	The Shuttleworth Collection, Old Warden	
C4994	Bristol M1C <R> (G-BLWM)	RAF Museum, Hendon	
C5430	RAF SE5a <R> (G-CCXG) [V]	Privately owned, Wrexham	
C6468	RAF SE5a <R> (G-CEKL) [A]	Privately owned, RAF Halton	
C8996	RAF SE5a (G-ECAE/A2-25)	Privately owned, Milden	
C9533	RAF SE5a <R> (G-BUWE) [M]	Privately owned, Boscombe Down	
D276	RAF SE5a <R> (BAPC 208) [A]	Prince's Mead Shopping Centre, Farnborough	
D5649	Airco DH9	Imperial War Museum, Duxford	
D7560	Avro 504K	Science Museum, South Kensington	
D8096	Bristol F2b Fighter (G-AEPH) [D]	The Shuttleworth Collection, Old Warden	
E449	Avro 504K (G-EBJE/9205M)	RAF Museum, Hendon	
E2466	Bristol F2b Fighter (BAPC 165) [I]	RAF Museum, Hendon	
E2581	Bristol F2b Fighter [13]	Imperial War Museum, Duxford	
E8894	Airco DH9 (G-CDLI)	Aero Vintage, Westfield, Sussex	

Notes	Serial	Type (code/other identity)	Owner/operator location or fate
	F141	RAF SE5a <R> (G-SEVA) [G]	Privately owned, Boscombe Down
	F235	RAF SE5a <R> (G-BMDB) [B]	Privately owned, Boscombe Down
	F904	RAF SE5a (G-EBIA)	The Shuttleworth Collection, Old Warden
	F904	RAF SE5a <R>	Aeroventure, Doncaster
	F938	RAF SE5a (G-EBIC/9208M)	RAF Museum, Hendon
	F943	RAF SE5a <R> (G-BIHF) [S]	Privately owned, White Waltham
	F943	RAF SE5a <R> (G-BKDT)	Yorkshire Air Museum, Elvington
	F1010	Airco DH9A [C]	RAF Museum, Hendon
	F3556	RAF RE8	Imperial War Museum, Duxford
	F5447	RAF SE5a <R> (G-BKER) [N]	Privately owned, Bridge of Weir
	F5459	RAF SE5a <R> (G-INNY) [Y]	Privately owned, North Coates
	F5475	RAF SE5a <R> (BAPC 250)	Brooklands Museum, Weybridge
	F6314	Sopwith 1F.1 Camel (9206M) [B]	RAF Museum, Hendon
	F8010	RAF SE5a <R> (G-BDWJ) [Z]	Privately owned, Langport, Somerset
	F8614	Vickers FB27A Vimy IV <R> (G-AWAU)	RAF Museum, Hendon
	H1968	Avro 504K <R> (BAPC 42)	Yorkshire Air Museum, stored Elvington
	H5199	Avro 504K (BK892/3118M/ G-ACNB/G-ADEV)	The Shuttleworth Collection, Old Warden
	J7326	DH53 Humming Bird (G-EBQP)	Mosquito Aircraft Museum, London Colney
	J8067	Westland Pterodactyl 1a	Science Museum, South Kensington
	J9941	Hawker Hart 2 (G-ABMR)	RAF Museum, Hendon
	K1786	Hawker Tomtit (G-AFTA)	The Shuttleworth Collection, Old Warden
	K2046	Isaacs Fury II (G-AYJY)	Privately owned, Little Rissington
	K2048	Isaacs Fury II (G-BZNW)	Privately owned, Linton-on-Ouse
	K2050	Isaacs Fury II (G-ASCM)	Privately owned, Little Rissington
	K2059	Isaacs Fury II (G-PFAR)	Privately owned, Netherthorpe
	K2060	Isaacs Fury II (G-BKZM)	Privately owned stored, Limetree, Ireland
	K2075	Isaacs Fury II (G-BEER)	Privately owned, Combrook, Warks
	K2227	Bristol 105 Bulldog IIA (G-ABBB)	RAF Museum, Hendon
	K2567	DH82A Tiger Moth (DE306/7035M/ G-MOTH)	Privately owned, Tadlow
	K2572	DH82A Tiger Moth (NM129/G-AOZH)	Privately owned, Wanborough, Wilts
	K2585	DH82A Tiger Moth II (T6818/G-ANKT)	The Shuttleworth Collection, Old Warden
	K2587	DH82A Tiger Moth <R> (G-BJAP)	Privately owned, Shobdon
	K3241	Avro 621 Tutor (K3215/G-AHSA)	The Shuttleworth Collection, Old Warden
	K3661	Hawker Nimrod II (G-BURZ) [562]	Aero Vintage, Duxford
	K3731	Isaacs Fury <R> (G-RODI)	Privately owned, Hailsham
	K4232	Avro 671 Rota I (SE-AZB)	RAF Museum, Hendon
	K4259	DH82A Tiger Moth (G-ANMO) [71]	Privately owned, Sywell
	K4972	Hawker Hart Trainer IIA (1764M)	RAF Museum, Hendon
	K5054	Supermarine Spitfire <R> (BAPC 190/ EN398)	Privately owned, Hawkinge
	K5054	Supermarine Spitfire <R> (BAPC 214)	Tangmere Military Aviation Museum
	K5054	Supermarine Spitfire <R> (G-BRDV)	Privately owned, Kent
	K5054	Supermarine Spitfire <R>	Kent Battle of Britain Museum, Hawkinge
	K5054	Supermarine Spitfire <R>	Southampton Airport, on display
	K5409	Hawker Hind	Privately owned, Hastings
	K5414	Hawker Hind (G-AENP/BAPC 78) [XV]	The Shuttleworth Collection, Old Warden
	K5462	Hawker Hind	Privately owned, Hastings
	K5554	Hawker Hind	Privately owned, Hastings
	K5600	Hawker Audax I (2015M/G-BVVI)	Aero Vintage, Westfield, Sussex
	K5673	Isaacs Fury II (G-BZAS)	Privately owned, Morpeth
	K5673	Hawker Fury I <R> (BAPC 249)	Brooklands Museum, Weybridge
	K5674	Hawker Fury I (G-CBZP)	Aero Vintage, Duxford
	K6035	Westland Wallace II (2361M)	RAF Museum, Hendon

Serial	Type (code/other identity)	Owner/operator location or fate	Notes
K6618	Hawker Hind	Privately owned, Hastings	
K6833	Hawker Hind	Privately owned, Hastings	
K7271	Hawker Fury II <R> (BAPC 148)	Shropshire Wartime Aircraft Recovery Grp Mus, Sleap	
K7271	Isaacs Fury II <R> (G-CCKV)	Privately owned, Roche, Cornwall	
K7985	Gloster Gladiator I (L8032/G-AMRK)	The Shuttleworth Collection, Old Warden	
K8042	Gloster Gladiator II (8372M)	RAF Museum, Hendon	
K8203	Hawker Demon I (G-BTVE/2292M)	Demon Displays, Hatch	
K8303	Isaacs Fury II (G-BWWN) [D]	Privately owned, RAF Henlow	
K9926	VS300 Spitfire I <R> (BAPC 217) [JH-C]	RAF Bentley Priory, on display	
K9942	VS300 Spitfire I (8383M) [SD-D]	RAF Museum, Cosford	
K9998	VS300 Spitfire I <R> [QJ-K]	RAF Biggin Hill, on display	
L1067	VS300 Spitfire I <R> (BAPC 227) [XT-D]	Edinburgh Airport, on display	
L1592	Hawker Hurricane I [KW-Z]	Science Museum, South Kensington	
L1639	Hawker Hurricane I	Cambridge Fighter & Bomber Society, Little Gransden	
L1679	Hawker Hurricane I <R> (BAPC 241) [JX-G]	Tangmere Military Aviation Museum	
L1684	Hawker Hurricane I <R> (BAPC 219)	RAF Northolt, on display	
L1710	Hawker Hurricane I <R> (BAPC 219) [AL-D]	Repainted as L1684	
L2301	VS Walrus I (G-AIZG)	FAA Museum, RNAS Yeovilton	
L2940	Blackburn Skua I	FAA Museum, RNAS Yeovilton	
L5343	Fairey Battle I	RAF Museum, Hendon	
L6906	Miles M14A Magister I (G-AKKY/T9841/ BAPC 44)	Museum of Berkshire Aviation, Woodley	
L7005	Boulton Paul P82 Defiant I <R> [PS-B]	Boulton Paul Association, Wolverhampton	
L7181	Hawker Hind (G-CBLK)	Aero Vintage, Duxford	
L7191	Hawker Hind	Privately owned, Hastings	
L7775	Vickers Wellington B IC <ff>	Lincolnshire Avn Heritage Centre, E Kirkby	
L8756	Bristol 149 Bolingbroke IVT (RCAF 10001) [XD-E]	RAF Museum, Hendon	
N248	Supermarine S6A (S1596)	Solent Sky, Southampton	
N500	Sopwith LC-1T Triplane <R> (G-PENY/ G-BWRA)	Privately owned, Yarcombe, Devon/RNAS Yeovilton	
N546	Wright Quadruplane 1 <R> (BAPC 164)	Solent Sky, Southampton	
N1671	Boulton Paul P82 Defiant I (8370M) [EW-D]	Medway Aircraft Preservation Society, Rochester	
N1854	Fairey Fulmar II (G-AIBE)	FAA Museum, RNAS Yeovilton	
N2078	Sopwith Baby (8214/8215)	FAA Museum, stored RNAS Yeovilton	
N2532	Hawker Hurricane I <R> (BAPC 272) [GZ-H]	Kent Battle of Britain Museum, Hawkinge	
N2980	Vickers Wellington IA [R]	Brooklands Museum, Weybridge	
N3194	VS300 Spitfire I <R> (BAPC 220) [GR-Z]	Privately owned, Hixon, Staffs	
N3200	VS300 Spitfire IA (G-CFGJ) (fuselage)	Airframe Assemblies Ltd, Sandown	
N3289	VS300 Spitfire I <R> (BAPC 65) [DW-K]	Kent Battle of Britain Museum, Hawkinge	
N3290	VS300 Spitfire I <R> [AI-H]	Privately owned, St Mawgan	
N3310	VS361 Spitfire IX [A] <R>	Privately owned, Abingdon	
N3313	VS300 Spitfire I <R> (MH314/BAPC 69) [KL-B]	Kent Battle of Britain Museum, Hawkinge	
N3378	Boulton Paul P82 Defiant I	Boulton Paul Association, Wolverhampton	
N3788	Miles M14A Magister I (V1075/G-AKPF)	Privately owned, Leicester	
N4389	Fairey Albacore (N4172) [4M]	FAA Museum, stored RNAS Yeovilton	
N4877	Avro 652A Anson I (G-AMDA) [MK-V]	Imperial War Museum, Duxford	
N5137	DH82A Tiger Moth (N6638/G-BNDW)	Caernarfon Air World	
N5177	Sopwith 1½ Strutter <R>	Privately owned, Sedgensworth, Hants	
N5182	Sopwith Pup <R> (G-APUP/9213M)	RAF Museum, Hendon	
N5195	Sopwith Pup (G-ABOX)	Museum of Army Flying, Middle Wallop	
N5199	Sopwith Pup <R> (G-BZND)	Privately owned, Yarcombe, Devon	
N5459	Sopwith Triplane <R> (BAPC 111)	FAA Museum, RNAS Yeovilton	
N5518	Gloster Sea Gladiator	FAA Museum, RNAS Yeovilton	

N5628-P9373

Notes	Serial	Type (code/other identity)	Owner/operator location or fate
	N5628	Gloster Gladiator II	RAF Museum, Hendon
	N5719	Gloster Gladiator II (G-CBHO)	Privately owned, Dursley, Glos
	N5903	Gloster Gladiator II (N2276/G-GLAD)	The Fighter Collection, Duxford
	N5912	Sopwith Triplane (8385M)	RAF Museum, Hendon
	N6290	Sopwith Triplane <R> (G-BOCK)	The Shuttleworth Collection, Old Warden
	N6452	Sopwith Pup <R> (G-BIAU)	FAA Museum, RNAS Yeovilton
	N6466	DH82A Tiger Moth (G-ANKZ)	Privately owned, Compton Abbas
	N6473	DH82A Tiger Moth (G-AOBO)	Privately owned, Orbigny, France
	N6537	DH82A Tiger Moth (G-AOHY)	Privately owned, Wickenby
	N6635	DH82A Tiger Moth (comp G-APAO & G-APAP) [25]	Imperial War Museum, Duxford
	N6720	DH82A Tiger Moth (G-BYTN/7014M) [VX]	Privately owned, Wickenby
	N6797	DH82A Tiger Moth (G-ANEH)	Privately owned, Swyncombe
	N6812	Sopwith 2F.1 Camel	Imperial War Museum, Lambeth
	N6847	DH82A Tiger Moth (G-APAL)	Privately owned, Great Casterton, Rutland
	N6965	DH82A Tiger Moth (G-AJTW) [FL-J]	Privately owned, Tibenham
	N7033	Noorduyn AT-16 Harvard IIB (FX442)	Kent Battle of Britain Museum, Hawkinge
	N9191	DH82A Tiger Moth (G-ALND)	Privately owned, Pontypool
	N9192	DH82A Tiger Moth (G-DHZF) [RCO-N]	Privately owned, Sywell
	N9389	DH82A Tiger Moth (G-ANJA)	Privately owned, Thruxton
	N9899	Supermarine Southampton I (fuselage)	RAF Museum, Hendon
	P1344	HP52 Hampden I (9175M) [PL-K]	RAF Museum Restoration Centre, Cosford
	P2617	Hawker Hurricane I (8373M) [AF-F]	RAF Museum, Hendon
	P2725	Hawker Hurricane I (wreck)	Imperial War Museum, Lambeth
	P2725	Hawker Hurricane I <R> (BAPC 68) [TM-B]	Privately owned, Delabole, Cornwall
	P2793	Hawker Hurricane I <R> (BAPC 236) [SD-M]	Eden Camp Theme Park, Malton, North Yorkshire
	P2902	Hawker Hurricane I (G-ROBT)	Privately owned, Milden
	P2921	Hawker Hurricane I <R> (BAPC 273) [GZ-L]	Kent Battle of Britain Museum, Hawkinge
	P2921	Hawker Hurricane I <R> [GZ-L]	RAF Biggin Hill, on display
	P2954	Hawker Hurricane I <R> (BAPC 267) [WX-E]	Imperial War Museum, Duxford
	P2970	Hawker Hurricane I <R> (BAPC 291) [US-X]	Battle of Britain Memorial, Capel le Ferne, Kent
	P3059	Hawker Hurricane I <R> (BAPC 64) [SD-N]	Kent Battle of Britain Museum, Hawkinge
	P3144	Hawker Hurricane I <R> [CZ-B]	Privately owned, Tonbridge, Kent
	P3175	Hawker Hurricane I (wreck)	RAF Museum, Hendon
	P3179	Hawker Hurricane I <ff>	Tangmere Military Aviation Museum
	P3208	Hawker Hurricane I <R> (BAPC 63/L1592) [SD-T]	Kent Battle of Britain Museum, Hawkinge
	P3386	Hawker Hurricane I <R> (BAPC 218) [FT-A]	RAF Bentley Priory, on display
	P3395	Hawker Hurricane IV (KX829)(JX-B]	Thinktank, Birmingham
	P3398	Supermarine Aircraft Spitfire 26 (G-CEPL)	Privately owned, Thurrock
	P3554	Hawker Hurricane I (composite)	The Air Defence Collection, Salisbury
	P3679	Hawker Hurricane I <R> (BAPC 278) [GZ-K]	Kent Battle of Britain Museum, Hawkinge
	P3717	Hawker Hurricane I (composite) (DR348/G-HITT)	Privately owned, Milden
	P3873	Hawker Hurricane I <R> (BAPC 265) [YO-H]	Yorkshire Air Museum, Elvington
	P3901	Hawker Hurricane I <R> [RF-E]	Battle of Britain Bunker, Uxbridge
	P4139	Fairey Swordfish II (HS618) [5H]	FAA Museum, RNAS Yeovilton
	P6382	Miles M14A Hawk Trainer 3 (G-AJRS) [C]	The Shuttleworth Collection, Old Warden
	P7350	VS329 Spitfire IIA (G-AWIJ) [EB-G]	RAF BBMF, Coningsby
	P7540	VS329 Spitfire IIA [DU-W]	Dumfries & Galloway Avn Mus, Ripon (on rebuild)
	P7666	VS329 Spitfire II <R> [EB-Z]	RAF High Wycombe, on display
	P7966	VS329 Spitfire II <R> [D-B]	Manx Aviation & Military Museum, Ronaldsway
	P8140	VS329 Spitfire II <R> (P9390/BAPC 71) [ZF-K]	Norfolk & Suffolk Avn Museum, Flixton
	P8208	VS329 Spitfire IIB (G-RRFF)	Privately owned, Oxon
	P8448	VS329 Spitfire II <R> (BAPC 225) [UM-D]	RAF Cranwell, on display
	P9373	VS300 Spitfire IA (G-CFGN) (wreck)	Privately owned, Duxford

Serial	Type (code/other identity)	Owner/operator location or fate	Notes
P9374	VS300 Spitfire IA (G-MKIA) [J]	Privately owned, Duxford	
P9398	Supermarine Aircraft Spitfire 26 (G-CEPL) [KL-B]	Privately owned, Audley End	
P9444	VS300 Spitfire IA [RN-D]	Science Museum, South Kensington	
P9637	Supermarine Aircraft Spitfire 26 (G-RORB) [GR-B]	Privately owned, Perth	
R1914	Miles M14A Magister (G-AHUJ)	Privately owned, Strathallan	
R3821	Bristol 149 Bolingbroke IVT (G-BPIV/Z5722) [UX-N]	Blenheim(Duxford) Ltd, Duxford (on rebuild)	
R4118	Hawker Hurricane I (G-HUPW) [UP-W]	Privately owned, Didcot, Oxon	
R4922	DH82A Tiger Moth II (G-APAO)	Privately owned, Henlow	
R4959	DH82A Tiger Moth II (G-ARAZ) [59]	Privately owned, Temple Bruer, Lincs	
R5136	DH82A Tiger Moth II (G-APAP)	Privately owned, Henlow	
R5172	DH82A Tiger Moth II (G-AOIS) [FIJ-E]	Privately owned, Breighton	
R5246	DH82A Tiger Moth II (G-AMIV) [40]	Privately owned, Germany	
R5868	Avro 683 Lancaster I (7325M) [PO-S]	RAF Museum, Hendon	
R6690	VS300 Spitfire I <R> (BAPC 254) [PR-A]	Yorkshire Air Museum, Elvington	
R6775	VS300 Spitfire I <R> (BAPC 299) [YT-J]	Battle of Britain Memorial, Capel le Ferne, Kent	
R6904	VS300 Spitfire I <R> [BT-K]	Privately owned, Cornwall	
R6915	VS300 Spitfire I	Imperial War Museum, Lambeth	
R9125	Westland Lysander III (8377M)[LX-L]	RAF Museum, Hendon	
S1287	Fairey Flycatcher <R> (G-BEYB)	FAA Museum, stored RNAS Yeovilton	
S1579	Hawker Nimrod I <R> (G-BBVO) [571]	Privately owned, stored Felixkirk	
S1581	Hawker Nimrod I (G-BWWK) [573]	The Fighter Collection, Duxford	
S1595	Supermarine S6B [1]	Science Museum, South Kensington	
S1615	Isaacs Fury II (G-BMEU)	Privately owned, stored Netherthorpe	
T5298	Bristol 156 Beaufighter I (4552M) <ff>	Midland Air Museum, Coventry	
T5424	DH82A Tiger Moth II (G-AJOA)	Privately owned, Swindon	
T5854	DH82A Tiger Moth II (G-ANKK)	Privately owned, Baxterley	
T5879	DH82A Tiger Moth II (G-AXBW) [RUC-W]	Privately owned, Frensham	
T6296	DH82A Tiger Moth II (8387M)	RAF Museum, Hendon	
T6562	DH82A Tiger Moth II (G-ANTE)	Privately owned, Sywell	
T6953	DH82A Tiger Moth II (G-ANNI)	Privately owned, Compton Abbas	
T6991	DH82A Tiger Moth II (DE694/HB-UPY)	Privately owned, Lausanne, Switzerland	
T7281	DH82A Tiger Moth II (G-ARTL)	Privately owned, Egton, nr Whitby	
T7793	DH82A Tiger Moth II (G-ANKV)	Privately owned, Booker	
T7842	DH82A Tiger Moth II (G-AMTF)	Privately owned, Westfield, Surrey	
T7909	DH82A Tiger Moth II (G-ANON)	Privately owned, Sherburn-in-Elmet	
T7997	DH82A Tiger Moth II (NL750/G-AHUF)	Privately owned, Wickenby	
T8191	DH82A Tiger Moth II (G-BWMK)	Privately owned, stored Sleap	
T9707	Miles M14A Magister I (G-AKKR/8378M/T9708)	Museum of Army Flying, Middle Wallop	
T9738	Miles M14A Magister I (G-AKAT)	Privately owned, Breighton	
V3388	Airspeed AS10 Oxford I (G-AHTW)	Imperial War Museum, Duxford	
V6028	Bristol 149 Bolingbroke IVT (G-MKIV) [GB-D] <rf>	The Aircraft Restoration Co, stored Duxford	
V6555	Hawker Hurricane I <R> [DT-A]	Privately owned,	
V6799	Hawker Hurricane I <R> (BAPC 72/V7767) [SD-X]	Gloucestershire Avn Coll, stored Gloucester	
V7313	Hawker Hurricane I <R> [US-F]	Privately owned, North Weald, on display	
V7350	Hawker Hurricane I (fuselage)	Brenzett Aeronautical Museum	
V7467	Hawker Hurricane I <R> (BAPC 223) [LE-D]	RAF High Wycombe, on display	
V7467	Hawker Hurricane I <R> (BAPC 288) [LE-D]	Wonderland Pleasure Park, Farnsfield, Notts	
V7497	Hawker Hurricane I (G-HRLI)	Hawker Restorations, Milden	

Notes	Serial	Type (code/other identity)	Owner/operator location or fate
	V9367	Westland Lysander IIIA (G-AZWT) [MA-B]	The Shuttleworth Collection, Old Warden
	V9673	Westland Lysander IIIA (V9300/G-LIZY) [MA-J]	Imperial War Museum, Duxford
	V9723	Westland Lysander IIIA (V9546/OO-SOT) [MA-D]	SABENA Old Timers, Brussels, Belgium
	V9312	Westland Lysander IIIA (G-CCOM)	The Aircraft Restoration Co, Duxford
	W1048	HP59 Halifax II (8465M) [TL-S]	RAF Museum, Hendon
	W2068	Avro 652A Anson I (9261M/VH-ASM) [68]	RAF Museum, Hendon
	W2718	VS Walrus I (G-RNLI)	Privately owned, Audley End
	W3850	VS349 Spitfire V <R> [PR-A]	Privately owned, Cheshire
	W4041	Gloster E28/39	Science Museum, South Kensington
	W4041	Gloster E28/39 <R>	Gloucestershire Avn Coll, Gloucester
	W4050	DH98 Mosquito	Mosquito Aircraft Museum, London Colney
	W5856	Fairey Swordfish II (G-BMGC) [A2A]	RN Historic Flight, Yeovilton
	W9385	DH87B Hornet Moth (G-ADND) [YG-L,3]	Privately owned, Hullavington
	X4276	VS300 Spitfire I (G-CDGU)	Privately owned, Sandown
	X4474	VS509 Spitfire T9 (PV202/H-98/G-CCCA) [QV-I]	Historic Flying Ltd, Duxford
	X4590	VS300 Spitfire I (8384M) [PR-F]	RAF Museum, Hendon
	X4650	VS300 Spitfire I (G-CGUK) [KL-A]	Privately owned, Biggin Hill
	X4683	Jurca MJ10 Spitfire (G-CDPM) [EB-N]	Privately owned, Fishburn
	X7688	Bristol 156 Beaufighter I (3858M/G-DINT)	Privately owned, Hatch
	Z1206	Vickers Wellington IV (fuselage)	Privately owned, Kenilworth
	Z2033	Fairey Firefly I (G-ASTL) [275/N]	FAA Museum, RNAS Yeovilton
	Z2315	Hawker Hurricane IIA [JU-E]	Imperial War Museum, Duxford
	Z2389	Hawker Hurricane IIA [XR-T]	Brooklands Museum, Weybridge
	Z3427	Hawker Hurricane IIC <R> (BAPC 205) [AV-R]	RAF Museum, Hendon
	Z5140	Hawker Hurricane XIIA (Z7381/G-HURI) [HA-C]	Historic Aircraft Collection, Duxford
	Z5207	Hawker Hurricane IIB (G-BYDL)	Privately owned, Thruxton
	Z5252	Hawker Hurricane IIB (G-BWHA/Z5053) [GO-B]	Privately owned, Milden
	Z7015	Hawker Sea Hurricane IB (G-BKTH) [7-L]	The Shuttleworth Collection, Old Warden
	Z7197	Percival P30 Proctor III (G-AKZN/8380M)	RAF Museum Reserve Collection, Stafford
	Z7258	DH89A Dragon Rapide (NR786/G-AHGD)	Privately owned, Membury (wreck)
	AB196	Supermarine Aircraft Spitfire 26 (G-CCGH)	Privately owned, Hawarden
	AB550	VS349 Spitfire VB <R> (BAPC 230/AA908) [GE-P]	Eden Camp Theme Park, Malton, North Yorkshire
	AB910	VS349 Spitfire VB (G-AISU) [RF-D]	RAF BBMF, Coningsby
	AD540	VS349 Spitfire VB (wreck)	Kennet Aviation, Tollerton (on rebuild)
	AE436	HP52 Hampden I [PL-J] (parts)	Lincolnshire Avn Heritage Centre, E Kirkby
	AL246	Grumman Martlet I	FAA Museum, RNAS Yeovilton
	AP506	Cierva C30A (G-ACWM)	The Helicopter Museum, Weston-super-Mare
	AP507	Cierva C30A (G-ACWP) [KX-P]	Science Museum, South Kensington
	AR213	VS300 Spitfire IA (K9853/G-AIST) [JZ-E]	Privately owned, Duxford
	AR501	VS349 Spitfire LF VC (G-AWII/AR4474) [NN-A]	The Shuttleworth Collection, Old Warden
	AV511	EHI-101 Merlin <R> [511]	SFDO, RNAS Culdrose
	BB697	DH82A Tiger Moth (G-ADGT)	Repainted as G-ADGT, 2010
	BB803	DH82A Tiger Moth (G-ADWJ) [75]	Privately owned, Henstridge
	BB807	DH82A Tiger Moth (G-ADWO)	Solent Sky, Southampton
	BD713	Hawker Hurricane IIB	Privately owned, Taunton

Serial	Type (code/other identity)	Owner/operator location or fate	Notes
BE505	Hawker Hurricane IIB (RCAF 5403/G-HHII) [XP-L]	Hangar 11 Collection, North Weald	
BL614	VS349 Spitfire VB (4354M) [ZD-F]	RAF Museum, Hendon	
BL655	VS349 Spitfire VB (wreck)	Lincolnshire Avn Heritage Centre, East Kirkby	
BL924	VS349 Spitfire VB <R> (BAPC 242) [AZ-G]	Tangmere Military Aviation Museum	
BL927	Supermarine Aircraft Spitfire 26 (G-CGWI) [YH-I]	Privately owned, Perth	
BM481	VS349 Spitfire VB <R> [YO-T] (also wears PK651/RAO-B)	Thornaby Aerodrome Memorial	
BM539	VS349 Spitfire LF VB (G-CGBI)	Privately owned, Hastings	
BM597	VS349 Spitfire LF VB (5718M/G-MKVB) [JH-C]	Historic Aircraft Collection, Duxford	
BM631	VS349 Spitfire VB <R> (BAPC 269) [XR-C]	RAF Lakenheath, on display	
BN230	Hawker Hurricane IIC (LF751/5466M) [FT-A]	RAF Manston, Memorial Pavilion	
BP926	VS353 Spitfire PR IV (G-PRIV)	Privately owned, Newport Pagnell	
BR600	VS361 Spitfire IX <R> (BAPC 222) [SH-V]	Repainted as BS239	
BS239	VS361 Spitfire IX <R> (BAPC 222) [5R-E]	Battle of Britain Bunker, Uxbridge	
BS410	VS361 Spitfire IXC (G-TCHI)	Airframe Assemblies Ltd, Sandown	
BS435	VS361 Spitfire IX <R> [FY-F]	Privately owned, Lytham St Annes	
BW853	Hawker Hurricane XIIA (G-BRKE) (fuselage)	Privately owned, Cotswold Airport	
DD931	Bristol 152 Beaufort VIII (9131M) [L]	RAF Museum, Hendon	
DE208	DH82A Tiger Moth II (G-AGYU)	Privately owned, Treswell, Notts	
DE470	DH82A Tiger Moth II (G-ANMY) [16]	Privately owned, RAF Cosford	
DE623	DH82A Tiger Moth II (G-ANFI)	Privately owned, Cardiff	
DE673	DH82A Tiger Moth II (6948M/G-ADNZ)	Privately owned, Tibenham	
DE992	DH82A Tiger Moth II (G-AXXV)	Privately owned, Upavon	
DF112	DH82A Tiger Moth II (G-ANRM)	Privately owned, Clacton/Duxford	
DF128	DH82A Tiger Moth II (G-AOJJ) [RCO-U]	Privately owned, White Waltham	
DF155	DH82A Tiger Moth II (G-ANFV)	Privately owned, Shempston Farm, Lossiemouth	
DF198	DH82A Tiger Moth II (G-BBRB)	Privately owned, Biggin Hill	
DG202	Gloster F9/40 (5758M)	RAF Museum, Hendon	
DG590	Miles M2H Hawk Major (8379M/G-ADMW)	RAF Museum Reserve Collection, Stafford	
DP872	Fairey Barracuda II <ff>	FAA Museum, RNAS Yeovilton	
DV372	Avro 683 Lancaster I <ff>	Imperial War Museum, Lambeth	
DZ313	DH98 Mosquito B IV <R>	Privately owned, Little Rissington	
EB518	Airspeed AS10 Oxford V	Privately owned, Kenilworth	
EE416	Gloster Meteor F3 <ff>	Martin Baker Aircraft, Chalgrove, fire section	
EE425	Gloster Meteor F3 <ff>	Gloucestershire Avn Coll, stored Gloucester	
EE531	Gloster Meteor F4 (7090M)	Midland Air Museum, Coventry	
EE549	Gloster Meteor F4 (7008M) [A]	Tangmere Military Aviation Museum	
EF545	VS349 Spitfire LF VC (G-CDGY)	Aero Vintage, Rye	
EJ693	Hawker Tempest V (N7027E) [SA-J]	Privately owned, Booker	
EJ922	Hawker Typhoon IB <ff>	Privately owned, Hawkinge	
EM720	DH82A Tiger Moth II (G-AXAN)	Privately owned, Treswell, Notts	
EM840	DH82A Tiger Moth II (G-ANBY)	Assault Glider Trust, Shawbury	
EN179	VS361 Spitfire F IX (G-TCHO)	Privately owned, Exeter	
EN224	VS366 Spitfire F XII (G-FXII)	Privately owned, Newport Pagnell	
EN343	VS365 Spitfire PR XI <R> (BAPC 226)	Repainted as PL904, 2011	
EN398	VS361 Spitfire F IX <R> (BAPC 184) [JE-J]	Privately owned, Tonbridge, Kent	
EN398	VS361 Spitfire F IX <R> [JE-J]	Shropshire Wartime Aircraft Recovery Grp Mus, Sleap	
EN526	VS361 Spitfire IX <R> (MH777/BAPC 221) [SZ-G]	RAF Northolt, on display	
EN961	Isaacs Spitfire <R> (G-CGIK) [SD-X]	Privately owned, Hawes, Cumbria	
EP120	VS349 Spitfire LF VB (5377M/8070M/ G-LFVB) [AE-A]	The Fighter Collection, Duxford	

Notes	Serial	Type (code/other identity)	Owner/operator location or fate
	EX976	NA AT-6D Harvard III (FAP 1657)	FAA Museum, RNAS Yeovilton
	FB226	Bonsall Mustang <R> (G-BDWM) [MT-A]	*Repainted in US markings as 414673, May 2011*
	FE695	Noorduyn AT-16 Harvard IIB (G-BTXI) [94]	The Fighter Collection, Duxford
	FE788	CCF Harvard IV (MM54137/G-CTKL)	Privately owned, Rochester
	FE905	Noorduyn AT-16 Harvard IIB (LN-BNM)	RAF Museum, Hendon
	FJ992	Boeing-Stearman PT-17 Kaydet (OO-JEH) [44]	Privately owned, Wevelgem, Belgium
	FK338	Fairchild 24W-41 Argus I (G-AJOZ)	Yorkshire Air Museum, Elvington
	FL586	Douglas C-47B Dakota (OO-SMA) [AI-N] (fuselage)	WWII Remembrance Museum, Handcross, W Sussex
	FR886	Piper L-4J Cub (G-BDMS)	Privately owned, Old Sarum
	FS628	Fairchild Argus 2 (43-14601/G-AIZE)	RAF Museum, Cosford
	FS728	Noorduyn AT-16 Harvard IIB (D-FRCP)	Privately owned, Gelnhausen, Germany
	FT118	Noorduyn AT-16 Harvard IIB (G-BZHL)	Privately owned, Wickenby
	FT323	NA AT-6D Harvard III (FAP 1513/G-CCOY)	Privately owned, Mendlesham, Suffolk
	FT391	Noorduyn AT-16 Harvard IIB (G-AZBN)	Privately owned, Shoreham
	FX301	NA AT-6D Harvard III (EX915/G-TXAN) [FD-NQ]	Privately owned, Bryngwyn Bach, Clwyd
	FX322	Noorduyn AT-16 Harvard IIB <ff>	Privately owned, Doncaster
	FX760	Curtiss P-40N Kittyhawk IV (A29-556/9150M) [GA-?]	RAF Museum, Hendon
	FZ626	Douglas Dakota III (KN566/G-AMPO) [YS-DH]	RAF Lyneham, on display
	HB275	Beech C-45 Expeditor II (RCAF 2324/G-BKGM)	Privately owned, Exeter
	HB751	Fairchild Argus III (G-BCBL)	Privately owned, Woolsery, Devon
	HG691	DH89A Dragon Rapide (G-AIYR)	Privately owned, Clacton/Duxford
	HH268	GAL48 Hotspur II (HH379/BAPC 261) [H]	Museum of Army Flying, Middle Wallop
	HJ711	DH98 Mosquito NF II [VI-C]	Night-Fighter Preservation Trm, Elvington
	HM580	Cierva C-30A (G-ACUU) [KX-K]	Imperial War Museum, Duxford
	HS503	Fairey Swordfish IV (BAPC 108)	RAF Museum Reserve Collection, Stafford
	IR206	Eurofighter Typhoon F2 <R> [IR]	RAF M&RU, Bottesford
	IR808	B-V Chinook HC2 <R>	RAF M&RU, Bottesford
	JF343	Supermarine Aircraft Spitfire 26 (G-CCZP) [JW-P]	Privately owned, Panshangar
	JG668	VS359 Spitfire LF VIIIC (A58-441/G-CFGA)	Privately owned, Haverfordwest
	JP843	Hawker Typhoon IB [Y]	Privately owned, Shrewsbury
	JR505	Hawker Typhoon IB <ff>	Midland Air Museum, Coventry
	JV482	Grumman Wildcat V	Ulster Aviation Society, Long Kesh
	JV579	Grumman FM-2 Wildcat (N4845V/G-RUMW) [F]	The Fighter Collection, Duxford
	JV928	Consolidated PBY-5A Catalina (N423RS) [Y]	Super Catalina Restoration, North Weald
	KB889	Avro 683 Lancaster B X (G-LANC) [NA-I]	Imperial War Museum, Duxford
	KB976	Avro 683 Lancaster B X <ff>	Brooklands Museum, Weybridge
	KB976	Avro 683 Lancaster B X (G-BCOH) <rf>	Aeroventure, Doncaster
	KB994	Avro 683 Lancaster B X (G-BVBP) <ff>	Privately owned,
	KD345	Goodyear FG-1D Corsair (88297/G-FGID) [130-A]	The Fighter Collection, Duxford
	KD431	CV Corsair IV [E2-M]	FAA Museum, RNAS Yeovilton
	KE209	Grumman Hellcat II	FAA Museum, RNAS Yeovilton
	KE418	Hawker Tempest <rf>	*Currently not known*
	KF183	Noorduyn AT-16 Harvard IIB [3]	MoD/AFD/QinetiQ, Boscombe Down
	KF388	Noorduyn AT-16 Harvard IIB (composite)	Bournemouth Aviation Museum

Serial	Type (code/other identity)	Owner/operator location or fate	Notes
KF435	Noorduyn AT-16 Harvard IIB <ff>	Privately owned, Swindon	
KF488	Noorduyn AT-16 Harvard IIB (comp KF388)	Repainted as KF388, April 2011	
KF532	Noorduyn AT-16 Harvard IIB <ff>	Newark Air Museum, Winthorpe	
KF584	CCF T-6J Texan (G-RAIX) [RAI-X]	Privately owned, Lee-on-Solent	
KF729	CCF T-6J Texan (G-BJST)	Privately owned, Thruxton	
KF741	Noorduyn AT-16 Harvard IIB <ff>	Privately owned, Kenilworth	
KG374	Douglas Dakota IV (KP208) [YS-DM]	Merville Barracks, Colchester, on display	
KG427	Douglas Dakota IV (KN353/G-AMYJ)	Repainted as KN353	
KG651	Douglas Dakota III (G-AMHJ)	Assault Glider Trust, Shawbury	
KJ351	Airspeed AS58 Horsa II (TL659/BAPC 80) [23]	Museum of Army Flying, Middle Wallop	
KJ994	Douglas Dakota III (F-AZTE)	Dakota et Cie, La Ferté Alais, France	
KK116	Douglas Dakota IV (G-AMPY)	Classic Flight, Coventry	
KK995	Sikorsky Hoverfly I [E]	RAF Museum, Hendon	
KL216	Republic P-47D Thunderbolt (45-49295/9212M) [RS-L]	RAF Museum, Hendon	
KN353	Douglas Dakota IV (G-AMYJ)	Yorkshire Air Museum, Elvington	
KN645	Douglas Dakota IV (KG374/8355M)	RAF Museum, Cosford	
KN751	Consolidated Liberator C VI (IAF HE807) [F]	RAF Museum, Hendon	
KP208	Douglas Dakota IV [YS]	Repainted as KG374, 2010	
KZ191	Hawker Hurricane IV (frame only)	Privately owned, East Garston, Bucks	
LA198	VS356 Spitfire F21 (7118M) [RAI-G]	Kelvingrove Art Gallery & Museum, Glasgow	
LA226	VS356 Spitfire F21 (7119M)	RAF Museum Reserve Collection, Stafford	
LA255	VS356 Spitfire F21 (6490M) [JX-U]	RAF, Coningsby	
LA543	VS474 Seafire F46 <ff>	The Air Defence Collection, Salisbury	
LA546	VS474 Seafire F46 (G-CFZJ)	Privately owned, Colchester	
LA564	VS474 Seafire F46 (G-FRSX)	Kennet Aviation, North Weald	
LB264	Taylorcraft Plus D (G-AIXA)	RAF Museum, Hendon	
LB294	Taylorcraft Plus D (G-AHWJ)	Museum of Army Flying, Whitchurch, Hants	
LB312	Taylorcraft Plus D (HH982/G-AHXE)	Privately owned, Netheravon	
LB323	Taylorcraft Plus D (G-AHSD)	Privately owned, Old Buckenham	
LB367	Taylorcraft Plus D (G-AHGZ)	Privately owned, Henstridge	
LB375	Taylorcraft Plus D (G-AHGW)	Privately owned, Coventry	
LF363	Hawker Hurricane IIC [YB-W]	RAF BBMF, Coningsby	
LF738	Hawker Hurricane IIC (5405M) [UH-A]	RAF Museum, Cosford	
LF789	DH82 Queen Bee (K3584/BAPC 186) [R2-K]	Mosquito Aircraft Museum, London Colney	
LF858	DH82 Queen Bee (G-BLUZ)	Privately owned, Henlow	
LH291	Airspeed AS51 Horsa I <R> (BAPC 279)	Assault Glider Trust, RAF Shawbury	
LS326	Fairey Swordfish II (G-AJVH) [L2]	RN Historic Flight, Yeovilton	
LV907	HP59 Halifax III (HR792) [NP-F]	Yorkshire Air Museum, Elvington	
LZ551	DH100 Vampire	FAA Museum, RNAS Yeovilton	
LZ766	Percival P34 Proctor III (G-ALCK)	Imperial War Museum, Duxford	
LZ842	VS361 Spitfire F IX [EF-D]	Privately owned, Sandown	
LZ844	VS349 Spitfire F VC [UP-X]	Privately owned, Cotswold Airport	
MA764	VS361 Spitfire F IX (G-MCDB)	Privately owned, Bentwaters	
MB293	VS357 Seafire IIC (G-CFGI) (wreck)	Privately owned, Duxford	
MD338	VS359 Spitfire LF VIII	Privately owned, Sandown	
MF628	Vickers Wellington T10 (9210M)	RAF Museum Restoration Centre, Cosford	
MH415	VS361 Spitfire IX <R> (MJ751/BAPC 209) [DU-V]	The Aircraft Restoration Co, Duxford	
MH434	VS361 Spitfire LF IXB (G-ASJV) [ZD-B]	The Old Flying Machine Company, Duxford	
MJ627	VS509 Spitfire T9 (G-BMSB) [9G-P]	Privately owned, RAF Waddington	
MJ832	VS361 Spitfire IX <R> (L1096/BAPC 229) [DN-Y]	RAF Digby, on display	
MK356	VS361 Spitfire LF IXC (5690M) [UF-Q]	RAF BBMF, Coningsby	
MK356	VS361 Spitfire LF IXC <R> [2I-V]	Kent Battle of Britain Museum, Hawkinge	

Notes	Serial	Type (code/other identity)	Owner/operator location or fate
	MK356	VS361 Spitfire LF IXC (BAPC 289) <R>	RAF Cosford, on display
	MK805	VS361 Spitfire IX <R> [SH]	Privately owned, Oulton Broad, Suffolk
	MK912	VS361 Spitfire LF IXC (G-BRRA) [SH-L]	Privately owned, Biggin Hill
	ML407	VS509 Spitfire T9 (G-LFIX) [OU-V]	Privately owned, Bentwaters
	ML411	VS361 Spitfire LF IXE (G-CBNU)	Privately owned, Ashford, Kent
	ML427	VS361 Spitfire IX (6457M) [HK-A]	Thinktank, Birmingham
	ML796	Short S25 Sunderland V [NS-F]	Imperial War Museum, Duxford
	ML824	Short S25 Sunderland V [NS-Z]	RAF Museum, Hendon
	MN235	Hawker Typhoon IB	RAF Museum, Hendon
	MP425	Airspeed AS10 Oxford I (G-AITB) [G]	RAF Museum, Hendon
	MS902	Miles M25 Martinet TT1 (TF-SHC)	Museum of Berkshire Aviation, Woodley
	MT197	Auster IV (G-ANHS)	Privately owned, Spanhoe
	MT255	Auster IV (G-ANHU)	Privately owned, Wickenby
	MT438	Auster III (G-AREI)	Privately owned, Eggesford
	MT818	VS502 Spitfire T8 (G-AIDN)	Privately owned, Booker
	MT847	VS379 Spitfire FR XIVE (6960M) [AX-H]	Museum of Science & Industry, Manchester
	MT928	VS359 Spitfire HF VIIIC (D-FEUR/MV154/AR654)[ZX-M]	Privately owned, Bremgarten, Germany
	MV268	VS379 Spitfire FR XIVE (MV293/G-SPIT) [JE-J]	The Fighter Collection, Duxford
	MW401	Hawker Tempest II (IAF HA604/G-PEST)	Privately owned, Wickenby
	MW404	Hawker Tempest II (IAF HA557)	Privately owned, stored Booker
	MW763	Hawker Tempest II (IAF HA586/G-TEMT) [HF-A]	Privately owned, Wickenby
	MW810	Hawker Tempest II (IAF HA591) <ff>	Privately owned, Bentwaters
	NF370	Fairey Swordfish III [NH-L]	Imperial War Museum, Duxford
	NF389	Fairey Swordfish III [D]	RN Historic Flight, Yeovilton
	NH238	VS361 Spitfire LF IXE (G-MKIX) [D-A]	Privately owned, stored Greenham Common
	NJ633	Auster 5D (G-AKXP)	Privately owned, English Bicknor
	NJ673	Auster 5D (G-AOCR)	Privately owned, Shenington, Oxon
	NJ695	Auster 4 (G-AJXV)	Privately owned, Newark
	NJ703	Auster 5 (G-AKPI)	Privately owned, Ellerton
	NJ719	Auster 5 (TW385/G-ANFU)	Newcastle Motor Museum
	NJ889	Auster 3 (G-AHLK)	Privately owned, Leicester East
	NL750	DH82A Tiger Moth II (T7997/G-AOBH)	Privately owned, Eaglescott
	NL985	DH82A Tiger Moth I (7015M/G-BWIK)	Privately owned, Sywell
	NM138	DH82A Tiger Moth I (G-ANEW) [44]	Privately owned, Kidlington
	NM181	DH82A Tiger Moth I (G-AZGZ)	Privately owned, Rush Green
	NP294	Percival P31 Proctor IV [TB-M]	Lincolnshire Avn Heritage Centre, E Kirkby
	NV778	Hawker Tempest TT5 (8386M)	RAF Museum, Hendon
	NX534	Auster III (G-BUDL)	Privately owned, Spanhoe
	NX611	Avro 683 Lancaster B VII (8375M/G-ASXX) [DX-C,LE-C]	Lincolnshire Avn Heritage Centre, E Kirkby
	PA474	Avro 683 Lancaster B I [BQ-B,HW-R]	RAF BBMF, Coningsby
	PD685	Slingsby T7 Cadet TX1	Boulton Paul Association, Wolverhampton
	PF179	HS Gnat T1 (XR541/8602M)	Privately owned, Bruntingthorpe
	PK624	VS356 Spitfire F22 (8072M)	The Fighter Collection, Duxford
	PK664	VS356 Spitfire F22 (7759M) [V6-B]	RAF Museum Reserve Collection, Stafford
	PK683	VS356 Spitfire F24 (7150M)	Solent Sky, Southampton
	PK724	VS356 Spitfire F24 (7288M)	RAF Museum, Hendon
	PL256	VS361 Spitfire IX <R> [TM-L]	Privately owned, Leicester
	PL279	VS361 Spitfire IX <R> (N3317/BAPC 268) [ZF-Z]	Privately owned, St Mawgan
	PL904	VS365 Spitfire PR XI <R> (BAPC 226)	RAF Benson, on display
	PL965	VS365 Spitfire PR XI (G-MKXI) [R]	Hangar 11 Collection, North Weald
	PL983	VS365 Spitfire PR XI (G-PRXI)	Privately owned, Duxford (on rebuild)

Serial	Type (code/other identity)	Owner/operator location or fate	Notes
PM631	VS390 Spitfire PR XIX	RAF BBMF, Coningsby	
PM651	VS390 Spitfire PR XIX (7758M) [X]	RAF Museum, Cosford	
PN323	HP Halifax VII <ff>	Imperial War Museum, Lambeth	
PP566	Fairey Firefly I <rf>	Privately owned, Newton Abbott, Devon	
PP972	VS358 Seafire LF IIIC (G-BUAR)	Privately owned, stored Greenham Common	
PR536	Hawker Tempest II (IAF HA457)[OQ-H]	RAF Museum, Hendon	
PS853	VS390 Spitfire PR XIX (G-RRGN) [C]	Rolls-Royce, East Midlands	
PS890	VS390 Spitfire PR XIX (F-AZJS) [UM-E]	Privately owned, Dijon, France	
PS915	VS390 Spitfire PR XIX (7548M/7711M)	RAF BBMF, Coningsby	
PT462	VS509 Spitfire T9 (G-CTIX/N462JC) [SW-A]	Privately owned, Caernarfon/Duxford	
PV303	Supermarine Aircraft Spitfire 26 (G-CCJL) [ON-B]	Privately owned, Perranporth	
PZ865	Hawker Hurricane IIC (G-AMAU) [JX-E]	RAF BBMF, Duxford (on overhaul)	
QQ100	Agusta A109E Power Elite	MoD/AFD/QinetiQ, Boscombe Down	
QQ101	BAE RJ.100 (G-BZAY)	MoD/AFD/QinetiQ, Boscombe Down	
QQ102	BAE RJ.70	MoD/AFD/QinetiQ, Boscombe Down	
RA848	Slingsby T7 Cadet TX1	Privately owned, Leeds	
RA854	Slingsby T7 Cadet TX1	Yorkshire Air Museum, Elvington	
RA897	Slingsby T7 Cadet TX1	Newark Air Museum, Winthorpe	
RA905	Slingsby T7 Cadet TX1 (BGA1143)	Trenchard Museum, RAF Halton	
RB142	Supermarine Aircraft Spitfire 26 (G-CEFC) [DW-B]	Privately owned, Basingstoke, Hants	
RB159	VS379 Spitfire F XIV <R> [DW-D]	Privately owned, Delabole, Cornwall	
RD220	Bristol 156 Beaufighter TF X	Royal Scottish Mus'm of Flight, stored E Fortune	
RD253	Bristol 156 Beaufighter TF X (7931M)	RAF Museum, Hendon	
RF398	Avro 694 Lincoln B II (8376M)	RAF Museum, Cosford	
RG333	Miles M38 Messenger IIA (G-AIEK)	Privately owned, Felton, Bristol	
RG904	VS Spitfire <R> [BT-K]	RAF Museum, Cosford	
RH746	Bristol 164 Brigand TF1 (fuselage)	RAF Museum Restoration Centre, Cosford	
RL962	DH89A Dominie II (G-AHED)	RAF Museum Reserve Collection, Stafford	
RM169	Percival P31 Proctor IV (SE-CEA) [4-47]	Privately owned, Great Oakley, Essex	
RM221	Percival P31 Proctor IV (G-ANXR)	Privately owned, Biggin Hill	
RM689	VS379 Spitfire F XIV (G-ALGT)	Rolls-Royce, stored Derby	
RM694	VS379 Spitfire F XIV (G-DBKL/6640M)	Privately owned, Booker	
RM927	VS379 Spitfire F XIV (G-JNMA)	Privately owned, Sandown	
RN218	Isaacs Spitfire <R> (G-BBJI) [N]	Privately owned, Builth Wells	
RR232	VS361 Spitfire HF IXC (G-BRSF)	Privately owned, Langford, Devon	
RT486	Auster 5 (G-AJGJ)	Privately owned, Lee-on-Solent	
RT520	Auster 5 (G-ALYB)	Aeroventure, Doncaster	
RT610	Auster 5A-160 (G-AKWS)	Privately owned, Shobdon	
RW382	VS361 Spitfire LF XVIE (7245M/8075M/G-PBIX)	Privately owned, Biggin Hill	
RW386	VS361 Spitfire LF XVIE (6944M/SE-BIR) [NG-D]	Privately owned, Angelholm, Sweden	
RW388	VS361 Spitfire LF XVIE (6946M) [U4-U]	Stoke-on-Trent City Museum, Hanley	
RX168	VS358 Seafire L IIIC (IAC 157/G-BWEM)	Privately owned, Exeter	
SL611	VS361 Spitfire LF XVIE	Supermarine Aero Engineering, Stoke-on-Trent	
SL674	VS361 Spitfire LF IX (8392M) [RAS-H]	RAF Museum Reserve Collection, Stafford	
SM520	VS509 Spitfire T9 (H-99/G-ILDA) [KJ-I]	Privately owned, Kidlington	
SN280	Hawker Tempest V <ff>	Aeroventure, Doncaster	
SX137	VS384 Seafire F XVII	FAA Museum, RNAS Yeovilton	
SX300	VS384 Seafire F XVII (G-RIPH)	Kennet Aviation, North Weald	
SX336	VS384 Seafire F XVII (G-KASX) [105/VL]	Kennet Aviation, Yeovilton	
TA122	DH98 Mosquito FB VI [UP-G]	Mosquito Aircraft Museum, London Colney	
TA634	DH98 Mosquito TT35 (G-AWJV) [8K-K]	Mosquito Aircraft Museum, London Colney	

Notes	Serial	Type (code/other identity)	Owner/operator location or fate
	TA639	DH98 Mosquito TT35 (7806M) [AZ-E]	RAF Museum, Cosford
	TA719	DH98 Mosquito TT35 (G-ASKC)	Imperial War Museum, Duxford
	TA805	VS361 Spitfire HF IX (G-PMNF) [FX-M]	Privately owned, Biggin Hill
	TB382	VS361 Spitfire LF XVIE (X4277/MK673)	RAF BBMF, stored Coningsby
	TB675	VS361 Spitfire LF XVIE (RW393/7293M) [4D-V]	RAF Museum Reserve Collection, Stafford
	TB752	VS361 Spitfire LF XVIE (8086M) [KH-Z]	RAF Manston, Memorial Pavilion
	TD248	VS361 Spitfire LF XVIE (7246M/G-OXVI) [CR-S]	Spitfire Limited, Humberside
	TD248	VS361 Spitfire LF XVIE [8Q-T] (fuselage)	Norfolk & Suffolk Avn Mus'm, Flixton
	TD314	VS361 Spitfire LF IX (G-CGYJ)	Privately owned, Biggin Hill
	TE184	VS361 Spitfire LF XVIE (6850M/G-MXVI) [EJC]	Privately owned, Bremgarten, Germany
	TE311	VS361 Spitfire LF XVIE (MK178/7241M) [4D-V]	RAF BBMF, Coningsby (on rebuild)
	TE462	VS361 Spitfire LF XVIE (7243M)	Royal Scottish Mus'm of Flight, E Fortune
	TE517	VS361 Spitfire LF IXE (G-JGCA) [HL-K]	Privately owned, Sussex
	TE566	VS361 Spitfire LF IXE (VH-IXT)	Privately owned, Cotswold Airport (wreck)
	TG263	Saro SR A1 (G-12-1)	Solent Sky, Southampton
	TG511	HP67 Hastings T5 (8554M) [511]	RAF Museum, Cosford
	TG517	HP67 Hastings T5 (517)	Newark Air Museum, Winthorpe
	TG528	HP67 Hastings C1A [528]	Imperial War Museum, Duxford
	TJ118	DH98 Mosquito TT35 <ff>	Mosquito Aircraft Museum, stored London Colney
	TJ138	DH98 Mosquito B35 (7607M) [VO-L]	RAF Museum, Hendon
	TJ343	Auster 5 (G-AJXC)	Privately owned, Hook
	TJ398	Auster AOP6 (BAPC 70)	North-East Aircraft Museum, Usworth
	TJ534	Auster 5 (G-AKSY)	Privately owned, Breighton
	TJ569	Auster 5 (G-AKOW)	Museum of Army Flying, Middle Wallop
	TJ652	Auster 5 (TJ565/G-AMVD)	Privately owned, Hardwick, Norfolk
	TJ672	Auster 5D (G-ANIJ) [TS-D]	Privately owned, Netheravon
	TK718	GAL59 Hamilcar I (fuselage)	The Tank Museum, Bovington
	TK777	GAL59 Hamilcar I (fuselage)	Museum of Army Flying, Middle Wallop
	TP298	VS394 Spitfire FR XVIII [UM-T]	Privately owned, Sandown
	TS291	Slingsby T7 Cadet TX1 (BGA852)	Royal Scottish Mus'm of Flight, stored Granton
	TS798	Avro 685 York C1 (G-AGNV/MW100)	RAF Museum, Cosford
	TV959	DH98 Mosquito T III [AF-V]	Sold to New Zealand, 2011
	TW439	Auster 5 (G-ANRP)	Privately owned, Lavenham, Suffolk
	TW467	Auster 5 (G-ANIE)	Privately owned, Spanhoe
	TW477	Auster 5 (OY-EFI)	Privately owned, Ringsted, Denmark
	TW511	Auster 5 (G-APAF)	Privately owned, Chisledon, Wilts
	TW536	Auster AOP6 (7704M/G-BNGE) [TS-V]	Privately owned, Netheravon
	TW591	Auster 6A (G-ARIH) [6]	Privately owned, Eaglescott
	TW641	Beagle A61 Terrier 2 (G-ATDN)	Privately owned, Biggin Hill
	TX213	Avro 652A Anson C19 (G-AWRS)	North-East Aircraft Museum, Usworth
	TX214	Avro 652A Anson C19 (7817M)	RAF Museum, Cosford
	TX226	Avro 652A Anson C19 (7865M)	Classic Flight, stored Compton Verney
	TX235	Avro 652A Anson C19	Classic Flight, stored Compton Verney
	TX310	DH89A Dragon Rapide 6 (G-AIDL)	Classic Flight, Coventry
	VF301	DH100 Vampire F1 (7060M) [RAL-G]	Midland Air Museum, Coventry
	VF512	Auster 6A (G-ARRX) [PF-M]	Privately owned, Popham
	VF516	Beagle A61 Terrier 2 (G-ASMZ)	Privately owned, Eggesford
	VF519	Auster AOP6 (G-ASYN)	Privately owned, Doncaster
	VF526	Auster 6A (G-ARXU) [T]	Privately owned, Netheravon
	VF557	Auster 6A (G-ARHM) [H]	Privately owned, Spanhoe
	VF560	Auster 6A (frame)	Aeroventure, Doncaster
	VF581	Beagle A61 Terrier 1 (G-ARSL) [G]	Privately owned, Eggesford
	VH127	Fairey Firefly TT4 [200/R]	FAA Museum, RNAS Yeovilton

Serial	Type (code/other identity)	Owner/operator location or fate	Notes
VL348	Avro 652A Anson C19 (G-AVVO)	Newark Air Museum, Winthorpe	
VL349	Avro 652A Anson C19 (G-AWSA) [V7-Q]	Norfolk & Suffolk Avn Mus'm, Flixton	
VM325	Avro 652A Anson C19	Privately owned, Carew Cheriton, Pembrokeshire	
VM360	Avro 652A Anson C19 (G-APHV)	Royal Scottish Mus'm of Flight, E Fortune	
VM684	Slingsby Cadet T2 (BGA791)	Currently not known	
VM687	Slingsby T8 Tutor (BGA794)	Privately owned, Lee-on-Solent	
VM791	Slingsby Cadet TX3 (XA312/8876M)	RAF Manston History Museum	
VN485	VS356 Spitfire F24 (7326M)	Imperial War Museum, Duxford	
VN799	EE Canberra T4 (WJ874/G-CDSX)	AIRBASE, Coventry	
VP293	Avro 696 Shackleton T4 [X] <ff>	Shackleton Preservation Trust, Coventry	
VP519	Avro 652A Anson C19 (G-AVVR) <ff>	Privately owned, Wolverhampton	
VP952	DH104 Devon C2 (8820M)	RAF Museum, Cosford	
VP955	DH104 Devon C2 (G-DVON)	Privately owned, Little Rissington	
VP957	DH104 Devon C2 (8822M) <ff>	No 1137 Sqn ATC, Belfast	
VP967	DH104 Devon C2 (G-KOOL)	Yorkshire Air Museum, Elvington	
VP975	DH104 Devon C2 [M]	Science Museum, Wroughton	
VP981	DH104 Devon C2 (G-DHDV)	Classic Flight, Coventry	
VR137	Westland Wyvern TF1	FAA Museum, stored RNAS Yeovilton	
VR192	Percival P40 Prentice T1 (G-APIT)	Privately owned, Cambs	
VR249	Percival P40 Prentice T1 (G-APIY) [FA-EL]	Newark Air Museum, Winthorpe	
VR259	Percival P40 Prentice T1 (G-APJB) [M]	Air Atlantique Classic Flight, Coventry	
VR930	Hawker Sea Fury FB11 (8382M) [110/Q]	RN Historic Flight, Yeovilton	
VS356	Percival P40 Prentice T1 (G-AOLU)	Privately owned, Montrose	
VS562	Avro 652A Anson T21 (8012M)	Privately owned, Market Drayton	
VS610	Percival P40 Prentice T1 (G-AOKL)[K-L]	The Shuttleworth Collection, Old Warden	
VS618	Percival P40 Prentice T1 (G-AOLK)	RAF Museum, Hendon	
VS623	Percival P40 Prentice T1 (G-AOKZ)[KQ-F]	Midland Air Museum, Coventry	
VT812	DH100 Vampire F3 (7200M) [N]	RAF Museum, Hendon	
VT935	Boulton Paul P111A (VT769)	Midland Air Museum, Coventry	
VT987	Auster AOP6 (G-BKXP)	Privately owned, Thruxton	
VV106	Supermarine 510 (7175M)	FAA Museum, stored RNAS Yeovilton	
VV217	DH100 Vampire FB5 (7323M)	Mosquito Aircraft Museum, stored London Colney	
VV400	EoN Olympia 2 (BGA1697)	Privately owned, Rivar Hill, Wilts	
VV401	EoN Olympia 2 (BGA1125) [99]	Privately owned, Ringmer, E Sussex	
VV612	DH112 Venom FB50 (J-1523/WE402/G-VENI)	Privately owned, Bournemouth	
VV901	Avro 652A Anson T21	Yorkshire Air Museum, Elvington	
VW453	Gloster Meteor T7 (8703M) [Z]	RAF Innsworth, on display	
VW957	DH103 Sea Hornet NF21 <rf>	Privately owned, Chelmsford	
VW993	Beagle A61 Terrier 2 (G-ASCD)	Yorkshire Air Museum, Elvington	
VX113	Auster AOP6 (G-ARNO) [36]	Privately owned, Eggesford	
VX147	Alon A2 Aircoupe (G-AVIL)	Privately owned, Eaglescott	
VX185	EE Canberra B(I)8 (7631M) <ff>	Royal Scottish Mus'm of Flight, E Fortune	
VX250	DH103 Sea Hornet NF21 [48] <rf>	Mosquito Aircraft Museum, London Colney	
VX272	Hawker P.1052 (7174M)	FAA Museum, stored RNAS Yeovilton	
VX275	Slingsby T21B Sedbergh TX1 (8884M/BGA572)	RAF Museum Reserve Collection, Stafford	
VX281	Hawker Sea Fury T20S (G-RNHF) [120/VL]	Naval Aviation Ltd, Yeovilton	
VX573	Vickers Valetta C2 (8389M)	RAF Museum, stored Cosford	
VX580	Vickers Valetta C2 [580]	Norfolk & Suffolk Avn Museum, Flixton	
VX595	WS51 Dragonfly HR1	FAA Museum, RNAS Yeovilton	
VX665	Hawker Sea Fury FB11 <rf>	RN Historic Flight, at BAE Systems Brough	
VX926	Auster T7 (G-ASKJ)	Privately owned, Gamlingay, Cambs	
VX927	Auster T7 (G-ASYG)	Privately owned, Wickenby	
VZ193	DH100 Vampire FB5 <ff>	Privately owned, Hooton Park	
VZ345	Hawker Sea Fury T20S	The Fighter Collection, Duxford	
VZ440	Gloster Meteor F8 (WA984) [X]	Tangmere Military Aviation Museum	
VZ477	Gloster Meteor F8 (7741M) <ff>	Midland Air Museum, Coventry	

Notes	Serial	Type (code/other identity)	Owner/operator location or fate
	VZ608	Gloster Meteor FR9	Newark Air Museum, Winthorpe
	VZ634	Gloster Meteor T7 (8657M)	Newark Air Museum, Winthorpe
	VZ638	Gloster Meteor T7 (G-JETM) [HF]	Gatwick Aviation Museum, Charlwood, Surrey
	VZ728	RS4 Desford Trainer (G-AGOS)	Snibston Discovery Park, stored Coalville
	VZ962	WS51 Dragonfly HR1 [904]	The Helicopter Museum, Weston-super-Mare
	WA346	DH100 Vampire FB5	RAF Museum, stored Cosford
	WA473	VS Attacker F1 [102/J]	FAA Museum, RNAS Yeovilton
	WA576	Bristol 171 Sycamore 3 (7900M/G-ALSS)	Dumfries & Galloway Avn Mus, Dumfries
	WA577	Bristol 171 Sycamore 3 (7718M/G-ALST)	North-East Aircraft Museum, Usworth
	WA591	Gloster Meteor T7 (7917M/G-BWMF) [FMK-Q]	Classic Flight, Coventry
	WA630	Gloster Meteor T7 [69] <ff>	Robertsbridge Aviation Society, Newhaven
	WA634	Gloster Meteor T7/8	RAF Museum, Cosford
	WA638	Gloster Meteor T7(mod)	Martin Baker Aircraft, Chalgrove
	WA662	Gloster Meteor T7	Aeroventure, Doncaster
	WA984	Gloster Meteor F8 [X]	Repainted as VZ440, 2010
	WB188	Hawker Hunter F3 (7154M)	Tangmere Military Aviation Museum
WB188	Hawker Hunter GA11 (WV256/G-BZPB)	AIRBASE, Coventry
WB188	Hawker Hunter GA11 (XF300/G-BZPC)	Privately owned, Melksham, Wilts
	WB440	Fairey Firefly AS6 <ff>	Privately owned, Newton Abbott, Devon
	WB491	Avro 706 Ashton 2 (TS897/G-AJJW) <ff>	Newark Air Museum, Winthorpe
	WB555	DHC1 Chipmunk T10 <ff>	Privately owned, Ellerton
	WB556	DHC1 Chipmunk T10 (fuselage) [O-C,P]	Privately owned, New Milton, Hants
	WB560	DHC1 Chipmunk T10 (comp WG403)	Privately owned, South Molton, Devon
	WB565	DHC1 Chipmunk T10 (G-PVET) [X]	Privately owned, Rendcomb
	WB569	DHC1 Chipmunk T10 (G-BYSJ) [R]	Privately owned, Cotswold Airport
	WB571	DHC1 Chipmunk T10 (G-AOSF) [34]	Privately owned, Trier, Germany
	WB584	DHC1 Chipmunk T10 (comp WG303/7706M)	Newcastle Aviation Academy
	WB585	DHC1 Chipmunk T10 (G-AOSY) [M]	Privately owned, Audley End
	WB588	DHC1 Chipmunk T10 (G-AOTD) [D]	Privately owned, Old Sarum
	WB615	DHC1 Chipmunk T10 (G-BXIA) [E]	Privately owned, Blackpool
	WB624	DHC1 Chipmunk T10	Newark Air Museum, Winthorpe
	WB626	DHC1 Chipmunk T10 <ff>	No 1365 Sqn ATC, Aylesbury
	WB627	DHC1 Chipmunk T10 (9248M) (fuselage) [N]	Dulwich College CCF
	WB654	DHC1 Chipmunk T10 (G-BXGO) [U]	Privately owned, Booker
	WB657	DHC1 Chipmunk T10 [908]	RN Historic Flight, Yeovilton
	WB670	DHC1 Chipmunk T10 (comp WG303) (comp WG303) (8361M)	Newcastle Aviation Academy
	WB671	DHC1 Chipmunk T10 (G-BWTG) [910]	Privately owned, Teuge, The Netherlands
	WB685	DHC1 Chipmunk T10 (comp WP969/G-ATHC)	Mosquito Aircraft Museum, London Colney
	WB685	DHC1 Chipmunk T10 <rf>	North-East Aircraft Museum, stored Usworth
	WB697	DHC1 Chipmunk T10 (G-BXCT) [95]	Privately owned, Wickenby
	WB702	DHC1 Chipmunk T10 (G-AOFE)	Privately owned, Goodwood
	WB703	DHC1 Chipmunk T10 (G-ARMC)	Privately owned, Compton Abbas
	WB711	DHC1 Chipmunk T10 (G-APPM)	Privately owned, Sywell
	WB726	DHC1 Chipmunk T10 (G-AOSK) [E]	Privately owned, Halton
	WB733	DHC1 Chipmunk T10 (comp WG422)	Aeroventure, Doncaster
	WB763	DHC1 Chipmunk T10 (G-BBMR) [14]	Privately owned, Bodmin
	WB922	Slingsby T21B Sedbergh TX1 (BGA4366)	Privately owned, Hullavington
	WB924	Slingsby T21B Sedbergh TX1 (BGA3901)	Privately owned, Dunstable
	WB943	Slingsby T21B Sedbergh TX1 (BGA2941)	Privately owned, Rufforth
	WB944	Slingsby T21B Sedbergh TX1 (BGA3160)	Privately owned, Bicester
	WB945	Slingsby T21B Sedbergh TX1 (BGA1254)	Privately owned, Lasham

Serial	Type (code/other identity)	Owner/operator location or fate	Notes
WB971	Slingsby T21B Sedbergh TX1 (BGA3324)	Privately owned, Tibenham	
WB975	Slingsby T21B Sedbergh TX1 (BGA3288) [FJB]	Privately owned, Shipdham	
WB980	Slingsby T21B Sedbergh TX1 (BGA3290)	Privately owned, Husbands Bosworth	
WB981	Slingsby T21B Sedbergh TX1 (BGA3238)	Privately owned, Keevil	
WD286	DHC1 Chipmunk T10 (G-BBND)	Privately owned, Little Gransden	
WD292	DHC1 Chipmunk T10 (G-BCRX)	Privately owned, White Waltham	
WD293	DHC1 Chipmunk T10 (7645M) <ff>	Privately owned, St Athan	
WD305	DHC1 Chipmunk T10 (G-ARGG)	Repainted in Irish markings as 169, March 2011	
WD310	DHC1 Chipmunk T10 (G-BWUN) [B]	Privately owned, Deanland	
WD319	DHC1 Chipmunk T10 (OY-ATF)	Privately owned, Stauning, Denmark	
WD325	DHC1 Chipmunk T10 [N]	AAC Historic Aircraft Flight, Middle Wallop	
WD331	DHC1 Chipmunk T10 (G-BXDH) [J]	Privately owned, Enstone	
WD355	DHC1 Chipmunk T10 (WD335/G-CBAJ)	Privately owned, Eastleigh	
WD363	DHC1 Chipmunk T10 (G-BCIH) [5]	Privately owned, Audley End	
WD370	DHC1 Chipmunk T10 <ff>	No 225 Sqn ATC, Brighton	
WD373	DHC1 Chipmunk T10 (G-BXDI) [12]	Privately owned, Bicester	
WD377	DHC1 Chipmunk T10 <ff>	Privately owned, Lancs	
WD386	DHC1 Chipmunk T10 (comp WD377)	Privately owned, Lisburn, Northern Ireland	
WD388	DHC1 Chipmunk T10 (D-EPAK) [68]	Quax Flieger, Hamm, Germany	
WD390	DHC1 Chipmunk T10 (G-BWNK) [68]	Privately owned, Wickenby	
WD413	Avro 652A Anson T21 (7881M/G-VROE)	Classic Flight, Coventry	
WD615	Gloster Meteor TT20 (WD646/8189M) [R]	RAF Manston History Museum	
WD686	Gloster Meteor NF11 [S]	Muckleburgh Collection, Weybourne	
WD790	Gloster Meteor NF11 (8743M)<ff>	North-East Aircraft Museum, Usworth	
WD889	Fairey Firefly AS5 (comp VT809)	Privately owned, Newton Abbot, Devon	
WD931	EE Canberra B2 <ff>	RAF Museum, stored Cosford	
WD935	EE Canberra B2 (8440M) <ff>	Aeroventure, Doncaster	
WD954	EE Canberra B2 <ff>	Privately owned, St Mawgan	
WE113	EE Canberra B2 <ff>	Privately owned, Privately owned, Tangmere	
WE122	EE Canberra TT18 [845] <ff>	Blyth Valley Aviation Collection, Walpole, Suffolk	
WE139	EE Canberra PR3 (8369M)	RAF Museum, Hendon	
WE168	EE Canberra PR3 (8049M) <ff>	Norfolk & Suffolk Avn Museum, Flixton	
WE173	EE Canberra PR3 (8740M) <ff>	Robertsbridge Aviation Society, Mayfield	
WE188	EE Canberra T4	Solway Aviation Society, Carlisle	
WE192	EE Canberra T4 <ff>	Blyth Valley Aviation Collection, Walpole, Suffolk	
WE275	DH112 Venom FB50 (J-1601/G-VIDI)	BAE Systems Hawarden, Fire Section	
WE569	Auster T7 (G-ASAJ)	Privately owned, Benson	
WE570	Auster T7 (G-ASBU)	Privately owned, Stonehaven	
WE591	Auster T7 (F-AZTJ)	Privately owned, Toussus-le-Noble, France	
WE600	Auster T7 Antarctic (7602M)	RAF Museum, Cosford	
WE724	Hawker Sea Fury FB11 (VX653/G-BUCM) [062]	The Fighter Collection, Duxford	
WE982	Slingsby T30B Prefect TX1 (8781M)	RAF Museum, stored Cosford	
WE987	Slingsby T30B Prefect TX1 (BGA2517)	Aeroventure, Doncaster	
WE990	Slingsby T30B Prefect TX1 (BGA2583)	Privately owned, stored Beds	
WE992	Slingsby T30B Prefect TX1 (BGA2692)	Privately owned, Hullavington	
WF118	Percival P57 Sea Prince T1 (G-DACA)	Gatwick Aviation Museum, Charlwood, Surrey	
WF122	Percival P57 Sea Prince T1 [575/CU]	Aeroventure, Doncaster	
WF128	Percival P57 Sea Prince T1 (8611M)	Norfolk & Suffolk Avn Museum, Flixton	
WF137	Percival P57 Sea Prince C1	Privately owned, Booker	
WF145	Hawker Sea Hawk F1 <ff>	Privately owned, Newton Abbot, Devon	
WF219	Hawker Sea Hawk F1 <rf>	FAA Museum, stored RNAS Yeovilton	
WF225	Hawker Sea Hawk F1 [CU]	RNAS Culdrose, at main gate	
WF259	Hawker Sea Hawk F2 [171/A]	Royal Scottish Mus'm of Flight, E Fortune	
WF369	Vickers Varsity T1 [F]	Newark Air Museum, Winthorpe	

Notes	Serial	Type (code/other identity)	Owner/operator location or fate
	WF372	Vickers Varsity T1 [A]	Brooklands Museum, Weybridge
	WF408	Vickers Varsity T1 (8395M) <ff>	Privately owned, Ashford, Kent
	WF643	Gloster Meteor F8 [P]	Norfolk & Suffolk Avn Museum, Flixton
	WF714	Gloster Meteor F8 (WK914)	Sold to Malta, April 2011
	WF784	Gloster Meteor T7 (7895M)	Gloucestershire Avn Coll, stored Gloucester
	WF825	Gloster Meteor T7 (8359M) [A]	Montrose Air Station Heritage Centre
	WF911	EE Canberra B2 [CO] <ff>	Gloster Aviation Club, Gloucester
	WF922	EE Canberra PR3	Midland Air Museum, Coventry
	WG303	DHC1 Chipmunk T10 (8208M) <ff>	Privately owned, Stamford
	WG308	DHC1 Chipmunk T10 (G-BYHL) [8]	Privately owned, Syerston
	WG316	DHC1 Chipmunk T10 (G-BCAH)	Privately owned, Church Fenton
	WG321	DHC1 Chipmunk T10 (G-DHCC)	Privately owned, Wevelgem, Belgium
	WG348	DHC1 Chipmunk T10 (G-BBMV)	Privately owned, Biggin Hill
	WG350	DHC1 Chipmunk T10 (G-BPAL)	Privately owned, Cascais, Portugal
	WG362	DHC1 Chipmunk T10 (8437M/8630M/WX643) <ff>	No 1094 Sqn ATC, Ely
	WG407	DHC1 Chipmunk T10 (G-BWMX) [67]	Privately owned, Croydon, Cambs
	WG418	DHC1 Chipmunk T10 (8209M/G-ATDY) <ff>	No 1940 Sqn ATC, Levenshulme, Gr Manchester
	WG419	DHC1 Chipmunk T10 (8206M) <ff>	Sywell Aviation Museum
	WG422	DHC1 Chipmunk T10 (8394M/G-BFAX) [16]	Privately owned, Eggesford
	WG432	DHC1 Chipmunk T10 [L]	Museum of Army Flying, Middle Wallop
	WG458	DHC1 Chipmunk T10 (N458BG) [2]	Privately owned, Breighton
	WG465	DHC1 Chipmunk T10 (G-BCEY)	Privately owned, White Waltham
	WG469	DHC1 Chipmunk T10 (G-BWJY) [72]	Privately owned, Sligo, Eire
	WG471	DHC1 Chipmunk T10 (8210M) <ff>	Thameside Aviation Museum, East Tilbury
	WG472	DHC1 Chipmunk T10 (G-AOTY)	Privately owned, Bryngwyn Bach, Clwyd
	WG477	DHC1 Chipmunk T10 (8362M/G-ATDP) <ff>	No 281 Sqn ATC, Birkdale, Merseyside
	WG486	DHC1 Chipmunk T10 [G]	RAF BBMF, Coningsby
	WG498	Slingsby T21B Sedbergh TX1 (BGA3245)	Privately owned, Aston Down
	WG511	Avro 696 Shackleton T4 (fuselage)	Flambards Village Theme Park, Helston
	WG655	Hawker Sea Fury T20 (NX20MD) [910/GN]	The Fighter Collection, Duxford
	WG719	WS51 Dragonfly HR5 (G-BRMA)	The Helicopter Museum, Weston-super-Mare
	WG724	WS51 Dragonfly HR5 [932]	North-East Aircraft Museum, Usworth
	WG751	WS51 Dragonfly HR5 [710/GJ]	World Naval Base, Chatham
	WG760	EE P1A (7755M)	RAF Museum, Cosford
	WG763	EE P1A (7816M)	Museum of Science & Industry, Manchester
	WG768	Short SB5 (8005M)	RAF Museum, Cosford
	WG774	BAC 221	Science Museum, at FAA Museum, RNAS Yeovilton
	WG777	Fairey FD2 (7986M)	RAF Museum, Cosford
	WG789	EE Canberra B2/6 <ff>	Norfolk & Suffolk Avn Museum, Flixton
	WH132	Gloster Meteor T7 (7906M) [J]	RAF Leconfield, for display
	WH166	Gloster Meteor T7 (8052M) [A]	Privately owned, Birlingham, Worcs
	WH291	Gloster Meteor F8	Privately owned, Liverpool Airport
	WH301	Gloster Meteor F8 (7930M) [T]	RAF Museum, Hendon
	WH364	Gloster Meteor F8 (8169M)	Gloucestershire Avn Coll, stored Gloucester
	WH453	Gloster Meteor D16 [L]	Bentwaters Cold War Air Museum
	WH646	EE Canberra T17A <ff>	Midland Air Museum, Coventry
	WH657	EE Canberra B2 <ff>	Brenzett Aeronautical Museum
	WH725	EE Canberra B2	Imperial War Museum, Duxford
	WH734	EE Canberra B2(mod) <ff>	Privately owned, Pershore
	WH739	EE Canberra B2 <ff>	No 2475 Sqn ATC, Ammanford, Dyfed
	WH740	EE Canberra T17 (8762M) [K]	East Midlands Airport Aeropark
	WH773	EE Canberra PR7 (8696M)	Gatwick Aviation Museum, Charlwood, Surrey
	WH775	EE Canberra PR7 (8128M/8868M) <ff>	Privately owned, Welshpool
	WH779	EE Canberra PR7 <ff>	Newark Air Museum, Winthorpe

Serial	Type (code/other identity)	Owner/operator location or fate	Notes
WH779	EE Canberra PR7 [BP] <rf>	RAF, stored Shawbury	
WH792	EE Canberra PR7 (WH791/8165M/ 8176M/8187M)	Newark Air Museum, Winthorpe	
WH798	EE Canberra PR7 (8130M) <ff>	Privately owned, Kesgrave, Suffolk	
WH840	EE Canberra T4 (8350M)	Privately owned, Flixton	
WH846	EE Canberra T4	Yorkshire Air Museum, Elvington	
WH850	EE Canberra T4 <ff>	Privately owned, Narborough	
WH863	EE Canberra T17 (8693M) <ff>	Newark Air Museum, Winthorpe	
WH876	EE Canberra B2(mod) <ff>	Boscombe Down Aviation Collection	
WH887	EE Canberra TT18 [847] <ff>	Privately owned, Upwood, Cambs	
WH903	EE Canberra B2 <ff>	Yorkshire Air Museum, Elvington	
WH904	EE Canberra T19	Newark Air Museum, Winthorpe	
WH953	EE Canberra B6(mod) <ff>	Blyth Valley Aviation Collection, Walpole, Suffolk	
WH957	EE Canberra E15 (8869M) <ff>	Lincolnshire Avn Heritage Centre, East Kirkby	
WH960	EE Canberra B15 (8344M) <ff>	Rolls-Royce Heritage Trust, Derby	
WH964	EE Canberra E15 (8870M) <ff>	Privately owned, Lewes	
WH984	EE Canberra B15 (8101M) <ff>	City of Norwich Aviation Museum	
WH991	WS51 Dragonfly HR3	Yorkshire Helicopter Preservation Group, Elvington	
WJ231	Hawker Sea Fury FB11 (WE726) [115/O]	FAA Museum, RNAS Yeovilton	
WJ306	Slingsby T21B Sedbergh TX1 (BGA3240)	Privately owned, Weston-on-the-Green	
WJ306	Slingsby T21B Sedbergh TX1 (WB957/BGA2720)	Privately owned, Parham Park, Sussex	
WJ358	Auster AOP6 (G-ARYD)	Museum of Army Flying, Middle Wallop	
WJ368	Auster AOP6 (G-ASZX)	Privately owned, Eggesford	
WJ404	Auster AOP6 (G-ASOI)	Privately owned, Bidford-on-Avon, Warks	
WJ476	Vickers Valetta T3 <ff>	Aeroventure, Doncaster	
WJ565	EE Canberra T17 (8871M) <ff>	Aeroventure, Doncaster	
WJ567	EE Canberra B2 <ff>	Privately owned, Houghton, Cambs	
WJ576	EE Canberra T17 <ff>	Boulton Paul Association, Wolverhampton	
WJ633	EE Canberra T17 <ff>	City of Norwich Aviation Museum	
WJ639	EE Canberra TT18 [39]	North-East Aircraft Museum, Usworth	
WJ676	EE Canberra B2 (7796M) <ff>	*To Australia, 2011*	
WJ677	EE Canberra B2 <ff>	Privately owned, Redruth	
WJ717	EE Canberra TT18 (9052M) <ff>	RAF St Athan, Fire Section	
WJ721	EE Canberra TT18 [21] <ff>	No 2405 Det Flt ATC, Gairloch	
WJ731	EE Canberra B2T [BK] <ff>	Privately owned, Golders Green	
WJ775	EE Canberra B6 (8581M) <ff>	Privately owned, Upwood, Cambs	
WJ821	EE Canberra PR7 (8668M)	Army, Bassingbourn, on display	
WJ865	EE Canberra T4	Boscombe Down Aviation Collection	
WJ866	EE Canberra T4	*Currently not known*	
WJ880	EE Canberra T4 (8491M) <ff>	Dumfries & Galloway Avn Mus, Dumfries	
WJ903	Vickers Varsity T1 <ff>	Aeroventure, Doncaster	
WJ945	Vickers Varsity T1 (G-BEDV) [21]	Imperial War Museum, Duxford	
WJ975	EE Canberra T19 <ff>	Aeroventure, Doncaster	
WJ992	EE Canberra T4	Bournemouth Airport Fire Section	
WK001	Thales Watchkeeper 450 UAV (4X-USC)	Thales, for Army	
WK002	Thales Watchkeeper 450 UAV	Thales, for Army	
WK003	Thales Watchkeeper 450 UAV	Thales, for Army	
WK004	Thales Watchkeeper 450 UAV	Thales, for Army	
WK005	Thales Watchkeeper 450 UAV	Thales, for Army	
WK006	Thales Watchkeeper 450 UAV	Thales, for Army	
WK007	Thales Watchkeeper 450 UAV	Thales, for Army	
WK008	Thales Watchkeeper 450 UAV	Thales, for Army	
WK009	Thales Watchkeeper 450 UAV	Thales, for Army	
WK010	Thales Watchkeeper 450 UAV	Thales, for Army	
WK011	Thales Watchkeeper 450 UAV	Thales, for Army	

Notes	Serial	Type (code/other identity)	Owner/operator location or fate
	WK012	Thales Watchkeeper 450 UAV	Thales, for Army
	WK013	Thales Watchkeeper 450 UAV	Thales, for Army
	WK014	Thales Watchkeeper 450 UAV	Thales, for Army
	WK015	Thales Watchkeeper 450 UAV	Thales, for Army
	WK016	Thales Watchkeeper 450 UAV	Thales, for Army
	WK017	Thales Watchkeeper 450 UAV	Thales, for Army
	WK018	Thales Watchkeeper 450 UAV	Thales, for Army
	WK019	Thales Watchkeeper 450 UAV	Thales, for Army
	WK020	Thales Watchkeeper 450 UAV	Thales, for Army
	WK021	Thales Watchkeeper 450 UAV	Thales, for Army
	WK022	Thales Watchkeeper 450 UAV	Thales, for Army
	WK023	Thales Watchkeeper 450 UAV	Thales, for Army
	WK024	Thales Watchkeeper 450 UAV	Thales, for Army
	WK025	Thales Watchkeeper 450 UAV	Thales, for Army
	WK026	Thales Watchkeeper 450 UAV	Thales, for Army
	WK027	Thales Watchkeeper 450 UAV	Thales, for Army
	WK028	Thales Watchkeeper 450 UAV	Thales, for Army
	WK029	Thales Watchkeeper 450 UAV	Thales, for Army
	WK030	Thales Watchkeeper 450 UAV	Thales, for Army
	WK031	Thales Watchkeeper 450 UAV	Thales, for Army
	WK032	Thales Watchkeeper 450 UAV	Thales, for Army
	WK033	Thales Watchkeeper 450 UAV	Thales, for Army
	WK034	Thales Watchkeeper 450 UAV	Thales, for Army
	WK035	Thales Watchkeeper 450 UAV	Thales, for Army
	WK036	Thales Watchkeeper 450 UAV	Thales, for Army
	WK037	Thales Watchkeeper 450 UAV	Thales, for Army
	WK038	Thales Watchkeeper 450 UAV	Thales, for Army
	WK039	Thales Watchkeeper 450 UAV	Thales, for Army
	WK040	Thales Watchkeeper 450 UAV	Thales, for Army
	WK060	Thales Watchkeeper 450 UAV	Thales, for Army
	WK102	EE Canberra T17 (8780M) <ff>	Privately owned, Welshpool
	WK118	EE Canberra TT18 <ff>	Hawker Hunter Aviation Ltd, Scampton
	WK122	EE Canberra TT18 <ff>	Lakes Lightnings, Spark Bridge, Cumbria
	WK124	EE Canberra TT18 (9093M) [CR]	MoD DFTDC, Manston
	WK126	EE Canberra TT18 (N2138J) [843]	Gloucestershire Avn Coll, stored Gloucester
	WK127	EE Canberra TT18 (8985M) <ff>	Privately owned, Peterborough
	WK146	EE Canberra B2 <ff>	Gatwick Aviation Museum, Charlwood, Surrey
	WK163	EE Canberra B2/6 (G-BVWC)	AIRBASE, Coventry
	WK198	VS Swift F4 (7428M) (fuselage)	Brooklands Museum, Weybridge
	WK275	VS Swift F4	Privately owned, Upper Hill, nr Leominster
	WK277	VS Swift FR5 (7719M) [N]	Newark Air Museum, Winthorpe
	WK281	VS Swift FR5 (7712M) [S]	Tangmere Military Aviation Museum
	WK393	DH112 Venom FB1 <ff>	Aeroventure, stored Doncaster
	WK436	DH112 Venom FB50 (J-1614/G-VENM)	Classic Flight, Coventry
	WK512	DHC1 Chipmunk T10 (G-BXIM) [A]	Privately owned, South Cerney
	WK514	DHC1 Chipmunk T10 (G-BBMO)	Privately owned, Wellesbourne Mountford
	WK517	DHC1 Chipmunk T10 (G-ULAS)	Privately owned, Denham
	WK518	DHC1 Chipmunk T10 [K]	RAF BBMF, Coningsby
	WK522	DHC1 Chipmunk T10 (G-BCOU)	Privately owned, Duxford
	WK549	DHC1 Chipmunk T10 (G-BTWF)	Privately owned, Sturgate
	WK562	DHC1 Chipmunk T10 (F-AZUR) [91]	Privately owned, La Baule, France
	WK570	DHC1 Chipmunk T10 (8211M) <ff>	No 424 Sqn ATC, Solent Sky, Southampton
	WK576	DHC1 Chipmunk T10 (8357M) <ff>	No 1206 Sqn ATC, Lichfield
	WK577	DHC1 Chipmunk T10 (G-BCYM)	Privately owned, Oaksey Park
	WK584	DHC1 Chipmunk T10 (7556M) <ff>	No 511 Sqn ATC, Ramsey, Cambs
	WK585	DHC1 Chipmunk T10 (9265M/G-BZGA)	Privately owned, Duxford
	WK586	DHC1 Chipmunk T10 (G-BXGX) [V]	Privately owned, Slinfold
	WK590	DHC1 Chipmunk T10 (G-BWVZ) [69]	Privately owned, Spanhoe

Serial	Type (code/other identity)	Owner/operator location or fate	Notes
WK608	DHC1 Chipmunk T10 [906]	RN Historic Flight, Yeovilton	
WK609	DHC1 Chipmunk T10 (G-BXDN) [93]	Privately owned, Booker	
WK611	DHC1 Chipmunk T10 (G-ARWB)	Privately owned, Thruxton	
WK620	DHC1 Chipmunk T10 [T] (fuselage)	Privately owned, Twyford, Bucks	
WK622	DHC1 Chipmunk T10 (G-BCZH)	Privately owned, Horsford	
WK624	DHC1 Chipmunk T10 (G-BWHI)	Privately owned, Woodvale	
WK626	DHC1 Chipmunk T10 (8213M) <ff>	Aeroventure, stored Doncaster	
WK628	DHC1 Chipmunk T10 (G-BBMW)	Privately owned, Goodwood	
WK630	DHC1 Chipmunk T10 (G-BXDG)	Privately owned, Felthorpe	
WK633	DHC1 Chipmunk T10 (G-BXEC) [A]	Privately owned, Redhill	
WK635	DHC1 Chipmunk T10 (G-HFRH)	Privately owned, Henley-on-Thames	
WK638	DHC1 Chipmunk T10 (G-BWJZ) (fuselage)	Privately owned, South Marston, Swindon	
WK640	DHC1 Chipmunk T10 (G-BWUV) [C]	Privately owned, Bagby	
WK642	DHC1 Chipmunk T10 (G-BXDP) [94]	Privately owned, Kilrush, Eire	
WK654	Gloster Meteor F8 (8092M) [B]	City of Norwich Aviation Museum	
WK800	Gloster Meteor D16 [Z]	Boscombe Down Aviation Collection	
WK864	Gloster Meteor F8 (WL168/7750M) [C]	Yorkshire Air Museum, Elvington	
WK935	Gloster Meteor Prone Pilot (7869M)	RAF Museum, Cosford	
WK991	Gloster Meteor F8 (7825M)	Imperial War Museum, Duxford	
WL131	Gloster Meteor F8 (7751M) <ff>	Aeroventure, Doncaster	
WL181	Gloster Meteor F8 [X]	North-East Aircraft Museum, Usworth	
WL332	Gloster Meteor T7 [888]	Privately owned, Long Marston	
WL345	Gloster Meteor T7	St Leonard's Motors, Hollington, E Sussex	
WL349	Gloster Meteor T7	Gloucestershire Airport, Staverton, on display	
WL375	Gloster Meteor T7(mod)	Dumfries & Galloway Avn Mus, Dumfries	
WL405	Gloster Meteor T7	Hooton Park Trust	
WL419	Gloster Meteor T7(mod)	Martin Baker Aircraft, Chalgrove	
WL505	DH100 Vampire FB9 (7705M/G-FBIX)	Currently not known	
WL626	Vickers Varsity T1 (G-BHDD) [P]	East Midlands Airport Aeropark	
WL627	Vickers Varsity T1 (8488M) [D] <ff>	Privately owned, Preston, E Yorkshire	
WL679	Vickers Varsity T1 (9155M)	RAF Museum, Cosford	
WL732	BP P108 Sea Balliol T21	RAF Museum, stored Cosford	
WL795	Avro 696 Shackleton MR2C (8753M) [T]	RAF St Mawgan, on display	
WL798	Avro 696 Shackleton MR2C (8114M) <ff>	Privately owned, Elgin	
WM145	AW Meteor NF11 <ff>	Privately owned, Over Dinsdale, N Yorks	
WM167	AW Meteor NF11 (G-LOSM)	Classic Flight, Coventry	
WM224	AW Meteor TT20 (WM311/8177M)	East Midlands Airport Aeropark	
WM267	AW Meteor NF11 <ff>	City of Norwich Aviation Museum	
WM292	AW Meteor TT20 [841]	FAA Museum, stored RNAS Yeovilton	
WM366	AW Meteor NF13 (4X-FNA) (comp VZ462)	Gloucestershire Avn. Coll, stored Gloucester	
WM367	AW Meteor NF13 <ff>	East Midlands Airport Aeropark	
WM571	DH112 Sea Venom FAW21 [VL]	Solent Sky, stored Romsey	
WM729	DH113 Vampire NF10 <ff>	Mosquito Aircraft Museum, stored London Colney	
WM913	Hawker Sea Hawk FB5 (8162M) [456/J]	Newark Air Museum, Winthorpe	
WM961	Hawker Sea Hawk FB5 [J]	Caernarfon Air World	
WM969	Hawker Sea Hawk FB5 [10/Z]	Imperial War Museum, Duxford	
WN105	Hawker Sea Hawk FB3 (WF299/8164M)	Privately owned, Birlingham, Worcs	
WN108	Hawker Sea Hawk FB5 [033]	Ulster Aviation Society, Long Kesh	
WN149	BP P108 Balliol T2 [AT]	Boulton Paul Association, Wolverhampton	
WN411	Fairey Gannet AS1 (fuselage)	Privately owned, Sholing, Hants	
WN493	WS51 Dragonfly HR5	FAA Museum, RNAS Yeovilton	
WN499	WS51 Dragonfly HR5	Aeroventure, Doncaster	
WN516	BP P108 Balliol T2 <ff>	Staffs Aircraft Restoration Team, Baxterley	
WN534	BP P108 Balliol T2 <ff>	Staffs Aircraft Restoration Team, Baxterley	
WN890	Hawker Hunter F2 <ff>	Air Defence Collection, Boscombe Down	

Notes	Serial	Type (code/other identity)	Owner/operator location or fate
	WN904	Hawker Hunter F2 (7544M)	RE 39 Regt, Waterbeach, on display
	WN907	Hawker Hunter F2 (7416M) <ff>	Robertsbridge Aviation Society, Newhaven
	WN957	Hawker Hunter F5 <ff>	Privately owned, Stockport
	WP185	Hawker Hunter F5 (7583M)	Privately owned, Great Dunmow, Essex
	WP190	Hawker Hunter F5	Tangmere Military Aviation Museum
		(7582M/8473M/WP180) [K]	
	WP255	DH113 Vampire NF10 <ff>	Aeroventure, stored Doncaster
	WP269	EoN Eton TX1 (BGA3214)	Privately owned, stored Keevil
	WP270	EoN Eton TX1 (8598M)	RAF Museum Reserve Collection, Stafford
	WP308	Percival P57 Sea Prince T1	Gatwick Aviation Museum, Charlwood, Surrey
		(G-GACA) [572/CU]	
	WP313	Percival P57 Sea Prince T1 [568/CU]	FAA Museum, stored RNAS Yeovilton
	WP314	Percival P57 Sea Prince T1	Privately owned, Carlisle Airport
		(8634M) [573/CU]	
	WP321	Percival P57 Sea Prince T1	Privately owned, Bournemouth
		(G-BRFC) [750/CU]	
	WP772	DHC1 Chipmunk T10 [Q] (wreck)	RAF Manston History Museum
	WP784	DHC1 Chipmunk T10 <ff>	East Midlands Airport Aeropark
	WP788	DHC1 Chipmunk T10 (G-BCHL)	Privately owned, Sleap
	WP790	DHC1 Chipmunk T10 (G-BBNC) [T]	Mosquito Aircraft Museum, London Colney
	WP795	DHC1 Chipmunk T10 (G-BVZZ) [901]	Privately owned, Lee-on-Solent
	WP800	DHC1 Chipmunk T10 (G-BCXN) [2]	Privately owned, Halton
	WP803	DHC1 Chipmunk T10 (G-HAPY) [G]	Privately owned, Booker
	WP805	DHC1 Chipmunk T10 (G-MAJR) [D]	Privately owned, Lee-on-Solent
	WP808	DHC1 Chipmunk T10 (G-BDEU)	Privately owned, Prestwick
	WP809	DHC1 Chipmunk T10 (G-BVTX) [78]	Privately owned, Husbands Bosworth
	WP835	DHC1 Chipmunk T10 (D-ERTY)	Privately owned, Teuge, The Netherlands
	WP840	DHC1 Chipmunk T10 (G-BXDM) [9]	Privately owned, Reims, France
	WP844	DHC1 Chipmunk T10 (G-BWOX) [85]	Privately owned, Shobdon
	WP857	DHC1 Chipmunk T10 (G-BDRJ) [24]	Privately owned, Prestwick
	WP859	DHC1 Chipmunk T10 (G-BXCP) [E]	Privately owned, Fishburn
	WP860	DHC1 Chipmunk T10 (G-BXDA) [6]	Privately owned, Kirknewton
	WP863	DHC1 Chipmunk T10 (8360M/G-ATJI) <ff>	No 1011 Sqn ATC, Boscombe Down
	WP869	DHC1 Chipmunk T10 (8215M) <ff>	Mosquito Aircraft Museum, London Colney
	WP870	DHC1 Chipmunk T10 (G-BCOI) [12]	Privately owned, Rayne Hall Farm, Essex
	WP896	DHC1 Chipmunk T10 (G-BWVY)	Privately owned, RAF Halton
	WP901	DHC1 Chipmunk T10 (G-BWNT) [B]	Privately owned, East Midlands Airport
	WP903	DHC1 Chipmunk T10 (G-BCGC)	Privately owned, Henlow
	WP912	DHC1 Chipmunk T10 (8467M)	RAF Museum, Cosford
	WP921	DHC1 Chipmunk T10 (G-ATJJ) <ff>	Privately owned, Brooklands
	WP925	DHC1 Chipmunk T10 (G-BXHA) [C]	Privately owned, Seppe, The Netherlands
	WP927	DHC1 Chipmunk T10 (8216M/G-ATJK) <ff>	Privately owned, St Neots, Cambs
	WP928	DHC1 Chipmunk T10 (G-BXGM) [D]	Privately owned, Shoreham
	WP929	DHC1 Chipmunk T10 (G-BXCV) [F]	Privately owned, Duxford
	WP930	DHC1 Chipmunk T10 (G-BXHF) [J]	Privately owned, Redhill
	WP962	DHC1 Chipmunk T10 (9287M) [C]	RAF Museum, Hendon
	WP971	DHC1 Chipmunk T10 (G-ATHD)	Privately owned, Denham
	WP977	DHC1 Chipmunk T10 (G-BHRD) <ff>	Privately owned, Yateley, Hants
	WP983	DHC1 Chipmunk T10 (G-BXNN) [B]	Privately owned, Eggesford
	WP984	DHC1 Chipmunk T10 (G-BWTO) [H]	Privately owned, Little Gransden
	WR360	DH112 Venom FB50 (J-1626/G-DHSS) [K]	Privately owned, Bournemouth
	WR410	DH112 Venom FB50	Privately owned, Bournemouth
		(J-1539/G-DHUU/WE410)	
	WR410	DH112 Venom FB54 (J-1790/G-BLKA) [N]	Mosquito Aircraft Museum, London Colney
	WR421	DH112 Venom FB50 (J-1611/G-DHTT)	Privately owned, Bournemouth
	WR470	DH112 Venom FB50 (J-1542/G-DHVM)	Classic Flight, Coventry

Serial	Type (code/other identity)	Owner/operator location or fate	Notes
WR539	DH112 Venom FB4 (8399M) <ff>	Mosquito Aircraft Museum, stored London Colney	
WR960	Avro 696 Shackleton AEW2 (8772M)	Museum of Science & Industry, Manchester	
WR963	Avro 696 Shackleton AEW2 [B-M]	AIRBASE, Coventry	
WR971	Avro 696 Shackleton MR3 (8119M) [Q]	Fenland & W Norfolk Aviation Museum, Wisbech	
WR974	Avro 696 Shackleton MR3 (8117M) [K]	Gatwick Aviation Museum, Charlwood, Surrey	
WR977	Avro 696 Shackleton MR3 (8186M) [B]	Newark Air Museum, Winthorpe	
WR982	Avro 696 Shackleton MR3 (8106M) [J]	Gatwick Aviation Museum, Charlwood, Surrey	
WR985	Avro 696 Shackleton MR3 (8103M) [H]	Privately owned, Long Marston	
WS103	Gloster Meteor T7 [709]	FAA Museum, stored RNAS Yeovilton	
WS692	Gloster Meteor NF12 (7605M) [C]	Newark Air Museum, Winthorpe	
WS726	Gloster Meteor NF14 (7960M) [H]	No 1855 Sqn ATC, Royton, Gr Manchester	
WS739	Gloster Meteor NF14 (7961M)	Newark Air Museum, Winthorpe	
WS760	Gloster Meteor NF14 (7964M)	East Midlands Airport Aeropark	
WS776	Gloster Meteor NF14 (7716M) [K]	Bournemouth Aviation Museum	
WS788	Gloster Meteor NF14 (7967M) [Z]	Yorkshire Air Museum, Elvington	
WS792	Gloster Meteor NF14 (7965M) [K]	Brighouse Bay Caravan Park, Borgue, D&G	
WS807	Gloster Meteor NF14 (7973M) [N]	Gloucestershire Avn Coll, stored Gloucester	
WS832	Gloster Meteor NF14	Solway Aviation Society, Carlisle	
WS838	Gloster Meteor NF14 [D]	Midland Air Museum, Coventry	
WS843	Gloster Meteor NF14 (7937M) [J]	RAF Museum, Cosford	
WT121	Douglas Skyraider AEW1 [415/CU]	FAA Museum, stored RNAS Yeovilton	
WT205	EE Canberra B15 <ff>	RAF Manston History Museum	
WT308	EE Canberra B(I)6	RN, Predannack Fire School	
WT309	EE Canberra B(I)6 <ff>	Farnborough Air Sciences Trust, Farnborough	
WT319	EE Canberra B(I)6 <ff>	Aeroventure, Doncaster	
WT333	EE Canberra B6(mod) (G-BVXC)	Privately owned, Bruntingthorpe	
WT339	EE Canberra B(I)8 (8198M)	RAF Barkston Heath Fire Section	
WT486	EE Canberra T4 (8102M) <ff>	Privately owned, Newtownards	
WT507	EE Canberra PR7 (8131M/8548M) [44] <ff>	No 384 Sqn ATC, Mansfield	
WT520	EE Canberra PR7 (8094M/8184M) <ff>	No 967 Sqn ATC, Warton	
WT525	EE Canberra T22 [855] <ff>	Privately owned, St Mawgan	
WT532	EE Canberra PR7 (8728M/8890M) <ff>	Bournemouth Aviation Museum	
WT534	EE Canberra PR7 (8549M) [43] <ff>	Privately owned, Upwood	
WT536	EE Canberra PR7 (8063M) <ff>	Privately owned, Shirrell Heath, Hants	
WT537	EE Canberra PR7	*Sold to Greece, 2011*	
WT555	Hawker Hunter F1 (7499M)	Vanguard Haulage, Greenford, London	
WT569	Hawker Hunter F1 (7491M)	No 2117 Sqn ATC, Kenfig Hill, Mid-Glamorgan	
WT612	Hawker Hunter F1 (7496M)	RAF Henlow, on display	
WT619	Hawker Hunter F1 (7525M)	RAF Museum, stored Cosford	
WT648	Hawker Hunter F1 (7530M) <ff>	Air Defence Collection, Boscombe Down	
WT651	Hawker Hunter F1 (7532M) [C]	Newark Air Museum, Winthorpe	
WT660	Hawker Hunter F1 (7421M) [C]	Highland Aviation Museum, Inverness	
WT680	Hawker Hunter F1 (7533M) [J]	Privately owned, Holbeach, Lincs	
WT684	Hawker Hunter F1 (7422M) <ff>	Privately owned, Olney, Bucks	
WT694	Hawker Hunter F1 (7510M)	Caernarfon Air World	
WT711	Hawker Hunter GA11 [833/DD]	Lakes Lightnings, Spark Bridge, Cumbria	
WT720	Hawker Hunter F51 (RDAF E-408/8565M) [B]	Privately owned, North Scarle, Lincs	
WT722	Hawker Hunter T8C (G-BWGN) [878/VL]	AIRBASE, Coventry	
WT741	Hawker Hunter GA11 [791] <ff>	Privately owned, Doncaster	
WT744	Hawker Hunter GA11 [868/VL]	Privately owned, Ilfracombe	
WT804	Hawker Hunter GA11 [831/DD]	FETC, Moreton-in-Marsh, Glos	
WT806	Hawker Hunter GA11	Privately owned, Bruntingthorpe	
WT859	Supermarine 544 <ff>	Boscombe Down Aviation Collection	
WT867	Slingsby T31B Cadet TX3	Privately owned, Eaglescott	

Notes	Serial	Type (code/other identity)	Owner/operator location or fate
	WT877	Slingsby T31B Cadet TX3	Staffs Aircraft Restoration Team, Baxterley
	WT900	Slingsby T31B Cadet TX3 (BGA33372)	Privately owned, Lee-on-Solent
	WT905	Slingsby T31B Cadet TX3	Privately owned, Keevil
	WT908	Slingsby T31B Cadet TX3 (BGA3487)	Privately owned, Dunstable
	WT910	Slingsby T31B Cadet TX3 (BGA3953)	Privately owned, Llantisilio
	WT914	Slingsby T31B Cadet TX3 (BGA3194) (fuselage)	Privately owned, Tibenham
	WT933	Bristol 171 Sycamore 3 (G-ALSW/7709M)	Newark Air Museum, Winthorpe
	WV106	Douglas Skyraider AEW1 [427/C]	FAA Museum, stored RNAS Yeovilton
	WV198	Sikorsky S55 Whirlwind HAR21 (G-BJWY) [K]	Solway Aviation Society, Carlisle
	WV318	Hawker Hunter T7B (9236M/G-FFOX)	WV318 Group, Cotswold Airport
	WV322	Hawker Hunter T8C (G-BZSE/9096M) [Y]	Hunter Flying Ltd, Exeter
	WV332	Hawker Hunter F4 (7673M) <ff>	Tangmere Military Aircraft Museum
	WV372	Hawker Hunter T7 (G-BXFI) [R]	Privately owned, St Athan
	WV381	Hawker Hunter GA11 [732] <ff>	Privately owned, Chiltern Park, Wallingford
	WV382	Hawker Hunter GA11 [830/VL]	East Midlands Airport Aeropark
	WV383	Hawker Hunter T7	Farnborough Air Sciences Trust, Farnborough
	WV396	Hawker Hunter T8C (9249M) [91]	RAF Valley, at main gate
	WV486	Percival P56 Provost T1 (7694M) [N-D]	Privately owned, Thatcham, Berks
	WV493	Percival P56 Provost T1 (G-BDYG/7696M) [29]	Royal Scottish Mus'm of Flight, stored E Fortune
	WV499	Percival P56 Provost T1 (G-BZRF/7698M) [P-G]	Privately owned, Westonzoyland, Somerset
	WV514	Percival P56 Provost T51 (G-BLIW) [N-C]	Privately owned, Shoreham
	WV562	Percival P56 Provost T1 (7606M) [P-C]	RAF Museum, Cosford
	WV605	Percival P56 Provost T1 [T-B]	Norfolk & Suffolk Avn Museum, Flixton
	WV606	Percival P56 Provost T1 (7622M)[P-B]	Newark Air Museum, Winthorpe
	WV679	Percival P56 Provost T1 (7615M) [O-J]	Wellesbourne Wartime Museum
	WV705	Percival P66 Pembroke C1 <ff>	Privately owned, Awbridge, Hants
	WV740	Percival P66 Pembroke C1 (G-BNPH)	Privately owned, Bournemouth
	WV746	Percival P66 Pembroke C1 (8938M)	RAF Museum, Cosford
	WV781	Bristol 171 Sycamore HR12 (G-ALTD/7839M) <ff>	Caernarfon Air World
	WV783	Bristol 171 Sycamore HR12 (G-ALSP/7841M)	RAF Museum, Hendon
	WV787	EE Canberra B2/8 (8799M)	Newark Air Museum, Winthorpe
	WV795	Hawker Sea Hawk FGA6 (8151M)	Privately owned, Dunsfold
	WV797	Hawker Sea Hawk FGA6 (8155M) [491/J]	Midland Air Museum, Coventry
	WV798	Hawker Sea Hawk FGA6 [026/CU]	Privately owned, Booker
	WV838	Hawker Sea Hawk FGA4 [182] <ff>	Norfolk & Suffolk Avn Museum, Flixton
	WV856	Hawker Sea Hawk FGA6 [163]	FAA Museum, RNAS Yeovilton
	WV903	Hawker Sea Hawk FGA4 (8153M) [128] <ff>	Privately owned, Mold, Flintshire
	WV903	Hawker Sea Hawk FGA4 (8153M) [C] <rf>	Privately owned, Booker
	WV908	Hawker Sea Hawk FGA6 (8154M) [188/A]	RN Historic Flight, Yeovilton
	WV910	Hawker Sea Hawk FGA6 <ff>	Boscombe Down Aviation Collection
	WV911	Hawker Sea Hawk FGA4 [115/C]	RN Historic Flight, stored Yeovilton
	WW138	DH112 Sea Venom FAW22 [227/Z]	FAA Museum, stored RNAS Yeovilton
	WW145	DH112 Sea Venom FAW22 [680/LM]	Royal Scottish Mus'm of Flight, E Fortune
	WW217	DH112 Sea Venom FAW22 [351]	Newark Air Museum, Winthorpe
	WW388	Percival P56 Provost T1 (7616M) [O-F]	Privately owned, stored Hinstock, Shrops
	WW421	Percival P56 Provost T1 (WW450/G-BZRE/7689M) [P-B]	Bournemouth Aviation Museum
	WW442	Percival P56 Provost T1 (7618M) [N]	Gatwick Aviation Museum, Charlwood, Surrey
	WW444	Percival P56 Provost T1 [D]	Privately owned, Brownhills, Staffs
	WW447	Percival P56 Provost T1 [F]	Privately owned, Shoreham

Serial	Type (code/other identity)	Owner/operator location or fate	Notes
WW453	Percival P56 Provost T1 (G-TMKI) [W-S]	Privately owned, Westonzoyland, Somerset	
WW654	Hawker Hunter GA11 [834/DD]	Privately owned, Ford, W Sussex	
WW664	Hawker Hunter F4 <ff>	Privately owned, Spanhoe	
WX788	DH112 Venom NF3	Aeroventure, stored Doncaster	
WX853	DH112 Venom NF3 (7443M)	Mosquito Aircraft Museum, stored London Colney	
WX905	DH112 Venom NF3 (7458M)	Newark Air Museum, Winthorpe	
WZ425	DH115 Vampire T11	Privately owned, Birlingham, Worcs	
WZ450	DH115 Vampire T11 <ff>	Privately owned, Corscombe, Dorset	
WZ507	DH115 Vampire T11 (G-VTII) [74]	Privately owned, North Weald	
WZ515	DH115 Vampire T11 [60]	Solway Aviation Society, Carlisle	
WZ518	DH115 Vampire T11 [B]	North-East Aircraft Museum, Usworth	
WZ549	DH115 Vampire T11 (8118M) [F]	Ulster Aviation Society, Long Kesh	
WZ553	DH115 Vampire T11 (G-DHYY) <ff>	Privately owned, Stockton, Warks	
WZ557	DH115 Vampire T11	Privately owned, Over Dinsdale, N Yorks	
WZ572	DH115 Vampire T11 (8124M) [65] <ff>	Privately owned, Sholing, Hants	
WZ581	DH115 Vampire T11 <ff>	The Vampire Collection, Hemel Hempstead	
WZ584	DH115 Vampire T11 (G-BZRC) [K]	Privately owned, Cantley, Norfolk	
WZ589	DH115 Vampire T11 [19]	Privately owned, Rochester	
WZ589	DH115 Vampire T55 (U-1230/LN-DHZ)	Privately owned, Norway	
WZ590	DH115 Vampire T11 [19]	Imperial War Museum, Duxford	
WZ662	Auster AOP9 (G-BKVK)	Privately owned, Eggesford	
WZ706	Auster AOP9 (7851M/G-BURR)	Privately owned, Eggesford	
WZ711	Auster AOP9/Beagle E3 (G-AVHT)	Privately owned, Spanhoe	
WZ721	Auster AOP9	Museum of Army Flying, Middle Wallop	
WZ724	Auster AOP9 (7432M)	AAC Middle Wallop, at main gate	
WZ729	Auster AOP9 (G-BXON)	Privately owned, Newark-on-Trent	
WZ736	Avro 707A (7868M)	Museum of Science & Industry, Manchester	
WZ744	Avro 707C (7932M)	RAF Museum, Cosford	
WZ753	Slingsby T38 Grasshopper TX1	Solent Sky, Southampton	
WZ755	Slingsby T38 Grasshopper TX1 (BGA3481)	Boulton Paul Association, Wolverhampton	
WZ757	Slingsby T38 Grasshopper TX1 (comp XK820)	Privately owned, Kirton-in-Lindsey, Lincs	
WZ767	Slingsby T38 Grasshopper TX1	North-East Aircraft Museum, stored Usworth	
WZ772	Slingsby T38 Grasshopper TX1	Trenchard Museum, RAF Halton	
WZ773	Slingsby T38 Grasshopper TX1	Edinburgh Academy	
WZ784	Slingsby T38 Grasshopper TX1	Privately owned, stored Southend	
WZ791	Slingsby T38 Grasshopper TX1 (8944M)	RAF Museum, Hendon	
WZ793	Slingsby T38 Grasshopper TX1	Privately owned, Keevil	
WZ796	Slingsby T38 Grasshopper TX1	Privately owned, stored Nympsfield	
WZ798	Slingsby T38 Grasshopper TX1	Privately owned, stored Hullavington	
WZ816	Slingsby T38 Grasshopper TX1 (BGA3979)	Privately owned, Redhill	
WZ818	Slingsby T38 Grasshopper TX1 (BGA4361)	Privately owned, Nympsfield	
WZ819	Slingsby T38 Grasshopper TX1 (BGA3498)	Privately owned, Halton	
WZ820	Slingsby T38 Grasshopper TX1	Sywell Aviation Museum	
WZ822	Slingsby T38 Grasshopper TX1	Aeroventure, stored Doncaster	
WZ824	Slingsby T38 Grasshopper TX1	Solway Aviation Society, Carlisle	
WZ826	Vickers Valiant B(K)1 (XD826/7872M) <ff>	Privately owned, Rayleigh, Essex	
WZ828	Slingsby T38 Grasshopper TX1 (BGA4421)	Privately owned, Hullavington	
WZ831	Slingsby T38 Grasshopper TX1	Privately owned, stored Nympsfield, Glos	
WZ846	DHC1 Chipmunk T10 (G-BCSC/8439M)	No 2427 Sqn ATC, Biggin Hill	
WZ847	DHC1 Chipmunk T10 (G-CPMK) [F]	Privately owned, Sleap	
WZ869	DHC1 Chipmunk T10 (8019M) <ff>	Privately owned, Leicester	
WZ872	DHC1 Chipmunk T10 (G-BZGB) [E]	Privately owned, Blackpool	
WZ876	DHC1 Chipmunk T10 (G-BBWN) <ff>	Privately owned, Yateley, Hants	
WZ879	DHC1 Chipmunk T10 (G-BWUT) [X]	Privately owned, Duxford	
WZ882	DHC1 Chipmunk T10 (G-BXGP) [K]	Privately owned, Eaglescott	

Notes	Serial	Type (code/other identity)	Owner/operator location or fate
	XA109	DH115 Sea Vampire T22	Montrose Air Station Heritage Centre
	XA127	DH115 Sea Vampire T22 <ff>	FAA Museum, RNAS Yeovilton
	XA129	DH115 Sea Vampire T22	FAA Museum, stored RNAS Yeovilton
	XA225	Slingsby T38 Grasshopper TX1	Privately owned, Keevil
	XA226	Slingsby T38 Grasshopper TX1	Norfolk & Suffolk Avn Museum, Flixton
	XA228	Slingsby T38 Grasshopper TX1	Royal Scottish Mus'm of Flight, stored Granton
	XA230	Slingsby T38 Grasshopper TX1 (BGA4098)	Privately owned, Henlow
	XA231	Slingsby T38 Grasshopper TX1 (8888M)	RAF Manston History Museum
	XA240	Slingsby T38 Grasshopper TX1 (BGA4556)	Privately owned, Portmoak, Perth & Kinross
	XA241	Slingsby T38 Grasshopper TX1	Shuttleworth Collection, Old Warden
	XA243	Slingsby T38 Grasshopper TX1 (8886M)	Privately owned, Gransden Lodge, Cambs
	XA244	Slingsby T38 Grasshopper TX1	Privately owned, Keevil
	XA282	Slingsby T31B Cadet TX3	Caernarfon Air World
	XA289	Slingsby T31B Cadet TX3	Privately owned, Eaglescott
	XA290	Slingsby T31B Cadet TX3	Privately owned, Portmoak, Perth & Kinross
	XA293	Slingsby T31B Cadet TX3 <ff>	Privately owned, Breighton
	XA295	Slingsby T31B Cadet TX3 (BGA3336)	Privately owned, Aston Down
	XA302	Slingsby T31B Cadet TX3 (BGA3786)	RAF Museum, Hendon
	XA310	Slingsby T31B Cadet TX3 (BGA4963)	Privately owned, Hullavington
	XA459	Fairey Gannet ECM6 [E]	Privately owned, White Waltham
	XA460	Fairey Gannet ECM6 [768/BY]	Ulster Aviation Society, Long Kesh
	XA466	Fairey Gannet COD4 [777/LM]	FAA Museum, stored RNAS Yeovilton
	XA508	Fairey Gannet T2 [627/GN]	FAA Museum, at Midland Air Museum, Coventry
	XA564	Gloster Javelin FAW1 (7464M)	RAF Museum, Cosford
	XA634	Gloster Javelin FAW4 (7641M)	RAF Leeming, on display
	XA699	Gloster Javelin FAW5 (7809M)	Midland Air Museum, Coventry
	XA847	EE P1B (8371M)	Privately owned, Stowmarket, Suffolk
	XA862	WS55 Whirlwind HAR1 (G-AMJT) <ff>	Yorkshire Helicopter Preservation Group, Elvington
	XA864	WS55 Whirlwind HAR1	FAA Museum, stored RNAS Yeovilton
	XA870	WS55 Whirlwind HAR1 [911]	Aeroventure, Doncaster
	XA880	DH104 Devon C2 (G-BVXR)	Privately owned, Little Rissington
	XA893	Avro 698 Vulcan B1 (8591M) <ff>	RAF Museum, Cosford
	XA903	Avro 698 Vulcan B1 <ff>	Privately owned, Stoneykirk, D&G
	XA917	HP80 Victor B1 (7827M) <ff>	Privately owned, Cupar, Fife
	XB259	Blackburn B101 Beverley C1 (G-AOAI)	Fort Paull Armoury
	XB261	Blackburn B101 Beverley C1 <ff>	Newark Air Museum, Winthorpe
	XB446	Grumman TBM-3 Avenger ECM6B	FAA Museum, Yeovilton
	XB480	Hiller HT1 [537]	FAA Museum, stored RNAS Yeovilton
	XB812	Canadair CL-13 Sabre F4 (9227M) [U]	RAF Museum, Cosford
	XD145	Saro SR53	RAF Museum, Cosford
	XD163	WS55 Whirlwind HAR10 (8645M) [X]	The Helicopter Museum, Weston-super-Mare
	XD165	WS55 Whirlwind HAR10 (8673M)	Caernarfon Airfield Fire Section
	XD215	VS Scimitar F1 <ff>	Privately owned, Cheltenham
	XD235	VS Scimitar F1 <ff>	Privately owned, Olney, Bucks
	XD317	VS Scimitar F1 [112/R]	FAA Museum, RNAS Yeovilton
	XD332	VS Scimitar F1 [194/C]	Solent Sky, stored Romsey
	XD375	DH115 Vampire T11 (7887M)	Privately owned, Elland, W Yorks
	XD377	DH115 Vampire T11 (8203M) <ff>	Aeroventure, stored Doncaster
	XD425	DH115 Vampire T11 <ff>	Privately owned, Newcastle
	XD434	DH115 Vampire T11 [25]	Fenland & W Norfolk Aviation Museum, Wisbech
	XD445	DH115 Vampire T11 [51]	Privately owned, Abbots Bromley
	XD447	DH115 Vampire T11 [50]	East Midlands Airport Aeropark
	XD452	DH115 Vampire T11 (7990M) [66] <ff>	Privately owned, Dursley, Glos
	XD459	DH115 Vampire T11 [63] <ff>	Aeroventure, stored Doncaster
	XD506	DH115 Vampire T11 (7983M)	Gloucestershire Avn Coll, stored Gloucester
	XD515	DH115 Vampire T11 (7998M/XM515)	RAF Museum Restoration Centre, Cosford

Serial	Type (code/other identity)	Owner/operator location or fate	Notes
XD534	DH115 Vampire T11 [41]	East Midlands Airport Aeropark	
XD542	DH115 Vampire T11 (7604M) [N]	Montrose Air Station Heritage Centre	
XD547	DH115 Vampire T11 [Z] (composite)	Privately owned, Leeming	
XD593	DH115 Vampire T11	Newark Air Museum, Winthorpe	
XD595	DH115 Vampire T11 <ff>	Privately owned, Glentham, Lincs	
XD596	DH115 Vampire T11 (7939M)	Solent Sky, Southampton	
XD599	DH115 Vampire T11 [A] <ff>	Sywell Aviation Museum	
XD602	DH115 Vampire T11 (7737M) <ff>	Privately owned, Ripon	
XD616	DH115 Vampire T11 [56]	Mosquito Aircraft Museum, stored Gloucester	
XD622	DH115 Vampire T11 (8160M)	No 2214 Sqn ATC, Usworth	
XD624	DH115 Vampire T11	Privately owned, Hooton Park	
XD626	DH115 Vampire T11 [Q]	Midland Air Museum, stored Coventry	
XD674	Hunting Jet Provost T1 (7570M)	RAF Museum, Cosford	
XD693	Hunting Jet Provost T1 (XM129/G-AOBU) [Z-Q]	Kennet Aviation, North Weald	
XD816	Vickers Valiant B(K)1 <ff>	Brooklands Museum, Weybridge	
XD818	Vickers Valiant B(K)1 (7894M)	RAF Museum, Cosford	
XD857	Vickers Valiant B(K)1 <ff>	Norfolk & Suffolk Aviation Museum, Flixton	
XD875	Vickers Valiant B(K)1 <ff>	Highland Aviation Museum, Inverness	
XE317	Bristol 171 Sycamore HR14 (G-AMWO) [S-N]	Aeroventure, stored Doncaster	
XE339	Hawker Sea Hawk FGA6 (8156M) [149] <ff>	Privately owned, Glos	
XE339	Hawker Sea Hawk FGA6 (8156M) [E] <rf>	Privately owned, Booker	
XE340	Hawker Sea Hawk FGA6 [131/Z]	FAA Museum, stored RNAS Yeovilton	
XE364	Hawker Sea Hawk FGA6 (G-JETH) (comp WM983) [485/J]	Gatwick Aviation Museum, Charlwood, Surrey	
XE368	Hawker Sea Hawk FGA6 [200/J]	Privately owned, Barrow-in-Furness	
XE521	Fairey Rotodyne Y (parts)	The Helicopter Museum, Weston-super-Mare	
XE584	Hawker Hunter FGA9 <ff>	Privately owned, Hooton Park	
XE597	Hawker Hunter FGA9 (8874M) <ff>	Privately owned, Halfpenny Green	
XE601	Hawker Hunter FGA9 (G-ETPS)	Apache Aviation, Istres, France	
XE606	Hawker Hunter F6A (XJ673/8841M)	RAF Cottesmore, preserved	
XE624	Hawker Hunter FGA9 (8875M) [G]	Metheringham Airfield Visitors Centre	
XE627	Hawker Hunter F6A [T]	Imperial War Museum, Duxford	
XE643	Hawker Hunter FGA9 (8586M) <ff>	RAF M&RU, Aldergrove	
XE650	Hawker Hunter FGA9 (G-9-449) <ff>	Farnborough Air Sciences Trust, Farnborough	
XE664	Hawker Hunter F4 <ff>	Gloucestershire Avn Coll, stored Gloucester	
XE665	Hawker Hunter T8C (G-BWGM) [876/VL]	Classic Flight, Coventry	
XE668	Hawker Hunter GA11 [832/DD]	Hamburger Hill Paintball, Marksbury, Somerset	
XE670	Hawker Hunter F4 (7762M/8585M) <ff>	RAF Museum, Cosford	
XE683	Hawker Hunter F51 (RDAF E-409) [G]	City of Norwich Aviation Museum	
XE685	Hawker Hunter GA11 (G-GAII) [861/VL]	Privately owned, Exeter	
XE689	Hawker Hunter GA11 (G-BWGK) <ff>	Privately owned, Cotswold Airport	
XE707	Hawker Hunter GA11 (N707XE) [863]	Bentwaters Cold War Museum	
XE786	Slingsby T31B Cadet TX3 (BGA4033)	Privately owned, Arbroath	
XE793	Slingsby T31B Cadet TX3 (8666M)	Privately owned, Tamworth	
XE799	Slingsby T31B Cadet TX3 (8943M) [R]	Privately owned, Abbots Bromley	
XE802	Slingsby T31B Cadet TX3 (BGA5283)	Privately owned, Shipdham	
XE849	DH115 Vampire T11 (7928M) [V3]	Privately owned, Barton	
XE852	DH115 Vampire T11 [H]	No 2247 Sqn ATC, Hawarden	
XE855	DH115 Vampire T11	Midland Air Museum, stored Coventry	
XE856	DH115 Vampire T11 (G-DUSK) [V]	Bournemouth Aviation Museum	
XE864	DH115 Vampire T11 (comp XD435) <ff>	Privately owned, Ingatstone, Essex	
XE872	DH115 Vampire T11 [62]	Midland Air Museum, Coventry	
XE874	DH115 Vampire T11 (8582M)	Paintball Commando, Birkin, W Yorks	
XE897	DH115 Vampire T11 (XD403)	Privately owned, Errol, Tayside	

Notes	Serial	Type (code/other identity)	Owner/operator location or fate
	XE921	DH115 Vampire T11 [64] <ff>	Privately owned, St Mawgan
	XE935	DH115 Vampire T11	Aeroventure, Doncaster
	XE946	DH115 Vampire T11 (7473M) <ff>	RAF Cranwell Aviation Heritage Centre
	XE956	DH115 Vampire T11 (G-OBLN)	De Havilland Aviation, stored Rochester
	XE979	DH115 Vampire T11 [54]	Privately owned, Birlingham, Worcs
	XE982	DH115 Vampire T11 (7564M) [01]	Privately owned, Weston, Eire
	XE985	DH115 Vampire T11 (WZ476)	Privately owned, New Inn, Torfaen
	XE993	DH115 Vampire T11 (8161M) <ff>	Privately owned, Staffs
	XE998	DH115 Vampire T11 (U-1215)	Painted in Swiss markings
	XF113	VS Swift F7 [19] <ff>	Boscombe Down Aviation Collection
	XF114	VS Swift F7 (G-SWIF)	Solent Sky, stored Romsey
	XF314	Hawker Hunter F51 (RDAF E-412) [N]	Brooklands Museum, Weybridge
	XF321	Hawker Hunter T7 <ff>	Privately owned, Welshpool
	XF321	Hawker Hunter T7 <rf>	Phoenix Aviation, Bruntingthorpe
	XF375	Hawker Hunter F6A (8736M/G-BUEZ) [05]	Boscombe Down Aviation Collection
	XF382	Hawker Hunter F6A [15]	Midland Air Museum, Coventry
	XF383	Hawker Hunter F6 (8706M) <ff>	Gloster Aviation Club, Gloucester
	XF418	Hawker Hunter F51 (RDAF E-430)	Gatwick Aviation Museum, Charlwood, Surrey
	XF506	Hawker Hunter F4 (WT746/7770M) [A]	Dumfries & Galloway Avn Mus, Dumfries
	XF509	Hawker Hunter F6 (8708M)	Fort Paull Armoury
	XF522	Hawker Hunter F6 <ff>	Herts & Bucks ATC Wing, RAF Halton
	XF526	Hawker Hunter F6 (8679M) [78/E]	Privately owned, Birlingham, Worcs
	XF527	Hawker Hunter F6 (8680M)	RAF Halton, on display
	XF545	Percival P56 Provost T1 (7957M) [O-K]	Privately owned, Thatcham
	XF597	Percival P56 Provost T1 (G-BKFW) [AH]	Privately owned, Brimpton, Berks
	XF603	Percival P56 Provost T1 (G-KAPW)	Shuttleworth Collection, Old Warden
	XF690	Percival P56 Provost T1 (8041M/G-MOOS)	Kennet Aviation, Yeovilton
	XF708	Avro 716 Shackleton MR3 [C]	Imperial War Museum, Duxford
	XF785	Bristol 173 (7648M/G-ALBN)	Bristol Aero Collection, Cotswold Airport
	XF836	Percival P56 Provost T1)	Privately owned, Thatcham
		(8043M/G-AWRY [JG]	
	XF926	Bristol 188 (8368M)	RAF Museum, Cosford
	XF940	Hawker Hunter F4 <ff>	Privately owned, Kew Stoke, Somerset
	XF994	Hawker Hunter T8C (G-CGHU) [873/VL]	Hawker Hunter Aviation, Scampton
	XF995	Hawker Hunter T8B (G-BZSF/9237M) [K]	Hawker Hunter Aviation, Scampton
	XG154	Hawker Hunter FGA9 (8863M) [54]	RAF Museum, Hendon
	XG160	Hawker Hunter F6A (8831M/G-BWAF) [U]	Bournemouth Aviation Museum
	XG164	Hawker Hunter F6 (8681M)	Privately owned, Wellington, Somerset
	XG168	Hawker Hunter F6A (XG172/8832M) [10]	City of Norwich Aviation Museum
	XG190	Hawker Hunter F51 (RDAF E-425) [C]	Solway Aviation Society, Carlisle
	XG193	Hawker Hunter FGA9 (XG297)	Aeroventure, Doncaster
		comp with WT741) <ff>	
	XG194	Hawker Hunter PR11 (WT723/G-PRII) [N]	Hunter Flying Ltd, St Athan
	XG195	Hawker Hunter FGA9 <ff>	Privately owned, Lewes
	XG196	Hawker Hunter F6A (8702M) [31]	Army, Mytchett, Surrey, on display
	XG209	Hawker Hunter F6 (8709M) <ff>	Privately owned, Kingston-on-Thames
	XG210	Hawker Hunter F6	Privately owned, Beck Row, Suffolk
	XG225	Hawker Hunter F6A (8713M)	DCAE Cosford, at main gate
	XG226	Hawker Hunter F6A (8800M) <ff>	RAF Manston History Museum
	XG252	Hawker Hunter FGA9 (8840M) [U]	Privately owned, Bosbury, Hereford
	XG254	Hawker Hunter FGA9 (8881M)	Norfolk & Suffolk Avn Museum, Flixton
	XG274	Hawker Hunter F6 (8710M) [71]	Privately owned, Newmarket
	XG290	Hawker Hunter F6 (8711M) <ff>	Air Defence Collection, Boscombe Down
	XG290	Hawker Hunter T7 (comp XL578 & XL586)	Privately owned, Kirkstead, Lincs
	XG297	Hawker Hunter FGA9 <ff>	Aeroventure, Doncaster
	XG325	EE Lightning F1 <ff>	Privately owned,

Serial	Type (code/other identity)	Owner/operator location or fate	Notes
XG329	EE Lightning F1 (8050M)	Privately owned, Flixton	
XG331	EE Lightning F1 <ff>	Privately owned, Glos	
XG337	EE Lightning F1 (8056M) [M]	RAF Museum, Cosford	
XG452	Bristol 192 Belvedere HC1 (7997M/G-BRMB)	The Helicopter Museum, Weston-super-Mare	
XG454	Bristol 192 Belvedere HC1 (8366M)	Museum of Science & Industry, Manchester	
XG462	Bristol 192 Belvedere HC1 <ff>	The Helicopter Museum, stored Weston-super-Mare	
XG474	Bristol 192 Belvedere HC1 (8367M) [O]	RAF Museum, Hendon	
XG502	Bristol 171 Sycamore HR14	Museum of Army Flying, Middle Wallop	
XG518	Bristol 171 Sycamore HR14 (8009M) [S-E]	Norfolk & Suffolk Avn Museum, Flixton	
XG523	Bristol 171 Sycamore HR14 <ff> [V]	Norfolk & Suffolk Avn Museum, Flixton	
XG574	WS55 Whirlwind HAR3 [752/PO]	FAA Museum, stored RNAS Yeovilton	
XG588	WS55 Whirlwind HAR3 (G-BAMH/VR-BEP)	East Midlands Airport Aeropark	
XG592	WS55 Whirlwind HAS7 [54]	Task Force Adventure Park, Cowbridge, S Glam	
XG594	WS55 Whirlwind HAS7 [517]	FAA Museum, stored Yeovilton	
XG596	WS55 Whirlwind HAS7 [66]	The Helicopter Museum, Weston-super-Mare	
XG613	DH112 Sea Venom FAW21	Imperial War Museum, Duxford	
XG629	DH112 Sea Venom FAW22	Privately owned, Stone, Staffs	
XG680	DH112 Sea Venom FAW22 [438]	North-East Aircraft Museum, Usworth	
XG692	DH112 Sea Venom FAW22 [668/LM]	Privately owned, Stockport	
XG730	DH112 Sea Venom FAW22 [499/A]	Mosquito Aircraft Museum, London Colney	
XG736	DH112 Sea Venom FAW22	Privately owned, East Midlands	
XG737	DH112 Sea Venom FAW22 [220/Z]	East Midlands Airport Aeropark	
XG743	DH115 Sea Vampire T22 [597/LM]	Imperial War Museum, Duxford	
XG797	Fairey Gannet ECM6 [277]	Imperial War Museum, Duxford	
XG831	Fairey Gannet ECM6 [396]	Davidstow Airfield & Cornwall At War Museum	
XG882	Fairey Gannet T5 (8754M) [771/LM]	Privately owned, Errol, Tayside	
XG883	Fairey Gannet T5 [773/BY]	FAA Museum, at Museum of Berkshire Aviation, Woodley	
XG900	Short SC1	Science Museum, South Kensington	
XG905	Short SC1	Ulster Folk & Transport Mus, Holywood, Co Down	
XH131	EE Canberra PR9	Ulster Aviation Society, Long Kesh	
XH134	EE Canberra PR9 (G-OMHD)	Privately owned, Cotswold Airport	
XH135	EE Canberra PR9	Privately owned, Cotswold Airport	
XH136	EE Canberra PR9 (8782M) [W] <ff>	Privately owned, Ashford, Kent	
XH165	EE Canberra PR9 <ff>	Blyth Valley Aviation Collection, Walpole	
XH168	EE Canberra PR9	RAF Marham Fire Section	
XH169	EE Canberra PR9	RAF Marham, on display	
XH170	EE Canberra PR9 (8739M)	RAF Wyton, on display	
XH171	EE Canberra PR9 (8746M) [U]	RAF Museum, Cosford	
XH174	EE Canberra PR9 <ff>	Privately owned, Staffs	
XH175	EE Canberra PR9 <ff>	Privately owned, Bewdley, Worcs	
XH177	EE Canberra PR9 <ff>	Newark Air Museum, Winthorpe	
XH278	DH115 Vampire T11 (8595M/7866M) [42]	Yorkshire Air Museum, Elvington	
XH313	DH115 Vampire T11 (G-BZRD) [E]	Tangmere Military Aviation Museum	
XH318	DH115 Vampire T11 (7761M) [64]	Privately owned, Sholing, Hants	
XH328	DH115 Vampire T11 <ff>	Privately owned, Norfolk	
XH330	DH115 Vampire T11 [73]	Privately owned, Camberley, Surrey	
XH537	Avro 698 Vulcan B2MRR (8749M) <ff>	Privately owned, Bournemouth	
XH558	Avro 698 Vulcan B2 (G-VLCN)	Vulcan To The Sky Trust, Doncaster Sheffield Airport	
XH560	Avro 698 Vulcan K2 <ff>	Privately owned, Foulness	
XH563	Avro 698 Vulcan B2MRR <ff>	Privately owned, Over Dinsdale, N Yorks	
XH584	EE Canberra T4 (G-27-374) <ff>	Aeroventure, Doncaster	
XH592	HP80 Victor B1A (8429M) <ff>	Phoenix Aviation, Bruntingthorpe	
XH648	HP80 Victor K1A	Imperial War Museum, Duxford	
XH669	HP80 Victor K2 (9092M) <ff>	Privately owned, Foulness	
XH670	HP80 Victor SR2 <ff>	Privately owned, Foulness	

Notes	Serial	Type (code/other identity)	Owner/operator location or fate
	XH672	HP80 Victor K2 (9242M)	RAF Museum, Cosford
	XH673	HP80 Victor K2 (8911M)	RAF Marham, on display
	XH767	Gloster Javelin FAW9 (7955M) [L]	Yorkshire Air Museum, Elvington
	XH783	Gloster Javelin FAW7 (7798M) <ff>	Privately owned, Catford
	XH837	Gloster Javelin FAW7 (8032M) <ff>	Caernarfon Air World
	XH892	Gloster Javelin FAW9R (7982M) [J]	Norfolk & Suffolk Avn Museum, Flixton
	XH897	Gloster Javelin FAW9	Imperial War Museum, Duxford
	XH903	Gloster Javelin FAW9 (7938M)	Gloucester Airport, on display
	XH992	Gloster Javelin FAW8 (7829M) [P]	Newark Air Museum, Winthorpe
	XJ314	RR Thrust Measuring Rig	Science Museum, South Kensington
	XJ380	Bristol 171 Sycamore HR14 (8628M)	Boscombe Down Aviation Collection
	XJ389	Fairey Jet Gyrodyne (XD759/G-AJJP)	Museum of Berkshire Aviation, Woodley
	XJ398	WS55 Whirlwind HAR10 (XD768/G-BDBZ)	Aeroventure, Doncaster
	XJ435	WS55 Whirlwind HAR10 (XD804/8671M) [V]	RAF Manston History Museum, spares use
	XJ476	DH110 Sea Vixen FAW1 <ff>	Boscombe Down Aviation Collection
	XJ481	DH110 Sea Vixen FAW1 [VL]	FAA Museum, stored RNAS Yeovilton
	XJ482	DH110 Sea Vixen FAW1 [713/VL]	Norfolk & Suffolk Avn Museum, Flixton
	XJ488	DH110 Sea Vixen FAW1 <ff>	Robertsbridge Aviation Society, Mayfield
	XJ494	DH110 Sea Vixen FAW2 (121/E]	Privately owned, Bruntingthorpe
	XJ560	DH110 Sea Vixen FAW2 (8142M) [243/H]	Newark Air Museum, Winthorpe
	XJ565	DH110 Sea Vixen FAW2 [127/E]	Mosquito Aircraft Museum, London Colney
	XJ571	DH110 Sea Vixen FAW2 (8140M) [242/R]	Solent Sky, Southampton
	XJ575	DH110 Sea Vixen FAW2 <ff> [SAH-13]	Wellesbourne Wartime Museum
	XJ579	DH110 Sea Vixen FAW2 <ff>	Midland Air Museum, Coventry
	XJ580	DH110 Sea Vixen FAW2 [131/E]	Tangmere Military Aviation Museum
	XJ714	Hawker Hunter FR10 (comp XG226)	East Midlands Airport Aeropark
	XJ723	WS55 Whirlwind HAR10	Privately owned, Newcastle upon Tyne
	XJ726	WS55 Whirlwind HAR10	Caernarfon Air World
	XJ727	WS55 Whirlwind HAR10 (8661M) [L]	Privately owned, Ramsgate
	XJ758	WS55 Whirlwind HAR10 (8464M) <ff>	Privately owned, Welshpool
	XJ771	DH115 Vampire T55 (U-1215/G-HELV)	Classic Flight, Coventry
	XJ772	DH115 Vampire T11 [H]	Mosquito Aircraft Museum, London Colney
	XJ823	Avro 698 Vulcan B2A	Solway Aviation Society, Carlisle
	XJ824	Avro 698 Vulcan B2A	Imperial War Museum, Duxford
	XJ917	Bristol 171 Sycamore HR14 [H-S]	Bristol Sycamore Group, stored Cotswold Airport
	XJ918	Bristol 171 Sycamore HR14 (8190M)	RAF Museum, Cosford
	XK416	Auster AOP9 (7855M/G-AYUA)	Privately owned, Widmerpool
	XK417	Auster AOP9 (G-AVXY)	Privately owned, Messingham, Lincs
	XK418	Auster AOP9 (7976M)	93rd Bomb Group Museum, Hardwick, Norfolk
	XK421	Auster AOP9 (8365M) (frame)	Privately owned, South Molton, Devon
	XK488	Blackburn NA39 Buccaneer S1	FAA Museum, stored RNAS Yeovilton
	XK526	Blackburn NA39 Buccaneer S2 (8648M)	RAF Honington, at main gate
	XK527	Blackburn NA39 Buccaneer S2D (8818M) <ff>	Privately owned, North Wales
	XK532	Blackburn NA39 Buccaneer S1 (8867M) [632/LM]	Highland Aviation Museum, Inverness
	XK533	Blackburn NA39 Buccaneer S1 <ff>	Royal Scottish Mus'm of Flight, stored Granton
	XK590	DH115 Vampire T11 [V]	Wellesbourne Wartime Museum
	XK623	DH115 Vampire T11 (G-VAMP) [56]	Caernarfon Air World
	XK624	DH115 Vampire T11 [32]	Norfolk & Suffolk Avn Museum, Flixton
	XK625	DH115 Vampire T11 [14]	Brenzett Aeronautical Museum
	XK627	DH115 Vampire T11 <ff>	Davidstow Airfield & Cornwall At War Museum
	XK632	DH115 Vampire T11 <ff>	Privately owned, Greenford, London
	XK637	DH115 Vampire T11 [56]	Privately owned, Gr Manchester

Serial	Type (code/other identity)	Owner/operator location or fate	Notes
XK695	DH106 Comet C2(RC) (G-AMXH/9164M) <ff>	Mosquito Aircraft Museum, London Colney	
XK699	DH106 Comet C2 (7971M) [699]	RAF Lyneham on display	
XK724	Folland Gnat F1 (7715M)	RAF Museum, Cosford	
XK740	Folland Gnat F1 (8396M)	Solent Sky, Southampton	
XK776	ML Utility 1	Museum of Army Flying, Middle Wallop	
XK789	Slingsby T38 Grasshopper TX1	Midland Air Museum, stored Coventry	
XK790	Slingsby T38 Grasshopper TX1	Privately owned, stored Husbands Bosworth	
XK819	Slingsby T38 Grasshopper TX1	Privately owned, Breighton	
XK822	Slingsby T38 Grasshopper TX1	Privately owned, Partridge Green, W Sussex	
XK885	Percival P66 Pembroke C1 (8452M/N46EA)	Gatwick Aviation Museum, Charlwood, Surrey	
XK895	DH104 Sea Devon C20 (G-SDEV) [19/CU]	Classic Flight, Coventry	
XK907	WS55 Whirlwind HAS7	Midland Air Museum, stored Coventry	
XK911	WS55 Whirlwind HAS7 [519/PO]	Privately owned, Shepherds Bush	
XK936	WS55 Whirlwind HAS7 [62]	Imperial War Museum, Duxford	
XK940	WS55 Whirlwind HAS7 (G-AYXT) [911]	The Helicopter Museum, Weston-super-Mare	
XK970	WS55 Whirlwind HAR10 (8789M)	Army, Bramley, Hants	
XL149	Blackburn B101 Beverley C1 (7988M) <ff>	Aeroventure, Doncaster	
XL160	HP80 Victor K2 (8910M) <ff>	Norfolk & Suffolk Avn Museum, Flixton	
XL164	HP80 Victor K2 (9215M) <ff>	Gatwick Aviation Museum, Charlwood, Surrey	
XL190	HP80 Victor K2 (9216M) <ff>	RAF Manston History Museum	
XL231	HP80 Victor K2	Yorkshire Air Museum, Elvington	
XL318	Avro 698 Vulcan B2 (8733M)	RAF Museum, Hendon	
XL319	Avro 698 Vulcan B2	North-East Aircraft Museum, Usworth	
XL360	Avro 698 Vulcan B2A	Midland Air Museum, Coventry	
XL388	Avro 698 Vulcan B2 <ff>	Aeroventure, Doncaster	
XL426	Avro 698 Vulcan B2 (G-VJET)	Vulcan Restoration Trust, Southend	
XL445	Avro 698 Vulcan K2 (8811M) <ff>	Norfolk & Suffolk Avn Museum, Flixton	
XL449	Fairey Gannet AEW3 <ff>	Privately owned, Camberley, Surrey	
XL472	Fairey Gannet AEW3 [044/R]	Gatwick Aviation Museum, Charlwood, Surrey	
XL497	Fairey Gannet AEW3 [041/R]	Dumfries & Galloway Avn Mus, Dumfries	
XL500	Fairey Gannet AEW3 (G-KAEW) [CU]	Hunter Flying Ltd, Exeter	
XL502	Fairey Gannet AEW3 (8610M/G-BMYP)	Yorkshire Air Museum, Elvington	
XL503	Fairey Gannet AEW3 [070/E]	FAA Museum, RNAS Yeovilton	
XL563	Hawker Hunter T7 (9218M)	Privately owned, Southmoor, Oxon	
XL564	Hawker Hunter T7 <ff>	Privately owned, South Molton, Devon	
XL565	Hawker Hunter T7 (parts of WT745) [Y]	Privately owned, Bruntingthorpe	
XL568	Hawker Hunter T7A (9224M) [X]	RAF Museum, Cosford	
XL569	Hawker Hunter T7 (8833M)	East Midlands Airport Aeropark	
XL571	Hawker Hunter T7 (XL572/8834M/G-HNTR) [V]	Yorkshire Air Museum, Elvington	
XL573	Hawker Hunter T7 (G-BVGH)	Hunter Flying Ltd, St Athan	
XL577	Hawker Hunter T7 (G-BXKF/8676M) [V]	Privately owned, Cotswold Airport	
XL580	Hawker Hunter T8M [723]	FAA Museum, RNAS Yeovilton	
XL586	Hawker Hunter T7 (comp XL578)	Action Park, Wickford, Essex	
XL587	Hawker Hunter T7 (8807M/G-HPUX) [Z]	Hawker Hunter Aviation, stored Scampton	
XL591	Hawker Hunter T7	Gatwick Aviation Museum, Charlwood, Surrey	
XL592	Hawker Hunter T7 (8836M) [Y]	Privately owned, Booker	
XL601	Hawker Hunter T7 (G-BZSR) [874/VL]	Classic Fighters, Brustem, Belgium	
XL602	Hawker Hunter T8M (G-BWFT)	'Hunter Flying, St Athan	
XL609	Hawker Hunter T7 <ff>	Privately owned, South Molton, Devon	
XL612	Hawker Hunter T7 [2]	Privately owned, Swansea	
XL618	Hawker Hunter T7 (8892M)	Caernarfon Air World	
XL621	Hawker Hunter T7 (G-BNCX)	Privately owned, Dunsfold	
XL623	Hawker Hunter T7 (8770M)	The Planets Leisure Centre, Woking	
XL629	EE Lightning T4	MoD/QinetiQ Boscombe Down, at main gate	

Notes	Serial	Type (code/other identity)	Owner/operator location or fate
	XL703	SAL Pioneer CC1 (8034M)	RAF Museum, Cosford
	XL714	DH82A Tiger Moth II (T6099/G-AOGR)	Privately owned, Boughton, Lincs
	XL716	DH82A Tiger Moth II (T7363/G-AOIL)	*Crashed 15 May 2011, Moor Crichel, Dorset*
	XL738	Saro Skeeter AOP12 (7860M)	Privately owned, Aeroventure, Doncaster
	XL739	Saro Skeeter AOP12	AAC, stored Wattisham
	XL762	Saro Skeeter AOP12 (8017M)	Royal Scottish Mus'm of Flight, E Fortune
	XL763	Saro Skeeter AOP12	Privately owned, Aeroventure, Doncaster
	XL764	Saro Skeeter AOP12 (7940M) [J]	Newark Air Museum, Winthorpe
	XL765	Saro Skeeter AOP12	Privately owned, Melksham, Wilts
	XL767	Saro Skeeter AOP12 <ff>	The Helicopter Museum, Weston-super-Mare
	XL770	Saro Skeeter AOP12 (8046M)	Solent Sky, Southampton
	XL809	Saro Skeeter AOP12 (G-BLIX)	Privately owned, Wilden, Beds
	XL811	Saro Skeeter AOP12	The Helicopter Museum, Weston-super-Mare
	XL812	Saro Skeeter AOP12 (G-SARO)	AAC Historic Aircraft Flight, stored Middle Wallop
	XL813	Saro Skeeter AOP12	Museum of Army Flying, Middle Wallop
	XL814	Saro Skeeter AOP12	AAC Historic Aircraft Flight, Middle Wallop
	XL824	Bristol 171 Sycamore HR14 (8021M)	RAF Museum Reserve Collection, Stafford
	XL829	Bristol 171 Sycamore HR14	The Helicopter Museum, Weston-super-Mare
	XL840	WS55 Whirlwind HAS7	Privately owned, Bawtry
	XL853	WS55 Whirlwind HAS7 [PO]	FAA Museum, stored RNAS Yeovilton
	XL875	WS55 Whirlwind HAR9	Perth Technical College
	XL929	Percival P66 Pembroke C1 (G-BNPU)	Classic Flight, stored Compton Verney
	XL954	Percival P66 Pembroke C1 (9042M/N4234C/G-BXES)	Classic Flight, Coventry
	XL993	SAL Twin Pioneer CC1 (8388M)	RAF Museum, Cosford
	XM135	BAC Lightning F1 [B]	Imperial War Museum, Duxford
	XM144	BAC Lightning F1 (8417M) <ff>	Lakes Lightnings, Spark Bridge, Cumbria
	XM169	BAC Lightning F1A (8422M) <ff>	Highland Aviation Museum, Inverness
	XM172	BAC Lightning F1A (8427M)	Lakes Lightnings, Spark Bridge, Cumbria
	XM173	BAC Lightning F1A (8414M) [A]	MSS Holdings, Kirkham, Lancs
	XM191	BAC Lightning F1A (7854M/8590M) <ff>	RAF M&RU, Bottesford
	XM192	BAC Lightning F1A (8413M) [K]	Thorpe Camp Preservation Group, Lincs
	XM223	DH104 Devon C2 (G-BWWC) [J]	Air Atlantique Classic Flight, stored Compton Verney
	XM279	EE Canberra B(I)8 <ff>	Privately owned, Flixton
	XM300	WS58 Wessex HAS1	Privately owned, Nantgarw, Rhondda
	XM328	WS58 Wessex HAS3 [653/PO]	The Helicopter Museum, Weston-super-Mare
	XM330	WS58 Wessex HAS1	The Helicopter Museum, Weston-super-Mare
	XM350	Hunting Jet Provost T3A (9036M) [89]	Aeroventure, Doncaster
	XM351	Hunting Jet Provost T3 (8078M) [Y]	RAF Museum, Cosford
	XM355	Hunting Jet Provost T3 (8229M) [D]	Privately owned, Newcastle
	XM358	Hunting Jet Provost T3A (8987M) [53]	Privately owned, Newbridge, Powys
	XM362	Hunting Jet Provost T3 (8230M)	DCAE, No 1 SoTT, Cosford
	XM365	Hunting Jet Provost T3A (G-BXBH) [37]	Privately owned, Bruntingthorpe
	XM369	Hunting Jet Provost T3 (8084M) [C]	*Sold to The Netherlands*
	XM370	Hunting Jet Provost T3 (G-BVSP) [10]	*Repainted as G-BVSP*
	XM373	Hunting Jet Provost T3 (7726M) [2] <ff>	Yorkshire Air Museum, Elvington
	XM383	Hunting Jet Provost T3A [90]	Newark Air Museum, Winthorpe
	XM402	Hunting Jet Provost T3 (8055AM) [18]	Fenland & W Norfolk Aviation Museum, Wisbech
	XM404	Hunting Jet Provost T3 (8055BM)	FETC, Moreton-in-Marsh, Glos
	XM409	Hunting Jet Provost T3 (8082M) <ff>	Air Scouts, Guernsey Airport
	XM410	Hunting Jet Provost T3 (8054AM) [B]	Privately owned, Gillingham, Kent
	XM411	Hunting Jet Provost T3 (8434M) <ff>	Aeroventure, Doncaster
	XM412	Hunting Jet Provost T3A (9011M) [41]	Privately owned, Balado Bridge, Scotland
	XM414	Hunting Jet Provost T3A (8996M)	Ulster Aviation Society, Long Kesh
	XM417	Hunting Jet Provost T3 (8054BM) [D] <ff>	Privately owned, Cannock
	XM419	Hunting Jet Provost T3A (8990M) [102]	Privately owned, Newcastle
	XM425	Hunting Jet Provost T3A (8995M) [88]	Privately owned, Longton, Staffs

Serial	Type (code/other identity)	Owner/operator location or fate	Notes
XM463	Hunting Jet Provost T3A [38] (fuselage)	RAF Museum, Hendon	
XM468	Hunting Jet Provost T3 (8081M) <ff>	Privately owned, Terrington St Clement, Norfolk	
XM473	Hunting Jet Provost T3A (8974M/G-TINY)	Bedford College, instructional use	
XM474	Hunting Jet Provost T3 (8121M) <ff>	No 2517 Sqn ATC, Levenshulme	
XM479	Hunting Jet Provost T3A (G-BVEZ)	Privately owned, Newcastle	
XM480	Hunting Jet Provost T3 (8080M)	4x4 Car Centre, Chesterfield	
XM496	Bristol 253 Britannia C1 (EL-WXA) [496]	Britannia Preservation Society, Cotswold Airport	
XM497	Bristol 175 Britannia 312F (G-AOVF) [497]	RAF Museum, Cosford	
XM529	Saro Skeeter AOP12 (7979M/G-BDNS)	Privately owned, Handforth	
XM553	Saro Skeeter AOP12 (G-AWSV)	Yorkshire Air Museum, Elvington	
XM555	Saro Skeeter AOP12 (8027M)	RAF Museum Reserve Collection, Stafford	
XM557	Saro Skeeter AOP12 <ff>	The Helicopter Museum, Weston-super-Mare	
XM569	Avro 698 Vulcan B2 <ff>	Gloucestershire Avn Coll, stored Gloucester	
XM575	Avro 698 Vulcan B2A (G-BLMC)	East Midlands Airport Aeropark	
XM594	Avro 698 Vulcan B2	Newark Air Museum, Winthorpe	
XM597	Avro 698 Vulcan B2	Royal Scottish Mus'm of Flight, E Fortune	
XM598	Avro 698 Vulcan B2 (8778M)	RAF Museum, Cosford	
XM602	Avro 698 Vulcan B2 (8771M) <ff>	Manchester Museum of Science & Industry, stored	
XM603	Avro 698 Vulcan B2	Avro Aircraft Heritage Society, Woodford	
XM607	Avro 698 Vulcan B2 (8779M)	RAF Waddington, on display	
XM612	Avro 698 Vulcan B2	City of Norwich Aviation Museum	
XM651	Saro Skeeter AOP12 (XM561/7980M)	Aeroventure, Doncaster	
XM652	Avro 698 Vulcan B2 <ff>	Privately owned, Welshpool	
XM655	Avro 698 Vulcan B2 (G-VULC)	Privately owned, Wellesbourne Mountford	
XM685	WS55 Whirlwind HAS7 (G-AYZJ) [513/PO]	Newark Air Museum, Winthorpe	
XM692	HS Gnat T1 <ff>	Privately owned, Welshpool	
XM693	HS Gnat T1 (7891M)	BAE Systems Hamble, on display	
XM697	HS Gnat T1 (G-NAAT)	Reynard Garden Centre, Carluke, S Lanarkshire	
XM708	HS Gnat T1 (8573M)	Privately owned, Lytham St Annes	
XM715	HP80 Victor K2	Cold War Jets Collection, Bruntingthorpe	
XM717	HP80 Victor K2 <ff>	RAF Museum, Hendon	
XM819	Lancashire EP9 Prospector (G-APXW)	Museum of Army Flying, Middle Wallop	
XM833	WS58 Wessex HAS3	North-East Aircraft Museum, Usworth	
XN126	WS55 Whirlwind HAR10 (8655M) [S]	Pinewood Studios, Elstree	
XN137	Hunting Jet Provost T3 <ff>	Privately owned, Little Addington, Notts	
XN156	Slingsby T21B Sedbergh TX1 (BGA3250)	Privately owned, Portmoak	
XN157	Slingsby T21B Sedbergh TX1 (BGA3255)	Privately owned, stored Long Mynd	
XN185	Slingsby T21B Sedbergh TX1 (8942M/BGA4077)	RAF Museum Reserve Collection, Stafford	
XN186	Slingsby T21B Sedbergh TX1 (BGA3905) [HFG]	Privately owned, Watton	
XN187	Slingsby T21B Sedbergh TX1 (BGA3903)	Privately owned, Halton	
XN198	Slingsby T31B Cadet TX3	Privately owned, Bodmin	
XN238	Slingsby T31B Cadet TX3 <ff>	Aeroventure, Doncaster	
XN239	Slingsby T31B Cadet TX3 (8889M) [G]	Imperial War Museum, Duxford	
XN246	Slingsby T31B Cadet TX3	Solent Sky, Southampton	
XN258	WS55 Whirlwind HAR9 [589/CU]	North-East Aircraft Museum, Usworth	
XN297	WS55 Whirlwind HAR9 (XN311) [12]	Privately owned, Hull	
XN298	WS55 Whirlwind HAR9 [810/LS]	Privately owned	
XN299	WS55 Whirlwind HAS7 [758]	Tangmere Military Aviation Museum	
XN304	WS55 Whirlwind HAS7 [WW/B]	Norfolk & Suffolk Avn Museum, Flixton	
XN332	Saro P531 (G-APNV) [759]	FAA Museum, stored RNAS Yeovilton	
XN334	Saro P531	FAA Museum, stored RNAS Yeovilton	
XN341	Saro Skeeter AOP12 (8022M)	Stondon Transport Mus & Garden Centre, Beds	
XN344	Saro Skeeter AOP12 (8018M)	Science Museum, South Kensington	
XN345	Saro Skeeter AOP12 <ff>	The Helicopter Museum, Weston-super-Mare	
XN351	Saro Skeeter AOP12 (G-BKSC)	Privately owned, Ipswich	

Notes	Serial	Type (code/other identity)	Owner/operator location or fate
	XN380	WS55 Whirlwind HAS7	RAF Manston History Museum
	XN385	WS55 Whirlwind HAS7	Battleground Paintball, Yarm, Cleveland
	XN386	WS55 Whirlwind HAR9 [435/ED]	Aeroventure, Doncaster
	XN412	Auster AOP9	Auster 9 Group, Melton Mowbray
	XN437	Auster AOP9 (G-AXWA)	Privately owned, North Weald
	XN441	Auster AOP9 (G-BGKT)	Privately owned, Eggesford
	XN458	Hunting Jet Provost T3 (8234M/XN594)	Privately owned, Northallerton
	XN459	Hunting Jet Provost T3A (G-BWOT)	Transair(UK) Ltd, North Weald
	XN462	Hunting Jet Provost T3A [17]	FAA Museum, stored RNAS Yeovilton
	XN466	Hunting Jet Provost T3A [29] <ff>	No 1005 Sqn ATC, Radcliffe, Gr Manchester
	XN492	Hunting Jet Provost T3 (8079M) <ff>	No 2434 Sqn ATC, Linton-on-Ouse
	XN493	Hunting Jet Provost T3A (XN137) <ff>	Privately owned, Camberley
	XN494	Hunting Jet Provost T3A (9012M) [43]	Gatwick Aviation Museum, Charlwood, Surrey
	XN500	Hunting Jet Provost T3A	Norfolk & Suffolk Avn Museum, Flixton
	XN503	Hunting Jet Provost T3 <ff>	Boscombe Down Aviation Collection
	XN508	Hunting Jet Provost T3A <ff>	MoD/DSG, St Athan
	XN511	Hunting Jet Provost T3 [64] <ff>	Aeroventure, Doncaster
	XN549	Hunting Jet Provost T3 (8235M) <ff>	Privately owned, Warrington
	XN551	Hunting Jet Provost T3A (8984M)	Privately owned, Felton Common, Bristol
	XN554	Hunting Jet Provost T3 (8436M) [K]	Gunsmoke Paintball, Hadleigh, Suffolk
	XN573	Hunting Jet Provost T3 [E] <ff>	Newark Air Museum, Winthorpe
	XN579	Hunting Jet Provost T3A (9137M) [14]	Gunsmoke Paintball, Hadleigh, Suffolk
	XN582	Hunting Jet Provost T3A (8957M) [95,H]	Privately owned, Bruntingthorpe
	XN584	Hunting Jet Provost T3A (9014M) [E]	Phoenix Aviation, Bruntingthorpe
	XN586	Hunting Jet Provost T3A (9039M) [91,S]	Brooklands Technical College
	XN589	Hunting Jet Provost T3A (9143M) [46]	RAF Linton-on-Ouse, on display
	XN597	Hunting Jet Provost T3 (7984M) <ff>	Lakes Lightnings, Spark Bridge, Cumbria
	XN607	Hunting Jet Provost T3 <ff>	Highland Aviation Museum, Inverness
	XN623	Hunting Jet Provost T3 (XN632/8352M)	Privately owned, Birlingham, Worcs
	XN629	Hunting Jet Provost T3A (G-BVEG/G-KNOT) [49]	Bentwaters Cold War Museum
	XN634	Hunting Jet Provost T3A <ff>	Privately owned, Preston, Lancs
	XN634	Hunting Jet Provost T3A [53] <rf>	BAE Systems Warton Fire Section
	XN637	Hunting Jet Provost T3 (G-BKOU) [03]	Privately owned, North Weald
	XN647	DH110 Sea Vixen FAW2 <ff>	'Privately owned, Staverton
	XN650	DH110 Sea Vixen FAW2 [456] <ff>	Privately owned, Spanhoe
	XN651	DH110 Sea Vixen FAW2 <ff>	Privately owned, Olney, Bucks
	XN685	DH110 Sea Vixen FAW2 (8173M) [703/VL]	Midland Air Museum, Coventry
	XN696	DH110 Sea Vixen FAW2 [751] <ff>	North-East Aircraft Museum, Unsworth
	XN714	Hunting H126	RAF Museum, Cosford
	XN726	EE Lightning F2A (8545M) <ff>	Boscombe Down Aviation Collection
	XN728	EE Lightning F2A (8546M) <ff>	Privately owned, Lincoln
	XN774	EE Lightning F2A (8551M) <ff>	Privately owned, Boston
	XN776	EE Lightning F2A (8535M) [C]	Royal Scottish Mus'm of Flight, E Fortune
	XN795	EE Lightning F2A <ff>	Privately owned, Foulness
	XN817	AW660 Argosy C1	*Scrapped at West Freugh, 20 July 2011*
	XN819	AW660 Argosy C1 (8205M) <ff>	Newark Air Museum, Winthorpe
	XN923	HS Buccaneer S1 [13]	Gatwick Aviation Museum, Charlwood, Surrey
	XN928	HS Buccaneer S1 (8179M) <ff>	Privately owned, Gravesend
	XN957	HS Buccaneer S1 [630/LM]	FAA Museum, RNAS Yeovilton
	XN964	HS Buccaneer S1 [118/V]	Newark Air Museum, Winthorpe
	XN967	HS Buccaneer S1 [233] <ff>	City of Norwich Aviation Museum
	XN972	HS Buccaneer S1 (8183M/XN962) <ff>	RAF Museum, Cosford
	XN974	HS Buccaneer S2A	Yorkshire Air Museum, Elvington
	XN979	HS Buccaneer S2 <ff>	Aeroventure, Doncaster
	XN981	HS Buccaneer S2B (fuselage)	Privately owned, Errol
	XN983	HS Buccaneer S2B <ff>	Fenland & W Norfolk Aviation Museum, Wisbech

Serial	Type (code/other identity)	Owner/operator location or fate	Notes
XP110	WS58 Wessex HAS3 (A2636)	DCAE AESS, HMS Sultan, Gosport	
XP137	WS58 Wessex HAS3 [11/DD]	RN, Predannack Fire School	
XP142	WS58 Wessex HAS3	FAA Museum, stored RNAS Yeovilton	
XP150	WS58 Wessex HAS3 [LS]	FETC, Moreton-in-Marsh, Glos	
XP165	WS Scout AH1	The Helicopter Museum, Weston-super-Mare	
XP190	WS Scout AH1	Aeroventure, Doncaster	
XP191	WS Scout AH1	Privately owned, Prenton, The Wirral	
XP226	Fairey Gannet AEW3	Newark Air Museum, Winthorpe	
XP241	Auster AOP9 (G-CEHR)	Privately owned, Eggesford	
XP242	Auster AOP9 (G-BUCI)	AAC Historic Aircraft Flight, Middle Wallop	
XP244	Auster AOP9 (7864M/M7922)	Privately owned, Stretton on Dunsmore	
XP248	Auster AOP9 (7863M/WZ679)	Privately owned, Coventry	
XP254	Auster AOP11 (G-ASCC)	Privately owned, Widmerpool	
XP279	Auster AOP9 (G-BWKK)	Privately owned, Popham	
XP280	Auster AOP9	Snibston Discovery Park, Coalville	
XP281	Auster AOP9	Imperial War Museum, Duxford	
XP286	Auster AOP9	Privately owned, Eggesford	
XP299	WS55 Whirlwind HAR10 (8726M)	RAF Museum, Hendon	
XP328	WS55 Whirlwind HAR10 (G-BKHC)	Privately owned, Tattershall Thorpe (wreck)	
XP330	WS55 Whirlwind HAR10	CAA Fire School, Durham/Tees Valley	
XP344	WS55 Whirlwind HAR10 (8764M) [H723]	RAF North Luffenham Training Area	
XP345	WS55 Whirlwind HAR10 (8792M) [N]	Yorkshire Helicopter Preservation Group, Doncaster	
XP346	WS55 Whirlwind HAR10 (8793M)	Privately owned, Long Marston	
XP350	WS55 Whirlwind HAR10	Privately owned, Bassetts Pole, Staffs	
XP351	WS55 Whirlwind HAR10 (8672M) [Z]	Gatwick Aviation Museum, Charlwood, Surrey	
XP355	WS55 Whirlwind HAR10 (8463M/G-BEBC)	City of Norwich Aviation Museum	
XP360	WS55 Whirlwind HAR10 [V]	Privately owned, Bicton, nr Leominster	
XP398	WS55 Whirlwind HAR10 (8794M)	Gatwick Aviation Museum, Charlwood, Surrey	
XP404	WS55 Whirlwind HAR10 (8682M)	The Helicopter Museum, Weston-super-Mare	
XP411	AW660 Argosy C1 (8442M) [C]	RAF Museum, Cosford	
XP454	Slingsby T38 Grasshopper TX1	Privately owned, Sywell	
XP459	Slingsby T38 Grasshopper TX1	Privately owned, stored Nayland, Suffolk	
XP463	Slingsby T38 Grasshopper TX1 (BGA4372)	Privately owned, Lasham	
XP488	Slingsby T38 Grasshopper TX1	Privately owned, Keevil	
XP490	Slingsby T38 Grasshopper TX1 (BGA4552)	Privately owned, stored Watton	
XP492	Slingsby T38 Grasshopper TX1 (BGA3480)	Privately owned, Gallows Hill, Dorset	
XP493	Slingsby T38 Grasshopper TX1	Privately owned, stored Aston Down	
XP494	Slingsby T38 Grasshopper TX1	Privately owned, Wolverhampton	
XP502	HS Gnat T1 (8576M)	Privately owned, Cotswold Airport	
XP505	HS Gnat T1	Science Museum, Wroughton	
XP516	HS Gnat T1 (8580M) [16]	Farnborough Air Sciences Trust, Farnborough	
XP540	HS Gnat T1 (8608M) [62]	Privately owned, North Weald	
XP542	HS Gnat T1 (8575M)	Solent Sky, Southampton	
XP556	Hunting Jet Provost T4 (9027M) [B]	RAF Cranwell Aviation Heritage Centre	
XP557	Hunting Jet Provost T4 (8494M) [72]	Dumfries & Galloway Avn Mus, Dumfries	
XP558	Hunting Jet Provost T4 (8627M) <ff>	Privately owned, Stoneykirk, D&G	
XP558	Hunting Jet Provost T4 (8627M)[20] <rf>	Privately owned, Sproughton	
XP563	Hunting Jet Provost T4 (9028M) [C]	Privately owned, Sproughton	
XP568	Hunting Jet Provost T4	East Midlands Airport Aeropark	
XP573	Hunting Jet Provost T4 (8236M) [19]	Jersey Airport Fire Section	
XP585	Hunting Jet Provost T4 (8407M) [24]	NE Wales Institute, Wrexham	
XP627	Hunting Jet Provost T4	North-East Aircraft Museum, stored Usworth	
XP629	Hunting Jet Provost T4 (9026M) [P]	Gunsmoke Paintball, Hadleigh, Suffolk	
XP640	Hunting Jet Provost T4 (8501M) [M]	Yorkshire Air Museum, Elvington	
XP642	Hunting Jet Provost T4 <ff>	Privately owned, Welshpool	
XP672	Hunting Jet Provost T4 (8458M/G-RAFI) 03]	Privately owned, Bruntingthorpe	
XP680	Hunting Jet Provost T4 (8460M)	FETC, Moreton-in-Marsh, Glos	

Notes	Serial	Type (code/other identity)	Owner/operator location or fate
	XP686	Hunting Jet Provost T4 (8401M/8502M) [G]	Gunsmoke Paintball, Hadleigh, Suffolk
	XP701	BAC Lightning F3 (8924M) <ff>	Robertsbridge Aviation Society, Mayfield
	XP703	BAC Lightning F3 <ff>	Lightning Preservation Group, Bruntingthorpe
	XP706	BAC Lightning F3 (8925M)	Aeroventure, Doncaster
	XP743	BAC Lightning F3 <ff>	Wattisham Airfield Museum
	XP745	BAC Lightning F3 (8453M) <ff>	Vanguard Haulage, Greenford, London
	XP765	BAC Lightning F6 (XS897) [A]	Lakes Lightnings, RAF Coningsby
	XP820	DHC2 Beaver AL1	AAC Historic Aircraft Flight, Middle Wallop
	XP821	DHC2 Beaver AL1 [MCO]	Museum of Army Flying, Middle Wallop
	XP822	DHC2 Beaver AL1	Museum of Army Flying, Middle Wallop
	XP831	Hawker P.1127 (8406M)	Science Museum, South Kensington
	XP841	Handley-Page HP115	FAA Museum, RNAS Yeovilton
	XP847	WS Scout AH1	Museum of Army Flying, Middle Wallop
	XP848	WS Scout AH1	DCAE Arborfield, on display
	XP853	WS Scout AH1	Privately owned, Sutton, Surrey
	XP854	WS Scout AH1 (7898M/TAD 043)	Mayhem Paintball, Abridge, Essex
	XP855	WS Scout AH1	DCAE SEAE, Arborfield
	XP856	WS Scout AH1	Scrapped
	XP883	WS Scout AH1	Privately owned, Bruntingthorpe
	XP884	WS Scout AH1	AAC, stored Middle Wallop
	XP885	WS Scout AH1	AAC Wattisham, instructional use
	XP886	WS Scout AH1	The Helicopter Museum, Weston-super-Mare
	XP888	WS Scout AH1	Privately owned, Sproughton
	XP890	WS Scout AH1 [G] (fuselage)	Privately owned, Ipswich
	XP893	WS Scout AH1	AAC Middle Wallop, BDRT
	XP895	WS Scout AH1	Privately owned, Woodley, Berks
	XP899	WS Scout AH1 [D]	DCAE SEAE, Arborfield
	XP900	WS Scout AH1	AAC Wattisham, instructional use
	XP902	WS Scout AH1 <ff>	Aeroventure, Doncaster
	XP905	WS Scout AH1	Privately owned, stored Sproughton
	XP907	WS Scout AH1 (G-SROE)	Privately owned, Wattisham
	XP910	WS Scout AH1	Museum of Army Flying, Middle Wallop
	XP924	DH110 Sea Vixen D3 (G-CVIX) [134/E]	Privately owned, Bournemouth
	XP925	DH110 Sea Vixen FAW2 [752] <ff>	No 1268 Sqn ATC, Haslemere, Surrey
	XP980	Hawker P.1127	FAA Museum, RNAS Yeovilton
	XP984	Hawker P.1127	Brooklands Museum, Weybridge
	XR220	BAC TSR2 (7933M)	RAF Museum, Cosford
	XR222	BAC TSR2	Imperial War Museum, Duxford
	XR232	Sud Alouette AH2 (F-WEIP)	Museum of Army Flying, Middle Wallop
	XR239	Auster AOP9	Privately owned, Stretton on Dunsmore
	XR240	Auster AOP9 (G-BDFH)	Privately owned, Yeovilton
	XR241	Auster AOP9 (G-AXRR)	Privately owned, Eggesford
	XR244	Auster AOP9	AAC Historic Aircraft Flight, Middle Wallop
	XR246	Auster AOP9 (7862M/G-AZBU)	Privately owned, Melton Mowbray
	XR267	Auster AOP9 (G-BJXR)	Privately owned, Hucknall
	XR271	Auster AOP9	Royal Artillery Experience, Woolwich
	XR346	Northrop Shelduck D1 (comp XW578)	Bournemouth Aviation Museum
	XR371	SC5 Belfast C1	RAF Museum, Cosford
	XR379	Sud Alouette AH2	AAC Historic Aircraft Flight, Middle Wallop
	XR453	WS55 Whirlwind HAR10 (8873M) [A]	RAF Odiham, on gate
	XR458	WS55 Whirlwind HAR10 (8662M) [H]	Privately owned, Orton, Northants
	XR485	WS55 Whirlwind HAR10 [Q]	Norfolk & Suffolk Avn Museum, Flixton
	XR486	WS55 Whirlwind HCC12 (8727M/G-RWWW)	The Helicopter Museum, Weston-super-Mare
	XR498	WS58 Wessex HC2 (9342M) [X]	DCAE, No 1 SoTT, Cosford
	XR501	WS58 Wessex HC2	Army, Keogh Barracks, Aldershot, instructional use
	XR502	WS58 Wessex HC2 (G-CCUP) [Z]	Privately owned, Badgers Mount, Kent

Serial	Type (code/other identity)	Owner/operator location or fate	Notes
XR503	WS58 Wessex HC2	MoD DFTDC, Manston	
XR506	WS58 Wessex HC2 (9343M) [V]	Army, Longmoor Camp, Hants, instructional use	
XR516	WS58 Wessex HC2 (9319M) [V]	RAF Shawbury, on display	
XR517	WS58 Wessex HC2 [N]	Ulster Aviation Society, Long Kesh	
XR518	WS58 Wessex HC2	DCAE AESS, HMS Sultan, Gosport	
XR523	WS58 Wessex HC2 [M]	RN HMS Raleigh, Torpoint, instructional use	
XR525	WS58 Wessex HC2 [G]	RAF Museum, Cosford	
XR526	WS58 Wessex HC2 (8147M)	The Helicopter Museum, Weston-super-Mare	
XR528	WS58 Wessex HC2	Privately owned, Little Rissington (GI use)	
XR529	WS58 Wessex HC2 (9268M) [E]	RAF Aldergrove, on display	
XR534	HS Gnat T1 (8578M) [65]	Newark Air Museum, Winthorpe	
XR537	HS Gnat T1 (8642M/G-NATY)	Privately owned, Bournemouth	
XR538	HS Gnat T1 (8621M/G-RORI) [01]	Heritage Aircraft Trust, North Weald	
XR571	HS Gnat T1 (8493M)	RAF Red Arrows, Scampton, on display	
XR574	HS Gnat T1 (8631M) [72]	Trenchard Museum, Halton	
XR595	WS Scout AH1 (G-BWHU) [M]	Privately owned, North Weald	
XR601	WS Scout AH1	Army Whittington Barracks, Lichfield, on display	
XR627	WS Scout AH1 [X]	Privately owned, Townhill, Fife	
XR628	WS Scout AH1	Privately owned, Ipswich	
XR629	WS Scout AH1 (fuselage)	Privately owned, Ipswich	
XR635	WS Scout AH1	Coventry University, instructional use	
XR650	Hunting Jet Provost T4 (8459M) [28]	Boscombe Down Aviation Collection	
XR654	Hunting Jet Provost T4 <ff>	Privately owned, Chester	
XR658	Hunting Jet Provost T4 (8192M)	Deeside College, Connah's Quay, Clwyd	
XR662	Hunting Jet Provost T4 (8410M) [25]	Boulton Paul Association, Wolverhampton	
XR673	Hunting Jet Provost T4 (G-BXLO/9032M) [L]	Privately owned, Church Fenton	
XR681	Hunting Jet Provost T4 (8588M) <ff>	Robertsbridge Aviation Society, Mayfield	
XR700	Hunting Jet Provost T4 (8589M) <ff>	RAF Aldergrove	
XR713	BAC Lightning F3 (8935M) [C]	RAF Leuchars, on display	
XR718	BAC Lightning F6 (8932M) [DA]	Privately owned, Over Dinsdale, N Yorks	
XR724	BAC Lightning F6 (G-BTSY)	The Lightning Association, Binbrook	
XR725	BAC Lightning F6	Privately owned, Binbrook	
XR726	BAC Lightning F6 <ff>	Privately owned, Harrogate	
XR728	BAC Lightning F6 [JS]	Lightning Preservation Grp, Bruntingthorpe	
XR747	BAC Lightning F6 <ff>	Privately owned, Cubert, Cornwall	
XR749	BAC Lightning F3 (8934M) [DA]	Privately owned, Peterhead	
XR751	BAC Lightning F3 <ff>	Privately owned, Thorpe Wood, N Yorks	
XR753	BAC Lightning F6 (8969M) [XI]	RAF Coningsby on display	
XR753	BAC Lightning F53 (ZF578) [A]	Tangmere Military Aviation Museum	
XR754	BAC Lightning F6 (8972M) <ff>	Aeroventure, Doncaster	
XR755	BAC Lightning F3	Privately owned, Callington, Cornwall	
XR757	BAC Lightning F6 <ff>	RAF Scampton Historical Museum	
XR759	BAC Lightning F6 <ff>	Privately owned, Haxey, Lincs	
XR770	BAC Lightning F6 [AA]	RAF Waddington, for display	
XR771	BAC Lightning F6 [BF]	Midland Air Museum, Coventry	
XR806	BAC VC10 C1K (9285M) <ff>	RAF Brize Norton, BDRT	
XR808	BAC VC10 C1K [R]	RAF No 101 Sqn, Brize Norton	
XR810	BAC VC10 C1K <ff>	Privately owned, Crondall, Hants	
XR944	Wallis WA116 (G-ATTB)	Privately owned, Reymerston Hall, Norfolk	
XR977	HS Gnat T1 (8640M) [3]	RAF Museum, Cosford	
XR991	HS Gnat T1 (8624M/XS102/G-MOUR)	Heritage Aircraft Trust, North Weald	
XR993	HS Gnat T1 (8620M/XP534/G-BVPP)	Privately owned, Bruntingthorpe	
XS100	HS Gnat T1 (8561M) <ff>	Privately owned, London SW3	
XS100	HS Gnat T1 (8561M) <rf>	Privately owned, Fyfield, Essex	
XS104	HS Gnat T1 (8604M/G-FRCE)	Privately owned, North Weald	
XS111	HS Gnat T1 (8618M/XP504/G-TIMM)	Heritage Aircraft Trust, North Weald	
XS149	WS58 Wessex HAS3 [661/GL]	The Helicopter Museum, Weston-super-Mare	

Notes	Serial	Type (code/other identity)	Owner/operator location or fate
	XS176	Hunting Jet Provost T4 (8514M) <ff>	Highland Aviation Museum, Inverness
	XS177	Hunting Jet Provost T4 (9044M) [N]	Metheringham Airfield Visitors Centre
	XS179	Hunting Jet Provost T4 (8237M) [20]	Museum of Science & Industry, stored Manchester
	XS180	Hunting Jet Provost T4 (8238M/8338M) [21]	MoD, Boscombe Down
	XS181	Hunting Jet Provost T4 (9033M) <ff>	Lakes Lightnings, Spark Bridge, Cumbria
	XS183	Hunting Jet Provost T4 <ff>	Privately owned, Plymouth
	XS186	Hunting Jet Provost T4 (8408M) [M]	Metheringham Airfield Visitors Centre
	XS209	Hunting Jet Provost T4 (8409M)	Solway Aviation Society, Carlisle
	XS216	Hunting Jet Provost T4 <ff>	Aeroventure, Doncaster
	XS218	Hunting Jet Provost T4 (8508M) <ff>	No 447 Sqn ATC, Henley-on-Thames, Berks
	XS231	BAC Jet Provost T5 (G-ATAJ)	Boscombe Down Aviation Collection
	XS235	DH106 Comet 4C (G-CPDA)	Cold War Jets Collection, Bruntingthorpe
	XS238	Auster AOP9 (TAD 200)	Newark Air Museum, stored Winthorpe
	XS416	BAC Lightning T5	Privately owned, New York, Lincs
	XS417	BAC Lightning T5 [DZ]	Newark Air Museum, Winthorpe
	XS420	BAC Lightning T5	Lakes Lightnings, FAST, Farnborough
	XS421	BAC Lightning T5 <ff>	Privately owned, Foulness
	XS456	BAC Lightning T5 [DX]	Skegness Water Leisure Park
	XS457	BAC Lightning T5 <ff>	Privately owned, Binbrook
	XS458	BAC Lightning T5 [T]	T5 Projects, Cranfield
	XS459	BAC Lightning T5 [AW]	Fenland & W Norfolk Aviation Museum, Wisbech
	XS463	WS Wasp HAS1 (XT431)	Gatwick Aviation Museum, Charlwood, Surrey
	XS481	WS58 Wessex HU5	Aeroventure, Doncaster
	XS482	WS58 Wessex HU5	RAF Manston History Museum
	XS486	WS58 Wessex HU5 (9272M) [524/CU,F]	The Helicopter Museum, Weston-super-Mare
	XS488	WS58 Wessex HU5 (9056M) [F]	DCAE AESS, HMS Sultan, Gosport
	XS489	WS58 Wessex HU5 [R]	Privately owned, Westerham, Kent
	XS493	WS58 Wessex HU5	Vector Aerospace, stored Fleetlands
	XS496	WS58 Wessex HU5 [625/PO]	DCAE AESS, HMS Sultan, Gosport
	XS507	WS58 Wessex HU5	RAF Benson, for display
	XS508	WS58 Wessex HU5	FAA Museum, stored RNAS Yeovilton
	XS510	WS58 Wessex HU5 [626/PO]	No 1414 Sqn ATC, Crowborough, Sussex
	XS511	WS58 Wessex HU5 [M]	Tangmere Military Aircraft Museum
	XS513	WS58 Wessex HU5	RNAS Yeovilton Fire Section
	XS514	WS58 Wessex HU5 (A2740) [L/PO]	DCAE AESS, HMS Sultan, Gosport
	XS515	WS58 Wessex HU5 [N]	Army, Keogh Barracks, Aldershot, instructional use
	XS516	WS58 Wessex HU5 [Q]	Privately owned, Redruth, Cornwall
	XS520	WS58 Wessex HU5 [F]	RN, Predannack Fire School
	XS522	WS58 Wessex HU5 [ZL]	Blackball Paintball, Truro, Cornwall
	XS527	WS Wasp HAS1	FAA Museum, stored RNAS Yeovilton
	XS529	WS Wasp HAS1	Privately owned, Redruth, Cornwall
	XS539	WS Wasp HAS1 [435]	Vector Aerospace Fleetlands Apprentice School
	XS567	WS Wasp HAS1 [434/E]	Imperial War Museum, Duxford
	XS568	WS Wasp HAS1 (A2715) [441]	DCAE AESS, HMS Sultan, Gosport
	XS570	WS Wasp HAS1 [445/P]	Warship Preservation Trust, Birkenhead
	XS574	Northrop Shelduck D1 <R>	FAA Museum, stored RNAS Yeovilton
	XS576	DH110 Sea Vixen FAW2 [125/E]	Imperial War Museum, Duxford
	XS587	DH110 Sea Vixen FAW(TT)2 (8828M/G-VIXN)	Gatwick Aviation Museum, Charlwood, Surrey
	XS590	DH110 Sea Vixen FAW2 [131/E]	FAA Museum, RNAS Yeovilton
	XS596	HS Andover C1(PR)	MoD, Boscombe Down (wfu)
	XS598	HS Andover C1 (fuselage)	FETC, Moreton-in-Marsh, Glos
	XS606	HS Andover C1	MoD/ETPS, Boscombe Down
	XS639	HS Andover E3A (9241M)	RAF Museum, Cosford
	XS641	HS Andover C1PR (9198M) (fuselage)	Privately owned, Sandbach, Cheshire
	XS643	HS Andover E3A (9278M) <ff>	Privately owned, Stock, Essex
	XS646	HS Andover C1(mod)	RAF/AWC/No 206(R) Sqn, Boscombe Down

Serial	Type (code/other identity)	Owner/operator location or fate	Notes
XS651	Slingsby T45 Swallow TX1 (BGA1211)	Privately owned, Keevil	
XS652	Slingsby T45 Swallow TX1 (BGA1107)	Privately owned, Chipping, Lancs	
XS674	WS58 Wessex HC2 [R]	Privately owned, Biggin Hill	
XS695	HS Kestrel FGA1	RAF Museum Restoration Centre, Cosford	
XS709	HS125 Dominie T1 [M]	RAF Museum, Cosford	
XS710	HS125 Dominie T1 (9259M) [O]	RAF Cranwell Fire Section	
XS711	HS125 Dominie T1 (fuselage)	MoD, Boscombe Down	
XS712	HS125 Dominie T1 [A]	Sold as N19CQ, May 2011	
XS713	HS125 Dominie T1 [C]	RAF Shawbury Fire Section	
XS714	HS125 Dominie T1 (9246M) [P]	MoD DFTDC, Manston	
XS726	HS125 Dominie T1 (9273M) [T]	Privately owned, Sproughton	
XS727	HS125 Dominie T1 [D]	RAF Cranwell (wfu)	
XS728	HS125 Dominie T1 [E]	Sold as N19CU, May 2011	
XS730	HS125 Dominie T1 [H]	Sold as N19UG, May 2011	
XS731	HS125 Dominie T1 [J]	Sold as N19XY, May 2011	
XS733	HS125 Dominie T1 (9276M) [Q]	Privately owned, Sproughton	
XS734	HS125 Dominie T1 (9260M) [N]	Privately owned, Sproughton	
XS735	HS125 Dominie T1 (9264M) [R]	Absolute Adventure, Craig-y-nos, Powys	
XS736	HS125 Dominie T1 [S]	Privately owned, Winterbourne Gunner, Wilts	
XS737	HS125 Dominie T1 [K]	Sold as N19EK, May 2011	
XS738	HS125 Dominie T1 (9274M) [U]	RN, Predannack Fire School	
XS739	HS125 Dominie T1 [F]	Sold as N19UK, May 2011	
XS743	Beagle B206Z	MoD/ETPS, Boscombe Down	
XS765	Beagle B206 Basset CC1 (G-BSET)	MoD, QinetiQ, Boscombe Down (spares use)	
XS770	Beagle B206 Basset CC1 (G-HRHI)	MoD, QinetiQ, Boscombe Down (spares use)	
XS790	HS748 Andover CC2 <ff>	Boscombe Down Aviation Collection	
XS791	HS748 Andover CC2 (fuselage)	Privately owned, Stock, Essex	
XS863	WS58 Wessex HAS1 [304]	Imperial War Museum, Duxford	
XS876	WS58 Wessex HAS1 [523/PO]	East Midlands Airport Aeropark	
XS885	WS58 Wessex HAS1 [512/DD]	RN, Predannack Fire School	
XS886	WS58 Wessex HAS1 [527/CU]	Privately owned, Ditchling, E Sussex	
XS887	WS58 Wessex HAS1 [403/FI]	Aeroventure, Doncaster	
XS888	WS58 Wessex HAS1 [521]	Guernsey Airport Fire Section	
XS897	BAC Lightning F6	Repainted as XP765, November 2011	
XS898	BAC Lightning F6 <ff>	Privately owned, Lavendon, Bucks	
XS899	BAC Lightning F6 <ff>	Privately owned, Binbrook	
XS903	BAC Lightning F6 [BA]	Yorkshire Air Museum, Elvington	
XS904	BAC Lightning F6 [BQ]	Lightning Preservation Grp, Bruntingthorpe	
XS919	BAC Lightning F6	Privately owned, stored Dinton Wilts	
XS922	BAC Lightning F6 (8973M) <ff>	Lakes Lightnings, Spark Bridge, Cumbria	
XS923	BAC Lightning F6 <ff>	Privately owned, Welshpool	
XS925	BAC Lightning F6 (8961M) [BA]	RAF Museum, Hendon	
XS928	BAC Lightning F6 [AD]	BAE Systems Warton, on display	
XS932	BAC Lightning F6 <ff>	Privately owned, Walcott, Lincs	
XS933	BAC Lightning F6 <ff>	Privately owned, Farnham	
XS933	BAC Lightning F53 (ZF594) [BF]	North-East Aircraft Museum, Usworth	
XS936	BAC Lightning F6	Castle Motors, Liskeard, Cornwall	
XT108	Agusta-Bell 47G-3 Sioux AH1 [U]	Museum of Army Flying, Middle Wallop	
XT123	WS Sioux AH1 (XT827) [D]	AAC Middle Wallop, at main gate	
XT131	Agusta-Bell 47G-3 Sioux AH1 [B]	AAC Historic Aircraft Flight, Middle Wallop	
XT140	Agusta-Bell 47G-3 Sioux AH1	Perth Technical College	
XT141	Agusta-Bell 47G-3 Sioux AH1	Privately owned, Newcastle	
XT150	Agusta-Bell 47G-3 Sioux AH1 (7883M) [R]	Privately owned, Aeroventure, Doncaster	
XT151	WS Sioux AH1	Museum of Army Flying, stored Middle Wallop	
XT176	WS Sioux AH1 [U]	FAA Museum, stored RNAS Yeovilton	
XT190	WS Sioux AH1	The Helicopter Museum, Weston-super-Mare	
XT200	WS Sioux AH1 [F]	Newark Air Museum, Winthorpe	

Notes	Serial	Type (code/other identity)	Owner/operator location or fate
	XT208	WS Sioux AH1 (wreck)	Blessingbourne Museum, Fivemiletown, Co Tyrone, NI
	XT223	WS Sioux AH1 (G-XTUN)	Privately owned, Sherburn-in-Elmet
	XT236	WS Sioux AH1 (frame only)	Aeroventure, Doncaster
	XT242	WS Sioux AH1 (composite) [12]	Aeroventure, Doncaster
	XT257	WS58 Wessex HAS3 (8719M)	Bournemouth Aviation Museum
	XT277	HS Buccaneer S2A (8853M) <ff>	Privately owned, Welshpool
	XT280	HS Buccaneer S2A <ff>	Dumfries & Galloway Avn Mus, Dumfries
	XT284	HS Buccaneer S2A (8855M) <ff>	Privately owned, Felixstowe
	XT288	HS Buccaneer S2B (9134M)	Royal Scottish Museum of Flight, stored E Fortune
	XT420	WS Wasp HAS1 (G-CBUI) [606]	Privately owned, Thruxton
	XT427	WS Wasp HAS1 [606]	FAA Museum, stored RNAS Yeovilton
	XT434	WS Wasp HAS1 (G-CGGK) [455]	Privately owned, Breighton
	XT435	WS Wasp HAS1 (NZ3907/G-RIMM) [430]	Privately owned, Badwell Green, Suffolk
	XT437	WS Wasp HAS1 [423]	Boscombe Down Aviation Collection
	XT439	WS Wasp HAS1 [605]	Privately owned, Hemel Hempstead
	XT443	WS Wasp HAS1 [422/AU]	The Helicopter Museum, Weston-super-Mare
	XT453	WS58 Wessex HU5 (A2756) [B/PO]	DCAE AESS, HMS Sultan, Gosport
	XT455	WS58 Wessex HU5 (A2654) [U]	DCAE AESS, HMS Sultan, Gosport
	XT456	WS58 Wessex HU5 (8941M) [XZ]	RAF Aldergrove, BDRT
	XT458	WS58 Wessex HU5 (A2768) [P/VL]	RNAS Yeovilton
	XT466	WS58 Wessex HU5 (A2617/8921M) [XV]	Army Whittington Barracks, Lichfield, on display
	XT467	WS58 Wessex HU5 (8922M) [BF]	Gunsmoke Paintball, Hadleigh, Suffolk
	XT469	WS58 Wessex HU5 (8920M)	MSS Holdings, Kirkham, Lancs
	XT472	WS58 Wessex HU5 [XC]	The Helicopter Museum, Weston-super-Mare
	XT480	WS58 Wessex HU5 [468/RG]	Rednal Paintball, Shropshire
	XT482	WS58 Wessex HU5 [ZM/VL]	FAA Museum, RNAS Yeovilton
	XT484	WS58 Wessex HU5 (A2742) [H]	DCAE AESS, HMS Sultan, Gosport
	XT485	WS58 Wessex HU5 (A2680)	DCAE AESS, HMS Sultan, Gosport
	XT486	WS58 Wessex HU5 (8919M)	Dumfries & Galloway Avn Mus, Dumfries
	XT550	WS Sioux AH1 [D]	AAC, stored Middle Wallop
	XT575	Vickers Viscount 837 <ff>	Brooklands Museum, Weybridge
	XT581	Northrop Shelduck D1	Imperial War Museum, Duxford
	XT583	Northrop Shelduck D1	Royal Artillery Experience, Woolwich
	XT596	McD F-4K Phantom FG1	FAA Museum, RNAS Yeovilton
	XT597	McD F-4K Phantom FG1	Boscombe Down Aviation Collection
	XT601	WS58 Wessex HC2 (9277M) (composite)	RAF Odiham, BDRT
	XT604	WS58 Wessex HC2	East Midlands Airport Aeropark
	XT617	WS Scout AH1	AAC Wattisham, on display
	XT621	WS Scout AH1	Defence Academy of the UK, Shrivenham
	XT623	WS Scout AH1	DCAE SEAE, Arborfield
	XT626	WS Scout AH1 [Q]	AAC Historic Aircraft Flt, Middle Wallop
	XT630	WS Scout AH1 (G-BXRL) [X]	Privately owned, Bruntingthorpe
	XT631	WS Scout AH1 [D]	Privately owned, Ipswich
	XT633	WS Scout AH1	DCAE SEAE, Arborfield
	XT634	WS Scout AH1 (G-BYRX) [T]	Privately owned, Tollerton
	XT638	WS Scout AH1 [N]	AAC Middle Wallop, at gate
	XT640	WS Scout AH1	Privately owned, Sproughton
	XT643	WS Scout AH1 [Z]	Army, Thorpe Camp, East Wretham
	XT672	WS58 Wessex HC2 [WE]	RAF Stafford, on display
	XT681	WS58 Wessex HC2 (9279M) [U] <ff>	Privately owned, Wallingford, Oxon
	XT761	WS58 Wessex HU5	DCAE AESS, HMS Sultan, Gosport
	XT762	WS58 Wessex HU5	Hamburger Hill Paintball, Marksbury, Somerset
	XT765	WS58 Wessex HU5 [J]	FAA Museum, RNAS Yeovilton
	XT769	WS58 Wessex HU5 [823]	FAA Museum, RNAS Yeovilton
	XT771	WS58 Wessex HU5 [620/PO]	DCAE AESS, HMS Sultan, Gosport
	XT773	WS58 Wessex HU5 (9123M)	RAF Shawbury Fire Section
	XT778	WS Wasp HAS1 [430]	FAA Museum, stored RNAS Yeovilton
	XT780	WS Wasp HAS1 [636]	Fareham Tertiary College, Hants

Serial	Type (code/other identity)	Owner/operator location or fate	Notes
XT787	WS Wasp HAS1 (NZ3905/G-KAXT)	Kennet Aviation, Old Warden	
XT788	WS Wasp HAS1 (G-BMIR) [474]	Privately owned, Dunkeswell	
XT793	WS Wasp HAS1 (G-BZPP) [456]	Privately owned, Thruxton (wreck)	
XT852	McD YF-4M Phantom FGR2	*Scrapped at West Freugh, 20 July 2011*	
XT863	McD F-4K Phantom FG1 <ff>	Privately owned, Cowes, IOW	
XT864	McD F-4K Phantom FG1 (8998M/XT684) [BJ]	RAF Leuchars on display	
XT891	McD F-4M Phantom FGR2 (9136M) [P]	RAF Coningsby, at main gate	
XT903	McD F-4M Phantom FGR2 <ff>	RAF Museum Restoration Centre, Cosford	
XT905	McD F-4M Phantom FGR2 (9286M) [P]	RAF North Luffenham Training Area	
XT907	McD F-4M Phantom FGR2 (9151M) [W]	DEODS, Chattenden, Kent	
XT914	McD F-4M Phantom FGR2 (9269M) [Z]	RAF Brampton, Cambs, on display	
XV101	BAC VC10 K1 [S]	Privately owned, Bruntingthorpe	
XV102	BAC VC10 C1K [T]	Privately owned, Bruntingthorpe	
XV104	BAC VC10 C1K [U]	RAF No 101 Sqn, Brize Norton	
XV105	BAC VC10 C1K [V]	Privately owned, Bruntingthorpe	
XV106	BAC VC10 C1K [W]	MoD/DSG, St Athan	
XV107	BAC VC10 C1K [X]	Privately owned, Bruntingthorpe	
XV108	BAC VC10 C1K [Y]	RAF No 101 Sqn, Brize Norton	
XV109	BAC VC10 C1K <ff>	Privately owned, Bruntingthorpe	
XV118	WS Scout AH1 (9141M)	Kennet Aviation, North Weald	
XV122	WS Scout AH1 [D]	Defence Academy of the UK, Shrivenham	
XV123	WS Scout AH1	RAF Shawbury, on display	
XV124	WS Scout AH1 [W]	*Sold to Greece, 2011*	
XV127	WS Scout AH1	Museum of Army Flying, Middle Wallop	
XV130	WS Scout AH1 (G-BWJW) [R]	Privately owned, Tollerton	
XV131	WS Scout AH1 [Y]	AAC 70 Aircraft Workshops, Middle Wallop, BDRT	
XV134	WS Scout AH1 (G-BWLX) [P]	*Sold as N438VC, March 2011*	
XV136	WS Scout AH1 [X]	AAC Netheravon, on display	
XV137	WS Scout AH1 (G-CRUM)	Privately owned, Chiseldon, Wilts	
XV137	WS Scout AH1 (XV139)	Aeroventure, stored Doncaster	
XV138	WS Scout AH1 (G-SASM)	Privately owned, Thruxton	
XV141	WS Scout AH1	REME Museum, Arborfield	
XV148	HS Nimrod MR1(mod) <ff>	Privately owned, Malmesbury	
XV161	HS Buccaneer S2B (9117M) <ff>	Dundonald Aviation Centre	
XV165	HS Buccaneer S2B <ff>	Privately owned, Ashford, Kent	
XV168	HS Buccaneer S2B [AF]	BAE Systems Brough, on display	
XV177	Lockheed C-130K Hercules C3A [177]	RAF No 47 Sqn, Brize Norton	
XV188	Lockheed C-130K Hercules C3A [188]	RAF No 47 Sqn, Brize Norton	
XV196	Lockheed C-130K Hercules C1 [196]	RAF No 47 Sqn, Brize Norton	
XV197	Lockheed C-130K Hercules C3 [197]	Privately owned, Hixon, Staffs	
XV200	Lockheed C-130K Hercules C1 [200]	RAF No 47 Sqn, Brize Norton	
XV201	Lockheed C-130K Hercules C1K <ff>	Marshalls, Cambridge	
XV202	Lockheed C-130K Hercules C3 [202]	RAF Museum, Cosford	
XV208	Lockheed C-130K Hercules W2	Marshalls, Cambridge (wfu)	
XV209	Lockheed C-130K Hercules C3A [209]	RAF No 47 Sqn, Brize Norton	
XV212	Lockheed C-130K Hercules C3 [212]	MoD/Marshalls, stored Cambridge, for disposal	
XV214	Lockheed C-130K Hercules C3A [214]	RAF No 47 Sqn, Brize Norton	
XV217	Lockheed C-130K Hercules C3	Privately owned, Hixon, Staffs	
XV220	Lockheed C-130K Hercules C3	Privately owned, Hixon, Staffs	
XV221	Lockheed C-130K Hercules C3 [221]	Privately owned, Bruntingthorpe	
XV226	HS Nimrod MR2 $	Cold War Jets Collection, Bruntingthorpe	
XV229	HS Nimrod MR2 [29]	MoD DFTDC, Manston	
XV231	HS Nimrod MR2 [31]	Aviation Viewing Park, Manchester	
XV232	HS Nimrod MR2 [32]	AIRBASE, Coventry	
XV235	HS Nimrod MR2 [35] <ff>	Privately owned, Kinloss	
XV240	HS Nimrod MR2 [40] <ff>	Privately owned, Spey Bay, Moray	

Notes	Serial	Type (code/other identity)	Owner/operator location or fate
	XV241	HS Nimrod MR2 [41] <ff>	Royal Scottish Mus'm of Flight, E Fortune
	XV244	HS Nimrod MR2 [44] <ff>	RAF Kinloss
	XV246	HS Nimrod MR2	*Scrapped at Woodford, January 2011*
	XV248	HS Nimrod MR2	*Scrapped at Kinloss, July 2010*
	XV249	HS Nimrod R1 $	RAF Museum, Cotswold Airport (for Cosford)
	XV250	HS Nimrod MR2 [50]	Yorkshire Air Museum, Elvington
	XV252	HS Nimrod MR2 [52] <ff>	Privately owned, Cullen, Moray
	XV253	HS Nimrod MR2 (9118M)	*Scrapped at Woodford, May 2009*
	XV254	HS Nimrod MR2 [54] <ff>	Highland Aviation Museum, Inverness
	XV255	HS Nimrod MR2 [55]	City of Norwich Aviation Museum
	XV259	BAe Nimrod AEW3 <ff>	Privately owned, Carlisle
	XV263	BAe Nimrod AEW3P (8967M) <ff>	BAE Systems, Brough
	XV263	BAe Nimrod AEW3P (8967M) <rf>	MoD/BAE Systems, Woodford
	XV268	DHC2 Beaver AL1 (G-BVER)	Privately owned, Cumbernauld
	XV277	HS P.1127(RAF)	Royal Scottish Mus'm of Flight, E Fortune
	XV279	HS P.1127(RAF) (8566M)	RAF Wittering
	XV280	HS P.1127(RAF) <ff>	RNAS Yeovilton Fire Section
	XV290	Lockheed C-130K Hercules C3 [290]	*Scrapped at Lyneham, August 2011*
	XV294	Lockheed C-130K Hercules C3 [294]	MoD/Marshalls, stored Cambridge, for disposal
	XV295	Lockheed C-130K Hercules C1 [295]	Marshalls, Cambridge (wfu)
	XV299	Lockheed C-130K Hercules C3 [299]	*Scrapped at Cambridge, 6 December 2011*
	XV301	Lockheed C-130K Hercules C3 [301]	Privately owned, Bruntingthorpe
	XV302	Lockheed C-130K Hercules C3 [302]	Marshalls, Cambridge, fatigue test airframe
	XV303	Lockheed C-130K Hercules C3A [303]	RAF No 47 Sqn, Brize Norton
	XV304	Lockheed C-130K Hercules C3A	RAF Brize Norton, instructional use
	XV305	Lockheed C-130K Hercules C3 $	Privately owned, Hixon, Staffs
	XV307	Lockheed C-130K Hercules C3 (G-52-40) [307]	MoD/Marshalls, stored Cambridge, for disposal
	XV328	BAC Lightning T5 <ff>	Phoenix Aviation, Bruntingthorpe
	XV333	HS Buccaneer S2B [234/H]	FAA Museum, RNAS Yeovilton
	XV344	HS Buccaneer S2C	QinetiQ Farnborough, on display
	XV350	HS Buccaneer S2B	East Midlands Airport Aeropark
	XV352	HS Buccaneer S2B <ff>	RAF Manston History Museum
	XV359	HS Buccaneer S2B [035/R]	Privately owned, Topsham, Devon
	XV361	HS Buccaneer S2B	Ulster Aviation Society, Long Kesh
	XV370	Sikorsky SH-3D (A2682) [260]	DCAE AESS, HMS Sultan, Gosport
	XV371	WS61 Sea King HAS1(DB) [61/DD]	SFDO, RNAS Culdrose
	XV372	WS61 Sea King HAS1	RAF, St Mawgan, instructional use
	XV383	Northrop Shelduck D1 (fuselage)	Privately owned, Wimborne, Dorset
	XV401	McD F-4M Phantom FGR2 [I]	Boscombe Down Aviation Collection
	XV402	McD F-4M Phantom FGR2 <ff>	Privately owned, Kent
	XV406	McD F-4M Phantom FGR2 (9098M) [CK]	Solway Aviation Society, Carlisle
	XV408	McD F-4M Phantom FGR2 (9165M) [Z]	Tangmere Military Aviation Museum
	XV411	McD F-4M Phantom FGR2 (9103M) [L]	MoD DFTDC, Manston
	XV415	McD F-4M Phantom FGR2 (9163M) [E]	RAF Boulmer, on display
	XV424	McD F-4M Phantom FGR2 (9152M) [I]	RAF Museum, Hendon
	XV426	McD F-4M Phantom FGR2 <ff>	City of Norwich Aviation Museum
	XV426	McD F-4M Phantom FGR2 [P] <rf>	RAF Coningsby, BDRT
	XV460	McD F-4M Phantom FGR2 <ff>	No 2214 Sqn ATC, Usworth
	XV474	McD F-4M Phantom FGR2 [T]	The Old Flying Machine Company, Duxford
	XV490	McD F-4M Phantom FGR2 [R] <ff>	Wattisham Airfield Museum
	XV497	McD F-4M Phantom FGR2 (9295M) [D]	RAF Waddington, (preserved)
	XV499	McD F-4M Phantom FGR2	RAF Leeming, WLT
	XV581	McD F-4K Phantom FG1 (9070M) <ff>	No 2481 Sqn ATC, Bridge of Don
	XV582	McD F-4K Phantom FG1 (9066M) [M]	RAF Leuchars, on display
	XV586	McD F-4K Phantom FG1 (9067M) [AJ]	RAF Leuchars, on display
	XV591	McD F-4K Phantom FG1 [013] <ff>	RAF Museum, Cosford
	XV625	WS Wasp HAS1 (A2649) [471]	DCAE AESS, HMS Sultan, Gosport

Serial	Type (code/other identity)	Owner/operator location or fate	Notes
XV631	WS Wasp HAS1 (fuselage)	Farnborough Air Sciences Trust, Farnborough	
XV642	WS61 Sea King HAS2A (A2614) [259]	DCAE AESS, HMS Sultan, Gosport	
XV643	WS61 Sea King HAS6 [262]	DCAE, No 1 SoTT, Cosford	
XV647	WS61 Sea King HU5 [28]	MoD/Vector Aerospace, Fleetlands	
XV648	WS61 Sea King HU5 [18/CU]	RN No 771 NAS, Culdrose	
XV649	WS61 Sea King ASaC7 [180]	RN No 857 NAS, Culdrose	
XV651	WS61 Sea King HU5	MoD/AFD/QinetiQ, Boscombe Down	
XV653	WS61 Sea King HAS6 (9326M) [63/CU]	DCAE, No 1 SoTT, Cosford	
XV654	WS61 Sea King HAS6 [05/DD] (wreck)	SFDO, RNAS Culdrose	
XV655	WS61 Sea King HAS6 [270/N]	DCAE AESS, HMS Sultan, Gosport	
XV656	WS61 Sea King ASaC7 [185]	MoD/Vector Aerospace, Fleetlands	
XV657	WS61 Sea King HAS5 (ZA135) [32/DD]	SFDO, RNAS Culdrose	
XV659	WS61 Sea King HAS6 (9324M) [62/CU]	DCAE, No 1 SoTT, Cosford	
XV660	WS61 Sea King HAS6 [69/N]	DCAE AESS, HMS Sultan, Gosport	
XV661	WS61 Sea King HU5 [26]	MoD/Vector Aerospace, stored Fleetlands	
XV663	WS61 Sea King HAS6	DCAE, stored HMS Sultan, Gosport	
XV664	WS61 Sea King ASaC7 [190]	RN No 857 NAS, Culdrose	
XV665	WS61 Sea King HAS6 [507/CU]	DCAE AESS, HMS Sultan, Gosport	
XV666	WS61 Sea King HU5 [21]	RN No 771 NAS, Culdrose	
XV670	WS61 Sea King HU5 [17]	RN No 771 NAS, Culdrose	
XV671	WS61 Sea King ASaC7 [183]	RN No 854 NAS, Culdrose	
XV672	WS61 Sea King ASaC7 [187]	MoD/Vector Aerospace, Fleetlands	
XV673	WS61 Sea King HU5 [27/CU]	RN No 771 NAS, Culdrose	
XV675	WS61 Sea King HAS6 [701/PW]	DCAE AESS, HMS Sultan, Gosport	
XV676	WS61 Sea King HC6 [ZE]	DCAE, stored HMS Sultan, Gosport	
XV677	WS61 Sea King HAS6 [269]	Aeroventure, Doncaster	
XV696	WS61 Sea King HAS6 [267/L]	DCAE AESS, HMS Sultan, Gosport	
XV697	WS61 Sea King ASaC7 [181]	RN No 849 NAS, Culdrose	
XV699	WS61 Sea King HU5 [823/PW]	RN No 771 NAS, Prestwick	
XV700	WS61 Sea King HC6 [ZC]	DCAE, stored HMS Sultan, Gosport	
XV701	WS61 Sea King HAS6 [268/N,64]	DCAE, No 1 SoTT, Cosford	
XV703	WS61 Sea King HC6 [ZD]	DCAE, stored HMS Sultan, Gosport	
XV705	WS61 Sea King HAR5 [29]	RN No 771 NAS, Culdrose	
XV706	WS61 Sea King HAS6 (9344M) [017/L]	RN ETS, Culdrose	
XV707	WS61 Sea King ASaC7 [184]	MoD/AFD/QinetiQ, Boscombe Down	
XV708	WS61 Sea King HAS6 [501/CU]	DCAE AESS, HMS Sultan, Gosport	
XV709	WS61 Sea King HAS6 (9303M) [263]	RAF Valley, instructional use	
XV711	WS61 Sea King HAS6 [15/CW]	DCAE AESS, HMS Sultan, Gosport	
XV712	WS61 Sea King HAS6 [66]	Imperial War Museum, Duxford	
XV713	WS61 Sea King HAS6 (A2646) [018/L]	DCAE AESS, HMS Sultan, Gosport	
XV714	WS61 Sea King ASaC7 [188]	RN No 849 NAS, Culdrose	
XV720	WS58 Wessex HC2 (A2701)	DCAE AESS, HMS Sultan, Gosport	
XV722	WS58 Wessex HC2 (8805M) [WH]	Privately owned, Badgers Mount, Kent	
XV724	WS58 Wessex HC2	DCAE AESS, HMS Sultan, Gosport	
XV725	WS58 Wessex HC2 [C]	MoD DFTDC, Manston	
XV726	WS58 Wessex HC2 [J]	Privately owned, Biggin Hill	
XV728	WS58 Wessex HC2 [A]	Newark Air Museum, Winthorpe	
XV731	WS58 Wessex HC2 [Y]	Privately owned, Badgers Mount, Kent	
XV732	WS58 Wessex HCC4	RAF Museum, Hendon	
XV733	WS58 Wessex HCC4	The Helicopter Museum, Weston-super-Mare	
XV741	HS Harrier GR3 (A2608) [41/DD]	DCAE AESS, HMS Sultan, Gosport	
XV744	HS Harrier GR3 (9167M) [3K]	Defence Academy of the UK, Shrivenham	
XV748	HS Harrier GR3 [3D]	Yorkshire Air Museum, Elvington	
XV751	HS Harrier GR3	Gatwick Aviation Museum, Charlwood	
XV752	HS Harrier GR3 (9075M) [B]	Aeroventure, Doncaster	
XV753	HS Harrier GR3 (9078M) [53/DD]	RN, Predannack Fire School	
XV755	HS Harrier GR3 [M]	RNAS Yeovilton Fire Section	
XV759	HS Harrier GR3 [O] <ff>	Privately owned, Hitchin, Herts	

Notes	Serial	Type (code/other identity)	Owner/operator location or fate
	XV760	HS Harrier GR3 <ff>	Solent Sky, Southampton
	XV779	HS Harrier GR3 (8931M)	RAF Wittering
	XV783	HS Harrier GR3 [83/DD]	RN, Predannack Fire School
	XV784	HS Harrier GR3 (8909M) <ff>	Boscombe Down Aviation Collection
	XV786	HS Harrier GR3 <ff>	RNAS Culdrose
	XV786	HS Harrier GR3 [S] <rf>	RN, Predannack Fire School
	XV798	HS Harrier GR1(mod)	Bristol Aero Collection, stored Cotswold Airport
	XV804	HS Harrier GR3 (9280M) [O]	RAF North Luffenham Training Area
	XV806	HS Harrier GR3 <ff>	Privately owned, Worksop
	XV808	HS Harrier GR3 (9076M/A2687) [08/DD]	DCAE AESS, HMS Sultan, Gosport
	XV810	HS Harrier GR3 (9038M) [K]	Privately owned, Bruntingthorpe
	XV814	DH106 Comet 4 (G-APDF) <ff>	Privately owned, Chipping Campden
	XV863	HS Buccaneer S2B (9115M/9139M/9145M) [S]	Privately owned, Weston, Eire
	XV864	HS Buccaneer S2B (9234M)	MoD DFTDC, Manston
	XV865	HS Buccaneer S2B (9226M)	Imperial War Museum, Duxford
	XV867	HS Buccaneer S2B <ff>	Highland Aviation Museum, Inverness
	XW175	HS Harrier T4(VAAC)	MoD, Boscombe Down (wfu)
	XW198	WS Puma HC1	RAF No 33 Sqn/No 230 Sqn, Benson
	XW199	WS Puma HC1	RAF No 33 Sqn/No 230 Sqn, Benson
	XW200	WS Puma HC1 (wreck)	RAF, stored Shawbury
	XW201	WS Puma HC1	RAF Benson, BDRT
	XW202	WS Puma HC1	RAF, stored Shawbury
	XW204	WS Puma HC2	MoD/Eurocopter, Brasov, Romania (conversion)
	XW206	WS Puma HC1	AgustaWestland, Yeovil
	XW207	WS Puma HC1	RAF No 33 Sqn/No 230 Sqn, Benson
	XW208	WS Puma HC2	MoD/Eurocopter, Marseilles, France (conversion)
	XW209	WS Puma HC2	MoD/Eurocopter, Brasov, Romania (conversion)
	XW210	WS Puma HC1 (comp XW215)	RAF No 33 Sqn/No 230 Sqn, Benson
	XW211	WS Puma HC1	Crashed 6 July 2011, Andover
	XW212	WS Puma HC1	RAF No 33 Sqn/No 230 Sqn, Benson
	XW213	WS Puma HC1	RAF No 33 Sqn/No 230 Sqn, Benson
	XW214	WS Puma HC1	RAF No 33 Sqn/No 230 Sqn, Benson
	XW216	WS Puma HC2	MoD/Eurocopter, Oxford (conversion)
	XW217	WS Puma HC1	RAF No 33 Sqn/No 230 Sqn, Benson
	XW218	WS Puma HC1 (wreck)	RAF, stored Shawbury
	XW219	WS Puma HC1	RAF No 33 Sqn/No 230 Sqn, Benson
	XW220	WS Puma HC1	AgustaWestland, Yeovil
	XW222	WS Puma HC1	RAF No 33 Sqn/No 230 Sqn, Benson
	XW223	WS Puma HC1	RAF No 33 Sqn/No 230 Sqn, Benson
	XW224	WS Puma HC2	MoD/Eurocopter, Brasov, Romania (conversion)
	XW226	WS Puma HC1	RAF No 33 Sqn/No 230 Sqn, Benson
	XW227	WS Puma HC1	Privately owned, Colsterworth, Leics
	XW229	WS Puma HC2	MoD/Eurocopter, Brasov, Romania (conversion)
	XW231	WS Puma HC2	MoD/Eurocopter, Brasov, Romania (conversion)
	XW232	WS Puma HC2 (F-ZWDE)	MoD/Eurocopter, Marseilles, France
	XW235	WS Puma HC2	MoD/Eurocopter, Brasov, Romania (conversion)
	XW236	WS Puma HC1	RAF No 33 Sqn/No 230 Sqn, Benson
	XW237	WS Puma HC1	RAF No 33 Sqn/No 230 Sqn, Benson
	XW241	Sud SA330E Puma	Farnborough Air Sciences Trust, Farnborough
	XW264	HS Harrier T2 <ff>	Gloucestershire Avn Coll, stored Gloucester
	XW265	HS Harrier T4A (9258M) <ff>	No 2345 Sqn ATC, RAF Leuchars
	XW265	HS Harrier T4A (9258M) <rf>	DSG, St Athan
	XW267	HS Harrier T4 (9263M) [SA]	Territorial Army, Toton, Notts
	XW268	HS Harrier T4N	City of Norwich Aviation Museum
	XW269	HS Harrier T4	Privately owned, Thorpe Wood, N Yorks
	XW270	HS Harrier T4 (fuselage)	Coventry University, instructional use

Serial	Type (code/other identity)	Owner/operator location or fate	Notes
XW271	HS Harrier T4 [71/DD]	RN, Predannack Fire School	
XW272	HS Harrier T4 (8783M) (fuselage) (comp XV281)	Privately owned, Cannock, Staffs	
XW276	Aérospatiale SA341 Gazelle (F-ZWRI)	Newark Air Museum, Winthorpe	
XW281	WS Scout AH1 (G-BYNZ) [T]	Privately owned, Wembury, Devon	
XW283	WS Scout AH1 [U]	RM, stored Yeovilton	
XW289	BAC Jet Provost T5A (G-BVXT/G-JPVA) [73]	Kennet Aviation, Yeovilton	
XW290	BAC Jet Provost T5A (9199M) [41,MA]	DCAE, No 1 SoTT, Cosford	
XW293	BAC Jet Provost T5 (G-BWCS) [Z]	Privately owned, Bournemouth	
XW299	BAC Jet Provost T5A (9146M) [60,MB]	DCAE, No 1 SoTT, Cosford	
XW301	BAC Jet Provost T5A (9147M) [63,MC]	DCAE, No 1 SoTT, Cosford	
XW303	BAC Jet Provost T5A (9119M) [127]	RAF Halton	
XW304	BAC Jet Provost T5 (9172M) [MD]	Privately owned, Eye, Suffolk	
XW309	BAC Jet Provost T5 (9179M) [V,ME]	Hartlepool College of Further Education	
XW311	BAC Jet Provost T5 (9180M) [W,MF]	Privately owned, North Weald	
XW315	BAC Jet Provost T5A <ff>	Privately owned, Wolverhampton	
XW318	BAC Jet Provost T5A (9190M) [78,MG]	DCAE, No 1 SoTT, Cosford	
XW320	BAC Jet Provost T5A (9015M) [71]	DCAE, No 1 SoTT, Cosford	
XW321	BAC Jet Provost T5A (9154M) [62,MH]	DCAE, No 1 SoTT, Cosford	
XW323	BAC Jet Provost T5A (9166M) [86]	RAF Museum, Hendon	
XW324	BAC Jet Provost T5 (G-BWSG) [U]	Privately owned, East Midlands	
XW325	BAC Jet Provost T5B (G-BWGF) [E]	Privately owned, Woodvale	
XW327	BAC Jet Provost T5A (9130M) [62]	DCAE, No 1 SoTT, Cosford	
XW328	BAC Jet Provost T5A (9177M) [75,MI]	DCAE, No 1 SoTT, Cosford	
XW330	BAC Jet Provost T5A (9195M) [82,MJ]	DCAE, No 1 SoTT, Cosford	
XW333	BAC Jet Provost T5A (G-BVTC)	Global Aviation, Humberside	
XW353	BAC Jet Provost T5A (9090M) [3]	RAF Cranwell, on display	
XW354	BAC Jet Provost T5A (XW355/G-JPTV)	Privately owned, Church Fenton	
XW358	BAC Jet Provost T5A (9181M) [59,MK]	Currently not known	
XW360	BAC Jet Provost T5A (9153M) [61,ML]	DCAE, No 1 SoTT, Cosford	
XW361	BAC Jet Provost T5A (9192M) [81,MM]	DCAE, No 1 SoTT, Cosford	
XW363	BAC Jet Provost T5A [36]	Dumfries & Galloway Avn Mus, Dumfries	
XW364	BAC Jet Provost T5A (9188M) [35,MN]	DCAE, No 1 SoTT, Cosford	
XW367	BAC Jet Provost T5A (9193M) [64,MO]	DCAE, No 1 SoTT, Cosford	
XW370	BAC Jet Provost T5A (9196M) [72,MP]	DCAE, No 1 SoTT, Cosford	
XW375	BAC Jet Provost T5A (9149M) [52]	DCAE, No 1 SoTT, Cosford	
XW404	BAC Jet Provost T5A (9049M) [77]	Hartlepool FE College	
XW405	BAC Jet Provost T5A (9187M) [J,MQ]	Hartlepool FE College, stored	
XW409	BAC Jet Provost T5A (9047M)	Privately owned, Hawarden	
XW410	BAC Jet Provost T5A (9125M) [80,MR]	DCAE, No 1 SoTT, Cosford	
XW416	BAC Jet Provost T5A (9191M) [84,MS]	DCAE, No 1 SoTT, Cosford	
XW418	BAC Jet Provost T5A (9173M) [MT]	DCAE, No 1 SoTT, Cosford	
XW419	BAC Jet Provost T5A (9120M) [125]	Privately owned, Bournemouth	
XW420	BAC Jet Provost T5A (9194M) [83,MU]	DCAE, No 1 SoTT, Cosford	
XW422	BAC Jet Provost T5A (G-BWEB) [3]	Privately owned, Cotswold Airport	
XW423	BAC Jet Provost T5A (G-BWUW) [14]	Deeside College, Connah's Quay, Clwyd	
XW425	BAC Jet Provost T5A (9200M) [H,MV]	DCAE, No 1 SoTT, Cosford	
XW430	BAC Jet Provost T5A (9176M) [77,MW]	DCAE, No 1 SoTT, Cosford	
XW432	BAC Jet Provost T5A (9127M) [76,MX]	DCAE, No 1 SoTT, Cosford	
XW433	BAC Jet Provost T5A (G-JPRO)	Classic Flight, Coventry	
XW434	BAC Jet Provost T5A (9091M) [78,MY]	DCAE, No 1 SoTT, Cosford	
XW436	BAC Jet Provost T5A (9148M) [68]	DCAE, No 1 SoTT, Cosford	
XW530	HS Buccaneer S2B [530]	Buccaneer Service Station, Elgin	
XW541	HS Buccaneer S2B (8858M) <ff>	Privately owned, Lavendon, Bucks	
XW544	HS Buccaneer S2B (8857M) [O]	Privately owned, Bruntingthorpe	
XW547	HS Buccaneer S2B (9095M/9169M) [R]	RAF Museum, Hendon	
XW550	HS Buccaneer S2B <ff>	Privately owned, West Horndon, Essex	
XW560	SEPECAT Jaguar S <ff>	Boscombe Down Aviation Collection	

Notes	Serial	Type (code/other identity)	Owner/operator location or fate
	XW563	SEPECAT Jaguar S (XX822/8563M)	County Hall, Norwich, on display
	XW566	SEPECAT Jaguar B	Farnborough Air Sciences Trust, Farnborough
	XW612	WS Scout AH1 (G-BXRR)	Privately owned, Thruxton
	XW613	WS Scout AH1 (G-BXRS)	Privately owned, New Milton, Hants
	XW616	WS Scout AH1	AAC Dishforth, instructional use
	XW630	HS Harrier GR3	RNAS Yeovilton, Fire Section
	XW635	Beagle D5/180 (G-AWSW)	Privately owned, Spanhoe
	XW664	HS Nimrod R1	East Midlands Airport Aeropark
	XW665	HS Nimrod R1 <ff>	To Germany, August 2011
	XW666	HS Nimrod R1 <ff>	Aeroventure, Doncaster
	XW763	HS Harrier GR3 (9002M/9041M) <ff>	Privately owned, Wigston, Leics
	XW768	HS Harrier GR3 (9072M) [N]	MoD DFTDC, Manston
	XW784	Mitchell-Procter Kittiwake I (G-BBRN) [VL]	Privately owned, RNAS Yeovilton
	XW795	WS Scout AH1	Blessingbourne Museum, Fivemiletown, Co Tyrone, NI
	XW796	WS Scout AH1	Gunsmoke Paintball, Hadleigh, Suffolk
	XW838	WS Lynx (TAD 009)	DCAE SEAE, Arborfield
	XW839	WS Lynx	The Helicopter Museum, Weston-super-Mare
	XW844	WS Gazelle AH1	Vector Aerospace Fleetlands Apprentice School
	XW846	WS Gazelle AH1	AAC No 665 Sqn/5 Regt, Aldergrove
	XW847	WS Gazelle AH1	AAC GDSH, Middle Wallop
	XW848	WS Gazelle AH1 [D]	Privately owned, Colsterworth, Leics
	XW849	WS Gazelle AH1 [G]	AAC GDSH, Middle Wallop
	XW851	WS Gazelle AH1	Privately owned, Durham
	XW852	WS Gazelle HCC4 (9331M)	DCAE, No 1 SoTT, Cosford
	XW854	WS Gazelle HT2 (G-TIZZ) [46/CU]	Privately owned, Redhill
	XW855	WS Gazelle HCC4	RAF Museum, Hendon
	XW858	WS Gazelle HT3 (G-ONNE) [C]	Privately owned, Murton, York
	XW860	WS Gazelle HT2 (TAD 021)	DCAE SEAE, Arborfield
	XW862	WS Gazelle HT3 (G-CBKC) [D]	Privately owned, Fowlmere
	XW863	WS Gazelle HT2 (TAD 022)	Privately owned, Fairoaks
	XW864	WS Gazelle HT2 [54/CU]	FAA Museum, stored RNAS Yeovilton
	XW865	WS Gazelle AH1 [5C]	AAC No 29 Flt, BATUS, Suffield, Canada
	XW866	WS Gazelle HT3 (G-BXTH) [E]	Repainted as G-BXTH
	XW870	WS Gazelle AH1 (9299M) [F]	MoD DFTDC, Manston
	XW888	WS Gazelle AH1 (TAD 017)	DCAE SEAE, Arborfield
	XW889	WS Gazelle AH1 (TAD 018)	Currently not known
	XW890	WS Gazelle HT2	RNAS Yeovilton, on display
	XW892	WS Gazelle AH1 (G-CGJX/9292M) [C]	Privately owned, Babcary, Somerset
	XW897	WS Gazelle AH1	DCAE, No 1 SoTT, Cosford
	XW899	WS Gazelle AH1 [Z]	DCAE, No 1 SoTT, Cosford
	XW900	WS Gazelle AH1 (TAD 900)	Army, Bramley, Hants
	XW902	WS Gazelle HT3 (G-CGJY) [H]	Privately owned, Hurstbourne Tarrant, Hants
	XW904	WS Gazelle AH1 [H]	AAC GDSH, Middle Wallop
	XW906	WS Gazelle HT3 [J]	QinetiQ Boscombe Down, Apprentice School
	XW908	WS Gazelle AH1 [A]	QinetiQ, Boscombe Down (spares use)
	XW909	WS Gazelle AH1	Privately owned, Colsterworth, Leics
	XW912	WS Gazelle AH1 (TAD 019)	DCAE SEAE, Arborfield
	XW913	WS Gazelle AH1	Privately owned, Colsterworth, Leics
	XW917	HS Harrier GR3 (8975M)	Privately owned, Swanwick
	XW922	HS Harrier GR3 (8885M)	MoD DFTDC, Manston
	XW923	HS Harrier GR3 (8724M) <ff>	RAF Wittering, Fire Section
	XW924	HS Harrier GR3 (9073M) [G]	RAF Coningsby, preserved
	XW927	HS Harrier T4 <ff>	Privately owned, South Molton, Devon
	XW934	HS Harrier T4 [Y]	Farnborough Air Sciences Trust, Farnborough
	XW994	Northrop Chukar D1	FAA Museum, stored RNAS Yeovilton
	XW999	Northrop Chukar D1	Davidstow Airfield & Cornwall At War Museum
	XX105	BAC 1-11/201AC (G-ASJD)	Scrapped at Boscombe Down, 17 December 2011

Serial	Type (code/other identity)	Owner/operator location or fate	Notes
XX108	SEPECAT Jaguar GR1(mod)	Imperial War Museum, Duxford	
XX109	SEPECAT Jaguar GR1 (8918M) [GH]	City of Norwich Aviation Museum	
XX110	SEPECAT Jaguar GR1 (8955M) [EP]	DCAE, No 1 SoTT, Cosford	
XX110	SEPECAT Jaguar GR1 <R> (BAPC 169)	DCAE, No 1 SoTT, Cosford	
XX112	SEPECAT Jaguar GR3A [EA]	DCAE, No 1 SoTT, Cosford	
XX115	SEPECAT Jaguar GR1 (8821M) (fuselage)	DCAE, No 1 SoTT, Cosford	
XX116	SEPECAT Jaguar GR3A [EO]	MoD DFTDC, Manston	
XX117	SEPECAT Jaguar GR3A [ES]	DCAE, No 1 SoTT, Cosford	
XX119	SEPECAT Jaguar GR3A (8898M) [AI]$	DCAE, No 1 SoTT, Cosford	
XX121	SEPECAT Jaguar GR1 [EQ]	Privately owned, Charlwood, Surrey	
XX139	SEPECAT Jaguar T4 [PT]	Privately owned, Sproughton	
XX140	SEPECAT Jaguar T2 (9008M) <ff>	Privately owned, Chesterfield	
XX141	SEPECAT Jaguar T2A (9297M) [Y]	DCAE, TCF, RAFC Cranwell	
XX144	SEPECAT Jaguar T2A [U]	Privately owned, Sproughton	
XX145	SEPECAT Jaguar T2A	RAFC Cranwell Fire Section	
XX146	SEPECAT Jaguar T4 [GT]	Privately owned, Sproughton	
XX150	SEPECAT Jaguar T4 [FY]	Privately owned, Bentwaters	
XX153	WS Lynx AH1 (9320M)	Museum of Army Flying, Middle Wallop	
XX154	HS Hawk T1	MoD/ETPS, Boscombe Down	
XX156	HS Hawk T1 [156]	RAF No 4 FTS/208(R) Sqn, Valley	
XX157	HS Hawk T1A $	RN FRADU, Culdrose	
XX158	HS Hawk T1A [158]	RAF No 4 FTS/208(R) Sqn, Valley	
XX159	HS Hawk T1A $	RN FRADU, Culdrose	
XX160	HS Hawk T1 [160]	RN, stored Shawbury	
XX161	HS Hawk T1W [161]	RAF, stored Shawbury	
XX162	HS Hawk T1	RAF Centre of Aviation Medicine, Boscombe Down	
XX165	HS Hawk T1 [165]	RN FRADU, Culdrose	
XX167	HS Hawk T1W [167]	RAF No 4 FTS/208(R) Sqn, Valley	
XX168	HS Hawk T1 [168]	RN, stored Shawbury	
XX169	HS Hawk T1 [169]	RN, stored Shawbury	
XX170	HS Hawk T1 [170]	RN FRADU, Culdrose (on repair)	
XX171	HS Hawk T1 [171]	RAF, stored Shawbury	
XX172	HS Hawk T1 [172]	RN, stored Shawbury	
XX173	HS Hawk T1	RN, stored Shawbury	
XX174	HS Hawk T1 [174]	RAF No 4 FTS/208(R) Sqn, Valley	
XX175	HS Hawk T1 [175]	RAF, stored Shawbury	
XX176	HS Hawk T1W [176]	RN FRADU, Culdrose	
XX177	HS Hawk T1	RAF Red Arrows, Scampton	
XX178	HS Hawk T1W [178]	RAF No 4 FTS/208(R) Sqn, Valley	
XX179	HS Hawk T1W	Crashed 20 August 2011, Throop, Dorset	
XX181	HS Hawk T1W [181]	RAF No 4 FTS/208(R) Sqn, Valley	
XX184	HS Hawk T1 [CQ]	RAF No 100 Sqn, Leeming	
XX185	HS Hawk T1 [185]	RAF, stored Shawbury	
XX187	HS Hawk T1A [187]	RAF No 4 FTS/208(R) Sqn, Valley	
XX188	HS Hawk T1A [188]	RAF No 4 FTS/208(R) Sqn, Valley	
XX189	HS Hawk T1A [CR]	RAF No 100 Sqn, Leeming	
XX190	HS Hawk T1A [CN]	RAF, stored Shawbury	
XX191	HS Hawk T1A [191]	RAF, stored Shawbury	
XX194	HS Hawk T1A [194]	RAF No 4 FTS/208(R) Sqn, Valley	
XX195	HS Hawk T1W [195]	RAF, stored Shawbury	
XX198	HS Hawk T1A [CG]	RAF No 100 Sqn, Leeming	
XX199	HS Hawk T1A [199]	RAF No 4 FTS/208(R) Sqn, Valley	
XX200	HS Hawk T1A [CG]	RAF Valley	
XX201	HS Hawk T1A	RAF No 4 FTS/208(R) Sqn, Valley	
XX202	HS Hawk T1A [CF]	RAF No 100 Sqn, Leeming	
XX203	HS Hawk T1A [CC]	RAF No 100 Sqn, Leeming	
XX204	HS Hawk T1A [204]	RAF No 4 FTS/208(R) Sqn, Valley	
XX205	HS Hawk T1A $	RN FRADU, Culdrose	

Notes	Serial	Type (code/other identity)	Owner/operator location or fate
	XX217	HS Hawk T1A [217]	RN FRADU, Culdrose
	XX218	HS Hawk T1A [218]	RAF No 4 FTS/208(R) Sqn, Valley
	XX219	HS Hawk T1A [219]	RAF, stored Shawbury
	XX220	HS Hawk T1A [220]	RAF, stored Shawbury
	XX221	HS Hawk T1A [221]	RN FRADU, Culdrose (on repair)
	XX222	HS Hawk T1 [CI]	RAF, stored Shawbury
	XX223	HS Hawk T1 <ff>	Privately owned, Charlwood, Surrey
	XX224	HS Hawk T1W [224]	RAF No 4 FTS/208(R) Sqn, Valley
	XX225	HS Hawk T1 [225]	RN, stored Shawbury
	XX226	HS Hawk T1 [226]	RN, stored Shawbury
	XX227	HS Hawk T1 <R> (*XX226*/BAPC 152)	RAF M&RU, Bottesford
	XX227	HS Hawk T1A	RAF Red Arrows, Scampton
	XX228	HS Hawk T1A [CG]	RAF, stored Shawbury
	XX230	HS Hawk T1A [230]	RAF No 4 FTS/208(R) Sqn, Valley
	XX231	HS Hawk T1W [213]	RAF, stored Shawbury
	XX232	HS Hawk T1 [232]	RAF, stored Shawbury
	XX234	HS Hawk T1 [234]	RAF, stored Shawbury
	XX235	HS Hawk T1W [235]	RAF, stored Shawbury
	XX236	HS Hawk T1W [236]	RAF No 4 FTS/208(R) Sqn, Valley
	XX237	HS Hawk T1	RAF, stored Shawbury
	XX238	HS Hawk T1 [238]	RAF, stored Shawbury
	XX239	HS Hawk T1W [239]	RAF, stored Shawbury
	XX240	HS Hawk T1 [240]	RN FRADU, Culdrose
	XX242	HS Hawk T1	RAF Red Arrows, Scampton
	XX244	HS Hawk T1 $	RAF No 4 FTS/208(R) Sqn, Valley
	XX245	HS Hawk T1 [245] $	RAF No 4 FTS/208(R) Sqn, Valley
	XX246	HS Hawk T1A [CA]	RAF No 100 Sqn, Leeming
	XX247	HS Hawk T1A [247]	RAF, stored Shawbury
	XX248	HS Hawk T1A [CJ]	RAF, stored Shawbury
	XX250	HS Hawk T1 [250]	RAF Valley
	XX253	HS Hawk T1A	RAF Scampton, for display
	XX254	HS Hawk T1A <ff>	MoD/DSG, St Athan
	XX254	HS Hawk T1A	MoD/BAE Systems, stored Scampton
	XX254	HS Hawk T1A <R>	Privately owned, Marlow, Bucks
	XX255	HS Hawk T1A [CL]	RAF No 100 Sqn, Leeming
	XX256	HS Hawk T1A	RAF Valley (on repair)
	XX257	HS Hawk T1A (fuselage)	Privately owned, Charlwood, Surrey
	XX258	HS Hawk T1A [CE]	RAF No 100 Sqn, Leeming
	XX260	HS Hawk T1A	RAF, stored Shawbury
	XX261	HS Hawk T1A $	RN FRADU, Culdrose
	XX263	HS Hawk T1A $	RAF No 4 FTS/208(R) Sqn, Valley
	XX264	HS Hawk T1A	RAF Red Arrows, Scampton
	XX265	HS Hawk T1A [265]	RAF, stored Shawbury
	XX266	HS Hawk T1A	RAF Red Arrows, Scampton
	XX278	HS Hawk T1A	RAF, Valley
	XX280	HS Hawk T1A [CM]	RAF No 100 Sqn, Leeming
	XX281	HS Hawk T1A	RN FRADU, Culdrose
	XX283	HS Hawk T1W [283]	RAF No 4 FTS/208(R) Sqn, Valley
	XX284	HS Hawk T1A [CA]	RAF Red Arrows, Scampton
	XX285	HS Hawk T1A [CB]	RAF No 100 Sqn, Leeming
	XX286	HS Hawk T1A [286]	RAF No 4 FTS/208(R) Sqn, Valley
	XX287	HS Hawk T1A [287]	RAF No 4 FTS/208(R) Sqn, Valley
	XX289	HS Hawk T1A [CO]	RAF No 100 Sqn, Leeming
	XX290	HS Hawk T1W [CU]	RAF, stored Shawbury
	XX292	HS Hawk T1	RAF, stored Shawbury
	XX294	HS Hawk T1	RAF, stored Shawbury
	XX295	HS Hawk T1W [295]	RAF, stored Shawbury
	XX296	HS Hawk T1 [296]	RAF, stored Shawbury

Serial	Type (code/other identity)	Owner/operator location or fate	Notes
XX299	HS Hawk T1W [299]	RAF, stored Shawbury	
XX301	HS Hawk T1A $	RN FRADU, Culdrose	
XX303	HS Hawk T1A	RN FRADU, Culdrose	
XX304	HS Hawk T1A <rf>	Cardiff International Airport Fire Section	
XX306	HS Hawk T1A	RAF Red Arrows, Scampton	
XX307	HS Hawk T1 [307]	RAF No 4 FTS/208(R) Sqn, Valley	
XX308	HS Hawk T1	RAF Red Arrows, Scampton	
XX308	HS Hawk T1 <R> (XX263/BAPC 171)	RAF M&RU, Bottesford	
XX309	HS Hawk T1	RAF, stored Shawbury	
XX310	HS Hawk T1W [310]	RAF, stored Shawbury	
XX311	HS Hawk T1 [311]	RAF, stored Shawbury	
XX312	HS Hawk T1W	RAF No 4 FTS/208(R) Sqn, Valley	
XX313	HS Hawk T1W [313]	RAF No 4 FTS/208(R) Sqn, Valley	
XX314	HS Hawk T1W [314]	RAF, stored Shawbury	
XX315	HS Hawk T1A [315]	RAF No 4 FTS/208(R) Sqn, Valley	
XX316	HS Hawk T1A [316]	RN FRADU, Culdrose	
XX317	HS Hawk T1A [317]	RAF No 4 FTS/208(R) Sqn, Valley	
XX318	HS Hawk T1A [CN]	RAF No 100 Sqn, Leeming	
XX319	HS Hawk T1A	RAF Red Arrows, Scampton	
XX320	HS Hawk T1A <ff>	RAF Scampton Historical Aviation Museum	
XX321	HS Hawk T1A [CI]	RAF No 100 Sqn, Leeming	
XX322	HS Hawk T1A	RAF Red Arrows, Scampton	
XX323	HS Hawk T1A [323]	RAF Red Arrows, Cranwell	
XX324	HS Hawk T1A	RAF, stored Shawbury	
XX325	HS Hawk T1A [325] $	RAF, stored Shawbury	
XX326	HS Hawk T1A <ff>	MoD/DSG, St Athan	
XX326	HS Hawk T1A	MoD/BAE Systems, Brough (on rebuild)	
XX327	HS Hawk T1	RAF Centre of Aviation Medicine, Boscombe Down	
XX329	HS Hawk T1A [CJ]	RAF No 100 Sqn, Leeming	
XX330	HS Hawk T1A [330]	RN FRADU, Culdrose	
XX331	HS Hawk T1A [331]	RN, stored Shawbury	
XX332	HS Hawk T1A [CD]	RAF No 100 Sqn, Leeming	
XX335	HS Hawk T1A [335]	RAF, stored Shawbury	
XX337	HS Hawk T1A	RN FRADU, Culdrose	
XX338	HS Hawk T1	RAF No 4 FTS/208(R) Sqn, Valley	
XX339	HS Hawk T1A [CK]	RAF No 100 Sqn, Leeming	
XX341	HS Hawk T1 ASTRA	MoD/ETPS, Boscombe Down	
XX342	HS Hawk T1 [2]	MoD/ETPS, Boscombe Down	
XX343	HS Hawk T1 [3] (wreck)	Boscombe Down Aviation Collection	
XX345	HS Hawk T1A [CE]	RAF, stored Shawbury	
XX346	HS Hawk T1A [CH]	RAF No 100 Sqn, Leeming	
XX348	HS Hawk T1A [348]	RAF Leeming, RTP	
XX349	HS Hawk T1W	RAF Valley (for display)	
XX350	HS Hawk T1A [350]	RAF, stored Shawbury	
XX351	HS Hawk T1A	RAF, stored Shawbury	
XX371	WS Gazelle AH1	Privately owned, Colsterworth, Leics	
XX372	WS Gazelle AH1	MoD/QinetiQ, Boscombe Down	
XX375	WS Gazelle AH1	Privately owned, Shepherds Bush	
XX378	WS Gazelle AH1 [Q]	AAC, stored Shawbury	
XX379	WS Gazelle AH1 [Y]	AAC, stored Shawbury	
XX380	WS Gazelle AH1 [A]	Wattisham Airfield Museum	
XX381	WS Gazelle AH1	Privately owned, Welbeck	
XX383	WS Gazelle AH1 [D]	Privately owned, Colsterworth, Leics	
XX384	WS Gazelle AH1	AAC Dishforth, instructional use	
XX386	WS Gazelle AH1	Privately owned, Colsterworth, Leics	
XX387	WS Gazelle AH1 (TAD 014)	Privately owned, stored Cranfield	
XX392	WS Gazelle AH1	Army, Middle Wallop, preserved	
XX394	WS Gazelle AH1 [X]	Privately owned, Colsterworth, Leics	

Notes	Serial	Type (code/other identity)	Owner/operator location or fate
	XX396	WS Gazelle HT3 (8718M) [N]	DCAE, TCF, RAFC Cranwell
	XX398	WS Gazelle AH1	Privately owned, Colsterworth, Leics
	XX399	WS Gazelle AH1 [B]	AAC, stored Shawbury
	XX403	WS Gazelle AH1 [U]	AAC, stored Shawbury
	XX405	WS Gazelle AH1	AAC No 665 Sqn/5 Regt, Aldergrove
	XX406	WS Gazelle HT3 (G-CBSH) [P]	Privately owned, Rochester
	XX409	WS Gazelle AH1	Privately owned, Colsterworth, Leics
	XX411	WS Gazelle AH1 [X]	Aeroventure, Doncaster
	XX411	WS Gazelle AH1 <rf>	FAA Museum, RNAS Yeovilton
	XX412	WS Gazelle AH1 [B]	DCAE, No 1 SoTT, Cosford
	XX414	WS Gazelle AH1 [V]	Privately owned, Badgers Mount, Kent
	XX416	WS Gazelle AH1	Privately owned, Colsterworth, Leics
	XX418	WS Gazelle AH1	Privately owned, Hurstbourne Tarrant, Hants
	XX419	WS Gazelle AH1	AAC GDSH, Middle Wallop
	XX431	WS Gazelle HT2 (9300M) [43/CU]	RAF Shawbury, for display
	XX433	WS Gazelle AH1 <ff>	Privately owned, Hurstbourne Tarrant, Hants
	XX435	WS Gazelle AH1 (fuselage)	QinetiQ, Boscombe Down (spares use)
	XX437	WS Gazelle AH1	Privately owned, Colsterworth, Leics
	XX438	WS Gazelle AH1 [F]	Privately owned, Colsterworth, Leics
	XX439	WS Gazelle AH1	Privately owned, Colsterworth, Leics
	XX440	WS Gazelle AH1 (G-BCHN)	Privately owned
	XX442	WS Gazelle AH1 [E]	AAC, stored Shawbury
	XX443	WS Gazelle AH1 [Y]	DCAE, stored HMS Sultan, Gosport
	XX444	WS Gazelle AH1	Wattisham Airfield Museum
	XX445	WS Gazelle AH1 [T]	Privately owned, Colsterworth, Leics
	XX447	WS Gazelle AH1 [D1]	AAC, stored Shawbury
	XX449	WS Gazelle AH1	MoD/QinetiQ, Boscombe Down
	XX453	WS Gazelle AH1	MoD/QinetiQ, Boscombe Down
	XX454	WS Gazelle AH1 (TAD 023) (fuselage)	DCAE SEAE, Arborfield
	XX455	WS Gazelle AH1	Privately owned, Colsterworth, Leics
	XX456	WS Gazelle AH1	Privately owned, Colsterworth, Leics
	XX457	WS Gazelle AH1 (TAD 001)	East Midlands Airport Aeropark
	XX460	WS Gazelle AH1	AAC, stored Shawbury
	XX462	WS Gazelle AH1 [W]	Privately owned, Colsterworth, Leics
	XX466	HS Hunter T66B/T7	Guernsey Airport Fire Section
	XX467	HS Hunter T66B/T7 (XL605/G-TVII) [86]	Privately owned, Bruntingthorpe
	XX476	HP137 Jetstream T2 (N1037S) [561/CU]	*Sold to Germany, July 2011*
	XX477	HP137 Jetstream T1 (G-AXXS/8462M) <ff>	Aeroventure, Doncaster
	XX478	HP137 Jetstream T2 (G-AXXT) [564/CU]	Privately owned, Sproughton
	XX479	HP137 Jetstream T2 (G-AXUR)	RN, Predannack Fire School
	XX481	HP137 Jetstream T2 (G-AXUP) [560/CU]	Privately owned, Sproughton
	XX482	SA Jetstream T1 [J]	Privately owned, Hixon, Staffs
	XX483	SA Jetstream T2 [562] <ff>	Dumfries & Galloway Avn Mus, Dumfries
	XX484	SA Jetstream T2 [566/CU]	*Sold to Italy, September 2011*
	XX486	SA Jetstream T2 [567/CU]	Privately owned, Sproughton
	XX487	SA Jetstream T2 [568/CU]	Barry Technical College, instructional use
	XX491	SA Jetstream T1 [K]	Northbrook College, Shoreham, instructional use
	XX492	SA Jetstream T1 [A]	Newark Air Museum, Winthorpe
	XX494	SA Jetstream T1 [B]	Privately owned, Bruntingthorpe
	XX495	SA Jetstream T1 [C]	Bedford College, instructional use
	XX496	SA Jetstream T1 [D]	RAF Museum, Cosford
	XX499	SA Jetstream T1 [G]	Brooklands Museum, Weybridge
	XX500	SA Jetstream T1 [H]	Privately owned, Pinewood Studios
	XX510	WS Lynx HAS2 [69/DD]	SFDO, RNAS Culdrose
	XX513	SA Bulldog T1 (G-KKKK) [10]	Privately owned, Meppershall
	XX515	SA Bulldog T1 (G-CBBC) [4]	Privately owned, Blackbushe
	XX518	SA Bulldog T1 (G-UDOG) [S]	Privately owned, North Weald
	XX520	SA Bulldog T1 (9288M) [A]	No 172 Sqn ATC, Haywards Heath

Serial	Type (code/other identity)	Owner/operator location or fate	Notes
XX521	SA Bulldog T1 (G-CBEH) [H]	Privately owned, East Dereham, Norfolk	
XX522	SA Bulldog T1 (G-DAWG) [06]	Privately owned, Barton	
XX524	SA Bulldog T1 (G-DDOG) [04]	Privately owned, Malaga, Spain	
XX525	SA Bulldog T1 (G-CBJJ) [03]	Privately owned, Kortrijk, Belgium	
XX528	SA Bulldog T1 (G-BZON) [D]	Privately owned, Earls Colne	
XX530	SA Bulldog T1 (XX637/9197M) [F]	No 2175 Sqn ATC, RAF Kinloss	
XX534	SA Bulldog T1 (G-EDAV) [B]	Privately owned, Tollerton	
XX537	SA Bulldog T1 (G-CBCB) [C]	Privately owned, RAF Halton	
XX538	SA Bulldog T1 (G-TDOG) [O]	Privately owned, Shobdon	
XX539	SA Bulldog T1 [L]	Privately owned, Derbyshire	
XX543	SA Bulldog T1 (G-CBAB) [F]	Privately owned, Duxford	
XX546	SA Bulldog T1 (G-WINI) [03]	Privately owned, Farnborough	
XX549	SA Bulldog T1 (G-CBID) [6]	Privately owned, White Waltham	
XX550	SA Bulldog T1 (G-CBBL) [Z]	Privately owned, Fenland	
XX551	SA Bulldog T1 (G-BZDP) [E]	Privately owned, Hullavington	
XX554	SA Bulldog T1 (G-BZMD) [09]	Privately owned, Wellesbourne Mountford	
XX557	SA Bulldog T1	Privately owned, stored Fort Paull, Yorks	
XX561	SA Bulldog T1 (G-BZEP) [7]	Privately owned, Biggin Hill	
XX611	SA Bulldog T1 (G-CBDK) [7]	Privately owned, Coventry	
XX612	SA Bulldog T1 (G-BZXC) [A,03]	Ayr College, instructional use	
XX614	SA Bulldog T1 (G-GGRR) [V]	Privately owned, White Waltham	
XX619	SA Bulldog T1 (G-CBBW) [T]	Privately owned, Coventry	
XX621	SA Bulldog T1 (G-CBEF) [H]	Privately owned, Leicester	
XX622	SA Bulldog T1 (G-CBGX) [B]	Privately owned, Shoreham	
XX623	SA Bulldog T1 [M]	Privately owned, Hurstbourne Tarrant, Hants	
XX624	SA Bulldog T1 (G-KDOG) [E]	Privately owned, North Weald	
XX626	SA Bulldog T1 (9290M/G-CDVV) [W,02]	Privately owned, Wellesbourne Mountford	
XX628	SA Bulldog T1 (G-CBFU) [9]	Privately owned, Faversham	
XX629	SA Bulldog T1 (G-BZXZ) [V]	Privately owned, Wellesbourne Mountford	
XX630	SA Bulldog T1 (G-SIJW) [5]	Privately owned, Cranfield	
XX631	SA Bulldog T1 (G-BZXS) [W]	Privately owned, Sligo, Eire	
XX633	SA Bulldog T1 [X]	Privately owned, Diseworth, Leics	
XX634	SA Bulldog T1 [T]	Newark Air Museum, Winthorpe	
XX636	SA Bulldog T1 (G-CBFP) [Y]	Privately owned, Cranfield	
XX638	SA Bulldog T1 (G-DOGG)	Privately owned, Hurstbourne Tarrant, Hants	
XX639	SA Bulldog T1 (F-AZTF) [D]	Privately owned, La Baule, France	
XX653	SA Bulldog T1 [E]	*Scrapped*	
XX654	SA Bulldog T1 [3]	RAF Museum, Cosford	
XX655	SA Bulldog T1 (9294M) [V] <ff>	Aeroventure, Doncaster	
XX656	SA Bulldog T1 [C]	Privately owned, Derbyshire	
XX658	SA Bulldog T1 (G-BZPS) [07]	Privately owned, Wellesbourne Mountford	
XX659	SA Bulldog T1 [E]	Privately owned, Derbyshire	
XX664	SA Bulldog T1 (F-AZTV) [04]	Privately owned, Pontoise, France	
XX665	SA Bulldog T1 (9289M)	No 2409 Sqn ATC, Halton	
XX667	SA Bulldog T1 (G-BZFN) [16]	Privately owned, Ronaldsway, IoM	
XX668	SA Bulldog T1 (G-CBAN) [1]	Privately owned, St Athan	
XX669	SA Bulldog T1 (8997M) [B]	Aeroventure, Doncaster	
XX671	SA Bulldog T1 [D]	Privately owned, Diseworth, Leics	
XX687	SA Bulldog T1 [F]	Barry Technical College, Cardiff Airport	
XX690	SA Bulldog T1 [A]	James Watt College, Greenock	
XX692	SA Bulldog T1 (G-BZMH) [A]	Privately owned, Wellesbourne Mountford	
XX693	SA Bulldog T1 (G-BZML) [07]	Privately owned, Elmsett	
XX694	SA Bulldog T1 (G-CBBS) [E]	Privately owned, Newcastle	
XX695	SA Bulldog T1 (G-CBBT) [3]	Privately owned, Sherburn-in-Elmet	
XX698	SA Bulldog T1 (G-BZME) [9]	Privately owned, Breighton	
XX699	SA Bulldog T1 (G-CBCV) [F]	Privately owned, North Coates	
XX700	SA Bulldog T1 (G-CBEK) [17]	Privately owned, Blackbushe	
XX702	SA Bulldog T1 (G-CBCR) [π]	Privately owned, Egginton	

Notes	Serial	Type (code/other identity)	Owner/operator location or fate
	XX704	SA122 Bulldog (G-BCUV/G-112)	Privately owned, Bournemouth
	XX705	SA Bulldog T1 [5]	QinetiQ Boscombe Down, Apprentice School
	XX707	SA Bulldog T1 (G-CBDS) [4]	Privately owned, Caernarfon
	XX711	SA Bulldog T1 (G-CBBU) [X]	Privately owned, stored Fishburn
	XX720	SEPECAT Jaguar GR3A [FL]	Privately owned, Sproughton
	XX722	SEPECAT Jaguar GR1 (9252M) <ff>	RAF St Athan, instructional use
	XX723	SEPECAT Jaguar GR3A [EU]	DCAE, No 1 SoTT, Cosford
	XX724	SEPECAT Jaguar GR3A [EC]	DCAE, No 1 SoTT, Cosford
	XX725	SEPECAT Jaguar GR3A [T]	DCAE, No 1 SoTT, Cosford
	XX726	SEPECAT Jaguar GR1 (8947M) [EB]	DCAE, No 1 SoTT, Cosford
	XX727	SEPECAT Jaguar GR1 (8951M) [ER]	DCAE, No 1 SoTT, Cosford
	XX729	SEPECAT Jaguar GR3A [EL]	DCAE, No 1 SoTT, Cosford
	XX733	SEPECAT Jaguar GR1B [EB] (wreck)	Privately owned, Faygate
	XX734	SEPECAT Jaguar GR1 (8816M)	Gatwick Aviation Museum, Charlwood
	XX736	SEPECAT Jaguar GR1 (9110M) <ff>	Aeroventure, Doncaster
	XX738	SEPECAT Jaguar GR3A [ED]	DCAE, No 1 SoTT, Cosford
	XX739	SEPECAT Jaguar GR1 (8902M) [I]	RAF Syerston, instructional use
	XX741	SEPECAT Jaguar GR1A [04]	Bentwaters Cold War Museum
	XX743	SEPECAT Jaguar GR1 (8949M) [EG]	DCAE, No 1 SoTT, Cosford
	XX744	SEPECAT Jaguar GR1 (9251M)	Mayhem Paintball, Abridge, Essex
	XX745	SEPECAT Jaguar GR1A [GV]	MoD/QinetiQ, Boscombe Down
	XX746	SEPECAT Jaguar GR1 (8895M) [S]	DCAE, No 1 SoTT, Cosford
	XX747	SEPECAT Jaguar GR1 (8903M)	DCAE, TCF, RAFC Cranwell
	XX748	SEPECAT Jaguar GR3A [EG]	DCAE, No 1 SoTT, Cosford
	XX751	SEPECAT Jaguar GR1 (8937M) [10]	RAF Syerston, instructional use
	XX752	SEPECAT Jaguar GR3A [EK]	DCAE, No 1 SoTT, Cosford
	XX753	SEPECAT Jaguar GR1 (9087M) <ff>	Newark Air Museum, Winthorpe
	XX756	SEPECAT Jaguar GR1 (8899M) [W]	DCAE, No 1 SoTT, Cosford
	XX757	SEPECAT Jaguar GR1 (8948M) [CU]	DCAE, No 1 SoTT, Cosford
	XX761	SEPECAT Jaguar GR1 (8600M) <ff>	Boscombe Down Aviation Collection
	XX763	SEPECAT Jaguar GR1 (9009M)	Bournemouth Aviation Museum
	XX764	SEPECAT Jaguar GR1 (9010M)	Privately owned, Woodmancote, W Sussex
	XX765	SEPECAT Jaguar ACT	RAF Museum, Cosford
	XX766	SEPECAT Jaguar GR3A [EF]	DCAE, No 1 SoTT, Cosford
	XX767	SEPECAT Jaguar GR3A [FK]	DCAE, No 1 SoTT, Cosford
	XX818	SEPECAT Jaguar GR1 (8945M) [DE]	DCAE, No 1 SoTT, Cosford
	XX819	SEPECAT Jaguar GR1 (8923M) [CE]	DCAE, No 1 SoTT, Cosford
	XX821	SEPECAT Jaguar GR1 (8896M) [P]	DCAE, TCF, RAFC Cranwell
	XX824	SEPECAT Jaguar GR1 (9019M) [AD]	DCAE, No 1 SoTT, Cosford
	XX825	SEPECAT Jaguar GR1 (9020M) [BN]	DCAE, No 1 SoTT, Cosford
	XX826	SEPECAT Jaguar GR1 (9021M) [34,JH]	Privately owned, Welshpool
	XX829	SEPECAT Jaguar T2A [GZ]	Privately owned, Sproughton
	XX830	SEPECAT Jaguar T2 <ff>	City of Norwich Aviation Museum
	XX832	SEPECAT Jaguar T2A [EZ]	Privately owned, Bentwaters
	XX833	SEPECAT Jaguar T2B	DCAE, No 1 SoTT, Cosford
	XX835	SEPECAT Jaguar T4 [EX]	DCAE, No 1 SoTT, Cosford
	XX836	SEPECAT Jaguar T2A [X]	Privately owned, Sproughton
	XX837	SEPECAT Jaguar T2 (8978M) [Z]	DCAE, TCF, RAFC Cranwell
	XX838	SEPECAT Jaguar T4 [FZ]	Privately owned, Bentwaters
	XX840	SEPECAT Jaguar T4 [EY]	DCAE, No 1 SoTT, Cosford
	XX841	SEPECAT Jaguar T4	Privately owned, Tunbridge Wells
	XX842	SEPECAT Jaguar T2A [FX]	Privately owned, Bentwaters
	XX845	SEPECAT Jaguar T4 [EV]	RN, Predannack Fire School
	XX847	SEPECAT Jaguar T4 [EZ]	DCAE, No 1 SoTT, Cosford
	XX885	HS Buccaneer S2B (9225M/G-HHAA)	Hawker Hunter Aviation, Scampton
	XX888	HS Buccaneer S2B <ff>	Privately owned, Barnstaple
	XX889	HS Buccaneer S2B [T]	Blackburn Buccaneer Society, Bruntingthorpe
	XX892	HS Buccaneer S2B <ff>	Privately owned, Perthshire

Serial	Type (code/other identity)	Owner/operator location or fate	Notes
XX893	HS Buccaneer S2B <ff>	*To Germany, 2011*	
XX894	HS Buccaneer S2B [020/R]	Buccaneer Supporters Club, Bruntingthorpe	
XX897	HS Buccaneer S2B(mod)	Privately owned, Bournemouth	
XX899	HS Buccaneer S2B <ff>	Midland Air Museum, Coventry	
XX900	HS Buccaneer S2B [900]	Cold War Jets Collection, Bruntingthorpe	
XX901	HS Buccaneer S2B	Yorkshire Air Museum, Elvington	
XX907	WS Lynx AH1	Privately owned, Stoke-on-Trent	
XX910	WS Lynx HAS2	The Helicopter Museum, Weston-super-Mare	
XX914	BAC VC10/1103 (8777M) <rf>	RAF Defence Movements School, Brize Norton	
XX919	BAC 1-11/402AP (PI-C1121) <ff>	Boscombe Down Aviation Collection	
XX946	Panavia Tornado (P02) (8883M) [WT]	RAF Museum, Cosford	
XX947	Panavia Tornado (P03) (8797M)	Shoreham Airport, on display	
XX958	SEPECAT Jaguar GR1 (9022M) [BK]	DCAE, No 1 SoTT, Cosford	
XX959	SEPECAT Jaguar GR1 (8953M) [CJ]	DCAE, No 1 SoTT, Cosford	
XX965	SEPECAT Jaguar GR1A (9254M) [C]	DCAE, TCF, RAFC Cranwell	
XX967	SEPECAT Jaguar GR1 (9006M) [AC]	DCAE, No 1 SoTT, Cosford	
XX968	SEPECAT Jaguar GR1 (9007M) [AJ]	DCAE, No 1 SoTT, Cosford	
XX969	SEPECAT Jaguar GR1 (8897M) [01]	DCAE, No 1 SoTT, Cosford	
XX970	SEPECAT Jaguar GR3A [EH]	DCAE, No 1 SoTT, Cosford	
XX974	SEPECAT Jaguar GR3 [FE]	Privately owned, Sproughton	
XX975	SEPECAT Jaguar GR1 (8905M) [07]	DCAE, No 1 SoTT, Cosford	
XX976	SEPECAT Jaguar GR1 (8906M) [BD]	DCAE, No 1 SoTT, Cosford	
XX977	SEPECAT Jaguar GR1 (9132M) [DL,05] <rf>	Privately owned, Sproughton	
XX979	SEPECAT Jaguar GR1A (9306M) <ff>	Air Defence Radar Museum, Neatishead	
XZ103	SEPECAT Jaguar GR3A [EF]	DCAE, No 1 SoTT, Cosford	
XZ104	SEPECAT Jaguar GR3A [FM]	DCAE, No 1 SoTT, Cosford	
XZ106	SEPECAT Jaguar GR3A [FD,FW]	RAF Manston History Museum	
XZ107	SEPECAT Jaguar GR3A [FH]	Privately owned, Bentwaters	
XZ109	SEPECAT Jaguar GR3A [EN]	DCAE, No 1 SoTT, Cosford	
XZ112	SEPECAT Jaguar GR3A [GW]	DCAE, No 1 SoTT, Cosford	
XZ113	SEPECAT Jaguar GR3 [FD]	Privately owned, Bentwaters	
XZ114	SEPECAT Jaguar GR3 [EO]	DCAE, No 1 SoTT, Cosford	
XZ115	SEPECAT Jaguar GR3 [ER]	DCAE, No 1 SoTT, Cosford	
XZ117	SEPECAT Jaguar GR3 [ES]	DCAE, No 1 SoTT, Cosford	
XZ118	SEPECAT Jaguar GR3	Slimelight, Islington	
XZ119	SEPECAT Jaguar GR1A (9266M) [FG]	Royal Scottish Mus'm of Flight, E Fortune	
XZ130	HS Harrier GR3 (9079M) [A]	No 1034 Sqn ATC, Tolworth, Surrey	
XZ131	HS Harrier GR3 (9174M) <ff>	Privately owned, Spark Bridge, Cumbria	
XZ132	HS Harrier GR3 (9168M) [C]	DCAE, TCF, RAFC Cranwell	
XZ133	HS Harrier GR3 [10]	Imperial War Museum, Duxford	
XZ135	HS Harrier GR3 (8848M) <ff>	*Sold to Germany, December 2011*	
XZ138	HS Harrier GR3 (9040M) <ff>	RAFC Cranwell, Trenchard Hall	
XZ145	HS Harrier T4 [45/DD]	RN, Predannack Fire School	
XZ146	HS Harrier T4 (9281M) [S]	RAF Wittering	
XZ166	WS Lynx HAS2 <ff>	Farnborough Air Sciences Trust, Farnborough	
XZ170	WS Lynx AH9	DCAE SEAE, Arborfield	
XZ171	WS Lynx AH7	Army, Salisbury Plain	
XZ172	WS Lynx AH7	DCAE SEAE, Arborfield	
XZ173	WS Lynx AH7 <ff>	Privately owned, Hixon, Staffs	
XZ174	WS Lynx AH7 <ff>	MoD Police, Gosport, instructional use	
XZ175	WS Lynx AH7	Privately owned,	
XZ176	WS Lynx AH7	AAC No 1 Regt, Gütersloh	
XZ177	WS Lynx AH7	RM No 847 NAS, Yeovilton	
XZ178	WS Lynx AH7 <ff>	Privately owned,	
XZ179	WS Lynx AH7	AAC No 1 Regt, Gütersloh	
XZ180	WS Lynx AH7	RM No 847 NAS, Yeovilton	
XZ181	WS Lynx AH1	AAC Middle Wallop Fire Section	

Notes	Serial	Type (code/other identity)	Owner/operator location or fate
	XZ182	WS Lynx AH7	AAC No 1 Regt, Gütersloh
	XZ183	WS Lynx AH7 <ff>	MoD/Vector Aerospace, stored Fleetlands
	XZ184	WS Lynx AH7 [Z]	AAC No 9 Regt, Dishforth
	XZ185	WS Lynx AH7	AAC No 1 Regt, Gütersloh
	XZ187	WS Lynx AH7	DCAE SEAE, Arborfield
	XZ188	WS Lynx AH7	DCAE SEAE, Arborfield
	XZ190	WS Lynx AH7	AAC No 671 Sqn/7 Regt, Middle Wallop
	XZ191	WS Lynx AH7	AAC No 9 Regt, Dishforth
	XZ192	WS Lynx AH7	RM No 847 NAS, Yeovilton
	XZ193	WS Lynx AH7 <ff>	Privately owned,
	XZ194	WS Lynx AH7 [V]	AAC No 671 Sqn/7 Regt, Middle Wallop
	XZ195	WS Lynx AH7 <ff>	Privately owned, Hixon, Staffs
	XZ196	WS Lynx AH7 [T]	ACC 671 Sqn/7 Regt, Middle Wallop
	XZ197	WS Lynx AH7 <ff>	MoD/Vector Aerospace, stored Fleetlands
	XZ198	WS Lynx AH7 <ff>	MoD/Vector Aerospace, stored Fleetlands
	XZ203	WS Lynx AH7 [F]	AAC GDSH, Middle Wallop
	XZ205	WS Lynx AH7 <ff>	AAC GDSH, Middle Wallop
	XZ206	WS Lynx AH7 <ff>	Privately owned, Hixon, Staffs
	XZ207	WS Lynx AH7 <rf>	DCAE SEAE, Arborfield
	XZ208	WS Lynx AH7	AAC No 671 Sqn/7 Regt, Middle Wallop
	XZ209	WS Lynx AH7 <ff>	MoD JARTS, Boscombe Down
	XZ210	WS Lynx AH7	*Crashed 1 December 2011, Gütersloh*
	XZ211	WS Lynx AH7	AAC No 1 Regt, Gütersloh
	XZ212	WS Lynx AH7 [X]	AAC No 9 Regt, Dishforth
	XZ213	WS Lynx AH1 (TAD 213)	Vector Aerospace Fleetlands Apprentice School
	XZ214	WS Lynx AH7	AAC No 657 Sqn, Odiham
	XZ215	WS Lynx AH7	AAC No 9 Regt, Dishforth
	XZ216	WS Lynx AH7	AAC No 1 Regt, Gütersloh
	XZ217	WS Lynx AH7	Privately owned,
	XZ218	WS Lynx AH7	Warfighters R6 Centre, Barby, Northants
	XZ219	WS Lynx AH7 <ff>	MoD/Vector Aerospace, stored Fleetlands
	XZ220	WS Lynx AH7 [U]	Privately owned, Hixon, Staffs
	XZ221	WS Lynx AH7 [Z]	AAC No 671 Sqn/7 Regt, Middle Wallop
	XZ222	WS Lynx AH7	AAC No 657 Sqn, Odiham
	XZ228	WS Lynx HAS3GMS [313]	RN Lynx RTP, Yeovilton
	XZ229	WS Lynx HAS3GMS [360/MC]	Privately owned, Hixon, Staffs
	XZ230	WS Lynx HAS3GMS <ff>	Privately owned,
	XZ232	WS Lynx HAS3GMS	MoD/Vector Aerospace, stored Fleetlands
	XZ233	WS Lynx HAS3S [635] $	RN, Yeovilton (wfu)
	XZ234	WS Lynx HAS3S [630]	AAC GDSH, Middle Wallop
	XZ235	WS Lynx HAS3S(ICE) [630]	RN, Yeovilton (wfu)
	XZ236	WS Lynx HMA8 [LST-1]	RN ETS, Yeovilton, GI use
	XZ237	WS Lynx HAS3S [631]	RN No 702 NAS, Yeovilton
	XZ238	WS Lynx HAS3S(ICE) [633]	RN No 702 NAS, Yeovilton
	XZ239	WS Lynx HAS3GMS [633]	Privately owned, Hixon, Staffs
	XZ245	WS Lynx HAS3GMS [632]	RN No 702 NAS, Yeovilton
	XZ246	WS Lynx HAS3S(ICE) [434/EE]	MoD/Vector Aerospace, stored Fleetlands
	XZ248	WS Lynx HAS3S [666]	SFDO, RNAS Culdrose
	XZ250	WS Lynx HAS3S [426/PO] $	RN, Portland, Dorset, on display
	XZ252	WS Lynx HAS3S	Privately owned, Hixon, Staffs
	XZ254	WS Lynx HAS3S	Privately owned, Hixon, Staffs
	XZ255	WS Lynx HMA8SRU [314]	RN No 815 NAS, HQ Flt, Yeovilton
	XZ257	WS Lynx HAS3S <ff>	Privately owned, Hixon, Staffs
	XZ287	BAe Nimrod AEW3 (9140M) (fuselage)	RAF TSW, Stafford
	XZ290	WS Gazelle AH1	AAC GDSH, Middle Wallop
	XZ291	WS Gazelle AH1	Privately owned, Colsterworth, Leics
	XZ292	WS Gazelle AH1	Privately owned, Colsterworth, Leics
	XZ294	WS Gazelle AH1 [X]	AAC, stored Shawbury

Serial	Type (code/other identity)	Owner/operator location or fate	Notes
XZ295	WS Gazelle AH1	AAC, stored Shawbury	
XZ296	WS Gazelle AH1 [V]	Privately owned, Colsterworth, Leics	
XZ298	WS Gazelle AH1 <ff>	AAC, Middle Wallop	
XZ303	WS Gazelle AH1	AAC, stored Shawbury	
XZ304	WS Gazelle AH1	Privately owned, Colsterworth, Leics	
XZ305	WS Gazelle AH1 (TAD 020)	DCAE AESS HMS Sultan, Gosport	
XZ307	WS Gazelle AH1 (G-CHBN)	Privately owned, Stapleford Tawney	
XZ308	WS Gazelle AH1	QinetiQ, Boscombe Down (spares use)	
XZ311	WS Gazelle AH1 [U]	AAC, stored Shawbury	
XZ312	WS Gazelle AH1	RAF Henlow, instructional use	
XZ313	WS Gazelle AH1 <ff>	AAC GDSH, Middle Wallop	
XZ314	WS Gazelle AH1 [A]	Privately owned, Colsterworth, Leics	
XZ315	WS Gazelle AH1 <ff>	Privately owned, Babcary, Somerset	
XZ316	WS Gazelle AH1 [B]	DCAE SEAE, Arborfield	
XZ318	WS Gazelle AH1 (fuselage)	Tong Paintball Park, Shropshire	
XZ320	WS Gazelle AH1	AAC No 665 Sqn/5 Regt, Aldergrove	
XZ322	WS Gazelle AH1 (9283M) [N]	DCAE, No 1 SoTT, Cosford	
XZ323	WS Gazelle AH1 [J]	AAC, stored Shawbury	
XZ324	WS Gazelle AH1	Privately owned, Colsterworth, Leics	
XZ325	WS Gazelle AH1 [T]	DCAE SEAE, Arborfield	
XZ326	WS Gazelle AH1	AAC GDSH, Middle Wallop	
XZ327	WS Gazelle AH1	AAC Middle Wallop (recruiting aid)	
XZ328	WS Gazelle AH1 [C]	AAC, stored Shawbury	
XZ329	WS Gazelle AH1 (G-BZYD) [J]	Privately owned, East Harston, Bucks	
XZ330	WS Gazelle AH1 [Y]	AAC Wattisham, instructional use	
XZ331	WS Gazelle AH1 [D]	AAC, stored Shawbury	
XZ332	WS Gazelle AH1 [O]	DCAE SEAE, Arborfield	
XZ333	WS Gazelle AH1 [A]	REME Museum, Arborfield	
XZ334	WS Gazelle AH1	AAC GDSH, Middle Wallop	
XZ335	WS Gazelle AH1	North-East Aircraft Museum, Usworth	
XZ337	WS Gazelle AH1 [Z]	AAC, stored Shawbury	
XZ338	WS Gazelle AH1 [Y]	Privately owned, Colsterworth, Leics	
XZ340	WS Gazelle AH1	AAC No 29 Flt, BATUS, Suffield, Canada	
XZ341	WS Gazelle AH1	AAC, Middle Wallop	
XZ342	WS Gazelle AH1	AAC No 8 Flt, Credenhill	
XZ343	WS Gazelle AH1	AAC, stored Shawbury	
XZ344	WS Gazelle AH1 [Y]	Privately owned, Colsterworth, Leics	
XZ345	WS Gazelle AH1 [M]	AAC No 671 Sqn/7 Regt, Middle Wallop	
XZ346	WS Gazelle AH1	AAC Netheravon, at main gate	
XZ347	WS Gazelle AH1	Privately owned, Hurstbourne Tarrant, Hants	
XZ349	WS Gazelle AH1	Privately owned,	
XZ356	SEPECAT Jaguar GR3A [FU]	Privately owned, Welshpool	
XZ358	SEPECAT Jaguar GR1A (9262M) [L]	DCAE, TCF, RAFC Cranwell	
XZ360	SEPECAT Jaguar GR3 [FN]	Privately owned, Bentwaters	
XZ363	SEPECAT Jaguar GR1A <R>	RAF M&RU, Bottesford	
	(XX824/BAPC 151) [A]		
XZ364	SEPECAT Jaguar GR3A <ff>	Privately owned, Tunbridge Wells	
XZ366	SEPECAT Jaguar GR3A [FC]	Privately owned, Bentwaters	
XZ367	SEPECAT Jaguar GR3 [GP]	DCAE, No 1 SoTT, Cosford	
XZ368	SEPECAT Jaguar GR1 [8900M] [E]	DCAE, No 1 SoTT, Cosford	
XZ369	SEPECAT Jaguar GR3A [EU]	Privately owned, Bentwaters	
XZ370	SEPECAT Jaguar GR1 (9004M) [JB]	DCAE, No 1 SoTT, Cosford	
XZ371	SEPECAT Jaguar GR1 (8907M) [AP]	DCAE, No 1 SoTT, Cosford	
XZ372	SEPECAT Jaguar GR3 [FV]	Aberdeen Airport, on display	
XZ374	SEPECAT Jaguar GR1 (9005M) [JC]	DCAE, stored Cosford	
XZ375	SEPECAT Jaguar GR1A (9255M) <ff>	City of Norwich Aviation Museum	
XZ377	SEPECAT Jaguar GR3A [EP]	DCAE, No 1 SoTT, Cosford	
XZ378	SEPECAT Jaguar GR1A [EP]	Privately owned, Topsham, Devon	

Notes	Serial	Type (code/other identity)	Owner/operator location or fate
	XZ382	SEPECAT Jaguar GR1 (8908M)	Cold War Jets Collection, Bruntingthorpe
	XZ383	SEPECAT Jaguar GR1 (8901M) [AF]	DCAE, No 1 SoTT, Cosford
	XZ384	SEPECAT Jaguar GR1 (8954M) [BC]	DCAE, No 1 SoTT, Cosford
	XZ385	SEPECAT Jaguar GR3A [FT]	Privately owned, Bentwaters
	XZ389	SEPECAT Jaguar GR1 (8946M) [BL]	DCAE, No 1 SoTT, Cosford
	XZ390	SEPECAT Jaguar GR1 (9003M) [DM]	DCAE, No 1 SoTT, Cosford
	XZ391	SEPECAT Jaguar GR3A [ET]	DCAE, No 1 SoTT, Cosford
	XZ392	SEPECAT Jaguar GR3A [EM]	DCAE, No 1 SoTT, Cosford
	XZ394	SEPECAT Jaguar GR3 [FG]	Privately owned, Bentwaters
	XZ396	SEPECAT Jaguar GR3A [EQ]	Privately owned, Bentwaters
	XZ398	SEPECAT Jaguar GR3A [EQ]	DCAE, No 1 SoTT, Cosford
	XZ399	SEPECAT Jaguar GR3A [EJ]	DCAE, No 1 SoTT, Cosford
	XZ400	SEPECAT Jaguar GR3A [FQ]	Privately owned, Bentwaters
	XZ431	HS Buccaneer S2B (9233M) <ff>	Privately owned, Market Drayton, Shropshire
	XZ440	BAe Sea Harrier FA2 [40/DD]	SFDO, RNAS Culdrose
	XZ455	BAe Sea Harrier FA2 [001] (wreck)	Privately owned, Thorpe Wood, N Yorks
	XZ457	BAe Sea Harrier FA2 [104/VL]	Boscombe Down Aviation Collection
	XZ459	BAe Sea Harrier FA2 [126]	Privately owned, Sussex
	XZ492	BAe Sea Harrier FA2 (wreck)	Privately owned, Faygate
	XZ493	BAe Sea Harrier FRS1 (comp XV760) [001/N]	FAA Museum, RNAS Yeovilton
	XZ493	BAe Sea Harrier FRS1 <ff>	RN Yeovilton, Fire Section
	XZ494	BAe Sea Harrier FA2 [128]	Privately owned, Wedmore, Somerset
	XZ497	BAe Sea Harrier FA2 [126]	Privately owned, Charlwood
	XZ499	BAe Sea Harrier FA2 [003]	FAA Museum, RNAS Yeovilton
	XZ559	Slingsby T61F Venture T2 (G-BUEK)	Privately owned, Tibenham
	XZ570	WS61 Sea King HAS5(mod)	RN, Predannack Fire School
	XZ574	WS61 Sea King HAS6	FAA Museum, RNAS Yeovilton
	XZ575	WS61 Sea King HU5	MoD/AFD/QinetiQ, Boscombe Down
	XZ576	WS61 Sea King HAS6	DCAE AESS, HMS Sultan, Gosport
	XZ578	WS61 Sea King HU5	MoD/Vector Aerospace, Fleetlands
	XZ579	WS61 Sea King HAS6 [707/PW]	DCAE AESS, HMS Sultan, Gosport
	XZ580	WS61 Sea King HC6 [ZB]	DCAE, stored HMS Sultan, Gosport
	XZ581	WS61 Sea King HAS6 [69/CU]	DCAE AESS, HMS Sultan, Gosport
	XZ585	WS61 Sea King HAR3 [A]	RAF No 202 Sqn, A Flt, Boulmer
	XZ586	WS61 Sea King HAR3 [B]	RAF SKAMG, RNAS Yeovilton
	XZ587	WS61 Sea King HAR3 [C]	RAF No 202 Sqn, A Flt, Boulmer
	XZ588	WS61 Sea King HAR3 [D]	RAF No 202 Sqn, D Flt, Lossiemouth
	XZ589	WS61 Sea King HAR3 [E] $	RAF No 202 Sqn, D Flt, Lossiemouth
	XZ590	WS61 Sea King HAR3 [F]	MoD/Vector Aerospace, Fleetlands
	XZ591	WS61 Sea King HAR3 [G]	RAF No 1564 Flt, Mount Pleasant, Fl
	XZ592	WS61 Sea King HAR3 [H]	RAF SKAMG, RNAS Yeovilton
	XZ593	WS61 Sea King HAR3 [I]	MoD/Vector Aerospace, Fleetlands
	XZ594	WS61 Sea King HAR3	MoD/Vector Aerospace, Fleetlands
	XZ595	WS61 Sea King HAR3 [K]	RAF No 22 Sqn, C Flt/No 203(R) Sqn, Valley
	XZ596	WS61 Sea King HAR3 [L]	RAF No 22 Sqn, C Flt/No 203(R) Sqn, Valley
	XZ597	WS61 Sea King HAR3 [M]	RAF No 1564 Flt, Mount Pleasant, Fl
	XZ598	WS61 Sea King HAR3	RAF No 22 Sqn, C Flt/No 203(R) Sqn, Valley
	XZ599	WS61 Sea King HAR3 [P]	RAF No 202 Sqn, E Flt, Leconfield
	XZ605	WS Lynx AH7 [L]	MoD/Vector Aerospace, Fleetlands
	XZ606	WS Lynx AH7	AAC No 9 Regt, Dishforth
	XZ607	WS Lynx AH7 <ff>	MoD/Vector Aerospace, Fleetlands
	XZ608	WS Lynx AH7	MoD/Vector Aerospace, Fleetlands
	XZ609	WS Lynx AH7	AAC No 1 Regt, Gütersloh
	XZ611	WS Lynx AH7 <ff>	Privately owned, Hixon, Staffs
	XZ612	WS Lynx AH7	AAC No 671 Sqn/7 Regt, Middle Wallop
	XZ613	WS Lynx AH7 [F]	AAC Stockwell Hall, Middle Wallop
	XZ615	WS Lynx AH7 <ff>	Privately owned,

Serial	Type (code/other identity)	Owner/operator location or fate	Notes
XZ616	WS Lynx AH7	AAC No 657 Sqn, Odiham	
XZ617	WS Lynx AH7	RM No 847 NAS, Yeovilton	
XZ630	Panavia Tornado GR1 (8976M)	RAF Halton, on display	
XZ631	Panavia Tornado GR1	Yorkshire Air Museum, Elvington	
XZ641	WS Lynx AH7	AAC No 657 Sqn, Odiham	
XZ642	WS Lynx AH7	AAC No 667 Sqn/7 Regt, Middle Wallop	
XZ643	WS Lynx AH7 [C]	AAC No 671 Sqn/7 Regt, Middle Wallop	
XZ645	WS Lynx AH7	AAC No 657 Sqn, Odiham	
XZ646	WS Lynx AH7 <ff>	MoD JARTS, Boscombe Down	
XZ646	WS Lynx AH7 (really XZ649)	Bristol University, instructional use	
XZ647	WS Lynx AH7 <ff>	Currently not known	
XZ648	WS Lynx AH7 <ff>	Privately owned,	
XZ651	WS Lynx AH7	AAC No 657 Sqn, Odiham	
XZ652	WS Lynx AH7	MoD/Vector Aerospace, Fleetlands	
XZ653	WS Lynx AH7	RM No 847 NAS, Yeovilton	
XZ654	WS Lynx AH7	AAC No 9 Regt, Dishforth	
XZ655	WS Lynx AH7 <ff>	Privately owned,	
XZ661	WS Lynx AH7 [V]	AAC GDSH, Middle Wallop	
XZ663	WS Lynx AH7 <ff>	Privately owned, Hixon, Staffs	
XZ664	WS Lynx AH7	Warfighters R6 Centre, Barby, Northants	
XZ665	WS Lynx AH7	Warfighters R6 Centre, Barby, Northants	
XZ666	WS Lynx AH7	DCAE SEAE, Arborfield	
XZ669	WS Lynx AH7 [I]	AAC No 671 Sqn/7 Regt, Middle Wallop	
XZ670	WS Lynx AH7	AAC No 1 Regt, Gütersloh	
XZ671	WS Lynx AH7 <ff>	AgustaWestland, Yeovil, instructional use	
XZ672	WS Lynx AH7 <ff>	AAC GDSH, Middle Wallop	
XZ673	WS Lynx AH7	AAC No 1 Regt, Gütersloh	
XZ674	WS Lynx AH7	AAC No 1 Regt, Gütersloh	
XZ675	WS Lynx AH7 [H]	Museum of Army Flying, Middle Wallop	
XZ676	WS Lynx AH7 [N]	AAC GDSH, Middle Wallop	
XZ677	WS Lynx AH7	AAC No 9 Regt, Dishforth	
XZ678	WS Lynx AH7	RM No 847 NAS, Yeovilton	
XZ679	WS Lynx AH7	AAC No 1 Regt, Gütersloh	
XZ680	WS Lynx AH7 [E]	AAC No 671 Sqn/7 Regt, Middle Wallop	
XZ689	WS Lynx HMA8SRU [451/DA]	RN No 815 NAS, *Daring* Flt, Yeovilton	
XZ690	WS Lynx HMA8SRU [452]	RN No 815 NAS, *Dauntless* Flt, Yeovilton	
XZ691	WS Lynx HMA8SRU [365/AY]	RN No 815 NAS, *Argyll* Flt, Yeovilton	
XZ692	WS Lynx HMA8SRU [641] $	RN No 702 NAS, Yeovilton	
XZ693	WS Lynx HAS3S [311]	*RN, Yeovilton (wfu)*	
XZ694	WS Lynx HAS3GMS [434]	*Currently not known*	
XZ696	WS Lynx HAS3GMS [633]	Privately owned, Hixton, Staffs	
XZ697	WS Lynx HMA8SRU	MoD/Vector Aerospace, Fleetlands	
XZ698	WS Lynx HMA8SRU [348/SU]	RN No 815 NAS, *Sutherland* Flt, Yeovilton	
XZ699	WS Lynx HAS2	FAA Museum, RNAS Yeovilton	
XZ719	WS Lynx HMA8SRU [316]	RN No 815 NAS, HQ Flt, Yeovilton	
XZ720	WS Lynx HAS3GMS [410/GC]	RN Lynx RTP, Yeovilton	
XZ721	WS Lynx HAS3GMS [322]	RN No 815 NAS, HQ Flt, Yeovilton	
XZ722	WS Lynx HMA8SRU [645]$	RN No 702 NAS, Yeovilton	
XZ723	WS Lynx HMA8SRU [643]	RN No 702 NAS, Yeovilton	
XZ725	WS Lynx HMA8SRU [415]	RN No 815 NAS, *Monmouth* Flt, Yeovilton	
XZ726	WS Lynx HMA8SRU [411/EN]	RN No 815 NAS, *Edinburgh* Flt, Yeovilton	
XZ727	WS Lynx HAS3S [634]	RN No 702 NAS, Yeovilton	
XZ728	WS Lynx HMA8 [326/AW]	RNAS Yeovilton, on display	
XZ729	WS Lynx HMA8SRU [350]	MoD/Vector Aerospace, Fleetlands	
XZ730	WS Lynx HAS3S	RN, Yeovilton, GI use	
XZ731	WS Lynx HMA8SRU [332/LP]	RN No 815 NAS, *Liverpool* Flt, Yeovilton	
XZ732	WS Lynx HMA8SRU [302/DT]	RN No 815 NAS, HQ Flt, Yeovilton	
XZ733	WS Lynx HAS3GMS [305]	Privately owned, Hixon, Staffs	

Notes	Serial	Type (code/other identity)	Owner/operator location or fate
	XZ735	WS Lynx HAS3GMS [404]	MoD/Vector Aerospace, stored Fleetlands
	XZ736	WS Lynx HMA8SRU [304/DA]	MoD/Vector Aerospace, Fleetlands
	XZ791	Northrop Shelduck D1	Davidstow Airfield & Cornwall At War Museum
	XZ795	Northrop Shelduck D1	Museum of Army Flying, Middle Wallop
	XZ920	WS61 Sea King HU5 [707/PW]	RN No 771 NAS, Prestwick
	XZ921	WS61 Sea King HAS6 [269/N]	DCAE, stored HMS Sultan, Gosport
	XZ922	WS61 Sea King HC6 [ZA]	DCAE, stored HMS Sultan, Gosport
	XZ930	WS Gazelle HT3 (A2713) [Q]	DCAE AESS, HMS Sultan, Gosport
	XZ934	WS Gazelle HT3 (G-CBSI) [U]	Privately owned, Babcary, Somerset
	XZ935	WS Gazelle HCC4	DCAE SEAE, Arborfield
	XZ936	WS Gazelle HT2 [6]	MoD/ETPS, Boscombe Down
	XZ936	WS Gazelle HT3 (XZ933/G-CGJZ)	Privately owned, Hurstbourne Tarrant, Hants
	XZ939	WS Gazelle HT2 [9]	MoD/ETPS, Boscombe Down
	XZ941	WS Gazelle HT2 (9301M) [B]	DCAE, No 1 SoTT, Cosford
	XZ942	WS Gazelle HT2 (9305M) [42/CU]	Preserved at Suffield, Canada
	XZ964	BAe Harrier GR3 [D]	Royal Engineers Museum, Chatham
	XZ966	BAe Harrier GR3 (9221M) [G]	MoD DFTDC, Manston
	XZ968	BAe Harrier GR3 (9222M) [3G]	Muckleborough Collection, Weybourne
	XZ969	BAe Harrier GR3 [69/DD]	RN, Predannack Fire School
	XZ971	BAe Harrier GR3 (9219M)	HQ DSDA, Donnington, Shropshire, on display
	XZ987	BAe Harrier GR3 (9185M) [C]	RAF Stafford, at main gate
	XZ990	BAe Harrier GR3 <ff>	Currently not known
	XZ990	BAe Harrier GR3 <rf>	RAF Wittering, derelict
	XZ991	BAe Harrier GR3 (9162M) [3A]	DCAE, No 1 SoTT, Cosford
	XZ993	BAe Harrier GR3 (9240M) <ff>	Privately owned, Welshpool
	XZ994	BAe Harrier GR3 (9170M) [U]	RAF Defence Movements School, Brize Norton
	XZ995	BAe Harrier GR3 (9220M/G-CBGK) [3G]	Privately owned, Dunboyne, Eire
	XZ996	BAe Harrier GR3 [96/DD]	RN, Predannack Fire School
	XZ997	BAe Harrier GR3 (9122M) [V]	RAF Museum, Hendon
	ZA101	BAe Hawk 100 (G-HAWK) Training Centre	BAE Systems Warton, Overseas Customer
	ZA105	WS61 Sea King HAR3 [Q]	MoD/Vector Aerospace, Fleetlands
	ZA110	BAe Jetstream T2 (F-BTMI) [563/CU]	Privately owned, Sproughton
	ZA111	BAe Jetstream T2 (9Q-CTC) [565/CU]	SFDO, RNAS Culdrose
	ZA126	WS61 Sea King ASaC7 [191]	RN No 849 NAS, Culdrose
	ZA127	WS61 Sea King HAS6 [509/CU]	DCAE, stored HMS Sultan, Gosport
	ZA128	WS61 Sea King HAS6 [010]	DCAE, stored HMS Sultan, Gosport
	ZA130	WS61 Sea King HU5 [19]	RN No 771 NAS, Prestwick
	ZA131	WS61 Sea King HAS6 [271/N]	DCAE, No 1 SoTT, Cosford
	ZA133	WS61 Sea King HAS6 [831/CU]	MoD/Vector Aerospace, Fleetlands, GI use
	ZA134	WS61 Sea King HU5	MoD/Vector Aerospace, Fleetlands
	ZA135	WS61 Sea King HAS6	Privately owned, Hixon, Staffs
	ZA136	WS61 Sea King HAS6 [018]	DCAE, AESS, HMS Sultan, Gosport (wreck)
	ZA137	WS61 Sea King HU5 [20]	RN No 771 NAS, Culdrose
	ZA144	BAe VC10 K2 (G-ARVC) <ff>	MoD JARTS, Boscombe Down
	ZA147	BAe VC10 K3 (5H-MMT) [F]	MoD/DSG, St Athan
	ZA148	BAe VC10 K3 (5Y-ADA) [G]	RAF No 161 Sqn, Brize Norton
	ZA149	BAe VC10 K3 (5X-UVJ) [H]	MoD/DSG, St Athan
	ZA150	BAe VC10 K3 (5H-MOG) [J]	MoD/DSG, St Athan
	ZA166	WS61 Sea King HU5 [16/CU]	RN No 771 NAS, Culdrose
	ZA167	WS61 Sea King HU5 [22/CU]	RN No 771 NAS, Culdrose
	ZA168	WS61 Sea King HAS6 [830/CU]	DCAE, AESS, HMS Sultan, Gosport
	ZA169	WS61 Sea King HAS6 [515/CW]	DCAE, No 1 SoTT, Cosford
	ZA170	WS61 Sea King HAS5	DCAE, stored HMS Sultan, Gosport
	ZA175	BAe Sea Harrier FA2	Norfolk & Suffolk Avn Museum, Flixton
	ZA176	BAe Sea Harrier FA2 [126/R]	Newark Air Museum, Winthorpe
	ZA195	BAe Sea Harrier FA2	Tangmere Military Aviation Museum

Serial	Type (code/other identity)	Owner/operator location or fate	Notes
ZA209	Short MATS-B	Museum of Army Flying, Middle Wallop	
ZA220	Short MATS-B	Privately owned, Awbridge, Hants	
ZA250	BAe Harrier T52 (G-VTOL)	Brooklands Museum, Weybridge	
ZA254	Panavia Tornado F2 (9253M) (fuselage)	RAF Marham, instructional use	
ZA267	Panavia Tornado F2 (9284M)	RAF Marham, instructional use	
ZA291	WS61 Sea King HC4 [N]	RN No 845 NAS, Yeovilton	
ZA292	WS61 Sea King HC4 [WU]	RN SKAMG, Yeovilton	
ZA293	WS61 Sea King HC4 [A]	RN No 845 NAS, Yeovilton	
ZA295	WS61 Sea King HC4 [U]	RN No 846 NAS, Yeovilton	
ZA296	WS61 Sea King HC4 [Q]	RN SKAMG, Yeovilton	
ZA297	WS61 Sea King HC4 [W]	RN No 846 NAS, Yeovilton	
ZA298	WS61 Sea King HC4 (G-BJNM) [Y]	MoD/Vector Aerospace, Fleetlands (damaged)	
ZA299	WS61 Sea King HC4 [D]	MoD/AugustaWestland, Yeovil	
ZA310	WS61 Sea King HC4 [B]	RN No 845 NAS, Yeovilton	
ZA312	WS61 Sea King HC4	MoD/Vector Aerospace, Fleetlands	
ZA313	WS61 Sea King HC4 [M]	RN SKAMG, Yeovilton	
ZA314	WS61 Sea King HC4 [WT]	RN No 848 NAS, Yeovilton	
ZA319	Panavia Tornado GR1 (9315M)	DSDA, Bicester, on display	
ZA320	Panavia Tornado GR1 (9314M) [TAW]	DCAE, No 1 SoTT, Cosford	
ZA323	Panavia Tornado GR1 [TAZ]	DCAE, No 1 SoTT, Cosford	
ZA325	Panavia Tornado GR1 <ff>	RAF Manston History Museum	
ZA325	Panavia Tornado GR1 [TAX] <rf>	RAF, stored Shawbury	
ZA326	Panavia Tornado GR1P	MoD, Boscombe Down (wfu)	
ZA327	Panavia Tornado GR1 <ff>	BAE Systems, Warton	
ZA328	Panavia Tornado GR1	Marsh Lane Technical School, Preston	
ZA353	Panavia Tornado GR1 [B-53]	Privately owned, Thorpe Wood, N Yorks	
ZA354	Panavia Tornado GR1	Yorkshire Air Museum, Elvington	
ZA355	Panavia Tornado GR1 (9310M) [TAA]	RAF, stored Lossiemouth	
ZA356	Panavia Tornado GR1 <ff>	RAF Marham, instructional use	
ZA357	Panavia Tornado GR1 [TTV]	DCAE, No 1 SoTT, Cosford	
ZA359	Panavia Tornado GR1 Training Centre	BAE Systems Warton, Overseas Customer	
ZA360	Panavia Tornado GR1 (9318M) <ff>	RAF Marham, instructional use	
ZA361	Panavia Tornado GR1 [TD]	Privately owned, New York, Lincs	
ZA362	Panavia Tornado GR1 [AJ-F]	Highland Aviation Museum, Inverness	
ZA365	Panavia Tornado GR4 [001]	RAF, Lossiemouth Wing	
ZA367	Panavia Tornado GR4 [002,KC-N]	RAF, Lossiemouth Wing	
ZA369	Panavia Tornado GR4A [003] $	RAF, Marham Wing	
ZA370	Panavia Tornado GR4A [004]	RAF, Lossiemouth Wing	
ZA371	Panavia Tornado GR4A [005]	RAF CMU, stored Marham	
ZA372	Panavia Tornado GR4A [006]	RAF, Lossiemouth Wing	
ZA373	Panavia Tornado GR4A [007,H]	RAF, Lossiemouth Wing	
ZA375	Panavia Tornado GR1 (9335M) [AJ-W]	RAF Marham, Fire Section	
ZA393	Panavia Tornado GR4A [008]	RAF Marham, Wing	
ZA395	Panavia Tornado GR4A [009]	RAF, Lossiemouth Wing	
ZA398	Panavia Tornado GR4A [010,AJ-N]	RAF, Marham Wing	
ZA399	Panavia Tornado GR1 (9316M) [AJ-C]	DCAE, No 1 SoTT, Cosford	
ZA400	Panavia Tornado GR4A [011]	RAF, Marham Wing	
ZA401	Panavia Tornado GR4A [012]	RAF, Marham Wing	
ZA402	Panavia Tornado GR4A	MoD/BAE Systems, Warton	
ZA404	Panavia Tornado GR4A [013]	RAF, Marham Wing	
ZA405	Panavia Tornado GR4A [014]	RAF, Lossiemouth Wing	
ZA406	Panavia Tornado GR4 [015]	RAF, Marham Wing	
ZA407	Panavia Tornado GR1 (9336M) [AJ-N]	RAF Marham, on display	
ZA409	Panavia Tornado GR1 [VII]	RAF Lossiemouth (wfu)	
ZA410	Panavia Tornado GR4 [016]	RAF, Lossiemouth Wing	
ZA411	Panavia Tornado GR1 [TT]	MoD/BAE Systems, Warton	
ZA412	Panavia Tornado GR4 [017]	RAF, Marham Wing	

Notes	Serial	Type (code/other identity)	Owner/operator location or fate
	ZA446	Panavia Tornado GR4 [018]	RAF, stored Shawbury
	ZA447	Panavia Tornado GR4 [EB-R]	RAF AWC/FJWOEU/No 41(R) Sqn, Coningsby
	ZA449	Panavia Tornado GR4 [020]	RAF, Lossiemouth Wing
	ZA450	Panavia Tornado GR1 (9317M) [TH]	DCAE, No 1 SoTT, Cosford
	ZA452	Panavia Tornado GR4 [021]	RAF, Marham Wing
	ZA453	Panavia Tornado GR4 [022]	RAF, Lossiemouth Wing
	ZA456	Panavia Tornado GR4 [023]	RAF, Marham Wing
	ZA457	Panavia Tornado GR1 [AJ-J]	RAF Museum, Hendon
	ZA458	Panavia Tornado GR4 [024]	RAF, Lossiemouth Wing
	ZA459	Panavia Tornado GR4 [F] $	RAF, Marham Wing
	ZA461	Panavia Tornado GR4 [026]	RAF, Lossiemouth Wing
	ZA462	Panavia Tornado GR4 [027]	RAF, Lossiemouth Wing
	ZA463	Panavia Tornado GR4 [028]	RAF, Lossiemouth Wing
	ZA465	Panavia Tornado GR1 [FF]	Imperial War Museum, Duxford
	ZA469	Panavia Tornado GR4 [029] $	RAF, Lossiemouth Wing
	ZA470	Panavia Tornado GR4	RAF, stored Shawbury
	ZA472	Panavia Tornado GR4 [031]	RAF, Marham Wing
	ZA473	Panavia Tornado GR4 [032]	RAF, Marham, Wing
	ZA474	Panavia Tornado GR1 (9312M)	RAF, stored Lossiemouth
	ZA475	Panavia Tornado GR1 (9311M) [AJ-G]	RAF Lossiemouth, on display
	ZA492	Panavia Tornado GR4 [033]	RAF, Lossiemouth Wing
	ZA541	Panavia Tornado GR4 [034]	RAF CMU, Marham
	ZA542	Panavia Tornado GR4 [035]	RAF CMU, Marham
	ZA543	Panavia Tornado GR4 [036]	RAF CMU, Marham
	ZA544	Panavia Tornado GR4 [037]	RAF Marham, WLT
	ZA546	Panavia Tornado GR4 [038]	RAF, Lossiemouth Wing
	ZA547	Panavia Tornado GR4 [039] $	RAF CMU, Marham
	ZA548	Panavia Tornado GR4 [040]	RAF Marham, Wing
	ZA549	Panavia Tornado GR4 [041]	RAF, stored Marham
	ZA550	Panavia Tornado GR4 [042]	RAF TEF, Lossiemouth
	ZA551	Panavia Tornado GR4 [043]	RAF Marham Wing
	ZA552	Panavia Tornado GR4 [044]	RAF TEF, Lossiemouth
	ZA553	Panavia Tornado GR4 [045]	RAF Marham Wing
	ZA554	Panavia Tornado GR4 [046]	RAF Marham, Wing
	ZA556	Panavia Tornado GR4 [047]	RAF TEF, Lossiemouth
	ZA556	Panavia Tornado GR1 <R> (ZA368/BAPC 155) [Z]	RAF M&RU, Bottesford
	ZA557	Panavia Tornado GR4 [048]	RAF CMU, Marham
	ZA559	Panavia Tornado GR4 [049]	RAF Marham Wing
	ZA560	Panavia Tornado GR4 [050]	RAF TEF, Lossiemouth
	ZA562	Panavia Tornado GR4 [051]	RAF TEF, Lossiemouth
	ZA563	Panavia Tornado GR4	RAF, stored Shawbury
	ZA564	Panavia Tornado GR4 $	RAF, Marham Wing
	ZA585	Panavia Tornado GR4 [054]	RAF TEF, Lossiemouth
	ZA587	Panavia Tornado GR4 [055]	RAF, Marham Wing
	ZA588	Panavia Tornado GR4 [056]	RAF, Lossiemouth Wing
	ZA589	Panavia Tornado GR4 [057]	RAF TEF, Lossiemouth
	ZA591	Panavia Tornado GR4 [058]	RAF, Lossiemouth Wing
	ZA592	Panavia Tornado GR4 [059]	RAF CMU, Marham
	ZA594	Panavia Tornado GR4 [060]	RAF CMU, Marham
	ZA595	Panavia Tornado GR4 [061]	RAF Marham, Wing
	ZA597	Panavia Tornado GR4 [063]	RAF, Lossiemouth Wing
	ZA598	Panavia Tornado GR4 [064]	RAF, Lossiemouth Wing
	ZA600	Panavia Tornado GR4 [EB-G] $	RAF AWC/FJWOEU/No 41(R) Sqn, Coningsby
	ZA601	Panavia Tornado GR4 [AJ-G,066]	MoD/BAE Systems, Warton
	ZA602	Panavia Tornado GR4 [067]	RAF CMU, stored Marham
	ZA604	Panavia Tornado GR4 [068]	RAF, Lossiemouth Wing
	ZA606	Panavia Tornado GR4 [069]	RAF, Marham Wing

Serial	Type (code/other identity)	Owner/operator location or fate	Notes
ZA607	Panavia Tornado GR4 [070]	RAF CMU, Marham	
ZA608	Panavia Tornado GR4	RAF, stored Shawbury	
ZA609	Panavia Tornado GR4 [072]	RAF TEF, Lossiemouth	
ZA611	Panavia Tornado GR4 [073]	RAF Marham, Wing	
ZA612	Panavia Tornado GR4 [IV]	MoD/BAE Systems, Warton	
ZA613	Panavia Tornado GR4 [075]	RAF TEF, Lossiemouth	
ZA614	Panavia Tornado GR4 [076]	RAF, Lossiemouth Wing	
ZA630	Slingsby T61F Venture T2 (G-BUGL)	Privately owned, Tibenham	
ZA634	Slingsby T61F Venture T2 (G-BUHA) [C]	Privately owned, Saltby, Leics	
ZA652	Slingsby T61F Venture T2 (G-BUDC)	Privately owned, Enstone	
ZA670	B-V Chinook HC2 (N37010) [AA]	RAF No 1310 Flt, Kandahar, Afghanistan	
ZA671	B-V Chinook HC2 (N37011) [AB]	RAF Odiham Wing	
ZA674	B-V Chinook HC2 (N37019)	RAF Odiham Wing	
ZA675	B-V Chinook HC2 (N37020) [AE]	RAF Odiham Wing	
ZA676	B-V Chinook HC1 (N37021/9230M) [FG] (wreck)	Scrapped	
ZA677	B-V Chinook HC4 (N37022) [AF]	MoD/AFD/QinetiQ, Boscombe Down	
ZA678	B-V Chinook HC1 (N37023/9229M) [EZ] (wreck)	RAF Odiham, BDRT	
ZA679	B-V Chinook HC2 (N37025) [AG]	RAF Odiham Wing	
ZA680	B-V Chinook HC2 (N37026) [AH]	RAF Odiham Wing	
ZA681	B-V Chinook HC2 (N37027) [AI]	RAF No 1310 Flt, Kandahar, Afghanistan	
ZA682	B-V Chinook HC2 (N37029) [AJ]	MoD/Vector Aerospace, Fleetlands	
ZA683	B-V Chinook HC4 (N37030) [AK]	MoD/AFD/QinetiQ, Boscombe Down	
ZA684	B-V Chinook HC2 (N37031) [AL]	RAF Odiham Wing	
ZA704	B-V Chinook HC2 (N37033) [AM]	RAF Odiham Wing	
ZA705	B-V Chinook HC2 (N37035) [AN]	RAF Odiham Wing	
ZA707	B-V Chinook HC2 (N37040) [AO]	RAF Odiham Wing	
ZA708	B-V Chinook HC2 (N37042) [AP]	RAF Odiham Wing	
ZA710	B-V Chinook HC2 (N37044) [AR]	MoD/Vector Aerospace, Fleetlands	
ZA711	B-V Chinook HC2 (N37046) $	MoD/Vector Aerospace, Fleetlands	
ZA712	B-V Chinook HC2 (N37047) [AT]	MoD/Vector Aerospace, Fleetlands	
ZA713	B-V Chinook HC2 (N37048) [AU]	RAF No 1310 Flt, Kandahar, Afghanistan	
ZA714	B-V Chinook HC2 (N37051) [AV] $	RAF Odiham Wing	
ZA717	B-V Chinook HC1 (N37056/9238M) (wreck)	RAF M&RU, Bottesford	
ZA718	B-V Chinook HC2 (N37058) [BN]	RAF Odiham Wing	
ZA720	B-V Chinook HC2 (N37060) [AW]	RAF Odiham Wing	
ZA726	WS Gazelle AH1 [F1]	Privately owned, Colsterworth, Leics	
ZA728	WS Gazelle AH1 [E]	Privately owned, Colsterworth, Leics	
ZA729	WS Gazelle AH1	AAC Wattisham, BDRT	
ZA731	WS Gazelle AH1	AAC No 29 Flt, BATUS, Suffield, Canada	
ZA733	WS Gazelle AH1 (G-CHBR)	Privately owned, Stapleford Tawney	
ZA735	WS Gazelle AH1	DCAE SEAE, Arborfield	
ZA736	WS Gazelle AH1	AAC No 29 Flt, BATUS, Suffield, Canada	
ZA737	WS Gazelle AH1	Museum of Army Flying, Middle Wallop	
ZA766	WS Gazelle AH1	AAC No 665 Sqn/5 Regt, Aldergrove	
ZA768	WS Gazelle AH1 [F] (wreck)	MoD/Vector Aerospace, stored Fleetlands	
ZA769	WS Gazelle AH1 [K]	DCAE SEAE, Arborfield	
ZA771	WS Gazelle AH1	DCAE, No 1 SoTT, Cosford	
ZA772	WS Gazelle AH1	AAC GDSH, Middle Wallop	
ZA773	WS Gazelle AH1 [F]	AAC, stored Shawbury	
ZA774	WS Gazelle AH1	Privately owned, Babcary, Somerset	
ZA775	WS Gazelle AH1	AAC, stored Shawbury	
ZA776	WS Gazelle AH1 [F]	Privately owned, Colsterworth, Leics	
ZA804	WS Gazelle HT3	Privately owned, Solstice Park, Amesbury, Wilts	
ZA935	WS Puma HC2	MoD/Eurocopter, Brasov, Romania (conversion)	
ZA936	WS Puma HC2	MoD/Eurocopter, Brasov, Romania (conversion)	
ZA937	WS Puma HC1	RAF No 33 Sqn/No 230 Sqn, Benson	

Notes	Serial	Type (code/other identity)	Owner/operator location or fate
	ZA939	WS Puma HC1	RAF No 33 Sqn/No 230 Sqn, Benson
	ZA940	WS Puma HC2	MoD/Eurocopter, Oxford (conversion)
	ZA947	Douglas Dakota C3	RAF BBMF, Coningsby
	ZB500	WS Lynx 800 (G-LYNX/ZA500)	The Helicopter Museum, Weston-super-Mare
	ZB506	WS61 Sea King Mk 4X	MoD/AFD/QinetiQ, Boscombe Down
	ZB507	WS61 Sea King HC4 [F]	RN No 845 NAS, Yeovilton
	ZB601	BAe Harrier T4 (fuselage)	RNAS Yeovilton, Fire Section
	ZB603	BAe Harrier T8 [T03/DD]	SFDO, RNAS Culdrose
	ZB604	BAe Harrier T8 [722]	RNAS Yeovilton
	ZB615	SEPECAT Jaguar T2A	DCAE, TCF, RAFC Cranwell
	ZB625	WS Gazelle HT3 [N]	MoD/AFD/QinetiQ, Boscombe Down
	ZB627	WS Gazelle HT3 (G-CBSK) [A]	Privately owned, Hurstbourne Tarrant, Hants
	ZB646	WS Gazelle HT2 (G-CBGZ) [59/CU]	Privately owned, Knebworth
	ZB647	WS Gazelle HT2 (G-CBSF) [40]	Privately owned, Redhill
	ZB665	WS Gazelle AH1	AAC, stored Shawbury
	ZB667	WS Gazelle AH1	AAC No 665 Sqn/5 Regt, Aldergrove
	ZB668	WS Gazelle AH1 (TAD 015)	DCAE SEAE, Arborfield
	ZB669	WS Gazelle AH1	AAC No 665 Sqn/5 Regt, Aldergrove
	ZB670	WS Gazelle AH1	AAC Dishforth, on display
	ZB671	WS Gazelle AH1	AAC No 29 Flt, BATUS, Suffield, Canada
	ZB672	WS Gazelle AH1	Army Training Regiment, Winchester
	ZB673	WS Gazelle AH1 [P]	Privately owned, Colsterworth, Leics
	ZB674	WS Gazelle AH1	AAC, stored Shawbury
	ZB677	WS Gazelle AH1 [5B]	AAC No 29 Flt, BATUS, Suffield, Canada
	ZB678	WS Gazelle AH1	AAC No 665 Sqn/5 Regt, Aldergrove
	ZB679	WS Gazelle AH1	AAC, stored Shawbury
	ZB682	WS Gazelle AH1	AAC, stored Dishforth
	ZB683	WS Gazelle AH1	AAC No 665 Sqn/5 Regt, Aldergrove
	ZB684	WS Gazelle AH1	RAF Defence Movements School, Brize Norton
	ZB686	WS Gazelle AH1 <ff>	The Helicopter Museum, Weston-super-Mare
	ZB688	WS Gazelle AH1	Privately owned, Colsterworth, Leics
	ZB689	WS Gazelle AH1	AAC No 665 Sqn/5 Regt, Aldergrove
	ZB690	WS Gazelle AH1	MoD, stored Shawbury
	ZB691	WS Gazelle AH1 [S]	AAC No 671 Sqn/7 Regt, Middle Wallop
	ZB692	WS Gazelle AH1 [Y]	AAC No 671 Sqn/7 Regt, Middle Wallop
	ZB693	WS Gazelle AH1	AAC No 665 Sqn/5 Regt, Aldergrove
	ZD230	BAC Super VC10 K4 (G-ASGA) <ff>	Privately owned, Crondall, Hants
	ZD240	BAC Super VC10 K4 (G-ASGL) <ff>	Privately owned, Crondall, Hants
	ZD241	BAC Super VC10 K4 (G-ASGM) [N]	RAF No 101 Sqn, Brize Norton
	ZD242	BAC Super VC10 K4 (G-ASGP) [P]	*Scrapped at Boscombe Down, February 2011*
	ZD249	WS Lynx HAS3S [637]	MoD/Vector Aerospace, Fleetlands
	ZD250	WS Lynx HAS3S [636]	RN Lynx RTP, Yeovilton
	ZD251	WS Lynx HAS3S	*Scrapped*
	ZD252	WS Lynx HMA8SRU [335/WL]	MoD/Vector Aerospace, Fleetlands
	ZD254	WS Lynx HAS3S [306]	DCAE AESS, HMS Sultan, Gosport
	ZD255	WS Lynx HAS3GMS [316]	MoD/Vector Aerospace, stored Fleetlands
	ZD257	WS Lynx HMA8SRU [642]	RN No 702 NAS, Yeovilton
	ZD258	WS Lynx HMA8SRU [444]	RN No 815 NAS, *Montrose* Flt, Yeovilton
	ZD259	WS Lynx HMA8SRU [404/IR]	MoD/Vector Aerospace, Fleetlands
	ZD260	WS Lynx HMA8SRU [315]	RN No 815 NAS, HQ Flt, Yeovilton
	ZD261	WS Lynx HMA8SRU [407]	RN No 815 NAS, *York* Flt, Yeovilton
	ZD262	WS Lynx HMA8SRU [301]	RN No 815 NAS, HQ Flt, Yeovilton
	ZD263	WS Lynx HAS3S	RN Lynx RTP, Yeovilton
	ZD264	WS Lynx HAS3GMS [407]	*Scrapped*
	ZD265	WS Lynx HMA8SRU [644]	RN No 702 NAS, Yeovilton
	ZD266	WS Lynx HMA8SRU [640]	RN No 702 NAS, Yeovilton

Serial	Type (code/other identity)	Owner/operator location or fate	Notes
ZD267	WS Lynx HMA8 (comp XZ672) [LST-2]	RN ETS, Yeovilton, GI use	
ZD268	WS Lynx HMA8SRU [643]	MoD/Vector Aerospace, Fleetlands	
ZD272	WS Lynx AH7 [W]	AAC GDSH, Middle Wallop	
ZD273	WS Lynx AH7 <ff>	AAC GDSH, Middle Wallop	
ZD274	WS Lynx AH7 [E]	AAC No 671 Sqn/7 Regt, Middle Wallop	
ZD276	WS Lynx AH7	Mayhem Paintball, Abridge, Essex	
ZD277	WS Lynx AH7 [U]	MoD/Vector Aerospace, Fleetlands	
ZD278	WS Lynx AH7 [F]	AAC No 671 Sqn/7 Regt, Middle Wallop	
ZD279	WS Lynx AH7 <ff>	Privately owned,	
ZD280	WS Lynx AH7	AAC No 9 Regt, Dishforth	
ZD281	WS Lynx AH7 [K]	AAC No 671 Sqn/7 Regt, Middle Wallop	
ZD282	WS Lynx AH7	RM No 847 NAS, Yeovilton	
ZD283	WS Lynx AH7 [D]	AAC No 671 Sqn/7 Regt, Middle Wallop	
ZD284	WS Lynx AH7	AAC No 9 Regt, Dishforth	
ZD285	WS Lynx AH7	MoD/AFD/QinetiQ, Boscombe Down	
ZD318	BAe Harrier GR7	RAF HM&SF, Cottesmore (wfu)	
ZD319	BAe Harrier GR7A	*Sold to the USA, December 2011*	
ZD320	BAe Harrier GR9 [21]	RAF HM&SF, Cottesmore (wfu)	
ZD321	BAe Harrier GR9 [02]	RAF HM&SF, Cottesmore (wfu)	
ZD322	BAe Harrier GR9A [03A]	*Sold to the USA, December 2011*	
ZD323	BAe Harrier GR7 [04]	*Sold to the USA, December 2011*	
ZD327	BAe Harrier GR9 [08A,SH-M]	RAF HM&SF, Cottesmore (wfu)	
ZD328	BAe Harrier GR9 [09]	RAF HM&SF, Cottesmore (wfu)	
ZD329	BAe Harrier GR9A [10]	RAF HM&SF, Cottesmore (wfu)	
ZD330	BAe Harrier GR9 $	RAF HM&SF, Cottesmore (wfu)	
ZD346	BAe Harrier GR9 [13]	RAF HM&SF, Cottesmore (wfu)	
ZD347	BAe Harrier GR9A [14]	RAF HM&SF, Cottesmore (wfu)	
ZD348	BAe Harrier GR9A [15A]	RAF HM&SF, Cottesmore (wfu)	
ZD351	BAe Harrier GR9A $	RAF HM&SF, Cottesmore (wfu)	
ZD352	BAe Harrier GR9 [19]	RAF HM&SF, Cottesmore (wfu)	
ZD353	BAe Harrier GR5 (fuselage)	BAE Systems, Brough	
ZD354	BAe Harrier GR9 [21]	RAF HM&SF, Cottesmore (wfu)	
ZD375	BAe Harrier GR9 [23]	RAF HM&SF, Cottesmore (wfu)	
ZD376	BAe Harrier GR7A [24A]	RAF HM&SF, Cottesmore (wfu)	
ZD378	BAe Harrier GR9A [26A]	RAF HM&SF, Cottesmore (wfu)	
ZD379	BAe Harrier GR9 [27]	RAF HM&SF, Cottesmore (wfu)	
ZD380	BAe Harrier GR9A [28A]	*Sold to the USA, December 2011*	
ZD401	BAe Harrier GR9 [30]	RAF HM&SF, Cottesmore (wfu)	
ZD402	BAe Harrier GR9 [31]	RAF HM&SF, Cottesmore (wfu)	
ZD403	BAe Harrier GR9 [32,JX-B]	RAF HM&SF, Cottesmore (wfu)	
ZD404	BAe Harrier GR7A [33A]	RAF HM&SF, Cottesmore (wfu)	
ZD405	BAe Harrier GR9 [34]	RAF HM&SF, Cottesmore (wfu)	
ZD406	BAe Harrier GR9 $	RAF HM&SF, Cottesmore (wfu)	
ZD407	BAe Harrier GR7 [36]	RAF HM&SF, Cottesmore (wfu)	
ZD409	BAe Harrier GR9 [38]	RAF HM&SF, Cottesmore (wfu)	
ZD410	BAe Harrier GR9 $	RAF HM&SF, Cottesmore (wfu)	
ZD411	BAe Harrier GR7 [40]	RAF HM&SF, Cottesmore (wfu)	
ZD412	BAe Harrier GR5 (fuselage)	Privately owned, Charlwood	
ZD431	BAe Harrier GR7A [43A]	RAF HM&SF, Cottesmore (wfu)	
ZD433	BAe Harrier GR9A [45A]	FAA Museum, stored Yeovilton	
ZD435	BAe Harrier GR9 [47]	RAF HM&SF, Cottesmore (wfu)	
ZD436	BAe Harrier GR9A [48A]	RAF HM&SF, Cottesmore (wfu)	
ZD437	BAe Harrier GR9 [EB-J]	RAF HM&SF, Cottesmore (wfu)	
ZD438	BAe Harrier GR9 [50]	RAF HM&SF, Cottesmore (wfu)	
ZD461	BAe Harrier GR9A [51A]	RAF HM&SF, Cottesmore (wfu)	
ZD462	BAe Harrier GR7 (9302M) [52]	Privately owned, Sproughton	
ZD463	BAe Harrier GR7 [53]	RAF HM&SF, Cottesmore (wfu)	
ZD465	BAe Harrier GR9 [55]	RAF Wittering	

Notes	Serial	Type (code/other identity)	Owner/operator location or fate
	ZD466	BAe Harrier GR7 [56]	RAF HM&SF, Cottesmore (wfu)
	ZD467	BAe Harrier GR9A [57A]	RAF HM&SF, Cottesmore (wfu)
	ZD468	BAe Harrier GR9 [58]	RAF HM&SF, Cottesmore (wfu)
	ZD469	BAe Harrier GR7A	RAF Wittering, on display
	ZD470	BAe Harrier GR9 [60]	RAF HM&SF, Cottesmore (wfu)
	ZD476	WS61 Sea King HC4 [WZ]	MoD/Vector Aerospace, Fleetlands
	ZD477	WS61 Sea King HC4 [E]	RN No 845 NAS, Yeovilton
	ZD478	WS61 Sea King HC4 [J]	DCAE, stored HMS Sultan, Gosport
	ZD479	WS61 Sea King HC4 [WQ]	RN No 848 NAS, Yeovilton
	ZD480	WS61 Sea King HC4 [J]	RN SKAMG, Yeovilton
	ZD559	WS Lynx AH5X	MoD/AFD/QinetiQ, Boscombe Down
	ZD560	WS Lynx AH7	MoD/ETPS, Boscombe Down
	ZD565	WS Lynx HMA8SRU [410/GC]	MoD/Vector Aerospace, Fleetlands
	ZD566	WS Lynx HMA8SRU [407]	MoD/Vector Aerospace, Fleetlands
	ZD574	B-V Chinook HC2 (N37077) [DB]	RAF Odiham Wing
	ZD575	B-V Chinook HC4 (N37078) [DC]	MoD/Vector Aerospace, Fleetlands
	ZD578	BAe Sea Harrier FA2 [000,122]	RNAS Yeovilton, at main gate
	ZD579	BAe Sea Harrier FA2 [79/DD]	SFDO, RNAS Culdrose
	ZD580	BAe Sea Harrier FA2 [710]	Privately owned, Cheshire
	ZD581	BAe Sea Harrier FA2 [124]	RN, Predannack Fire School
	ZD582	BAe Sea Harrier FA2 [002/N]	Privately owned, Banbury, Oxon
	ZD607	BAe Sea Harrier FA2	DCAE AESS, HMS Sultan, Gosport
	ZD610	BAe Sea Harrier FA2 [006/N]	Privately owned, Dunsfold
	ZD611	BAe Sea Harrier FA2	RNAS Culdrose Fire Section
	ZD612	BAe Sea Harrier FA2	Privately owned, Topsham, Devon
	ZD613	BAe Sea Harrier FA2 [127/R]	Privately owned, Cross Green, Leeds
	ZD614	BAe Sea Harrier FA2 [122/R]	Privately owned, Sproughton
	ZD620	BAe 125 CC3	RAF No 32(The Royal) Sqn, Northolt
	ZD621	BAe 125 CC3	RAF No 32(The Royal) Sqn, Northolt
	ZD625	WS61 Sea King HC4 [P]	RN No 848 NAS, Yeovilton
	ZD626	WS61 Sea King HC4 [S]	RN SKAMG, Yeovilton
	ZD627	WS61 Sea King HC4 [WO]	RN No 845 NAS, Yeovilton
	ZD630	WS61 Sea King HAS6 [012/L]	DCAE, stored HMS Sultan, Gosport
	ZD631	WS61 Sea King HAS6 [66] (fuselage)	Privately owned, St Agnes, Cornwall
	ZD633	WS61 Sea King HAS6 [014/L]	DCAE, stored HMS Sultan, Gosport
	ZD634	WS61 Sea King HAS6 [503]	DCAE, stored HMS Sultan, Gosport
	ZD636	WS61 Sea King ASaC7 [182/CU]	RN No 857 NAS, Culdrose
	ZD637	WS61 Sea King HAS6 [700/PW]	DCAE, AESS, HMS Sultan, Gosport
	ZD667	BAe Harrier GR3 (9201M) [67/DD]	RN, Predannack Fire School
	ZD703	BAe 125 CC3	RAF No 32(The Royal) Sqn, Northolt
	ZD704	BAe 125 CC3	RAF No 32(The Royal) Sqn, Northolt
	ZD707	Panavia Tornado GR4 [077]	RAF Lossiemouth Wing
	ZD708	Panavia Tornado GR4	RAF, stored Shawbury
	ZD709	Panavia Tornado GR4 [078]	RAF CMU, Marham
	ZD710	Panavia Tornado GR1 <ff>	Privately owned, Ruthin, Denbighshire
	ZD711	Panavia Tornado GR4 [079]	RAF CMU, Marham
	ZD712	Panavia Tornado GR4 [080] $	RAF, Lossiemouth Wing
	ZD713	Panavia Tornado GR4 [081]	RAF, Marham Wing
	ZD714	Panavia Tornado GR4 [082]	RAF, Lossiemouth Wing
	ZD715	Panavia Tornado GR4 [083]	RAF, Marham Wing
	ZD716	Panavia Tornado GR4 [084]	RAF TEF, Lossiemouth
	ZD719	Panavia Tornado GR4 [085]	RAF, Marham Wing
	ZD720	Panavia Tornado GR4 [086]	RAF, Marham Wing
	ZD739	Panavia Tornado GR4 [087]	RAF, Marham Wing
	ZD740	Panavia Tornado GR4 [088]	RAF, Lossiemouth Wing
	ZD741	Panavia Tornado GR4 [089]	RAF TEF, stored Lossiemouth (damaged)
	ZD742	Panavia Tornado GR4 [090]	RAF TEF, Lossiemouth
	ZD743	Panavia Tornado GR4 [091]	RAF, Lossiemouth Wing

Serial	Type (code/other identity)	Owner/operator location or fate	Notes
ZD744	Panavia Tornado GR4 [092]	RAF CMU, Marham	
ZD745	Panavia Tornado GR4 [093]	RAF, Lossiemouth Wing	
ZD746	Panavia Tornado GR4 [094]	RAF, Marham Wing	
ZD747	Panavia Tornado GR4 [095]	RAF CMU, Marham	
ZD748	Panavia Tornado GR4 [096] $	RAF CMU, Marham	
ZD749	Panavia Tornado GR4 [097]	RAF, Marham Wing	
ZD788	Panavia Tornado GR4 [098]	RAF, Marham Wing	
ZD790	Panavia Tornado GR4 [099]	RAF CMU, Marham	
ZD792	Panavia Tornado GR4 [100] $	RAF, Marham Wing	
ZD793	Panavia Tornado GR4 [101]	RAF TEF, Lossiemouth	
ZD810	Panavia Tornado GR4 [102]	RAF CMU, Marham	
ZD811	Panavia Tornado GR4 [103]	RAF, Marham Wing	
ZD812	Panavia Tornado GR4 [104]	RAF TEF, Lossiemouth	
ZD842	Panavia Tornado GR4 [105]	RAF, Marham Wing	
ZD843	Panavia Tornado GR4 [106]	RAF, Lossiemouth Wing	
ZD844	Panavia Tornado GR4 [107]	RAF CMU, Marham	
ZD847	Panavia Tornado GR4 [108]	RAF, Marham Wing	
ZD848	Panavia Tornado GR4 [109]	RAF, Marham Wing	
ZD849	Panavia Tornado GR4 [110]	RAF, Marham Wing	
ZD850	Panavia Tornado GR4 [111]	RAF, Marham Wing	
ZD851	Panavia Tornado GR4 [112]	RAF, Marham Wing	
ZD890	Panavia Tornado GR4 [113]	RAF, Marham Wing	
ZD892	Panavia Tornado GR4 [TG]	RAF, stored Shawbury	
ZD895	Panavia Tornado GR4 [115]	RAF CMU, Marham	
ZD899	Panavia Tornado F2	MoD, Boscombe Down, spares use	
ZD902	Panavia Tornado F2A(TIARA)	MoD/AFD/QinetiQ, Boscombe Down	
ZD906	Panavia Tornado F2 (comp ZE294) <ff>	RAF Leuchars, BDRT	
ZD932	Panavia Tornado F2 (comp ZE255) (9308M) (fuselage)	Privately owned, Thorpe Wood, N Yorks	
ZD934	Panavia Tornado F2 (comp ZE786) <ff>	Currently not known	
ZD936	Panavia Tornado F2 (comp ZE251) <ff>	Boscombe Down Aviation Collection	
ZD938	Panavia Tornado F2 (comp ZE295) <ff>	Aeroventure, Doncaster	
ZD939	Panavia Tornado F2 (comp ZE292) <ff>	DCAE Cosford, instructional use	
ZD948	Lockheed TriStar KC1 (G-BFCA)	RAF No 216 Sqn, Brize Norton	
ZD949	Lockheed TriStar K1 (G-BFCB)	MoD/Marshalls, stored Cambridge	
ZD950	Lockheed TriStar KC1 (G-BFCC)	RAF No 216 Sqn, Brize Norton	
ZD951	Lockheed TriStar K1 (G-BFCD)	RAF No 216 Sqn, Brize Norton	
ZD952	Lockheed TriStar KC1 (G-BFCE)	RAF No 216 Sqn, Brize Norton	
ZD953	Lockheed TriStar KC1 (G-BFCF)	RAF No 216 Sqn, Brize Norton	
ZD980	B-V Chinook HC2 (N37082) [DD]	RAF No 1310 Flt, Kandahar, Afghanistan	
ZD981	B-V Chinook HC4 (N37083)	MoD/AFD/QinetiQ, Boscombe Down	
ZD982	B-V Chinook HC2 (N37085) [DF]	RAF No 1310 Flt, Kandahar, Afghanistan	
ZD983	B-V Chinook HC2 (N37086) [DG]	MoD/Vector Aerospace, Fleetlands	
ZD984	B-V Chinook HC4 (N37088) [DH]	MoD/Vector Aerospace, Fleetlands (conversion)	
ZD990	BAe Harrier T8 [T90/DD]	SFDO, RNAS Culdrose	
ZD992	BAe Harrier T8 [724] (fuselage)	Privately owned, Sproughton	
ZD993	BAe Harrier T8 [723/VL]	MoD, Boscombe Down (spares use)	
ZD996	Panavia Tornado GR4A [EB-B]	RAF AWC/FJWOEU/No 41(R) Sqn, Coningsby	
ZE116	Panavia Tornado GR4A [116]	RAF, Marham Wing	
ZE157	Panavia Tornado F3 [TY]	Scrapped at Leeming, October 2009	
ZE163	Panavia Tornado F3 (comp ZG753) [HY]	RAF Leeming, for scrapping	
ZE164	Panavia Tornado F3 [HO]	RAF Leeming, for scrapping	
ZE165	Panavia Tornado F3 [GE]	RAF, stored Shawbury	
ZE168	Panavia Tornado F3 [HH]	RAF Leeming, for scrapping	
ZE200	Panavia Tornado F3 [HN]	Scrapped at Leeming	
ZE201	Panavia Tornado F3 [HU]	RAF Leeming, for scrapping	
ZE203	Panavia Tornado F3 [GA]	MoD/AFD/QinetiQ, Boscombe Down	

Notes	Serial	Type (code/other identity)	Owner/operator location or fate
	ZE204	Panavia Tornado F3 [FC]	RAF, stored Shawbury
	ZE250	Panavia Tornado F3 [TR]	*Scrapped at Leeming*
	ZE256	Panavia Tornado F3 [TP]	Privately owned, Thorpe Wood, N Yorks
	ZE288	Panavia Tornado F3 (comp ZD940) [HA] $	RAF Leeming, for scrapping
	ZE292	Panavia Tornado F3 (comp ZD939) [FE]	*Scrapped at Leeming, December 2010*
	ZE338	Panavia Tornado F3 [GJ]	RAF Leeming, for scrapping
	ZE339	Panavia Tornado F3 <ff>	*Scrapped*
	ZE340	Panavia Tornado F3 (ZE758/9298M) [GO]	DCAE, No 1 SoTT, Cosford
	ZE341	Panavia Tornado F3 [HI]	RAF Leeming, for scrapping
	ZE342	Panavia Tornado F3 [HP]	RAF Leeming, for scrapping
	ZE343	Panavia Tornado F3 (comp ZD900) [DZ]	*Scrapped at Leeming*
	ZE350	McD F-4J(UK) Phantom (9080M) <ff>	Privately owned, Shrewsbury
	ZE352	McD F-4J(UK) Phantom (9086M) <ff>	Privately owned, Hooton Park
	ZE360	McD F-4J(UK) Phantom (9059M) [O]	MoD DFTDC, Manston
	ZE368	WS61 Sea King HAR3 [R] $	RAF No 22 Sqn, C Flt/No 203(R) Sqn, Valley
	ZE369	WS61 Sea King HAR3 [S]	RAF No 22 Sqn, C Flt/No 203(R) Sqn, Valley
	ZE370	WS61 Sea King HAR3 [T]	RAF No 202 Sqn, E Flt, Leconfield
	ZE375	WS Lynx AH9A	MoD/Vector Aerospace, Fleetlands
	ZE376	WS Lynx AH9A	MoD/AgustaWestland, Yeovil (conversion)
	ZE378	WS Lynx AH7	AAC No 657 Sqn, Odiham
	ZE379	WS Lynx AH7	AAC Dishforth, BDRT
	ZE380	WS Lynx AH9A	AAC No 657 Sqn, Odiham
	ZE381	WS Lynx AH7 [X]	DCAE SEAE, Arborfield
	ZE395	BAe 125 CC3	RAF No 32(The Royal) Sqn, Northolt
	ZE396	BAe 125 CC3	RAF No 32(The Royal) Sqn, Northolt
	ZE410	Agusta A109A (AE-334)	Museum of Army Flying, stored Middle Wallop
	ZE411	Agusta A109A (AE-331)	FAA Museum, stored RNAS Yeovilton
	ZE412	Agusta A109A	DCAE SEAE, Arborfield
	ZE413	Agusta A109A	Army Whittington Barracks, Lichfield, GI use
	ZE416	Agusta A109E Power Elite (G-ESLH)	MoD/ETPS, Boscombe Down
	ZE418	WS61 Sea King ASaC7 [186]	RN No 857 NAS, Culdrose
	ZE420	WS61 Sea King ASaC7 [189]	RN No 849 NAS, Culdrose
	ZE422	WS61 Sea King ASaC7 [192]	RN No 849 NAS, Culdrose
	ZE425	WS61 Sea King HC4 [WR]	RN No 848 NAS, Yeovilton
	ZE426	WS61 Sea King HC4 [WX]	RN No 848 NAS, Yeoviltonn
	ZE427	WS61 Sea King HC4 [K]	RN No 845 NAS, Yeovilton
	ZE428	WS61 Sea King HC4 [H]	MoD/AgustaWestland, Yeovil
	ZE432	BAC 1-11/479FU (DQ-FBV)	MoD, Boscombe Down (wfu)
	ZE433	BAC 1-11/479FU (DQ-FBQ)	MoD, Boscombe Down (wfu)
	ZE438	BAe Jetstream T3 [76]	*Sold as N437UH, February 2011*
	ZE439	BAe Jetstream T3 [77]	*Sold as N437SS, February 2011*
	ZE440	BAe Jetstream T3 [78]	*Sold as N437ZZ, April 2011*
	ZE441	BAe Jetstream T3 [79]	*Sold as N437TH, February 2011*
	ZE449	SA330L Puma HC1 (9017M/PA-12)	RAF PDSH, Benson (wreck)
	ZE477	WS Lynx 3	The Helicopter Museum, Weston-super-Mare
	ZE495	Grob G103 Viking T1 (BGA3000) [VA]	RAF No 625 VGS, Hullavington
	ZE496	Grob G103 Viking T1 (BGA3001) [VB]	RAF No 661 VGS, Kirknewton
	ZE498	Grob G103 Viking T1 (BGA3003) [VC]	RAF No 614 VGS, Wethersfield
	ZE499	Grob G103 Viking T1 (BGA3004) [VD]	RAF ACCGS/No 643 VGS, Syerston
	ZE502	Grob G103 Viking T1 (BGA3007) [VF]	RAF No 614 VGS, Wethersfield
	ZE503	Grob G103 Viking T1 (BGA3008) [VG]	RAF CGMF, Syerston
	ZE504	Grob G103 Viking T1 (BGA3009) [VH]	RAF No 614 VGS, Wethersfield
	ZE520	Grob G103 Viking T1 (BGA3010) [VJ]	RAF No 661 VGS, Kirknewton
	ZE521	Grob G103 Viking T1 (BGA3011) [VK]	RAF No 626 VGS, Predannack
	ZE522	Grob G103 Viking T1 (BGA3012) [VL]	RAF No 625 VGS, Hullavington
	ZE524	Grob G103 Viking T1 (BGA3014) [VM]	RAF No 611 VGS, Watton
	ZE526	Grob G103 Viking T1 (BGA3016) [VN]	RAF No 625 VGS, Hullavington
	ZE527	Grob G103 Viking T1 (BGA3017) [VP]	RAF No 626 VGS, Predannack

Serial	Type (code/other identity)	Owner/operator location or fate	Notes
ZE528	Grob G103 Viking T1 (BGA3018) [VQ]	RAF CGMF, Syerston	
ZE529	Grob G103 Viking T1 (BGA3019) (comp ZE655) [VR]	RAF CGMF, stored Syerston	
ZE530	Grob G103 Viking T1 (BGA3020) [VS]	RAF ACCGS/No 643 VGS, Syerston	
ZE531	Grob G103 Viking T1 (BGA3021) [VT]	RAF No 622 VGS, Upavon	
ZE532	Grob G103 Viking T1 (BGA3022) [VU]	RAF No 615 VGS, Kenley	
ZE533	Grob G103 Viking T1 (BGA3023) [VV]	RAF No 661 VGS, Kirknewton	
ZE550	Grob G103 Viking T1 (BGA3025) [VX]	RAF CGMF, Syerston (damaged)	
ZE551	Grob G103 Viking T1 (BGA3026) [VY]	RAF No 614 VGS, Wethersfield	
ZE552	Grob G103 Viking T1 (BGA3027) [VZ]	RAF No 615 VGS, Kenley	
ZE553	Grob G103 Viking T1 (BGA3028) [WA]	RAF No 615 VGS, Kenley	
ZE554	Grob G103 Viking T1 (BGA3029) [WB]	RAF No 615 VGS, Kenley	
ZE555	Grob G103 Viking T1 (BGA3030) [WC]	RAF No 611 VGS, Watton	
ZE556	Grob G103 Viking T1 (BGA3031) <ff>	No 1360 Sqn ATC, Nottingham	
ZE557	Grob G103 Viking T1 (BGA3032) [WE]	RAF No 621 VGS, Hullavington	
ZE558	Grob G103 Viking T1 (BGA3033) [WF]	RAF CGMF, Syerston	
ZE559	Grob G103 Viking T1 (BGA3034) [WG]	RAF No 661 VGS, Kirknewton	
ZE560	Grob G103 Viking T1 (BGA3035) [WH]	RAF No 625 VGS, Hullavington	
ZE561	Grob G103 Viking T1 (BGA3036) [WJ]	RAF No 621 VGS, Hullavington	
ZE562	Grob G103 Viking T1 (BGA3037) [WK]	RAF CGMF, Syerston	
ZE563	Grob G103 Viking T1 (BGA3038) [WL]	RAF CGMF, stored Syerston	
ZE564	Grob G103 Viking T1 (BGA3039) [WN]	RAF No 625 VGS, Hullavington	
ZE584	Grob G103 Viking T1 (BGA3040) [WP]	RAF CGMF, stored Syerston	
ZE585	Grob G103 Viking T1 (BGA3041) [WQ]	RAF No 614 VGS, Wethersfield	
ZE586	Grob G103 Viking T1 (BGA3042) [WR]	RAF ACCGS/No 643 VGS, Syerston	
ZE587	Grob G103 Viking T1 (BGA3043) [WS]	RAF No 621 VGS, Hullavington	
ZE590	Grob G103 Viking T1 (BGA3046) [WT]	RAF No 661 VGS, Kirknewton	
ZE591	Grob G103 Viking T1 (BGA3047) [WU]	RAF No 662 VGS, Arbroath	
ZE592	Grob G103 Viking T1 (BGA3048) <ff>	RAFGSA, stored Henlow	
ZE593	Grob G103 Viking T1 (BGA3049) [WW]	RAF No 615 VGS, Kenley	
ZE594	Grob G103 Viking T1 (BGA3050) [WX]	RAF No 662 VGS, Arbroath	
ZE595	Grob G103 Viking T1 (BGA3051) [WY]	RAF No 661 VGS, Kirknewton	
ZE600	Grob G103 Viking T1 (BGA3052) [WZ]	RAF No 622 VGS, Upavon	
ZE601	Grob G103 Viking T1 (BGA3053) [XA]	RAF No 626 VGS, Predannack	
ZE602	Grob G103 Viking T1 (BGA3054) [XB]	RAF No 662 VGS, Arbroath	
ZE603	Grob G103 Viking T1 (BGA3055) [XC]	RAF No 614 VGS, Wethersfield	
ZE604	Grob G103 Viking T1 (BGA3056) [XD]	RAF No 621 VGS, Hullavington	
ZE605	Grob G103 Viking T1 (BGA3057) [XE]	RAF No 626 VGS, Predannack	
ZE606	Grob G103 Viking T1 (BGA3058) [XF]	RAF No 621 VGS, Hullavington	
ZE607	Grob G103 Viking T1 (BGA3059) [XG]	RAF No 622 VGS, Upavon	
ZE608	Grob G103 Viking T1 (BGA3060) [XH]	RAF ACCGS/No 643 VGS, Syerston	
ZE609	Grob G103 Viking T1 (BGA3061) [XJ]	RAF CGMF, stored Syerston	
ZE610	Grob G103 Viking T1 (BGA3062) [XK]	RAF No 614 VGS, Wethersfield	
ZE611	Grob G103 Viking T1 (BGA3063) [XL]	RAF No 611 VGS, Watton	
ZE613	Grob G103 Viking T1 (BGA3065) [XM]	RAF No 621 VGS, Hullavington	
ZE614	Grob G103 Viking T1 (BGA3066) [XN]	RAF CGMF, Syerston	
ZE625	Grob G103 Viking T1 (BGA3067) [XP]	RAF No 625 VGS, Hullavington	
ZE626	Grob G103 Viking T1 (BGA3068) [XQ]	RAF No 626 VGS, Predannack	
ZE627	Grob G103 Viking T1 (BGA3069) [XR]	RAF ACCGS/No 643 VGS, Syerston	
ZE628	Grob G103 Viking T1 (BGA3070) [XS]	RAF No 622 VGS, Upavon	
ZE629	Grob G103 Viking T1 (BGA3071) [XT]	RAF No 662 VGS, Arbroath	
ZE630	Grob G103 Viking T1 (BGA3072) [XU]	RAF No 662 VGS, Arbroath	
ZE631	Grob G103 Viking T1 (BGA3073) [XV]	RAF No 615 VGS, Kenley	
ZE632	Grob G103 Viking T1 (BGA3074) [XW]	RAF No 662 VGS, Arbroath	
ZE633	Grob G103 Viking T1 (BGA3075) [XX]	RAF CGMF, Syerston	
ZE636	Grob G103 Viking T1 (BGA3078) [XZ]	RAF No 611 VGS, Watton	
ZE637	Grob G103 Viking T1 (BGA3079) [YA]	RAF No 615 VGS, Kenley	
ZE650	Grob G103 Viking T1 (BGA3080) [YB]	RAF CGMF, Syerston	

Notes	Serial	Type (code/other identity)	Owner/operator location or fate
	ZE651	Grob G103 Viking T1 (BGA3081) [YC]	RAF No 621 VGS, Hullavington
	ZE652	Grob G103 Viking T1 (BGA3082) [YD]	RAF CGMF, Syerston
	ZE653	Grob G103 Viking T1 (BGA3083) [YE]	RAF No 625 VGS, Hullavington
	ZE656	Grob G103 Viking T1 (BGA3086) [YH]	RAF No 611 VGS, Watton
	ZE657	Grob G103 Viking T1 (BGA3087) [YJ]	RAF ACCGS/No 643 VGS, Syerston
	ZE658	Grob G103 Viking T1 (BGA3088) [YK]	RAF ACCGS/No 643 VGS, Syerston
	ZE677	Grob G103 Viking T1 (BGA3090) [YM]	RAF No 615 VGS, Kenley
	ZE678	Grob G103 Viking T1 (BGA3091) [YN]	RAF ACCGS/No 643 VGS, Syerston
	ZE679	Grob G103 Viking T1 (BGA3092) [YP]	RAF No 621 VGS, Hullavington
	ZE680	Grob G103 Viking T1 (BGA3093) [YQ]	RAF ACCGS/No 643 VGS, Syerston
	ZE681	Grob G103 Viking T1 (BGA3094) <ff>	RAF Hullavington
	ZE682	Grob G103 Viking T1 (BGA3095) [YS]	RAF No 662 VGS, Arbroath
	ZE683	Grob G103 Viking T1 (BGA3096) [YT]	RAF CGMF, Syerston
	ZE684	Grob G103 Viking T1 (BGA3097) [YU]	RAF No 611 VGS, Watton
	ZE685	Grob G103 Viking T1 (BGA3098) [YV]	RAF ACCGS/No 643 VGS, Syerston
	ZE686	Grob G103 Viking T1 (BGA3099) <ff>	RAF Museum, Hendon
	ZE690	BAe Sea Harrier FA2 [90/DD]	SFDO, RNAS Culdrose
	ZE691	BAe Sea Harrier FA2 [710]	Classic Autos, Winsford, Cheshire
	ZE692	BAe Sea Harrier FA2 [92/DD]	SFDO, RNAS Culdrose
	ZE693	BAe Sea Harrier FA2 [717]	Privately owned, Sproughton
	ZE694	BAe Sea Harrier FA2 [004]	Midland Air Museum, Coventry
	ZE695	BAe Sea Harrier FA2	Slimelight, Islington
	ZE697	BAe Sea Harrier FA2 [006]	Privately owned, Binbrook
	ZE698	BAe Sea Harrier FA2 [001]	Privately owned, Charlwood
	ZE700	BAe 146 CC2 (G-6-021)	RAF No 32(The Royal) Sqn, Northolt
	ZE701	BAe 146 CC2 (G-6-029)	RAF No 32(The Royal) Sqn, Northolt
	ZE704	Lockheed TriStar C2 (N508PA)	RAF No 216 Sqn, Brize Norton
	ZE705	Lockheed TriStar C2 (N509PA)	RAF No 216 Sqn, Brize Norton
	ZE706	Lockheed TriStar C2A (N503PA)	RAF No 216 Sqn, Brize Norton
	ZE734	Panavia Tornado F3 [JU]$	RAF Leeming, for scrapping
	ZE737	Panavia Tornado F3 [GK]	RAF, stored Shawbury
	ZE757	Panavia Tornado F3 $	*Scrapped at Leeming, May 2010*
	ZE760	Panavia Tornado F3 (MM7206) [AP]	RAF Coningsby, on display
	ZE763	Panavia Tornado F3 [HD]	RAF Leeming, for scrapping
	ZE764	Panavia Tornado F3 [HK]	*Scrapped at Leeming, December 2010*
	ZE785	Panavia Tornado F3 [HS]	*Scrapped at Leeming, November 2010*
	ZE788	Panavia Tornado F3 [HV]	RAF Leeming, for scrapping
	ZE790	Panavia Tornado F3 [HC]	RAF Leeming, for scrapping
	ZE791	Panavia Tornado F3 $	RAF Leeming, for scrapping
	ZE794	Panavia Tornado F3 [FL]	MoD/AFD/QinetiQ, Boscombe Down
	ZE808	Panavia Tornado F3 [HJ]	*Scrapped at Leeming, August 2011*
	ZE810	Panavia Tornado F3 [GG]	RAF Leeming, for scrapping
	ZE831	Panavia Tornado F3 [GN]	RAF Leeming, for scrapping
	ZE834	Panavia Tornado F3 [HA]	RAF Leeming, for scrapping
	ZE837	Panavia Tornado F3 (MM55057) [TD]	*Scrapped*
	ZE838	Panavia Tornado F3 [GH]	RAF Leeming, for scrapping
	ZE887	Panavia Tornado F3 [GF] $	RAF Museum, Hendon
	ZE934	Panavia Tornado F3 [TA]	Royal Scottish Mus'm of Flight, E Fortune
	ZE936	Panavia Tornado F3 [HE]	RAF Leeming, for scrapping
	ZE961	Panavia Tornado F3 [HB]	MoD/AFD/QinetiQ, Boscombe Down
	ZE963	Panavia Tornado F3 [YT]	*Scrapped at Leeming, July 2010*
	ZE965	Panavia Tornado F3 [HZ]	RAF Leeming, for scrapping
	ZE966	Panavia Tornado F3 [VT]	Museum of Science & Industry, stored Manchester
	ZE967	Panavia Tornado F3 [UT]	RAF Leuchars, at main gate
	ZE968	Panavia Tornado F3	RAF Leeming, for scrapping
	ZE969	Panavia Tornado F3 [FH]	*Scrapped at Leeming, April 2011*
	ZE983	Panavia Tornado F3 [HL]	RAF Leeming, for scrapping

Serial	Type (code/other identity)	Owner/operator location or fate	Notes
ZF115	WS61 Sea King HC4 [R,WV]	RN No 848 NAS, Yeovilton	
ZF116	WS61 Sea King HC4 [WP]	RN SKAMG, Yeovilton	
ZF117	WS61 Sea King HC4 [X]	RN No 846 NAS, Yeovilton	
ZF118	WS61 Sea King HC4 [O]	RN SKAMG, Yeovilton	
ZF119	WS61 Sea King HC4 [WY]	RN No 848 NAS, Yeovilton	
ZF120	WS61 Sea King HC4 [Z]	RN SKAMG, Yeovilton	
ZF121	WS61 Sea King HC4 [T]	RN No 846 NAS, Yeovilton	
ZF122	WS61 Sea King HC4 [V]	RN No 846 NAS, Yeovilton	
ZF123	WS61 Sea King HC4 [WW]	RN No 848 NAS, Yeovilton	
ZF124	WS61 Sea King HC4 [L]	RN No 846 NAS, Yeovilton	
ZF135	Shorts Tucano T1 [135]	RAF, stored Linton-on-Ouse	
ZF137	Shorts Tucano T1 [137]	RAF, stored Linton-on-Ouse	
ZF139	Shorts Tucano T1 [139]	RAF No 1 FTS, Linton-on-Ouse	
ZF140	Shorts Tucano T1 [140]	RAF No 1 FTS/207(R) Sqn, Linton-on-Ouse	
ZF142	Shorts Tucano T1 [142]	RAF No 1 FTS, Linton-on-Ouse	
ZF143	Shorts Tucano T1 [143]	RAF No 1 FTS, Linton-on-Ouse	
ZF144	Shorts Tucano T1 [144]	RAF No 1 FTS, Linton-on-Ouse	
ZF145	Shorts Tucano T1 [145]	RAF, stored Linton-on-Ouse	
ZF160	Shorts Tucano T1 [160]	RAF, stored Shawbury	
ZF161	Shorts Tucano T1 [161]	RAF, stored Shawbury	
ZF163	Shorts Tucano T1 [163]	RAF, stored Shawbury	
ZF166	Shorts Tucano T1 [166]	RAF, stored Shawbury	
ZF167	Shorts Tucano T1 (fuselage)	Shorts, Belfast	
ZF169	Shorts Tucano T1 [169]	RAF No 1 FTS/72(R) Sqn, Linton-on-Ouse	
ZF170	Shorts Tucano T1 [MP-A]	RAF No 1 FTS, Linton-on-Ouse	
ZF171	Shorts Tucano T1 [171]	RAF No 1 FTS, Linton-on-Ouse	
ZF172	Shorts Tucano T1 [MP-D]	RAF No 1 FTS, Linton-on-Ouse	
ZF202	Shorts Tucano T1 [202]	RAF Linton-on-Ouse, on display	
ZF203	Shorts Tucano T1 [203]	RAF, stored Shawbury	
ZF204	Shorts Tucano T1 [204]	RAF No 1 FTS/207(R) Sqn, Linton-on-Ouse	
ZF205	Shorts Tucano T1 [205]	RAF No 1 FTS/72(R) Sqn, Linton-on-Ouse	
ZF209	Shorts Tucano T1 [209]	RAF No 1 FTS/72(R) Sqn, Linton-on-Ouse	
ZF210	Shorts Tucano T1 [210]	RAF No 1 FTS, Linton-on-Ouse	
ZF211	Shorts Tucano T1 [211]	RAF, stored Shawbury	
ZF212	Shorts Tucano T1 [212]	RAF, stored Shawbury	
ZF239	Shorts Tucano T1 [239,MP-T]	RAF No 1 FTS, Linton-on-Ouse	
ZF240	Shorts Tucano T1 [240]	RAF No 1 FTS/207(R) Sqn, Linton-on-Ouse	
ZF242	Shorts Tucano T1 [242]	RAF, stored Shawbury	
ZF243	Shorts Tucano T1 [243]	RAF No 1 FTS/207(R) Sqn, Linton-on-Ouse	
ZF244	Shorts Tucano T1 [244]	RAF No 1 FTS/72(R) Sqn, Linton-on-Ouse	
ZF263	Shorts Tucano T1 [263]	RAF, stored Shawbury	
ZF264	Shorts Tucano T1 [MP-Q]	RAF No 1 FTS, Linton-on-Ouse	
ZF267	Shorts Tucano T1 [267]	Privately owned, Norwich	
ZF268	Shorts Tucano T1 [268]	RAF, stored Shawbury	
ZF269	Shorts Tucano T1 [MP-O]	RAF No 1 FTS, Linton-on-Ouse	
ZF286	Shorts Tucano T1 [286]	RAF, stored Shawbury	
ZF287	Shorts Tucano T1 [287]	RAF No 1 FTS/72(R) Sqn, Linton-on-Ouse	
ZF288	Shorts Tucano T1 [288]	RAF, stored Shawbury	
ZF289	Shorts Tucano T1 [289]	RAF No 1 FTS, Linton-on-Ouse	
ZF290	Shorts Tucano T1 [290]	RAF No 1 FTS/207(R) Sqn, Linton-on-Ouse	
ZF291	Shorts Tucano T1 [291]	RAF No 1 FTS, Linton-on-Ouse	
ZF292	Shorts Tucano T1 [292]	RAF No 1 FTS, Linton-on-Ouse	
ZF293	Shorts Tucano T1 [293]	RAF No 1 FTS/207(R) Sqn, Linton-on-Ouse	
ZF294	Shorts Tucano T1 [294]	RAF No 1 FTS/207(R) Sqn, Linton-on-Ouse	
ZF295	Shorts Tucano T1 [295] $	RAF No 1 FTS/72(R) Sqn, Linton-on-Ouse	
ZF315	Shorts Tucano T1 [315]	RAF, stored Shawbury	
ZF317	Shorts Tucano T1 [317]	RAF No 1 FTS, Linton-on-Ouse	
ZF318	Shorts Tucano T1 [318] $	RAF, stored Shawbury	

Notes	Serial	Type (code/other identity)	Owner/operator location or fate
	ZF319	Shorts Tucano T1 [319]	RAF, stored Linton-on-Ouse
	ZF338	Shorts Tucano T1 [338, MP-W]	RAF No 1 FTS, Linton-on-Ouse
	ZF339	Shorts Tucano T1 [339]	RAF No 1 FTS/72(R) Sqn, Linton-on-Ouse
	ZF341	Shorts Tucano T1 [341]	MoD/AFD/QinetiQ, Boscombe Down
	ZF342	Shorts Tucano T1 [342]	RAF No 1 FTS, Linton-on-Ouse
	ZF343	Shorts Tucano T1 [343]	RAF No 1 FTS/72(R) Sqn, Linton-on-Ouse
	ZF345	Shorts Tucano T1 [345]	RAF, stored Shawbury
	ZF347	Shorts Tucano T1 [347]	RAF No 1 FTS, Linton-on-Ouse
	ZF348	Shorts Tucano T1 [348]	RAF No 1 FTS, Linton-on-Ouse
	ZF349	Shorts Tucano T1 [349]	RAF No 1 FTS/207(R) Sqn, Linton-on-Ouse
	ZF350	Shorts Tucano T1 [350]	RAF, stored Shawbury
	ZF372	Shorts Tucano T1 [372]	RAF, stored Shawbury
	ZF374	Shorts Tucano T1 [374]	RAF No 1 FTS, Linton-on-Ouse
	ZF376	Shorts Tucano T1 [376]	RAF, stored Shawbury
	ZF377	Shorts Tucano T1 [377]	RAF No 1 FTS, Linton-on-Ouse
	ZF378	Shorts Tucano T1 [378] $	RAF No 1 FTS, Linton-on-Ouse
	ZF379	Shorts Tucano T1 [379]	RAF No 1 FTS, Linton-on-Ouse
	ZF380	Shorts Tucano T1 [380]	RAF, stored Shawbury
	ZF405	Shorts Tucano T1 [405]	RAF, stored Shawbury
	ZF406	Shorts Tucano T1 [406]	RAF No 1 FTS, Linton-on-Ouse
	ZF407	Shorts Tucano T1 [407]	RAF No 1 FTS, Linton-on-Ouse
	ZF408	Shorts Tucano T1 [408]	RAF, stored Shawbury
	ZF409	Shorts Tucano T1 [409]	RAF, stored Linton-on-Ouse (wreck)
	ZF410	Shorts Tucano T1 [410]	RAF, stored Shawbury
	ZF412	Shorts Tucano T1 [412]	RAF, stored Shawbury
	ZF414	Shorts Tucano T1 [414]	RAF, stored Shawbury
	ZF416	Shorts Tucano T1 [416]	RAF, stored Shawbury
	ZF417	Shorts Tucano T1 [417]	RAF No 1 FTS/207(R) Sqn, Linton-on-Ouse
	ZF418	Shorts Tucano T1 [418]	RAF, stored Shawbury
	ZF446	Shorts Tucano T1 [446]	RAF, stored Shawbury
	ZF447	Shorts Tucano T1 [447]	RAF, stored Shawbury
	ZF448	Shorts Tucano T1 [448] $	RAF No 1 FTS/72(R) Sqn, Linton-on-Ouse
	ZF449	Shorts Tucano T1 [449]	RAF, stored Shawbury
	ZF483	Shorts Tucano T1 [483]	RAF, stored Shawbury
	ZF484	Shorts Tucano T1 [484]	RAF, stored Shawbury
	ZF485	Shorts Tucano T1 (G-BULU) [485]	RAF, stored Linton-on-Ouse
	ZF486	Shorts Tucano T1 [486]	RAF, stored Shawbury
	ZF487	Shorts Tucano T1 [487]	RAF, stored Shawbury
	ZF488	Shorts Tucano T1 [488]	RAF, stored Shawbury
	ZF489	Shorts Tucano T1 [489]	RAF No 1 FTS/207(R) Sqn, Linton-on-Ouse
	ZF490	Shorts Tucano T1 [490]	RAF, stored Shawbury
	ZF491	Shorts Tucano T1 [491]	RAF No 1 FTS, Linton-on-Ouse
	ZF492	Shorts Tucano T1 [492]	RAF, stored Shawbury
	ZF510	Shorts Tucano T1 [510]	MoD/AFD/QinetiQ, Boscombe Down
	ZF511	Shorts Tucano T1 [511]	MoD/AFD/QinetiQ, Boscombe Down
	ZF512	Shorts Tucano T1 [512]	RAF No 1 FTS/72(R) Sqn, Linton-on-Ouse
	ZF513	Shorts Tucano T1 [513]	RAF, stored Shawbury
	ZF514	Shorts Tucano T1 [514]	RAF, stored Shawbury
	ZF515	Shorts Tucano T1 [515]	RAF, stored Linton-on-Ouse
	ZF516	Shorts Tucano T1 [516]	RAF, stored Shawbury
	ZF534	BAe EAP	Loughborough University
	ZF537	WS Lynx AH9A	AAC No 9 Regt, Dishforth
	ZF538	WS Lynx AH9A	AAC No 9 Regt, Dishforth
	ZF539	WS Lynx AH9A	MoD/Vector Aerospace, Fleetlands
	ZF540	WS Lynx AH9A	MoD/AgustaWestland, Yeovil
	ZF557	WS Lynx HMA8SRU [453/DM]	RN No 815 NAS, *Diamond* Flt, Yeovilton
	ZF558	WS Lynx HMA8SRU [372]	RN No 815 NAS, *Northumberland* Flt, Yeovilton
	ZF560	WS Lynx HMA8SRU [412]	MoD/Vector Aerospace, Fleetlands

Serial	Type (code/other identity)	Owner/operator location or fate	Notes
ZF562	WS Lynx HMA8SRU [360/MC]	RN No 815 NAS, *Manchester* Flt, Yeovilton	
ZF563	WS Lynx HMA8SRU [303]	RN No 815 NAS, HQ Flt, Yeovilton	
ZF573	PBN 2T Islander CC2 (G-SRAY)	RAF Northolt Station Flight	
ZF579	BAC Lightning F53	Gatwick Aviation Museum, Charlwood	
ZF580	BAC Lightning F53	BAE Systems Samlesbury, at main gate	
ZF581	BAC Lightning F53	Cold War Jets Museum, Bentwaters	
ZF582	BAC Lightning F53 <ff>	Bournemouth Aviation Museum	
ZF583	BAC Lightning F53	Solway Aviation Society, Carlisle	
ZF584	BAC Lightning F53	Dumfries & Galloway Avn Mus, Dumfries	
ZF587	BAC Lightning F53 <ff>	Lashenden Air Warfare Museum, Headcorn	
ZF588	BAC Lightning F53 [L]	East Midlands Airport Aeropark	
ZF590	BAC Lightning F53 <ff>	Privately owned, Upwood, Cambs	
ZF595	BAC Lightning T55 (fuselage)	Privately owned, Binbrook	
ZF596	BAC Lightning T55 <ff>	Lakes Lightnings, Spark Bridge, Cumbria	
ZF622	Piper PA-31 Navajo Chieftain 350 (N3548Y)	MoD/AFD/QinetiQ, Boscombe Down	
ZF641	EHI-101 [PP1]	SFDO, RNAS Culdrose	
ZF649	EHI-101 Merlin (A2714) [PP5]	DCAE AESS, HMS Sultan, Gosport	
ZG101	EHI-101 (mock-up) [GB]	AgustaWestland, Yeovil	
ZG347	Northrop Chukar D2	Davidstow Airfield & Cornwall At War Museum	
ZG471	BAe Harrier GR7 [61A]	RAF HM&SF, Cottesmore (wfu)	
ZG472	BAe Harrier GR9A [62]	RAF HM&SF, Cottesmore (wfu)	
ZG474	BAe Harrier GR9 [64]	RAF HM&SF, Cottesmore (wfu)	
ZG477	BAe Harrier GR9 $	RAF Museum, Cosford	
ZG478	BAe Harrier GR9 (fuselage)	Privately owned, Sproughton	
ZG479	BAe Harrier GR9A [69A]	RAF HM&SF, Cottesmore (wfu)	
ZG480	BAe Harrier GR9 [70]	RAF HM&SF, Cottesmore (wfu)	
ZG500	BAe Harrier GR9 [71]	RAF HM&SF, Cottesmore (wfu)	
ZG501	BAe Harrier GR9 [EB-Q]	RAF HM&SF, Cottesmore (wfu)	
ZG502	BAe Harrier GR9 $	RAF HM&SF, Cottesmore (wfu)	
ZG503	BAe Harrier GR9 [EB-Z]	RAF HM&SF, Cottesmore (wfu)	
ZG504	BAe Harrier GR9A [75A]	RAF HM&SF, Cottesmore (wfu)	
ZG505	BAe Harrier GR9 [76]	RAF HM&SF, Cottesmore (wfu)	
ZG506	BAe Harrier GR9A $	RAF HM&SF, Cottesmore (wfu)	
ZG507	BAe Harrier GR9 [78]	RAF HM&SF, Cottesmore (wfu)	
ZG508	BAe Harrier GR9 [79]	RAF HM&SF, Cottesmore (wfu)	
ZG509	BAe Harrier GR7 [80]	RAF HM&SF, Cottesmore (wfu)	
ZG510	BAe Harrier GR9A [EB-Y]	*Sold to the USA, December 2011*	
ZG511	BAe Harrier GR9A [82A]	RAF HM&SF, Cottesmore (wfu)	
ZG530	BAe Harrier GR9 [84]	RAF HM&SF, Cottesmore (wfu)	
ZG531	BAe Harrier GR9 [85]	RAF HM&SF, Cottesmore (wfu)	
ZG631	Northrop Chukar D2	Farnborough Air Sciences Trust, Farnborough	
ZG705	Panavia Tornado GR4A [118]	RAF TEF, Lossiemouth	
ZG706	Panavia Tornado GR1A [E]	MoD/DSG, stored St Athan	
ZG707	Panavia Tornado GR4A [EB-Z]	RAF AWC/FJWOEU/No 41(R) Sqn, Coningsby	
ZG709	Panavia Tornado GR4A [120]	RAF, Lossiemouth Wing	
ZG712	Panavia Tornado GR4A [122]	RAF, Lossiemouth Wing	
ZG713	Panavia Tornado GR4A [123]	RAF, Marham Wing	
ZG714	Panavia Tornado GR4A [124]	RAF, Lossiemouth Wing	
ZG726	Panavia Tornado GR4A [125]	RAF CMU, stored Marham	
ZG727	Panavia Tornado GR4A [126]	MoD/BAE Systems, Warton	
ZG729	Panavia Tornado GR4A [127]	RAF TEF, stored Lossiemouth	
ZG750	Panavia Tornado GR4 [128]	RAF, Lossiemouth Wing	
ZG751	Panavia Tornado F3 [HI]	*Scrapped at Leeming, November 2010*	
ZG752	Panavia Tornado GR4 [129]	RAF CMU, stored Marham	
ZG753	Panavia Tornado F3 [H]	*Scrapped at Leeming, January 2010*	
ZG754	Panavia Tornado GR4 [130]	RAF, Lossiemouth Wing	

Notes	Serial	Type (code/other identity)	Owner/operator location or fate
	ZG755	Panavia Tornado F3 [F]	*Scrapped at Leeming, January 2010*
	ZG756	Panavia Tornado GR4 [131]	RAF Lossiemouth Wing
	ZG769	Panavia Tornado GR4	RAF, stored Shawbury (damaged)
	ZG771	Panavia Tornado GR4 [133]	RAF, Lossiemouth Wing
	ZG773	Panavia Tornado GR4	MoD/BAE Systems, Warton
	ZG774	Panavia Tornado F3 [HM]	RAF Leeming, for scrapping
	ZG775	Panavia Tornado GR4 [134]	RAF, Marham Wing
	ZG777	Panavia Tornado GR4 [EB-Q]	RAF CMU Marham
	ZG779	Panavia Tornado GR4 [136]	RAF, Marham Wing
	ZG791	Panavia Tornado GR4 [137]	RAF CMU, stored Marham
	ZG794	Panavia Tornado GR4 [TN]	RAF, stored Lossiemouth
	ZG797	Panavia Tornado F3 [D]	*Scrapped at Leeming, November 2009*
	ZG798	Panavia Tornado F3 [GQ]	*Scrapped at Leeming, August 2008*
	ZG816	WS61 Sea King HAS6 [014/L]	DCAE, stored HMS Sultan, Gosport
	ZG817	WS61 Sea King HAS6 [702/PW]	DCAE AESS, HMS Sultan, Gosport
	ZG818	WS61 Sea King HAS6 [707/PW]	DCAE, stored HMS Sultan, Gosport
	ZG819	WS61 Sea King HAS6 [265/N]	DCAE AESS, HMS Sultan, Gosport
	ZG820	WS61 Sea King HC4 [I]	MoD/Vector Aerospace, Fleetlands
	ZG821	WS61 Sea King HC4 [G]	RN No 846 NAS, Yeovilton
	ZG822	WS61 Sea King HC4 [WS]	RN No 848 NAS, Yeovilton
	ZG844	PBN 2T Islander AL1 (G-BLNE)	AAC No 651 Sqn/5 Regt, Aldergrove
	ZG845	PBN 2T Islander AL1 (G-BLNT)	AAC No 651 Sqn/5 Regt, Aldergrove
	ZG846	PBN 2T Islander AL1 (G-BLNU)	AAC No 651 Sqn/5 Regt, Aldergrove
	ZG847	PBN 2T Islander AL1 (G-BLNV)	AAC, stored Shawbury
	ZG848	PBN 2T Islander AL1 (G-BLNY)	AAC No 651 Sqn/5 Regt, Aldergrove
	ZG857	BAe Harrier GR9 [EB-Z]	RAF HM&SF, Cottesmore (wfu)
	ZG858	BAe Harrier GR9 $	RAF HM&SF, Cottesmore (wfu)
	ZG859	BAe Harrier GR9A [91A]	RAF HM&SF, Cottesmore (wfu)
	ZG860	BAe Harrier GR9	RAF HM&SF, Cottesmore (wfu)
	ZG862	BAe Harrier GR9 [94]	RAF HM&SF, Cottesmore (wfu)
	ZG875	WS61 Sea King HAS6 [013/L]	DCAE, stored HMS Sultan, Gosport (damaged)
	ZG884	WS Lynx AH9A	RM No 847 NAS, Yeovilton
	ZG885	WS Lynx AH9A	AAC No 9 Regt, Dishforth
	ZG886	WS Lynx AH9A	AAC No 667 Sqn/7 Regt, Middle Wallop
	ZG887	WS Lynx AH9A	AAC No 9 Regt, Dishforth
	ZG888	WS Lynx AH9A	MoD/Vector Aerospace, Fleetlands
	ZG889	WS Lynx AH9A	MoD/Vector Aerospace, Fleetlands
	ZG914	WS Lynx AH9A	AAC No 9 Regt, Dishforth
	ZG915	WS Lynx AH9A	MoD/AgustaWestland, Yeovil
	ZG916	WS Lynx AH9A	MoD/Vector Aerospace stored, Fleetlands
	ZG917	WS Lynx AH9A	AAC No 667 Sqn/7 Regt, Middle Wallop
	ZG918	WS Lynx AH9A	AAC No 9 Regt, Dishforth
	ZG919	WS Lynx AH9A	AAC No 667 Sqn/7 Regt, Middle Wallop
	ZG920	WS Lynx AH9A	AAC No 9 Regt, Dishforth
	ZG921	WS Lynx AH9A	AAC No 667 Sqn/7 Regt, Middle Wallop
	ZG922	WS Lynx AH9	Privately owned, Staverton, GI use
	ZG923	WS Lynx AH9A	MoD/AgustaWestland, Yeovil
	ZG969	Pilatus PC-9 (HB-HQE)	BAE Systems Warton
	ZG989	PBN 2T Islander ASTOR (G-DLRA)	MoD/Britten-Norman, Bembridge
	ZG993	PBN 2T Islander AL1 (G-BOMD)	AAC, stored Shawbury
	ZG994	PBN 2T Islander AL1 (G-BPLN) (fuselage)	Britten-Norman, stored Bembridge
	ZG995	PBN 2T Defender AL1 (G-SURV)	AAC No 651 Sqn/5 Regt, Aldergrove
	ZG996	PBN 2T Defender AL2 (G-BWPR)	AAC No 651 Sqn/5 Regt, Aldergrove
	ZG997	PBN 2T Defender AL2 (G-BWPV)	AAC No 651 Sqn/5 Regt, Aldergrove
	ZG998	PBN 2T Defender AL1 (G-BWPX)	AAC No 651 Sqn/5 Regt, Aldergrove
	ZH001	PBN 2T Defender AL2 (G-CEIO)	AAC No 651 Sqn/5 Regt, Aldergrove
	ZH002	PBN 2T Defender AL2 (G-CEIP)	AAC No 651 Sqn/5 Regt, Aldergrove

Serial	Type (code/other identity)	Owner/operator location or fate	Notes
ZH003	PBN 2T Defender AL2 (G-CEIR)	AAC No 651 Sqn/5 Regt, Aldergrove	
ZH004	PBN 2T Defender T3 (G-BWPO)	AAC No 651 Sqn/5 Regt, Aldergrove	
ZH005	PBN 2T Defender AL2 (G-CGVB)	AAC No 651 Sqn/5 Regt, Aldergrove	
ZH006	PBN 2T Defender AL2 (G-CGTC)	DE&S/Britten-Norman, for AAC	
ZH101	Boeing E-3D Sentry AEW1 [01]	RAF No 8 Sqn, Waddington	
ZH102	Boeing E-3D Sentry AEW1 [02]	RAF No 8 Sqn, Waddington	
ZH103	Boeing E-3D Sentry AEW1 [03]	RAF No 8 Sqn, Waddington	
ZH104	Boeing E-3D Sentry AEW1 [04]	MoD/Northrop Grumman, Lake Charles, USA	
ZH105	Boeing E-3D Sentry AEW1 [05]	RAF, stored Waddington	
ZH106	Boeing E-3D Sentry AEW1 [06]	RAF No 8 Sqn, Waddington	
ZH107	Boeing E-3D Sentry AEW1 [07]	RAF No 8 Sqn, Waddington	
ZH115	Grob G109B Vigilant T1 [TA]	RAF No 642 VGS, Linton-on-Ouse	
ZH116	Grob G109B Vigilant T1 [TB]	RAF No 618 VGS, Odiham	
ZH117	Grob G109B Vigilant T1 [TC]	RAF No 642 VGS, Linton-on-Ouse	
ZH118	Grob G109B Vigilant T1 [TD]	RAF No 664 VGS, Newtownards	
ZH119	Grob G109B Vigilant T1 [TE]	RAF No 632 VGS, Ternhill	
ZH120	Grob G109B Vigilant T1 [TF]	RAF No 632 VGS, Ternhill	
ZH121	Grob G109B Vigilant T1 [TG]	RAF CGMF, Syerston	
ZH122	Grob G109B Vigilant T1 [TH]	RAF No 616 VGS, Henlow	
ZH123	Grob G109B Vigilant T1 [TJ]	RAF No 637 VGS, Little Rissington	
ZH124	Grob G109B Vigilant T1 [TK]	RAF No 631 VGS, Woodvale	
ZH125	Grob G109B Vigilant T1 [TL]	RAF ACCGS/No 644 VGS, Syerston	
ZH126	Grob G109B Vigilant T1 (D-KGRA) [TM]	RAF No 631 VGS, Woodvale	
ZH127	Grob G109B Vigilant T1 (D-KEEC) [TN]	RAF No 616 VGS, Henlow	
ZH128	Grob G109B Vigilant T1 [TP]	RAF CGMF, Syerston	
ZH129	Grob G109B Vigilant T1 [TQ]	RAF No 632 VGS, Ternhill	
ZH139	BAe Harrier GR7 <R> (BAPC 191/*ZD472*)	RAF M&RU, Bottesford (wfu)	
ZH144	Grob G109B Vigilant T1 [TR]	RAF No 635 VGS, Topcliffe	
ZH145	Grob G109B Vigilant T1 [TS]	RAF No 624 VGS, Chivenor RMB	
ZH146	Grob G109B Vigilant T1 [TT]	RAF No 642 VGS, Linton-on-Ouse	
ZH147	Grob G109B Vigilant T1 [TU]	RAF ACCGS/No 644 VGS, Syerston	
ZH148	Grob G109B Vigilant T1 [TV]	RAF No 645 VGS, Topcliffe	
ZH184	Grob G109B Vigilant T1 [TW]	RAF No 632 VGS, Ternhill	
ZH185	Grob G109B Vigilant T1 [TX]	RAF No 636 VGS, Swansea	
ZH186	Grob G109B Vigilant T1 [TY]	RAF No 616 VGS, Henlow	
ZH187	Grob G109B Vigilant T1 [TZ]	RAF No 664 VGS, Newtownards	
ZH188	Grob G109B Vigilant T1 [UA]	RAF No 633 VGS, Cosford	
ZH189	Grob G109B Vigilant T1 [UB]	RAF No 636 VGS, Swansea	
ZH190	Grob G109B Vigilant T1 [UC]	RAF CGMF, Syerston	
ZH191	Grob G109B Vigilant T1 [UD]	RAF No 613 VGS, Halton	
ZH192	Grob G109B Vigilant T1 [UE]	RAF No 633 VGS, Cosford	
ZH193	Grob G109B Vigilant T1 [UF]	RAF No 631 VGS, Woodvale	
ZH194	Grob G109B Vigilant T1 [UG]	RAF CGMF, Syerston	
ZH195	Grob G109B Vigilant T1 [UH]	RAF No 624 VGS, Chivenor RMB	
ZH196	Grob G109B Vigilant T1 [UJ]	RAF No 663 VGS, Kinloss	
ZH197	Grob G109B Vigilant T1 [UK]	RAF No 618 VGS, Odiham	
ZH200	BAe Hawk 200	BAE Systems, stored Brough	
ZH205	Grob G109B Vigilant T1 [UL]	RAF No 635 VGS, Topcliffe	
ZH206	Grob G109B Vigilant T1 [UM]	RAF No 631 VGS, Woodvale	
ZH207	Grob G109B Vigilant T1 [UN]	RAF ACCGS/No 644 VGS, Syerston	
ZH208	Grob G109B Vigilant T1 [UP]	RAF No 645 VGS, Topcliffe	
ZH209	Grob G109B Vigilant T1 [UQ]	RAF No 634 VGS, St Athan	
ZH211	Grob G109B Vigilant T1 [UR]	RAF No 616 VGS, Henlow	
ZH247	Grob G109B Vigilant T1 [US]	RAF No 635 VGS, Topcliffe	
ZH248	Grob G109B Vigilant T1 [UT]	RAF No 618 VGS, Odiham	
ZH249	Grob G109B Vigilant T1 [UU]	RAF No 634 VGS, St Athan	
ZH257	B-V CH-47C Chinook (9217M) (fuselage)	RAF Odiham, BDRT	
ZH263	Grob G109B Vigilant T1 [UV]	RAF No 637 VGS, Little Rissington	

Notes	Serial	Type (code/other identity)	Owner/operator location or fate
	ZH264	Grob G109B Vigilant T1 [UW]	RAF No 613 VGS, Halton
	ZH265	Grob G109B Vigilant T1 [UX]	RAF No 612 VGS, Abingdon
	ZH266	Grob G109B Vigilant T1 [UY]	RAF No 633 VGS, Cosford
	ZH267	Grob G109B Vigilant T1 [UZ]	RAF CGMF, Syerston
	ZH268	Grob G109B Vigilant T1 [SA]	RAF No 612 VGS, Abingdon
	ZH269	Grob G109B Vigilant T1 [SB]	RAF No 663 VGS, Kinloss
	ZH270	Grob G109B Vigilant T1 [SC]	RAF No 616 VGS, Henlow
	ZH271	Grob G109B Vigilant T1 [SD]	RAF No 637 VGS, Little Rissington
	ZH278	Grob G109B Vigilant T1 (D-KAIS) [SF]	RAF No 616 VGS, Henlow
	ZH279	Grob G109B Vigilant T1 (D-KNPS) [SG]	RAF No 664 VGS, Newtownards
	ZH536	PBN 2T Islander CC2 (G-BSAH)	RAF Northolt Station Flight
	ZH537	PBN 2T Islander CC2 (G-SELX)	RAF Northolt Station Flight
	ZH540	WS61 Sea King HAR3A	RAF No 22 Sqn, B Flt, Wattisham
	ZH541	WS61 Sea King HAR3A [V]	RAF No 22 Sqn, B Flt, Wattisham
	ZH542	WS61 Sea King HAR3A [W] $	RAF No 22 Sqn, A Flt, Chivenor RMB
	ZH543	WS61 Sea King HAR3A [X]	RAF No 22 Sqn, A Flt, Chivenor RMB
	ZH544	WS61 Sea King HAR3A	RAF No 22 Sqn, A Flt, Chivenor RMB
	ZH545	WS61 Sea King HAR3A $	RAF No 22 Sqn, B Flt, Wattisham
	ZH552	Panavia Tornado F3 [HW]	MoD/AFD/QinetiQ, Boscombe Down
	ZH553	Panavia Tornado F3 [RT]	RAF, stored Shawbury
	ZH554	Panavia Tornado F3 [HX,JU-C]	RAF Leeming, for scrapping
	ZH555	Panavia Tornado F3 [PT]	RAF Leeming, for scrapping
	ZH557	Panavia Tornado F3 [NT]	Scrapped at Leeming, June 2010
	ZH588	Eurofighter Typhoon (DA2)	RAF Museum, Hendon
	ZH590	Eurofighter Typhoon (DA4)	Imperial War Museum, Duxford
	ZH653	BAe Harrier T10	Sold to the USA, December 2011
	ZH654	BAe Harrier T10 <ff>	RAF, Cottesmore
	ZH657	BAe Harrier T12 [105]	RAF HM&SF, Cottesmore (wfu)
	ZH658	BAe Harrier T10 [106]	RAF HM&SF, Cottesmore (wfu)
	ZH659	BAe Harrier T12 [107]	RAF HM&SF, Cottesmore (wfu)
	ZH660	BAe Harrier T12 [108]	RAF HM&SF, Cottesmore (wfu)
	ZH661	BAe Harrier T12 [109]	RAF HM&SF, Cottesmore (wfu)
	ZH662	BAe Harrier T10 [110]	RAF HM&SF, Cottesmore (wfu)
	ZH663	BAe Harrier T12 [111]	RAF HM&SF, Cottesmore (wfu)
	ZH664	BAe Harrier T12 [112]	RAF HM&SF, Cottesmore (wfu)
	ZH665	BAe Harrier T12A [113]	RAF HM&SF, Cottesmore (wfu)
	ZH763	BAC 1-11/539GL (G-BGKE)	RAF/AWC/No 206(R) Sqn, Boscombe Down
	ZH775	B-V Chinook HC2 (N7424J) [HB]	RAF Odiham Wing
	ZH776	B-V Chinook HC2 (N7424L) [HC]	RAF Odiham Wing
	ZH777	B-V Chinook HC2 (N7424M) [HE]	MoD/Vector Aerospace, Fleetlands
	ZH796	BAe Sea Harrier FA2 [001/L]	SFDO, RNAS Culdrose
	ZH797	BAe Sea Harrier FA2 [97/DD]	SFDO, RNAS Culdrose
	ZH798	BAe Sea Harrier FA2 [98/DD]	SFDO, RNAS Culdrose
	ZH799	BAe Sea Harrier FA2 [730]	Privately owned, Tunbridge Wells
	ZH800	BAe Sea Harrier FA2 (ZH801) [123]	RNAS Yeovilton
	ZH801	BAe Sea Harrier FA2 (ZH800) [001]	RNAS Yeovilton
	ZH802	BAe Sea Harrier FA2 [02/DD]	SFDO, RNAS Culdrose
	ZH803	BAe Sea Harrier FA2 [03/DD]	SFDO, RNAS Culdrose
	ZH804	BAe Sea Harrier FA2 [003/L]	RN, stored Culdrose
	ZH806	BAe Sea Harrier FA2 [007]	Privately owned, Bentwaters
	ZH807	BAe Sea Harrier FA2 <ff>	Privately owned, Newport, Isle of Wight
	ZH810	BAe Sea Harrier FA2 [125]	Privately owned, Sproughton
	ZH811	BAe Sea Harrier FA2 [002/L]	RN, stored Culdrose
	ZH812	BAe Sea Harrier FA2 [005/L]	Privately owned, Sproughton
	ZH813	BAe Sea Harrier FA2 [13/DD]	SFDO, RNAS Culdrose
	ZH814	Bell 212HP AH1 (G-BGMH)	AAC No 7 Flt, Brunei
	ZH815	Bell 212HP AH1 (G-BGCZ)	AAC No 7 Flt, Brunei
	ZH816	Bell 212HP AH1 (G-BGMG)	AAC No 7 Flt, Brunei

Serial	Type (code/other identity)	Owner/operator location or fate	Notes
ZH821	EHI-101 Merlin HM1	AgustaWestland, Yeovil, Fire Section	
ZH822	EHI-101 Merlin HM1	RN, stored Shawbury	
ZH823	EHI-101 Merlin HM1	RN, stored Shawbury	
ZH824	EHI-101 Merlin HM1 [65]	RN No 814 NAS, Culdrose	
ZH825	EHI-101 Merlin HM1 [583]	MoD/AgustaWestland, Yeovil	
ZH826	EHI-101 Merlin HM2	MoD/AgustaWestland, Yeovil	
ZH827	EHI-101 Merlin HM1 [10]	RN No 820 NAS, Culdrose	
ZH828	EHI-101 Merlin HM1 [14]	RN No 820 NAS, Culdrose	
ZH829	EHI-101 Merlin HM2 [CU]	MoD/AgustaWestland, Yeovil	
ZH830	EHI-101 Merlin HM1	MoD/AFD/QinetiQ, Boscombe Down	
ZH831	EHI-101 Merlin HM2	MoD/AgustaWestland, Yeovil (conversion)	
ZH832	EHI-101 Merlin HM1	MoD/AgustaWestland, Yeovil	
ZH833	EHI-101 Merlin HM1 [85]	RN MDMF, Culdrose	
ZH834	EHI-101 Merlin HM2 [86]	MoD/AgustaWestland, Yeovil (conversion)	
ZH835	EHI-101 Merlin HM1 [87/CU]	RN No 824 NAS, Culdrose	
ZH836	EHI-101 Merlin HM1 [68]	RN No 814 NAS, Culdrose	
ZH837	EHI-101 Merlin HM1 [503/LA]	RN No 829 NAS, Culdrose	
ZH838	EHI-101 Merlin HM1 [86]	RN No 824 NAS, Culdrose	
ZH839	EHI-101 Merlin HM1 [67]	RN No 814 NAS, Culdrose	
ZH840	EHI-101 Merlin HM1 [11]	RN No 820 NAS, Culdrose	
ZH841	EHI-101 Merlin HM1 [502]	RN No 829 NAS, Culdrose	
ZH842	EHI-101 Merlin HM1 [88]	RN No 824 NAS, Culdrose	
ZH843	EHI-101 Merlin HM2	MoD/AgustaWestland, Yeovil	
ZH845	EHI-101 Merlin HM1	RN No 814 NAS, Culdrose	
ZH846	EHI-101 Merlin HM1 [16]	RN No 820 NAS, Culdrose	
ZH847	EHI-101 Merlin HM1 [67]	RN No 814 NAS, Culdrose	
ZH848	EHI-101 Merlin HM1	RN No 829 NAS, Culdrose	
ZH849	EHI-101 Merlin HM1	RN No 829 NAS, Culdrose	
ZH850	EHI-101 Merlin HM1 [12]	RN No 820 NAS, Culdrose	
ZH851	EHI-101 Merlin HM1 [13]	RN No 820 NAS, Culdrose	
ZH852	EHI-101 Merlin HM1	RN No 829 NAS, Culdrose	
ZH853	EHI-101 Merlin HM1 [68]	MoD/AgustaWestland, Yeovil	
ZH854	EHI-101 Merlin HM1 [84]	RN No 824 NAS, Culdrose	
ZH855	EHI-101 Merlin HM1 [83]	RN MDMF, Culdrose	
ZH856	EHI-101 Merlin HM1 [82]	RN No 824 NAS, Culdrose	
ZH857	EHI-101 Merlin HM1 [CU]	RN No 814 NAS, Culdrose	
ZH858	EHI-101 Merlin HM1 [14]	RN MDMF, Culdrose	
ZH859	EHI-101 Merlin HM1 [68]	RN No 814 NAS, Culdrose	
ZH860	EHI-101 Merlin HM1 [81]	RN No 824 NAS, Culdrose	
ZH861	EHI-101 Merlin HM1	RN No 829 NAS, Culdrose	
ZH862	EHI-101 Merlin HM1	RN No 829 NAS, Culdrose	
ZH863	EHI-101 Merlin HM1 [17]	RN No 820 NAS, Culdrose	
ZH864	EHI-101 Merlin HM1 [17]	RN No 820 NAS, Culdrose	
ZH865	Lockheed C-130J-30 Hercules C4 (N130JA) [865]	RAF No 24 Sqn/No 30 Sqn, Brize Norton	
ZH866	Lockheed C-130J-30 Hercules C4 (N130JE) [866]	RAF No 24 Sqn/No 30 Sqn, Brize Norton	
ZH867	Lockheed C-130J-30 Hercules C4 (N130JJ) [867]	RAF No 24 Sqn/No 30 Sqn, Brize Norton	
ZH868	Lockheed C-130J-30 Hercules C4 (N130JN) [868]	RAF No 24 Sqn/No 30 Sqn, Brize Norton	
ZH869	Lockheed C-130J-30 Hercules C4 (N130JV) [869]	RAF No 24 Sqn/No 30 Sqn, Brize Norton	
ZH870	Lockheed C-130J-30 Hercules C4 (N78235) [870]	RAF No 24 Sqn/No 30 Sqn, Brize Norton	
ZH871	Lockheed C-130J-30 Hercules C4 (N73238) [871]	RAF No 24 Sqn/No 30 Sqn, Brize Norton	
ZH872	Lockheed C-130J-30 Hercules C4 (N4249Y) [872]	RAF No 24 Sqn/No 30 Sqn, Brize Norton	

Notes	Serial	Type (code/other identity)	Owner/operator location or fate
	ZH873	Lockheed C-130J-30 Hercules C4 (N4242N) [873]	RAF No 24 Sqn/No 30 Sqn, Brize Norton
	ZH874	Lockheed C-130J-30 Hercules C4 (N41030) [874]	RAF No 24 Sqn/No 30 Sqn, Brize Norton
	ZH875	Lockheed C-130J-30 Hercules C4 (N4099R) [875]	RAF No 24 Sqn/No 30 Sqn, Brize Norton
	ZH877	Lockheed C-130J-30 Hercules C4 (N4081M) [877]	RAF No 24 Sqn/No 30 Sqn, Brize Norton
	ZH878	Lockheed C-130J-30 Hercules C4 (N73232) [878]	RAF No 24 Sqn/No 30 Sqn, Brize Norton
	ZH879	Lockheed C-130J-30 Hercules C4 (N4080M) [879]	RAF No 24 Sqn/No 30 Sqn, Brize Norton
	ZH880	Lockheed C-130J Hercules C5 (N73238) [880]	RAF No 1312 Flt, Mount Pleasant, FI
	ZH881	Lockheed C-130J Hercules C5 (N4081M) [881]	RAF No 24 Sqn/No 30 Sqn, Brize Norton
	ZH882	Lockheed C-130J Hercules C5 (N4099R) [882]	RAF No 24 Sqn/No 30 Sqn, Brize Norton
	ZH883	Lockheed C-130J Hercules C5 (N4242N) [883]	RAF No 24 Sqn/No 30 Sqn, Brize Norton
	ZH884	Lockheed C-130J Hercules C5 (N4249Y) [884]	RAF No 24 Sqn/No 30 Sqn, Brize Norton
	ZH885	Lockheed C-130J Hercules C5 (N41030) [885]	RAF No 24 Sqn/No 30 Sqn, Brize Norton .
	ZH886	Lockheed C-130J Hercules C5 (N73235) [886]	RAF No 24 Sqn/No 30 Sqn, Brize Norton
	ZH887	Lockheed C-130J Hercules C5 (N4187W) [887]	RAF No 24 Sqn/No 30 Sqn, Brize Norton
	ZH888	Lockheed C-130J Hercules C5 (N4187) [888]	RAF No 24 Sqn/No 30 Sqn, Brize Norton
	ZH889	Lockheed C-130J Hercules C5 (N4099R) [889]	RAF No 24 Sqn/No 30 Sqn, Brize Norton
	ZH890	Grob G109B Vigilant T1 [SE]	RAF No 612 VGS, Abingdon
	ZH891	B-V Chinook HC2A (N20075) [HF]	MoD/Vector Aerospace, Fleetlands
	ZH892	B-V Chinook HC2A (N2019V) [HG]	RAF No 1310 Flt, Kandahar, Afghanistan
	ZH893	B-V Chinook HC2A (N2025L) [HH]	MoD/Vector Aerospace, Fleetlands
	ZH894	B-V Chinook HC2A (N2026E) [HI]	RAF Odiham Wing
	ZH895	B-V Chinook HC2A (N2034K) [HJ] $	RAF Odiham Wing
	ZH896	B-V Chinook HC2A (N2038G) [HK]	MoD/Vector Aerospace, Fleetlands
	ZH897	B-V Chinook HC3R (N2045G) [HL]	RAF Odiham Wing
	ZH898	B-V Chinook HC3R (N2057Q)	RAF Odiham Wing
	ZH899	B-V Chinook HC3R (N2057R)	RAF Odiham Wing
	ZH900	B-V Chinook HC3R (N2060H)	MoD/AFD/QinetiQ, Boscombe Down
	ZH901	B-V Chinook HC3R (N2060M)	RAF Odiham Wing
	ZH902	B-V Chinook HC3R (N2064W)	RAF Odiham Wing
	ZH903	B-V Chinook HC3R (N20671) [HR]	RAF Odiham Wing
	ZH904	B-V Chinook HC3R (N2083K)	RAF Odiham Wing
	ZH917	Panavia Tornado IDS (RSAF 6631)	MoD/BAE Systems, Warton
	ZJ100	BAe Hawk 102D	MoD/BAE Systems, stored Brough
	ZJ117	EHI-101 Merlin HC3	MoD/AgustaWestland, Yeovil
	ZJ118	EHI-101 Merlin HC3 [B]	RAF MDMF, RNAS Culdrose
	ZJ119	EHI-101 Merlin HC3 [C]	RAF No 28 Sqn/No 78 Sqn, Benson
	ZJ120	EHI-101 Merlin HC3 [D]	RAF No 28 Sqn/No 78 Sqn, Benson
	ZJ121	EHI-101 Merlin HC3 [E]	RAF No 28 Sqn/No 78 Sqn, Benson
	ZJ122	EHI-101 Merlin HC3 [F]	RAF No 28 Sqn/No 78 Sqn, Benson
	ZJ123	EHI-101 Merlin HC3 [G]	RAF No 1419 Flt, Kandahar, Afghanistan
	ZJ124	EHI-101 Merlin HC3 [H]	RAF No 28 Sqn/No 78 Sqn, Benson

Serial	Type (code/other identity)	Owner/operator location or fate	Notes
ZJ125	EHI-101 Merlin HC3 [J]	RAF No 1419 Flt, Kandahar, Afghanistan	
ZJ126	EHI-101 Merlin HC3 [K]	RAF No 28 Sqn/No 78 Sqn, Benson	
ZJ127	EHI-101 Merlin HC3 [L]	RAF No 1419 Flt, Kandahar, Afghanistan	
ZJ128	EHI-101 Merlin HC3 [M]	RAF No 28 Sqn/No 78 Sqn, Benson	
ZJ129	EHI-101 Merlin HC3 [N]	RAF MDMF, RNAS Culdrose	
ZJ130	EHI-101 Merlin HC3 [O]	RAF No 1419 Flt, Kandahar, Afghanistan	
ZJ131	EHI-101 Merlin HC3 [P]	RAF No 1419 Flt, Kandahar, Afghanistan	
ZJ132	EHI-101 Merlin HC3 [Q]	MoD/AgustaWestland, Yeovil	
ZJ133	EHI-101 Merlin HC3 [R]	RAF No 28 Sqn/No 78 Sqn, Benson	
ZJ134	EHI-101 Merlin HC3 [S]	RAF MDMF, RNAS Culdrose	
ZJ135	EHI-101 Merlin HC3 [T]	RAF MDMF, RNAS Culdrose	
ZJ136	EHI-101 Merlin HC3 [U]	RAF No 1419 Flt, Kandahar, Afghanistan	
ZJ137	EHI-101 Merlin HC3 [W]	RAF MDMF, RNAS Culdrose	
ZJ138	EHI-101 Merlin HC3 [X]	DCAE, stored HMS Sultan, Gosport	
ZJ164	AS365N-2 Dauphin 2 (G-BTLC)	RN/Bond Helicopters, Newquay	
ZJ165	AS365N-2 Dauphin 2 (G-NTOO)	RN/Bond Helicopters, Newquay	
ZJ166	WAH-64 Apache AH1 (N9219G)	AAC No 673 Sqn/7 Regt, Middle Wallop	
ZJ167	WAH-64 Apache AH1 (N3266B)	AAC No 4 Regt, Wattisham	
ZJ168	WAH-64 Apache AH1 (N3123T)	AAC No 3 Regt, Wattisham	
ZJ169	WAH-64 Apache AH1 (N3114H)	AAC No 4 Regt, Wattisham	
ZJ170	WAH-64 Apache AH1 (N3065U)	AAC No 673 Sqn/7 Regt, Middle Wallop	
ZJ171	WAH-64 Apache AH1 (N3266T)	AAC No 4 Regt, Wattisham	
ZJ172	WAH-64 Apache AH1	AAC, stored Wattisham	
ZJ173	WAH-64 Apache AH1 (N3266W)	AAC No 673 Sqn/7 Regt, Middle Wallop	
ZJ174	WAH-64 Apache AH1	AAC No 4 Regt, Wattisham	
ZJ175	WAH-64 Apache AH1 (N3218V)	AAC No 4 Regt, Wattisham	
ZJ176	WAH-64 Apache AH1	AAC No 4 Regt, Wattisham	
ZJ177	WAH-64 Apache AH1	AAC, stored Wattisham (damaged)	
ZJ178	WAH-64 Apache AH1	AAC No 4 Regt, Wattisham	
ZJ179	WAH-64 Apache AH1	AAC No 3 Regt, Wattisham	
ZJ180	WAH-64 Apache AH1	AAC No 673 Sqn/7 Regt, Middle Wallop	
ZJ181	WAH-64 Apache AH1	AAC No 4 Regt, Wattisham	
ZJ182	WAH-64 Apache AH1	AAC No 3 Regt, Wattisham	
ZJ183	WAH-64 Apache AH1	AAC No 4 Regt, Wattisham	
ZJ184	WAH-64 Apache AH1	AAC No 4 Regt, Wattisham	
ZJ185	WAH-64 Apache AH1	AAC No 3 Regt, Wattisham	
ZJ186	WAH-64 Apache AH1	AAC No 3 Regt, Wattisham	
ZJ187	WAH-64 Apache AH1	AAC No 3 Regt, Wattisham	
ZJ188	WAH-64 Apache AH1	AAC No 3 Regt, Wattisham	
ZJ189	WAH-64 Apache AH1	AAC No 3 Regt/No 4 Regt, Wattisham	
ZJ190	WAH-64 Apache AH1	AAC No 3 Regt, Wattisham	
ZJ191	WAH-64 Apache AH1	AAC No 4 Regt, Wattisham	
ZJ192	WAH-64 Apache AH1	AAC No 673 Sqn/7 Regt, Middle Wallop	
ZJ193	WAH-64 Apache AH1	AAC No 3 Regt, Wattisham	
ZJ194	WAH-64 Apache AH1	AAC No 3 Regt, Wattisham	
ZJ195	WAH-64 Apache AH1	AAC No 4 Regt, Wattisham	
ZJ196	WAH-64 Apache AH1	AAC No 4 Regt, Wattisham	
ZJ197	WAH-64 Apache AH1	AAC No 3 Regt, Wattisham	
ZJ198	WAH-64 Apache AH1	AAC No 4 Regt, Wattisham	
ZJ199	WAH-64 Apache AH1	MoD/AgustaWestland, Yeovil	
ZJ200	WAH-64 Apache AH1	AAC No 4 Regt, Wattisham	
ZJ202	WAH-64 Apache AH1	AAC No 4 Regt, Wattisham	
ZJ203	WAH-64 Apache AH1	AAC No 3 Regt, Wattisham	
ZJ204	WAH-64 Apache AH1	AAC No 3 Regt, Wattisham	
ZJ205	WAH-64 Apache AH1	AAC No 3 Regt, Wattisham	
ZJ206	WAH-64 Apache AH1	AAC No 673 Sqn/7 Regt, Middle Wallop	
ZJ207	WAH-64 Apache AH1	AAC No 4 Regt, Wattisham	
ZJ208	WAH-64 Apache AH1	AAC No 3 Regt, Wattisham	

Notes	Serial	Type (code/other identity)	Owner/operator location or fate
	ZJ209	WAH-64 Apache AH1	AAC No 3 Regt, Wattisham
	ZJ210	WAH-64 Apache AH1	AAC No 3 Regt, Wattisham
	ZJ211	WAH-64 Apache AH1	AAC No 4 Regt, Wattisham
	ZJ212	WAH-64 Apache AH1	AAC No 673 Sqn/7 Regt, Middle Wallop
	ZJ213	WAH-64 Apache AH1	AAC No 673 Sqn/7 Regt, Middle Wallop
	ZJ214	WAH-64 Apache AH1	AAC No 673 Sqn/7 Regt, Middle Wallop
	ZJ215	WAH-64 Apache AH1	AAC No 673 Sqn/7 Regt, Middle Wallop
	ZJ216	WAH-64 Apache AH1	AAC No 3 Regt, Wattisham
	ZJ217	WAH-64 Apache AH1	AAC No 4 Regt, Wattisham
	ZJ218	WAH-64 Apache AH1	AAC No 4 Regt, Wattisham
	ZJ219	WAH-64 Apache AH1	AAC No 673 Sqn/7 Regt, Middle Wallop
	ZJ220	WAH-64 Apache AH1	AAC No 4 Regt, Wattisham
	ZJ221	WAH-64 Apache AH1	AAC No 673 Sqn/7 Regt, Middle Wallop
	ZJ222	WAH-64 Apache AH1	AAC No 4 Regt, Wattisham
	ZJ223	WAH-64 Apache AH1	AAC No 673 Sqn/7 Regt, Middle Wallop
	ZJ224	WAH-64 Apache AH1	AAC No 3 Regt, Wattisham
	ZJ225	WAH-64 Apache AH1	AAC No 3 Regt, Wattisham
	ZJ226	WAH-64 Apache AH1	MoD/AgustaWestland, Yeovil
	ZJ227	WAH-64 Apache AH1	AAC, stored Wattisham
	ZJ228	WAH-64 Apache AH1	AAC No 3 Regt, Wattisham
	ZJ229	WAH-64 Apache AH1	AAC No 3 Regt, Wattisham
	ZJ230	WAH-64 Apache AH1	AAC No 4 Regt, Wattisham
	ZJ231	WAH-64 Apache AH1	AAC No 3 Regt, Wattisham
	ZJ232	WAH-64 Apache AH1	AAC No 4 Regt, Wattisham
	ZJ233	WAH-64 Apache AH1	AAC No 4 Regt, Wattisham
	ZJ234	Bell 412EP Griffin HT1 (G-BWZR) [S]	DHFS No 60(R) Sqn, RAF Shawbury
	ZJ235	Bell 412EP Griffin HT1 (G-BXBF) [I]	DHFS No 60(R) Sqn, RAF Shawbury
	ZJ236	Bell 412EP Griffin HT1 (G-BXBE) [X]	DHFS No 60(R) Sqn, RAF Shawbury
	ZJ237	Bell 412EP Griffin HT1 (G-BXFF) [T]	DHFS No 60(R) Sqn, RAF Shawbury
	ZJ238	Bell 412EP Griffin HT1 (G-BXHC) [Y]	DHFS No 60(R) Sqn, RAF Shawbury
	ZJ239	Bell 412EP Griffin HT1 (G-BXFH) [R]	DHFS No 60(R) Sqn RAF Shawbury
	ZJ240	Bell 412EP Griffin HT1 (G-BXIR) [U]	DHFS No 60(R) Sqn, RAF Shawbury
	ZJ241	Bell 412EP Griffin HT1 (G-BXIS) [L]	DHFS No 60(R) Sqn/SARTU, RAF Valley
	ZJ242	Bell 412EP Griffin HT1 (G-BXDK) [E]	DHFS No 60(R) Sqn, RAF Shawbury
	ZJ243	AS350BA Squirrel HT2 (G-BWZS) [43]	DHFS, RAF Shawbury
	ZJ244	AS350BA Squirrel HT2 (G-BXMD) [44]	School of Army Aviation/No 670 Sqn, Middle Wallop
	ZJ245	AS350BA Squirrel HT2 (G-BXME) [45]	School of Army Aviation/No 670 Sqn, Middle Wallop
	ZJ246	AS350BA Squirrel HT2 (G-BXMJ) [46]	School of Army Aviation/No 670 Sqn, Middle Wallop
	ZJ248	AS350BA Squirrel HT2 (G-BXNE) [48]	School of Army Aviation/No 670 Sqn, Middle Wallop
	ZJ249	AS350BA Squirrel HT2 (G-BXNJ) [49]	School of Army Aviation/No 670 Sqn, Middle Wallop
	ZJ250	AS350BA Squirrel HT2 (G-BXNY) [50]	School of Army Aviation/No 670 Sqn, Middle Wallop
	ZJ251	AS350BA Squirrel HT2 (G-BXOG) [51]	School of Army Aviation/No 670 Sqn, Middle Wallop
	ZJ252	AS350BA Squirrel HT2 (G-BXOK) [52]	School of Army Aviation/No 670 Sqn, Middle Wallop
	ZJ253	AS350BA Squirrel HT2 (G-BXPG) [53]	School of Army Aviation/No 670 Sqn, Middle Wallop
	ZJ254	AS350BA Squirrel HT2 (G-BXPJ) [54]	School of Army Aviation/No 670 Sqn, Middle Wallop
	ZJ255	AS350BB Squirrel HT1 (G-BXAG) [55]	DHFS, RAF Shawbury
	ZJ256	AS350BB Squirrel HT1 (G-BXCE) [56]	DHFS, RAF Shawbury
	ZJ257	AS350BB Squirrel HT1 (G-BXDJ) [57]	DHFS, RAF Shawbury
	ZJ258	AS350BB Squirrel HT1 (G-BXEO) [58]	RAF Shawbury (wreck)
	ZJ260	AS350BB Squirrel HT1 (G-BXGB) [60]	DHFS, RAF Shawbury
	ZJ261	AS350BB Squirrel HT1 (G-BXGJ) [61]	DHFS, RAF Shawbury
	ZJ262	AS350BB Squirrel HT1 (G-BXHB) [62]	DHFS, RAF Shawbury
	ZJ264	AS350BB Squirrel HT1 (G-BXHW) [64]	DHFS, RAF Shawbury
	ZJ265	AS350BB Squirrel HT1 (G-BXHX) [65]	DHFS, RAF Shawbury
	ZJ266	AS350BB Squirrel HT1 (G-BXIL) [66]	DHFS, RAF Shawbury
	ZJ267	AS350BB Squirrel HT1 (G-BXIP) [67]	DHFS, RAF Shawbury
	ZJ268	AS350BB Squirrel HT1 (G-BXJE) [68]	DHFS, RAF Shawbury
	ZJ269	AS350BB Squirrel HT1 (G-BXJN) [69]	DHFS, RAF Shawbury

Serial	Type (code/other identity)	Owner/operator location or fate	Notes
ZJ270	AS350BB Squirrel HT1 (G-BXJR) [70]	DHFS, RAF Shawbury	
ZJ271	AS350BB Squirrel HT1 (G-BXKE) [71]	DHFS, RAF Shawbury	
ZJ272	AS350BB Squirrel HT1 (G-BXKN) [72]	DHFS, RAF Shawbury	
ZJ273	AS350BB Squirrel HT1 (G-BXKP) [73]	DHFS, RAF Shawbury	
ZJ274	AS350BB Squirrel HT1 (G-BXKR) [74]	DHFS, RAF Shawbury	
ZJ275	AS350BB Squirrel HT1 (G-BXLB) [75]	DHFS, RAF Shawbury	
ZJ276	AS350BB Squirrel HT1 (G-BXLE) [76]	DHFS, RAF Shawbury	
ZJ277	AS350BB Squirrel HT1 (G-BXLH) [77]	DHFS, RAF Shawbury	
ZJ278	AS350BB Squirrel HT1 (G-BXMB) [78]	DHFS, RAF Shawbury	
ZJ279	AS350BB Squirrel HT1 (G-BXMC) [79]	DHFS, RAF Shawbury	
ZJ280	AS350BB Squirrel HT1 (G-BXMI) [80]	DHFS, RAF Shawbury	
ZJ369	GEC Phoenix UAV	Defence Academy of the UK, Shrivenham	
ZJ385	GEC Phoenix UAV	Muckleburgh Collection, Weybourne, Norfolk	
ZJ449	GEC Phoenix UAV	REME Museum, Arborfield	
ZJ452	GEC Phoenix UAV	Science Museum, Wroughton	
ZJ489	GAF Jindivik 800 (A92-809)	Caernarfon Air World	
ZJ493	GAF Jindivik 800 (A92-814)	RAF Stafford	
ZJ496	GAF Jindivik 900 (A92-901)	Farnborough Air Sciences Trust, Farnborough	
ZJ514	BAE Systems Nimrod MRA4 (XV251) [PA-4] [A]	*Scrapped at Warton, February 2011*	
ZJ515	BAE Systems Nimrod MRA4 (XV258) <ff>	Cranfield University, instructional use	
ZJ516	BAE Systems Nimrod MRA4 (XV247) [PA-1]	*Scrapped at Woodford, March 2011*	
ZJ518	BAE Systems Nimrod MRA4 (XV234) [PA-2]	*Scrapped at Woodford, March 2011*	
ZJ519	BAE Systems Nimrod MRA4 (XZ284) [PA-6]	*Scrapped at Woodford, February 2011*	
ZJ520	BAE Systems Nimrod MRA4 (XV233) [PA-7]	*Scrapped at Woodford, February 2011*	
ZJ521	BAE Systems Nimrod MRA4 (XV227) [PA-8]	*Scrapped at Woodford, February 2011*	
ZJ523	BAE Systems Nimrod MRA4 (XV228) [PA-10]	*Scrapped at Woodford, February 2011*	
ZJ645	D-BD Alpha Jet (98+62) [45]	MoD/AFD/QinetiQ, Boscombe Down	
ZJ646	D-BD Alpha Jet (98+55) [46]	MoD/AFD/QinetiQ, Boscombe Down	
ZJ647	D-BD Alpha Jet (98+71) [47]	MoD/AFD/QinetiQ, Boscombe Down	
ZJ648	D-BD Alpha Jet (98+09) [48]	MoD/AFD/QinetiQ, Boscombe Down	
ZJ649	D-BD Alpha Jet (98+73) [49]	MoD/ETPS, Boscombe Down	
ZJ650	D-BD Alpha Jet (98+35)	MoD/QinetiQ, stored Boscombe Down	
ZJ651	D-BD Alpha Jet (41+42) [51]	MoD/ETPS, Boscombe Down	
ZJ652	D-BD Alpha Jet (41+09)	MoD/QinetiQ Boscombe Down, spares use	
ZJ653	D-BD Alpha Jet (40+22)	MoD/QinetiQ Boscombe Down, spares use	
ZJ654	D-BD Alpha Jet (41+02)	MoD/QinetiQ Boscombe Down, spares use	
ZJ655	D-BD Alpha Jet (41+19)	MoD/QinetiQ Boscombe Down, spares use	
ZJ656	D-BD Alpha Jet (41+40)	MoD/QinetiQ Boscombe Down, spares use	
ZJ690	Bombardier Sentinel R1 (C-GJRG)	RAF No 5 Sqn, Waddington	
ZJ691	Bombardier Sentinel R1 (C-FZVM)	RAF No 5 Sqn, Waddington	
ZJ692	Bombardier Sentinel R1 (C-FZWW)	RAF No 5 Sqn, Waddington	
ZJ693	Bombardier Sentinel R1 (C-FZXC)	RAF No 5 Sqn, Waddington	
ZJ694	Bombardier Sentinel R1 (C-FZYL)	RAF No 5 Sqn, Waddington	
ZJ699	Eurofighter Typhoon (PT001)	MoD/BAE Systems, Warton	
ZJ700	Eurofighter Typhoon (PS002)	MoD/BAE Systems, Warton	
ZJ703	Bell 412EP Griffin HAR2 (G-CBST) [Spades,3]	DHFS No 60(R) Sqn/SARTU, RAF Valley	
ZJ704	Bell 412EP Griffin HAR2 (G-CBWT) [Clubs,4]	RAF No 84 Sqn, Akrotiri	
ZJ705	Bell 412EP Griffin HAR2 (G-CBXL) [Hearts,5]	RAF No 84 Sqn, Akrotiri	
ZJ706	Bell 412EP Griffin HAR2 (G-CBYR) [Diamonds,6]	RAF No 84 Sqn, Akrotiri	
ZJ707	Bell 412EP Griffin HT1 (G-CBUB) [O]	DHFS No 60(R) Sqn, RAF Shawbury	
ZJ708	Bell 412EP Griffin HT1 (G-CBVP) [K]	DHFS No 60(R) Sqn, RAF Shawbury	
ZJ780	AS365N-3 Dauphin II (G-CEXT)	AAC No 8 Flt, Credenhill	
ZJ781	AS365N-3 Dauphin II (G-CEXU)	AAC No 8 Flt, Credenhill	

89

Notes	Serial	Type (code/other identity)	Owner/operator location or fate
	ZJ782	AS365N-3 Dauphin II (G-CEXV)	AAC No 8 Flt, Credenhill
	ZJ783	AS365N-3 Dauphin II (G-CEXW)	AAC No 8 Flt, Credenhill
	ZJ785	AS365N-3 Dauphin II (G-CFFW)	AAC No 8 Flt, Credenhill'
	ZJ800	Eurofighter Typhoon T3 [BC]	RAF No 29(R) Sqn, Coningsby
	ZJ801	Eurofighter Typhoon T3 [BJ]	RAF No 29(R) Sqn, Coningsby
	ZJ802	Eurofighter Typhoon T3 [QO-B]	RAF No 3 Sqn, Coningsby
	ZJ803	Eurofighter Typhoon T3 [BA]	RAF TMF, Coningsby
	ZJ804	Eurofighter Typhoon T3 [BM]	RAF No 29(R) Sqn, Coningsby
	ZJ805	Eurofighter Typhoon T3 [BD]	MoD/BAE Systems, Warton (conversion)
	ZJ806	Eurofighter Typhoon T3 [BE]	RAF No 29(R) Sqn, Coningsby
	ZJ807	Eurofighter Typhoon T3 [BF]	MoD/BAE Systems, Warton (conversion)
	ZJ808	Eurofighter Typhoon T3 [DW]	RAF No 11 Sqn, Coningsby
	ZJ809	Eurofighter Typhoon T3 [BH]	RAF No 29(R) Sqn, Coningsby
	ZJ810	Eurofighter Typhoon T3 [BI]	MoD/BAE Systems, Warton (conversion)
	ZJ811	Eurofighter Typhoon T3 [BP]	RAF No 29(R) Sqn, Coningsby
	ZJ812	Eurofighter Typhoon T3 [BK]	RAF No 29(R) Sqn, Coningsby
	ZJ813	Eurofighter Typhoon T3 [BL]	RAF No 29(R) Sqn, Coningsby
	ZJ814	Eurofighter Typhoon T3 [QO-Z]	MoD/BAE Systems, Warton (conversion)
	ZJ815	Eurofighter Typhoon T3 [BN]	RAF No 29(R) Sqn, Coningsby
	ZJ910	Eurofighter Typhoon FGR4 [BV]	RAF No 29(R) Sqn, Coningsby
	ZJ911	Eurofighter Typhoon FGR4 [BZ]	RAF TMF, Coningsby
	ZJ912	Eurofighter Typhoon FGR4 [AB]	RAF No 17(R) Sqn, Coningsby
	ZJ913	Eurofighter Typhoon FGR4 [AC]	RAF TMF, Coningsby
	ZJ914	Eurofighter Typhoon FGR4 [AF]	RAF No 17(R) Sqn, Coningsby
	ZJ915	Eurofighter Typhoon FGR4 [BY]	RAF No 29(R) Sqn, Coningsby
	ZJ916	Eurofighter Typhoon FGR4 [QO-U]	RAF No 3 Sqn, Coningsby
	ZJ917	Eurofighter Typhoon FGR4 [QO-G]	RAF No 3 Sqn, Coningsby
	ZJ918	Eurofighter Typhoon FGR4 [QO-L]	RAF No 3 Sqn, Coningsby
	ZJ919	Eurofighter Typhoon FGR4 [DC]	RAF No 11 Sqn, Coningsby
	ZJ920	Eurofighter Typhoon FGR4 [QO-A]	RAF No 3 Sqn, Coningsby
	ZJ921	Eurofighter Typhoon FGR4 [QO-H]	RAF No 3 Sqn, Coningsby
	ZJ922	Eurofighter Typhoon FGR4 [QO-C]	RAF No 3 Sqn, Coningsby
	ZJ923	Eurofighter Typhoon FGR4 [DM]	RAF No 11 Sqn, Coningsby
	ZJ924	Eurofighter Typhoon FGR4 [DD]	RAF No 11 Sqn, Coningsby
	ZJ925	Eurofighter Typhoon FGR4 [QO-R]	RAF No 3 Sqn, Coningsby
	ZJ926	Eurofighter Typhoon FGR4 [QO-Y]	RAF No 3 Sqn, Coningsby
	ZJ927	Eurofighter Typhoon FGR4 [QO-M]	RAF No 3 Sqn, Coningsby
	ZJ928	Eurofighter Typhoon FGR4 [BX]	RAF No 29(R) Sqn, Coningsby
	ZJ929	Eurofighter Typhoon FGR4 [DL]	MoD/BAE Systems, Warton
	ZJ930	Eurofighter Typhoon FGR4 [AA]	RAF No 17(R) Sqn, Coningsby
	ZJ931	Eurofighter Typhoon FGR4 [DA]	MoD/BAE Systems, Warton (conversion)
	ZJ932	Eurofighter Typhoon FGR4 [DB]	RAF No 11 Sqn, Coningsby
	ZJ933	Eurofighter Typhoon FGR4 [DF]	RAF No 11 Sqn, Coningsby
	ZJ934	Eurofighter Typhoon FGR4 [QO-T]	MoD/BAE Systems, Warton (conversion)
	ZJ935	Eurofighter Typhoon FGR4 [DJ]	RAF No 11 Sqn, Coningsby
	ZJ936	Eurofighter Typhoon F2 [QO-S]	RAF No 29(R) Sqn, Coningsby
	ZJ937	Eurofighter Typhoon FGR4 [QO-W]	MoD/BAE Systems, Warton (conversion)
	ZJ938	Eurofighter Typhoon FGR4	MoD/BAE Systems, Warton
	ZJ939	Eurofighter Typhoon FGR4 [DXI]	RAF No 11 Sqn, Coningsby
	ZJ940	Eurofighter Typhoon FGR4	RAF, stored Coningsby
	ZJ941	Eurofighter Typhoon FGR4 [QO-J]	RAF No 3 Sqn, Coningsby
	ZJ942	Eurofighter Typhoon FGR4 [DH]	RAF No 11 Sqn, Coningsby
	ZJ943	Eurofighter Typhoon FGR4 [DK]	RAF, stored Coningsby (wreck)
	ZJ944	Eurofighter Typhoon FGR4 [F]	RAF No 1435 Flt, Mount Pleasant, FI
	ZJ945	Eurofighter Typhoon FGR4	RAF, stored Coningsby
	ZJ946	Eurofighter Typhoon FGR4 [AG]	RAF No 17(R) Sqn, Coningsby
	ZJ947	Eurofighter Typhoon FGR4 [AH]	RAF No 17(R) Sqn, Coningsby
	ZJ948	Eurofighter Typhoon FGR4	RAF, stored Coningsby

Serial	Type (code/other identity)	Owner/operator location or fate	Notes
ZJ949	Eurofighter Typhoon FGR4 [H]	RAF No 1435 Flt, Mount Pleasant, FI	
ZJ950	Eurofighter Typhoon FGR4 [C]	RAF No 1435 Flt, Mount Pleasant, FI	
ZJ951	BAE Systems Hawk 120D	MoD/BAE Systems, stored Brough	
ZJ954	SA330H Puma HC2 (SAAF 144)	MoD/Eurocopter, Marseilles, France (conversion)	
ZJ955	SA330H Puma HC1 (SAAF 148)	RAF No 33 Sqn/No 230 Sqn, Benson	
ZJ956	SA330H Puma HC2 (SAAF 172)	MoD/Eurocopter, Brasov, Romania (conversion)	
ZJ957	SA330H Puma HC2 (SAAF 169)	MoD/Eurocopter, Marseilles, France (conversion)	
ZJ958	SA330H Puma (SAAF 173)	DE&S, stored Bicester	
ZJ959	SA330H Puma (SAAF 184)	DE&S, stored Bicester	
ZJ960	Grob G109B Vigilant T1 (D-KSMU) [SH]	RAF No 642 VGS, Linton-on-Ouse	
ZJ961	Grob G109B Vigilant T1 (D-KLCW) [SJ]	RAF ACCGS/No 644 VGS, Syerston	
ZJ962	Grob G109B Vigilant T1 (D-KBEU) [SK]	RAF No 634 VGS, St Athan	
ZJ963	Grob G109B Vigilant T1 (D-KMSN) [SL]	RAF No 635 VGS, Topcliffe	
ZJ964	Bell 212HP AH2 (G-BJGV) [A]	AAC No 25 Flt, Middle Wallop	
ZJ966	Bell 212HP AH2 (G-BJJO) [C]	AAC No 25 Flt, Middle Wallop	
ZJ967	Grob G109B Vigilant T1 (G-DEWS) [SM]	RAF No 612 VGS, Abingdon	
ZJ968	Grob G109B Vigilant T1 (N109BT) [SN]	RAF No 631 VGS, Woodvale	
ZJ969	Bell 212HP AH1 (G-BGLJ) [K]	AAC No 25 Flt, Middle Wallop	
ZJ990	EHI-101 Merlin HC3A (M-501) [AA]	RAF No 28 Sqn/No 78 Sqn, Benson	
ZJ992	EHI-101 Merlin HC3A (M-503) [AB]	RAF No 28 Sqn/No 78 Sqn, Benson	
ZJ994	EHI-101 Merlin HC3A (M-505) [AC]	RAF No 28 Sqn/No 78 Sqn, Benson	
ZJ995	EHI-101 Merlin HC3A (M-506) [AD]	RAF No 28 Sqn/No 78 Sqn, Benson	
ZJ998	EHI-101 Merlin HC3A (M-509) [AE]	RAF No 28 Sqn/No 78 Sqn, Benson	
ZK001	EHI-101 Merlin HC3A (M-511) [AF]	RAF MDMF, RNAS Culdrose	
ZK005	Grob G109B Vigilant T1 (OH-797) [SP]	RAF CGMF, Syerston	
ZK010	BAE Systems Hawk T2	RAF No 4 FTS/4(R) Sqn, Valley	
ZK011	BAE Systems Hawk T2	RAF No 4 FTS/4(R) Sqn, Valley	
ZK012	BAE Systems Hawk T2 [C]	RAF No 4 FTS/4(R) Sqn, Valley	
ZK013	BAE Systems Hawk T2	RAF No 4 FTS/4(R) Sqn, Valley	
ZK014	BAE Systems Hawk T2	RAF No 4 FTS/4(R) Sqn, Valley	
ZK015	BAE Systems Hawk T2	RAF No 4 FTS/4(R) Sqn, Valley	
ZK016	BAE Systems Hawk T2	RAF No 4 FTS/4(R) Sqn, Valley	
ZK017	BAE Systems Hawk T2	MoD/BAE Systems, Warton	
ZK018	BAE Systems Hawk T2	MoD/BAE Systems, Warton	
ZK019	BAE Systems Hawk T2	RAF No 4 FTS/4(R) Sqn, Valley	
ZK020	BAE Systems Hawk T2	MoD/BAE Systems, Warton	
ZK021	BAE Systems Hawk T2	MoD/BAE Systems, Warton	
ZK022	BAE Systems Hawk T2 [M]	RAF No 4 FTS/4(R) Sqn, Valley	
ZK023	BAE Systems Hawk T2	RAF No 4 FTS/4(R) Sqn, Valley	
ZK024	BAE Systems Hawk T2	RAF No 4 FTS/4(R) Sqn, Valley	
ZK025	BAE Systems Hawk T2 [P]	RAF No 4 FTS/4(R) Sqn, Valley	
ZK026	BAE Systems Hawk T2	RAF No 4 FTS/4(R) Sqn, Valley	
ZK027	BAE Systems Hawk T2	RAF No 4 FTS/4(R) Sqn, Valley	
ZK028	BAE Systems Hawk T2	RAF No 4 FTS/4(R) Sqn, Valley	
ZK029	BAE Systems Hawk T2	RAF No 4 FTS/4(R) Sqn, Valley	
ZK030	BAE Systems Hawk T2	MoD/BAE Systems, Warton	
ZK031	BAE Systems Hawk T2	RAF No 4 FTS/4(R) Sqn, Valley	
ZK032	BAE Systems Hawk T2	RAF No 4 FTS/4(R) Sqn, Valley	
ZK033	BAE Systems Hawk T2	RAF No 4 FTS/4(R) Sqn, Valley	
ZK034	BAE Systems Hawk T2	RAF No 4 FTS/4(R) Sqn, Valley	
ZK035	BAE Systems Hawk T2	RAF No 4 FTS/4(R) Sqn, Valley	
ZK036	BAE Systems Hawk T2	RAF No 4 FTS/4(R) Sqn, Valley	
ZK037	BAE Systems Hawk T2	RAF No 4 FTS/4(R) Sqn, Valley	
ZK045	BAE Systems Hawk T2	Reservation for RAF	
ZK046	BAE Systems Hawk T2	Reservation for RAF	
ZK047	BAE Systems Hawk T2	Reservation for RAF	
ZK048	BAE Systems Hawk T2	Reservation for RAF	

Notes	Serial	Type (code/other identity)	Owner/operator location or fate
	ZK049	BAE Systems Hawk T2	Reservation for RAF
	ZK050	BAE Systems Hawk T2	Reservation for RAF
	ZK051	BAE Systems Hawk T2	Reservation for RAF
	ZK052	BAE Systems Hawk T2	Reservation for RAF
	ZK053	BAE Systems Hawk T2	Reservation for RAF
	ZK054	BAE Systems Hawk T2	Reservation for RAF
	ZK055	BAE Systems Hawk T2	Reservation for RAF
	ZK056	BAE Systems Hawk T2	Reservation for RAF
	ZK057	BAE Systems Hawk T2	Reservation for RAF
	ZK058	BAE Systems Hawk T2	Reservation for RAF
	ZK059	BAE Systems Hawk T2	Reservation for RAF
	ZK067	Bell 212HP AH3 (G-BFER)	AAC JHC/No 7 Regt, Middle Wallop
	ZK079	Eurofighter Typhoon	*To R Saudi AF as 311, 31 March 2011*
	ZK080	Eurofighter Typhoon	*To R Saudi AF as 312, 31 March 2011*
	ZK081	Eurofighter Typhoon	*To R Saudi AF as 313, 29 June 2011*
	ZK082	Eurofighter Typhoon	*To R Saudi AF as 314, 29 June 2011*
	ZK083	Eurofighter Typhoon	*To R Saudi AF as 315, 22 September 2011*
	ZK084	Eurofighter Typhoon	*To R Saudi AF as 316, 22 September 2011*
	ZK113	Panavia Tornado IDS (RSAF 6606)	MoD/BAE Systems, Warton
	ZK114	M2370 UAV	QinetiQ
	ZK119	Pilatus PC-9 (HB-HQU/RSAF 2204)	MoD/BAE Systems, Warton
	ZK120*	Lockheed Martin Desert Hawk DH1+ UAV	Army
	ZK150*	Lockheed Martin Desert Hawk UAV	Army
	ZK155*	Honeywell T-Hawk UAV	Army
	ZK182	AgustaWestland Super Lynx Mk.130	*To Algeria as AN08, 10 February 2011*
	ZK184	AgustaWestland Super Lynx Mk.130	AgustaWestland, for Algeria as AN10
	ZK205	Grob G109B Vigilant T1 (D-KBRU) [SS]	RAF No 624 VGS, Chivenor RMB
	ZK206	Bell 212EP AH2 (G-CFXE) [A]	AAC JHC/No 7 Regt, Middle Wallop
	ZK210	BAE Systems Mantis UAV	MoD/BAE Systems, Warton
	ZK300	Eurofighter Typhoon FGR4 [EJ]	RAF No 6 Sqn, Leuchars
	ZK301	Eurofighter Typhoon FGR4 [D]	RAF No 1435 Flt, Mount Pleasant, FI
	ZK302	Eurofighter Typhoon FGR4 [EA]	RAF No 6 Sqn, Leuchars
	ZK303	Eurofighter Typhoon T3 [AX]	MoD/BAE Systems, Warton
	ZK304	Eurofighter Typhoon FGR4 [EB]	RAF No 6 Sqn, Leuchars
	ZK305	Eurofighter Typhoon FGR4 [DE]	RAF No 11 Sqn, Coningsby
	ZK306	Eurofighter Typhoon FGR4 [BT]	RAF No 29(R) Sqn, Coningsby
	ZK307	Eurofighter Typhoon FGR4 [BU]	RAF No 29(R) Sqn, Coningsby
	ZK308	Eurofighter Typhoon FGR4 [BW]	RAF No 29(R) Sqn, Coningsby
	ZK309	Eurofighter Typhoon FGR4 [Q-OP]	RAF No 3 Sqn, Coningsby
	ZK310	Eurofighter Typhoon FGR4 [EL]	RAF No 6 Sqn, Leuchars
	ZK311	Eurofighter Typhoon FGR4 [EK]	RAF No 6 Sqn, Leuchars
	ZK312	Eurofighter Typhoon FGR4 [EM]	RAF No 6 Sqn, Leuchars
	ZK313	Eurofighter Typhoon FGR4 [EN]	RAF No 6 Sqn, Leuchars
	ZK314	Eurofighter Typhoon FGR4 [EO]	RAF No 6 Sqn, Leuchars
	ZK315	Eurofighter Typhoon FGR4	MoD/BAE Systems, Warton
	ZK316	Eurofighter Typhoon FGR4 [ER]	RAF No 6 Sqn, Leuchars
	ZK317	Eurofighter Typhoon FGR4 [ES]	RAF No 6 Sqn, Leuchars
	ZK318	Eurofighter Typhoon FGR4 [ET]	RAF No 6 Sqn, Leuchars
	ZK319	Eurofighter Typhoon FGR4 [EW]	RAF No 6 Sqn, Leuchars
	ZK320	Eurofighter Typhoon FGR4 [EV]	RAF No 6 Sqn, Leuchars
	ZK321	Eurofighter Typhoon FGR4 [EU]	RAF No 6 Sqn, Leuchars
	ZK322	Eurofighter Typhoon FGR4 [EZ]	RAF No 6 Sqn, Leuchars
	ZK323	Eurofighter Typhoon FGR4 [EH]	RAF No 6 Sqn, Leuchars
	ZK324	Eurofighter Typhoon FGR4 [EI]	RAF No 6 Sqn, Leuchars
	ZK325	Eurofighter Typhoon FGR4 [EQ]	RAF No 6 Sqn, Leuchars
	ZK326	Eurofighter Typhoon FGR4 [EP]	RAF No 6 Sqn, Leuchars
	ZK327	Eurofighter Typhoon FGR4	RAF TMF, Coningsby
	ZK328	Eurofighter Typhoon FGR4 [BS]	RAF No 29(R) Sqn, Coningsby

Serial	Type (code/other identity)	Owner/operator location or fate	Notes
ZK329	Eurofighter Typhoon FGR4	MoD/BAE Systems, Warton	
ZK330	Eurofighter Typhoon FGR4	MoD/BAE Systems, Warton	
ZK331	Eurofighter Typhoon FGR4	MoD/BAE Systems, Warton	
ZK332	Eurofighter Typhoon FGR4	MoD/BAE Systems, Warton	
ZK333	Eurofighter Typhoon FGR4	MoD/BAE Systems, Warton	
ZK334	Eurofighter Typhoon FGR4	MoD/BAE Systems, Warton	
ZK335	Eurofighter Typhoon FGR4	MoD/BAE Systems, Warton	
ZK336	Eurofighter Typhoon FGR4	MoD/BAE Systems, Warton	
ZK337	Eurofighter Typhoon FGR4	MoD/BAE Systems, Warton	
ZK338	Eurofighter Typhoon FGR4	MoD/BAE Systems, Warton	
ZK379	Eurofighter Typhoon T3 [EX]	RAF No 6 Sqn, Leuchars	
ZK380	Eurofighter Typhoon T3	RAF, stored Coningsby	
ZK381	Eurofighter Typhoon T3	MoD/BAE Systems, Warton	
ZK382	Eurofighter Typhoon T3	MoD/BAE Systems, Warton	
ZK383	Eurofighter Typhoon T3	MoD/BAE Systems, Warton	
ZK450	Beech King Air B200 (G-RAFJ) [J]	SERCO/RAF No 3 FTS/45(R) Sqn, Cranwell	
ZK451	Beech King Air B200 (G-RAFK) [K]	SERCO/RAF No 3 FTS/45(R) Sqn, Cranwell	
ZK452	Beech King Air B200 (G-RAFL) [L]	SERCO/RAF No 3 FTS/45(R) Sqn, Cranwell	
ZK453	Beech King Air B200 (G-RAFM) [M]	SERCO/RAF No 3 FTS/45(R) Sqn, Cranwell	
ZK454	Beech King Air B200 (G-RAFN) [N]	SERCO/RAF No 3 FTS/45(R) Sqn, Cranwell	
ZK455	Beech King Air B200 (G-RAFO) [O]	SERCO/RAF No 3 FTS/45(R) Sqn, Cranwell	
ZK456	Beech King Air B200 (G-RAFP) [P]	SERCO/RAF No 3 FTS/45(R) Sqn, Cranwell	
ZK457	Beech King Air B200 (G-ROWN)	MoD/Foreign & Commonwealth Office, Afghanistan	
ZK458	Hawker Beechcraft King Air B200GT (G-RAFD) [D]	SERCO/RAF No 3 FTS/45(R) Sqn, Cranwell	
ZK459	Hawker Beechcraft King Air B200GT (G-RAFX) [X]	SERCO/RAF No 3 FTS/45(R) Sqn, Cranwell	
ZK460	Hawker Beechcraft King Air B200GT (G-RAFU) [U]	SERCO/RAF No 3 FTS/45(R) Sqn, Cranwell	
ZK501	Elbit Hermes 450 UAV	Army 32 Regt Royal Artillery, Larkhill	
ZK502	Elbit Hermes 450 UAV	Army 32 Regt Royal Artillery, Larkhill	
ZK503	Elbit Hermes 450 UAV	Army 32 Regt Royal Artillery, Larkhill	
ZK504	Elbit Hermes 450 UAV	Army 32 Regt Royal Artillery, Larkhill	
ZK505	Elbit Hermes 450 UAV	Army 32 Regt Royal Artillery, Larkhill	
ZK506	Elbit Hermes 450 UAV	Army 32 Regt Royal Artillery, Larkhill	
ZK507	Elbit Hermes 450 UAV	Army 32 Regt Royal Artillery, Larkhill	
ZK508	Elbit Hermes 450 UAV	Army 32 Regt Royal Artillery, Larkhill	
ZK509	Elbit Hermes 450 UAV	Army 32 Regt Royal Artillery, Larkhill	
ZK510	Elbit Hermes 450 UAV	Army 32 Regt Royal Artillery, Larkhill	
ZK511	Elbit Hermes 450 UAV	Army 32 Regt Royal Artillery, Larkhill	
ZK512	Elbit Hermes 450 UAV	Army 32 Regt Royal Artillery, Larkhill	
ZK513	Elbit Hermes 450 UAV	Army 32 Regt Royal Artillery, Larkhill	
ZK514	Elbit Hermes 450 UAV	Army 32 Regt Royal Artillery, Larkhill	
ZK515	Elbit Hermes 450 UAV	Army 32 Regt Royal Artillery, Larkhill	
ZK516	Elbit Hermes 450 UAV	Army 32 Regt Royal Artillery, Larkhill	
ZK517	Elbit Hermes 450 UAV	Army 32 Regt Royal Artillery, Larkhill	
ZK518	Elbit Hermes 450 UAV	Army 32 Regt Royal Artillery, Larkhill	
ZK519	Elbit Hermes 450 UAV	Army 32 Regt Royal Artillery, Larkhill	
ZK520	Elbit Hermes 450 UAV	Army 32 Regt Royal Artillery, Larkhill	
ZK521	Elbit Hermes 450 UAV	Army 32 Regt Royal Artillery, Larkhill	
ZK522	Elbit Hermes 450 UAV	Army 32 Regt Royal Artillery, Larkhill	
ZK523	Elbit Hermes 450 UAV	Army 32 Regt Royal Artillery, Larkhill	
ZK524	Elbit Hermes 450 UAV	Army 32 Regt Royal Artillery, Larkhill	
ZK525	Elbit Hermes 450 UAV	Army 32 Regt Royal Artillery, Larkhill	
ZK531	BAe Hawk T53 (LL-5306)	MoD/BAE Systems, stored Brough	
ZK532	BAe Hawk T53 (LL-5315)	MoD/BAE Systems, stored Brough	
ZK533	BAe Hawk T53 (LL-5317)	Aircraft Maintenance Training Academy, Doncaster	
ZK534	BAe Hawk T53 (LL-5319)	BAE Systems, Brough, systems rig	

Notes	Serial	Type (code/other identity)	Owner/operator location or fate
	ZK535	BAe Hawk T53 (LL-5320)	Aircraft Maintenance Training Academy, Doncaster
	ZK550	Boeing Chinook HC6	Boeing, for RAF
	ZK551	Boeing Chinook HC6	Boeing, for RAF
	ZK552	Boeing Chinook HC6	Boeing, for RAF
	ZK553	Boeing Chinook HC6	Boeing, for RAF
	ZK554	Boeing Chinook HC6	Boeing, for RAF
	ZK555	Boeing Chinook HC6	Boeing, for RAF
	ZK556	Boeing Chinook HC6	Boeing, for RAF
	ZK557	Boeing Chinook HC6	Boeing, for RAF
	ZK558	Boeing Chinook HC6	Boeing, for RAF
	ZK559	Boeing Chinook HC6	Boeing, for RAF
	ZK560	Boeing Chinook HC6	Boeing, for RAF
	ZK561	Boeing Chinook HC6	Boeing, for RAF
	ZK562	Boeing Chinook HC6	Boeing, for RAF
	ZK563	Boeing Chinook HC6	Boeing, for RAF
	ZM135	Lockheed Martin F-35C Lightning II	Reservation for RAF/RN
	ZM136	Lockheed Martin F-35C Lightning II	Reservation for RAF/RN
	ZM137	Lockheed Martin F-35C Lightning II	Reservation for RAF/RN
	ZM138	Lockheed Martin F-35C Lightning II	Reservation for RAF/RN
	ZM139	Lockheed Martin F-35C Lightning II	Reservation for RAF/RN
	ZM140	Lockheed Martin F-35C Lightning II	Reservation for RAF/RN
	ZM141	Lockheed Martin F-35C Lightning II	Reservation for RAF/RN
	ZM142	Lockheed Martin F-35C Lightning II	Reservation for RAF/RN
	ZM143	Lockheed Martin F-35C Lightning II	Reservation for RAF/RN
	ZM144	Lockheed Martin F-35C Lightning II	Reservation for RAF/RN
	ZM145	Lockheed Martin F-35C Lightning II	Reservation for RAF/RN
	ZM146	Lockheed Martin F-35C Lightning II	Reservation for RAF/RN
	ZM147	Lockheed Martin F-35C Lightning II	Reservation for RAF/RN
	ZM148	Lockheed Martin F-35C Lightning II	Reservation for RAF/RN
	ZM149	Lockheed Martin F-35C Lightning II	Reservation for RAF/RN
	ZM150	Lockheed Martin F-35C Lightning II	Reservation for RAF/RN
	ZM151	Lockheed Martin F-35C Lightning II	Reservation for RAF/RN
	ZM152	Lockheed Martin F-35C Lightning II	Reservation for RAF/RN
	ZM153	Lockheed Martin F-35C Lightning II	Reservation for RAF/RN
	ZM154	Lockheed Martin F-35C Lightning II	Reservation for RAF/RN
	ZM155	Lockheed Martin F-35C Lightning II	Reservation for RAF/RN
	ZM156	Lockheed Martin F-35C Lightning II	Reservation for RAF/RN
	ZM157	Lockheed Martin F-35C Lightning II	Reservation for RAF/RN
	ZM158	Lockheed Martin F-35C Lightning II	Reservation for RAF/RN
	ZM159	Lockheed Martin F-35C Lightning II	Reservation for RAF/RN
	ZM160	Lockheed Martin F-35C Lightning II	Reservation for RAF/RN
	ZM161	Lockheed Martin F-35C Lightning II	Reservation for RAF/RN
	ZM162	Lockheed Martin F-35C Lightning II	Reservation for RAF/RN
	ZM163	Lockheed Martin F-35C Lightning II	Reservation for RAF/RN
	ZM164	Lockheed Martin F-35C Lightning II	Reservation for RAF/RN
	ZM165	Lockheed Martin F-35C Lightning II	Reservation for RAF/RN
	ZM166	Lockheed Martin F-35C Lightning II	Reservation for RAF/RN
	ZM167	Lockheed Martin F-35C Lightning II	Reservation for RAF/RN
	ZM168	Lockheed Martin F-35C Lightning II	Reservation for RAF/RN
	ZM169	Lockheed Martin F-35C Lightning II	Reservation for RAF/RN
	ZM170	Lockheed Martin F-35C Lightning II	Reservation for RAF/RN
	ZM171	Lockheed Martin F-35C Lightning II	Reservation for RAF/RN
	ZM172	Lockheed Martin F-35C Lightning II	Reservation for RAF/RN
	ZM173	Lockheed Martin F-35C Lightning II	Reservation for RAF/RN
	ZM174	Lockheed Martin F-35C Lightning II	Reservation for RAF/RN
	ZM175	Lockheed Martin F-35C Lightning II	Reservation for RAF/RN
	ZM176	Lockheed Martin F-35C Lightning II	Reservation for RAF/RN

Serial	Type (code/other identity)	Owner/operator location or fate	Notes
ZM177	Lockheed Martin F-35C Lightning II	Reservation for RAF/RN	
ZM178	Lockheed Martin F-35C Lightning II	Reservation for RAF/RN	
ZM179	Lockheed Martin F-35C Lightning II	Reservation for RAF/RN	
ZM180	Lockheed Martin F-35C Lightning II	Reservation for RAF/RN	
ZM181	Lockheed Martin F-35C Lightning II	Reservation for RAF/RN	
ZM182	Lockheed Martin F-35C Lightning II	Reservation for RAF/RN	
ZM183	Lockheed Martin F-35C Lightning II	Reservation for RAF/RN	
ZM184	Lockheed Martin F-35C Lightning II	Reservation for RAF/RN	
ZM185	Lockheed Martin F-35C Lightning II	Reservation for RAF/RN	
ZM186	Lockheed Martin F-35C Lightning II	Reservation for RAF/RN	
ZM187	Lockheed Martin F-35C Lightning II	Reservation for RAF/RN	
ZM188	Lockheed Martin F-35C Lightning II	Reservation for RAF/RN	
ZM189	Lockheed Martin F-35C Lightning II	Reservation for RAF/RN	
ZM190	Lockheed Martin F-35C Lightning II	Reservation for RAF/RN	
ZM191	Lockheed Martin F-35C Lightning II	Reservation for RAF/RN	
ZM192	Lockheed Martin F-35C Lightning II	Reservation for RAF/RN	
ZM193	Lockheed Martin F-35C Lightning II	Reservation for RAF/RN	
ZM194	Lockheed Martin F-35C Lightning II	Reservation for RAF/RN	
ZM195	Lockheed Martin F-35C Lightning II	Reservation for RAF/RN	
ZM196	Lockheed Martin F-35C Lightning II	Reservation for RAF/RN	
ZM197	Lockheed Martin F-35C Lightning II	Reservation for RAF/RN	
ZM198	Lockheed Martin F-35C Lightning II	Reservation for RAF/RN	
ZM199	Lockheed Martin F-35C Lightning II	Reservation for RAF/RN	
ZM200	Lockheed Martin F-35C Lightning II	Reservation for RAF/RN	
ZM400	Airbus A400M Atlas C1	Reservation for RAF	
ZM401	Airbus A400M Atlas C1 (F-WWMZ)	Airbus Military, Toulouse, for RAF	
ZM402	Airbus A400M Atlas C1	Reservation for RAF	
ZM403	Airbus A400M Atlas C1	Reservation for RAF	
ZM404	Airbus A400M Atlas C1	Reservation for RAF	
ZM405	Airbus A400M Atlas C1	Reservation for RAF	
ZM406	Airbus A400M Atlas C1	Reservation for RAF	
ZM407	Airbus A400M Atlas C1	Reservation for RAF	
ZM408	Airbus A400M Atlas C1	Reservation for RAF	
ZM409	Airbus A400M Atlas C1	Reservation for RAF	
ZM410	Airbus A400M Atlas C1	Reservation for RAF	
ZM411	Airbus A400M Atlas C1	Reservation for RAF	
ZM412	Airbus A400M Atlas C1	Reservation for RAF	
ZM413	Airbus A400M Atlas C1	Reservation for RAF	
ZM414	Airbus A400M Atlas C1	Reservation for RAF	
ZM415	Airbus A400M Atlas C1	Reservation for RAF	
ZM416	Airbus A400M Atlas C1	Reservation for RAF	
ZM417	Airbus A400M Atlas C1	Reservation for RAF	
ZM418	Airbus A400M Atlas C1	Reservation for RAF	
ZM419	Airbus A400M Atlas C1	Reservation for RAF	
ZM420	Airbus A400M Atlas C1	Reservation for RAF	
ZM421	Airbus A400M Atlas C1	Reservation for RAF	
ZR283	AgustaWestland AW139 (G-FBHA)	FBS Helicopters/RAF DHFS, Valley	
ZR321	Agusta A109E Power Elite (G-CDVB)	Sold as G-CDVB, 20 April 2011	
ZR322	Agusta A109E Power Elite (G-CDVC)	RAF No 32(The Royal) Sqn, Northolt	
ZR323	Agusta A109E Power Elite (G-CDVE)	RAF No 32(The Royal) Sqn, Northolt	
ZR324	Agusta A109E Power (G-EMHB)	DHFS, RAF Shawbury	
ZR325	Agusta A109E Power (G-BZEI)	DHFS, RAF Shawbury	
ZR326	AgustaWestland AW139 (G-CFUO) [F]	FBS Helicopters/RAF DHFS, Valley	
ZR327	AgustaWestland AW139 (G-CFVD) [B]	FBS Helicopters/RAF DHFS, Valley	
ZR328	AgustaWestland AW101 Mk.610	AgustaWestland, for Algeria	
ZR329	AgustaWestland AW101 Mk.610	AgustaWestland, for Algeria	
ZR330	AgustaWestland AW101 Mk.610	AgustaWestland, for Algeria	

Notes	Serial	Type (code/other identity)	Owner/operator location or fate
	ZR331	AgustaWestland AW101 Mk.610	AgustaWestland, for Algeria
	ZR332	AgustaWestland AW101 Mk.610	AgustaWestland, for Algeria
	ZR333	AgustaWestland AW101 Mk.610	To Algeria as AN06, 31 July 2011
	ZR334	AgustaWestland AW101 Mk.640	AgustaWestland, for Saudi Arabia
	ZR335	AgustaWestland AW101 Mk.640	AgustaWestland, for Saudi Arabia
	ZR336	AgustaWestland AW101 Mk.643 [015]	AgustaWestland, for Turkmenistan
	ZR337	AgustaWestland AW101 Mk.643	AgustaWestland, for Turkmenistan
	ZR338	AgustaWestland AW101 Mk.641	AgustaWestland, for India
	ZR339	AgustaWestland AW101 Mk.641	AgustaWestland, for India
	ZR340	AgustaWestland AW101 Mk.641	AgustaWestland, for India
	ZR341	AgustaWestland AW101 Mk.641	AgustaWestland, for India
	ZR342	AgustaWestland AW101 Mk.641	AgustaWestland, for India
	ZR343	AgustaWestland AW101 Mk.641	AgustaWestland, for India
	ZR344	AgustaWestland AW101 Mk.641	AgustaWestland, for India
	ZR345	AgustaWestland AW101 Mk.641	AgustaWestland, for India
	ZR346	AgustaWestland AW101 Mk.641	AgustaWestland, for India
	ZR347	AgustaWestland AW101 Mk.641	AgustaWestland, for India
	ZR348	AgustaWestland AW101 Mk.641	AgustaWestland, for India
	ZR349	AgustaWestland AW101 Mk.641	AgustaWestland, for India
	ZT800	WS Super Lynx Mk 300	MoD/AgustaWestland, Yeovil
	ZZ171	Boeing C-17A Globemaster III (00-201/N171UK)	RAF No 99 Sqn, Brize Norton
	ZZ172	Boeing C-17A Globemaster III (00-202/N172UK)	RAF No 99 Sqn, Brize Norton
	ZZ173	Boeing C-17A Globemaster III (00-203/N173UK)	RAF No 99 Sqn, Brize Norton
	ZZ174	Boeing C-17A Globemaster III (00-204/N174UK)	RAF No 99 Sqn, Brize Norton
	ZZ175	Boeing C-17A Globemaster III (06-0205/N9500Z)	RAF No 99 Sqn, Brize Norton
	ZZ176	Boeing C-17A Globemaster III (08-0206/N9500B)	RAF No 99 Sqn, Brize Norton
	ZZ177	Boeing C-17A Globemaster III (09-8207/N9500B) $	RAF No 99 Sqn, Brize Norton
	ZZ190	Hawker Hunter F58 (J-4066/G-HHAE)	Hawker Hunter Aviation, Scampton
	ZZ191	Hawker Hunter F58 (J-4058/G-HHAD)	Hawker Hunter Aviation, Scampton
	ZZ192	Grob G109B Vigilant T1 (D-KLVI) [SQ]	RAF No 618 VGS, Odiham
	ZZ193	Grob G109B Vigilant T1 (D-KBLO) [SR]	RAF No 613 VGS, Halton
	ZZ201	General Atomics Reaper UAV (07-111)	RAF No 39 Sqn, Creech AFB, Nevada, USA
	ZZ202	General Atomics Reaper UAV (07-117)	RAF No 39 Sqn, Creech AFB, Nevada, USA
	ZZ203	General Atomics Reaper UAV (08-133)	RAF No 39 Sqn, Creech AFB, Nevada, USA
	ZZ204	General Atomics Reaper UAV (10-0157)	RAF No 39 Sqn, Creech AFB, Nevada, USA
	ZZ205	General Atomics Reaper UAV (10-0162)	RAF No 39 Sqn, Creech AFB, Nevada, USA
	ZZ206	General Atomics Reaper UAV	General Atomics, for RAF
	ZZ207	General Atomics Reaper UAV	General Atomics, for RAF
	ZZ208	General Atomics Reaper UAV	General Atomics, for RAF
	ZZ209	General Atomics Reaper UAV	General Atomics, for RAF
	ZZ210	General Atomics Reaper UAV	General Atomics, for RAF
	ZZ211	General Atomics Reaper UAV	General Atomics, for RAF
	ZZ212	General Atomics Reaper UAV	General Atomics, for RAF
	ZZ213	General Atomics Reaper UAV	General Atomics, for RAF
	ZZ250	BAE Systems Taranis UAV	BAE Systems, Warton
	ZZ251	BAE Systems HERTI UAV	BAE Systems, Warton
	ZZ252	BAE Systems HERTI UAV	BAE Systems, Warton
	ZZ253	BAE Systems HERTI UAV	BAE Systems, Warton
	ZZ254	BAE Systems HERTI UAV	BAE Systems, Warton

Serial	Type (code/other identity)	Owner/operator location or fate	Notes
ZZ330	Airbus A330 Voyager KC2 (G-VYGA)	RAF/Air Tanker Ltd, Brize Norton	
ZZ331	Airbus A330 Voyager KC2/KC3	DE&S/Airbus, for RAF	
ZZ332	Airbus A330 Voyager KC2/KC3	DE&S/Airbus, for RAF	
ZZ333	Airbus A330 Voyager KC2/KC3	DE&S/Airbus, for RAF	
ZZ334	Airbus A330 Voyager KC2/KC3	Reservation for RAF	
ZZ335	Airbus A330 Voyager KC2/KC3	Reservation for RAF	
ZZ336	Airbus A330 Voyager KC2/KC3	Reservation for RAF	
ZZ337	Airbus A330 Voyager KC2/KC3	Reservation for RAF	
ZZ338	Airbus A330 Voyager KC2/KC3	Reservation for RAF	
ZZ339	Airbus A330 Voyager KC2/KC3	Reservation for RAF	
ZZ340	Airbus A330 Voyager KC2/KC3	Reservation for RAF	
ZZ341	Airbus A330 Voyager KC2/KC3	Reservation for RAF	
ZZ342	Airbus A330 Voyager KC2/KC3	Reservation for RAF	
ZZ343	Airbus A330 Voyager KC2/KC3	Reservation for RAF	
ZZ349	AgustaWestland AW159 Lynx Wildcat	For RN/AAC	
ZZ350	AgustaWestland AW159 Lynx Wildcat	For RN/AAC	
ZZ351	AgustaWestland AW159 Lynx Wildcat	For RN/AAC	
ZZ352	AgustaWestland AW159 Lynx Wildcat	For RN/AAC	
ZZ353	AgustaWestland AW159 Lynx Wildcat	For RN/AAC	
ZZ354	AgustaWestland AW159 Lynx Wildcat	For RN/AAC	
ZZ355	AgustaWestland AW159 Lynx Wildcat	For RN/AAC	
ZZ356	AgustaWestland AW159 Lynx Wildcat	For RN/AAC	
ZZ357	AgustaWestland AW159 Lynx Wildcat	For RN/AAC	
ZZ358	AgustaWestland AW159 Lynx Wildcat	For RN/AAC	
ZZ359	AgustaWestland AW159 Lynx Wildcat	For RN/AAC	
ZZ360	AgustaWestland AW159 Lynx Wildcat	For RN/AAC	
ZZ361	AgustaWestland AW159 Lynx Wildcat	For RN/AAC	
ZZ362	AgustaWestland AW159 Lynx Wildcat	For RN/AAC	
ZZ363	AgustaWestland AW159 Lynx Wildcat	For RN/AAC	
ZZ364	AgustaWestland AW159 Lynx Wildcat	For RN/AAC	
ZZ365	AgustaWestland AW159 Lynx Wildcat	For RN/AAC	
ZZ366	AgustaWestland AW159 Lynx Wildcat	For RN/AAC	
ZZ367	AgustaWestland AW159 Lynx Wildcat	For RN/AAC	
ZZ368	AgustaWestland AW159 Lynx Wildcat	For RN/AAC	
ZZ369	AgustaWestland AW159 Lynx Wildcat	For RN/AAC	
ZZ370	AgustaWestland AW159 Lynx Wildcat	For RN/AAC	
ZZ371	AgustaWestland AW159 Lynx Wildcat	For RN/AAC	
ZZ372	AgustaWestland AW159 Lynx Wildcat	For RN/AAC	
ZZ373	AgustaWestland AW159 Lynx Wildcat	For RN/AAC	
ZZ374	AgustaWestland AW159 Lynx Wildcat	For RN/AAC	
ZZ375	AgustaWestland AW159 Lynx Wildcat	For RN/AAC	
ZZ376	AgustaWestland AW159 Lynx Wildcat	For RN/AAC	
ZZ377	AgustaWestland AW159 Lynx Wildcat	For RN/AAC	
ZZ378	AgustaWestland AW159 Lynx Wildcat	For RN/AAC	
ZZ379	AgustaWestland AW159 Lynx Wildcat	For RN/AAC	
ZZ380	AgustaWestland AW159 Lynx Wildcat	For RN/AAC	
ZZ381	AgustaWestland AW159 Lynx Wildcat	For RN/AAC	
ZZ382	AgustaWestland AW159 Lynx Wildcat	For RN/AAC	
ZZ383	AgustaWestland AW159 Lynx Wildcat	For RN/AAC	
ZZ384	AgustaWestland AW159 Lynx Wildcat	For RN/AAC	
ZZ385	AgustaWestland AW159 Lynx Wildcat	For RN/AAC	
ZZ386	AgustaWestland AW159 Lynx Wildcat	For RN/AAC	
ZZ387	AgustaWestland AW159 Lynx Wildcat	For RN/AAC	
ZZ388	AgustaWestland AW159 Lynx Wildcat	For RN/AAC	
ZZ389	AgustaWestland AW159 Lynx Wildcat	For RN/AAC	
ZZ390	AgustaWestland AW159 Lynx Wildcat	For RN/AAC	
ZZ391	AgustaWestland AW159 Lynx Wildcat	For RN/AAC	
ZZ392	AgustaWestland AW159 Lynx Wildcat	For RN/AAC	

Notes	Serial	Type (code/other identity)	Owner/operator location or fate
	ZZ393	AgustaWestland AW159 Lynx Wildcat	For RN/AAC
	ZZ394	AgustaWestland AW159 Lynx Wildcat	For RN/AAC
	ZZ395	AgustaWestland AW159 Lynx Wildcat	For RN/AAC
	ZZ396	AgustaWestland AW159 Lynx Wildcat HMA1	For RN
	ZZ397	AgustaWestland AW159 Lynx Wildcat HMA1	For RN
	ZZ398	AgustaWestland AW159 Lynx Wildcat AH1	MoD/AgustaWestland, Yeovil
	ZZ399	AgustaWestland AW159 Lynx Wildcat AH1	MoD/AgustaWestland, Yeovil
	ZZ400	AgustaWestland AW159 Lynx Wildcat	MoD/AgustaWestland, Yeovil
	ZZ401	AgustaWestland AW159 Lynx Wildcat	MoD/AgustaWestland, Yeovil
	ZZ402	AgustaWestland AW159 Lynx Wildcat	MoD/AgustaWestland, Yeovil
	ZZ403	AgustaWestland AW159 Lynx Wildcat HMA1	MoD/AFD/QinetiQ, Boscombe Down
	ZZ404	AgustaWestland AW159 Lynx Wildcat AH1	MoD/AgustaWestland, Yeovil
	ZZ405	AgustaWestland AW159 Lynx Wildcat AH1	MoD/AgustaWestland, Yeovil
	ZZ406	AgustaWestland AW159 Lynx Wildcat AH1	For AAC
	ZZ407	AgustaWestland AW159 Lynx Wildcat AH1	For AAC
	ZZ408	AgustaWestland AW159 Lynx Wildcat AH1	For AAC
	ZZ409	AgustaWestland AW159 Lynx Wildcat AH1	For AAC
	ZZ410	AgustaWestland AW159 Lynx Wildcat AH1	For AAC
	ZZ413	AgustaWestland AW159 Lynx Wildcat HMA1	For RN
	ZZ414	AgustaWestland AW159 Lynx Wildcat HMA1	For RN
	ZZ415	AgustaWestland AW159 Lynx Wildcat HMA1	For RN
	ZZ416	Hawker Beechcraft Shadow R1 (G-JENC)	RAF No 14 Sqn, Waddington
	ZZ417	Hawker Beechcraft Shadow R1 (G-NICY)	RAF No 14 Sqn, Waddington
	ZZ418	Hawker Beechcraft Shadow R1 (G-JIMG)	RAF No 14 Sqn, Waddington
	ZZ419	Hawker Beechcraft Shadow R1 (G-OTCS)	RAF No 14 Sqn, Waddington
	ZZ500	Hawker Beechcraft Avenger T1 (G-MFTA)	RN No 750 NAS, Culdrose
	ZZ501	Hawker Beechcraft Avenger T1 (G-MFTB)	RN No 750 NAS, Culdrose
	ZZ502	Hawker Beechcraft Avenger T1 (G-MFTC)	RN No 750 NAS, Culdrose
	ZZ503	Hawker Beechcraft Avenger T1 (G-MFTD)	RN No 750 NAS, Culdrose
	ZZ504	Hawker Beechcraft Shadow R1 (G-CGUM)	RAF No 14 Sqn, Waddington
	ZZ664	Boeing RC-135W (64-14833)	Boeing, for RAF
	ZZ665	Boeing RC-135W (64-14838)	Boeing, for RAF
	ZZ666	Boeing RC-135W (64-14830)	Boeing, for RAF

After a lengthy restoration, it is good to see the RN Historic Flight's Swordfish II, LS326, back in the air again.

Spitfire PR XIX PM631 is one of the RAF's Battle of Britain Memorial Flight fleet, based at Coningsby.

VF581 is a Beagle A61 Terrier 1 with civil registration G-ARSL. It is based at Eggesford in Devon.

Lightning F6 XS904 is one of two owned and regularly taxied by the Lightning Preservation Group at Bruntingthorpe.

2011 saw the retirement of the Nimrod from RAF service. MR2 XV226 was the first of the breed

Jaguar T4 XX845 still wears the 6 Squadron 'Flying Can Openers' badge and lingers on at Predannack.

Buccaneer S2B(mod) XX897 has a nose designed to take the Foxhunter radar for the Tornado ADV. It is now kept at Bournemouth in red, white and silver markings.

Lynx AH7 XZ192 is one of a small number operated by the Royal Marines of 847 NAS at Yeovilton and is seen performing in the spectacular finale of the Air Day held here.

Sea King HC4 ZA314 is coded WT and operated by 848 NAS from Yeovilton.

Merlin HM1 ZH845 is seen here in the markings of 820 NAS, based at Culdrose in Cornwall.

Chinook HC2A ZH895 is coded HJ and based at Odiham. It wears special markings commemorating 30 years of RAF Chinook operations.

ZJ120 is a Merlin HM3, coded D and operated jointly by 28 Squadron and 78 Squadron from RAF Benson in Oxfordshire.

ZJ649 is an Alpha Jet, one of a small number based at Boscombe Down with QinetiQ. Notice the serial placed, unusually, on the air brake on this type.

Typhoon ZJ700 is one of a small number kept by BAE Systems for trials at Warton. It is seen here at Fairford about to perform a magnificent display with a full weapons load.

ZZ177 is the latest of the RAF's Globemaster IIIs to be delivered, to 99 Squadron, based at Brize Norton. It wears markings celebrating 10 years of RAF Globemaster service.

The Airbus Voyager is the RAF's next tanker and this one, KC2 EC-337, became ZZ330. Externally it wore MRTT017 on the tail and under the wings

Serial	Type (code/other identity)	Owner/operator location or fate	Notes
G-BYUA	Grob G.115E Tutor	VT Aerospace/No 1 EFTS, Barkston Heath	
G-BYUB	Grob G.115E Tutor	VT Aerospace/East Midlands Universities AS/ No 16(R) Sqn/No 115(R) Sqn, Cranwell	
G-BYUC	Grob G.115E Tutor	VT Aerospace/East Midlands Universities AS/ No 16(R) Sqn/No 115(R) Sqn, Cranwell	
G-BYUD	Grob G.115E Tutor	VT Aerospace/No 1 EFTS, Barkston Heath	
G-BYUE	Grob G.115E Tutor	VT Aerospace/East Midlands Universities AS/ No 16(R) Sqn/No 115(R) Sqn, Cranwell	
G-BYUF	Grob G.115E Tutor	VT Aerospace/Northumbrian Universities AS, Leeming	
G-BYUG	Grob G.115E Tutor	VT Aerospace/Cambridge UAS/University of London AS/No 57(R) Sqn, Wyton	
G-BYUH	Grob G.115E Tutor	VT Aerospace/Southampton UAS, Boscombe Down	
G-BYUI	Grob G.115E Tutor	VT Aerospace/No 1 EFTS, Barkston Heath	
G-BYUJ	Grob G.115E Tutor	VT Aerospace/Yorkshire Universities AS, Church Fenton	
G-BYUK	Grob G.115E Tutor	VT Aerospace/No 1 EFTS, Barkston Heath	
G-BYUL	Grob G.115E Tutor	VT Aerospace/No 1 EFTS, Middle Wallop	
G-BYUM	Grob G.115E Tutor	VT Aerospace/No 1 EFTS, Barkston Heath	
G-BYUN	Grob G.115E Tutor	VT Aerospace/No 1 EFTS, Barkston Heath	
G-BYUO	Grob G.115E Tutor	VT Aerospace/Cambridge UAS/University of London AS/No 57(R) Sqn, Wyton	
G-BYUP	Grob G.115E Tutor	VT Aerospace/East Midlands Universities AS/ No 16(R) Sqn/No 115(R) Sqn, Cranwell	
G-BYUR	Grob G.115E Tutor	VT Aerospace/No 1 EFTS, Barkston Heath	
G-BYUS	Grob G.115E Tutor	VT Aerospace/Cambridge UAS/University of London AS/No 57(R) Sqn, Wyton	
G-BYUU	Grob G.115E Tutor	VT Aerospace/Cambridge UAS/University of London AS/No 57(R) Sqn, Wyton	
G-BYUV	Grob G.115E Tutor	VT Aerospace/Bristol UAS, Colerne	
G-BYUW	Grob G.115E Tutor	VT Aerospace/Cambridge UAS/University of London AS/No 57(R) Sqn, Wyton	
G-BYUX	Grob G.115E Tutor	VT Aerospace/No 1 EFTS, Barkston Heath	
G-BYUY	Grob G.115E Tutor	VT Aerospace/East Midlands Universities AS/ No 16(R) Sqn/No 115(R) Sqn, Cranwell	
G-BYUZ	Grob G.115E Tutor	VT Aerospace/No 1 EFTS, Barkston Heath	
G-BYVA	Grob G.115E Tutor	VT Aerospace/No 1 EFTS, Middle Wallop	
G-BYVB	Grob G.115E Tutor	VT Aerospace/Oxford UAS, Benson	
G-BYVC	Grob G.115E Tutor	VT Aerospace/Cambridge UAS/University of London AS/No 57(R) Sqn, Wyton	
G-BYVD	Grob G.115E Tutor	VT Aerospace/No 1 EFTS, Barkston Heath	
G-BYVE	Grob G.115E Tutor	VT Aerospace/Cambridge UAS/University of London AS/No 57(R) Sqn, Wyton	
G-BYVF	Grob G.115E Tutor	VT Aerospace/RN No 727 NAS, Yeovilton	
G-BYVG	Grob G.115E Tutor	VT Aerospace/Cambridge UAS/University of London AS/No 57(R) Sqn, Wyton	
G-BYVH	Grob G.115E Tutor	VT Aerospace/No 1 EFTS, Barkston Heath	
G-BYVI	Grob G.115E Tutor	VT Aerospace/Cambridge UAS/University of London AS/No 57(R) Sqn, Wyton	
G-BYVJ	Grob G.115E Tutor	VT Aerospace/Yorkshire Universities AS, Church Fenton	
G-BYVK	Grob G.115E Tutor	VT Aerospace/RN No 727 NAS, Yeovilton	
G-BYVL	Grob G.115E Tutor	VT Aerospace/Oxford UAS, Benson	
G-BYVM	Grob G.115E Tutor	VT Aerospace/No 1 EFTS, Barkston Heath	
G-BYVO	Grob G.115E Tutor	VT Aerospace/No 1 EFTS, Barkston Heath	
G-BYVP	Grob G.115E Tutor	VT Aerospace/Cambridge UAS/University of London AS/No 57(R) Sqn, Wyton	
G-BYVR	Grob G.115E Tutor	VT Aerospace/East Midlands Universities AS/ No 16(R) Sqn/No 115(R) Sqn, Cranwell	
G-BYVS	Grob G.115E Tutor	VT Aerospace/East Midlands Universities AS/ No 16(R) Sqn/No 115(R) Sqn, Cranwell	
G-BYVT	Grob G.115E Tutor	VT Aerospace/Cambridge UAS/University of London AS/No 57(R) Sqn, Wyton	
G-BYVU	Grob G.115E Tutor	VT Aerospace/No 1 EFTS, Middle Wallop	

Notes	Serial	Type (code/other identity)	Owner/operator location or fate
	G-BYVV	Grob G.115E Tutor	VT Aerospace/Northumbrian Universities AS, Leeming
	G-BYVW	Grob G.115E Tutor	VT Aerospace/University of Wales AS, St Athan
	G-BYVX	Grob G.115E Tutor	VT Aerospace/Yorkshire Universities AS, Church Fenton
	G-BYVY	Grob G.115E Tutor	VT Aerospace/No 1 EFTS, Middle Wallop
	G-BYVZ	Grob G.115E Tutor	VT Aerospace/No 1 EFTS, Barkston Heath
	G-BYWA	Grob G.115E Tutor	VT Aerospace/University of Wales AS, St Athan
	G-BYWB	Grob G.115E Tutor	VT Aerospace/East Midlands Universities AS/ No 16(R) Sqn/No 115(R) Sqn, Cranwell
	G-BYWC	Grob G.115E Tutor	VT Aerospace/Bristol UAS, Colerne
	G-BYWD	Grob G.115E Tutor	VT Aerospace/University of Wales AS, St Athan
	G-BYWE	Grob G.115E Tutor	VT Aerospace/Bristol UAS, Colerne
	G-BYWF	Grob G.115E Tutor	VT Aerospace/East Midlands Universities AS/ No 16(R) Sqn/No 115(R) Sqn, Cranwell
	G-BYWG	Grob G.115E Tutor	VT Aerospace/East Midlands Universities AS/ No 16(R) Sqn/No 115(R) Sqn, Cranwell
	G-BYWH	Grob G.115E Tutor	VT Aerospace/Cambridge UAS/University of London AS/No 57(R) Sqn, Wyton
	G-BYWI	Grob G.115E Tutor	VT Aerospace/No 1 EFTS, Barkston Heath
	G-BYWJ	Grob G.115E Tutor	VT Aerospace/No 1 EFTS, Barkston Heath
	G-BYWK	Grob G.115E Tutor	VT Aerospace/Bristol UAS, Colerne
	G-BYWL	Grob G.115E Tutor	VT Aerospace/East Midlands Universities AS/ No 16(R) Sqn/No 115(R) Sqn, Cranwell
	G-BYWM	Grob G.115E Tutor	VT Aerospace/RN No 727 NAS, Yeovilton
	G-BYWN	Grob G.115E Tutor	VT Aerospace/No 1 EFTS, Barkston Heath
	G-BYWO	Grob G.115E Tutor	VT Aerospace/Cambridge UAS/University of London AS/No 57(R) Sqn, Wyton
	G-BYWP	Grob G.115E Tutor	VT Aerospace/Yorkshire Universities AS, Church Fenton
	G-BYWR	Grob G.115E Tutor	VT Aerospace/Cambridge UAS/University of London AS/No 57(R) Sqn, Wyton
	G-BYWS	Grob G.115E Tutor	VT Aerospace/No 1 EFTS, Barkston Heath
	G-BYWT	Grob G.115E Tutor	Aerospace/Northumbrian Universities AS, Leeming
	G-BYWU	Grob G.115E Tutor	VT Aerospace/Oxford UAS, Benson
	G-BYWV	Grob G.115E Tutor	VT Aerospace/Yorkshire Universities AS, Church Fenton
	G-BYWW	Grob G.115E Tutor	VT Aerospace/Southampton UAS, Boscombe Down
	G-BYWX	Grob G.115E Tutor	VT Aerospace/Cambridge UAS/University of London AS/No 57(R) Sqn, Wyton
	G-BYWY	Grob G.115E Tutor	VT Aerospace/East Midlands Universities AS/ No 16(R) Sqn/No 115(R) Sqn, Cranwell
	G-BYWZ	Grob G.115E Tutor	VT Aerospace/East Midlands Universities AS/ No 16(R) Sqn/No 115(R) Sqn, Cranwell
	G-BYXA	Grob G.115E Tutor	VT Aerospace/Oxford UAS, Benson
	G-BYXB	Grob G.115E Tutor	VT Aerospace/Bristol UAS, Colerne
	G-BYXC	Grob G.115E Tutor	VT Aerospace/Oxford UAS, Benson
	G-BYXD	Grob G.115E Tutor	VT Aerospace/Southampton UAS, Boscombe Down
	G-BYXE	Grob G.115E Tutor	VT Aerospace/Southampton UAS, Boscombe Down
	G-BYXF	Grob G.115E Tutor	VT Aerospace/No 1 EFTS, Middle Wallop
	G-BYXG	Grob G.115E Tutor	VT Aerospace/Yorkshire Universities AS, Church Fenton
	G-BYXH	Grob G.115E Tutor	VT Aerospace/Bristol UAS, Colerne
	G-BYXI	Grob G.115E Tutor	VT Aerospace/Southampton UAS, Boscombe Down
	G-BYXJ	Grob G.115E Tutor	VT Aerospace/Southampton UAS, Boscombe Down
	G-BYXK	Grob G.115E Tutor	VT Aerospace/RN No 727 NAS, Yeovilton
	G-BYXL	Grob G.115E Tutor	VT Aerospace/Oxford UAS, Benson
	G-BYXM	Grob G.115E Tutor	VT Aerospace/East Midlands Universities AS/ No 16(R) Sqn/No 115(R) Sqn, Cranwell
	G-BYXN	Grob G.115E Tutor	VT Aerospace/East Midlands Universities AS/ No 16(R) Sqn/No 115(R) Sqn, Cranwell
	G-BYXO	Grob G.115E Tutor	VT Aerospace/East Midlands Universities AS/ No 16(R) Sqn/No 115(R) Sqn, Cranwell
	G-BYXP	Grob G.115E Tutor	VT Aerospace/Cambridge UAS/University of London AS/No 57(R) Sqn, Wyton

Serial	Type (code/other identity)	Owner/operator location or fate	Notes
G-BYXS	Grob G.115E Tutor	VT Aerospace/RN No 727 NAS, Yeovilton	
G-BYXT	Grob G.115E Tutor	VT Aerospace/Cambridge UAS/University of London AS/No 57(R) Sqn, Wyton	
G-BYXX	Grob G.115E Tutor	VT Aerospace/No 1 EFTS, Barkston Heath	
G-BYXY	Grob G.115E Tutor	VT Aerospace/Cambridge UAS/University of London AS/No 57(R) Sqn, Wyton	
G-BYXZ	Grob G.115E Tutor	VT Aerospace/East Midlands Universities AS/ No 16(R) Sqn/No 115(R) Sqn, Cranwell	
G-BYYA	Grob G.115E Tutor	VT Aerospace/Northumbrian Universities AS, Leeming	
G-BYYB	Grob G.115E Tutor	VT Aerospace/No 1 EFTS, Barkston Heath	
G-CEYO	AS350BB Squirrel HT3 [00]	DHFS, RAF Shawbury	
G-CGKA	Grob G.115E Tutor	VT Aerospace/East Midlands Universities AS/ No 16(R) Sqn/No 115(R) Sqn, Cranwell	
G-CGKB	Grob G.115E Tutor	VT Aerospace/East Midlands Universities AS/ No 16(R) Sqn/No 115(R) Sqn, Cranwell	
G-CGKC	Grob G.115E Tutor	VT Aerospace/East Midlands Universities AS/ No 16(R) Sqn/No 115(R) Sqn, Cranwell	
G-CGKD	Grob G.115E Tutor	VT Aerospace/University of Birmingham AS, Cosford	
G-CGKE	Grob G.115E Tutor	VT Aerospace/University of Birmingham AS, Cosford	
G-CGKF	Grob G.115E Tutor	VT Aerospace/University of Birmingham AS, Cosford	
G-CGKG	Grob G.115E Tutor	VT Aerospace/University of Birmingham AS, Cosford	
G-CGKH	Grob G.115E Tutor	VT Aerospace/University of Birmingham AS, Cosford	
G-CGKI	Grob G.115E Tutor	VT Aerospace/East of Scotland UAS, Leuchars	
G-CGKJ	Grob G.115E Tutor	VT Aerospace/East of Scotland UAS, Leuchars	
G-CGKK	Grob G.115E Tutor	VT Aerospace/East of Scotland UAS, Leuchars	
G-CGKL	Grob G.115E Tutor	VT Aerospace/East of Scotland UAS, Leuchars	
G-CGKM	Grob G.115E Tutor	VT Aerospace/East of Scotland UAS, Leuchars	
G-CGKN	Grob G.115E Tutor	VT Aerospace/Universities of Glasgow & Strathclyde AS, Glasgow	
G-CGKO	Grob G.115E Tutor	VT Aerospace/Universities of Glasgow & Strathclyde AS, Glasgow	
G-CGKP	Grob G.115E Tutor	VT Aerospace/Liverpool UAS/Manchester and Salford Universities AS, Woodvale	
G-CGKR	Grob G.115E Tutor	VT Aerospace/Liverpool UAS/Manchester and Salford Universities AS, Woodvale	
G-CGKS	Grob G.115E Tutor	VT Aerospace/Liverpool UAS/Manchester and Salford Universities AS, Woodvale	
G-CGKT	Grob G.115E Tutor	VT Aerospace/Liverpool UAS/Manchester and Salford Universities AS, Woodvale	
G-CGKU	Grob G.115E Tutor	VT Aerospace/Liverpool UAS/Manchester and Salford Universities AS, Woodvale	
G-CGKV	Grob G.115E Tutor	VT Aerospace/Liverpool UAS/Manchester and Salford Universities AS, Woodvale	
G-CGKW	Grob G.115E Tutor	VT Aerospace/Liverpool UAS/Manchester and Salford Universities AS, Woodvale	
G-CGKX	Grob G.115E Tutor	VT Aerospace/Liverpool UAS/Manchester and Salford Universities AS, Woodvale	
G-DOIT	AS350BB Squirrel HT3 [99]	DHFS, RAF Shawbury	
G-FFRA	Dassault Falcon 20DC (N902FR)	Cobham Leasing Ltd, Bournemouth	
G-FRAD	Dassault Falcon 20E	Cobham Leasing Ltd, Bournemouth	
G-FRAF	Dassault Falcon 20E (N911FR)	Cobham Leasing Ltd, Bournemouth	
G-FRAH	Dassault Falcon 20DC (N900FR)	Cobham Leasing Ltd, Durham/Tees Valley	
G-FRAI	Dassault Falcon 20E (N901FR)	Cobham Leasing Ltd, Bournemouth	
G-FRAJ	Dassault Falcon 20E (N903FR)	Cobham Leasing Ltd, Bournemouth	
G-FRAK	Dassault Falcon 20DC (N905FR)	Cobham Leasing Ltd, Durham/Tees Valley	
G-FRAL	Dassault Falcon 20DC (N904FR)	Cobham Leasing Ltd, Durham/Tees Valley	
G-FRAO	Dassault Falcon 20DC (N906FR)	Cobham Leasing Ltd, Bournemouth	
G-FRAP	Dassault Falcon 20DC (N908FR)	Cobham Leasing Ltd, Bournemouth	
G-FRAR	Dassault Falcon 20DC (N909FR)	Cobham Leasing Ltd, Bournemouth	
G-FRAS	Dassault Falcon 20C (117501)	Cobham Leasing Ltd, Durham/Tees Valley	
G-FRAT	Dassault Falcon 20C (117502)	Cobham Leasing Ltd, Durham/Tees Valley	
G-FRAU	Dassault Falcon 20C (117504)	Cobham Leasing Ltd, Durham/Tees Valley	
G-FRAW	Dassault Falcon 20ECM (117507)	Cobham Leasing Ltd, Durham/Tees Valley	

2015M/K5600	7532M/WT651	7862M/XR246	8054AM/XM410
2292M/K8203	7533M/WT680	7863M/XP248	8054BM/XM417
2361M/K6035	7544M/WN904	7864M/XP244	8055AM/XM402
3118M/H5199/(BK892)	7548M/PS915	7865M/TX226	8055BM/XM404
3858M/X7688	7556M/WK584	7866M/XH278	8056M/XG337
4354M/BL614	7564M/XE982	7868M/WZ736	8057M/XR243
4552M/T5298	7570M/XD674	7869M/WK935	8063M/WT536
5377M/EP120	7582M/WP190	7872M/WZ826/(XD826)	8070M/EP120
5405M/LF738	7583M/WP185	7881M/WD413	8072M/PK624
5466M/BN230/(LF751)	7602M/WE600	7883M/XT150	8073M/TB252
5690M/MK356	7605M/WS692	7887M/XD375	8075M/RW382
5718M/BM597	7606M/WV562	7891M/XM693	8078M/XM351
5758M/DG202	7607M/TJ138	7894M/XD818	8080M/XM480
6457M/ML427	7615M/WV679	7895M/WF784	8081M/XM468
6490M/LA255	7616M/WW388	7898M/XP854	8082M/XM409
6640M/RM694	7618M/WW442	7900M/WA576	8086M/TB752
6850M/TE184	7622M/WV606	7906M/WH132	8092M/WK654
6946M/RW388	7631M/VX185	7917M/WA591	8094M/WT520
6948M/DE673	7641M/XA634	7928M/XE849	8097M/XN492
6960M/MT847	7645M/WD293	7930M/WH301	8101M/WH984
7008M/EE549	7648M/XF785	7931M/RD253	8102M/WT486
7014M/N6720	7673M/WV332	7932M/WZ744	8103M/WR985
7015M/NL985	7689M/WW421/(WW450)	7933M/XR220	8106M/WR982
7035M/K2567/(DE306)	7694M/WV486	7937M/WS843	8114M/WL798
7060M/VF301	7696M/WV493	7938M/XH903	8117M/WR974
7090M/EE531	7698M/WV499	7939M/XD596	8118M/WZ549
7118M/LA198	7704M/TW536	7940M/XL764	8119M/WR971
7119M/LA226	7705M/WL505	7955M/XH767	8121M/XM474
7150M/PK683	7706M/WB584	7957M/XF545	8124M/WZ572
7154M/WB188	7709M/WT933	7960M/WS726	8128M/WH775
7174M/VX272	7711M/PS915	7961M/WS739	8130M/WH798
7175M/VV106	7712M/WK281	7964M/WS760	8131M/WT507
7200M/VT812	7715M/XK724	7965M/WS792	8140M/XJ571
7241M/TE311/(MK178)	7716M/WS776	7967M/WS788	8142M/XJ560
7243M/TE462	7718M/WA577	7971M/XK699	8147M/XR526
7245M/RW382	7719M/WR277	7973M/WS807	8151M/WV795
7246M/TD248	7726M/XM373	7979M/XM529	8153M/WV903
7256M/TB752	7737M/XD602	7980M/XM561	8154M/WV908
7257M/TB252	7741M/VZ477	7982M/XH892	8155M/WV797
7279M/TB752	7750M/WK864/(WL168)	7983M/XD506	8156M/XE339
7281M/TB252	7751M/WL131	7984M/XN597	8158M/XE369
7288M/PK724	7755M/WG760	7986M/WG777	8160M/XD622
7293M/TB675/(RW393)	7758M/PM651	7988M/XL149	8161M/XE993
7323M/VV217	7759M/PK664	7990M/XD452	8162M/WM913
7325M/R5868	7761M/XH318	7997M/XG452	8164M/WN105/(WF299)
7326M/VN485	7762M/XE670	7998M/XM515/(XD515)	8165M/WH791
7362M/475081/(VP546)	7764M/XH318	8005M/WG768	8169M/WH364
7416M/WN907	7770M/XF506/(WT746)	8009M/XG518	8173M/XN685
7421M/WT660	7793M/XG523	8010M/XG547	8176M/WH791
7422M/WT684	7798M/XH783	8012M/VS562	8177M/WM224
7428M/WK198	7806M/TA639	8017M/XL762	8179M/XN928
7432M/WZ724	7809M/XA699	8018M/XN344	8183M/XN972/(XN962)
7438M/18671/(WP905)	7816M/WG763	8019M/WZ869	8184M/WT520
7443M/WX853	7817M/TX214	8021M/XL824	8186M/WR977
7458M/WX905	7825M/WK991	8022M/XN341	8187M/WH791
7464M/XA564	7827M/XA917	8027M/XM555	8189M/WD615 (WD646)
7470M/XA553	7829M/XH992	8032M/XH837	8190M/XJ918
7473M/XE946	7839M/WV781	8034M/XL703	8192M/XR658
7491M/WT569	7841M/WV783	8041M/XF690	8198M/WT339
7496M/WT612	7851M/WZ706	8043M/XF836	8203M/XD377
7499M/WT555	7854M/XM191	8046M/XL770	8205M/XN819
7510M/WT694	7855M/XK416	8049M/WE168	8206M/WG419
7525M/WT619	7859M/XP283	8050M/XG329	8208M/WG303
7530M/WT648	7860M/XL738	8052M/WH166	8209M/WG418

8210M/WG471	8458M/XP672	8618M/XS111/(XP504)	8783M/XW272
8211M/WK570	8459M/XR650	8620M/XP534	8785M/XS642
8213M/WK626	8460M/XP680	8621M/XR538	8789M/XK970
8215M/WP869	8462M/XX477	8624M/XR991/(XS102)	8792M/XP345
8216M/WP927	8463M/XP355	8627M/XP558	8793M/XP346
8229M/XM355	8464M/XJ758	8628M/XJ380	8794M/XP398
8230M/XM362	8465M/W1048	8630M/WG362	8796M/XK943
8234M/XN458	8466M/L-866	8631M/XR574	8797M/XX947
8235M/XN549	8467M/WP912	8633M/3W-17/MK732	8799M/WV787
8236M/XP573	8468M/MM5701/(BT474)	8634M/WP314	8800M/XG226
8237M/XS179	8469M/100503	8640M/XR977	8805M/XV722
8238M/XS180	8470M/584219	8642M/XR537	8807M/XL587
8338M/XS180	8471M/701152	8645M/XD163	8810M/XJ825
8344M/WH960	8472M/120227/(VN679)	8648M/XK526	8816M/XX734
8350M/WH840	8473M/WP190	8653M/XS120	8818M/XK527
8352M/XN632	8474M/494083	8655M/XN126	8820M/VP952
8355M/KN645	8475M/360043/(PJ876)	8656M/XP405	8821M/XX115
8357M/WK576	8476M/24	8657M/VZ634	8822M/VP957
8359M/WF825	8477M/4101/(DG200)	8661M/XJ727	8828M/XS587
8361M/WB670	8478M/10639	8662M/XR458	8830M/N-294/(XF515)
8362M/WG477	8479M/730301	8666M/XE793	8831M/XG160
8364M/WG464	8481M/191614	8668M/WJ821	8832M/XG168/(XG172)
8365M/XK421	8482M/112372/(VK893)	8671M/XJ435	8833M/XL569
8366M/XG454	8483M/420430	8672M/XP351	8834M/XL571
8367M/XG474	8484M/5439	8673M/XD165	8836M/XL592
8368M/XF926	8485M/997	8676M/XL577	8838M/34037/(429356)
8369M/WE139	8486M/BAPC 99	8679M/XF526	8839M/69/(XG194)
8370M/N1671	8487M/J-1172	8680M/XF527	8840M/XG252
8371M/XA847	8488M/WL627	8681M/XG164	8841M/XE606
8372M/K8042	8491M/WJ880	8682M/XP404	8848M/XZ135
8373M/P2617	8493M/XR571	8693M/WH863	8853M/XT277
8375M/NX611	8494M/XP557	8696M/WH773	8855M/XT284
8376M/RF398	8501M/XP640	8702M/XG196	8857M/XW544
8377M/R9125	8502M/XP686	8703M/VW453	8858M/XW541
8378M/T9707	8508M/XS218	8706M/XF383	8863M/XG154
8379M/DG590	8509M/XT141	8708M/XF509	8867M/XK532
8380M/Z7197	8514M/XS176	8709M/XG209	8868M/WH775
8382M/VR930	8535M/XN776	8710M/XG274	8869M/WH957
8383M/K9942	8538M/XN781	8711M/XG290	8870M/WH964
8384M/X4590	8545M/XN726	8713M/XG225	8871M/WJ565
8385M/N5912	8546M/XN728	8718M/XX396	8873M/XR453
8386M/NV778	8548M/WT507	8719M/XT257	8874M/XE597
8387M/T6296	8549M/WT534	8724M/XW923	8875M/XE624
8388M/XL993	8554M/TG511	8726M/XP299	8876M/VM791/(XA312)
8389M/VX573	8561M/XS100	8727M/XR486	8880M/XF435
8392M/SL674	8563M/XX822/(XW563)	8728M/WT532	8881M/XG254
8394M/WG422	8565M/WT720/(E-408)	8729M/WJ815	8883M/XX946
8395M/WF408	8566M/XV279	8733M/XL318	8884M/VX275
8396M/XK740	8573M/XM708	8736M/XF375	8885M/XW922
8399M/WR539	8575M/XP542	8739M/XH170	8886M/XA243
8401M/XP686	8576M/XP502	8740M/WE173	8888M/XA231
8406M/XP831	8578M/XR534	8741M/XW329	8889M/XN239
8407M/XP585	8581M/WJ775	8743M/WD790	8890M/WT532
8408M/XS186	8582M/XE874	8746M/XH171	8892M/XL618
8409M/XS209	8583M/BAPC 94	8749M/XH537	8895M/XX746
8410M/XR662	8585M/XE670	8751M/XT255	8896M/XX821
8413M/XM192	8586M/XE643	8753M/WL795	8897M/XX969
8414M/XM173	8588M/XR681	8762M/WH740	8898M/XX119
8417M/XM144	8589M/XR700	8764M/XP344	8899M/XX756
8422M/XM169	8590M/XM191	8768M/A-522	8900M/XZ368
8427M/XM172	8591M/XA813	8769M/A-528	8901M/XZ383
8429M/XH592	8595M/XH278	8770M/XL623	8902M/XX739
8434M/XM411	8598M/WP270	8771M/XM602	8903M/XX747
8436M/XN554	8600M/XX761	8772M/WR960	8905M/XX975
8437M/WG362	8602M/PF179/(XR541)	8777M/XX914	8906M/XX976
8439M/WZ846	8604M/XS104	8778M/XM598	8907M/XZ371
8440M/WD935	8606M/XP530	8779M/XM607	8908M/XZ382
8442M/XP411	8608M/XP540	8780M/WK102	8909M/XV784
8452M/XK885	8610M/XL502	8781M/WE982	8910M/XL160
8453M/XP745	8611M/WF128	8782M/XH136	8911M/XH673

RAF Maintenance Command Cross-Reference

8918M/XX109	9038M/XV810	9170M/XZ994	9265M/WK585
8919M/XT486	9039M/XN586	9172M/XW304	9266M/XZ119
8920M/XT469	9040M/XZ138	9173M/XW418	9267M/XW269
8921M/XT466	9041M/XW763	9174M/XZ131	9268M/XR529
8922M/XT467	9042M/XL954	9175M/P1344	9269M/XT914
8923M/XX819	9044M/XS177	9176M/XW430	9270M/XZ145
8924M/XP701	9047M/XW409	9177M/XW328	9272M/XS486
8925M/XP706	9048M/XM403	9179M/XW309	9273M/XS726
8931M/XV779	9049M/XW404	9180M/XW311	9274M/XS738
8932M/XR718	9052M/WJ717	9181M/XW358	9275M/XS729
8934M/XR749	9056M/XS488	9185M/XZ987	9276M/XS733
8935M/XR713	9059M/ZE360	9187M/XW405	9277M/XT601
8937M/XX751	9066M/XV582	9188M/XW364	9278M/XS643
8938M/WV746	9067M/XV586	9190M/XW318	9279M/XT681
8941M/XT456	9070M/XV581	9191M/XW416	9280M/XW804
8942M/XN185	9072M/XW768	9192M/XW361	9281M/XZ146
8943M/XE799	9073M/XW924	9193M/XW367	9283M/XZ322
8944M/WZ791	9075M/XV752	9194M/XW420	9284M/ZA267
8945M/XX818	9076M/XV808	9195M/XW330	9285M/XR806
8946M/XZ389	9078M/XV753	9196M/XW370	9286M/XT905
8947M/XX726	9079M/XZ130	9197M/XX530/(XX637)	9287M/WP962
8948M/XX757	9080M/ZE350	9198M/XS641	9288M/XX520
8949M/XX743	9086M/ZE352	9199M/XW290	9289M/XX665
8951M/XX727	9087M/XX753	9200M/XW425	9290M/XX626
8953M/XX959	9090M/XW353	9201M/ZD667	9292M/XW892
8954M/XZ384	9091M/XW434	9203M/3066	9293M/XX830
8955M/XX110	9092M/XH669	9205M/E449	9294M/XX655
8957M/XN582	9093M/WK124	9206M/F6314	9295M/XV497
8961M/XS925	9095M/XW547	9207M/8417/18	9298M/ZE340
8967M/XV263	9096M/WV322	9208M/F938	9299M/XW870
8969M/XR753	9098M/XV406	9210M/MF628	9300M/XX431
8972M/XR754	9103M/XV411	9211M/733682	9301M/XZ941
8973M/XS922	9110M/XX736	9212M/KL216/(45-49295)	9302M/ZD462
8974M/XM473	9111M/XW421	9213M/N5182	9303M/XV709
8975M/XW917	9115M/XV863	9215M/XL164	9305M/XZ942
8976M/XZ630	9117M/XV161	9216M/XL190	9306M/XX979
8978M/XX837	9119M/XW303	9217M/ZH257	9308M/ZD932
8984M/XN551	9120M/XW419	9218M/XL563	9310M/ZA355
8985M/WK127	9122M/XZ997	9219M/XZ971	9311M/ZA475
8986M/XV261	9123M/XT773	9221M/XZ966	9312M/ZA474
8987M/XM358	9125M/XW410	9222M/XZ968	9314M/ZA320
8990M/XM419	9127M/XW432	9224M/XL568	9315M/ZA319
8995M/XM425	9130M/XW327	9225M/XX885	9316M/ZA399
8996M/XM414	9131M/DD931	9226M/XV865	9317M/ZA450
8997M/XX669	9132M/XX977	9227M/XB812	9318M/ZA360
8998M/XT864	9133M/413573	9229M/ZA678	9319M/XR516
9002M/XW763	9134M/XT288	9233M/XZ431	9320M/XX153
9003M/XZ390	9136M/XT891	9234M/XV864	9321M/XZ367
9004M/XZ370	9137M/XN579	9236M/WV318	9322M/ZB686
9005M/XZ374	9139M/XV863	9237M/XF445	9323M/XV643
9006M/XX967	9140M/XZ287	9238M/ZA717	9324M/XV659
9007M/XX968	9141M/XV118	9239M/7198/18	9326M/XV653
9008M/XX140	9143M/XN589	9241M/XS639	9328M/ZD607
9009M/XX763	9145M/XV863	9242M/XH672	9329M/ZD578
9010M/XX764	9146M/XW299	9246M/XS714	9330M/ZB684
9011M/XM412	9147M/XW301	9248M/WB627	9331M/XW852
9012M/XN494	9148M/XW436	9249M/WV396	9332M/XZ935
9014M/XN584	9149M/XW375	9251M/XX744	9335M/ZA375
9015M/XW320	9150M/FX760	9252M/XX722	9336M/ZA407
9017M/ZE449	9151M/XT907	9253M/ZA254	9337M/ZA774
9019M/XX824	9152M/XV424	9254M/XX965	9338M/ZA325
9020M/XX825	9153M/XW360	9255M/XZ375	9339M/ZA323
9021M/XX826	9154M/XW321	9257M/XX962	9340M/XX745
9022M/XX958	9155M/WL679	9258M/XW265	9341M/ZA357
9026M/XP629	9162M/XZ991	9259M/XS710	9342M/XR498
9027M/XP556	9163M/XV415	9260M/XS734	9343M/XR506
9028M/XP563	9166M/XW323	9261M/W2068	9344M/XV706
9032M/XR673	9167M/XV744	9262M/XZ358	
9033M/XS181	9168M/XZ132	9263M/XW267	
9036M/XM350	9169M/XW547	9264M/XS735	

Ships' Numeric Code – Deck Letters Analysis

	0	1	2	3	4	5	6	7	8	9
33									CT	
34									CM	
36					AY	LB				
37			NL			SM				
38										
40					IR			YK		
41		EB	CW	CW		MM				
42		SU			KT	PD	SB			
43					EE	EE				
44					MR					
45		DA	DT	DM					LA	
46			WM							
47					RM					

RN Code - Squadron - Base - Aircraft Cross-check

Deck/Base Code Numbers	Letters	Unit	Location	Aircraft Type(s)
010 – 020	CU	820 NAS	Culdrose	Merlin HM1
180 – 190	CU	849 NAS	Culdrose	Sea King ASaC7
180 – 190	CU	854 NAS	Culdrose	Sea King ASaC7
180 – 190	CU	857 NAS	Culdrose	Sea King ASaC7
264 – 274	CU	814 NAS	Culdrose	Merlin HM1
300 – 308	VL	815 NAS	Yeovilton	Lynx HMA8
311 – 316	VL	815 NAS, MI Flight	Yeovilton	Lynx HMA8
321 – 474	*	815 NAS	Yeovilton	Lynx HMA8
500 – 515	CU	829 NAS	Culdrose	Merlin HM1
580 – 588	CU	824 NAS	Culdrose	Merlin HM1
630 – 645	VL	702 NAS	Yeovilton	Lynx HMA8
817 – 831	CU	771 NAS	Culdrose	Sea King HU5/HAS6

*See foregoing separate ships' Deck Letters Analysis
Note that only the 'last two' digits of the Code are worn by some aircraft types, especially helicopters.

Code	Deck Letters	Vesel name & Pennant No	Vessel Type & Unit
–	AB	HMS Albion (L14)	Assault
–	AS	RFA Argus (A135)	Aviation Training ship
365	AY	HMS Argyll (F231)	Type 23 (815 NAS)
–	BV	RFA Black Rover (A273)	Fleet tanker
–	CB	RFA Cardigan Bay (L3009)	Landing ship
348	CM	HMS Chatham (F87)	Type 22 (815 NAS)
338	CT	HMS Campbeltown (F86)	Type 22 (815 NAS)
–	CU	RNAS Culdrose (HMS Seahawk)	
412/3	CW	HMS Cornwall (F99)	Type 22 (815 NAS)
451	DA	HMS Daring (D32)	Type 45 (815 NAS)
–	DC	HMS Dumbarton Castle (P265)	Fishery protection
–	DG	RFA Diligence (A132)	Maintenance
453	DM	HMS Diamond (D34)	Type 45 (815 NAS)
–	DR	HMS Dragon (D35)	Type 45 (815 NAS)
452	DT	HMS Dauntless (D33)	Type 45 (815 NAS)
411	EB	HMS Edinburgh (D97)	Type 42 (815 NAS)
434/5	EE	HMS Endurance (A171)	Ice Patrol (815 NAS)
–	FA	RFA Fort Austin (A386)	Support ship
–	FE	RFA Fort Rosalie (A385)	Support ship
–	GV	RFA Gold Rover (A271)	Fleet tanker
404	IR	HMS Iron Duke (F234)	Type 23 (815 NAS)
425	KT	HMS Kent (F78)	Type 23 (815 NAS)
–	L	HMS Illustrious (R06)	Carrier
457	LA	HMS Lancaster (F229)	Type 23 (829 NAS)
366	LB	RFA Largs Bay (L3006)	Landing ship
–	LC	HMS Leeds Castle (P258)	Fishery protection
–	MB	RFA Mounts Bay (L3008)	Landing ship
415	MM	HMS Monmouth (F235)	Type 23 (829 NAS)
444	MR	HMS Montrose (F236)	Type 23 (815 NAS)
372	NL	HMS Northumberland (F238)	Type 23 (829 NAS)
–	O	HMS Ocean (L12)	Helicopter carrier
426	PD	HMS Portland (F79)	Type 23 (815 NAS)
474	RM	HMS Richmond (F239)	Type 23 (815 NAS)
427	SB	HMS St Albans (F83)	Type 23 (815 NAS)
375	SM	HMS Somerset (F82)	Type 23 (815 NAS)
422	SU	HMS Sutherland (F81)	Type 23 (815 NAS)
–	VL	RNAS Yeovilton (HMS Heron)	
462	WM	HMS Westminster (F237)	Type 23 (829 NAS)
407	YK	HMS York (D98)	Type 42 (815 NAS)
–	–	HMS Bulwark (L15)	Assault
–	–	HMS Defender (D36)	Type 45
–	–	HMS Duncan (D37)	Type 45
–	–	HMS Protector (A173)	Ice patrol
–	–	RFA Fort Victoria (A387)	Auxiliary Oiler
–	–	RFA Fort George (A388)	Auxiliary Oiler
–	–	RFA Lyme Bay (L3007)	Landing ship
–	–	RFA Wave Knight (A389)	Fleet tanker
–	–	RFA Wave Ruler (A390)	Fleet tanker

This table gives brief details of the markings worn by aircraft of RAF squadrons at the beginning of 2012. While this may help to identify the operator of a particular machine, it may not always give the true picture. For example, from time to time aircraft are loaned to other units while others wear squadron marks but are actually operated on a pool basis. Squadron badges are usually located on the front fuselage.

Squadron	Type(s) operated	Base(s)	Distinguishing marks & other comments
No 2 Sqn	Tornado GR4/GR4A	RAF Marham	Badge: A wake knot on a white circular background flanked on either side by black and white triangles. Tail fin has a black stripe with white triangles and the badge repeated on it.
No 3 Sqn	Typhoon T3/FGR4	RAF Coningsby	Badge: A blue cockatrice on a white circular background flanked by two green bars edged with yellow. Tail fin as a green stripe edged with yellow. Aircraft are coded QO-*
No 4(R) Sqn	Hawk T2	RAF Valley	Badge (on nose): A yellow lightning flash on a red background with IV superimposed. Aircraft carry a yellow lightning flash on a red and black background on the tail and this is repeated in bars either side of the roundel on the fuselage. Part of No 4 FTS.
No 5 Sqn	Sentinel R1	RAF Waddington	Badge (on tail): A green maple leaf on a white circle over a red horizontal band.
No 6 Sqn	Typhoon T3/FGR4	RAF Leuchars	Badge (on tail): A red, winged can opener on a blue shield, edged in red. The roundel is flanked by a red zigzag on a blue background. Aircraft are coded E*.
No 7 Sqn	Chinook HC2/HC2A/HC3R	RAF Odiham	Badge (on tail): A blue badge containing the seven stars of Ursa Major ('The Plough') in yellow. Aircraft pooled with No 18 Sqn and No 27 Sqn.
No 8 Sqn	Sentry AEW1	RAF Waddington	Badge (on tail): A grey, sheathed, Arabian dagger. Aircraft pooled with No 54(R) Sqn.
No 9 Sqn	Tornado GR4/GR4A	RAF Marham	Badge: A green bat on a black circular background, flanked by yellow and green horizontal stripes. The green bat also appears on the tail, edged in yellow.
No 11 Sqn	Typhoon T3/FGR4	RAF Coningsby	Badge (on tail): Two eagles in flight on a white shield. The roundel is flanked by yellow and black triangles. Aircraft are coded D*
No 12 Sqn	Tornado GR4/GR4A	RAF Lossiemouth	Roundel is superimposed on a green chevron. Tail fin has a black & white horizontal stripe with the squadron badge, a fox's head on a white circle, in the middle.
No 13 Sqn	Reaper	RAF Waddington	No markings worn.
No 14 Sqn	Shadow R1	RAF Waddington	No markings worn.
No 15(R) Sqn [NTOCU]	Tornado GR4/GR4A	RAF Lossiemouth	Roman numerals XV appear in white on the tail.
No 16(R) Sqn	Tutor	RAF Cranwell	No markings carried. Aircraft pooled with East Midlands UAS and No 115(R) Sqn.
No 17(R) Sqn	Typhoon T3/FGR4	RAF Coningsby	Badge (on tail): A gauntlet on a black and white shield. Roundel is flanked by two white bars which have a pair of jagged black lines running along them horizontally. Aircraft are coded A*.
No 18 Sqn	Chinook HC2/HC2A/HC3R	RAF Odiham	Badge (on tail): A red winged horse on a black circle. Aircraft pooled with No 7 Sqn and No 27 Sqn.

RAF Squadron Markings

Squadron	Type(s) operated	Base(s)	Distinguishing marks & other comments
No 22 Sqn	Sea King HAR3/HAR3A	A Flt: RMB Chivenor B Flt: Wattisham C Flt: RAF Valley	Badge: A black pi symbol in front of a white Maltese cross on a red circle.
No 24 Sqn	Hercules C4/C5	RAF Brize Norton	No squadron markings carried. Aircraft pooled with No 30 Sqn.
No 27 Sqn	Chinook HC2/HC2A/HC3R	RAF Odiham	Badge (on tail): An dark green elephant on a green circle, flanked by green and dark green stripes. Aircraft pooled with No 7 Sqn and No 18 Sqn.
No 28 Sqn	Merlin HC3/HC3A	RAF Benson	Badge: A winged horse above two white crosses on a red shield. Aircraft pooled with No 78 Sqn.
No 29(R) Sqn [TOCU]	Typhoon T3/FGR4	RAF Coningsby	Badge (on tail): An eagle in flight, preying on a buzzard, with three red Xs across the top. The roundel is flanked by two white bars outlined by a red line, each containing three red Xs. Aircraft are coded B*.
No 30 Sqn	Hercules C4/C5	RAF Brize Norton	No squadron markings carried. Aircraft pooled with No 24 Sqn.
No 31 Sqn	Tornado GR4/GR4A	RAF Marham	Badge: A gold, five-pointed star on a yellow circle flanked by yellow and green checks. The star is repeated on the tail.
No 32(The Royal) Sqn	BAe 125 CC3/146 CC2/ Agusta 109	RAF Northolt	No squadron markings carried but aircraft carry a distinctive livery with a red stripe, edged in blue along the middle of the fuselage and a red tail.
No 33 Sqn	Puma HC1	RAF Benson	Badge: A stag's head.
No 39 Sqn	Predator/ Reaper	Nellis AFB Creech AFB	No markings worn
No 41(R) Sqn [FJWOEU]	Tornado GR4	RAF Coningsby	Badge: A red, double armed cross, flanked by red and white horizontal stripes. Stripes repeated on tail.
No 45(R) Sqn	Super King Air 200/200GT	RAF Cranwell	Aircraft carry a dark blue stripe on the tail superimposed with red diamonds. Part of No 3 FTS.
No 47 Sqn	Hercules C1/C3/C3A	RAF Brize Norton	No squadron markings usually carried.
No 54(R) Sqn [ISTAR OCU]	Sentry AEW1	RAF Waddington	Based aircraft as required.
No 56(R) Sqn [ISTAR Test & Evaluation Sqn]	Shadow R1/ Sentry AEW1/ Sentinel R1	RAF Waddington	Based aircraft as required.
No 57(R) Sqn	Tutor	RAF Wyton	No markings carried. Aircraft pooled with Cambridge UAS and University of London AS.
No 60(R) Sqn	Griffin HT1	RAF Shawbury [DHFS] & RAF Valley [SARTU]	No squadron markings usually carried.
No 72(R) Sqn	Tucano T1	RAF Linton-on-Ouse	Badge: A black swift in flight on a red disk, flanked by blue bars edged with red. The blue bars edged with red also flank the roundel on the fuselage; part of No 1 FTS

Squadron	Type(s) operated	Base(s)	Distinguishing marks & other comments
No 78 Sqn	Merlin HC3/HC3A	RAF Benson	Badge: A yellow, heraldic tiger with two tails, on a black circle. Aircraft pooled with No 28 Sqn.
No 84 Sqn	Griffin HAR2	RAF Akrotiri	Badge (on tail): A scorpion on a playing card symbol (diamonds, clubs etc). Aircraft carry a vertical light blue stripe through the roundel on the fuselage.
No 99 Sqn	Globemaster III	RAF Brize Norton	Badge (on tail): A black puma leaping.
No 100 Sqn	Hawk T1A	RAF Leeming	Badge (on tail): A skull in front of two bones crossed. Aircraft are usually coded C*. Incorporates the Joint Forward Air Control Training and Standards Unit (JFACTSU)
No 101 Sqn	VC10 C1K/K3	RAF Brize Norton	Badge (on tail): A lion behind a castle turret.
No 115(R) Sqn	Tutor	RAF Cranwell	No markings carried. Aircraft pooled with East Midlands UAS and No 16(R) Sqn.
No 202 Sqn	Sea King HAR3	A Flt: RAF Boulmer D Flt: RAF Lossiemouth E Flt: RAF Leconfield	Badge: A mallard alighting on a white circle.
No 203(R) Sqn	Sea King HAR3	RAF Valley	Badge: A green sea horse on a white circle.
No 206(R) Sqn [HAT&ES]	Hercules C1/C3/C3A/C4 C5	RAF Brize Norton/ Boscombe Down	No squadron markings usually carried.
No 208(R) Sqn	Hawk T1/T1A/T1W	RAF Valley	Badge (on tail): A Sphinx inside a white circle, flanked by flashes of yellow. Aircraft also carry blue and yellow bars either side of the roundel on the fuselage and a blue and yellow chevron on the nose. Part of No 4 FTS.
No 216 Sqn	TriStar K1/KC1/C2/C2A	RAF Brize Norton	Badge (on tail): An eagle in flight with a bomb in its claws.
No 230 Sqn	Puma HC1	RAF Benson	Badge: A tiger in front of a palm tree on a black pentagon.
No 617 Sqn	Tornado GR4/GR4A	RAF Lossiemouth	Badge: Dam breached, flanked on either side by red lightning flashes on a black background. Tail fin is black with a red lightning flash.
No 1312 Flt	VC10 K3/K4 (101 Sqn) Hercules	Mount Pleasant, Fl	Badge (on tail): A red Maltese cross on a white circle, flanked by red and white horizontal bars.
No 1419 Flt	Merlin HC3	Afghanistan	No markings carried.
No 1435 Flt	Typhoon FGR4	Mount Pleasant, Fl	Badge (on tail): A red Maltese cross on a white circle, flanked by red and white horizontal bars.
No 1564 Flt	Chinook HC2/ Sea King HAR3	Mount Pleasant, Fl	No markings known.

Some UAS aircraft carry squadron badges and markings, usually on the tail. Squadron crests all consist of a white circle surrounded by a blue circle, topped with a red crown and having a yellow scroll beneath. Each differs by the motto on the scroll, the UAS name running around the blue circle & by the contents at the centre and it is the latter which are described below.

* All AEFs come under the administration of local UASs and these are listed here.

UAS	Base	Marks
Bristol UAS/ No 3 AEF	Colerne	A sailing ship on water.
Cambridge UAS/ No 5 AEF	RAF Wyton	A heraldic lion in front of a red badge. Aircraft pooled with University of London AS
East Midlands Universities AS/ No 7 AEF	RAF Cranwell	A yellow quiver, full of arrows.
East of Scotland UAS/ No 12 AEF	RAF Leuchars	An open book in front of a white diagonal cross edged in blue.
Liverpool UAS	RAF Woodvale	A bird atop an open book, holding a branch in its beak. Aircraft pooled with Manchester and Salford Universities AS
Manchester and Salford Universities AS/ No 10 AEF	RAF Woodvale	A bird of prey with a green snake in its beak. Aircraft pooled with Liverpool UAS
Northumbrian Universities AS/ No 11 AEF	RAF Leeming	A white cross on a blue background.
Oxford UAS/ No 6 AEF	RAF Benson	An open book in front of crossed swords.
Southampton UAS/ No 2 AEF	Boscombe Down	A red stag in front of a stone pillar.
Universities of Glasgow and Strathclyde AS/ No 4 AEF	Glasgow	A bird of prey in flight, holding a branch in its beak, in front of an upright sword.
University of Birmingham AS/ No 8 AEF	DCAE Cosford	A blue griffon with two heads.
University of London AS	RAF Wyton	A globe superimposed over an open book. Aircraft pooled with Cambridge UAS
University of Wales AS/ No 1 AEF	MoD St Athan	A red Welsh dragon in front of an open book, clasping a sword. Some aircraft have the dragon in front of white and green squares.
Yorkshire Universities AS/ No 9 AEF	RAF Church Fenton	An open book in front of a Yorkshire rose with leaves.

Fleet Air Arm Squadron Markings

This table gives brief details of the markings worn by aircraft of FAA squadrons. Squadron badges, when worn, are usually located on the front fuselage. All FAA squadron badges (other than 800 NAS) comprise a crown atop a circle edged in gold braid and so the badge details below list only what appears in the circular part.

Squadron	Type(s) operated	Base(s)	Distinguishing marks & other comments
No 702 NAS	Lynx HMA8	RNAS Yeovilton	Badge: A Lynx rearing up in front of a circle comprising alternate dark blue and white sectors.
No 727 NAS	Tutor	RNAS Yeovilton	Badge: The head of Britannia wearing a gold helmet on a background of blue and white waves.
No 750 NAS	Avenger T1	RNAS Culdrose	Badge: A Greek runner bearing a torch & sword on a background of blue and white waves.
No 771 NAS	Sea King HU5/HAS6	RNAS Culdrose & Prestwick	Badge: Three bees on a background of blue and white waves.
No 814 NAS	Merlin HM1	RNAS Culdrose	Badge: A winged tiger mask on a background of dark blue and white waves.
No 815 NAS	Lynx HMA8	RNAS Yeovilton	Badge: A winged, gold harpoon on a background of blue and white waves.
No 820 NAS	Merlin HM1	RNAS Culdrose	Badge: A flying fish on a background of blue and white waves.
No 824 NAS	Merlin HM1	RNAS Culdrose	Badge: A heron on a background of blue and white waves.
No 829 NAS	Merlin HM1	RNAS Culdrose	Badge: A kingfisher hovering on a background of blue and white waves.
No 845 NAS	Sea King HC4	RNAS Yeovilton	Badge: A dragonfly on a background of blue and white waves.
No 846 NAS	Sea King HC4	RNAS Yeovilton	Badge: A swordsman riding a winged horse whilst attacking a serpent on a background of blue and white waves. Aircraft are usually coded V*.
No 847 NAS	Lynx AH7	RNAS Yeovilton	Badge: A gold sea lion on a blue background.
No 848 NAS	Sea King HC4	RNAS Yeovilton	Badge: Inside a red circle, a hawk in flight with a torpedo in its claws above white and blue waves. Aircraft are usually coded W*.
No 849 NAS	Sea King ASaC7	RNAS Culdrose	Badge: A winged streak of lightning with an eye in front on a background of blue and white waves.
No 854 NAS	Sea King ASaC7	RNAS Culdrose	Badge: A winged lion in front of a sword.
No 857 NAS	Sea King ASaC7	RNAS Culdrose	Badge: A hand emerging from the waves, clutching a sword aloft.

This section lists the codes worn by some UK military aircraft and, alongside, the serial of the aircraft currently wearing this code. It should be pointed out that in some cases more than one aircraft wears the same code but the aircraft listed is the one believed to be in service with the unit concerned at the time of going to press. This list will be updated regularly and those with Internet access can download the latest version via the 'AirNet' Web Site, www.aviation-links.co.uk.

ROYAL AIR FORCE

AgustaWestland AW.139

B	ZR327
F	ZR326

BAC VC10

Code	Serial
F	ZA147
G	ZA148
H	ZA149
J	ZA150
N	ZD241
R	XR808
U	XV104
W	XV106
Y	XV108

Beech King Air 200

Code	Serial
D	ZK458
J	ZK450
K	ZK451
L	ZK452
M	ZK453
N	ZK454
O	ZK455
P	ZK456
U	ZK460
X	ZK459

Bell 412EP Griffin HT1

Code	Serial
E	ZJ242
I	ZJ235
K	ZJ708
L	ZJ241
O	ZJ707
R	ZJ239
S	ZJ234
T	ZJ237
U	ZJ240
X	ZJ236
Y	ZJ238

B-V Chinook

Code	Serial
AA	ZA670
AB	ZA671
AE	ZA675
AF	ZA677
AG	ZA679
AH	ZA680
AI	ZA681
AJ	ZA682
AK	ZA683
AL	ZA684
AM	ZA704
AN	ZA705
AO	ZA707
AP	ZA708
AR	ZA710
AT	ZA712
AU	ZA713
AV	ZA714

AW	ZA720
BN	ZA718
DB	ZD574
DC	ZD575
DD	ZD980
DF	ZD982
DG	ZD983
DH	ZD984
HB	ZH775
HC	ZH776
HE	ZH777
HF	ZH891
HG	ZH892
HH	ZH893
HI	ZH894
HJ	ZH895
HK	ZH896
HL	ZH897
HR	ZH903

EHI-101 Merlin

Code	Serial
B	ZJ118
C	ZJ119
D	ZJ120
E	ZJ121
F	ZJ122
G	ZJ123
H	ZJ124
J	ZJ125
K	ZJ126
L	ZJ127
M	ZJ128
N	ZJ129
O	ZJ130
P	ZJ131
Q	ZJ132
R	ZJ133
S	ZJ134
T	ZJ135
U	ZJ136
W	ZJ137
X	ZJ138
AA	ZJ990
AB	ZJ992
AC	ZJ994
AD	ZJ995
AE	ZJ998
AF	ZK001

Eurofighter Typhoon

Code	Serial
C	ZJ950
D	ZK301
F	ZJ944
H	ZJ949
AA	ZJ930
AB	ZJ912
AC	ZJ913
AF	ZJ914
AG	ZJ946
AH	ZJ947
AX	ZK303
BA	ZJ803

BD	ZJ805
BE	ZJ806
BH	ZJ809
BI	ZJ810
BJ	ZJ801
BK	ZJ812
BL	ZJ813
BM	ZJ804
BN	ZJ815
BP	ZJ811
BT	ZK306
BU	ZK307
BV	ZJ910
BW	ZK308
BX	ZJ928
BY	ZJ915
BZ	ZJ911
DA	ZJ931
DB	ZJ932
DC	ZJ919
DD	ZJ924
DE	ZK305
DF	ZJ933
DH	ZJ942
DJ	ZJ935
DL	ZJ929
DM	ZJ923
DN	ZJ947
DW	ZJ808
DXI	ZJ939
EA	ZK302
EB	ZK304
EH	ZK323
EI	ZK324
EJ	ZK300
EK	ZK311
EL	ZK310
EM	ZK312
EN	ZK313
EO	ZK314
EP	ZK326
EQ	ZK325
ER	ZK316
ES	ZK317
ET	ZK318
EU	ZK321
EV	ZK320
EW	ZK319
EX	ZK379
EZ	ZK322
QO-A	ZJ920
QO-B	ZJ802
QO-C	ZJ922
QO-G	ZJ917
QO-H	ZJ921
QO-J	ZJ941
QO-L	ZJ918
QO-M	ZJ927
QO-P	ZK309
QO-R	ZJ925
QO-S	ZJ936
QO-T	ZJ934
QO-U	ZJ916
QO-W	ZJ937

Code	Serial
QO-Y	ZJ926
QO-Z	ZJ814

BAE Hawk T1/T2

Code	Serial
M	ZK022
P	ZK025
CA	XX246
CB	XX285
CC	XX203
CD	XX332
CE	XX258
CF	XX202
CG	XX198
CH	XX346
CI	XX321
CJ	XX329
CK	XX339
CL	XX255
CM	XX280
CN	XX318
CO	XX289
CQ	XX184
CR	XX189

Panavia Tornado GR4

Code	Serial
001	ZA365
002	ZA367
003	ZA369
004	ZA370
005	ZA371
006	ZA372
007	ZA373
008	ZA393
009	ZA395
010	ZA398
011	ZA400
012	ZA401
013	ZA404
014	ZA405
015	ZA406
016	ZA410
017	ZA412
018	ZA446
020	ZA449
021	ZA452
022	ZA453
023	ZA456
024	ZA458
026	ZA461
027	ZA462
028	ZA463
029	ZA469
031	ZA472
032	ZA473
033	ZA492
034	ZA541
035	ZA542
036	ZA543
037	ZA544
038	ZA546
040	ZA548
041	ZA549
042	ZA550
043	ZA551
044	ZA552
045	ZA553
046	ZA554
047	ZA556
048	ZA557
049	ZA559

Code	Serial
050	ZA560
051	ZA562
054	ZA585
055	ZA587
056	ZA588
057	ZA589
058	ZA591
059	ZA592
060	ZA594
061	ZA595
062	ZA596
063	ZA597
064	ZA598
066	ZA601
067	ZA602
068	ZA604
069	ZA606
070	ZA607
072	ZA609
073	ZA611
075	ZA613
076	ZA614
077	ZD707
078	ZD709
079	ZD711
080	ZD712
081	ZD713
082	ZD714
083	ZD715
084	ZD716
085	ZD719
086	ZD720
087	ZD739
088	ZD740
089	ZD741
090	ZD742
091	ZD743
092	ZD744
093	ZD745
094	ZD746
095	ZD747
096	ZD748
097	ZD749
098	ZD788
099	ZD790
100	ZD792
101	ZD793
102	ZD810
103	ZD811
104	ZD812
105	ZD842
106	ZD843
107	ZD844
108	ZD847
109	ZD848
110	ZD849
111	ZD850
112	ZD851
113	ZD890
115	ZD895
116	ZE116
118	ZD705
120	ZG709
122	ZG712
123	ZG713
124	ZG714
125	ZG726
126	ZG727
128	ZG750
129	ZG752
130	ZG754
133	ZG771

Code	Serial
134	ZG775
136	ZG779
137	ZG791
C	ZA371
F	ZA459
H	ZA373
M	ZG729
IV	ZA612
TN	ZG794
AJ-G	ZA601
AJ-N	ZA398
EB-B	ZD996
EB-G	ZA600
EB-Q	ZG777
EB-R	ZA447
EB-Z	ZG707
KC-N	ZA367

Shorts Tucano T1

Code	Serial
MP-A	ZF170
MP-D	ZF172
MP-O	ZF269
MP-Q	ZF264
MP-T	ZF239
MP-W	ZF338

WS61 Sea King

Code	Serial
A	XZ585
B	XZ586
C	XZ587
D	XZ588
E	XZ589
F	XZ590
G	XZ591
H	XZ592
I	XZ593
K	XZ595
L	XZ596
M	XZ597
P	XZ599
Q	ZA105
R	ZE368
S	ZE369
T	ZE370
V	ZH541
W	ZH542
X	ZH543

ROYAL NAVY
EHI-101 Merlin

Code	Serial
10	ZH827
11	ZH840
12	ZH850
13	ZH851
14	ZH828
17	ZH864
65	ZH824
67	ZH847
68	ZH860
70	ZH857
81	ZH861
82	ZH856
83	ZH855
84	ZH854
85	ZH833
86	ZH838
87	ZH835
88	ZH842
502	ZH841

503   ZH837

WS Lynx

Code	Serial
301	ZD262
302	XZ732
303	ZF563
304	XZ736
314	XZ255
315	ZD260
316	XZ719
322	XZ721
332	XZ731
335	ZD252
348	XZ698
350	XZ729
365	XZ691
372	ZF558
404	ZD259
407	ZD261
410	ZD565
411	XZ726
412	ZF560
415	XZ725
444	ZD258
451	XZ689
452	XZ690
453	ZF557
631	XZ237
632	XZ245
633	XZ238
634	XZ727
635	XZ233
640	ZD266
641	XZ692
642	ZD257
643	XZ723
644	ZD265
645	XZ722

WS61 Sea King

Code	Serial
16	ZA166
17	XV670
18	XV648
19	ZA130
20	ZA137
21	XV666
22	ZA167
26	XV661
27	XV673
28	XV647
29	XV705
180	XV649
181	XV697
182	ZD636
183	XV671
184	XV707
185	XV656
186	ZE418
187	XV672
188	XV714
189	ZE420
190	XV664
191	ZA126
192	ZE422
707	XZ920
823	XV699
A	ZA293
B	ZA310
D	ZA299
E	ZD477
F	ZB507
G	ZG821
H	ZE428
I	ZG820
J	ZD480
K	ZE427
L	ZF124
M	ZA313
N	ZA291
O	ZF118
P	ZD625
Q	ZA296
R	ZF115
S	ZD626
T	ZF121
U	ZA295
V	ZF122
W	ZA297
X	ZF117
Y	ZA298
Z	ZF120
WO	ZD627
WP	ZF116
WQ	ZD479
WR	ZE425
WS	ZG822
WT	ZA314
WU	ZA292
WV	ZF115
WW	ZF123
WX	ZE426
WY	ZF119
WZ	ZD476
ZB	XZ580

ARMY AIR CORPS

WS Gazelle AH1

Code	Serial
M	XZ345
S	ZB691
Y	ZB692

WS Lynx AH7

Code	Serial
C	XZ643
D	ZD283
E	ZD274
F	ZD278
H	XZ675
I	XZ669
K	ZD281
L	XZ605
T	XZ196
U	ZD277
V	XZ194
W	ZD272
Z	XZ184 & XZ221

2011 celebrated the 40th Anniversary of the first flight of the Westland Lynx. To commemorate this, Lynx HAS3S XZ233 of 702 NAS was painted in the blue colour scheme worn by early Navy machines

Tornado GR4 ZA600 of 41(R) Squadron based at Coninsgby wears special markings to commemorate the squadron's 90th anniversary.

The BBMF's Dakota, ZA947, was repainted in 2011 in the markings of a 233 Squadron machine, named 'Kwicherbichen'.

Gazelle AH1 ZB692/Y is operated by the Army Air Corps' 671 Squadron, based at Middle Wallop. The Gazelle is another type that is slowly disappearing from UK service.

ZH545 is a Sea King HAR3A, operated by 22 Squadron from Wattisham. It wears markings commemorating 70 years of RAF Search And Rescue (1941 - 2011).

Some *historic*, *classic* and *warbird* aircraft carry the markings of overseas air arms and can be seen in the UK, mainly preserved in museums and collections or taking part in air shows.

Serial	Type (code/other identity)	Owner/operator location or fate	Notes
AFGHANISTAN			
-	Hawker Afghan Hind (BAPC 82)	RAF Museum, Cosford	
ARGENTINA			
-	Bell UH-1H Iroquois (AE-406/998-8888) [Z]	RAF Valley, instructional use	
0729	Beech T-34C Turbo Mentor	FAA Museum, stored RNAS Yeovilton	
0767	Aermacchi MB339AA	Rolls-Royce Heritage Trust, stored Derby	
A-515	FMA IA58 Pucara (ZD485)	RAF Museum, Cosford	
A-517	FMA IA58 Pucara (G-BLRP)	Privately owned, Channel Islands	
A-522	FMA IA58 Pucara (8768M)	FAA Museum, at NE Aircraft Museum, Usworth	
A-528	FMA IA58 Pucara (8769M)	Norfolk & Suffolk Avn Museum, Flixton	
A-533	FMA IA58 Pucara (ZD486) <ff>	Privately owned, Cheltenham	
A-549	FMA IA58 Pucara (ZD487)	Imperial War Museum, Duxford	
AE-409	Bell UH-1H Iroquois [656]	Museum of Army Flying, Middle Wallop	
AE-422	Bell UH-1H Iroquois	FAA Museum, stored RNAS Yeovilton	
AUSTRALIA			
369	Hawker Fury ISS (F-AZXL) [D]	Privately owned, Avignon, France	
A2-4	Supermarine Seagull V (VH-ALB)	RAF Museum, Hendon	
A16-199	Lockheed Hudson IIIA (G-BEOX) [SF-R]	RAF Museum, Hendon	
A17-48	DH82A Tiger Moth (G-BPHR)	Privately owned, Wanborough, Wilts	
A19-144	Bristol 156 Beaufighter XIc (JM135/A8-324)	The Fighter Collection, Duxford	
A92-255	GAF Jindivik 102	DPA/QinetiQ, Boscombe Down, apprentice use	
A92-664	GAF Jindivik 4A	Boscombe Down Aviation Collection	
A92-708	GAF Jindivik 4A	Bristol Aero Collection, stored Kemble	
A92-908	GAF Jindivik 900 (ZJ503)	No 2445 Sqn ATC, Llanbedr	
N6-766	DH115 Sea Vampire T22) (XG766/G-VYPO [808]	Privately owned, Bournemouth	
BELGIUM			
A-41	SA318C Alouette II	The Helicopter Museum, Weston-super-Mare	
FT-36	Lockheed T-33A Shooting Star	Dumfries & Galloway Avn Mus, Dumfries	
H-50	Noorduyn AT-16 Harvard IIB (OO-DAF)	Privately owned, Brasschaat, Belgium	
HD-75	Hanriot HD1 (G-AFDX)	RAF Museum, Hendon	
IF-68	Hawker Hunter F6 <ff>	Privately owned,	
L-44	Piper L-18C Super Cub (OO-SPQ)	Royal Aéro Para Club de Spa, Belgium	
L-47	Piper L-18C Super Cub (OO-SPG)	Aeroclub Brasschaat VZW, Brasschaat, Belgium	
L-156	Piper L-18C Super Cub (OO-LGB)	Aeroclub Brasschaat VZW, Brasschaat, Belgium	
MT-23	Fouga CM170 Magister	*To Belgium, 2011*	
V-4	SNCAN Stampe SV-4B (OO-EIR)	Antwerp Stampe Centre, Antwerp-Deurne, Belgium	
V-18	SNCAN Stampe SV-4B (OO-GWD)	Antwerp Stampe Centre, Antwerp-Deurne, Belgium	
V-29	SNCAN Stampe SV-4B (OO-GWB)	Antwerp Stampe Centre, Antwerp-Deurne, Belgium	
V-66	SNCAN Stampe SV-4C (OO-GWA)	Antwerp Stampe Centre, Antwerp-Deurne, Belgium	
BOLIVIA			
FAB184	SIAI-Marchetti SF.260W (G-SIAI)	Privately owned, Booker	
BRAZIL			
1317	Embraer T-27 Tucano	Shorts, Belfast (engine test bed)	
BURKINA FASO			
BF8431	SIAI-Marchetti SF.260 (G-NRRA) [31]	Privately owned, Oaksey Park	
CANADA			
-	Lockheed T-33A Shooting Star (17473)	Midland Air Museum, Coventry	
622	Piasecki HUP-3 Retriever (51-16622/N6699D)	The Helicopter Museum, Weston-super-Mare	
920	VS Stranraer (CF-BXO) [Q-N]	RAF Museum, Hendon	
3019	NA81 Harvard II (G-CPPM)	Beech Restorations, Bruntingthorpe	
3349	NA64 Yale (G-BYNF)	Privately owned, Duxford	
5487	Hawker Hurricane II (G-CBOE)	Privately owned, Thruxton	
9041	Bristol 149 Bolingbroke IV <ff>	Manx Aviation Museum, Ronaldsway	
9048	Bristol 149 Bolingbroke IV <ff>	Bristol Aero Collection, Cotswold Airport	
9048	Bristol 149 Bolingbroke IV <rf>	Bristol Aero Collection, stored Filton	
9754	Consolidated PBY-5A Catalina (VP-BPS) [P]	Privately owned, Lee-on-Solent	
9893	Bristol 149 Bolingbroke IVT	Imperial War Museum store, Duxford	

Historic Aircraft in Overseas Markings

Notes	Serial	Type (code/other identity)	Owner/operator location or fate
	9940	Bristol 149 Bolingbroke IVT	Royal Scottish Mus'm of Flight, E Fortune
	15195	Fairchild PT-19A Cornell	RAF Museum Reserve Collection, Stafford
	16693	Auster J/1N Alpha (G-BLPG) [693]	Privately owned, Clacton
	18393	Avro Canada CF-100 Canuck 4B (G-BCYK)	Imperial War Museum, Duxford
	18671	DHC1 Chipmunk 22	The Shuttleworth Collection, Old Warden
		(WP905/7438M/G-BNZC) [671]	
	20249	Noorduyn AT-16 Harvard IIB	Privately owned, Texel, The Netherlands
		(PH-KLU) [XS-249]	
	20310	CCF T-6J Texan (G-BSBG) [310]	Privately owned, Tatenhill
	21417	Canadair CT-133 Silver Star	Yorkshire Air Museum, Elvington
	23140	Canadair CL-13 Sabre [AX] <rf>	Midland Air Museum, Coventry
	23380	Canadair CL-13 Sabre <rf>	Privately owned, Haverigg
	FH153	Noorduyn AT-16 Harvard IIB (G-BBHK) [58]	Sold to Poland, July 2011
	FJ777	Boeing-Stearman PT-17D Kaydet	Privately owned, Rendcomb
		(41-8689/G-BIXN)	
	KN448	Douglas Dakota IV <ff>	Science Museum, South Kensington

CHINA

Notes	Serial	Type (code/other identity)	Owner/operator location or fate
	61762	Nanchang CJ-6A Chujiao (G-CGFS) [72]	Privately owned, Seething
	68	Nanchang CJ-6A Chujiao	Privately owned, White Waltham
		(2632016/G-BXZB)	
	68	Nanchang CJ-6A Chujiao	Privately owned, White Waltham
		(2751219/G-BVVG)	

CZECH REPUBLIC

Notes	Serial	Type (code/other identity)	Owner/operator location or fate
	3677	Letov S-103 (MiG-15bisSB) (613677)	Royal Scottish Mus'm of Flight, E Fortune
	3794	Letov S-102 (MiG-15) (623794)	Norfolk & Suffolk Avn Museum, Flixton
		(starboard side only, painted in Polish	
		marks as 1972 on port side)	
	9147	Mil Mi-4	The Helicopter Museum, Weston-super-Mare

DENMARK

Notes	Serial	Type (code/other identity)	Owner/operator location or fate
	A-011	SAAB A-35XD Draken	Privately owned, Westhoughton, Lancs
	AR-107	SAAB S-35XD Draken	Newark Air Museum, Winthorpe
	E-419	Hawker Hunter F51 (G-9-441)	North-East Aircraft Museum, Usworth
	E-420	Hawker Hunter F51 (G-9-442) <ff>	Privately owned, Walton-on-Thames
	E-421	Hawker Hunter F51 (G-9-443)	Brooklands Museum, Weybridge
	E-423	Hawker Hunter F51 (G-9-444)	To Abu Dhabi, 2011
	E-424	Hawker Hunter F51 (G-9-445)	Aeroventure, Doncaster
	ET-272	Hawker Hunter T7 <ff>	Boulton Paul Association, Wolverhampton
	K-682	Douglas C-47A Skytrain (OY-BPB)	Foreningen For Flyvende Mus, Vaerløse, Denmark
	L-866	Consolidated PBY-6A Catalina (8466M)	RAF Museum, Cosford
	P-129	DHC-1 Chipmunk 22 (OY-ATO)	Privately owned, Roskilde, Denmark
	R-756	Lockheed F-104G Starfighter	Midland Air Museum, Coventry
	S-881	Sikorsky S-55C	The Helicopter Museum, Weston-super-Mare
	S-882	Sikorsky S-55C	Skirmish Paintball, Portishead
	S-886	Sikorsky S-55C	Hamburger Hill Paintball, Marksbury, Somerset
	S-887	Sikorsky S-55C	The Helicopter Museum, Weston-super-Mare

ECUADOR

Notes	Serial	Type (code/other identity)	Owner/operator location or fate
	FAE 259	BAC Strikemaster 80A (G-UPPI) [T59]	Privately owned, Exeter

EGYPT

Notes	Serial	Type (code/other identity)	Owner/operator location or fate
	158	Heliopolis Gomhouria Mk 6	Privately owned, Breighton
	356	Heliopolis Gomhouria Mk 6	Privately owned, Breighton
	764	Mikoyan MiG-21SPS <ff>	Privately owned, Northampton
	773	WS61 Sea King 47 (WA.823)	RNAS Yeovilton Fire Section
	774	WS61 Sea King 47 (WA.822)	DCAE AESS, HMS Sultan, Gosport
	775	WS61 Sea King 47 (WA.824)	DCAE AESS, HMS Sultan, Gosport
	776	WS61 Sea King 47 (WA.825)	DCAE AESS, HMS Sultan, Gosport
	0446	Mikoyan MiG-21UM <ff>	Thameside Aviation Museum, Tilbury
	7907	Sukhoi Su-7 <ff>	Robertsbridge Aviation Society, Mayfield

FINLAND

Notes	Serial	Type (code/other identity)	Owner/operator location or fate
	GA-43	Gloster Gamecock II (G-CGYF)	Privately owned, Dursley, Glos
	GN-101	Folland Gnat F1 (XK741)	Midland Air Museum, Coventry
	VI-3	Valtion Viima 2 (OO-EBL)	Privately owned, Brasschaat, Belgium

FRANCE

Notes	Serial	Type (code/other identity)	Owner/operator location or fate
	1/4513	Spad XIII <R> (G-BFYO/S3398)	American Air Museum, Duxford
	37	Nord 3400 (G-ZARA) [MAB]	Privately owned, Swanton Morley
	54	SNCAN NC.856A Norvigie [AOM]	Privately owned, Spanhoe
	67	SNCAN 1101 Noralpha (F-GMCY) [CY]	Privately owned, la Ferté-Alais, France

Serial	Type (code/other identity)	Owner/operator location or fate	Notes
70	Dassault Mystère IVA	Midland Air Museum, Coventry	
78	Nord 3202B-1 (G-BIZK)	Privately owned, Norfolk	
79	Dassault Mystère IVA [2-EG]	Norfolk & Suffolk Avn Museum, Flixton	
82	Curtiss Hawk 75 (G-CCVH)	The Fighter Collection, Duxford	
82	NA T-28D Fennec (F-AZKG)	Privately owned, Strasbourg, France	
83	Dassault Mystère IVA	Newark Air Museum, Winthorpe	
83	Morane-Saulnier MS.733 Alcyon (F-AZKS)	Privately owned, Montlucon, France	
84	Dassault Mystère IVA [8-NF]	Lashenden Air Warfare Museum, Headcorn	
85	Dassault Mystère IVA [8-MV]	Cold War Jets Collection, Bruntingthorpe	
104	MH1521M Broussard (F-GHFG) [307-FG]	Privately owned, Montceau-les-Mines, France	
105	Nord N2501F Noratlas (F-AZVM) [62-SI]	Le Noratlas de Provence, Marseilles, France	
106	MH1521M Broussard (F-GKJT) [33-JT]	Privately owned, Montceau-les-Mines, France	
108	MH1521M Broussard (F-BNEX) [50S9]	Privately owned, Lelystad, The Netherlands	
108	SO1221 Djinn (FR108) [CDL]	The Helicopter Museum, Weston-super-Mare	
121	Dassault Mystère IVA [8-MY]	City of Norwich Aviation Museum	
128	Morane-Saulnier MS.733 Alcyon (F-BMMY)	Privately owned, St Cyr, France	
143	Morane-Saulnier MS.733 Alcyon (G-MSAL)	Privately owned, Spanhoe	
146	Dassault Mystère IVA [8-MC]	North-East Aircraft Museum, Usworth	
156	SNCAN Stampe SV-4B (G-NIFE)	Privately owned, Gloucester	
157	Morane-Saulnier MS.230 Et2 (G-AVEB) [M-573,01]	*Sold to the US, March 2011*	
208	MH1521C1 Broussard (G-YYYY) [IR]	Privately owned, Eggesford	
261	MH1521M Broussard (F-GIBN) [30-QA]	Privately owned, Rotterdam, The Netherlands	
282	Dassault MD311 Flamant (F-AZFX) [316-KY]	Memorial Flt Association, la Ferté-Alais, France	
290	Dewoitine D27 (F-AZJD)	Les Casques de Cuir, la Ferté-Alais, France	
316	MH1521M Broussard (F-GGKR) [315-SN]	Privately owned, Lognes, France	
318	Dassault Mystère IVA [8-NY]	Dumfries & Galloway Avn Mus, Dumfries	
319	Dassault Mystère IVA [8-ND]	Rebel Air Museum, Andrewsfield	
319	Grumman TBM-3E Avenger (HB-RDG) [4F.6]	Privately owned, Lausanne, Switzerland	
354	Morane-Saulnier MS315E-D2 (G-BZNK)	Privately owned, Hemswell	
394	SNCAN Stampe SV-4C (G-BIMO)	Privately owned, White Waltham	
538	Dassault Mirage IIIE [3-QH]	Yorkshire Air Museum, Elvington	
42157	NA F-100D Super Sabre [11-ML]	North-East Aircraft Museum, Usworth	
54439	Lockheed T-33A Shooting Star (55-4439) [WI]	North-East Aircraft Museum, Usworth	
63938	NA F-100F Super Sabre [11-EZ]	Lashenden Air Warfare Museum, Headcorn	
121748	Grumman F8F-2P Bearcat (F-AZRJ) [5834/P]	Privately owned, Anemasse, France	
125716	Douglas AD-4N Skyraider (F-AZFN) [22-DG]	Privately owned, Mélun, France	
127002	Douglas AD-4NA Skyraider (F-AZHK) [20-LN]	Privately owned, Avignon, France	
517692	NA T-28S Fennec (G-TROY) [142]	Privately owned, Duxford	
18-5395	Piper L-18C Super Cub (52-2436/G-CUBJ) [CDG]	Privately owned, Old Warden	
51-7545	NA T-28S Fennec (N14113)	Privately owned, Duxford	
C850	Salmson 2A2 <R>	Barton Aviation Heritage Society, Barton	
MS824	Morane-Saulnier Type N <R> (G-AWBU)	Privately owned, Booker	
N1977	Nieuport Scout 17/23 <R> (N1723/G-BWMJ) [8]	Privately owned, Popham	

GERMANY

Serial	Type (code/other identity)	Owner/operator location or fate	Notes
-	Fieseler Fi103R-IV (V-1) (BAPC 91)	Lashenden Air Warfare Museum, Headcorn	
-	Fokker Dr1 Dreidekker <R> (BAPC 88)	FAA Museum stored, RNAS Yeovilton	
-	Messerschmitt Bf109 <R> (6357/BAPC 74) [6]	Kent Battle of Britain Museum, Hawkinge	
1	Hispano HA 1.112M1L Buchón (G-AWHE)	Privately owned, Duxford	
1	Messerschmitt Bf109G <R> (BAPC 240)	Yorkshire Air Museum, Elvington	
2	Messerschmitt Bf109G-10 (151591/D-FDME)	*Repainted as 3, 2010*	
3	Messerschmitt Bf109G-10 (D-FDME)	Messerschmitt Stiftung, Manching, Germany	
3	SNCAN 1101 Noralpha (G-BAYV)	Barton Aviation Heritage Society, Barton	
6	Messerschmitt Bf109G-2/Trop (10639/8478M/G-USTV)	RAF Museum, Hendon	
7	Messerschmitt Bf109G-4 (D-FWME)	Messerschmitt Stiftung, Manching, Germany	
8	Focke-Wulf Fw190 <R> (G-WULF)	Privately owned, Halfpenny Green	
9	Focke-Wulf Fw190 <R> (G-CCFW)	Privately owned, Little Rissington	
10	Hispano HA 1.112M1L Buchón (C4K-102/G-BWUE)	Historic Flying Ltd, Duxford	
14	Messerschmitt Bf109 <R> (BAPC 67)	Kent Battle of Britain Museum, Hawkinge	
14	Nord 1002 (G-ETME)	Privately owned, White Waltham	
14	SNCAN 1101 Noralpha (G-BSMD)	Privately owned, Prestwick	
139	SNCAN 1101 Noralpha (G-BSMD)	Privately owned, Perth	
87	Heinkel He111 <R> <ff> (F-AZPQ)	Privately owned, East Kirkby	
152/17	Fokker Dr1 Dreidekker <R> (F-AZPQ)	Les Casques de Cuir, la Ferté-Alais, France	

Historic Aircraft in Overseas Markings

Notes	Serial	Type (code/other identity)	Owner/operator location or fate
	152/17	Fokker Dr1 Dreidekker <R> (G-BVGZ)	Privately owned, Breighton
	157/18	Fokker D.VIII <R> (BAPC 239)	Norfolk & Suffolk Air Museum, Flixton
	210/16	Fokker EIII (BAPC 56)	Science Museum, South Kensington
	403/17	Fokker Dr1 Dreidekker <R> (G-CDXR)	Privately owned, Popham
	416/15	Fokker EIII <R> (G-GSAL)	Privately owned, Aston Down
	422/15	Fokker EIII <R> (G-AVJO)	Privately owned, Booker
	422/15	Fokker EIII <R> (G-FOKR)	Privately owned, Damyn's Hall, Essex
	425/17	Fokker Dr1 Dreidekker <R> (BAPC 133)	Kent Battle of Britain Museum, Hawkinge
	477/17	Fokker Dr1 Dreidekker <R> (G-FOKK)	Privately owned, Sywell
	556/17	Fokker Dr1 Dreidekker <R> (G-CFHY)	Privately owned, Tibenham
	626/8	Fokker DVII <R> (N6268)	Privately owned, Booker
	764	Mikoyan MiG-21SPS <ff>	Privately owned, Booker
	959	Mikoyan MiG-21SPS	Midland Air Museum, Coventry
	1190	Messerschmitt Bf109E-3 [4]	Imperial War Museum, Duxford
	1480	Messerschmitt Bf109 <R> (BAPC 66) [6]	Kent Battle of Britain Museum, Hawkinge
	1801/18	Bowers Fly Baby 1A (G-BNPV)	Privately owned, Chessington
	1803/18	Bowers Fly Baby 1A (G-BUYU)	Privately owned, Chessington
	1983	Messerschmitt Bf109E-3 (G-EMIL)	Privately owned, Colchester
	2100	Focke-Wulf Fw189A-1 (G-BZKY) [V7+1H]	Privately owned, Sandown
	4034	Messerschmitt Bf109E (G-CDTI)	Privately owned,
	4101	Messerschmitt Bf109E-3 (DG200/8477M) [12]	RAF Museum, Hendon
	4477	CASA 1.131E Jungmann (G-RETA) [GD+EG]	The Shuttleworth Collection, Old Warden
	6234	Junkers Ju87R-4 (G-STUK)	Privately owned, Surrey
	7198/18	LVG CVI (G-AANJ/9239M)	RAF Museum Restoration Centre, Cosford
	8417/18	Fokker DVII (9207M)	RAF Museum, Hendon
	12802	Antonov An-2T (D-FOFM)	Historische Flugzeuge, Grossenhain, Germany
	100143	Focke-Achgelis Fa330A-1	Imperial War Museum, Duxford
	100502	Focke-Achgelis Fa330A-1	Privately owned, Millom
	100503	Focke-Achgelis Fa330A-1 (8469M)	RAF Museum, Cosford
	100509	Focke-Achgelis Fa330A-1	Science Museum, stored Wroughton
	100545	Focke-Achgelis Fa330A-1	FAA Museum, stored RNAS Yeovilton
	100549	Focke-Achgelis Fa330A-1	Lashenden Air Warfare Museum, Headcorn
	110451	Fieseler Fi156D Storch (G-STOR)	Privately owned, Surrey
	112372	Messerschmitt Me262A-2a (AM.51/VH893/8482M) [4]	RAF Museum, Hendon
	120076	Heinkel He162A-2 Salamander (VH523/AM.59) [4]	*Sold to Germany, August 2011*
	120227	Heinkel He162A-2 Salamander (VN679/AM.65/8472M) [2]	RAF Museum, Hendon
	120235	Heinkel He162A-1 Salamander (AM.68)	Imperial War Museum, Lambeth
	191316	Messerschmitt Me163B Komet	Science Museum, South Kensington
	191454	Messerschmitt Me163B Komet <R> (BAPC 271)	The Shuttleworth Collection, Old Warden
	191461	Messerschmitt Me163B Komet (191614/8481M) [14]	RAF Museum, Cosford
	191659	Messerschmitt Me163B Komet (8480M) [15]	Royal Scottish Mus'm of Flight, E Fortune
	280020	Flettner Fl282/B-V20 Kolibri (frame only)	Midland Air Museum, Coventry
	360043	Junkers Ju88R-1 (PJ876/8475M) [D5+EV]	RAF Museum, Hendon
	420430	Messerschmitt Me410A-1/U2 (AM.72/8483M) [3U+CC]	RAF Museum, Cosford
	475081	Fieseler Fi156C-7 Storch (VP546/AM.101/7362M)[GM+AK]	RAF Museum, Cosford
	494083	Junkers Ju87D-3 (8474M) [RI+JK]	RAF Museum, Hendon
	584219	Focke-Wulf Fw190F-8/U1 (AM.29/8470M) [38]	RAF Museum, Hendon
	701152	Heinkel He111H-23 (8471M) [NT+SL]	RAF Museum, Hendon
	730301	Messerschmitt Bf110G-4 (AM.34/8479M) [D5+RL]	RAF Museum, Hendon
	733682	Focke-Wulf Fw190A-8/R7 (AM.75/9211M)	Imperial War Museum, Lambeth
	980554	Flug Werk FW190A-8/N (G-FWAB)	Meier Motors, Bremgarten, Germany
	2+1	Focke-Wulf Fw190 <R> (G-SYFW) [7334]	Privately owned, Wickenby
	17+TF	CASA 1.133C Jungmeister (G-BZTJ)	Privately owned, Turweston
	22+35	Lockheed F-104G Starfighter	Privately owned, Bruntingthorpe
	22+57	Lockheed F-104G Starfighter	Privately owned, Thorpe Wood, N Yorks
	23.02	Albatros B.II <R> (D-EKGH)	Historischer Flugzeugbau, Fürstenwalde, Germany
	28+08	Aero L-39ZO Albatros (142/28+04)	Pinewood Studios, Bucks
	2E+RA	Fieseler Fi-156C-3 Storch (F-AZRA)	Amicale J-B Salis, la Ferté-Alais, France
	4+1	Focke-Wulf Fw190 <R> (G-BSLX)	Privately owned, Norwich
	4V+GH	Amiot AAC1/Ju52 (Port.AF 6316) [9]	Imperial War Museum, Duxford
	6G+ED	Slepcev Storch (G-BZOB) [5447]	Privately owned, Croydon, Cambs
	37+86	McD F-4F Phantom II <ff>	Privately owned, Bruntingthorpe

Serial	Type (code/other identity)	Owner/operator location or fate	Notes
58+89	Dornier Do28D-2 Skyservant (D-ICDY)	Privately owned, Uetersen, Germany	
80+39	MBB Bo.105M	Privately owned, Coney Park, Leeds	
80+40	MBB Bo.105M	Privately owned, Coney Park, Leeds	
80+55	MBB Bo.105M	Lufthansa Resource Technical Training, Cotswold Airport	
80+77	MBB Bo.105M	Lufthansa Resource Technical Training, Cotswold Airport	
81+00	MBB Bo.105M (D-HZYR)	The Helicopter Museum, Weston-super-Mare	
96+21	Mil Mi-24D (406)	Imperial War Museum, Duxford	
96+26	Mil Mi-24D (421)	The Helicopter Museum, Weston-super-Mare	
97+04	Putzer Elster B (G-APVF)	Privately owned, Wickenby	
98+14	Sukhoi Su-22M-4	Hawker Hunter Aviation Ltd, stored Scampton	
99+24	NA OV-10B Bronco (F-AZKM)	Privately owned, Montelimar, France	
99+32	NA OV-10B Bronco (G-BZGK)	Privately owned, Rotterdam, The Netherlands	
AZ+JU	CASA 3.52L (F-AZJU)	Amicale J-B Salis, la Ferté-Alais, France	
BU+CC	CASA 1.131E Jungmann (G-BUCC)	Privately owned, Sandown	
CF+HF	Morane-Saulnier MS502 (EI-AUY)	Imperial War Museum, Duxford	
D5397/17	Albatros DVA <R> (G-BFXL)	FAA Museum, stored RNAS Yeovilton	
DM+BK	Morane-Saulnier MS505 (G-BPHZ)	Historic Aircraft Collection, Duxford	
ES+BH	Messerschmitt Bf108B-2 (D-ESBH)	Messerschmitt Stiftung, Manching, Germany	
FI+S	Morane-Saulnier MS505 (G-BIRW)	Royal Scottish Mus'm of Flight, E Fortune	
FM+BB	Messerschmitt Bf109G-6 (D-FMBB)	Messerschmitt Stiftung, Manching, Germany	
FW+WC	Flug Werk Fw190A-8/N (D-FWWC)	Sold to New Zealand, 2011	
GL+SU	Bücker Bü1181B-1 Bestmann (D-EQXE)	Crashed 10 April 2011, Dortmund, Germany	
GM+AI	Fieseler Fi156A Storch (2088/G-STCH)	Privately owned, Old Warden	
LG+03	Bücker Bü133C Jungmeister (G-AEZX)	Privately owned, Milden	
NJ+C11	Nord 1002 (G-ATBG)	Privately owned, Audley End	
NQ+NR	Klemm Kl35D (D-EQXD)	Quax Flieger, Hamm, Germany	
NV+KG	Focke-Wulf Fw44J Stieglitz (D-ENAY)	Quax Flieger, Hamm, Germany	
S4+A07	CASA 1.131E Jungmann (G-BWHP)	Privately owned, Yarcombe, Devon	
S5+B06	CASA 1.131E Jungmann 2000 (G-BSFB)	Privately owned, Old Buckenham	
TP+WX	Heliopolis Gomhouria Mk 6 (G-TPWX)	Privately owned, Swanborough	

GHANA
G-102	SA122 Bulldog	To Hungary	
G-108	SA122 Bulldog (G-BCUP)	To Hungary	

GREECE
52-6541	Republic F-84F Thunderflash [541]	North-East Aircraft Museum, Usworth	
63-8418	Northrop F-5A	Martin-Baker Ltd, Chalgrove, Fire Section	

HONG KONG
HKG-5	SA128 Bulldog (G-BULL)	Privately owned, Cotswold Airport	
HKG-6	SA128 Bulldog (G-BPCL)	Privately owned, North Weald	
HKG-11	Slingsby T.67M Firefly 200 (G-BYRY)	Privately owned, Antwerp, Belgium	
HKG-13	Slingsby T.67M Firefly 200 (G-BXKW)	Privately owned, St Ghislain, Belgium	

HUNGARY
501	Mikoyan MiG-21PF	Imperial War Museum, Duxford	
503	Mikoyan MiG-21SMT (G-BRAM)	RAF Museum, Cosford	

INDIA
Q497	EE Canberra T4 (WE191) (fuselage)	Dumfries & Galloway Avn Mus, Dumfries	
HA561	Hawker Tempest II (MW743)	Privately owned, stored Wickenby	
IN609	BAe Sea Harrier FRS51	Returned to India, 3 February 2009	

INDONESIA
LL-5313	BAe Hawk T53	BAE Systems, Brough, on display	

IRAQ
333	DH115 Vampire T55 <ff>	Aeroventure, stored Doncaster	

ITALY
MM5701	Fiat CR42 (BT474/8468M) [13-95]	RAF Museum, Hendon	
MM52801	Fiat G46-3B (G-BBII) [4-97]	Privately owned, Sandown	
MM53692	CCF T-6G Texan	RAeS Medway Branch, Rochester	
MM53774	Fiat G59-4B (I-MRSV) [181]	Privately owned, Parma, Italy	
MM54099	NA T-6G Texan (G-BRBC) [RR-56]	Privately owned, Chigwell	
MM54532	SIAI-Marchetti SF.260AM (G-ITAF) [70-42]	Privately owned, Leicester	
MM57247	SIAI-Marchetti SM.1019 (G-SIMA)	Sold to the US, May 2010	
MM81205	Agusta A109A-2 SEM [GF-128]	The Helicopter Museum, Weston-super-Mare	
MM54-2372	Piper L-21B Super Cub	Privately owned, Kesgrave, Suffolk	

Notes	Serial	Type (code/other identity)	Owner/operator location or fate
	JAPAN		
	-	Yokosuka MXY 7 Ohka II (BAPC 159)	Imperial War Museum, stored Duxford
	24	Kawasaki Ki100-1B (8476M/BAPC 83)	RAF Museum, Cosford
	997	Yokosuka MXY 7 Ohka II (8485M/BAPC 98)	Museum of Science & Industry, Manchester
	5439	Mitsubishi Ki46-III (8484M/BAPC 84)	RAF Museum, Cosford
	15-1585	Yokosuka MXY 7 Ohka II (BAPC 58)	Science Museum, at FAA Museum, RNAS Yeovilton
	I-13	Yokosuka MXY 7 Ohka II (8486M/BAPC 99)	RAF Museum, Cosford
	Y2-176	Mitsubishi A6M3-2 Zero (3685) [76]	Imperial War Museum, Duxford
	JORDAN		
	408	SA125 Bulldog (G-BDIN)	Privately owned, Lasham
	KENYA		
	115	Dornier Do28D-2 Skyservant	Privately owned, stored Hibaldstow
	117	Dornier Do28D-2 Skyservant	Privately owned, stored Hibaldstow
	KUWAIT		
	113	BAC Strikemaster 80A (G-CFBK) [D]	Privately owned, North Weald
	MYANMAR		
	UB441	VS361 Spitfire IX (ML119/G-SDNI)	Privately owned, Sandown
	THE NETHERLANDS		
	16-218	Consolidated PBY-5A Catalina (2459/PH-PBY)	Neptune Association, Lelystad, The Netherlands
	174	Fokker S-11 Instructor (E-31/G-BEPV) [K]	Privately owned, Spanhoe
	179	Fokker S-11 Instructor (PH-ACG) [K]	Privately owned, Lelystad, The Netherlands
	197	Fokker S-11 Instructor (PH-GRY) [K]	KLu Historic Flt, Gilze-Rijen, The Netherlands
	204	Lockheed SP-2H Neptune [V]	RAF Museum, Cosford
	A-12	DH82A Tiger Moth (PH-TYG)	Privately owned, Gilze-Rijen, The Netherlands
	B-64	Noorduyn AT-16 Harvard IIB (PH-LSK)	KLu Historic Flt, Gilze-Rijen, The Netherlands
	B-71	Noorduyn AT-16 Harvard IIB (PH-MLM)	KLu Historic Flt, Gilze-Rijen, The Netherlands
	B-118	Noorduyn AT-16 Harvard IIB (PH-IIB)	KLu Historic Flt, Gilze-Rijen, The Netherlands
	B-182	Noorduyn AT-16 Harvard IIB (PH-TBR)	KLu Historic Flt, Gilze-Rijen, The Netherlands
	E-14	Fokker S-11 Instructor (PH-AFS)	Privately owned, Lelystad, The Netherlands
	E-15	Fokker S-11 Instructor (G-BIYU)	Privately owned, Bagby
	E-20	Fokker S-11 Instructor (PH-GRB)	Privately owned, Gilze-Rijen, The Netherlands
	E-27	Fokker S-11 Instructor (PH-HOL)	Privately owned, Lelystad, The Netherlands
	E-32	Fokker S-11 Instructor (PH-HOI)	Privately owned, Gilze-Rijen, The Netherlands
	E-39	Fokker S-11 Instructor (PH-HOG)	Privately owned, Lelystad, The Netherlands
	G-29	Beech D18S (PH-KHV)	KLu Historic Flt, Gilze-Rijen, The Netherlands
	MH424	VS361 Spitfire LFIXC (MJ271/H-53)	Privately owned, Duxford
	MK732	VS361 Spitfire LFIXC (8633M/PH-OUQ) [3W-17]	KLu Historic Flt, Gilze-Rijen, The Netherlands
	N-202	Hawker Hunter F6 [10] <ff>	Privately owned, Stockport
	N-250	Hawker Hunter F6 (G-9-185) <ff>	Imperial War Museum, Duxford
	N-268	Hawker Hunter FGA78 (Qatar QA-10)	Yorkshire Air Museum, Elvington
	N-294	Hawker Hunter F6A (XF515/G-KAXF)	Stichting Hawker Hunter Foundation, Leeuwarden, The Netherlands
	N-302	Hawker Hunter T7 (ET-273/G-9-431) <ff>	Aeroventure, Doncaster
	N-315	Hawker Hunter T7 (comp XM121)	Privately owned, Netherley, Aberdeenshire
	N-321	Hawker Hunter T8C (G-BWGL)	Stichting Hawker Hunter Foundation, Leeuwarden, The Netherlands
	N5-149	NA B-25J Mitchell (44-29507/HD346/PH-XXV) [232511]	KLu Historic Flt, Gilze-Rijen, The Netherlands
	R-18	Auster III (PH-NGK)	KLu Historic Flt, Gilze-Rijen, The Netherlands
	R-55	Piper L-18C Super Cub (52-2466/G-BLMI)	Privately owned, White Waltham
	R-109	Piper L-21B Super Cub (54-2337/PH-GAZ)	KLu Historic Flt, Gilze-Rijen, The Netherlands
	R-122	Piper L-21B Super Cub (54-2412/PH-PPW)	KLu Historic Flt, Gilze-Rijen, The Netherlands
	R-124	Piper L-21B Super Cub (54-2414/PH-APA)	Privately owned, Eindhoven, The Netherlands
	R-137	Piper L-21B Super Cub (54-2427/PH-PSC)	Privately owned, Gilze-Rijen, The Netherlands
	R-151	Piper L-21B Super Cub (54-2441/G-BIYR)	Privately owned, Yarcombe, Devon
	R-156	Piper L-21B Super Cub (54-2446/G-ROVE)	Privately owned, Headcorn
	R-163	Piper L-21B Super Cub (54-2453/G-BIRH)	*Repainted as G-BIRH*
	R-167	Piper L-21B Super Cub (54-2457/G-LION)	Privately owned, Turweston, Bucks
	R-170	Piper L-21B Super Cub (52-6222/PH-ENJ)	Privately owned, Midden Zealand, The Netherlands
	R-177	Piper L-21B Super Cub (54-2467/PH-KNR)	KLu Historic Flt, Gilze-Rijen, The Netherlands
	R-181	Piper L-21B Super Cub (54-2471/PH-GAU)	Privately owned, Gilze-Rijen, The Netherlands
	R-345	Piper J-3C Cub (PH-UCS)	Privately owned, Hilversum, The Netherlands
	S-9	DHC2 L-20A Beaver (55-4585/PH-DHC)	KLu Historic Flt, Gilze-Rijen, The Netherlands

Serial	Type (code/other identity)	Owner/operator location or fate	Notes
NEW ZEALAND			
NZ3909	WS Wasp HAS1 (XT782/G-KANZ)	Kennet Aviation, stored North Weald	
NZ6361	BAC Strikemaster 87 (OJ5/G-BXFP)	Privately owned, Chalgrove	
NORTH KOREA			
-	WSK Lim-2 (MiG-15) (01420/G-BMZF)	FAA Museum, RNAS Yeovilton	
NORTH VIETNAM			
1211	WSK Lim-5 (MiG-17F) (G-MIGG)	Privately owned, North Weald	
NORWAY			
848	Piper L-18C Super Cub (LN-ACL) [FA-N]	Privately owned, Norway	
56321	SAAB S91B Safir (G-BKPY)	Newark Air Museum, Winthorpe	
PX-K	DH100 Vampire FB6 (SE-DXS)	Privately owned, Rygge, Norway	
PX-M	DH115 Vampire T55 (LN-DHZ)	Privately owned, Rygge, Norway	
OMAN			
425	BAC Strikemaster 82A (G-SOAF)	Privately owned, Hawarden	
801	Hawker Hunter T66B <ff>	Privately owned, Exeter	
801	Hawker Hunter T66B <rf>	Privately owned, Hawarden	
853	Hawker Hunter FR10 (XF426)	RAF Museum, Hendon	
POLAND			
05	WSK SM-2 (Mi-2) (S2-03006)	The Helicopter Museum, Weston-super-Mare	
309	WSK SBLim-2A (MiG-15UTI) <ff>	R Scottish Mus'm of Flight, stored Granton	
458	Mikoyan MiG-23ML (04 red/024003607)	Newark Air Museum, Winthorpe	
618	Mil Mi-8P (10618)	The Helicopter Museum, Weston-super-Mare	
1018	WSK-PZL Mielec TS-11 Iskra (1H-1018/G-ISKA)	Cold War Jets Collection, Bruntingthorpe	
1120	WSK Lim-2 (MiG-15bis)	RAF Museum, Cosford	
1706	WSK-PZL Mielec TS-11 Iskra (1H-0408)	Midland Air Museum, Coventry	
1972	Letov S-102 (MiG-15) (623794) (port side only, painted in Czech marks as 3794 on starboard side)	Norfolk & Suffolk Avn Museum, Flixton	
PORTUGAL			
85	Isaacs Fury II (G-BTPZ)	Privately owned, Ormskirk	
1350	OGMA/DHC1 Chipmunk T20 (G-CGAO)	Privately owned, Spanhoe	
1360	OGMA/DHC1 Chipmunk T20 (G-BYYU) (fuselage)	Privately owned, Little Stoughton	
1365	OGMA/DHC1 Chipmunk T20 (G-DHPM)	Privately owned, Sywell	
1367	OGMA/DHC1 Chipmunk T20 (G-UANO)	Privately owned, Sherburn-in-Elmet	
1372	OGMA/DHC1 Chipmunk T20 (HB-TUM)	Privately owned, Switzerland	
1373	OGMA/DHC1 Chipmunk T20 (G-CBJG)	Privately owned, Winwick, Cambs	
1375	OGMA/DHC1 Chipmunk T20 (F-AZJV)	Privately owned, Valenciennes, France	
1377	DHC1 Chipmunk 22 (G-BARS)	Privately owned, Yeovilton	
1741	CCF T-6J Texan (G-HRVD)	Privately owned, Bruntingthorpe	
1747	CCF T-6J Texan (20385/G-BGPB)	The Aircraft Restoration Co, Duxford	
3303	MH1521M Broussard (G-CBGL)	Privately owned, Bruntingthorpe	
QATAR			
QA12	Hawker Hunter FGA78 <ff>	Privately owned, New Inn, Torfaen	
QP30	WS Lynx Mk 28 (G-BFDV/TD 013)	DCAE SEAE, Arborfield	
QP31	WS Lynx Mk 28	Vector Aerospace Fleetlands Apprentice School	
QP32	WS Lynx Mk 28 (TAD 016)	DCAE SEAE, Arborfield	
ROMANIA			
29	LET L-29 Delfin <ff>	Privately owned, Shropshire	
42	LET L-29 Delfin	Privately owned, Catshill, Worcs	
47	LET L-29 Delfin	Privately owned, Ashton-under-Lyne	
53	LET L-29 Delfin (99954)	Privately owned, Bruntingthorpe	
RUSSIA (& FORMER SOVIET UNION)			
-	LET L-29S Delfin (491273/YL-PAG)	Privately owned, Breighton	
-	Mil Mi-24D (3532461715415)	Privately owned, Dunsfold	
-	Mil Mi-24D (3532464505029)	Midland Air Museum, Coventry	
1 w	SPP Yak C-11 (171314/G-BZMY)	Privately owned, Coventry	
01 y	Yakovlev Yak-52 (9311709/G-YKSZ)	Privately owned, White Waltham	
03 bl	Yakovlev Yak-55M (910103/RA-01274)	Privately owned, Halfpenny Green	
03 w	Yakovlev Yak-18A (1160403/G-CEIB)	Privately owned, Breighton	
03 w	Yakovlev Yak-52 (899803/G-YAKR)	Privately owned, North Weald	
5 w	Yakovlev Yak-3UA (0470204/D-FYGJ)	Privately owned, Sleap	
07 y	WSK SM-1 (Mi-1) (Polish AF 2007)	The Helicopter Museum, Weston-super-Mare	

Notes	Serial	Type (code/other identity)	Owner/operator location or fate
07 y		Yakovlev Yak-18M (G-BMJY)	Privately owned, East Garston, Bucks
07 r		Yakovlev Yak-52 (9011407/G-HYAK)	Privately owned, Exeter
09 y		Yakovlev Yak-52 (9411809/G-BVMU)	Privately owned, Shipdham
9 w		SPP Yak C-11 (1701139/G-OYAK)	Privately owned, Little Gransden
9 y		Polikarpov Po-2 (0094/G-BSSY)	Repainted as 28 w
10 si		Yakovlev Yak-52 (9111205/G-YAKF)	Privately owned, Swansea
10 y		Yakovlev Yak-50 (801810/G-BTZB)	Privately owned, Lee-on-Solent
10 y		Yakovlev Yak-52 (822710/G-CBMD)	Repainted as G-CBMD
11 y		SPP Yak C-11 (G-YCII)	Privately owned, Woodchurch, Kent
12 r		LET L-29 Delfin (194555/ES-YLM/G-DELF)	Privately owned, Manston
15 w		SPP Yak C-11 (170103/D-FYAK)	Classic Aviation Company, Hannover, Germany
20 w		Lavochkin La-11	The Fighter Collection, Duxford
21 w		Yakovlev Yak-3UA (0470203/G-CDBJ)	Privately owned, Headcorn
21 w		Yakovlev Yak-9UM (0470403/D-FENK)	Privately owned, Magdeburg, Germany
23 y		Bell P-39Q Airacobra (44-2911)	Privately owned, Sussex
23 w		Mikoyan MiG-27D (83712515040)	Privately owned, Hawarden
26 bl		Yakovlev Yak-52 (9111306/G-BVXK)	Privately owned, White Waltham
27 w		Yakovlev Yak-3UTI-PW (9/04623/F-AZIM)	Privately owned, la Ferté-Alais, France
27 r		Yakovlev Yak-52 (9111307/G-YAKX)	Privately owned, Popham
28 w		Polikarpov Po-2 (0094/G-BSSY)	The Shuttleworth Collection, Old Warden
31 w		Yakovlev Yak-52 (9111311/G-YAKV)	Privately owned, Rendcomb
33 r		Yakovlev Yak-50 (853206/G-YAKZ)	Privately owned, White Waltham
33 w		Yakovlev Yak-52 (899915/G-YAKH)	Privately owned, White Waltham
35 r		Sukhoi Su-17M-3 (25102)	Privately owned, Hawarden
36 w		LET/Yak C-11 (171101/G-KYAK)	Privately owned, North Weald
36 r		Yakovlev Yak-52 (9111604/G-IUII)	Privately owned, North Weald
42 w		Yakovlev Yak-52 (888911/G-CBRU)	Privately owned, Enstone
43 bl		Yakovlev Yak-52 (877501/G-BWSV)	Privately owned, North Weald
48 bl		Yakovlev Yak-52 (9111413/G-CBSN)	Privately owned, Manston
49 r		Yakovlev Yak-50 (822305/G-YAKU)	Privately owned, Henstridge
50 bk		Yakovlev Yak-50 (812101/G-CBPM)	Privately owned, High Cross
50 gy		Yakovlev Yak-52 (9111415/G-CBRW)	Meier Motors, Bremgarten, Germany
51 r		LET L-29 Delfin (893019/G-BZNT)	Privately owned, Winkleigh, Devon
51 y		Yakovlev Yak-50 (812004/G-BWYK)	Privately owned, West Meon, Hants
52 w		Yakovlev Yak C-11 (171312/G-BTZE)	Privately owned, Booker
52 w		Yakovlev Yak-52 (9612001/G-CCJK)	Privately owned, White Waltham
52 y		Yakovlev Yak-52 (878202/G-BWVR)	Privately owned, Barton
54 r		Sukhoi Su-17M (69004)	Privately owned, Hawarden
55 y		Yakovlev Yak-52 (9111505/G-BVOK)	Privately owned, Shoreham
61 r		Yakovlev Yak-50 (842710/G-YAKM)	Privately owned, Henstridge
66 r		Yakovlev Yak-52 (855905/G-YAKN)	Privately owned, Henstridge
67 r		Yakovlev Yak-52 (822013/G-CBSL)	Privately owned, Church Fenton
69 r		Hawker Hunter FGA9 (8839M/XG194)	Wattisham Airfield Museum
69 bl		Yakovlev Yak-52 (899413/G-XYAK)	Privately owned, Old Buckenham
69 y		Yakovlev Yak-52 (888712/G-CCSU)	Privately owned, Germany
71 r		Mikoyan MiG-27K (61912507006)	Newark Air Museum, Winthorpe
74 w		Yakovlev Yak-52 (877404/G-LAOK) [JA-74, IV-62]	Privately owned, Tollerton
93 w		Yakovlev Yak-50 (853001/G-JYAK) [R]	Privately owned, North Weald
100 bl		Yakovlev Yak-52 (866904/G-YAKI)	Privately owned, Popham
100 w		Yakovlev Yak-3M (0470107/G-CGXG)	Privately owned, Bentwaters
139 y		Yakovlev Yak-52 (833810/G-BWOD)	Privately owned, Sywell
526 bk		Mikoyan MiG-29 (2960725887) <ff>	Fenland & West Norfolk Aviation Museum, Wisbech
	1342	Yakovlev Yak-1 (G-BTZD)	Privately owned, Westfield, Sussex
	1870710	Ilyushin Il-2 (G-BZVW)	Privately owned, Wickenby
	1878576	Ilyushin Il-2 (G-BZVX)	Privately owned, Wickenby
1-12		Yakovlev Yak-52 (9011013/RA-02293)	Privately owned, Halfpenny Green
(RK858)		VS361 Spitfire LFIX (G-CGJE)	The Fighter Collection, Duxford
(SM639)		VS361 Spitfire LFIX	Privately owned, Catfield
SAUDI ARABIA			
	1104	BAC Strikemaster 80 (G-SMAS)	Privately owned, Hawarden
	1112	BAC Strikemaster 80 (G-FLYY)	Privately owned, Hawarden
	1115	BAC Strikemaster 80A	Global Aviation, Humberside
	1120	BAC Strikemaster 80A (G-RSAF)	Privately owned, Hawarden
	1129	BAC Strikemaster 80A	Global Aviation, Humberside
	1130	BAC Strikemaster 80A (G-VPER)	Sold as ZK-VPR, May 2011
	1133	BAC Strikemaster 80A (G-BESY)	Imperial War Museum, Duxford
	53-686	BAC Lightning F53 (G-AWON/ZF592)	City of Norwich Aviation Museum
	55-713	BAC Lightning T55 (ZF598) [C]	Midland Air Museum, Coventry

Serial	Type (code/other identity)	Owner/operator location or fate	Notes
SINGAPORE			
311	BAC Strikemaster 84 (G-MXPH)	Privately owned, North Weald	
323	BAC Strikemaster 81 (N21419)	Privately owned, stored Hawarden	
SOUTH AFRICA			
91	Westland Wasp HAS1 (pod)	Privately owned, Oaksey Park	
92	Westland Wasp HAS1 (G-BYCX)	Privately owned, Chiseldon	
221	DH115 Vampire T55 <ff>	Privately owned, Hemel Hempstead	
6130	Lockheed Ventura II (AJ469)	RAF Museum, stored Cosford	
7429	NA AT-6D Harvard III (D-FASS)	Privately owned, Aachen, Germany	
SOUTH VIETNAM			
24550	Cessna L-19E Bird Dog (G-PDOG) [GP]	Privately owned, Lincs	
SPAIN			
B.2I-27	CASA 2.111B (He111H-16) (B.2I-103)	Imperial War Museum, stored Duxford	
C.4E-88	Messerschmitt Bf109E	Privately owned, East Garston, Bucks	
E.3B-143	CASA 1.131E Jungmann (G-JUNG)	Privately owned, White Waltham	
E.3B-153	CASA 1.131E Jungmann (G-BPTS) [781-75]	Privately owned, Egginton	
E.3B-350	CASA 1.131E Jungmann (G-BHPL) [05-97]	Privately owned, Henstridge	
(E.3B-369)	CASA 1.131E Jungmann (G-BPDM) [781-32]	Privately owned, Heighington	
E.3B-494	CASA 1.131E Jungmann (G-CDLC) [81-47]	Privately owned, Chiseldon	
E.3B-521	CASA 1.131E Jungmann [781-3]	RAF Museum, Hendon	
E.3B-599	CASA 1.131E Jungmann (G-CGTX) [31]	Privately owned, Archerfield, Lothian	
E.18-2	Piper PA-31P Navajo 425 [42-71]	Bentwaters Cold War Museum	
EM-01	DH60G Moth (G-AAOR)	Privately owned, Rendcomb	
ES.1-4	Bücker Bü133C Jungmeister (G-BUTX)	Privately owned, Breighton	
ES.1-16	CASA 1.133L Jungmeister	Privately owned, Stretton, Cheshire	
SWEDEN			
-	Thulin A/Bleriot XI (SE-XMC)	Privately owned, Loberod, Sweden	
081	CFM 01 Tummelisa <R> (SE-XIL)	Privately owned, Loberod, Sweden	
2542	Fiat CR42 (G-CBLS)	The Fighter Collection, Duxford	
5033	Klemm KI35D (SE-BPT) [78]	Privately owned, Barkaby, Sweden	
5060	Klemm KI35D (SE-BPU) [174]	Privately owned, Barkaby, Sweden	
05108	DH60 Moth	Privately owned, Langham	
17239	SAAB B-17A (SE-BYH) [7-J]	Flygvapenmuseum, Linköping, Sweden	
28693	DH100 Vampire FB6 (J-1184/SE-DXY) [9-G]	Scandinavian Historic Flight, Oslo, Norway	
29640	SAAB J-29F [20-08]	Midland Air Museum, Coventry	
29670	SAAB J-29F (SE-DXB) [10-R]	Flygvapenmuseum/F10 Wing, Angelholm, Sweden	
32028	SAAB 32A Lansen (G-BMSG)	Privately owned, Willenhall, Staffs	
34066	Hawker Hunter F58 (J-4089/LN-HNT) [9-G]	Scandinavian Historic Flight, Halmstad, Sweden	
35075	SAAB J-35A Draken [40]	Dumfries & Galloway Aviation Museum	
35515	SAAB J-35F Draken [49]	Airborne Systems, Llangeinor	
37918	SAAB AJSH-37 Viggen [57]	Newark Air Museum, Winthorpe	
60140	SAAB 105 (SE-DXG) [140-5]	Flygvapenmuseum/F10 Wing, Angelholm, Sweden	
91130	SAAB S91A Safir (SE-BNN) [10-30]	Privately owned, Barkaby, Sweden	
SWITZERLAND			
-	DH112 Venom FB54 (J-1758/N203DM)	Grove Technology Park, Wantage, Oxon	
A-10	CASA 1.131E Jungmann (G-BECW)	Privately owned, Rochester	
A-12	Bücker Bu131B Jungmann (G-CCHY)	Privately owned, Booker	
A-57	CASA 1.131E Jungmann (G-BECT)	Privately owned, Goodwood	
A-701	Junkers Ju52/3m (HB-HOS)	Ju-Air, Dubendorf, Switzerland	
A-702	Junkers Ju52/3m (HB-HOT)	Ju-Air, Dubendorf, Switzerland	
A-703	Junkers Ju52/3m (HB-HOP)	Ju-Air, Dubendorf, Switzerland	
A-806	Pilatus P3-03 (G-BTLL)	Privately owned, East Dereham, Norfolk	
A-815	Pilatus P3-03 (HB-RCQ)	Privately owned, Locarno, Switzerland	
A-818	Pilatus P3-03 (HB-RCH)	Privately owned, Ambri, Switzerland	
A-829	Pilatus P3-03 (HB-RCJ)	Privately owned, Locarno, Switzerland	
A-873	Pilatus P3-03 (HB-RCL)	Privately owned, Locarno, Switzerland	
C-552	EKW C-3605 (G-DORN)	Privately owned, Bournemouth	
C-558	EKW C-3605 (G-CCYZ)	Privately owned, Wickenby	
J-1008	DH100 Vampire FB6Cotswold Airport	Mosquito Aircraft Museum, London Colney	
J-1169	DH100 Vampire FB6	Privately owned, Henley-on-Thames	
J-1172	DH100 Vampire FB6 (8487M)	RAF Museum Reserve Collection, Stafford	
J-1573	DH112 Venom FB50 (G-VICI)	Privately owned, Bournemouth	
J-1605	DH112 Venom FB50 (G-BLID)	Gatwick Aviation Museum, Charlwood, Surrey	
J-1629	DH112 Venom FB50	Privately owned, Shropshire	
J-1649	DH112 Venom FB50 <ff>	AIRBASE, Coventry	
J-1704	DH112 Venom FB54	RAF Museum, Cosford	

Notes	Serial	Type (code/other identity)	Owner/operator location or fate
	J-1712	DH112 Venom FB54 <ff>	Privately owned, Connah's Quay, Flintshire
	J-1790	DH112 Venom FB50 (J-1632/G-VNOM)	Mosquito Aircraft Museum, London Colney
	J-4015	Hawker Hunter F58 (J-4040/HB-RVS)	Privately owned, St Stephan, Switzerland
	J-4021	Hawker Hunter F58 (G-HHAC)	Hawker Hunter Aviation Ltd, Scampton
	J-4064	Hawker Hunter F58 (HB-RVQ)	Fliegermuseum Altenrhein, Switzerland
	J-4083	Hawker Hunter F58 (G-EGHH)	Privately owned, Exeter
	J-4086	Hawker Hunter F58 (HB-RVU)	Privately owned, Altenrhein, Switzerland
	J-4201	Hawker Hunter T68 (HB-RVR)	Amici dell'Hunter, Sion, Switzerland
	J-4205	Hawker Hunter T68 (HB-RVP)	Fliegermuseum Altenrhein, Switzerland
	J-4206	Hawker Hunter T68 (HB-RVV)	Fliegermuseum Altenrhein, Switzerland
	U-80	Bücker Bü133D Jungmeister (G-BUKK)	Privately owned, Kirdford, W Sussex
	U-95	Bücker Bü133C Jungmeister (G-BVGP)	Privately owned, Booker
	U-99	Bücker Bü133C Jungmeister (G-AXMT)	Privately owned, Breighton
	U-110	Pilatus P-2 (G-PTWO)	Privately owned, Rochester
	U-1215	DH115 Vampire T11 (XE998)	Solent Sky, Southampton
	V-54	SE3130 Alouette II (G-BVSD)	Privately owned, Glos
	USA		
	-	Noorduyn AT-16 Harvard IIB (KLu B-168)	American Air Museum, Duxford
	001	Ryan ST-3KR Recruit (G-BYPY)	Privately owned, Old Warden
	14	Boeing-Stearman A75N-1 Kaydet (G-ISDN)	Privately owned, Oaksey Park
	23	Fairchild PT-23 (N49272)	Privately owned, Sleap
	26	Boeing-Stearman A75N-1 Kaydet (G-BAVO)	Privately owned, Enstone
	27	NA SNJ-7 Texan (90678/G-BRVG)	Privately owned, Goodwood
	43	Noorduyn AT-16 Harvard IIB (43-13064/G-AZSC) [SC]	Privately owned, North Weald
	44	Boeing-Stearman D75N-1 Kaydet (42-15852/G-RJAH)	Privately owned, Duxford
	85	WAR P-47 Thunderbolt <R> (G-BTBI)	Privately owned, Perth
	104	Boeing-Stearman PT-13D Kaydet (42-16931/N4712V) [W]	Privately owned, Hardwick, Norfolk
	112	Boeing-Stearman PT-13D Kaydet (42-17397/G-BSWC)	Privately owned, Staverton
	164	Boeing-Stearman PT-13B Kaydet (N60320)	Privately owned, Baldock, Herts
	284	Curtiss P-40B Warhawk (41-13297/G-CDWH) [18P]	The Fighter Collection, Duxford
	379	Boeing-Stearman PT-13D Kaydet (42-14865/G-ILLE)	Fliegermuseum Altenrhein, Switzerland
	399	Boeing-Stearman N2S-5 Kaydet (38495/N67193)	Privately owned, Gelnhausen, Germany
	441	Boeing-Stearman N2S-4 Kaydet (30010/G-BTFG)	Privately owned, Manston
	466	Boeing-Stearman PT-13A Kaydet (37-0089/N731)	Privately owned, Staverton
	540	Piper L-4H Grasshopper (43-29877/G-BCNX)	Privately owned, Monewden
	560	Bell UH-1H Iroquois (73-22077/G-HUEY)	Privately owned, North Weald
	578	Boeing-Stearman N2S-5 Kaydet (N1364V)	Privately owned, North Weald
	586	Boeing-Stearman N2S-3 Kaydet (07874/N74650)	Privately owned, Popham
	628	Beech D17S (44-67761/N18V)	Privately owned, stored East Garston, Bucks
	669	Boeing-Stearman A75N-1 Kaydet (37869/G-CCXA)	Privately owned, Old Buckenham
	671	Boeing-Stearman PT-13D Kaydet (61181/G-CGPY)	Privately owned, Staverton
	699	Boeing-Stearman N2S-3 Kaydet (38233/G-CCXB)	Privately owned, Goodwood
	716	Boeing-Stearman PT-13D Kaydet (42-17553/N1731B)	Privately owned, Compton Abbas
	718	Boeing-Stearman PT-13D Kaydet (42-17555/N5345N)	Privately owned, Tibenham
	744	Boeing-Stearman A75N-1 Kaydet (42-16532/OO-USN)	Privately owned, Wevelgem, Belgium
	805	Boeing-Stearman PT-17 Kaydet (42-17642/N3922B)	Privately owned, Tibenham
	854	Ryan PT-22 Recruit (42-17378/G-BTBH)	Privately owned, Old Warden
	855	Ryan PT-22 Recruit (41-15510/N56421)	Privately owned, Sleap
	897	Aeronca 11AC Chief (G-BJEV) [E]	Privately owned, English Bicknor, Glos
	985	Boeing-Stearman PT-13D Kaydet (42-16930/OO-OPS)	Privately owned, Antwerp, Belgium
	1102	Boeing-Stearman N2S-5 Kaydet (G-AZLE) [102]	Privately owned, Tongham
	1164	Beech D18S (G-BKGL)	The Aircraft Restoration Co, Duxford

Serial	Type (code/other identity)	Owner/operator location or fate	Notes
1180	Boeing-Stearman N2S-3 Kaydet (3403/G-BRSK)	Privately owned, Morley	
3072	NA T-6G Texan (49-3072/G-TEXN) [72]	Privately owned, Shoreham	
3397	Boeing-Stearman N2S-3 Kaydet G-OBEE) [174]	Privately owned, Old Buckenham	
3403	Boeing-Stearman N2S-3 Kaydet (N75TQ) [180]	Privately owned, Tibenham	
3583	Piper L-4B Grasshopper (45-0583/G-FINT) [44-D]	Privately owned, Redhill	
4406	Naval Aircraft Factory N3N-3 (G-ONAF) [12]	Privately owned, Sandown	
6136	Boeing-Stearman A75N-1 Kaydet (42-16136/G-BRUJ) [205]	Privately owned, Liverpool	
6171	NA F-86D Sabre (51-6171)	North-East Aircraft Museum, Usworth	
6771	Republic F-84F Thunderstreak (BAF FU-6)	RAF Museum, stored Cosford	
7797	Aeronca L-16A Grasshopper (47-0797/G-BFAF)	Privately owned, Finmere	
8084	NA AT-6D Texan (42-85068/LN-AMY)	The Old Flying Machine Company, Duxford	
8178	NA F-86A Sabre (48-0178/G-SABR) [FU-178]	Golden Apple Operations/ARC, Duxford	
8242	NA F-86A Sabre (48-0242) [FU-242]	Midland Air Museum, Coventry	
01532	Northrop F-5E Tiger II <R>	RAF Alconbury on display	
02538	Fairchild PT-19B (N33870)	Privately owned, Mendlesham, Suffolk	
07539	Boeing-Stearman N2S-3 Kaydet (N63590) [143]	Privately owned, Billericay	
14286	Lockheed T-33A Shooting Star (51-4286)	American Air Museum, Duxford	
0-14419	Lockheed T-33A Shooting Star (51-4419)	Midland Air Museum, Coventry	
14863	NA AT-6D Harvard III (41-33908/G-BGOR)	Privately owned, Rednal	
15154	Bell OH-58A Kiowa (70-15154)	Defence Academy of the UK, Shrivenham	
15372	Piper L-18C Super Cub (51-15372/N123SA) [372-A]	Privately owned, Anwick, Lincs	
15990	Bell AH-1F Hueycobra (70-15990)	Museum of Army Flying, Middle Wallop	
16011	Hughes OH-6A Cayuse (69-16011/G-OHGA)	Privately owned, Wesham, Lancs	
16037	Piper J-3C Cub 65 (G-BSFD)	Privately owned, Sleap	
16445	Bell AH-1F Hueycobra (69-16445)	Defence Academy of the UK, Shrivenham	
16506	Hughes OH-6A Cayuse (67-16506)	The Helicopter Museum, Weston-super-Mare	
16544	NA AT-6A Texan (41-16544/N13FY) [FY]	Privately owned, Hilversum, The Netherlands	
16579	Bell UH-1H Iroquois (66-16579)	The Helicopter Museum, Weston-super-Mare	
16718	Lockheed T-33A Shooting Star (51-6718)	City of Norwich Aviation Museum	
17962	Lockheed SR-71A Blackbird (61-7962)	American Air Museum, Duxford	
18263	Boeing-Stearman PT-17 Kaydet (41-8263/N38940) [822]	Privately owned, Tibenham	
19252	Lockheed T-33A Shooting Star (51-9252)	Tangmere Military Aviation Museum	
21509	Bell UH-1H Iroquois (72-21509/G-UHIH)	Privately owned, Blackpool	
21605	Bell UH-1H Iroquois (72-21605)	American Air Museum, Duxford	
24538	Kaman HH-43F Huskie (62-4535)	Midland Air Museum, Coventry	
24541	Cessna L-19E Bird Dog (N134TT)	Privately owned, Yarcombe, Devon	
24568	Cessna L-19E Bird Dog (LN-WNO)	Army Aviation Norway, Kjeller, Norway	
24582	Cessna L-19E Bird Dog (G-VDOG)	Privately owned, Stockbridge, Hants	
28521	CCF T-6J Texan(G-TVIJ) [TA-521]	Privately owned, Woodchurch, Kent	
30274	Piper AE-1 Cub Cruiser (N203SA)	Privately owned, Nangis, France	
30861	NA TB-25J Mitchell (44-30861/N9089Z)	Privately owned, Booker	
31145	Piper L-4B Grasshopper (43-1145/G-BBLH) [26-G]	Privately owned, Biggin Hill	
31171	NA B-25J Mitchell (44-31171/N7614C)	American Air Museum, Duxford	
31430	Piper L-4B Grasshopper (43-1430/G-BHVV)	Privately owned, Perranporth	
31952	Aeronca O-58B Defender (G-BRPR)	Privately owned, Belchamp Water	
34037	NA TB-25N Mitchell (44-29366/N9115Z/8838M)	RAF Museum, Hendon	
37414	McD F-4C Phantom II (63-7414)	Midland Air Museum, stored Coventry	
39624	Wag Aero Sport Trainer (G-BVMH) [39-D]	Privately owned, Temple Bruer	
40467	Grumman F6F-5K Hellcat (80141/G-BTCC) [19]	The Fighter Collection, Duxford	
41386	Thomas-Morse S4 Scout <R> (G-MJTD)	Privately owned, Lutterworth	
42165	NA F-100D Super Sabre (54-2165) [VM]	American Air Museum, Duxford	
42196	NA F-100D Super Sabre (54-2196)	Norfolk & Suffolk Avn Museum, Flixton	
43517	Boeing-Stearman N2S-5 Kaydet (G-NZSS) [227]	Privately owned, Woodchurch, Kent	
46214	Grumman TBM-3E Avenger (69327/CF-KCG) [X-3]	American Air Museum, Duxford	
54433	Lockheed T-33A Shooting Star (55-4433)	Norfolk & Suffolk Avn Museum, Flixton	

135

Historic Aircraft in Overseas Markings

Notes	Serial	Type (code/other identity)	Owner/operator location or fate
	54884	Piper L-4J Grasshopper (45-4884/N61787) [57-D]	Privately owned, Sywell
	56498	Douglas C-54Q Skymaster (N44914)	Privately owned, stored North Weald
	60312	McD F-101F Voodoo (56-0312)	Midland Air Museum, Coventry
60344		Ryan Navion (N4956C)	Privately owned, Earls Colne
	60689	Boeing B-52D Stratofortress (56-0689)	American Air Museum, Duxford
63000		NA F-100D Super Sabre (54-2212) [FW-000]	USAF Croughton, Oxon, at gate
63319		NA F-100D Super Sabre (54-2269) [FW-319]	RAF Lakenheath, on display
	66692	Lockheed U-2CT (56-6692)	American Air Museum, Duxford
	70270	McD F-101B Voodoo (57-270) (fuselage)	Midland Air Museum, Coventry
80105		Replica SE5a <R> (PH-WWI/G-CCBN) [19]	Privately owned, Thruxton
80995		Cessna 337D Super Skymaster (F-BRPQ)	Privately owned, Strasbourg, France
	82062	DHC U-6A Beaver (58-2062)	Midland Air Museum, Coventry
	93542	CCF T-6J Harvard IV (G-BRLV) [LTA-542]	Privately owned, North Weald
	96995	CV F4U-4 Corsair (OE-EAS) [BR-37]	Flying Bulls, Salzburg, Austria
111836		NA AT-6C Harvard IIA (41-33262/G-TSIX) [JZ-6]	Privately owned, Church Fenton
	111989	Cessna L-19A Bird Dog (51-11989/N33600)	Museum of Army Flying, Middle Wallop
	114700	NA T-6G Texan (51-14700/G-TOMC)	Privately owned, Netherthorpe
	115042	NA T-6G Texan (51-15042/G-BGHU) [TA-042]	Privately owned, Headcorn
	115227	NA T-6G Texan (51-15227/G-BKRA)	Privately owned, Staverton
	115302	Piper L-18C Super Cub (51-15302/G-BJTP) [TP]	Privately owned, Defford
	115373	Piper L-18C Super Cub (51-15373/G-AYPM) [A-373]	Privately owned, Coldridge, Devon
	115684	Piper L-21A Super Cub (51-15684/G-BKVM) [DC]	Privately owned, Strubby
	121714	Grumman F8F-2P Bearcat (G-RUMM) [201-B]	The Fighter Collection, Duxford
	124143	Douglas AD-4NA Skyraider (F-AZDP) [205-RM]	Amicale J-B Salis, la Ferté-Alais, France
124485		Boeing B-17G Flying Fortress (44-85784/G-BEDF)[DF-A]	B-17 Preservation Ltd, Duxford
	124541	CV F4U-5NL Corsair (F-AZYS) [16-WF]	Privately owned, Avignon, France
	124724	CV F4U-5NL Corsair (F-AZEG) [22]	Les Casques de Cuir, la Ferté-Alais, France
	126922	Douglas AD-4NA Skyraider (G-RADR) [503-H]	Kennet Aviation, North Weald
134076		NA AT-6D Texan (41-34671/F-AZSC) [TA076]	Privately owned, Yvetot, France
	138179	NA T-28A Trojan (OE-ESA) [BA]	The Flying Bulls, Salzburg, Austria
	138266	NA T-28B Trojan (HB-RCT) [266-CT]	Jet Alpine Fighter, Sion, Switzerland
	140547	NA T-28C Trojan (F-AZHN) [IF-28]	Privately owned, Toussus le Noble, France
	140566	NA T-28C Trojan (N556EB) [252]	Privately owned, la Ferté-Alais, France
	146289	NA T-28C Trojan (N99153) [2W]	Norfolk & Suffolk Avn Museum, Flixton
150225		WS58 Wessex 60 (G-AWOX) [123]	Privately owned, Lulsgate
	155529	McD F-4J(UK) Phantom II (ZE359) [AJ-114]	American Air Museum, Duxford
	155848	McD F-4S Phantom II [WT-11]	Royal Scottish Mus'm of Flight, E Fortune
	159233	HS AV-8A Harrier [CG-33]	Imperial War Museum North, Salford Quays
	162068	McD AV-8B Harrier II <ff>	Privately owned, Thorpe Wood, N Yorks
	162071	McD AV-8B Harrier II (fuselage)	Rolls-Royce, Filton
	162074	McD AV-8B Harrier II <ff>	Privately owned, South Molton, Devon
	162730	McD AV-8B Harrier II <ff>	Privately owned, Liverpool
	162737	McD AV-8B Harrier II (fuselage) [38]	MoD, Boscombe Down
	162958	McD AV-8B Harrier II <ff>	QinetiQ, Farnborough
	162964	McD AV-8B Harrier II <ff>	Tri Sim Ltd, Peterborough
	162964	McD AV-8B Harrier II <ff>	Privately owned, Charlwood, Surrey
	163205	McD AV-8B Harrier II (fuselage)	Privately owned, Thorpe Wood, N Yorks
	163423	McD AV-8B Harrier II <ff>	QinetiQ, Boscombe Down
	163423	McD AV-8B Harrier II <rf>	Privately owned, Sproughton
	210855	Curtiss P-40M Kittyhawk (43-5802/G-KITT)	Hangar 11 Collection, North Weald
	217786	Boeing-Stearman PT-17 Kaydet (41-8169/CF-EQS) [25]	American Air Museum, Duxford
224319		Douglas C-47B Skytrain (44-77047/G-AMSN) <ff>	Privately owned, Sussex
	225068	Republic TP-47G Thunderbolt (42-25068/G-CDVX) [WZ-D]	The Fighter Collection, Duxford
226413		Republic P-47D Thunderbolt (45-49192/N47DD) [ZU-N]	American Air Museum, Duxford

Serial	Type (code/other identity)	Owner/operator location or fate	Notes
231983	Boeing B-17G Flying Fortress (44-83735/F-BDRS)[IY-G]	American Air Museum, Duxford	
234539	Fairchild PT-19B Cornell (42-34539/N50429) [63]	Privately owned, Dunkeswell	
236657	Piper L-4A Grasshopper (42-36657/G-BGSJ) [72-D]	Privately owned, Langport	
238410	Piper L-4A Grasshopper (42-38410/G-BHPK) [44-A]	Privately owned, Tibenham	
241079	Waco CG-4A Hadrian <R>	Assault Glider Association, Shawbury	
243809	Waco CG-4A Hadrian (BAPC 185)	Museum of Army Flying, Middle Wallop	
252983	Schweizer TG-3A (42-52983/N66630)	Imperial War Museum, stored Duxford	
298177	Stinson L-5A Sentinel (42-98177/N6438C) [8-R]	Privately owned, Tibenham	
314887	Fairchild Argus III (43-14887/G-AJPI)	Privately owned, Eelde, The Netherlands	
315211	Douglas C-47A Skytrain (43-15211/N1944A) [J8-B]	*Sold to the US, July 2011*	
315509	Douglas C-47A Skytrain (43-15509/G-BHUB) [W7-S]	American Air Museum, Duxford	
319764	Waco CG-4A Hadrian (237123/BAPC 157) (fuselage)	Yorkshire Air Museum, Elvington	
329282	Piper J-3C Cub 65 (N46779)	Privately owned, Abbots Bromley	
329405	Piper L-4H Grasshopper (43-29405/G-BCOB) [23-A]	Privately owned, South Walsham, Norfolk	
329417	Piper L-4A Grasshopper (42-38400/G-BDHK)	Privately owned, English Bicknor, Glos	
329471	Piper L-4H Grasshopper (43-29471/G-BGXA) [44-F]	Privately owned, Martley, Worcs	
329601	Piper L-4H Grasshopper (43-29601/G-AXHR) [44-D]	Privately owned, Nayland	
329707	Piper L-4H Grasshopper (43-29707/G-BFBY) [44-S]	Privately owned, Old Buckenham	
329854	Piper L-4H Grasshopper (43-29854/G-BMKC) [44-R]	Privately owned, Newtownards	
329934	Piper L-4H Grasshopper (43-29934/G-BCPH) [72-B]	Privately owned, Thatcham	
330238	Piper L-4H Grasshopper (43-30238/G-LIVH) [24-A]	Privately owned, Yarcombe, Devon	
330244	Piper L-4H Grasshopper (43-30244/G-CGIY) [46-C]	Privately owned, Leeds	
330372	Piper L-4H Grasshopper (43-30372/G-AISX)	Privately owned, Booker	
330485	Piper L-4H Grasshopper (43-30485/G-AJES) [44-C]	Privately owned, Shifnal	
411622	NA P-51D Mustang (44-74427/F-AZSB) [G4-C]	Amicale J-B Salis, la Ferté-Alais, France	
413317	NA P-51D Mustang (44-74409/N51RT) [VF-B]	RAF Museum, Hendon	
413521	NA P-51D Mustang (44-13521/G-MRLL) [5Q-B]	Privately owned, Hardwick, Norfolk	
413573	NA P-51D Mustang (44-73415/9133M/N6526D) [B6-V]	RAF Museum, Cosford	
413704	NA P-51D Mustang (44-73149/G-BTCD) [B7-H]	The Old Flying Machine Company, Duxford	
414151	NA P-51D Mustang (44-73140/NL314BG) [HO-M]	*Sold to the USA*	
414419	NA P-51D Mustang (45-15118/G-MSTG) [LH-F]	Privately owned, Hardwick, Norfolk	
414450	NA P-51D Mustang (44-73877/N167F) [B6-S]	Nordic Warbirds, Västerås, Sweden	
414673	Bonsall Mustang <R> (G-BDWM) [LH-I]	Privately owned, Gamston	
433915	Consolidated PBV-1A Canso A (RCAF 11005/G-PBYA)	Privately owned, Duxford	
434602	Douglas A-26B Invader (44-34602/LN-IVA) [B]	Nordic Warbirds, Västerås, Sweden	
436021	Piper J/3C Cub 65 (G-BWEZ)	Privately owned, Strathaven, Strathclyde	
442268	Noorduyn AT-16 Harvard IIB (KF568/LN-TEX) [TA-268]	Scandinavian Historic Flight, Oslo, Norway	
454467	Piper L-4J Grasshopper (45-4467/G-BILI) [44-J]	Privately owned, White Waltham	
454537	Piper L-4J Grasshopper (45-4537/G-BFDL) [04-J]	Privately owned, Shempston Farm, Lossiemouth	
458811	NA B-25J Mitchell (45-8811/F-AZZU) [SB]	*Crashed 31 May 2011, Melun, France*	

Notes	Serial	Type (code/other identity)	Owner/operator location or fate
	461748	Boeing B-29A Superfortress (44-61748/G-BHDK) [Y]	American Air Museum, Duxford
	463209	NA P-51D Mustang <R> (BAPC 255) [WZ-S]	American Air Museum, Duxford
	472035	NA P-51D Mustang (44-72035/G-SIJJ)	Hangar 11 Collection, North Weald
	472216	NA P-51D Mustang (44-72216/G-BIXL) [HO-M]	Privately owned, East Garston, Bucks
	472218	CAC-18 Mustang 22 (A68-192/D-FBBD) [WZ-I]	Crashed 10 July 2011, Duxford
	472218	NA P-51D Mustang (44-73979) [WZ-I]	Imperial War Museum, Lambeth
	472218	Titan T-51 Mustang (G-MUZY) [WZ-I]	Privately owned, Damyns Hall, Essex
	472773	NA P-51D Mustang (44-72773/D-FPSI) [QP-M]	Meier Motors, Bremgarten, Germany
	473871	NA TF-51D Mustang (44-73871/D-FTSI) [TF-871]	Meier Motors, Bremgarten, Germany
	474008	Jurca MJ77 Gnatsum (G-PSIR) [VF-R]	Privately owned, Lewes
	474425	NA P-51D Mustang (44-74425/PH-PSI) [OC-G]	Privately owned, Lelystad, The Netherlands
	474923	NA P-51D Mustang (44-74923/PH-JAT)	Privately owned, Lelystad, The Netherlands
	479744	Piper L-4H Grasshopper (44-79744/G-BGPD) [49-M]	Privately owned, Marsh, Bucks
	479766	Piper L-4H Grasshopper (44-79766/G-BKHG) [63-D]	Privately owned, Frogland Cross
	479781	Piper L-4H Grasshopper (44-79781/G-AISS)	Privately owned, Insch (under restoration)
	479897	Piper L-4H Grasshopper (44-79897/G-BOXJ) [JD]	Privately owned, Rochester
	480015	Piper L-4H Grasshopper (44-80015/G-AKIB) [44-M]	Privately owned, Perranporth
	480133	Piper L-4J Grasshopper (44-80133/ G-BDCD) [44-B]	Privately owned, Slinfold
	480173	Piper L-4J Grasshopper (44-80609/G-RRSR) [57-H]	Privately owned, Wellesbourne Mountford
	480321	Piper L-4J Grasshopper (44-80321/G-FRAN) [44-H]	Privately owned, Rayne, Essex
	480480	Piper L-4J Grasshopper (44-80480/G-BECN) [44-E]	Privately owned, Rayne, Essex
	480551	Piper L-4J Grasshopper (44-80551/LN-KLT) [43-S]	Scandinavian Historic Flight, Oslo, Norway
	480636	Piper L-4J Grasshopper (44-80636/G-AXHP) [58-A]	Privately owned, Spanhoe
	480723	Piper L-4J Grasshopper (44-80723/G-BFZB) [E5-J]	Privately owned, Egginton
	480752	Piper L-4J Grasshopper (44-80752/G-BCXJ) [39-E]	Privately owned, Old Sarum
	483868	Boeing B-17G Flying Fortress (44-83868/N5237V) [A-N]	RAF Museum, Hendon
	493209	NA T-6G Texan (49-3209/G-DDMV/41)	Privately owned, Rochester
	511701A	Beech C-45H (51-11701/G-BSZC) [AF258]	Privately owned, Bryngwyn Bach
	779465	Hiller UH-12C (N5315V)	Privately owned, Lower Upham, Hants
	2100882	Douglas C-47A Skytrain (42-100882/N473DC) [3X-P]	Privately owned, Liverpool
	2100884	Douglas C-47A Skytrain (42-100884/N147DC) [L4-D]	Privately owned, Dunsfold
	2105915	Curtiss P-40N Kittyhawk (42-105915/F-AZKU) [12]	Privately owned, la Ferté-Alais, France
	00195700	Cessna F.150G (G-USAA)	Repainted as G-USAA
	03-08003	B-V CH-47F Chinook	RAF Odiham, instructional use
	3-1923	Aeronca O-58B Defender (43-1923/ G-BRHP)	Privately owned, Chiseldon
	18-2001	Piper L-18C Super Cub (52-2401/G-BIZV)	Privately owned, Wicklow, Ireland
	39-139	Beech YC-43 Traveler (N295BS)	Duke of Brabant AF, Eindhoven, The Netherlands
	40-2538	Fairchild PT-19A Cornell (N33870)	Privately owned, Great Oakley, Essex
	41-19393	Douglas A-20C Havoc (wreck)	WWII Remembrance Museum, Handcross, W Sussex
	41-19841	Curtiss P-40F Warhawk (GCCGZP) [X-17]	The Fighter Collection, Duxford
	41-33275	NA AT-6C Texan (G-BICE) [CE]	Privately owned, Great Oakley, Essex
	42-12417	Noorduyn AT-16 Harvard IIB (KLu. B-163)	Newark Air Museum, Winthorpe
	42-35870	Taylorcraft DCO-65 (G-BWLJ) [129]	Privately owned, Nayland
	42-58678	Taylorcraft DF-65 (G-BRIY) [IY]	Privately owned, Carlisle
	42-78044	Aeronca 11AC Chief (G-BRXL)	Privately owned, Andrewsfield
	42-84555	NA AT-6D Harvard III (FAP.1662/G-ELMH) [EP-H]	Privately owned, Hardwick, Norfolk
	42-93510	Douglas C-47A Skytrain [CM] <ff>	Privately owned, Kew
	43-9628	Douglas A-20G Havoc <ff>	Privately owned, Hinckley, Leics

Serial	Type (code/other identity)	Owner/operator location or fate	Notes
43-11137	Bell P-63C Kingcobra (wreck)	WWII Remembrance Museum, Handcross, W Sussex	
43-21664	Douglas A-20G Havoc (wreck)	WWII Remembrance Museum, Handcross, W Sussex	
43-35943	Beech 3N (G-BKRN) [943]	Beech Restorations, Bruntingthorpe	
43-36140	NA B-25J Mitchell <ff>	WWII Remembrance Museum, Handcross, W Sussex	
44-4315	Bell P-63C Kingcobra	WWII Remembrance Museum, Handcross, W Sussex	
44-4368	Bell P-63C Kingcobra	Privately owned, Surrey	
44-13954	NA P-51D Mustang (G-UAKE)	Mustang Restoration Co Ltd, Coventry	
44-14574	NA P-51D Mustang (fuselage)	East Essex Aviation Museum, Clacton	
44-42914	Douglas DC-4 (N31356)	Privately owned, stored North Weald	
44-51228	Consolidated B-24M Liberator [EC]	American Air Museum, Duxford	
44-79609	Piper L-4H Grasshopper (G-BHXY) [PR]	Privately owned, Bealbury, Cornwall	
44-80594	Piper L-4J Grasshopper (G-BEDJ)	Privately owned, White Waltham	
44-80647	Piper L-4J Grasshopper (D-EGAF)	The Vintage Aircraft Co, Fürstenwalde, Germany	
44-83184	Fairchild UC-61K Argus III (G-RGUS)	Privately owned, Snitterby	
51-9036	Lockheed T-33A Shooting Star	Newark Air Museum, Winthorpe	
51-15319	Piper L-18C Super Cub (G-FUZZ) [A-319]	Privately owned, Elvington	
51-15555	Piper L-18C Super Cub (G-OSPS)	Privately owned, Weston, Eire	
52-8543	CCF T-6J Texan (G-BUKY) [66]	Privately owned, Breighton	
54-005	NA F-100D Super Sabre (54-2163)	Dumfries & Galloway Avn Mus, Dumfries	
54-174	NA F-100D Super Sabre (54-2174) [SM]	Midland Air Museum, Coventry	
54-2223	NA F-100D Super Sabre	Newark Air Museum, Winthorpe	
54-2445	Piper L-21B Super Cub (G-OTAN) [A-445]	Privately owned, Andrewsfield	
54-2447	Piper L-21B Super Cub (G-SCUB)	Privately owned, Anwick	
62-428	Republic F-105G Thunderchief (62-4428) [WW]	USAF Croughton, Oxon, at gate	
63-699	McD F-4C Phantom II (63-7699) [CG]	Midland Air Museum, Coventry	
64-17657	Douglas B-26K Counter Invader (N99218) <ff>	WWII Remembrance Museum, Handcross, W Sussex	
65-777	McD F-4C Phantom II (63-7419) [SA]	RAF Lakenheath, on display	
67-120	GD F-111E Aardvark (67-0120) [UH]	American Air Museum, Duxford	
68-0060	GD F-111E Aardvark <ff>	Dumfries & Galloway Avn Mus, Dumfries	
68-8284	Sikorsky MH-53M Pave Low IV	RAF Museum, Cosford	
70-0389	GD F-111E Aardvark (68-0011) [LN]	RAF Lakenheath, on display	
72-1447	GD F-111F Aardvark <ff>	American Air Museum, Duxford	
72-448	GD F-111E Aardvark (68-0011) [LN]	Repainted as 70-0389	
74-0177	GD F-111F Aardvark [FN]	RAF Museum, Cosford	
76-020	McD F-15A Eagle (76-0020)	American Air Museum, Duxford	
76-124	McD F-15B Eagle (76-0124) [LN]	RAF Lakenheath, instructional use	
77-259	Fairchild A-10A Thunderbolt (77-0259) [AR]	American Air Museum, Duxford	
80-219	Fairchild GA-10A Thunderbolt (80-0219) [AR]	RAF Alconbury, on display	
82-23762	B-V CH-47D Chinook <ff>	RAF Odiham, instructional use	
83-24104	B-V CH-47D Chinook [BN] <ff>	RAF Museum, Hendon	
86-01677	B-V CH-47D Chinook	RAF Odiham, instructional use	
89-00159	B-V CH-47D Chinook	RAF Odiham, instructional use	
92-048	McD F-15A Eagle (74-0131) [LN]	RAF Lakenheath, on display	
146-11042	Wolf WII Boredom Fighter (G-BMZX) [7]	Privately owned, Tibenham	
146-11083	Wolf WII Boredom Fighter (G-BNAI) [5]	Privately owned, Haverfordwest	
CY-D	NA TF-51D Mustang (44-84847/N251RJ)	The Fighter Collection, Duxford	
G-57	Piper L-4A Grasshopper (42-36375/G-AKAZ)	Privately owned, Duxford	

YEMEN

| 104 | BAC Jet Provost T.52A (G-PROV) | Privately owned, North Weald | |

YUGOSLAVIA

30139	Soko P-2 Kraguj [139]	Privately owned, Biggin Hill	
30140	Soko P-2 Kraguj (G-RADA) [140]	Privately owned, Biggin Hill	
30146	Soko P-2 Kraguj (G-BSXD) [146]	Privately owned, Linton-on-Ouse	
30149	Soko P-2 Kraguj (G-SOKO) [149]	Privately owned, Fenland	
30151	Soko P-2 Kraguj [151]	Privately owned, Sopley, Hants	

Broussard G-CBGL is painted in false Portuguese markings as 3303 and based at Bruntingthorpe.

C-47A N1944A is painted in US markings as 315211 and was based at Kemble until it departed on sale to the USA in late July 2011.

480133 is an L-4J Grasshopper, based at Slinfold. It is on the UK civil register as G-BDCD.

Bruntingthorpe's former French Air Force Mystere, 85, was repainted in an unusual grey and blue camouflage scheme during 2011 and is seen here before markings were reapplied.

Notes	Serial	Type (code/other identity)	Owner/operator location or fate
	C7	Avro 631 Cadet (EI-AGO)	IAC, Baldonnel
	34	Miles M14A Magister I (N5392)	National Museum of Ireland, Dublin
	141	Avro 652A Anson C19	IAC Museum, Baldonnel
	164	DHC1 Chipmunk T20	IAC Museum, Baldonnel
	168	DHC1 Chipmunk T20	IAC Museum, Baldonnel
	169	DHC1 Chipmunk 22 (G-ARGG)	Privately owned, Ballyboy
	172	DHC1 Chipmunk T20	IAC, stored Baldonnel
	173	DHC1 Chipmunk T20	South East Aviation Enthusiasts, Dromod
	176	DH104 Dove 4 (VP-YKF)	South East Aviation Enthusiasts, Waterford
	183	Percival P56 Provost T51	IAC Museum, Baldonnel
	184	Percival P56 Provost T51	South East Aviation Enthusiasts, Dromod
	187	DH115 Vampire T55	South East Aviation Enthusiasts, Dromod
	191	DH115 Vampire T55	IAC Museum, Baldonnel
	192	DH115 Vampire T55	South East Aviation Enthusiasts, Dromod
	195	Sud SA316 Alouette III (F-WJDH)	IAC Museum, Baldonnel
	198	DH115 Vampire T11 (XE977)	National Museum of Ireland, Dublin
	199	DHC1 Chipmunk T22	IAC, stored Baldonnel
	202	Sud SA316 Alouette III	Ulster Aviation Society, Long Kesh
	203	Reims-Cessna FR172H	IAC No 104 Sqn/1 Operations Wing, Baldonnel
	205	Reims-Cessna FR172H	IAC No 104 Sqn/1 Operations Wing, Baldonnel
	206	Reims-Cessna FR172H	IAC No 104 Sqn/1 Operations Wing, Baldonnel
	207	Reims-Cessna FR172H	IAC, stored Waterford
	208	Reims-Cessna FR172H	IAC No 104 Sqn/1 Operations Wing, Baldonnel
	210	Reims-Cessna FR172H	IAC No 104 Sqn/1 Operations Wing, Baldonnel
	215	Fouga CM170 Super Magister	Dublin Institute of Technology
	216	Fouga CM170 Super Magister	National Museum of Ireland, Dublin
	218	Fouga CM170 Super Magister	Shannon Aerospace, Shannon Airport
	219	Fouga CM170 Super Magister	IAC Museum, Baldonnel
	220	Fouga CM170 Super Magister	Cork University, instructional use
	231	SIAI SF-260WE Warrior	IAC Museum, stored Baldonnel
	240	Beech Super King Air 200MR	IAC No 102 Sqn/1 Operations Wing, Baldonnel
	251	Grumman G1159C Gulfstream IV (N17584)	IAC No 102 Sqn/1 Operations Wing, Baldonnel
	252	Airtech CN.235 MPA Persuader	IAC No 101 Sqn/1 Operations Wing, Baldonnel
	253	Airtech CN.235 MPA Persuader	IAC No 101 Sqn/1 Operations Wing, Baldonnel
	254	PBN-2T Defender 4000 (G-BWPN)	IAC No 106 Sqn/1 Operations Wing, Baldonnel
	256	Eurocopter EC135T-1 (G-BZRM)	IAC No 106 Sqn/1 Operations Wing, Baldonnel
	258	Gates Learjet 45 (N5009T)	IAC No 102 Sqn/1 Operations Wing, Baldonnel
	260	Pilatus PC-9M (HB-HQS)	IAC Flying Training School, Baldonnel
	261	Pilatus PC-9M (HB-HQT)	IAC Flying Training School, Baldonnel
	262	Pilatus PC-9M (HB-HQU)	IAC Flying Training School, Baldonnel
	263	Pilatus PC-9M (HB-HQV)	IAC Flying Training School, Baldonnel
	264	Pilatus PC-9M (HB-HQW)	IAC Flying Training School, Baldonnel
	266	Pilatus PC-9M (HB-HQY)	IAC Flying Training School, Baldonnel
	267	Pilatus PC-9M (HB-HQZ)	IAC Flying Training School, Baldonnel
	268	Pilatus PC-9M	IAC (option)
	269	Pilatus PC-9M	IAC (option)
	270	Eurocopter EC135P-2	IAC No 302 Sqn/3 Operations Wing, Baldonnel
	271	Eurocopter EC135P-2	IAC No 302 Sqn/3 Operations Wing, Baldonnel
	272	Eurocopter EC135T-2 (G-CECT)	IAC No 106 Sqn/1 Operations Wing, Baldonnel
	273	Eurocopter EC135P-2	IAC, on order
	274	AgustaWestland AW139	IAC No 301 Sqn/3 Operations Wing, Baldonnel
	275	AgustaWestland AW139	IAC No 301 Sqn/3 Operations Wing, Baldonnel
	276	AgustaWestland AW139	IAC No 301 Sqn/3 Operations Wing, Baldonnel
	277	AgustaWestland AW139	IAC No 301 Sqn/3 Operations Wing, Baldonnel
	278	AgustaWestland AW139	IAC No 301 Sqn/3 Operations Wing, Baldonnel
	279	AgustaWestland AW139	IAC No 301 Sqn/3 Operations Wing, Baldonnel

Aircraft included in this section include those likely to be seen visiting UK civil and military airfields on transport flights, exchange visits, exercises and for air shows. It is not a comprehensive list of all aircraft operated by the air arms concerned.

ALGERIA
**Force Aérienne Algérienne/
Al Quwwat al Jawwiya al Jaza'eriya**
Airbus A.340-541
Ministry of Defence, Boufarik
7T-VPP

Ilyushin
Il-76MD/Il-76TD/Il-78
347 Escadron de Transport
 Strategique,
 Boufarik;
357 Escadron de
 Ravitaillement en Vol,
 Boufarik

7T-WIA	Il-76MD	347 Esc
7T-WIB	Il-76MD	347 Esc
7T-WIC	Il-76MD	347 Esc
7T-WID	Il-76TD	347 Esc
7T-WIE	Il-76TD	347 Esc
7T-WIF	Il-78	357 Esc
7T-WIG	Il-76TD	347 Esc
7T-WIL	Il-78	357 Esc
7T-WIM	Il-76TD	347 Esc
7T-WIN	Il-78	357 Esc
7T-WIP	Il-76TD	347 Esc
7T-WIQ	Il-78	357 Esc
7T-WIR	Il-76TD	347 Esc
7T-WIS	Il-78	357 Esc
7T-WIT	Il-76TD	347 Esc
7T-WIU	Il-76TD	347 Esc
7T-WIV	Il-76TD	347 Esc

Lockheed
C-130H Hercules
2 Escadre de Transport
 Tactique et Logistique, Boufarik
7T-WHE (4935)
7T-WHF (4934)
7T-WHI (4930)
7T-WHJ (4928)
7T-WHQ (4926)
7T-WHR (4924)
7T-WHS (4912)
7T-WHT (4911)
7T-WHY (4913)
7T-WHZ (4914)

Lockheed
C-130H-30 Hercules
2 Escadre de Transport
 Tactique et Logistique,
 Boufarik
7T-WHB (5224)
7T-WHD (4987)
7T-WHL (4989)
7T-WHM (4919)
7T-WHN (4894)
7T-WHO (4897)
7T-WHP (4921)

Grumman
G.1159C Gulfstream IVSP
Ministry of Defence, Boufarik
7T-VPC (1418)

7T-VPM (1421)
7T-VPR (1288)
7T-VPS (1291)

Gulfstream Aerospace
Gulfstream V
Ministry of Defence, Boufarik
7T-VPG (617)

ARMENIA
Armenian Government
Airbus A.319CJ-132
Armenian Government, Yerevan
EK-RA01

AUSTRALIA
Royal Australian Air Force
Airbus A.330-203 MRTT
33 Sqn, Amberley
A39-001 (on order)
A39-002
A39-003
A39-004
A39-005

Boeing
737-7DF/-7DT/-7ES AEW&C
34 Sqn, Canberra

A30-001	737-7ES
A30-002	737-7ES
A30-003	737-7ES
A30-004	737-7ES
A30-005	737-7ES
A30-006	737-7ES
A36-001	737-7DT
A36-002	737-7DF

Boeing
C-17A Globemaster III
36 Sqn, Amberley
A41-206
A41-207
A41-208
A41-209
A41-210
A41-211 (on order)

Canadair
CL.604 Challenger
34 Sqn, Canberra
A37-001
A37-002
A37-003

Lockheed
**C-130H Hercules/
C-130J-30 Hercules II**
37 Sqn, Richmond, NSW
C-130H
A97-002
A97-004
A97-005
A97-006
A97-007
A97-008$

A97-009
A97-011
C-130J-30
A97-440
A97-441
A97-442
A97-447
A97-448
A97-449
A97-450
A97-464
A97-465
A97-466
A97-467
A97-468

Lockheed
AP-3C Orion
10/11 Sqns, 92 Wing,
 Edinburgh, NSW

A9-656	10 Sqn
A9-657	11 Sqn
A9-658	10 Sqn
A9-659	11 Sqn
A9-660	10 Sqn
A9-661	10 Sqn
A9-662	11 Sqn
A9-663	11 Sqn
A9-664	11 Sqn
A9-665	10 Sqn
A9-751	11 Sqn
A9-752	10 Sqn
A9-753	10 Sqn
A9-755	11 Sqn
A9-756	11 Sqn
A9-757	10 Sqn
A9-758	10 Sqn
A9-759	10 Sqn
A9-760	10 Sqn

AUSTRIA
**Öesterreichische
Luftstreitkräfte**
**Agusta-Bell AB.212/
Bell 212***
1. & 2. leichte
Transporthubschrauberstaffel,
Linz
5D-HB
5D-HC
5D-HD
5D-HF
5D-HG
5D-HH
5D-HI
5D-HJ
5D-HK
5D-HL
5D-HN
5D-HO
5D-HP
5D-HQ
5D-HR
5D-HS
5D-HT

5D-HU
5D-HV
5D-HW
5D-HX
5D-HY*
5D-HZ $

Bell
OH-58B Kiowa
Mehrzweckhubschrauberstaffel,
Tulln
3C-OA
3C-OB
3C-OC
3C-OD
3C-OE
3C-OG
3C-OH
3C-OI
3C-OJ
3C-OK $
3C-OL

Eurofighter
EF.2000
Überwachungsgeschwader:
1.Staffel & 2.Staffel, Zeltweg
7L-WA
7L-WB
7L-WC $
7L-WD
7L-WE
7L-WF
7L-WG
7L-WH
7L-WI
7L-WJ
7L-WK
7L-WL
7L-WM
7L-WN
7L-WO

Lockheed
C-130K Hercules
Lufttransportstaffel, Linz
8T-CA
8T-CB
8T-CC

Pilatus
PC-6B/B2-H2 Turbo Porter/
PC-6B/B2-H4 Turbo Porter*
leichte Lufttransportstaffel, Tulln
3G-EA
3G-EB
3G-EC
3G-ED
3G-EE
3G-EF
3G-EG
3G-EH
3G-EJ
3G-EK
3G-EL
3G-EM
3G-EN*

Pilatus
PC-7 Turbo Trainer
Lehrabteilung Fläche, Zeltweg
3H-FA
3H-FB
3H-FC
3H-FD
3H-FE
3H-FF
3H-FG $
3H-FH
3H-FI
3H-FJ
3H-FK
3H-FL
3H-FM
3H-FN
3H-FO
3H-FP

SAAB 105ÖE
Überwachungsgeschwader:
Düsentrainerstaffel, Linz
(yellow)
B   (105402)
D   (105404)
E   (105405)
G   (105407)
I   (105409)
J   (105410)
(green)
B   (105412)
D   (105414)
GF-16 (105416)$
GG-17 (105417)
(red)
B   (105422)
C   (105423)
D   (105424)
E   (105425)
RF-26 (105426)$
G   (105427)
H   (105428)
I   (105429)
J   (105430)
(blue)
A   (105431)
B   (105432)
C   (105433)
D   (105434)
E   (105435)
F   (105436)
G   (105437)
J   (105440)

Sikorsky S-70A
mittlere Transporthubschrauberstaffel,
Tulln
6M-BA
6M-BB
6M-BC
6M-BD
6M-BE
6M-BF
6M-BG
6M-BH
6M-BI

BAHRAIN
BAE RJ.85/RJ.100*
Bahrain Defence Force

A9C-AWL*
A9C-BDF*
A9C-HWR

Boeing 747SP-Z5
Bahrain Amiri Flt
A9C-HAK

Boeing 747-4P8
Bahrain Amiri Flt
A9C-HMK

Boeing 767-4SFER
Bahrain Amiri Flt
A9C-HMH

Grumman
G.1159 Gulfstream IIIT/
G.1159C Gulfstream IV-SP
Govt of Bahrain
A9C-BAH Gulfstream IV-SP
A9C-BG Gulfstream IIIT

Gulfstream Aerospace
G.450
Govt of Bahrain
A9C-BHR

Gulfstream Aerospace
G.550
Govt of Bahrain
A9C-BRN

BELGIUM
Composante Aérienne Belge/
Belgische Luchtcomponent
D-BD Alpha Jet E
11 Smaldeel (1 Wg),
Cazaux, France (ET 02.008)
AT-01
AT-02
AT-03
AT-05
AT-06
AT-08
AT-10
AT-11
AT-12
AT-13
AT-14
AT-15
AT-17
AT-18
AT-19
AT-20
AT-21
AT-22
AT-23
AT-24
AT-25
AT-26
AT-27
AT-28
AT-29
AT-30
AT-31
AT-32$
AT-33

Airbus A.330-321
21 Smaldeel (15 Wg), Melsbroek
CS-TMT

Dassault
Falcon 900B
21 Smaldeel (15 Wg), Melsbroek
CD-01

Embraer
ERJ.135LR/ERJ.145LR*
21 Smaldeel (15 Wg), Melsbroek
CE-01
CE-02
CE-03* $
CE-04*

Lockheed
C-130H Hercules
20 Smaldeel (15 Wg), Melsbroek
CH-01
CH-03
CH-04
CH-05
CH-07 $
CH-08
CH-09
CH-10
CH-11
CH-12
CH-13

Dassault
Falcon 20-5
21 Smaldeel (15 Wg), Melsbroek
CM-01 $
CM-02

General Dynamics
F-16 MLU
1,350 Smaldeel (2 Wg),
  Florennes [FS];
31,349 Smaldeel, OCU (10 Wg),
  Kleine-Brogel [BL]

Reg	Type	Unit
FA-56	F-16A	2 Wg
FA-57	F-16A	2 Wg
FA-67	F-16A	2 Wg
FA-68	F-16A	2 Wg$
FA-69	F-16A	10 Wg
FA-70	F-16A	10 Wg
FA-71	F-16A	2 Wg
FA-72	F-16A	2 Wg$
FA-77	F-16A	2 Wg
FA-81	F-16A	10 Wg
FA-82	F-16A	10 Wg
FA-83	F-16A	2 Wg
FA-84	F-16A	2 Wg
FA-86	F-16A	10 Wg
FA-87	F-16A	10 Wg$
FA-89	F-16A	2 Wg
FA-91	F-16A	2 Wg
FA-92	F-16A	2 Wg
FA-94	F-16A	2 Wg$
FA-95	F-16A	2 Wg
FA-97	F-16A	10 Wg
FA-98	F-16A	2 Wg
FA-99	F-16A	10 Wg
FA-101	F-16A	10 Wg
FA-102	F-16A	10 Wg
FA-103	F-16A	10 Wg
FA-104	F-16A	10 Wg
FA-106	F-16A	2 Wg
FA-107	F-16A	10 Wg
FA-109	F-16A	2 Wg
FA-110	F-16A	2 Wg$
FA-114	F-16A	10 Wg
FA-116	F-16A	10 Wg
FA-117	F-16A	2 Wg
FA-118	F-16A	10 Wg
FA-119	F-16A	10 Wg
FA-121	F-16A	2 Wg
FA-123	F-16A	10 Wg
FA-124	F-16A	10 Wg
FA-126	F-16A	2 Wg
FA-127	F-16A	2 Wg
FA-128	F-16A	10 Wg
FA-129	F-16A	10 Wg
FA-130	F-16A	2 Wg
FA-131	F-16A	10 Wg$
FA-132	F-16A	10 Wg
FA-133	F-16A	10 Wg
FA-134	F-16A	10 Wg$
FA-135	F-16A	10 Wg
FA-136	F-16A	2 Wg
FB-12	F-16B	10 Wg
FB-14	F-16B	10 Wg
FB-15	F-16B	2 Wg
FB-17	F-16B	10 Wg
FB-18	F-16B	2 Wg$
FB-20	F-16B	10 Wg
FB-21	F-16B	2 Wg
FB-22	F-16B	2 Wg
FB-23	F-16B	10 Wg
FB-24	F-16B	10 Wg

Agusta A109HA/HO*
17 Smaldeel MRH (1 Wg),
  Beauvechain;
18 Smaldeel MRH (1 Wg),
  Beauvechain;
SLV (1 Wg), Beauvechain
H-01* SLV
H-02* 18 Sm MRH
H-05* 18 Sm MRH
H-07* 17 Sm MRH
H-20 17 Sm MRH
H-21 18 Sm MRH
H-22 17 Sm MRH
H-23 17 Sm MRH
H-24 17 Sm MRH$
H-25 18 Sm MRH
H-26 18 Sm MRH
H-27 18 Sm MRH
H-28 17 Sm MRH
H-29 18 Sm MRH
H-31 18 Sm MRH
H-33 18 Sm MRH
H-35 18 Sm MRH
H-36 17 Sm MRH
H-38 17 Sm MRH
H-40 18 Sm MRH
H-41 17 Sm MRH
H-42 SLV
H-44 17 Sm MRH
H-45 17 Sm MRH
H-46 17 Sm MRH

Piper L-21B Super Cub
Centre Militaire de Vol à Voile
Bases: Florennes, Goetsenhoeven
  & Zoersel
LB-01
LB-02
LB-03
LB-05

NH Industries
NH.90-NFH/NH.90-TTH*
40 Smaldeel, Koksijde
RN-01 (on order)
RN-02 (on order)
RN-03 (on order)
RN-04 (on order)
RN-05* (on order)
RN-06* (on order)
RN-07* (on order)
RN-08* (on order)

Westland Sea
King Mk48/48A*
40 Smaldeel, Koksijde
RS-02
RS-03*
RS-04
RS-05$

SIAI Marchetti
SF260D/SF260M+
Centre of Competence Air,
  Bevekom;
Red Devils *
ST-02 SF-260M+ *
ST-03 SF-260M+ *
ST-04 SF-260M+ *
ST-06 SF-260M+
ST-12 SF-260M+
ST-15 SF-260M+ *
ST-16 SF-260M+
ST-17 SF-260M+
ST-18 SF-260M+
ST-19 SF-260M+
ST-20 SF-260M+
ST-22 SF-260M+
ST-23 SF-260M+ *
ST-24 SF-260M+
ST-25 SF-260M+
ST-26 SF-260M+
ST-27 SF-260M+ *
ST-30 SF-260M+ $
ST-31 SF-260M+
ST-32 SF-260M+ *
ST-34 SF-260M+
ST-35 SF-260M+
ST-36 SF-260M+
ST-40 SF-260D $
ST-41 SF-260D *
ST-42 SF-260D
ST-43 SF-260D
ST-44 SF-260D
ST-45 SF-260D
ST-46 SF-260D
ST-47 SF-260D
ST-48 SF-260D $

Police Fédérale/Federal Politie
Cessna 182 Skylane
Luchsteundetachment, Melsbroek
G-01 C.182Q
G-04 C.182R

MDH
MD.520N
Luchsteundetachment, Melsbroek
G-14
G-15

MDH
MD.900/MD.902* Explorer
Luchsteundetachment, Melsbroek
G-10
G-11
G-12
G-16*

BOTSWANA
Botswana Defence Force
Bombardier Global Express
VIP Sqn, Sir Seretse Kharma IAP,
  Gaborone
OK1

Lockheed
C-130B Hercules
Z10 Sqn, Thebephatshwa
OM-1
OM-2
OM-3

BRAZIL
Força Aérea Brasileira
Boeing KC-137
2° GT, 2° Esq, Galeão
2401
2402
2403
2404

Embraer
EMB.190-190IGW (VC-2)
1° Grupo de Transport Especial,
  1° Esq, Brasilia
2590
2591
2592

Lockheed
C-130 Hercules
1° GT, 1° Esq, Galeão;
1° GTT, 1° Esq, Afonsos

2451	C-130E	1° GTT
2453	C-130M	1° GTT
2454	C-130E	1° GTT
2456	C-130E	1° GTT
2459	SC-130E	1° GTT
2461	KC-130H	1° GT
2462	KC-130H	1° GT
2463	C-130H	1° GT
2464	C-130H	1° GT
2465	C-130M	1° GT
2466	C-130H	1° GT
2467	C-130M	1° GT
2470	C-130M	1° GT
2472	C-130H	1° GT
2473	C-130H	1° GT
2474	C-130H	1° GT
2475	C-130H	1° GT
2476	C-130H	1° GT
2479	C-130H	1° GT

BRUNEI
Airbus A.340
Brunei Govt, Bandar Seri Bergawan
V8-BKH A.340-212

Boeing 747-430
Brunei Govt, Bandar Seri Bergawan
V8-ALI

Boeing 767-27GER
Brunei Govt, Bandar Seri Bergawan
V8-MHB

BULGARIA
Bulgarsky Voenno-Vazdushni Sily
Aeritalia C-27J Spartan
16 TAB, Sofia/Vrazhdebna
071
072
073

Antonov An-30
16 TAP, Sofia/Dobroslavtzi
055

Pilatus PC.XII/45
16 TAP, Sofia/Dobroslavtzi
020

Bulgarian Govt
Airbus A.319-112
Bulgarian Govt/BH Air, Sofia
LZ-AOA
LZ-AOB

Dassault Falcon 2000
Bulgarian Govt, Sofia
LZ-OOI

Tupolev Tu-154M
Bulgarian Govt, Sofia
LZ-BTZ

BURKINA FASO
Boeing 727-282
Govt of Burkina Faso,
  Ouagadougou
XT-BFA

CAMEROON
Grumman
G.1159A Gulfstream III
Govt of Cameroon, Yaounde
TJ-AAW

CANADA
Royal Canadian Air Force
Lockheed
CC-130 Hercules
CC-130E/CC-130E(SAR)*
413 Sqn, Greenwood (SAR)
  (14 Wing);
424 Sqn, Trenton (SAR) (8 Wing);
426 Sqn, Trenton (8 Wing);
435 Sqn, Winnipeg (17 Wing);
436 Sqn, Trenton (8 Wing)

130305*	14 Wing
130308*	8 Wing
130310*	8 Wing
130319	8 Wing
130323	8 Wing
130327	8 Wing
130328	8 Wing

CC-130H/CC-130H(SAR)+/
CC-130H(T)*

130332	8 Wing
130333+	8 Wing
130334+	14 Wing
130335	8 Wing
130336	8 Wing
130337	8 Wing
130338*	17 Wing
130339*	17 Wing
130340*	17 Wing
130341*	17 Wing
130342*	17 Wing

CC-130H-30

130343	8 Wing
130344	8 Wing

CC-130J Hercules II

130601	8 Wing
130602	8 Wing
130603	8 Wing
130604	8 Wing
130605	8 Wing
130606	8 Wing
130607	8 Wing
130608	8 Wing
130609	8 Wing
130610	8 Wing
130611	8 Wing
130612	8 Wing
130613	8 Wing
130614	(on order)
130615	(on order)
130616	(on order)
130617	(on order)

Lockheed
CP-140 Aurora
404 Sqn, Greenwood (14 Wing);
405 Sqn, Greenwood (14 Wing);
407 Sqn, Comox (19 Wing)

140101	14 Wing
140102	407 Sqn
140103	407 Sqn
140104	14 Wing
140105	14 Wing
140106	407 Sqn
140107	407 Sqn
140108	14 Wing
140109	14 Wing
140110	14 Wing
140111	14 Wing
14011	407 Sqn
140113	14 Wing
140114	14 Wing
140115	407 Sqn
140116	14 Wing
140117	407 Sqn
140118	407 Sqn

De Havilland Canada
CT-142
402 Sqn, Winnipeg
  (17 Wing)

142803	CT-142
142804	CT-142
142805	CT-142
142806	CT-142

Canadair
CC-144 Challenger
412 Sqn, Ottawa (8 Wing)

144601	CC-144A
144614	CC-144B
144615	CC-144B
144616	CC-144B
144617	CC-144C
144618	CC-144C

Airbus
CC-150 Polaris
(A310-304/A310-304F*)
437 Sqn, Trenton (8 Wing)
15001   [991]
15002* [992]
15003* [993]
15004* [994]
15005* [995]

Boeing
CC-177
(C-17A Globemaster III)
429 Sqn, Trenton (8 Wing)
177701
177702
177703
177704

CHAD
Boeing 737-74Q
Chad Government, N'djamena
TT-ABD

CHILE
Fuerza Aérea de Chile
Boeing 707
Grupo 10, Santiago
902   707-351C
903   707-330B
904   707-358C

Boeing 737
Grupo 10, Santiago
921   737-58N
922   737-330

Boeing 767-3Y0ER
Grupo 10, Santiago
985

Boeing
KC-135E Stratotanker
Grupo 10, Santiago
981
983

Extra EA-300L
Los Halcones
145   [2]
146   [5]
149   [1]
1268 [3]

Grumman
G.1159C Gulfstream IV
Grupo 10, Santiago
911

Lockheed
C-130H Hercules
Grupo 10, Santiago
995
996

CROATIA
Hrvatske Zračne Snage
Pilatus PC-9*/PC-9M
92 ZB, Pula;
93 ZB, Zadar
051*   93 ZB

052* 93 ZB
053* 93 ZB
054   93 ZB
055   93 ZB
056   93 ZB
057   93 ZB
058   93 ZB
059   93 ZB
060   93 ZB
061   93 ZB
062   93 ZB
063   93 ZB
064   93 ZB
065   93 ZB
066   93 ZB
067   92 ZB
068   93 ZB
069   93 ZB
070   93 ZB

Canadair
CL.601 Challenger
Croatian Govt, Zagreb
9A-CRO
9A-CRT

CZECH REPUBLIC
Ceske Vojenske Letectvo
Aero L-39/L-59 Albatros
222.TL/22.zL, Náměšt;
CLV, Pardubice
0103 L-39C CLV
0106 L-39C CLV
0107 L-39C CLV
0108 L-39C CLV
0113 L-39C CLV
0115 L-39C CLV
0441 L-39C CLV
0444 L-39C CLV
0445 L-39C CLV
2344 L-39ZA 222.TL/22.zL
2415 L-39ZA 222.TL/22.zL
2421 L-39ZA 222.TL/22.zL
2433 L-39ZA 222.TL/22.zL $
2436 L-39ZA 222.TL/22.zL
3903 L-39ZA 222.TL/22.zL
5015 L-39ZA 222.TL/22.zL
5017 L-39ZA 222.TL/22.zL
5019 L-39ZA 222.TL/22.zL

Aero
L-159A ALCA/L-159B/L-159T-1
212.TL/21.zTL, Cáslav;
LZO, Praha/Kbely
L-159A
6048 212.TL/21.zTL
6049 212.TL/21.zTL
6050 212.TL/21.zTL
6051 212.TL/21.zTL
6052 212.TL/21.zTL
6053 212.TL/21.zTL
6054 212.TL/21.zTL
6055 212.TL/21.zTL
6057 212.TL/21.zTL
6058 212.TL/21.zTL
6059 212.TL/21.zTL
6060 212.TL/21.zTL
6061 212.TL/21.zTL
6062 212.TL/21.zTL
6063 212.TL/21.zTL
6064 212.TL/21.zTL

6065 212.TL/21.zTL
6066 212.TL/21.zTL$
6068 212.TL/21.zTL
6070 212.TL/21.zTL
L-159B
5831 LZO
5832 LZO
6069 212.TL/21.zTL
6073 212.TL/21.zTL
L-159T-1
6046 212.TL/21.zTL
6047 212.TL/21.zTL
6067 212.TL/21.zTL$
6075 212.TL/21.zTL

Airbus A.319CJ-115X
241.dlt/24.zDL, Praha/Kbely
2801
3085

Canadair
CL.601-3A Challenger
241.dlt/24.zDL, Praha/Kbely
5105

CASA C-295M
242.dl/24.zDL, Praha/Kbely
0452
0453
0454
0455

Evektor
EV-55M Outback
Evektor, Kunovice
0458

LET 410 Turbolet
242.dl/24.zDL, Praha/Kbely;
CLV, Pardubice
0731 L-410UVP-T CLV
0928 L-410UVP-T CLV
1132 L-410UVP-T 242.dl
1134 L-410UVP-T 242.dl
1504 L-410UVP   242.dl
1525 L-410FG   242.dl
1526 L-410FG   242.dl
2312 L-410UVP-E 242.dl
2601 L-410UVP-E 242.dl
2602 L-410UVP-E 242.dl
2710 L-410UVP-E 242.dl

Mil Mi-17/
Mi-171Sh*
231.vrl/23.zVrL, Přerov;
CLV, Pardubice
0803 231.vrl/23.zVrL
0811 231.vrl/23.zVrL
0828 231.vrl/23.zVrL
0832 231.vrl/23.zVrL
0834 231.vrl/23.zVrL
0835 231.vrl/23.zVrL
0836 CLV
0837 CLV
0839 231.vrl/23.zVrL
0840 231.vrl/23.zVrL
0848 231.vrl/23.zVrL
0849 231.vrl/23.zVrL
0850 231.vrl/23.zVrL
9767* 231.vrl/23.zVrL
9774* 231.vrl/23.zVrL

9781*	231.vrl/23.zVrL	
9799*	231.vrl/23.zVrL	
9806*	231.vrl/23.zVrL	
9813*	231.vrl/23.zVrL	
9825*	231.vrl/23.zVrL	
9837*	231.vrl/23.zVrL	
9844*	231.vrl/23.zVrL	
9868*	231.vrl/23.zVrL	
9873*	231.vrl/23.zVrL	
9887*	231.vrl/23.zVrL	
9892*	231.vrl/23.zVrL	
9904*	231.vrl/23.zVrL	
9915*	231.vrl/23.zVrL	
9926*	231.vrl/23.zVrL	

Mil Mi-24/Mi-35
221.lbvr/22.zL, Náměšt

0702	Mi-24V1
0788	Mi-24V1
0790	Mi-24V1
0815	Mi-24V1
0835	Mi-24V2
0981	Mi-24V2
3361	Mi-35
3362	Mi-35
3365	Mi-35
3366	Mi-35
3367	Mi-35
3368	Mi-35
3369	Mi-35
3370	Mi-35
3371	Mi-35
6050	Mi-24V
7353	Mi-24V$
7354	Mi-24V
7355	Mi-24V
7356	Mi-24V
7357	Mi-24V
7358	Mi-24V
7360	Mi-24V

SAAB Gripen
211.TL/21.zTL, Cáslav
JAS 39C

9234
9235
9236
9237
9238
9239
9240
9241
9242
9243
9244
9245

JAS 39D

9819 $
9820 $

Yakovlev Yak-40
241.dlt/24.zDL, Praha/Kbely

0260	Yak-40
1257	Yak-40K

DENMARK
Flyvevåbnet
Lockheed
C-130J-30 Hercules II
Eskadrille 721, Aalborg

B-536

B-537
B-538
B-583

Canadair
CL.604 Challenger
Eskadrille 721, Aalborg

C-080
C-168 $
C-172

General Dynamics
F-16 MLU
Eskadrille 727, Skrydstrup;
Eskadrille 730, Skrydstrup;
416th FTS/412th TW, Edwards
AFB, USA

E-004	F-16A	Esk 730
E-005	F-16A	
E-006	F-16A	Esk 727
E-007	F-16A	Esk 730
E-008	F-16A	Esk 727
E-011	F-16A	Esk 727
E-016	F-16A	Esk 727
E-017	F-16A	Esk 730
E-018	F-16A	Esk 730
E-024	F-16A	Esk 730
E-070	F-16A	Esk 730
E-074	F-16A	Esk 730
E-075	F-16A	Esk 727
E-107	F-16A	Esk 727
E-188	F-16A	Esk 727
E-189	F-16A	Esk 730
E-190	F-16A	Esk 727
E-191	F-16A	Esk 730
E-194	F-16A	Esk 730
E-195	F-16A	Esk 727
E-203	F-16A	Esk 730
E-596	F-16A	Esk 730
E-597	F-16A	Esk 730
E-598	F-16A	Esk 727
E-599	F-16A	Esk 727
E-600	F-16A	Esk 727
E-601	F-16A	Esk 730
E-602	F-16A	Esk 727
E-603	F-16A	Esk 727
E-604	F-16A	Esk 730
E-605	F-16A	Esk 727
E-606	F-16A	Esk 730
E-607	F-16A	Esk 727
E-608	F-16A	Esk 730
E-609	F-16A	Esk 727
E-610	F-16A	Esk 730
E-611	F-16A	Esk 727
ET-022	F-16B	Esk 730
ET-197	F-16B	Esk 727
ET-198	F-16B	Esk 730
ET-199	F-16B	Esk 730
ET-207	F-16B	Esk 727
ET-208	F-16B	Esk 730
ET-210	F-16B	412th TW
ET-612	F-16B	Esk 727
ET-613	F-16B	Esk 727
ET-614	F-16B	Esk 727
ET-615	F-16B	Esk 727

AgustaWestland
EH.101 Mk.512
Eskadrille 722, Karup
Detachments at:
Aalborg, Roskilde, Ronne, Skrydstrup

M-502
M-504
M-507
M-508
M-510
M-512
M-513
M-514
M-515
M-516
M-517
M-518
M-519
M-520

Aérospatiale
AS.550C-2 Fennec
Eskadrille 724, Karup

P-090
P-234
P-254
P-275
P-276
P-287
P-288
P-319
P-320
P-339
P-352
P-369

Westland Lynx
Mk 90B
Eskadrille 723, Karup

S-134
S-142
S-170
S-175
S-181
S-191
S-249
S-256

SAAB
T-17 Supporter
Aalborg Stn Flt;
Eskadrille 721, Aalborg;
Flyveskolen, Karup (FLSK);
Skrydstrup Stn Flt

T-401	FLSK
T-402	Skrydstrup
T-403	FLSK
T-404	FLSK
T-405	Aalborg
T-407	Esk 721
T-409	FLSK
T-410	FLSK
T-411	FLSK
T-412	FLSK
T-413	Skrydstrup
T-414	Esk 721
T-415	FLSK
T-417	FLSK
T-418	Esk 721
T-419	FLSK
T-420	FLSK
T-421	Aalborg
T-423	FLSK
T-425	FLSK
T-426	FLSK
T-427	FLSK

T-428 Skrydstrup
T-429 FLSK
T-430 FLSK
T-431 Esk 721
T-432 Skrydstrup

ECUADOR
Fuerza Aérea Ecuatoriana
Embraer
ERJ.135 Legacy 600
Escuadrón de Transporte 1114,
   Quito
FAE-051

EGYPT
Al Quwwat al-Jawwiya
il Misriya
Lockheed
C-130H/C-130H-30* Hercules
16 Sqn, Cairo West
1271/SU-BAB
1273/SU-BAD
1274/SU-BAE
1275/SU-BAF
1277/SU-BAI
1278/SU-BAJ
1279/SU-BAK
1280/SU-BAL
1281/SU-BAM
1282/SU-BAN
1283/SU-BAP
1284/SU-BAQ
1285/SU-BAR
1286/SU-BAS
1287/SU-BAT
1288/SU-BAU
1289/SU-BAV
1290/SU-BEW
1291/SU-BEX
1292/SU-BEY
1293/SU-BKS*
1294/SU-BKT*
1295/SU-BKU*
1296
1297
1298

Egyptian Govt
Airbus A.340-211
Egyptian Govt, Cairo
SU-GGG

Cessna 680
Citation Sovereign
Egyptian Govt, Cairo
SU-BRF
SU-BRG

Grumman
G.1159A Gulfstream III/
G.1159C Gulfstream IV/
G.1159C Gulfstream IV-SP/
Gulfstream 400
Egyptian Air Force/Govt,
   Cairo
SU-BGM Gulfstream IV
SU-BGU Gulfstream III
SU-BGV Gulfstream III
SU-BNC Gulfstream IV
SU-BND Gulfstream IV
SU-BNO Gulfstream IV-SP

SU-BNP Gulfstream IV-SP
SU-BPE Gulfstream 400
SU-BPF Gulfstream 400

FINLAND
Suomen Ilmavoimat
CASA C-295M
Tukilentolaivue,
   Jyväskylä/Tikkakoski
CC-1
CC-2
CC-3 (on order)

Fokker
F.27 Friendship
Tukilentolaivue,
   Jyväskylä/Tikkakoski
FF-1 F.27-100
FF-3 F.27-400M

McDonnell Douglas
F-18 Hornet
Hävittäjälentolaivue 11,
   Roveniemi;
Hävittäjälentolaivue 21,
   Tampere/Pirkkala;
Hävittäjälentolaivue 31,
   Kuopio/Rissala;
Koelentokeskus,
   Halli

F-18C Hornet

HN-401	HavLLv 21
HN-402	HavLLv 11
HN-403	KoeLntk
HN-404	HavLLv 21
HN-405	HavLLv 31
HN-406	HavLLv 11
HN-407	HavLLv 21
HN-408	HavLLv 31
HN-409	HavLLv 11
HN-410	HavLLv 11
HN-411	HavLLv 11
HN-412	HavLLv 21
HN-413	HavLLv 21
HN-414	KoeLntk
HN-415	HavLLv 21
HN-416	HavLLv 11
HN-417	HavLLv 31
HN-418	HavLLv 31
HN-419	HavLLv 31
HN-420	KoeLntk
HN-421	HavLLv 21
HN-422	HavLLv 31
HN-423	HavLLv 11
HN-424	HavLLv 31
HN-425	HavLLv 11
HN-426	HavLLv 31
HN-427	HavLLv 31
HN-428	HavLLv 21
HN-429	HavLLv 11
HN-431	HavLLv 31
HN-432	HavLLv 11
HN-433	HavLLv 31
HN-434	HavLLv 21
HN-435	HavLLv 11
HN-436	HavLLv 31
HN-437	HavLLv 31
HN-438	HavLLv 31
HN-439	HavLLv 31
HN-440	HavLLv 21
HN-441	HavLLv 11

HN-442	HavLLv 21
HN-443	HavLLv 21
HN-444	HavLLv 31
HN-445	HavLLv 31
HN-446	HavLLv 11
HN-447	HavLLv 21
HN-448	HavLLv 31
HN-449	HavLLv 11
HN-450	HavLLv 21
HN-451	HavLLv 21
HN-452	HavLLv 11
HN-453	HavLLv 31
HN-454	HavLLv 21
HN-455	HavLLv 21
HN-456	HavLLv 11
HN-457	HavLLv 31

F-18D Hornet

HN-461	HavLLv 31
HN-462	KoeLntk
HN-463	HavLLv 21
HN-464	HavLLv 21
HN-465	HavLLv 11
HN-466	HavLLv 11
HN-467	HavLLv 21

BAe Hawk 51/51A/66
Hävittäjälentolaivue 41,
   Kauhava;
Koelentokeskus,
   Halli

Hawk 51

HW-301	HavLLv 41
HW-303	HavLLv 41
HW-304	HavLLv 41
HW-306	HavLLv 41
HW-307	HavLLv 41
HW-308	HavLLv 41
HW-309	HavLLv 41
HW-310	HavLLv 41
HW-311	HavLLv 41
HW-312	HavLLv 41
HW-314	HavLLv 41
HW-315	HavLLv 41
HW-316	HavLLv 41
HW-318	HavLLv 41
HW-319	KoeLntk
HW-320	HavLLv 41
HW-321	KoeLntk
HW-322	HavLLv 41
HW-326	HavLLv 41
HW-327	HavLLv 41
HW-328	HavLLv 41
HW-329	HavLLv 41
HW-330	HavLLv 41
HW-331	HavLLv 41
HW-332	HavLLv 41
HW-333	HavLLv 41
HW-334	HavLLv 41
HW-337	HavLLv 41
HW-338	HavLLv 41
HW-339	HavLLv 41
HW-340	HavLLv 41
HW-341	HavLLv 41
HW-342	KoeLntk
HW-343	HavLLv 41
HW-344	HavLLv 41
HW-345	HavLLv 41
HW-346	HavLLv 41
HW-347	HavLLv 41
HW-348	HavLLv 41
HW-349	HavLLv 41

HW-350	HavLLv 41	
Hawk 51A		
HW-351	HavLLv 41	
HW-352	HavLLv 41	
HW-353	HavLLv 41	
HW-354	HavLLv 41	
HW-355	HavLLv 41	
HW-356	HavLLv 41	
HW-357	HavLLv 41	
Hawk 66		
HW-360		
HW-361		
HW-362		
HW-363		
HW-364		
HW-365		
HW-366		
HW-367		
HW-368		
HW-369		
HW-370		
HW-371		
HW-372		
HW-373	HavLLv 41	
HW-374	HavLLv 41	
HW-375		
HW-376	HavLLv 41	
HW-377		

Gates
Learjet 35A
Tukilentolaivue,
 Jyväskylä/Tikkakoski;
Tukilentolaivue (Det.),
 Kuopio/Rissala*

LJ-1*	
LJ-2	
LJ-3	

FRANCE
Armée de l'Air
Airbus A.310-304
ET 03.060 *Esterel*,
 Paris/Charles de Gaulle

418	F-RADC
421	F-RADA
422	F-RADB

Airbus A.330-223
ETEC 00.065, Villacoublay

240	(F-RARF)

Airbus A.340-212
ET 03.060 *Esterel*,
 Paris/Charles de Gaulle

075	F-RAJA
081	F-RAJB

Airtech CN-235M-200/-300*
ET 01.062 *Vercours*, Creil;
ET 03.062 *Ventoux*, Creil;
ETOM 00.052 *La Tontouta*, Noumea;
ETOM 00.058 *Antilles*, Fort de France;
ETOM 00.082 *Maine*, Faaa-Tahiti

045	62-IB	01.062
065	82-IC	00.082
066	52-ID	00.052
071	62-IE	01.062
072	82-IF	00.082
105	52-IG	00.052
107	52-IH	00.052

111	62-II	01.062
114	62-IJ	01.062
123	62-IM	01.062
128	62-IK	01.062
129	62-IL	01.062
137	62-IN	01.058
141	62-IO	00.058
152	62-IP	01.062
156	62-IQ	01.062
158	62-IR	01.062
160	62-IS	01.062
165	62-IT	01.062
193*	62-HA	
194*	62-HB	
195*	62-HC	
*	62-HD	
*	62-HE	
*	62-HF	
*	62-HG	
*	62-HH	

Boeing C-135 Stratotanker
GRV 02.093 *Bretagne*, Istres

470	C-135FR	93-CA
471	C-135FR	93-CB
472	C-135FR	93-CC
474	C-135FR	93-CE
475	C-135FR	93-CF
497	KC-135R	93-CM$
525	KC-135R	93-CN
574	KC-135R	93-CP
735	C-135FR	93-CG
736	C-135FR	93-CH
737	C-135FR	93-CI
738	C-135FR	93-CJ
739	C-135FR	93-CK
740	C-135FR	93-CL

Boeing E-3F Sentry
EDCA 00.036, Avord (BA 702)

201	702-CA
202	702-CB
203	702-CC
204	702-CD

CASA 212-300 Aviocar
DGA EV, Cazaux & Istres

378	MP
386	MQ

Cessna 310
DGA EV, Cazaux & Istres

190	310N	BL
193	310N	BG
194	310N	BH
513	310N	BE
569	310R	CS
820	310Q	CL
981	310Q	BF

D-BD Alpha Jet
AMD-BA, Istres;
CEAM (EC 05.330),
 Mont-de-Marsan (BA 118);
DGA EV, Cazaux (BA 120) & Istres
 (BA 125);
EAC 00.314, Tours (BA 705);
EE 02.002 *Côte d'Or*,
 Luxeuil (BA 116);
EPNER, Istres (BA 125);
ETO 01.008 *Saintonge*

& ETO 02.008 *Nice*,
 Cazaux (BA 120);
GE 00.312, Salon de
 Provence (BA 701);
Patrouille de France (PDF)
 (EPAA 20.300),
 Salon de Provence (BA 701)

01	F-ZJTS	DGA EV
E1		
E3		
E4		DGA EV
E5	314-LV	00.314
E7	705-TU	00.314
E8		DGA EV
E9	102-LF	02.002
E10	314-UL	00.314
E11	102-UB	02.002
E12		DGA EV
E13	102-MM	05.002
E14	102-FG	02.002
E15		DGA EV
E17	705-AA	00.314
E18	705-AK	00.314
E19		
E20	705-MS	00.314
E21		
E22	705-LS	00.314
E23	314-UG	00.314
E24	8-MP	01.008
E25	705-TJ	00.314
E26	102-ND	02.008
E28	705-AB	00.314
E29	102-NB	02.008
E30	705-MD	00.314
E31	F-TERK	*PDF*
E32	102-FI	02.002
E33	120-FJ	01.008
E34		*PDF*
E35	120-MA	01.008
E36	314-UF	
E37	120-NL	02.008
E38	705-LH	00.314
E41	F-TERA	*PDF* [9]
E42	705-TA	00.314
E43		
E44	F-UHRE	*PDF* [6]
E45	705-TF	00.314
E46	F-UHRF	*PDF* [3]
E47	705-AC	00.314
E48	705-MH	00.314
E49	705-LB	00.314
E51	705-AD	00.314
E53	102-LI	02.002
E55		
E58	705-TK	00.314
E59	705-LY	00.314
E60		EPNER
E61	102-LQ	02.002
E63		
E64	314-TL	00.314
E65		
E66	8-ME	
E67	705-TB$	00.314
E68	8-MO	01.008
E69		
E72	705-LA	00.314
E73	120-NE	02.008
E74	8-MI	01.008
E75	705-AE	00.314
E76	102-RJ	02.002
E79	102-NA	02.008

E80		DGA EV
E81	705-FO	00.314
E82	705-LW	00.314
E83	705-TZ	00.314
E84	314-UK	00.314
E85	F-UGFF	PDF [1]
E86	102-FB	02.002
E87	102-LC	02.002
E88	314-LL	00.314
E89	118-LX	CEAM
E90	705-TH	00.314
E91	102-RL	02.002
E92	314-FL	00.314
E93	705-TX	00.314
E94	F-TERH	PDF
E95	F-TERQ	PDF
E96	705-TC	00.314
E97	102-MB	02.002
E98	705-MF	00.314
E99	102-AH	02.002
E100		
E101	314-TT	00.314
E102	120-LM	01.008
E103	118-UA	CEAM
E104	705-TG	00.314
E105	102-FM	02.002
E106		
E107	F-TEUD$	00.314
E108	120-AF	01.008
E109	102-AG	02.002
E110	705-AH	00.314
E112	705-AO	00.314
E113	705-TD	00.314
E114	F-TERR	PDF
E115	120-MR	01.008
E116	120-FN	01.008
E117	F-RCAI	PDF [5]
E118	314-LN	00.314
E119	118-FE	CEAM
E120	705-LG	00.314
E121	705-LE	00.314
E123	705-RM	00.314
E124	120-RX	01.008
E125	314-LK	00.314
E126		
E127	705-FK	00.314
E128	705-TM	00.314
E129	705-LP	00.314
E130	F-TERP	PDF [4]
E131		
E132	705-LZ	00.314
E133		
E134	F-TERM	PDF [0]
E135	705-RX	00.314
E136	120-RP	01.008
E137	705-LJ	00.314
E138	705-RQ	00.314
E139	705-FC	00.314
E140	102-FA	02.002
E141	120-NF	02.008
E142	314-LO	00.314
E143	8-MQ	01.008
E144	120-AK	01.008
E145		
E146	314-RR	00.314
E147	120-LT	01.008
E148	705-LU	00.314
E149	705-RS	00.314
E150		
E151	705-FD	00.314
E152	705-RT	00.314

E153	705-RU	00.314
E154	120-AL	01.008
E155	120-NP	02.008
E156	314-TI	00.314
E157	314-UC	00.314
E158	F-TERF	PDF [8]
E159		
E160	314-UH	00.314
E161		
E162	F-TERJ	PDF [7]
E163	F-TERE	PDF [2]
E164		
E165		
E166	705-RW	00.314
E167	120-NM	01.008
E168	102-FP	02.002
E169		
E170	705-RY	00.314
E171	314-LR	00.314
E173		
E176		

Dassault
Falcon 7X
ETEC 00.065, Villacoublay
68 F-RAFA
86 F-RAFB

Dassault
Falcon 20
DGA EV, Cazaux & Istres
Falcon 20C
79 CT
96 CB
104 CW
138 CR
188 CX
Falcon 20E
252 CA
263 CY
288 CX
Falcon 20F
342 CU
375 CZ

Dassault
Falcon 50
ETEC 00.065, Villacoublay
27 (F-RAFK)
34 (F-RAFL)
78 F-RAFJ

Dassault
Falcon 2000LX
ETEC 00.065, Villacoublay
231 (F-RAFC)

Dassault
Falcon 900
ETEC 00.065, Villacoublay
02 (F-RAFP)
004 (F-RAFQ)

Dassault
Mirage F.1
CEAM (ECE 05.330) *Côte d'Argent*, Mont-de-Marsan (BA 118);
DGA EV, Cazaux (BA 120) & Istres (BA 125);
ER 02.033 *Savoie*, Mont-de-Marsan (BA 118);

Mirage F.1CT		
223	118-QX	02.033
226	112-QS	02.033
227	330-AP	CEAM
229	112-QW	02.033
236	112-QR	02.033
242	112-QA	02.033
253	112-QU	02.033
256	112-SH	02.033
267	112-QC	02.033
271	112-QQ	02.033
273	112-QF	02.033
274	112-QJ	02.033
279	118-QL	02.033
280	118-QD	02.033
Mirage F.1B		
502	118-SW	02.033
507	112-SE	02.033
509	118-SD	02.033
510	112-SL	02.033
514	118-SA	02.033
516	112-SI	02.033
517	118-SC	02.033
519	118-MY	02.033
Mirage F.1CR		
602		DGA EV
603	112-NU	02.033
604	112-CF	
606	112-CU	02.033
607	112-ND	02.033
610	118-CI	CEAM
611	112-NM	02.033
612	33-NJ	02.033
613	112-CC	
614	112-NR	02.033
616	118-NX	02.033
617	118-NE	02.033
620	112-CT	02.033
622	112-FA	02.033
623	112-AW	
624	112-NY	02.033
627	112-NA	02.033
630	33-CN	
631	112-AA	02.033
632	112-CQ	02.033
634	118-CK	02.033
635	112-NP	02.033
636	112-NL	02.033
637	112-CP	02.033
638	118-CD	02.033
640	112-NV	02.033
641	112-NI	02.033
642	112-CG	02.033
643	118-CE	02.033
645	112-CH	
646	112-NW	02.033
647	112-CB	
649	118-CR	02.033
650	112-NZ	02.033
651		
653	112-CV	02.033
654	118-NC	CEAM
655	112-NG	02.033
656	112-CS	
657	112-CL	02.033
658	112-NQ	02.033
659	112-NT	02.033
660	112-CY	
661	118-NK	02.033
662	112-NF	

Dassault
Mirage 2000B

AMD-BA, Istres;
CEAM (ECE 05.330) *Côte d'Argent*, Mont-de-Marsan (BA 118);
DGA EV, Cazaux (BA 120) & Istres (BA 125);
EC 02.005 *Ile de France*, Orange (BA 115);
EC 01.012 *Cambrésis*, Cambrai (BA 103)

501	(BX1)	DGA EV
506	115-OD	02.005
510	115-OQ	02.005
523	115-KJ	02.005
524	115-OA	02.005
525	118-AM	CEAM
526	115-YP	02.005
527	115-OR	02.005
528	115-KS	02.005
529	115-OC	02.005
530	115-OL	02.005

Dassault
Mirage 2000C/2000-5F*

CEAM (ECE 05.330) *Côte d'Argent*, Mont-de-Marsan (BA 118);
DGA EV, Istres (BA 125);
GC 01.002 *Cigognes*, Luxeuil (BA 116);
EC 02.005 *Ile de France*, Orange (BA 115);
EC 03.011 *Corse*, Djibouti (BA 188);
EC 01.012 *Cambrésis*, Cambrai (BA 103);
EC 03.030 *Lorraine*, Al Dhafra, UAE (BA 104)

01*		DGA EV
2		DGA EV
3	115-OG	02.005
5	115-OT	02.005
11	5-OF	02.005
12	115-OH	02.005
16	115-OX	02.005
17	115-OZ	02.005
20	115-OB	02.005
38*	102-EI	02.005
40*	102-EX	01.002
41*	102-FZ	01.002
42*	102-EY	01.002
43*	102-EJ	01.002
44*	118-EQ$	CEAM
45*	116-EF	01.002
46*	116-EF	01.002
47*	102-EP	01.002
48*	102-EW	01.002
49*	102-EA	01.002
51*	330-AS	CEAM
52*	188-EH	03.011
53*		
54*	102-EZ	01.002
55*	116-EU	01.002
56*	188-EG	03.011
57*	116-ET	01.002
58*	116-EL	01.002
59*	116-EV	01.002
61*	102-ME	01.002
62*	102-ED	01.002
63*	116-EM	01.002
64	330-AQ	CEAM
65*	118-MG	CEAM
66*	116-EO	01.002
67*	104-MH	03.030
68*	102-ER	01.002
70*	102-AD	01.002
71*	116-EE	01.002
73*	116-ES	01.002
74*	116-MK	01.002
77*	118-AX	CEAM
78*	116-EC	01.002
79	115-LE	02.005
80	103-LI$	01.012
81	103-LB	01.012
82	115-YL	02.005
83	188-YC	03.011
85	103-LK	01.012
86	103-LL	01.012
87	103-LA	01.012
88	103-KV	01.012
89	115-KA	02.005
90	115-YS	02.005
91	188-YR	03.011
92	118-AW	CEAM
93	116-EM	01.002
94	115-KB	02.005
95	115-KM	02.005
96	103-KI	
97	115-YK	02.005
98	103-YU	01.012
99	115-YB	02.005
100	103-YF	01.012
101	103-KE	01.012
102	103-KR	
103	188-YN	03.011
104	188-KG	03.011
105	103-LJ	01.012
106	103-KL	
107	103-YD	01.012
108	103-LC	01.012
109	103-YH	01.012
111	115-KF	02.005
112	103-KQ	
113	115-YO	02.005
114	103-KU	01.012
115	115-YM	02.005
117	115-LD	02.005
118	115-YG	02.005
119		
120	103-KC	02.005
121	103-KN	01.012
122	103-YE	01.012
123	103-KD	01.012
124	103-YT	01.012

Dassault
Mirage 2000D

AMD-BA, Istres;
CEAM (ECE 05.330) *Côte d'Argent*, Mont-de-Marsan (BA 118);
DGA EV, Istres (BA 125);
EC 01.003 *Navarre*, EC 02.003 *Champagne* & ETED 02.007 *Argonne*, Nancy (BA 133);
EC 03.003 *Ardennes*, Istres (BA 125);
EC 03.011 *Corse*, Djibouti (BA 188)

601	133-JG	02.003
602	188-XJ	03.011
603	133-XL	03.003
604	133-IP	01.003
605	133-LF	02.003
606	133-JC	02.003
607		DGA EV
609	3-IF	01.003
610	133-XX	03.003
611	133-JP	02.003
613	133-MO	02.003
614	133-JU	02.003
615	133-JY	02.003
616	118-XH	CEAM
617	133-IS	01.003
618	3-XC	03.003
619	3-IM	01.003
620	188-IU	03.011
622	133-IL	01.003
623	133-MP	02.003
624	188-IT	03.011
625	133-XG	03.003
626	133-IC	01.003
627	133-JO	02.003
628	133-JL	01.003
629	133-XO	03.003
630	188-XD	03.011
631	133-IH	02.007
632	133-XE	03.003
634	133-JE	01.003
635	133-AS	01.003
636	133-JV	02.003
637	133-XQ	03.003
638	133-IJ	01.003
639	3-JJ	02.003
640	133-IN	01.003
641	133-JW	02.003
642	133-IE	01.003
643	133-JD	02.003
644		DGA EV
645		
646	133-MQ	03.003
647	133-IO	01.003
648	133-XT	03.003
649	133-XY	03.003
650	133-IA	02.003
651	133-LG	02.003
652	133-XN	03.003
653	118-AU	CEAM
654	133-ID	01.003
655	133-LH	01.003
657	133-JM	03.003
658	133-JN	02.003
659	133-XR	03.003
660	133-JF	01.033
661	133-XI	03.003
662	133-XA	01.003
664	133-IW	01.003
665	133-AF	01.003
666	118-IQ	CEAM
667	133-JZ	02.003
668	118-IG	CEAM
669	133-AL	02.007
670	133-XF	03.003
671	133-XK	03.003
672	133-XV	03.003
673		DGA EV
674	133-IR	01.003
675	133-JI	02.003
676		DGA EV
677	133-JT	01.003
678	133-JB	02.003
679	133-JX	01.003
680	133-XM	03.003
681	133-AG	01.003
682	133-JR	02.003

683	133-IV	01.003
684	3-IW	01.003
685	133-XZ	01.003
686	133-JH	02.003
D02		DGA EV

Dassault
Mirage 2000N
CEAM (ECE 05.330) *Côte d'Argent*,
  Mont-de-Marsan (BA 118);
DGA EV, Istres (BA 125)
EC 02.004 *Lafayette*,
  Istres (BA 125)

301		DGA EV
304	116-CA	02.004
305	116-CS	02.004
306	116-BL	02.004
307	116-CH	02.004
310	116-BE	02.004
311	116-AF	
313	116-BG	02.004
316	116-AU$	02.004
317	4-BP	02.004
319	4-AC	
320	125-CD	
322	116-CP	02.004
324	116-CX	
325	4-CC	
326	4-AS	
327	4-CJ	
329	4-BH	02.004
330	116-AT	
331	4-BO	02.004
332	116-BN	02.004
333	4-AB	02.004
334		
335	125-CI	02.004
336	116-BI	02.004
337	116-BF	
338	125-CG	02.004
339	116-AD	02.004
340	125-AA	
341	116-BT	02.004
342	125-BA	02.004
343	116-AH	02.004
344	116-BV	02.004
345	125-BU	02.004
348	125-AL	02.004
350	125-AJ	02.004
351	125-AQ	02.004
353	125-AM	02.004
354	125-BJ	02.004
355	125-AE	02.004
356	125-BX	02.004
357	125-CO	
358	116-BQ	02.004
359	125-AK$	02.004
360	125-CB	
361	125-CK	
362	125-CU	
364	116-BB	02.004
365	125-AI	02.004
366	125-BC	02.004
367	116-AW	
368	125-AR	02.004
369	125-AG	02.004
370	125-CQ	
371	125-BD	02.004
372	125-CM	02.004
373	125-CF	02.004
374	116-BS	02.004

375	125-CL	02.004

Dassault
Rafale-B
AMD-BA, Istres;
CEAM (ECE 05.330) *Côte d'Argent*,
  Mont-de-Marsan (BA 118);
DGA EV, Istres (BA 125);
EC 01.007 *Provence*,
  EC 01.091 *Gascogne*,
  ETR 02.092 *Aquitaine*,
  St Dizier (BA 113);
EC 02.030 *Normandie-Niémen*,
  Mont-de-Marsan (BA 118);
EC 03.030 *Lorraine*,
  Al Dhafra, UAE (BA 104)

301		DGA EV
302		DGA EV
303	118-EA	CEAM
304	118-EB$	CEAM
305	118-EC$	CEAM
306	113-IB	01.091
307	113-IA	01.091
308	113-HA	01.007
309	113-HB	01.007
310	113-HC	02.092
311	104-HD	03.030
312	113-HF	01.007
313	113-HI	01.007
314	104-HP	03.030
315	113-HK	01.091
317	113-HO	02.091
318	113-HM	01.007
319	113-HN	01.007
320	113-HV	01.091
321	113-HQ	01.007
322	113-HU	01.091
323	118-HT	CEAM
324	113-HW	01.007
325	113-HX	01.007
326	113-HY	01.007
327	113-HZ	01.007
328	113-IC	01.091
329	113-ID	01.091
330	113-IE	01.091
331	IF	CEAM
332	IG	CEAM
333	113-IH	01.091
334	113-II	01.091
335	113-IJ	01.091
336	113-IK	01.091
337	113-IL	01.091
338	113-IO	01.091
339		
340		
341		
342		
343		
344		
345		
B01		DGA EV

Dassault
Rafale-C
AMD-BA, Istres;
CEAM (ECE 05.330) *Côte d'Argent*,
  Mont-de-Marsan (BA 118);
DGA EV, Istres (BA 125);
EC 01.007 *Provence*,
  EC 01.091 *Gascogne*,
  ETR 02.092 *Aquitaine*,

St Dizier (BA 113);
EC 02.030 *Normandie-Niémen*,
  Mont-de-Marsan (BA 118);
EC 03.030 *Lorraine*,
  Al Dhafra, UAE (BA 104)

101		DGA EV
102	113-EF	01.007
103	113-HR	01.007
104	113-HH	01.007
105	113-HE	01.007
106	104-HG	03.030
107	113-HJ	01.007
108	113-HS	01.007
109	113-IM	01.091
110	113-IN	01.091
111	113-IP	01.091
112	113-IQ	01.091
113	118-IR	02.030
114	113-IS	01.091
115	113-IT	01.091
116	113-IU	01.091
117	113-IV	01.091
118	113-IW$	01.091
119	118-IX	02.030
120	113-IY	01.091
121	113-IZ$	01.091
122	113-GA	01.007
123	118-GB	02.030
124	104-GC	03.330
125	104-GD	03.330
126	113-GE	01.007
127	113-GF	01.007
128	113-GG	01.007
129	113-GH	02.030
130	113-GI	02.092
131		
132		
133		
134		
135		
136		
137		
138		
139		
140		
C01		DGA EV

DHC-6 Twin Otter 200/300*
GAM 00.056 *Vaucluse*, Evreux;
ETOM 00.058 *Guadeloupe*,
  Pointe-à-Pitre;
ETOM 00.068 *Guyane*,
  Cayenne

292	CC	00.056
298	F-RACD	00.056
300	F-RACE	00.056
730*	CA	00.058
745*	CV	00.056

Embraer
EMB.121AA/AN* Xingu
EAT 00.319,
  Capitaine Dartigues,
  Avord (BA 702)

054	YX	
055*	YZ	
064	YY	
066*	ZA	
69*		
070*	ZC	
072	YA	

073	YB
075	YC
076	YD
77*	ZD
078	YE
080	YF
082	YG
083*	ZE
084	YH
086	YI
089	YJ
090*	ZF
091	YK
092	YL
095	YM
096	YN
098	YO
099	YP
101	YR
102	YS
103	YT
105	YU
107	YV
108	YW
111	YQ

**Eurocopter
AS.332 Super Puma/
AS.532 Cougar/
EC.725AP Cougar/
EC.725R2 Cougar**
EH 01.044 Solenzara, Solenzara;
EH 01.067 Pyrénées, Cazaux;
EH 03.067 Parisis, Villacoublay;
EH 05.067 Alpilles, Orange
GAM 00.056 Vaucluse, Evreux;
CEAM, Mont-de-Marsan

2014	AS.332C	PN	05.067
2057	AS.332C	PO	00.082
2093	AS.332L	PP	05.067
2233	AS.332L-1	FY	00.056
2235	AS.332L-1	FZ	03.067
2244	AS.332C	PM	01.044
2342	AS.532UL	FX	00.056
2369	AS.532UL	FW	00.056
2375	AS.532UL	FV	00.056
2377	AS.532L-1	FU	03.067
2461	EC.725AP	SA	01.067
2549	EC.725AP	SB	01.067
2552	EC.725AP	SE	01.067
2555	EC.725AP	SF	01.067
2619	EC.725AP	SC	05.067
2626	EC.725AP	SD	01.067
2770	EC.725R2	SG	00.056
2772	EC.725R2	SH	00.056
2789	EC.725R2	SJ	00.056

Eurocopter AS.555AN Fennec
ETM 02.040 Médoc, Bordeaux;
ETOM 00.050 Réunion, St Denis;
ETOM 00.052 La Tontouta, Noumea;
ETOM 00.055 Ouessant, Dakar;
ETOM 00.058 Antilles, Fort de France;
EH 03.067 Parisis, Villacoublay;
EH 05.067 Alpilles, Orange;
EH 06.067 Solenzara, Solenzara;
ETOM 00.068 Guyane, Cayenne;
ETOM 00.082 Maine, Faaa-Tahiti

5361	UT	05.067
5368	UU	03.067
5382	UV	05.067
5386	UX	05.067
5387	UY	05.067
5390	UZ	02.040
5391	VA	
5392	VB	05.067
5393	VC	00.082
5396	VD	05.067
5397	VE	03.067
5398	VF	02.040
5399	VG$	00.050
5400	VH	05.067
5412	VI	05.067
5427	VJ	03.067
5430	VL	06.067
5431	VM	05.067
5440	VN	03.067
5441	VO	05.067
5444	VP	00.055
5445	VQ	05.067
5448	VR	03.067
5452	VS	05.067
5455	VT	00.058
5458	VV	05.067
5466	VW	03.067
5468	VX	03.067
5490	VY	05.067
5506	WA	05.067
5509	WB	05.067
5511	WC	05.067
5516	WD	03.067
5520	WE	05.067
5523	WF	03.067
5526	WG	05.067
5530	WH	05.067
5532	WI	05.067
5534	WJ	05.067
5536	WK	05.067
5559		05.067

Extra EA-330LC*/EA-330SC
EVAA, Salon de Provence
03* F-TGCH
04 F-TGCI
05 F-TGCJ

**Lockheed
C-130H/C-130H-30* Hercules**
ET 02.061 Franche-Comté, Orléans

4588	61-PM
4589	61-PN
5114	61-PA
5116	61-PB
5119	61-PC
5140	61-PD
5142*	61-PE
5144*	61-PF$
5150*	61-PG
5151*	61-PH
5152*	61-PI
5153*	61-PJ
5226*	61-PK
5227*	61-PL

**SOCATA
TB-30 Epsilon**
*Cartouche Dorée, (EPAA 00.315) Cognac (BA 709);
EPAA 00.315, Cognac (BA 709);
SOCATA, Tarbes
Please note: A large number of these machines are kept in temporary storage at Chateaudun

1	315-UA
4	315-UC
5	315-UD
6	315-UE
7	315-UF
8	315-UG
9	315-UH
10	315-UI
12	315-UK
13	315-UL
14	315-UM
16	315-UO
21	315-UT
26	315-UY
27	315-UZ
28	315-VA
30	315-VC
32	315-VE
34	315-VG
36	315-VI
39	315-VL
40	315-VM
41	315-VN
43	315-VP
44	315-VQ
46	315-VS
47	315-VT
50	315-VW
56	315-WA
57	F-ZVLB
61	315-WD
62	315-WE
63	315-WF
64	315-WG
65	315-WH
66	315-WI
67	315-WJ
68	315-WK
69	315-WL
70	315-WM
73	315-WP
74	315-WQ
77	315-WT
78	315-WU
79	315-WV
80	315-WW
82	315-WY
83	315-WZ
84	315-XA
85	315-XB
87	315-XD
89	315-XF
90	F-SEXG[O]*
91	315-XH

92	315-XI
93	315-XJ
95	315-XL
96	315-XM
97	315-XN
99	F-SEXP*
100	315-XQ
101	F-SEXR [1]*
102	F-SEXS [2]*
103	315-XT
104	F-SEXU [3]*
105	315-XV
106	315-XW
108	315-XY
110	315-YA
111	315-YB
112	315-YC
113	315-YD
114	315-YE
115	315-YF
116	315-YG
117	315-YH
118	315-YI
120	315-YK
121	315-YL
122	315-YM
125	315-YP
127	315-YR
129	315-YT
130	315-YU
131	315-YV
132	315-YW
133	315-YX
134	315-YY
136	315-ZA
138	315-ZC
139	315-ZD
140	315-ZE
141	F-SEZF [4]*
142	315-ZG
143	315-ZH
144	315-ZI
146	315-ZK
149	315-ZM
150	315-ZN
152	315-ZO
153	315-ZP
155	315-ZR
159	315-ZT

SOCATA TBM 700A
CEAM (EC 02.330),
Mont-de-Marsan;
DGA EV, Cazaux & Istres;
ETM 01.040 Moselle, Metz;
ET 00.043 Médoc,
Bordeaux (BA 106);
ETEC 00.065, Villacoublay;
EdC 00.070, Chateaudun

33	XA	00.043
77	XD	01.040
78	XE	CEAM
93	XL	00.065
95	XH	CEAM
103	XI	00.065
104	XJ	00.070
105	XK	00.065
106	MN	DGA EV
110	XP	01.040
111	XM	01.040
117	XN	01.040

125	XO	00.065
131	XQ	00.065
146	XR	00.065
147	XS	00.065

Transall
C-160NG GABRIEL*/
C-160R
CEAM (EET 06.330),
Mont-de-Marsan;
DGA EV, Cazaux & Istres;
EEA 00.054 Dunkerque,
Metz;
ET 01.061 Touraine &
ET 03.061 Poitou,
Orléans;
ET 01.064 Bearn &
ET 02.064 Anjou, Evreux;
ETOM 00.050 Réunion,
St Denis;
ETOM 00.055 Ouessant,
Dakar;
ETOM 00.058 Guadeloupe,
Pointe-à-Pitre;
ETOM 00.088 Larzac,
Djibouti

RA02	C-160R	61-MI	01.061
R2	C-160R	61-MB	00.050
R4	C-160R	61-MD	01.061
R11	C-160R	61-MF	01.061
R42	C-160R	61-MN	01.061
R51	C-160R	61-MW$	01.061
R54	C-160R	61-MZ	01.061
R55	C-160R	61-ZC	03.061
R86	C-160R	61-ZD	03.061
R87	C-160R	61-ZE	00.050
R89	C-160R	61-ZG	03.061
R90	C-160R	61-ZH	03.061
R91	C-160R	61-ZI	03.061
R93	C-160R	61-ZK	03.061
R94	C-160R	61-ZL	03.061
R95	C-160R	61-ZM	03.061
R96	C-160R	61-ZN	03.061
R97	C-160R	61-ZA	03.061
R99	C-160R	61-ZQ	03.061
R153	C-160R	61-ZS	03.061
R154	C-160R	61-ZT	03.061
R157	C-160R	61-ZW	03.061
R158	C-160R	61-ZX	03.061
R159	C-160R	61-ZY	03.061
R160	C-160R	61-ZZ	03.061
R201	C-160R	64-GA	01.064
R202	C-160R	64-GB	02.064
R203	C-160R	64-GC	01.064
R204	C-160R	64-GD	02.064
R205	C-160R	64-GE	01.064
R206	C-160R	64-GF	02.064
R207	C-160R	64-GG	01.064
R208	C-160R	64-GH$	02.064
R210	C-160R	64-GJ	02.064
R211	C-160R	64-GK	01.064
R212	C-160R	64-GL	01.064
R213	C-160R	64-GM	01.064
R214	C-160R	64-GN	01.064
R215	C-160R	64-GO	01.064
F216	C-160NG*	54-GT	00.054
R217	C-160R	64-GQ	01.064
R218	C-160R	64-GR$	02.064
F221	C-160NG*	GS	00.054
R223	C-160R	64-GW	01.064
R224	C-160R	64-GX	02.064
R225	C-160R	64-GY	01.064
R226	C-160R	64-GZ	02.064

Aéronavale/Marine
Dassault-Breguet
Atlantic 2
21 Flottille &
23 Flottille,
Lorient/Lann Bihoué

2	21F
3	21F
11	21F
12	23F
13	21F
14	23F
15	21F
16	21F
17	21F$
18	21F
19	23F
20	23F
21	21F
25	21F
26	21F
28	21F

Dassault
Falcon 10(MER)
ES 57, Landivisiau
32
101
129
133
143
185

Dassault
Falcon 20G Guardian
25 Flottille,
Papeete &
Tontouta
48
65
72
77
80

Dassault
Falcon 50 SURMAR
24 Flottille,
Lorient/Lann Bihoué
5
7
30
36
132

Dassault
Rafale-M
11 Flottille,
Landivisiau;
12 Flottille,
Landivisiau;
AMD-BA, Istres;
CEPA, Istres;
DGA EV, Istres;
ETR 02.092 Aquitaine,
St Dizier (BA 113)

M01	DGA EV
M02	DGA EV
1	DGA EV

11	12F
12	12F
13	11F
14	11F
15	12F
16	12F
17	11F
19	12F
20	12F
21	12F
23	12F
24	11F
26	12F
27	CEPA
28	11F
29	02.092
30	11F
31	11F
32	11F
33	
34	
35	
36	
37	
38	
39	
40	

Dassault
Super Etendard
17 Flottille, Landivisiau;
CEPA, Istres

1	17F
2	17F
4	17F
6	17F
8	17F
10	17F
11	17F
12	17F
13	17F
14	CEPA
16	17F
17	17F
18	17F
19	17F
30	17F
31	17F
32	17F
33	17F
35	17F
37	17F
39	17F
41	17F
43	17F
44	17F
46	17F
50	17F
51	17F
52	17F
55	17F
57	17F
61	17F
62	17F
65	17F
68	CEPA
69	17F

Embraer
EMB.121AN Xingu
24 Flottille,
  Lorient/Lann Bihoué;
28 Flottille, Hyères

30	24F
47	24F
65	28F
67	28F$
68	24F
69	24F$
71	28F
74	24F$
77	28F
79	28F
81	24F
85	24F
87	24F

Eurocopter
AS.365/AS.565 Panther
35 Flottille, Hyères,
  (with detachments at
  La Rochelle
  Le Touquet & Tahiti*)
36 Flottille, Hyères

17	AS.365N	35F
19	AS.365N	35F
24	AS.365N	35F
57	AS.365N	35F
81	AS.365N	35F
91	AS.365N	35F
157	AS.365N	35F
313	AS.365F1	35F
318	AS.365F1	35F
322	AS.365F1	35F
355	AS.565MA	36F
362	AS.565MA	35F
403	AS.565UA	36F
436	AS.565MA	36F
452	AS.565MA	36F
453	AS.565MA	35F
466	AS.565MA	36F
482	AS.565MA	36F
486	AS.565MA	36F
488	AS.565MA	36F
503	AS.565MA	35F
505	AS.565MA	36F
506	AS.565MA	35F
507	AS.565MA	36F
510	AS.365N3	35F
511	AS.565MA	36F
519	AS.565MA	36F
522	AS.565MA	36F$
524	AS.565MA	36F
542	AS.565MA	36F
6872	AS.365N3	35F*
6928	AS.365N3	35F*

Eurocopter
EC.225LP Super Puma 2+
32 Flottille,
  Lanvéoc/Poulmic & Cherbourg
2741
2752
2851

NH Industries
NH.90-NFH/NH.90-NHC* Caiman
31 Flottille, Hyères;
33 Flottille,

Lanvéoc/Poulmic
CEPA, Hyères

1	(F-ZWTO)
2	CEPA
3*	CEPA
4	33F
5	
6	CEPA
7	
8	CEPA

Northrop Grumman
E-2C Hawkeye
4 Flottille,
  Lorient/Lann Bihoué
1 (165455)
2 (165456)
3 (166417)
4 (on order)

Sud
SA.316B/SA.319B/SE.3160
Alouette III
35 Flottille, Hyères;
ES 22/ESHE, Lanvéoc/Poulmic

13	SE.3160	35F
14	SE.3160	22S
18	SE.3160	22S
41	SE.3160	22S
100	SA.319B	22S
114	SA.319B	22S
161	SA.319B	22S
237	SA.319B	22S·
244	SE.3160	35F
245	SE.3160	22S
268	SA.319B	22S
279	SE.3160	22S
302	SA.319B	22S
303	SA.319B	22S
309	SA.319B	22S
314	SA.319B	22S
347	SA.319B	22S
358	SA.319B	22S
731	SA.316B	22S
806	SA.316B	22S
809	SA.316B	22S
997	SA.319B	22S

Westland
Lynx HAS2(FN)/HAS4(FN)*
34 Flottille, Lanvéoc/Poulmic
  (with a detachment at Hyères)
CEPA, Hyères
260
263
264
267
269
270
271
272$
273
276
621
623
624
625
627
801*
802*
804*

806*		
807*		
808*		
810*		
811*		
812*		
813*		
814*		

Aviation Legére de l'Armée de Terre (ALAT)
Aérospatiale
SA.330Ba Puma
1 RHC, Phalsbourg;
3 RHC, Etain;
5 RHC, Pau;
4 RHFS, Pau;
EALAT, Dax & Le Luc;
ESAM, Bourges;
GAM/STAT, Valence;
GIH, Cazaux

1005	DCA	ESAM
1006	DAA	
1020	DAB	5 RHC
1036	DAC	1 RHC
1037	DAD	5 RHC
1049	DAE	5 RHC
1052	DCB	EALAT
1055	DAF	GIH
1056	DCC	GAM/STAT
1057	DCD	EALAT
1069	DAG	1 RHC
1071	DCE	EALAT
1073	DCF	
1078	DAH	3 RHC
1093	DCG	3 RHC
1100	DAJ	3 RHC
1102	DAK	
1107	DAL	1 RHC
1109	DAM	3 RHC
1114	DCH	3 RHC
1122	DCI	
1123	DCJ	5 RHC
1128	DAN	1 RHC
1130	DCK	5 RHC
1135	DCL	1 RHC
1136	DCM	1 RHC
1142	DCN	
1143	DAO	1 RHC
1145	DCO	3 RHC
1149	DAP	EALAT
1150	DCP	3 RHC
1155	DCQ	4 RHFS
1156	DAQ	1 RHC
1163	DCR	EALAT
1164	DCS	1 RHC
1165	DCT	1 RHC
1171	DCU	1 RHC
1172	DCV	1 RHC
1173	DAR	
1176	DAS	3 RHC
1177	DCW	3 RHC
1179	DCX	5 RHC
1182	DCY	1 RHC
1186	DCZ	5 RHC
1189	DAT	3 RHC
1190	DDA	1 RHC
1192	DDB	1 RHC
1196	DDC	EALAT
1197	DAU	5 RHC
1198	DDD	1 RHC

1204	DAV	1 RHC
1206	DDE	3 RHC
1211	DAW	
1213	DDF	1 RHC
1214	DAX	3 RHC
1217	DAY	
1219	DAZ	3 RHC
1222	DDG	1 RHC
1223	DDH	EALAT
1228	DDI	
1231	DDK	5 RHC
1232	DBA	1 RHC
1235	DDL	
1236	DDM	EALAT
1239	DDN	EALAT
1243	DBB	5 RHC
1244	DDO	5 RHC
1248	DBC	3 RHC
1252	DDP	EALAT
1255	DDQ	1 RHC
1256	DDR	GAM/STAT
1260	DDS	EALAT
1262	DBD	5 RHC
1269	DDT	5 RHC
1277	DBE	1 RHC
1411	DDU	1 RHC
1417	DBF	
1419	DDV	1 RHC
1438	DBG	GAM/STAT
1447	DDW	1 RHC
1451	DBH	1 RHC
1507	DBI	3 RHC
1510	DBJ	3 RHC
1512	DBK	
1519	DBL	3 RHC
1617	DBM	1 RHC
1632	DBN	
1634	DBO	3 RHC
1654	DBP	5 RHC
1662	DDX	EALAT
1663	DBQ	4 RHFS
5682	DBR	4 RHFS

Aérospatiale
SA.341/342 Gazelle
1 RHC, Phalsbourg;
3 RHC, Etain;
5 RHC, Pau;
4 RHFS, Pau;
COMALAT, Villacoublay;
EALAT, Dax & Le Luc;
EFA, Le Luc;
EHADT, Etain;
ESAM, Bourges;
GAM/STAT, Valence
SA.341F Gazelle

1119	GHA	EALAT
1129	GHB	EALAT
1131	GQG	
1149	GQH	1 RHC
1171	GQI	1 RHC
1194	GQJ	5 RHC
1198	GHD	EALAT
1267	GHE	EALAT
1285	GQK	4 RHFS
1291	GQA	EALAT
1353	GHF	EALAT
1369	GQL	1 RHC
1372	GQM	3 RHC
1383	GQN	5 RHC
1399	GQB	EALAT

1416	GQO	3 RHC
1419	GHG	EALAT
1420	GQP	3 RHC
1447	GQC	
1451	GQQ	1 RHC
1463	GQR	4 RHFS
1467	GHH	EALAT
1483	GQS	3 RHC
1487	GQT	4 RHFS
1501	GHI	EALAT
1504	GQD	EALAT
1508	GQW	1 RHC
1518	GQX	1 RHC
1519	GHJ	EALAT
1522	GQU	
1523	GQE	EALAT
1536	GHK	
1540	GHL	EALAT
1541	GHM	EALAT
1544	GQF	EALAT
1562	GQV	1 RHC
1565	GHN	EALAT
1593	GQY	3 RHC
1594	GHO	EALAT
1597	GHP	EALAT
1598	GHQ	EALAT
1607	GHR	EALAT
1608	GHS	EALAT
1611	GHT	EALAT
1612	GHU	EALAT
1619	GHV	EALAT
1657	GHX	EALAT
1659	GHY	EALAT
1672	GHZ	EALAT
1678	GIA	EALAT
1690	GIB	EALAT
1693	GIC	EALAT
1718	GQZ	3 RHC

SA.342L1 Gazelle

4205	GEA	EALAT
4206	GEB	EALAT
4207	GEC	3 RHC
4208	GED	GAM/STAT
4209	GEE	EALAT
4210	GEF	1 RHC
4211	GEG	EALAT
4212	GEH	ESAM
4214	GEI	EALAT
4215	GEJ	EALAT
4216	GEK	GAM/STAT
4217	GEL	1 RHC
4218	GEM	1 RHC
4219	GEN	4 RHFS
4220	GEO	1 RHC
4221	GEP	EALAT
4222	GEQ	EALAT
4223	GER	3 RHC
4224	GES	1 RHC
4225	GET	GAM/STAT
4226	GEU	GAM/STAT
4227	GEV	1 RHC
4228	GEW	1 RHC
4229	GEX	4 RHFS
4230	GEY	
4231	GEZ	1 RHC
4232	GFA	EALAT
4233	GFB	3 RHC
4234	GFC	

SA.342M Gazelle

1732	GJA	EALAT
3458	GNA	EALAT

3459	GAA	1 RHC
3476	GAB	4 RHFS
3477	GJB	1 RHC
3511	GJC	EALAT
3512	GAC	1 RHC
3513	GNB	EALAT
3529	GJD	EALAT
3530	GAD	4 RHFS
3531	GJE	EALAT
3546	GJF	EALAT
3547	GJG	EFA
3548	GAE	1 RHC
3549	GNC	EALAT
3564	GAF	3 RHC
3567	GMA	EALAT
3615	GJH	EALAT
3617	GND	COMALAT
3848	GAG	5 RHC
3849	GAH	5 RHC
3850	GAI	1 RHC
3851	GJI	EALAT
3852	GNE	1 RHC
3853	GNF	EALAT
3855	GJJ	EALAT
3856	GAJ	5 RHC
3857	GJK	EALAT
3858	GNG	EALAT
3859	GAK	4 RHFS
3862	GAL	1 RHC
3863	GAM	3 RHC
3864	GJL	ESAM
3865	GAN	EALAT
3867	GJM	EALAT
3868	GAO	1 RHC
3870	GME	
3896	GNJ	
3911	GAP	1 RHC
3921	GAQ	EALAT
3929	GJN	EALAT
3930	GMF	
3938	GAR	EALAT
3939	GMG	
3947	GAS	5 RHC
3948	GAT	1 RHC
3956	GNK	
3957	GAU	
3964	GAV	3 RHC
3965	GJO	EALAT
3992	GNM	EALAT
3996	GAW	5 RHC
4008	GNN	
4014	GJP	GAM/STAT
4018	GAX	3 RHC
4019	GAY	3 RHC
4020	GAZ	1 RHC
4022	GJQ	EALAT
4023	GMH	ESAM
4026	GBA	1 RHC
4032	GNO	EALAT
4034	GBB	1 RHC
4038	GJR	EALAT
4039	GBC	1 RHC
4042	GMB	EALAT
4047	GJS	EALAT
4048	GBD	EALAT
4049	GNP	EALAT
4053	GBE	1 RHC
4059	GBF	1 RHC
4060	GNQ	EALAT
4061	GBG	GAM/STAT
4065	GNR	EALAT
4066	GBH	3 RHC
4067	GJU	EALAT
4071	GNS	EHADT
4072	GBI	1 RHC
4078	GJV	EALAT
4079	GMC	EALAT
4083	GNT	EALAT
4084	GBJ	3 RHC
4095	GBL	3 RHC
4096	GNU	EALAT
4102	GJW	EALAT
4103	GJX	EALAT
4108	GBM	
4109	GBN	5 RHC
4114	GBO	EALAT
4115	GBP	3 RHC
4118	GNV	EALAT
4119	GBQ	1 RHC
4120	GBR	EALAT
4123	GJY	EALAT
4124	GBS	4 RHFS
4135	GNW	
4136	GBT	1 RHC
4140	GBU	1 RHC
4141	GBV	
4142	GBW	5 RHC
4143	GNX	EALAT
4144	GBX	1 RHC
4145	GBY	1 RHC
4146	GNY	EALAT
4151	GBZ	3 RHC
4155	GCA	3 RHC
4159	GNZ	EALAT
4160	GCC	1 RHC
4161	GCD	1 RHC
4162	GCE	5 RHC
4164	GCF	4 RHFS
4166	GJZ	EALAT
4168	GCG	5 RHC
4171	GMI	EALAT
4172	GCH	
4175	GCI	4 RHFS
4176	GKA	EALAT
4177	GKB	EALAT
4178	GOA	EALAT
4179	GCJ	1 RHC
4180	GCK	GAM/STAT
4181	GCL	3 RHC
4182	GKC	EALAT
4183	GOB	EALAT
4184	GOC	EALAT
4185	GKD	3 RHC
4186	GCM	1 RHC
4187	GKE	EALAT
4189	GCN	
4190	GMJ	EALAT
4191	GCO	4 RHFS
4192	GOD	
4194	GMD	EALAT
4195	GCP	3 RHC
4198	GCQ	3 RHC
4201	GMK	EALAT

Aérospatiale
AS.532UL Cougar
1 RHC, Phalsbourg;
4 RHFS, Pau;
GAM/STAT, Valence

2252	CGA	GAM/STAT
2267	CGC	4 RHFS
2272	CGE	1 RHC
2273	CGF	1 RHC
2282	CGG	
2285	CGH	
2290	CGI	1 RHC
2293	CGJ	4 RHFS
2299	CGK	4 RHFS
2300	CGL	1 RHC
2301	CGM	1 RHC
2303	CGN	1 RHC
2316	CGO	1 RHC
2323	CGQ	4 RHFS
2324	CGR	4 RHFS
2325	CGS	
2327	CGT	
2331	CGU	
2336	CGV	4 RHFS
2443	CGW	
2446	CGX	1 RHC

Eurocopter
EC.665 Tigre HAP/Tigre HAD
5 RHC, Pau;
EFA, Le Luc;
GAM/STAT, Valence

Tigre HAP

2001	BHH	EFA
2002	BHI	EFA
2003	BHJ	EFA
2004	BHK	EFA
2006	BHL	EFA
2009	BHB	EFA
2010	BHA	5 RHC
2011	BHM	5 RHC
2012	BHT	GAM/STAT
2013	BHC	GAM/STAT
2015	BHD	5 RHC
2016	BIB	5 RHC
2018	BHE	5 RHC
2019	BHF	5 RHC
2021	BHN$	EFA
2022	BHG	5 RHC
2023	BHP	5 RHC
2024	BHO	5 RHC
2025	BHQ	5 RHC
2026	BHR	GAM/STAT
2027	BHS	5 RHC
2028	BHU	5 RHC
2029	BHV	5 RHC
2031	BHX	5 RHC
2032	BHW	5 RHC
2033	BHZ	5 RHC
2034	BIB	5 RHC
2035	BIC	5 RHC
2036	BID	
2037	BIE	5 RHC
2038		
2040		

Tigre HAD
6001	(on order)	

Eurocopter
EC.725AP Cougar
GIH, Cazaux

2611	CAA
2628	CAB
2630	CAC
2631	CAD
2633	CAE
2638	CAF
2640	CAG
2642	CAH

NH Industries
NH.90-TTH
GAM/STAT, Valence
1239 EAA   GAM/STAT
1256 EAB   (on order)

Pilatus
PC-6B/B2-H4 Turbo Porter
1 GSALAT, Montauban
887   MCA
888   MCB
889   MCC
890   MCD
891   MCE

SOCATA
TBM 700A/TBM 700B*
EAAT, Rennes
35   ABW
80   ABY
94   ABZ
99   ABO
100 ABP
115 ABQ
136 ABR
139 ABS
156* ABT
159* ABU
160* ABV

French Govt
Aérospatiale
AS.350B Ecureuil
Gendarmerie;
Sécurité Civile*
F-MCSF (2225) AS.350B-1
F-MJCA (1028) AS.350BA
F-MJCB (1574) AS.350B
F-MJCC (1916) AS.350B-1
F-MJCD (1576) AS.350B
F-MJCE (1812) AS.350B
F-MJCF (1691) AS.350BA
F-MJCG (1753) AS.350B
F-MJCH (1756) AS.350B
F-MJCI (2222) AS.350B-1
F-MJCL (1811) AS.350B
F-MJCM (1952) AS.350B
F-MJCN (2044) AS.350BA
F-MJCO (1917) AS.350B-1
F-MJCP (2045) AS.350B
F-MJCQ (2057) AS.350BA
F-MJCR (2088) AS.350B
F-MJCS (1575) AS.350B
F-MJCT (2104) AS.350B
F-MJCU (2117) AS.350B
F-MJCV (2118) AS.350B
F-MJCW (2218) AS.350BA
F-MJCX (2219) AS.350B
F-MJCY (2221) AS.350B
F-MJCZ (1467) AS.350BA $
F-MJEB (1692) AS.350B
F-MJEC (1810) AS.350B
F-ZBBN   AS.350B*
F-ZBEA   AS.350B
F-ZBFC   AS.350B-1*
F-ZBFD   AS.350B-1*

Aérospatiale
AS.355 Twin Ecureuil
Douanes Francaises
F-ZBAD AS.355F-2

F-ZBEF AS.355F-1
F-ZBEK AS.355F-1
F-ZBEL AS.355F-1

Beech
Super King Air B200
Sécurité Civile
F-ZBFJ 98
F-ZBFK 96
F-ZBMB 97

Canadair CL-415
Sécurité Civile
F-ZBEG 39
F-ZBEU 42
F-ZBFN 33
F-ZBFP 31
F-ZBFS 32
F-ZBFV 37
F-ZBFW 38
F-ZBFX 34
F-ZBFY 35
F-ZBME 44
F-ZBMF 45
F-ZBMG 48

Cessna F.406 Caravan II
Douanes Francaises
F-ZBAB (0025)
F-ZBBB (0039)
F-ZBCE (0042)
F-ZBCF (0077)
F-ZBCG (0066)
F-ZBCH (0075)
F-ZBCI (0070)
F-ZBCJ (0074)
F-ZBEP (0006)
F-ZBES (0017)
F-ZBFA (0001)
F-ZBGA (0086)
F-ZBGD (0090)
F-ZBGE (0061)

Conair
Turbo Firecat
Sécurité Civile
F-ZBAA 22
F-ZBAP 12
F-ZBAZ 01
F-ZBCZ 23
F-ZBEH 20
F-ZBET 15
F-ZBEW 11
F-ZBEY 07
F-ZBMA 24

De Havilland Canada
DHC-8Q-402MR
Sécurité Civile
F-ZBMC 73
F-ZBMD 74

Eurocopter
EC.135T-2
Douanes Francaises*;
Gendarmerie
F-MJDA (0642)
F-MJDB (0654)
F-MJDC (0717)
F-MJDD (0727)
F-MJDE (0747)

F-MJDF (0757)
F-MJDG (0772)
F-MJDH (0787)
F-MJDI (0797)
F-MJDJ (0806)
F-MJDK (0857)
F-MJDL (0867)
F-ZBGF*
F-ZBGG*
F-ZBGH*
F-ZBGI*
F-ZBGJ*

Eurocopter
EC.145
Gendarmerie;
Sécurité Civile*
F-MJBA (9008) EC.145C-1
F-MJBB (9014) EC.145C-1
F-MJBC (9018) EC.145C-1
F-MJBD (9019) EC.145C-1
F-MJBE (9025) EC.145C-1
F-MJBF (9035) EC.145C-2
F-MJBG (9036) EC.145C-2
F-MJBH (9037) EC.145C-2
F-MJBI (9127) EC.145C-2
F-MJBJ (9140) EC.145C-2
F-MJBK (9162) EC.145C-2
F-MJBM (9113) EC.145C-2
F-MJBN (9173) EC.145C-2
F-MJBO (9124) EC.145C-2
F-MJBR (9169) EC.145C-2
F-MJBT (9173) EC.145C-2
F-ZBPA   EC.145C-1*
F-ZBPD   EC.145C-1*
F-ZBPE   EC.145C-1*
F-ZBPF   EC.145C-1*
F-ZBPG   EC.145C-1*
F-ZBPH   EC.145C-1*
F-ZBPI   EC.145C-1*
F-ZBPJ   EC.145C-1*
F-ZBPK   EC.145C-1*
F-ZBPL   EC.145C-1*
F-ZBPM   EC.145C-1*
F-ZBPN   EC.145C-1*
F-ZBPO   EC.145C-1*
F-ZBPP   EC.145C-2*
F-ZBPQ   EC.145C-2*
F-ZBPS   EC.145C-2*
F-ZBPT   EC.145C-2*
F-ZBPU   EC.145C-2*
F-ZBPV   EC.145C-2*
F-ZBPW   EC.145C-2*
F-ZBPX   EC.145C-2*
F-ZBPY   EC.145C-2*
F-ZBPZ   EC.145C-2*
F-ZBQA   EC.145C-2*
F-ZBQB   EC.145C-2*
F-ZBQC   EC.145C-2*
F-ZBQD   EC.145C-2*
F-ZBQE   EC.145C-2*
F-ZBQF   EC.145C-2*
F-ZBQG   EC.145C-2*
F-ZBQH   EC.145C-2*
F-ZBQI   EC.145C-2*
F-ZBQJ   EC.145C-2*
F-ZBQK   EC.145C-2*
F-ZBQL   EC.145C-2*

Hawker Beechcraft King Air B350ER
Douanes Francaises
F-ZBGK (FL-682)
F-ZBGL (FL-746)
F-ZBG. (on order)
F-ZBG. (on order)
F-ZBG. (on order)
F-ZBG. (on order)
F-ZBG. (on order)
F-ZBG. (on order)

Civil operated aircraft in military use
BAE Jetstream 41
AVDEF, Nimes/Garons
F-HAVD
F-HAVF

Dassault Falcon 20
AVDEF, Nimes/Garons
F-GJDB Falcon 20C
F-GPAA Falcon 20ECM
F-GPAB Falcon 20E
F-GPAD Falcon 20E

Grob G120A-F
EADS Cognac Aviation Training
  Services/EPAA 00.315, Cognac
F-GUKA
F-GUKB
F-GUKC
F-GUKD
F-GUKE
F-GUKF
F-GUKG
F-GUKH
F-GUKI
F-GUKJ
F-GUKK
F-GUKL
F-GUKM
F-GUKN
F-GUKO
F-GUKP
F-GUKQ
F-GUKR
F-GUKS
F-GUKV
F-GUKW
F-GUKX
F-GUKZ

GABON
Grumman
G.1159C Gulfstream IVSP
Gabonese Government, Libreville
TR-KSP

GERMANY
*Please note that German serials do not
officially include the '+' part in them
but aircraft wearing German markings
are often painted with a cross in the
middle, which is why it is included here.*

Luftwaffe, Marineflieger
Airbus A.310-304/MRTT*
1/FBS, Köln-Bonn
10+23
10+24*
10+25*
10+26*
10+27*

Bombardier Global 5000
3/FBS, Köln-Bonn
14+01
14+02
14+03
14+04

Airbus A.319CJ-115X
3/FBS, Köln-Bonn
15+01
15+02

Airbus A.340-313X
3/FBS, Köln-Bonn
16+01
16+02

Eurofighter
EF.2000GS/EF.2000GT*
EADS, Manching;
JbG-31 *Boelcke*,
  Nörvenich;
JG-73 *Steinhoff*, Laage;
JG-74 *Molders*, Neuburg/Donau;
TsLw-1, Kaufbeuren;
WTD-61, Ingolstadt
30+02* JG-74
30+03* JG-73
30+04 JG-73
30+05* JG-73
30+06 JG-74
30+07 TsLw-1
30+09 JbG-31
30+10* JG-74
30+11 JG-73
30+12 JG-73
30+14* JG-73
30+15 JG-73
30+17* JG-73
30+20* JG-73 $
30+22 EADS
30+23 JbG-31
30+24* JG-73
30+25 JG-74
30+26 TsLw-1
30+27* JG-73
30+28 JG-74
30+29 JG-74
30+30 JG-73
30+31* JbG-31
30+32 JG-74
30+33 JG-74
30+35* JG-74
30+38* JG-73
30+39 JG-74
30+40 JbG-31
30+42* JG-73
30+45 JG-73
30+46 JG-73
30+47 JG-73
30+48 JG-74 $
30+49 JG-73
30+50 JG-73
30+51 JG-73
30+52 JG-73
30+53 JG-73
30+54* JG-73
30+55 JG-73
30+56 JbG-31
30+57 JG-73
30+58 JG-74
30+59* JG-73

30+60 JG-73
30+61 JG-74
30+62 JG-73
30+63 JG-74
30+64 JG-74
30+65 JG-74
30+66 JbG-31
30+67* JG-73
30+68 JG-74
30+69 JG-74
30+70 JG-74
30+71* EADS
30+72 JbG-31
30+73 EADS
30+74 JG-74
30+75 JbG-31
30+76 JbG-31
30+77* JG-73
30+78 JbG-31
30+79 JbG-31
30+80 EADS
30+81 EADS
30+82 EADS
30+83 EADS
30+84* EADS
30+85 EADS
31+14 JbG-31
31+15 TsLw-1
31+16 JG-73
31+17 JG-73
31+18 JG-73
31+19 JG-73
31+20 JG-73
31+21 JG-73
31+22 JG-73
98+03* EADS
98+04 EADS
98+07 EADS
98+31* EADS

McD F-4F Phantom
JG-71 *Richthoven*, Wittmundhaven;
TsLw-1, Kaufbeuren;
WTD-61, Ingolstadt
37+01 JG-71
37+04 JG-71
37+15 WTD-61
37+22 JG-71
37+26 JG-71
37+48 JG-71 $
37+63 JG-71
37+65 JG-71
37+77 JG-71
37+79 JG-71
37+81 JG-71
37+84 JG-71
37+85 JG-71
37+89 JG-71
37+92 JG-71
37+96 JG-71
38+00 JG-71
38+01 JG-71
38+02 JG-71
38+10 JG-71
38+13 WTD-61
38+16 JG-71
38+26 JG-71
38+28 JG-71
38+29 JG-71
38+33 JG-71
38+37 JG-71

38+39	$
38+42	JG-71
38+43	JG-71
38+45	JG-71
38+46	JG-71
38+48	JG-71
38+50	JG-71
38+53	JG-71
38+57	JG-71
38+58	JG-71
38+60	JG-71
38+61	TsLw-1
38+62	JG-71
38+67	JG-71
38+70	JG-71
38+75	JG-71
99+91	WTD-61

Panavia
Tornado Strike/
Trainer[1]/ECR[2]
AkG-51 *Immelmann*,
 Schleswig/Jagel;
EADS, Manching;
GAFFTC, Holloman AFB, USA;
JbG-32, Lechfeld;
JbG-33, Büchel;
TsLw-1, Kaufbeuren;
WTD-61, Ingolstadt

43+01[1]	JbG-33
43+02[1]	JbG-33
43+07[1]	AkG-51
43+10[1]	JbG-33
43+20	JbG-33
43+23[1]	GAFFTC
43+25	JbG-33
43+29[1]	
43+31[1]	GAFFTC
43+32	
43+34	TsLw-1
43+35[1]	AkG-51
43+37[1]	JbG-32
43+38	JbG-32
43+42[1]	GAFFTC
43+45[1]	JbG-32
43+46	AkG-51
43+48	AkG-51
43+50	AkG-51
43+52	JbG-33
43+54	TsLw-1
43+59	TsLw-1
43+71	JbG-32
43+73	AkG-51
43+75	GAFFTC
43+87	JbG-33
43+92[1]	AkG-51
43+94[1]	GAFFTC
43+97[1]	AkG-51
43+98	AkG-51
44+00	GAFFTC
44+02	JbG-32
44+06	GAFFTC
44+16[1]	JbG-33
44+17	AkG-51
44+21	
44+23	JbG-33
44+26	JbG-33
44+29	JbG-33
44+30	GAFFTC
44+33	JbG-33
44+34	AkG-51

44+58	JbG-32
44+61	AkG-51
44+64	AkG-51
44+65	AkG-51
44+69	AkG-51
44+70	JbG-33
44+72[1]	GAFFTC
44+73[1]	WTD-61
44+77[1]	AkG-51
44+78	AkG-51
44+79	JbG-33
44+90	AkG-51
44+92	JbG-33
45+00	JbG-33
45+04	JbG-33
45+06	AkG-51 $
45+07	JbG-33
45+08	GAFFTC
45+09	JbG-33
45+10	JbG-33
45+13[1]	JbG-32
45+14[1]	JbG-32
45+15[1]	GAFFTC
45+16[1]	JbG-33
45+19	JbG-32
45+20	JbG-32
45+22	AkG-51
45+23	JbG-33
45+25	WTD-61
45+28	JbG-33
45+35	AkG-51
45+36	
45+39	JbG-32
45+40	JbG-33
45+45	JbG-33
45+50	AkG-51
45+52	JbG-33
45+53	TsLw-1
45+54	GAFFTC
45+57	AkG-51
45+59	JbG-33
45+60[1]	AkG-51
45+61[1]	AkG-51
45+64	AkG-51
45+66	GAFFTC
45+67	AkG-51
45+68	JbG-33
45+69	JbG-33
45+70[1]	JbG-33
45+71	GAFFTC
45+72	JbG-32
45+74	TsLw-1
45+76	JbG-33
45+77[1]	JbG-33
45+78	JbG-33
45+82	JbG-33
45+84	
45+85	AkG-51
45+86	JbG-33
45+88	
45+90	JbG-33
45+91	JbG-33
45+92	JbG-33
45+93	JbG-32
45+94	JbG-33
46+00[1]	GAFFTC
46+01	JbG-33
46+02	JbG-33
46+04[1]	GAFFTC
46+05[1]	WTD-61
46+07[1]	GAFFTC

46+08[1]	JbG-32
46+09[1]	GAFFTC
46+10	AkG-51
46+11	JbG-33
46+12	GAFFTC
46+13	AkG-51
46+14	AkG-51
46+15	AkG-51
46+18	JbG-33
46+20	AkG-51
46+21	JbG-33
46+22	AkG-51
46+23[2]	JbG-32 $
46+24[2]	JbG-32
46+25[2]	JbG-32
46+26[2]	JbG-32
46+28[2]	JbG-32
46+29[2]	JbG-32 $
46+30[2]	JbG-32
46+31[2]	JbG-32
46+32[2]	WTD-61
46+33[2]	JbG-32 $
46+34[2]	JbG-32
46+35[2]	JbG-32
46+36[2]	JbG-32
46+37[2]	JbG-32
46+38[2]	JbG-32
46+39[2]	JbG-32
46+40[2]	WTD-61
46+41[2]	JbG-32
46+42[2]	JbG-32
46+44[2]	JbG-32
46+45[2]	JbG-32
46+46[2]	JbG-32
46+48[2]	JbG-32
46+49[2]	JbG-32
46+50[2]	JbG-32
46+51[2]	JbG-32
46+52[2]	JbG-32
46+53[2]	JbG-32
46+54[2]	JbG-32
46+55[2]	JbG-32
46+56[2]	JbG-32
46+57[2]	JbG-32
98+59	WTD-61
98+60	WTD-61
98+77	WTD-61
98+79[2]	WTD-61

Transall C-160D
LTG-61 (1.LwDiv),
 Landsberg;
LTG-62 (1.LwDiv),
 Wunsdorf;
LTG-63 (4.LwDiv),
 Hohn;
WTD-61, Ingolstadt

50+06	LTG-63
50+07	LTG-61
50+08	LTG-61
50+09	LTG-61
50+10	LTG-62
50+17	LTG-63
50+29	LTG-62
50+33	LTG-62
50+34	LTG-63
50+36	LTG-62
50+37	LTG-62
50+38	LTG-61
50+40	LTG-63
50+41	LTG-62

50+42	LTG-63
50+44	LTG-61
50+45	LTG-63
50+46	LTG-62
50+47	LTG-61
50+48	LTG-61 $
50+49	LTG-61
50+51	LTG-61
50+53	LTG-61
50+54	LTG-61
50+55	LTG-62
50+57	LTG-62
50+58	LTG-63
50+59	LTG-63
50+60	LTG-62
50+61	LTG-62
50+62	LTG-62
50+64	LTG-61
50+65	LTG-62
50+66	LTG-61
50+67	LTG-63
50+68	LTG-61
50+69	LTG-63
50+70	LTG-62
50+71	LTG-63
50+72	LTG-61
50+73	LTG-62
50+74	LTG-61
50+75	LTG-61
50+76	LTG-63
50+77	LTG-62
50+78	LTG-62
50+79	LTG-63
50+81	LTG-62
50+82	LTG-63
50+83	LTG-62
50+84	LTG-61
50+85	LTG-63 $
50+86	LTG-61
50+87	LTG-63
50+88	LTG-61
50+89	LTG-62
50+90	LTG-62
50+91	LTG-62
50+92	LTG-63
50+93	LTG-63
50+94	LTG-63
50+95	LTG-63
50+96	LTG-61
50+97	LTG-61
51+00	LTG-62
51+01	LTG-62
51+02	LTG-63
51+03	LTG-62
51+04	LTG-61
51+05	LTG-62
51+06	LTG-63
51+08	WTD-61
51+09	LTG-63
51+10	LTG-62
51+12	LTG-63
51+13	LTG-61
51+14	LTG-61

Dornier Do.228LM/Do.228NG*
MFG-3, Nordholz
57+01	
57+04	
57+05*	

Lockheed
P-3C Orion
MFG-3, Nordholz
60+01	
60+02	
60+03	
60+04	
60+05	
60+06	
60+07	
60+08	

Eurocopter
AS.532U-2 Cougar
3/FBS, Berlin-Tegel
82+01	
82+02	
82+03	

Westland
Super Lynx Mk88A
MFG-3, Nordholz;
WTD-61, Ingolstadt
83+02	MFG-3
83+03	MFG-3
83+04	MFG-3
83+05	MFG-3
83+06	MFG-3
83+07	WTD-61
83+09	MFG-3
83+10	MFG-3
83+11$	MFG-3
83+12	MFG-3
83+13	MFG-3
83+15	MFG-3
83+17	MFG-3
83+18	MFG-3
83+19	MFG-3
83+20	MFG-3
83+21	MFG-3
83+22	MFG-3
83+23	MFG-3
83+24	MFG-3
83+25	MFG-3

Westland
Sea King HAS41
MFG-5, Kiel-Holtenau
89+50	
89+51	
89+52	
89+53	
89+54	
89+55	
89+56	
89+57	
89+58$	
89+60	
89+61	
89+62	
89+63	
89+64$	
89+65	
89+66	
89+67	
89+68	
89+69	
89+70	
89+71	

Northrop Grumman
RQ-4E Euro Hawk
WTD-61, Manching
99+01	WTD-61
..+..	(on order)
..+..	(on order)
..+..	(on order)
..+..	(on order)

Heeresfliegertruppe
Eurocopter
EC.665 Tiger UHT
Ecole Franco-Allemande, Le Luc,
  France;
KHR-36, Fritzlar;
TsLw-3, Fassberg;
WTD-61, Ingolstadt
74+02	Eurocopter
74+03	WTD-61
74+05	EFA
74+06	EFA
74+07	EFA
74+08	EFA
74+09	EFA
74+10	KHR-36
74+11	KHR-36
74+17	KHR-36
74+18	KHR-36
74+19	KHR-36
74+20	KHR-36
74+21	
74+22	
74+23	
74+24	
74+26	
74+27	
74+28	
74+29	
74+30	
74+31	
74+32	
74+34	
74+36	
74+37	
74+38	
74+39	
74+40	
74+41	
74+42	
98+14	
98+15	
98+16	
98+17	WTD-61
98+18	Eurocopter
98+19	Eurocopter
98+23	TsLw-3
98+24	Eurocopter
98+25	TsLw-3
98+26	Eurocopter
98+27	

NH Industries
NH.90-TTH
HFWS, Bückeburg;
HSG-64, Holzdorf;
THR-10, Fassberg:
WTD-61, Ingolstadt
78+01	HFWS
78+02	HFWS
78+03	HFWS
78+04	HFWS

78+05	
78+06	HFWS
78+07	HFWS
78+08	HFWS
78+09	HFWS
78+10	HFWS
78+11	HFWS
78+13	HFWS
78+14	THR-10
78+16	
78+17	
78+18	
78+19	
78+20	
78+21	
78+22	
78+23	
78+24	
78+25	
78+26	
78+27	
79+01	HSG-64
79+02	HSG-64
79+03	HSG-64
79+07	Eurocopter
79+10	
79+25	
79+26	
98+50	Eurocopter
98+90	
98+97	

Eurocopter EC.135P-1
HFWS, Bückeburg

82+51	
82+52	
82+53	
82+54	
82+55	
82+56	
82+57	
82+59	
82+60	
82+61	
82+62	
82+63	
82+64	
82+65	

Sikorsky/VFW
CH-53G/CH-53GA/CH-53GE/
CH-53GS
HFWS, Bückeburg;
MTHR-15, Rheine-Bentlage;
MTHR-25, Laupheim;
TsLw-3, Fassberg;
WTD-61, Ingolstadt

84+05	CH-53G	HFWS
84+06	CH-53G	MTHR-15
84+09	CH-53G	TsLw-3
84+10	CH-53G	HFWS
84+11	CH-53G	HFWS
84+12	CH-53G	MTHR-15
84+13	CH-53G	HFWS
84+14	CH-53GE	MTHR-15
84+15	CH-53GS	MTHR-15
84+16	CH-53G	HFWS
84+17	CH-53G	MTHR-25
84+18	CH-53G	HFWS
84+19	CH-53G	TsLw-3
84+24	CH-53G	MTHR-15
84+25	CH-53GS	MTHR-15

84+26	CH-53GE	MTHR-15
84+27	CH-53G	HFWS
84+28	CH-53G	MTHR-25
84+29	CH-53G	MTHR-15
84+30	CH-53GS	MTHR-15
84+31	CH-53G	MTHR-25
84+32	CH-53G	MTHR-25
84+34	CH-53G	MTHR-15
84+35	CH-53G	MTHR-25
84+37	CH-53G	HFWS
84+38	CH-53G	MTHR-25
84+39	CH-53G	MTHR-15
84+40	CH-53G	MTHR-25
84+41	CH-53G	HFWS
84+42	CH-53GS	HFWS
84+43	CH-53G	MTHR-25
84+44	CH-53G	MTHR-25
84+45	CH-53GS	MTHR-25
84+46	CH-53G	MTHR-15
84+47	CH-53G	MTHR-25
84+48	CH-53G	HFWS
84+49	CH-53G	HFWS
84+50	CH-53G	HFWS
84+51	CH-53GS	MTHR-25
84+52	CH-53GS	MTHR-25
84+53	CH-53GE	MTHR-25
84+54	CH-53G	MTHR-25
84+55	CH-53G	WTD-61
84+57	CH-53G	HFWS
84+58	CH-53G	MTHR-25
84+59	CH-53G	HFWS
84+60	CH-53G	MTHR-25
84+62	CH-53GS	MTHR-25
84+63	CH-53G	MTHR-25
84+64	CH-53GS	MTHR-25
84+65	CH-53G	HFWS
84+66	CH-53GS	MTHR-25
84+67	CH-53GS	MTHR-15
84+68	CH-53G	MTHR-25
84+69	CH-53G	HFWS
84+70	CH-53G	MTHR-15
84+71	CH-53G	MTHR-15
84+72	CH-53G	MTHR-15
84+73	CH-53GS	MTHR-15
84+74	CH-53G	HFWS
84+75	CH-53G	MTHR-15
84+76	CH-53G	HFWS
84+77	CH-53G	MTHR-15
84+78	CH-53GS	MTHR-15
84+79	CH-53GS	MTHR-15
84+80	CH-53G	HFWS
84+82	CH-53GE	MTHR-15
84+83	CH-53G	HFWS
84+84	CH-53G	MTHR-15
84+85	CH-53GS	MTHR-15
84+86	CH-53GA	Eurocopter
84+87	CH-53G	MTHR-15
84+88	CH-53G	MTHR-15
84+89	CH-53G	MTHR-15
84+90	CH-53G	MTHR-15
84+91	CH-53GS	MTHR-15
84+92	CH-53GE	MTHR-15
84+94	CH-53G	
84+95	CH-53G	MTHR-25
84+96	CH-53GE	MTHR-25
84+97	CH-53G	MTHR-25
84+98	CH-53GS	MTHR-15
84+99	CH-53G	HFWS
85+00	CH-53GS	MTHR-25
85+01	CH-53GS	MTHR-25
85+02	CH-53G	MTHR-15

85+03	CH-53G	MTHR-15
85+04	CH-53GA	MTHR-15
85+05	CH-53GS	MTHR-15
85+06	CH-53G	MTHR-25
85+07	CH-53GS	HFWS
85+08	CH-53G	MTHR-15
85+10	CH-53GS	MTHR-25
85+11	CH-53G	MTHR-25
85+12	CH-53GS	MTHR-15

MBB Bo.105P
Ecole Franco-Allemande,
 Le Luc, France;
HFUS-1, Holzdorf;
HFUS-7, Mendig;
HFVAS-100, Celle;
HFVAS-300, Mendig;
HFWS, Bückeburg;
KHR-26, Roth;
KHR-36, Fritzlar;
MTHR-15, Rheine-Bentlage;
MTHR-25, Laupheim;
THR-30, Niederstetten;
TsLw-3, Fassberg;
WTD-61, Ingolstadt

86+02	KHR-36
86+03	HFWS
86+04	HFWS
86+05	KHR-36
86+06	KHR-36
86+07	HFWS
86+08	HFWS
86+09	HFWS
86+10	HFVAS-100
86+11	MTHR-15
86+12	HFWS
86+13	THR-30
86+14	KHR-36
86+15	MTHR-25
86+16	KHR-36
86+17	HFWS
86+18	HFWS
86+19	HFWS
86+20	HFWS
86+21	HFVAS-100
86+23	TsLw-3
86+24	HFWS
86+25	HFVAS-100
86+26	HFWS
86+27	KHR-26
86+28	HFUS-1
86+29	HFWS
86+30	KHR-26
86+31	HFUS-1
86+32	HFWS
86+33	MTHR-25
86+34	HFVAS-100
86+35	KHR-26
86+36	HFVAS-100
86+38	KHR-36
86+39	HFWS
86+40	HFWS
86+41	HFVAS-100
86+42	KHR-26
86+44	HFWS
86+45	KHR-26
86+46	HFWS
86+47	HFVAS-100
86+48	HFVAS-100
86+49	KHR-36
86+50	KHR-36

86+51	HFWS	87+37	HFWS	4117
86+52	HFUS-1	87+39	KHR-36	4118
86+53	HFVAS-100	87+41	HFWS	4120
86+54	EFA	87+43	KHR-36	4121
86+55	KHR-36	87+44	HFUS-1	4122
86+56	THR-30	87+45	HFUS-1	4123
86+57	KHR-26	87+46	KHR-36	4124
86+58	KHR-36	87+47	HFWS	4125
86+59	HFVAS-100	87+48	HFVAS-100	
86+60	HFWS	87+49	HFWS	**Dassault Mirage 2000**
86+61	KHR-26	87+50	KHR-36	331 MAPK/114 PM, Tanagra;
86+62	HFWS	87+51	HFVAS-100	332 MAPK/114 PM, Tanagra
86+63	KHR-26	87+52	HFUS-1	**Mirage 2000BG**
86+64	KHR-26	87+53	KHR-36	201 332 MAPK
86+66	KHR-26	87+55	KHR-36	202 332 MAPK
86+67	HFVAS-100	87+56	TsLw-3	**Mirage 2000EG**
86+68	KHR-36	87+58	HFWS	210 332 MAPK
86+69	KHR-36	87+59	HFWS	212 332 MAPK
86+70	HFVAS-100	87+60	KHR-36	213 332 MAPK
86+71	KHR-36	87+61	HFWS	215 332 MAPK
86+72	TsLw-3	87+62	HFWS	216 332 MAPK
86+73	HFWS	87+63	HFWS	217 332 MAPK
86+74	KHR-36	87+64	HFWS	218 332 MAPK
86+76	KHR-26	87+65	KHR-36	219 332 MAPK
86+77	HFWS	87+66	KHR-36	220 332 MAPK
86+78	HFVAS-300	87+67	HFWS	221 332 MAPK
86+79	KHR-26	87+68	KHR-36	228 332 MAPK
86+80	HFVAS-100	87+70	KHR-26	231 332 MAPK
86+83	TsLw-3	87+71	HFWS	232 332 MAPK
86+84	KHR-26	87+72	THR-30	233 332 MAPK
86+85	HFUS-1	87+73	WTD-61	237 332 MAPK
86+86	HFVAS-100	87+75	KHR-26	239 332 MAPK
86+87		87+76	KHR-36	241 332 MAPK
86+88	KHR-26	87+77		242 332 MAPK
86+89	HFUS-1	87+78	HFUS-1	**Mirage 2000-5BG**
86+90	KHR-36	87+79		505 331 MAPK
86+92	KHR-36	87+80	HFUS-1	506 331 MAPK
86+93	HFWS	87+82	HFVAS-300	507 331 MAPK
86+95	HFUS-1	87+83	MTHR-25	508 331 MAPK
86+96	HFWS	87+85	HFWS	509 331 MAPK
86+97	KHR-36	87+87	HFVAS-100	**Mirage 2000-5EG**
86+98	MTHR-15	87+88	KHR-26	511 331 MAPK
86+99	HFWS	87+89	MTHR-25	514 331 MAPK
87+01	KHR-26	87+90	HFWS	527 331 MAPK
87+02	KHR-26	87+92	KHR-26	530 331 MAPK
87+03	KHR-26	87+97	HFVAS-100	534 331 MAPK
87+04	KHR-26	87+98	HFWS	535 331 MAPK
87+06	MTHR-25	87+99	KHR-36	536 331 MAPK
87+09	KHR-26	88+01	KHR-36	540 331 MAPK
87+10	KHR-26	88+02	THR-30	543 331 MAPK
87+11	KHR-36	88+04	KHR-36	545 331 MAPK
87+12	HFWS	88+05	HFWS	546 331 MAPK
87+13	KHR-36	88+06	KHR-36	547 331 MAPK
87+15	KHR-36	88+07	HFWS	548 331 MAPK
87+16	HFVAS-100	88+08	HFWS	549 331 MAPK
87+17	KHR-26	88+09		550 331 MAPK
87+18	KHR-36	88+10	THR-30	551 331 MAPK
87+19	KHR-36	88+11	MTHR-25	552 331 MAPK
87+20	KHR-26	88+12	HFVAS-100	553 331 MAPK
87+22				554 331 MAPK
87+23	HFVAS-100	**GHANA**		555 331 MAPK
87+24	HFUS-7	**Ghana Air Force**		
87+25	KHR-26	**Dassault**		
87+26	HFUS-1	**Falcon 900EASy**		**Embraer**
87+27	HFWS	VIP Flight, Accra		**ERJ-135BJ Legacy/ERJ.145H/**
87+28	HFVAS-100	9G-EXE		**ERJ.135LR**
87+29	HFWS			352 MMYP/112 PM, Elefsís;
87+30	KHR-36	**GREECE**		380 Mira/112 PM, Elefsís
87+31	HFWS	**Ellinikí Polemikí Aeroporía**		135L-484 ERJ-135BJ 352 MMYP
87+34	KHR-26	**Aeritalia C-27J Spartan**		145-209 ERJ-135LR 352 MMYP
87+35	KHR-26	354 Mira, Elefsís		145-374 ERJ-145H 380 Mira
				145-671 ERJ-145H 380 Mira

145-729	ERJ-145H	380 Mira
145-757	ERJ-145H	380 Mira

Gulfstream Aerospace
Gulfstream V
352 MMYP/112 PM, Elefsís
678

Lockheed
C-130H Hercules
356 MTM/112 PM, Elefsís
*ECM
741*
742
743
744
745
746
747*
749
751
752$

Lockheed
F-16C/F-16D*
Fighting Falcon
330 Mira/111 PM,
 Nea Ankhialos;
335 Mira/116 PM,
 Áraxos;
336 Mira/116 PM,
 Áraxos;
337 Mira/110 PM, Larissa;
340 Mira/115PM, Souda;
341 Mira/111 PM,
 Nea Ankhialos;
343 Mira/115PM, Souda;
347 Mira/111 PM,
 Nea Ankhialos

001	335 Mira
002	335 Mira
003	335 Mira
004	335 Mira
005	335 Mira
006	335 Mira
007	335 Mira
008	335 Mira
009	335 Mira
010	335 Mira
011	335 Mira
012	335 Mira
013	335 Mira
014	335 Mira
015	335 Mira
016	335 Mira
017	335 Mira
018	335 Mira
019	335 Mira
020	335 Mira
021*	335 Mira
022*	335 Mira
023*	335 Mira
024*	335 Mira
025*	335 Mira
026*	335 Mira
027*	335 Mira
028*	335 Mira
029*	335 Mira
030*	335 Mira
046	341 Mira
047	347 Mira

048	341 Mira
049	347 Mira
050	341 Mira
051	347 Mira
052	341 Mira
053	347 Mira
054	341 Mira
055	347 Mira
056	341 Mira
057	347 Mira
058	341 Mira
060	341 Mira
061	347 Mira
062	341 Mira
063	347 Mira
064	341 Mira
065	347 Mira
066	341 Mira
067	347 Mira
068	341 Mira
069	347 Mira
070	341 Mira
071	347 Mira
072	341 Mira
073	347 Mira
074	341 Mira
075	347 Mira
076	341 Mira
077*	341 Mira
078*	347 Mira
079*	347 Mira
080*	341 Mira
081*	347 Mira
082*	341 Mira
083*	347 Mira
084*	341 Mira
110	330 Mira
111	330 Mira
112	
113	330 Mira
114	
115	330 Mira
116	330 Mira
117	330 Mira
118	
119	330 Mira
120	
121	330 Mira
122	
124	
125	330 Mira
126	330 Mira
127	330 Mira
128	
129	330 Mira
130	
132	
133	330 Mira
134	
136	
138	
139	330 Mira
140	
141	330 Mira
143	330 Mira
144*	330 Mira
145*	330 Mira
146*	
147*	330 Mira
148*	
149*	

500	343 Mira
501	337 Mira
502	337 Mira
503	343 Mira
504	343 Mira
505	343 Mira
506	340 Mira
507	337 Mira
508	337 Mira
509	343 Mira
510	340/343 Mira
511	343 Mira
512	343 Mira
513	343 Mira
515	337 Mira
517	347 Mira
518	340 Mira
519	340 Mira
520	343 Mira
521	340 Mira
523	340 Mira
524	337 Mira
525	343 Mira
526	343 Mira
527	343 Mira
528	337 Mira
529	343 Mira
530	337 Mira
531	337 Mira
532	337 Mira
533	340 Mira
534	340 Mira
535	340 Mira
536	340 Mira
537	340 Mira
538	340 Mira
539	337 Mira
600*	343 Mira
601*	340 Mira
602*	340 Mira
603*	340 Mira
605*	340 Mira
606*	337 Mira
607*	343 Mira
608*	340 Mira
609*	337 Mira
610*	340 Mira
611*	337 Mira
612*	337 Mira
613*	343 Mira
614*	340/343 Mira
615*	343 Mira
616*	340/343 Mira
617*	343 Mira
618*	343 Mira
619*	337 Mira

LTV A-7 Corsair II
336 Mira/116 PM,
 Áraxos

154404	TA-7C	
155424	TA-7C	
154477	TA-7C	
155489	TA-7C	
155507	TA-7C	
155774	TA-7C	(156774)
156738	TA-7C	
156747	TA-7C	
156750	TA-7C	
156753	TA-7C	
156767	TA-7C	

156768	TA-7C
156790	TA-7C
156795	TA-7C
158021	A-7E
158824	A-7E
158825	A-7E$
159263	A-7E
159274	A-7E
159639	A-7E
159645	A-7E
159648	A-7E
159967	A-7E
159975	A-7E
160537	A-7E
160543	A-7E
160552	A-7E
160560	A-7E
160616	A-7E$
160617	A-7E
160710	A-7E
160717	A-7E
160728	A-7E
160736	A-7E
160857	A-7E
160862	A-7E
160865	A-7E
160866	A-7E

HUNGARY
Hungarian Defence Forces
Antonov An-26
59 Sz.D.REB, Kecskemét
110
405
406
407
603

Boeing
C-17A Globemaster III
Strategic Airlift Capability (SAC),
Pápa, Hungary
01 (08-0001)
02 (08-0002)
03 (08-0003)

SAAB 39C/39D* Gripen
59 Sz.D.REB, Kecskemét
30
31
32
33
34
35
36
37
38
39
40
41
42*
43*

ISRAEL
Heyl ha'Avir
Boeing 707
120 Sqn, Nevatim
120 RC-707
128 RC-707
137 RC-707
140 KC-707

248 KC-707
250 KC-707
255 EC-707
260 KC-707
264 KC-707
272 KC-707
275 KC-707
290 KC-707
Lockheed
C-130 Karnaf
103 Sqn & 131 Sqn, Nevatim

102	C-130H
208	C-130E
305	C-130E
309	C-130E
310	C-130E
314	C-130E
316	C-130E
318	C-130E
420	KC-130H
427	C-130H
428	C-130H
435	C-130H
436	C-130H
522	KC-130H
545	KC-130H
...	C-130J-30 (on order)
...	C-130J-30 (on order)
...	C-130J-30 (on order)

ITALY
Aeronautica Militare Italiana
Aeritalia G222/C-27J Spartan
9ª Brigata Aerea,
  Pratica di Mare:
    14° Stormo/8° Gruppo;
46ª Brigata Aerea, Pisa:
    98° Gruppo;
RSV, Pratica di Mare

G222RM

MM62139	14-20	8

G222TCM

MM62124	RS-46	RSV
MM62146	14-11	8

C-27J Spartan

CSX62127		Alenia
MM62214	46-84	98
MM62215	46-80	98
MM62217	46-81	98
MM62218	46-82	98
CSX62219	RS-50	RSV
MM62220	46-83	98
MM62221	46-85	98
MM62222	46-86	98
MM62223	46-88	98
MM62224	46-89	98
MM62225	46-90	98
MM62250	46-91	98

Aeritalia-EMB AMX/AMX-T*
32° Stormo, Amendola:
    13° Gruppo &
    101° Gruppo;
51° Stormo, Istrana:
    103° Gruppo &
    132° Gruppo;
RSV, Pratica di Mare

MM7101		
MM7114		
MM7115		
MM7125		
MM7126	$	

MM7129	32-15	13
MM7131	51-11	103
MM7141		
MM7143	51-21	103
MM7144	$	103
MM7146	51-25	103
MM7147	32-01$	13
MM7148	51-61	132
MM7149	32-24	13
MM7151	51-51	132
MM7152		
MM7155		
MM7156		
MM7157	$	
CSX7158	RS-12	RSV
MM7159	51-10$	103
MM7160		
MM7161	51-37	132
MM7162		
MM7163	32-25	13
MM7164	51-40	132
MM7165	32-16	13
MM7166	32-13	13
MM7167		
MM7168	51-55	132
MM7169	51-66	132
MM7170	32-05	13
MM7171	51-52	132
MM7172		
MM7173	51-63	132
MM7174	51-60	132
CSX7175		Alenia
MM7177	51-42	132
MM7176		
MM7178	51-43	132
MM7179	51-64	132
MM7180	32-20	13
MM7182	51-62	132
MM7183	51-41	132
MM7184	51-65	132
MM7185	51-67	132
MM7186	51-50	132
MM7189		
MM7190	51-57	132
MM7191	51-45	132
MM7192	32-02	13
MM7193	51-54	132
MM7194	32-21	13
CSX7195		Alenia
MM7196	32-07	13
MM7197	51-46	132
MM7198	51-44$	132
MM55029*	32-50$	101
MM55030*	32-41	101
MM55031*	32-40	101
CSX55034*	RS-18	RSV
MM55035*		
MM55036*	32-51	101
MM55037*	32-64	101
MM55038*	32-53	101
MM55039*	32-54	101
MM55040*	32-52	101
MM55041*	32-55	101
MM55042*	32-56	101
MM55043*	32-65	101
MM55044*	32-57	101
MM55046*	32-47	101
MM55047*	32-53	101
MM55049*	32-66	101
MM55051*	32-42	101

Italy

Aermacchi
MB339A/MB339CD*
32° Stormo, Amendola:
632ª SC;
36° Stormo, Gioia del Colle:
12° Gruppo;
51° Stormo, Istrana:
651ª SC;
61° Stormo, Lecce:
212° Gruppo &
213° Gruppo;
Aermacchi, Venegono;
Frecce Tricolori [FT]
(313° Gruppo), Rivolto
(MB339A/PAN);
RSV, Pratica di Mare

MM54443	61-50	
MM54446	61-01	
MM54452		
CSX54453	RS-11	RSV
MM54457	61-11	
MM54458	61-12	
MM54465	61-21	
MM54467	61-23	
MM54468	61-24	
MM54473		[FT]
MM54475		[FT]
MM54477	5	[FT]
MM54479	10	[FT]
MM54480	2	[FT]
MM54482	3	[FT]
MM54485	8	[FT]
MM54487		[FT]
MM54488	61-32	
MM54492		
MM54496	61-42	
MM54500		[FT]
MM54505	9	[FT]
MM54507	61-55	
MM54510	6	[FT]
MM54511	61-61	
MM54512	61-62	
MM54514	61-64	
MM54515	61-65	
MM54516	61-66	
MM54517	1	[FT]
MM54518		[FT]
MM54532		
MM54533	61-72	
MM54534	4	[FT]
MM54536		
MM54537		
MM54538	7	[FT]
MM54539	0	[FT]
MM54542		[FT]
CSX54544*	RS-30	
MM54547		[FT]
MM54548	61-106	
MM54549	61-107	
MM54551	11	[FT]
MM55052		[FT]
MM55054	61-15	
MM55055	61-20	
MM55058	61-41	
MM55059	61-26	
MM55062*	61-126	
MM55063*	61-127	
MM55064*	61-130	
MM55065*	61-131	
MM55066*	61-132	
MM55067*	61-133	
MM55068*	RS-33	RSV
MM55069*	61-135	
MM55070*	61-136	
MM55072*	61-140	
MM55073*	61-141	
MM55074*	36-06	
MM55075*	61-143	
MM55076*	36-04	
MM55077*	61-145	
MM55078*	61-146	
MM55079*	61-147	
MM55080*	61-150	
MM55081*	61-151	
MM55082*	61-152	
MM55084*	61-154	
MM55085*	61-155	
MM55086*	61-156	
MM55087*	61-167	
MM55088*	61-160	
MM55089*	32-161	
MM55090*	61-162	
MM55091*	RS-32	RSV

Aermacchi
M311
Aermacchi, Venegono
CPX619

Aermacchi
M-346/T-346A Master
Aermacchi, Venegono

CPX616	M-346	
CPX617	M-346	
CSX55144	T-346A	RSV
CSX55145	T-346A	

Aérospatiale
ATR.72-600MP

CSX62279	(on order)
CSX62280	(on order)
CSX62281	(on order)
CSX62282	(on order)

Agusta-Sikorsky
HH-3F Pelican
15° Stormo:
82° Centro SAR,
Trapani/Birgi;
83° Gruppo SAR,
Cervia;
84° Centro SAR,
Brindisi/Casale;
85° Centro SAR,
Pratica di Mare

MM80974	15-01	85
MM80975	15-02$	85
MM80977	15-04	83
MM80978	15-05	83
MM80979	15-06	85
MM80984	15-13	85
MM80985	15-14	85
MM80986	15-15	82
MM80988	15-19	85
MM80989	15-20	85
MM80990	15-21	85
MM80992	15-23	83
MM81337	15-25	83
MM81339	15-27	85
MM81341	15-29	83
MM81342	15-30	85
MM81343	15-31	85
MM81344	15-32	82
MM81345	15-33	84
MM81346	15-34	85
MM81347	15-35	84
MM81348	15-36	85
MM81349	15-37	85
MM81350	15-38	85

Airbus A.319CJ-115X
31° Stormo,
Roma-Ciampino:
306° Gruppo
MM62174
MM62209
MM62243

Boeing 767T/T (767-2EYER)
14° Stormo,
Pratica di Mare:
8° Gruppo

MM62226	14-01
MM62227	14-02
MM62228	14-03
MM62229	14-04

Breguet Br.1150 Atlantic
41° Stormo, Catania:
88° Gruppo

MM40114	41-76
MM40115	41-77
MM40116	41-01
MM40117	41-02
MM40121	41-06

Dassault Falcon 50
31° Stormo,
Roma-Ciampino:
93° Gruppo
MM62026
MM62029

Dassault
Falcon 900EX/900EX EASy*
31° Stormo,
Roma-Ciampino:
93° Gruppo
MM62171 $
MM62172
MM62210
MM62244*
MM62245*

Eurofighter
F-2000A/F-2000B* Typhoon
4° Stormo, Grosseto:
9° Gruppo & 20° Gruppo;
36° Stormo, Gioia del Colle:
12° Gruppo;
Alenia, Torino/Caselle;
RSV, Pratica di Mare

MMX602	RS-01	Alenia
MMX603	RMV-01	Alenia
MMX614*		RSV
MM7235	36-04	12
MM7270	4-1	9
MM7271	36-03	12
MM7272	36-14	12
MM7273		
MM7274	4-10	9
CSX7275	36-11	12
MM7276	4-21	9

Italy

MM7277		
MM7278	36-05	12
MM7279		
MM7280		
MM7281	4-14	9
MM7282	36-15	12
MM7284	36-10	12
MM7285	4-16	9
MM7286	36-02	12
MM7287	4-3	9
MM7288	4-4	9
MM7289	4-5	9
MM7290	4-7	9
MM7291	4-11	9
MM7292	4-12	9
MM7293	36-33	12
MM7294	4-13	9
MM7295	36-20	12
MM7296	36-22	12
MM7297	36-23	12
MM7298	36-24	12
MM7299	4-20	9
MM7300	36-12	12
MM7301	4-22	9
MM7302	36-25	12
MM7303	4-2	9
MM7304	36-21	12
MM7305		RSV
MM7306		RSV
MM7307	4-15	9
MM7308	36-36	12
CSX7309		
MM7310	36-32	12
MM7311	4-6	9
MM7312	36-34	12
MM7313	36-35	12
MM7314	36-37	12
MM7315		
MM7316		
MM7317		
MM7318		
MM7319		
MM55092*	4-25	20
MM55093*	4-31	20
MM55094*	4-27	20
MM55095*	4-23	20
MM55096*	4-30	20
MM55097*	4-24	20
MM55128*	4-26	20
MM55129*	4-32	20
MM55130*	4-33	20
MM55131*	4-34	20
MM55132*		
MM55133*		
MM55134*	4-35	20

Lockheed
C-130J/C-130J-30/KC-130J*
Hercules II
46ª Brigata Aerea, Pisa:
  2º Gruppo & 50º Gruppo
C-130J

MM62175	46-40
MM62177	46-42
MM62178	46-43
MM62179	46-44
MM62180	46-45
MM62181	46-46
MM62182	46-47
MM62183*	46-48
MM62184	46-49
MM62185	46-50
MM62186	46-51

C-130J-30

MM62187	46-53
MM62188	46-54
MM62189	46-55
MM62190	46-56
MM62191	46-57
MM62192	46-58
MM62193	46-59
MM62194	46-60
MM62195	46-61
MM62196	46-62

Lockheed (GD)
F-16A-ADF/F-16B*
37º Stormo, Trapani:
  18º Gruppo

MM7236	$
MM7239	
MM7240	$
MM7242	
MM7244	
MM7249	
MM7251	$
MM7254	
MM7257	
MM7259	
MM7262	
MM7268*	
MM7269*	

Panavia
Tornado Strike/
Trainer[1]/ECR[2]
6º Stormo, Ghedi:
  102º Gruppo &
  154º Gruppo &
  156º Gruppo;
50º Stormo, Piacenza:
  155º Gruppo;
RSV, Pratica di Mare

MM7003	6-43	102
MM7004	6-53	102
MM7005	$	156
MM7006	6-31$	102
MM7007	6-01	154
CSX7009		Alenia
MM7011	6-13	154
MM7013	36-156	156
MM7015	6-32$	102
MM7016	6-20	154
MM7019[2]	50-05	155
MM7020[2]	50-41	155
MM7021[2]	50-01	155
MM7022	6-23	154
MM7023	36-31	156
MM7024	36-41	156
MM7025	6-05	154
MM7026	6-35	102
MM7027[2]		
MM7028	50-52	155
MM7029		
MM7030[2]	50-04$	155
MM7031	6-61	102
MM7033	50-53	155
MM7034[2]		
MM7035	6-27	154
MM7036[2]		
MM7038	6-37	102
MM7039	6-02	154
CSX7041	RS-06	RSV
MM7042	50-57	155
MM7043	6-25	154
MM7044		Alenia
MM7046[2]	6-06	154
CSX7047[2]	RS-05	RSV
MM7048		
MM7049	6-64	102
MM7051[2]	50-45	155
MM7052[2]	50-02	155
MM7053[2]	50-07	155
MM7054[2]	50-40$	155
MM7055	50-42	155
MM7056	6-66	102
MM7057	6-04	154
MM7058	6-11	154
MM7059	50-47	155
MM7061	6-14	154
MM7062[2]	50-44	155
MM7063	6-26	154
MM7065	50-56	155
MM7066	50-03	155
MM7067	6-71	156
MM7068[2]	50-46	155
MM7070[2]	50-06	155
MM7071	6-12	154
MM7073[2]	6-34	102
MM7075	6-07	154
MM7078		
CMX7079[2]		Alenia
MM7080	6-33$	102
MM7081	6-57	102
MM7082[2]	50-54	155
MM7083	6-72	156
MM7084	6-03	154
CMX7085	36-50	Alenia
MM7086	6-60	102
MM7087	6-36	102
MM7088	6-10	154
MM55000[1]	6-51$	102
MM55002[1]	6-52$	102
MM55003[1]		
MM55006[1]	6-15	154
MM55007[1]	6-56	102
MM55008[1]	6-45	102
MM55009[1]	6-44	102
MM55010[1]	6-42	102

Piaggio
P-180AM Avanti
9ª Brigata Aerea,
  Pratica di Mare:
  71º Gruppo;
36º Stormo, Gioia del Colle:
  636º SC;
RSV, Pratica di Mare

MM62159	71
MM62161	71
MM62162	71
MM62163	71
MM62164	RSV
MM62199	636
MM62201	71
MM62202	71
MM62203	71
MM62204	71
MM62205	71
MM62206	71
MM62207	71

Aviazione dell'Esercito
Dornier Do.228-212
28° Gruppo Squadrone
 Cavalleria dell'Aria,
 Viterbo
MM62156 E.I.101
MM62157 E.I.102
MM62158 E.I.103

Piaggio
P-180AM Avanti
28° Gruppo Squadrone Det,
 Cavalleria dell'Aria,
 Roma/Ciampino
MM62167
MM62168
MM62169

Guardia Costiera
Aérospatiale
ATR.42-400MP/-500MP*
2° Nucleo, Catania;
3° Nucleo, Pescara
MM62170	10-01	3
MM62208	10-02	2
MM62270*	10-03	2

Guardia di Finanza
Aérospatiale
ATR.42-400MP
Gruppo Esplorazione Aeromarittima,
 Pratica di Mare
MM62165	GF-13
MM62166	GF-14
MM62230	GF-15
MM62251	GF-16

Piaggio
P-180AM Avanti
Gruppo Esplorazione Aeromarittima,
 Pratica di Mare
MM62248	GF-18
MM62249	GF-19

Marina Militare Italiana
AgustaWestland
EH.101
1° Grupelicot, La Spezia/Luni;
3° Grupelicot, Catania
Mk110 ASW
MM81480	2-01	3
MM81481	2-02	3
MM81482	2-03	3
MM81483	2-04	3
MM81484	2-05	3
MM81485	2-06	3
MM81486	2-07	3
MM81487	2-08	3
CSX81719	2-22	1
MM81726	2-23	1

Mk112 ASW
MM81488	2-09	1
MM81489	2-10	1
MM81490	2-11	1
MM81491	2-12	1

Mk410 UTY
MM81492	2-13	1
MM81493	2-14	1
MM81494	2-15	1
MM81495	2-16	1
MM81633	2-18	1
MM81634	2-19	1
MM81635	2-20	1
MM81636	2-21	1

McDonnell Douglas
AV-8B/TAV-8B Harrier II+
Gruppo Aerei Imbarcarti,
 Taranto/Grottaglie
AV-8B
MM7199	1-03
MM7200	1-04
MM7201	1-05
MM7212	1-06
MM7213	1-07
MM7214	1-08
MM7215	1-09
MM7217	1-11
MM7218	1-12
MM7219	1-13
MM7220	1-14
MM7222	1-16
MM7223	1-18
MM7224	1-19

TAV-8B
MM55032	1-01
MM55033	1-02

Piaggio
P-180AM Avanti
9ª Brigata Aerea, AMI,
 Pratica di Mare:
 71° Gruppo
MM62200	9-01
MM62211	9-02
MM62212	9-03
MM62213	

Italian Govt
Dassault Falcon 900
Italian Govt/Soc. CAI,
 Roma/Ciampino
I-CAEX
I-DIES

IVORY COAST
Boeing 727-2Y4
Ivory Coast Govt, Abidjan
TU-VAO

Fokker 100
Ivory Coast Govt, Abidjan
TU-VAA

Grumman
G.1159C Gulfstream IV
Ivory Coast Govt, Abidjan
TU-VAD

JAPAN
Japan Air Self Defence Force
Boeing 747-47C
701st Flight Sqn, Chitose
20-1101
20-1102

JORDAN
Al Quwwat al Jawwiya
al Malakiya al Urduniya
Extra EA-300LP
Royal Jordanian Falcons,
 Amman
JY-RFA
JY-RFB
JY-RFC
JY-RFD
JY-RFE

Lockheed C-130H Hercules
3 Sqn, Amman/Marka
344
345
346
347

Jordanian Govt
Airbus A.318-112
Jordanian Govt, Amman
VQ-BDD

Airbus A.340-642
Jordanian Govt, Amman
JY-ASX (on order)

Gulfstream Aerospace G.450
Jordanian Govt, Amman
VQ-BCE

KAZAKHSTAN
Airbus A.330-223
Govt of Kazakhstan, Almaty
UP-A3001

Boeing 757-2M6
Govt of Kazakhstan, Almaty
UP-B5701

KENYA
Kenyan Air Force
Fokker 70ER
Kenyan Govt, Nairobi
308

KUWAIT
Al Quwwat al Jawwiya
al Kuwaitiya
Lockheed
KC-130J Hercules II
KAF 3.. (on order)
KAF 3.. (on order)
KAF 3.. (on order)

Lockheed
L100-30 Hercules
41 Sqn, Kuwait International
KAF 323
KAF 324
KAF 325

Kuwaiti Govt
Airbus A.300C4-620
Kuwaiti Govt, Safat
9K-AHI

Airbus A.310-308
Kuwaiti Govt, Safat
9K-ALD

Airbus A.319CJ-115X
Kuwaiti Govt, Safat
9K-GEA

Airbus A.320-212
Kuwaiti Govt, Safat
9K-AKD

Airbus A.340-542
Kuwaiti Govt, Safat
9K-GBA (on order)
9K-GBB (on order)

Boeing 737-9BQER
Kuwaiti Govt, Safat
9K-GCC

Boeing 747-469
Kuwaiti Govt, Safat
9K-ADE

Gulfstream Aerospace G.550
Kuwaiti Govt, Safat
9K-GFA

Gulfstream Aerospace
Gulfstream V
Kuwaiti Govt/Kuwait Airways,
 Safat
9K-AJD
9K-AJE
9K-AJF

KYRGYZSTAN
Tupolev Tu-154M
Govt of Kyrgyzstan, Bishkek
EX-85718

LITHUANIA
Karines Oro Pajegos
Aeritalia C-27J Spartan
Transporto Eskadrile,
 Siauliai-Zokniai
06
07
08

Antonov An-26RV
Transporto Eskadrile,
 Siauliai-Zokniai
03
04
05

LET 410UVP Turbolet
Transporto Eskadrile,
 Siauliai-Zokniai
01

Mil Mi-8
Sraigtasparniu Eskadrile,
 Panevezys/Pajuostis
02 Mi-8T
09 Mi-8T
10 Mi-8T
11 Mi-8PS
21 Mi-8MTV-1
22 Mi-8MTV-1
28 Mi-8T

LUXEMBOURG
NATO
Boeing 757-28A
NATO, Geilenkirchen,
 Germany
OO-TFA

Boeing E-3A
NAEW&CF, Geilenkirchen,
 Germany
LX-N90442
LX-N90443$
LX-N90444
LX-N90445
LX-N90446
LX-N90447
LX-N90448
LX-N90449
LX-N90450
LX-N90451
LX-N90452
LX-N90453
LX-N90454
LX-N90455
LX-N90456
LX-N90458
LX-N90459

MACEDONIA
Macedonian Govt
Bombardier Lear 60
Macedonian Govt, Skopje
Z3-MKD

MALAYSIA
Royal Malaysian Air Force/
Tentera Udara Diraja Malaysia
Boeing 737-7H6
2 Sqn, Simpang
M53-01

Bombardier
BD.700-1A10 Global Express
2 Sqn, Simpang
M48-02

Dassault Falcon 900
2 Sqn, Simpang
M37-01

Lockheed
C-130 Hercules
14 Sqn, Labuan;
20 Sqn, Subang

M30-01	C-130T	20 Sqn
M30-02	C-130H	20 Sqn
M30-03	C-130H	14 Sqn
M30-04	C-130H-30	20 Sqn
M30-05	C-130H-30	14 Sqn
M30-06	C-130H-30	14 Sqn
M30-07	C-130T	20 Sqn
M30-08	C-130H(MP)	20 Sqn
M30-09	C-130H(MP)	20 Sqn
M30-10	C-130H-30	20 Sqn
M30-11	C-130H-30	20 Sqn
M30-12	C-130H-30	20 Sqn
M30-14	C-130H-30	20 Sqn
M30-15	C-130H-30	20 Sqn
M30-16	C-130H-30	20 Sqn

Malaysian Govt
Airbus A.319CJ-115X
9M-NAA

MALTA
Bombardier
Learjet 60
Govt of Malta, Luqa
9H-AFK

MEXICO
Fuerza Aérea Mexicana
Boeing 757-225
8° Grupo Aéreo, Mexico City
TP-01 (XC-UJM)

Armada de Mexico
Gulfstream Aerospace G.450
PRIMESCTRANS, Mexico City
AMT-205

MOROCCO
Force Aérienne Royaume
Marocaine/ Al Quwwat al
Jawwiya al Malakiya
Marakishiya
Aeritalia
C-27J Spartan
Escadrille de Transport 3,
 Kenitra
CN-AMN
CN-AMO
CN-AMP
CN-AMQ

Airtech
CN.235M-100
Escadrille de Transport 3,
 Kenitra
023 CNA-MA
024 CNA-MB
025 CNA-MC
026 CNA-MD
027 CNA-ME
028 CNA-MF
031 CNA-MG

CAP-232
Marche Verte
28 CN-ABP [2]
29 CN-ABQ [6]
31 CN-ABR [5]
36 CN-ABS [4]
37 CN-ABT [3]
41 CN-ABU [7]
42 CN-ABV [1]
43 CN-ABW
44 CN-ABX [8]

Lockheed
C-130H Hercules
Escadrille de Transport 3,
 Kenitra

4535	CNA-OA	C-130H
4551	CNA-OC	C-130H
4575	CNA-OD	C-130H
4581	CNA-OE	C-130H
4583	CNA-OF	C-130H
4713	CNA-OG	C-130H
4733	CNA-OI	C-130H
4738	CNA-OJ	C-130H
4739	CNA-OK	C-130H
4742	CNA-OL	C-130H
4875	CNA-OM	C-130H
4876	CNA-ON	C-130H
4877	CNA-OO	C-130H
4888	CNA-OP	C-130H
4907	CNA-OR	KC-130H
4909	CNA-OS	KC-130H

Govt of Morocco
Boeing 737-8KB
Govt of Morocco, Rabat
CN-MVI

Cessna 560 Citation V
Govt of Morocco, Rabat
CNA-NV
CNA-NW

Cessna
560XLS Citation Excel
Govt of Morocco, Rabat
CN-AMJ
CN-AMK

Dassault Falcon 50
Govt of Morocco, Rabat
CN-ANO

Grumman
G.1159 Gulfstream IIIT/
G.1159A Gulfstream III
Govt of Morocco, Rabat
CNA-NL Gulfstream IIIT
CNA-NU Gulfstream III

Gulfstream Aerospace G.550
Govt of Morocco, Rabat
CN-AMS

NAMIBIA
Dassault Falcon 7X
Namibian Govt, Windhoek
V5-GON

Dassault Falcon 900B
Namibian Govt, Windhoek
V5-NAM

NETHERLANDS
Koninklijke Luchtmacht
Agusta-Bell AB.412SP
303 Sqn, Leeuwarden
R-01
R-02
R-03

Boeing-Vertol
CH-47 Chinook
298 Sqn, Defence Helicopter
Command, Gilze-Rijen
CH-47D Chinook
D-101
D-102
D-103
D-106
D-661
D-662
D-663
D-664
D-665
D-666
D-667
CH-47F Chinook
D-890 (on order)
D-891 (on order)
D-892 (on order)
D-893 (on order)
D-894 (on order)
D-895 (on order)

Eurocopter
AS.532U-2 Cougar
300 Sqn, Defence Helicopter
Command, Gilze-Rijen
S-419
S-440
S-441
S-445
S-447
S-453
S-454
S-457

Fokker 50
334 Sqn, Eindhoven
U-05
U-06

General Dynamics
F-16
Now operated on a pool basis.
Squadron markings carried do not
necessarily reflect the squadron
operating.
312/313 Sqns, Volkel;
322/323 Sqns, Leeuwarden;
148th FS/162th FW,
TucsonInternational
Airport, Arizona, USA

Serial	Type	Unit
J-001	F-16AM	312 Sqn
J-002	F-16AM	312 Sqn
J-003	F-16AM	312 Sqn
J-004	F-16AM	148th FS
J-005	F-16AM	
J-006	F-16AM	
J-008	F-16AM	313 Sqn$
J-009	F-16AM	313 Sqn
J-010	F-16AM	148th FS
J-011	F-16AM	312 Sqn
J-013	F-16AM	312 Sqn
J-014	F-16AM	313 Sqn
J-015	F-16AM	323 Sqn $
J-016	F-16AM	312 Sqn
J-017	F-16AM	
J-018	F-16AM	313 Sqn
J-019	F-16AM	148th FS
J-020	F-16AM	322 Sqn
J-021	F-16AM	312 Sqn
J-055	F-16AM	313 Sqn
J-057	F-16AM	
J-060	F-16AM	322 Sqn
J-061	F-16AM	
J-062	F-16AM	313 Sqn
J-063	F-16AM	313 Sqn
J-064	F-16BM	322 Sqn
J-065	F-16BM	148th FS
J-066	F-16BM	323 Sqn
J-067	F-16BM	148th FS
J-135	F-16AM	322 Sqn
J-136	F-16AM	
J-142	F-16AM	323 Sqn
J-144	F-16AM	323 Sqn
J-145	F-16AM	148th FS
J-146	F-16AM	323 Sqn
J-193	F-16AM	323 Sqn
J-196	F-16AM	313 Sqn
J-197	F-16AM	
J-199	F-16AM	311 Sqn
J-201	F-16AM	322 Sqn
J-202	F-16AM	323 Sqn
J-208	F-16BM	148th FS
J-209	F-16BM	148th FS
J-210	F-16BM	323 Sqn
J-254	F-16AM	
J-362	F-16AM	323 Sqn
J-366	F-16AM	148th FS
J-367	F-16AM	312 Sqn $
J-368	F-16BM	148th FS
J-369	F-16BM	313 Sqn
J-508	F-16AM	313 Sqn
J-509	F-16AM	322 Sqn
J-511	F-16AM	313 Sqn $
J-512	F-16AM	313 Sqn
J-513	F-16AM	323 Sqn
J-514	F-16AM	313 Sqn
J-515	F-16AM	
J-516	F-16AM	322 Sqn
J-616	F-16AM	323 Sqn
J-623	F-16AM	148th FS
J-624	F-16AM	322 Sqn
J-628	F-16AM	322 Sqn
J-630	F-16AM	312 Sqn
J-631	F-16AM	323 Sqn
J-632	F-16AM	322 Sqn
J-635	F-16AM	312 Sqn
J-637	F-16AM	311 Sqn
J-638	F-16AM	
J-641	F-16AM	312 Sqn
J-642	F-16AM	
J-643	F-16AM	313 Sqn
J-644	F-16AM	313 Sqn
J-646	F-16AM	312 Sqn
J-866	F-16AM	
J-868	F-16AM	323 Sqn
J-871	F-16AM	323 Sqn
J-872	F-16AM	323 Sqn
J-873	F-16AM	323 Sqn
J-876	F-16AM	322 Sqn
J-877	F-16AM	323 Sqn
J-879	F-16AM	322 Sqn
J-881	F-16AM	323 Sqn
J-882	F-16BM	148th FS

Grumman
G.1159C Gulfstream IV
334 Sqn, Eindhoven
V-11

Lockheed
C-130H/C-130H-30* Hercules
336 Sqn, Eindhoven
G-273*
G-275*
G-781
G-988

MDH
AH-64D Apache Longbow
301 Sqn, Defence Helicopter
Command,
 Gilze-Rijen
Q-01
Q-02
Q-03
Q-04
Q-05
Q-06
Q-07
Q-08
Q-09
Q-10
Q-11

Q-12
Q-13
Q-14
Q-15
Q-16
Q-17 $
Q-18
Q-19 $
Q-21
Q-22
Q-23
Q-24
Q-25
Q-26
Q-27
Q-28
Q-29
Q-30

NH Industries
NH.90-NFH
7 Sqn, De Kooij
N-088 (on order)
N-102
N-110
N-147 (on order)
N-164
N-175
N-195
N-227 (on order)

McDonnell Douglas
DC-10*/KDC-10
334 Sqn, Eindhoven
T-235
T-255*
T-264

Pilatus
PC-7 Turbo Trainer
131 EMVO Sqn,
  Woensdrecht
L-01
L-02
L-03
L-04
L-05
L-06
L-07
L-08
L-09
L-10
L-11
L-12
L-13

Sud Alouette III
300 Sqn, Defence Helicopter
Command, Gilze-Rijen
A-247
A-275
A-292
A-301

Westland SH-14D Lynx
Defence Helicopter Command
  (7 Sqn & 860 Sqn), De Kooij
  (7 Sqn operates 860 Sqn aircraft
  on loan)
260
261

262
265
266
267
272
273
274
278
279
280
281
283

Kustwacht
Dornier Do.228-212
Base: Schiphol
PH-CGC
PH-CGN

Netherlands Govt
Fokker 70
Dutch Royal Flight, Schiphol
PH-KBX

NEW ZEALAND
Royal New Zealand Air Force
Boeing 757-2K2
40 Sqn, Whenuapai
NZ7571
NZ7572

Lockheed
C-130H Hercules
40 Sqn, Whenuapai
NZ7001
NZ7002
NZ7003
NZ7004
NZ7005

Lockheed
P-3K/P-3K2* Orion
5 Sqn, Whenuapai
NZ4201*
NZ4202
NZ4203
NZ4204*
NZ4205
NZ4206

NIGER
Government of Niger
Boeing 737-2N9C
Government of Niger, Niamey
5U-BAG

NIGERIA
Federal Nigerian Air Force
Lockheed
C-130H/C-130H-30* Hercules
88 MAG, Lagos
NAF-910
NAF-912
NAF-913
NAF-917*
NAF-918*

Nigerian Govt
Boeing 737-7N6
Federal Govt of Nigeria,
  Lagos
5N-FGT [001]

Dassault Falcon 7X
Federal Govt of Nigeria,
  Lagos
5N-FGU
5N-FGV

Dassault Falcon 900
Federal Govt of Nigeria,
  Lagos
5N-FGE

Gulfstream Aerospace G.550
Federal Govt of Nigeria,
  Lagos
5N-FGW

Gulfstream Aerospace
Gulfstream V
Federal Govt of Nigeria,
  Lagos
5N-FGS

NORWAY
Luftforsvaret
Bell 412HP*/412SP
339 Skv, Bardufoss;
720 Skv, Rygge
139   720 Skv
140   720 Skv
141   720 Skv
142   720 Skv
143   339 Skv
144   339 Skv
145*   720 Skv
146   339 Skv
147   720 Skv
148   339 Skv
161   339 Skv
162   339 Skv
163   720 Skv
164*   720 Skv
165   720 Skv
166   720 Skv
167   720 Skv
194   720 Skv

Dassault
Falcon 20 ECM
717 Skv, Rygge
  041
  053
  0125

General Dynamics
F-16 MLU
331 Skv, Bodø;
332 Skv, Bodø;
338 Skv, Ørland
[All operate from a pool
and belong to the FLO]
272 F-16A $
273 F-16A
275 F-16A
276 F-16A
277 F-16A
279 F-16A
281 F-16A
282 F-16A
284 F-16A
285 F-16A

286 F-16A
288 F-16A
289 F-16A
291 F-16A
292 F-16A
293 F-16A
295 F-16A
297 F-16A
298 F-16A $
299 F-16A
302 F-16B
304 F-16B
305 F-16B
306 F-16B
658 F-16A
659 F-16A
660 F-16A
661 F-16A
662 F-16A
663 F-16A
664 F-16A
665 F-16A
666 F-16A
667 F-16A
668 F-16A
669 F-16A
670 F-16A
671 F-16A $
672 F-16A
673 F-16A
674 F-16A
675 F-16A
677 F-16A
678 F-16A
680 F-16A
681 F-16A
682 F-16A
683 F-16A
686 F-16A
687 F-16A
688 F-16A
689 F-16B
690 F-16B
691 F-16B
692 F-16B $
693 F-16B
711 F-16B

Lockheed
C-130J-30 Hercules II
335 Skv, Gardermoen
5601
5607
5629
5630

Lockheed P-3C Orion
333 Skv, Andøya
3296
3297
3298
3299

Lockheed P-3N Orion
333 Skv, Andøya
4576
6603

NH Industries
NH.90-NFH
337 Skv, Bardufoss

013
049

Westland
Sea King Mk 43/
Mk 43A/Mk 43B
330 Skv:
 A Flt, Bodø;
 B Flt, Banak;
 C Flt, Ørland;
 D Flt, Sola
060 Mk 43
062 Mk 43
066 Mk 43
069 Mk 43
070 Mk 43
071 Mk 43B
072 Mk 43
073 Mk 43
074 Mk 43
189 Mk 43A
322 Mk 43B
329 Mk 43B
330 Mk 43B

Kystvakt (Coast Guard)
Westland Lynx Mk86
337 Skv, Bardufoss
207
216
228
232
235

OMAN
Royal Air Force of Oman
Airbus A.320-214X
4 Sqn, Seeb
554
555
556

Grumman
G.1159C Gulfstream IV
4 Sqn, Seeb
557
558

Lockheed
C-130H Hercules/
C-130J-30 Hercules II
16 Sqn, Seeb
501 C-130H
502 C-130H
503 C-130H
504 C-130J-30 (on order)

Omani Govt
Airbus A.320-233
Govt of Oman, Seeb
A4O-AA

Boeing 747-430
Govt of Oman, Seeb
A4O-OMN

Boeing 747SP-27
Govt of Oman, Seeb
A4O-SO

Gulfstream Aerospace G.550
Govt of Oman, Seeb
A4O-AD
A4O-AE

PAKISTAN
Pakistan Fiza'ya
Boeing 707-340C
12 Sqn, Islamabad
68-19866

Pakistani Govt
Airbus A.310-304
Govt of Pakistan, Karachi
AP-OOI

Boeing 737-33A
Govt of Pakistan, Karachi
AP-BEH

Cessna 560 Citation VI
Govt of Pakistan, Karachi
J-754

Gulfstream Aerospace
G.1159C Gulfstream IV-SP
Govt of Pakistan, Karachi
J-755

Gulfstream Aerospace
G.450
Govt of Pakistan, Karachi
J-756

POLAND
Sily Powietrzne RP
CASA C-295M
13 EL, Kraków
011
012 $
013
014
015
016
017
018
020
021
022

Lockheed
C-130E Hercules
14 ELTR, Powidz
1501
1502
1503
1504 (on order)
1505
1506
1508

Lockheed Martin (GD)
F-16C/F-16D* Fighting Falcon
3 ELT, Poznan/Krzesiny;
6 ELT, Poznan/Krzesiny;
10 ELT, Lask;
412th TW, Edwards AFB, USA
4040 412th TW
4041   6 ELT
4042   3 ELT
4043   3 ELT

Poland

4044	3 ELT	
4045	3 ELT	
4046	3 ELT	
4047	3 ELT	
4048	3 ELT	
4049	3 ELT	
4050	3 ELT	
4051	3 ELT	
4052	6 ELT	
4053	6 ELT	
4054	6 ELT	
4055	6 ELT	
4056	6 ELT	
4057	6 ELT	
4058	6 ELT	
4059	6 ELT	
4060	6 ELT	
4061	6 ELT	
4062	6 ELT	
4063	10 ELT	
4064	10 ELT	
4065	10 ELT	
4066	10 ELT	
4067	10 ELT	
4068	10 ELT	
4069	10 ELT	
4070	10 ELT	
4071	10 ELT	
4072	10 ELT	
4073	10 ELT	
4074	10 ELT	
4075	10 ELT	
4076*	3 ELT	
4077*	3 ELT	
4078*	3 ELT	
4079*	3 ELT	
4080*	3 ELT	
4081*	3 ELT	
4082*	6 ELT	
4083*	6 ELT	
4084*	6 ELT	
4085*	10 ELT	
4086*	10 ELT	
4087*	10 ELT	

Mikoyan MiG-29A/UB
1 ELT, Minsk/Mazowiecki;
41 ELT, Malbork

15*	1 ELT $	
28*	1 ELT	
38	1 ELT	
40	1 ELT	
42*	1 ELT	
54	1 ELT	
56	1 ELT	
59	1 ELT	
65	41 ELT	
66	41 ELT	
67	41 ELT	
70	41 ELT	
77	41 ELT	
83	1 ELT	
89	1 ELT	
92	41 ELT	
105	1 ELT	
108	1 ELT	
111	1 ELT	
114	1 ELT	
115	1 ELT	
4101	41 ELT	
4103	41 ELT	

4104	41 ELT	
4105	1 ELT	
4110*	41 ELT	
4113	41 ELT	
4116	41 ELT	
4120	41 ELT	
4121	41 ELT	
4122	41 ELT	
4123*	41 ELT	

PZL 130TC-I/TC-II* Orlik
2 OSL, Radom

012		
014		
015		
016		
017		
018		
019		
020		
022		
023		
024		
025		
026		
027		
029		
030		
031		
032		
033		
035		
036		
037*		
038		
040		
041		
042		
043		
044		
045		
046		
047*		
048		
049		
050		
051		
052		

PZL M28 Bryza
1 OSL, Deblin;
14 ELTR, Powidz;
15 EL, Powidz

0203	M28TD	1 OSL
0204	M28TD	1 OSL
0205	M28TD	1 OSL
0206	M28TD	
0207	M28TD	1 OSL
0208	M28TD	
0209	M28TD	14 ELTR
0210	M28TD	14 ELTR
0211	M28TD	14 ELTR
0212	M28TD	
0213	M28TD	
0214	M28PT	
0215	M28PT	
0216	M28PT	
0217	M28PT	1 OSL
0218	M28PT	
0219	M28PT	(on order)
0723	M28TD	14 ELTR

1003	M28TD	14 ELTR

Sukhoi
Su-22UM-3K*/Su-22M-4
8 ELT, Swidwin;
40 ELT, Swidwin

001*		
308*	40 ELT	
310*	8 ELT	
508*	40 ELT	
509*	40 ELT	
605*		
707*	8 ELT	
3203		
3215		
3304		
3306		
3508	$	
3509	40 ELT	
3612	40 ELT	
3710	40 ELT	
3713	40 ELT$	
3715	40 ELT	
3816	40 ELT	
3817	40 ELT	
3819		
3920	40 ELT	
4604		
7411	8 ELT	
7412	8 ELT	
8101	40 ELT	
8102		
8103		
8205	8 ELT	
8308		
8309	40 ELT	
8310	40 ELT	
8715	40 ELT	
8816	40 ELT	
8818	$	
8919	$	
8920		
9102	40 ELT$	
9615	40 ELT	
9616	8 ELT	

Lotnictwo Marynarki Wojennej
PZL M28 Bryza
28 EL, Gydnia/Babie Doly;
30 EL, Cewice/Siemirowice

0404	M28B-E	28 EL
0405	M28B-E	28 EL
0810	M28B-1R	30 EL
1006	M28B-1R	30 EL
1008	M28B-1R	30 EL
1017	M28B-1R	30 EL
1022	M28B-1R	30 EL
1114	M28B-1R	28 EL
1115	M28B-1R	30 EL
1116	M28B-1R	28 EL
1117	M28B-1	28 EL
1118	M28B-1	28 EL

Straz Graniczna (Polish Border Guard)
PZL M28 05 Skytruck
Base: Gdansk/Rebiechowo
SN-50YG
SN-60YG

Polish Government
Embraer
EMB.175-200LR
Polish Government, Warszawa
SP-LIG
SP-LIH

PORTUGAL
Força Aérea Portuguesa
Aérospatiale
TB-30 Epsilon
Esq 101, Sintra
11401
11402
11403
11404
11405 $
11406
11407
11409
11410
11411
11413
11414
11415
11416
11417
11418

CASA C-295M/
CASA C-295MPA*
Esq 502, Lisbon/Montijo
(with a detachment at Lajes)
16701
16702
16703
16704
16705
16706
16707
16708*
16709*
16710*
16711*
16712*

D-BD Alpha Jet
Esq 103, Beja;
Asas de Portugal, Beja*
15202*
15206*
15208*
15211 $
15220*
15225*
15226
15227*
15230
15231
15232*
15235
15236
15246
15247
15250*

Dassault
Falcon 50
Esq 504, Lisbon/Montijo
17401
17402
17403

EHI EH-101
Mk514/Mk515/Mk516
Esq 751, Lisbon/Montijo
Mk514
19601
19602
19603
19604
19605*
19606*
Mk515
19607
19608
Mk516
19609
19610
19611
19612

Lockheed
C-130H/C-130H-30* Hercules
Esq 501, Lisbon/Montijo
16801*
16802*
16803$
16804
16805
16806*

Lockheed Martin (GD)
F-16 Fighting Falcon
(MLU aircraft are marked
with a *)
Esq 201, Monte Real;
Esq 301, Monte Real
15101 F-16A*
15102 F-16A*
15103 F-16A*
15104 F-16A*
15105 F-16A*
15106 F-16A $
15107 F-16A*
15108 F-16A*
15109 F-16A*
15110 F-16A
15112 F-16A*
15113 F-16A*
15114 F-16A
15115 F-16A* $
15116 F-16A*
15117 F-16A*
15118 F-16B*
15119 F-16B*
15120 F-16B
15121 F-16A*
15122 F-16A*
15123 F-16A
15124 F-16A*
15125 F-16A*
15126 F-16A*
15127 F-16A*
15128 F-16A*
15129 F-16A*
15130 F-16A*
15131 F-16A
15132 F-16A
15133 F-16A*
15134 F-16A*
15135 F-16A*
15136 F-16A
15137 F-16B*

15138 F-16A*
15139 F-16B*
15141 F-16A

Lockheed
P-3C Orion
Esq 601, Beja
14807
14808 $
14809
14810
14811

Marinha
Westland
Super Lynx Mk 95
Esq de Helicopteros,
 Lisbon/Montijo
19201
19202
19203
19204
19205

QATAR
Qatar Emiri Air Force
Boeing
C-17A Globemaster III
Qatar Emiri Air Force, Al-Udeid
MAA (08-0201)
MAB (08-0202)
MAC (on order)
MAD (on order)

Lockheed
C-130J-30 Hercules II
Qatar Emiri Air Force, Al-Udeid
MAH (08-0211)
MAI (08-0212)
MAJ (08-0213)
MAK (08-0214)

Qatar Government
Airbus A.310-308
Qatari Govt, Doha
A7-AFE

Airbus A.319-115X/
A.319CJ-133*
Qatari Govt, Doha
A7-HHJ*
A7-MED*
A7-MHH

Airbus A.320-232
Qatari Govt, Doha
A7-AAG
A7-MBK

Airbus A.330-202/-203*
Qatari Govt, Doha
A7-HHM*
A7-HJJ

Airbus A.340-211/-313X/-541
Qatari Govt, Doha
A7-AAH A.340-313X
A7-HHH A.340-541
A7-HHK A.340-211

Boeing 747-8KB
Qatari Govt, Doha
A7-HHE

Bombardier
Global Express
Qatari Govt/Qatar Airways, Doha
A7-AAM

ROMANIA
Fortele Aeriene Romania
Alenia C-27J Spartan
Escadrilla 902,
  Bucharest/Otopeni
2701
2702
2703
2704 (on order)
2705 (on order)
2706 (on order)
2707 (on order)

Antonov An-26
Escadrilla 902,
  Bucharest/Otopeni
801
808
809
810

Lockheed
C-130B/C-130H* Hercules
Escadrilla 901,
  Bucharest/Otopeni
5927
5930
6150
6166*
6191*

Romanian Govt
Boeing 707-3K1C
Romanian Govt,
  Bucharest/Otopeni
YR-ABB

RUSSIA
Voenno-Vozdushniye Sily Rossioki
Federatsii (Russian Air Force)
Antonov An-30B
(Open Skies)
Base: Chalovskiy
01 black

Sukhoi Su-27
TsAGI, Gromov Flight
  Institute, Zhukhovsky
595 Su-27P
597 Su-30
598 Su-27P

Russian Govt
Ilyushin Il-62M
Russian Govt, Moscow
RA-86466
RA-86467
RA-86468
RA-86539
RA-86540
RA-86559
RA-86561
RA-86712

Ilyushin Il-96-300
Russian Govt, Moscow
RA-96012
RA-96016
RA-96018
RA-96019

Tupolev Tu-134A
Russian Govt, Moscow
RA-65904

Tupolev Tu-154M
Russian Govt, Moscow;
Open Skies*
RA-85155
RA-85631
RA-85655*
RA-85666

Tupolev Tu-2140N
(Open Skies)
Base: Chalovskiy
RA-64519
RA-64520

Tupolev Tu-214SR
Russian Govt, Moscow
RA-64515
RA-64516

SAUDI ARABIA
Al Quwwat al Jawwiya
as Sa'udiya
Airbus A.330-203 MRTT
2401 (on order)
2402 (on order)
2403 (on order)

BAe 125-800/-800B*
1 Sqn, Riyadh
HZ-105
HZ-109*
HZ-110*
HZ-130*

Boeing 737-7DP/-8DP*
1 Sqn, Riyadh
HZ-101
HZ-102*

Boeing
E-3A/KE-3A/RE-3A/RE-3B
Sentry
18 Sqn, Al Kharj;
19 Sqn, Al Kharj

1801	E-3A	18 Sqn
1802	E-3A	18 Sqn
1803	E-3A	18 Sqn
1804	E-3A	18 Sqn
1805	E-3A	18 Sqn
1811	KE-3A	18 Sqn
1812	KE-3A	18 Sqn
1813	KE-3A	18 Sqn
1814	KE-3A	18 Sqn
1815	KE-3A	18 Sqn
1816	KE-3A	18 Sqn
1818	KE-3A	18 Sqn
1901	RE-3A	19 Sqn
1902	RE-3B	19 Sqn

Cessna 550 Citation II
1 Sqn, Riyadh
HZ-133
HZ-134
HZ-135
HZ-136

Grumman
G.1159C Gulfstream IV
1 Sqn, Riyadh
HZ-103

Lockheed
C-130/L.100 Hercules
1 Sqn, Riyadh;
4 Sqn, Jeddah;
16 Sqn, Jeddah;
32 Sqn, Al Kharj

111	VC-130H	1 Sqn
112	VC-130H	1 Sqn
464	C-130H	4 Sqn
465	C-130H	4 Sqn
466	C-130H	4 Sqn
467	C-130H	4 Sqn
468	C-130H	4 Sqn
472	C-130H	4 Sqn
473	C-130H	4 Sqn
474	C-130H	4 Sqn
475	C-130H	4 Sqn
477	C-130H	4 Sqn
478	C-130H	4 Sqn
482	C-130H	4 Sqn
483	C-130H	4 Sqn
1601	C-130H	16 Sqn
1602	C-130H	16 Sqn
1604	C-130H	16 Sqn
1605	C-130H	16 Sqn
1615	C-130H	16 Sqn
1622	C-130H-30	16 Sqn
1623	C-130H	16 Sqn
1624	C-130H	16 Sqn
1625	C-130H	16 Sqn
1626	C-130H	16 Sqn
1627	C-130H	16 Sqn
1628	C-130H	16 Sqn
1629	C-130H	16 Sqn
1630	C-130H-30	16 Sqn
1631	C-130H-30	16 Sqn
1632	L.100-30	16 Sqn
3201	KC-130H	32 Sqn
3202	KC-130H	32 Sqn
3203	KC-130H	32 Sqn
3204	KC-130H	32 Sqn
3205	KC-130H	32 Sqn
3206	KC-130H	32 Sqn
3207	KC-130H	32 Sqn
HZ-114	VC-130H	1 Sqn
HZ-115	VC-130H	1 Sqn
HZ-116	VC-130H	1 Sqn
HZ-117	L.100-30	1 Sqn
HZ-128	L.100-30	1 Sqn
HZ-129	L.100-30	1 Sqn
HZ-132	L.100-30	1 Sqn

Saudi Govt
Boeing 747-3G1/468*
Saudi Royal Flight, Jeddah
HZ-HM1A
HZ-HM1*

Boeing 747SP-68
Saudi Govt, Jeddah;
Saudi Royal Flight, Jeddah
HZ-AIF   Govt
HZ-AIJ   Royal Flight
HZ-HM1B   Royal Flight

Boeing 757-23A
Saudi Govt, Jeddah
HZ-HMED

Boeing MD-11
Saudi Royal Flight, Jeddah
HZ-AFAS
HZ-HM7

Dassault Falcon 900
Saudi Govt, Jeddah
HZ-AFT
HZ-AFZ

Grumman
G.1159A Gulfstream III
Armed Forces Medical
  Services, Riyadh;
Saudi Govt, Jeddah
HZ-AFN Govt
HZ-AFR Govt
HZ-MS3 AFMS

Grumman
G.1159C Gulfstream IV/
Gulfstream IV-SP*
Armed Forces Medical
  Services, Riyadh;
Saudi Govt, Jeddah
HZ-AFU Govt
HZ-AFV Govt
HZ-AFW Govt
HZ-AFX Govt
HZ-AFY Govt
HZ-MFL Govt
HZ-MS4* AFMS

Gulfstream Aerospace
Gulfstream V
Armed Forces Medical
  Services, Riyadh
HZ-MS5A
HZ-MS5B

Lockheed
C-130H/L.100 Hercules
Armed Forces Medical
  Services, Riyadh
HZ-MS2   C-130H
HZ-MS06 L.100-30
HZ-MS07 C-130H
HZ-MS09 L.100-30

SERBIA
Dassault Falcon 50
Govt of Serbia,
  Belgrade
YU-BNA

SINGAPORE
Republic of Singapore Air Force
Boeing
KC-135R Stratotanker
112 Sqn, Changi
750
751
752
753

Lockheed
C-130 Hercules
122 Sqn, Paya Labar
720   KC-130B
721   KC-130B
724   KC-130B
725   KC-130B
730   C-130H
731   C-130H
732   C-130H
733   C-130H
734   KC-130H
735   C-130H

SLOVAKIA
Slovenské Vojenske Letectvo
Aero L-39 Albatros
Zmiešané Letecké Kridlo
  'Otta Smika', Sliač:
  2 Stíhacia Letka [SL]
1701 L-39ZAM
1730 L-39ZAM
4703 L-39ZAM
4707 L-39ZA
5251 L-39CM
5252 L-39CM
5253 L-39CM
5254 L-39CM
5301 L-39CM
5302 L-39CM

Antonov An-26
Dopravniho Kridlo 'Generála
  Milana Ratislava Štefánika',
  Malacky:
  1 Dopravná Roj
2506
3208

LET 410 Turbolet
Dopravniho Kridlo 'Generála
  Milana Ratislava Štefánika',
  Malacky:
  2 Dopravná Roj
1133 L-410T
1521 L-410FG
2311 L-410UVP
2421 L-410UVP
2718 L-401UVP-E
2721 L-401UVP-E

Mikoyan MiG-29AS/UBS
Zmiešané Letecké Kridlo
  'Otta Smika', Sliač:
  1 Stíhacia Letka [SL]
0619 MiG-29AS
0921 MiG-29AS
1303 MiG-29UBS $
2123 MiG-29AS
3709 MiG-29AS
3911 MiG-29AS

5304 MiG-29UBS
6124 MiG-29AS
6425 MiG-29AS
6526 MiG-29AS
6627 MiG-29AS
6728 MiG-29AS

Mil M-17/M-17M*
Vrtulnikové Letcecké Kridlo
  'Generálplukovníka Jána
  Ambrusa', Prešov:
  2 Bitevná Vrtul'nikova
  Letka
0807
0808
0812
0820
0821
0823*
0824
0826
0827
0841
0842
0844
0845
0846
0847

Slovak Govt
Yakovlev Yak-40
Slovak Govt,
  Bratislava/Ivanka
OM-BYE
OM-BYL

SLOVENIA
Slovene Army
LET 410UVP-E
LTO, Brnik
L4-01

Pilatus PC-9/PC-9M*
1/2/3 OSBL, Cerklje
L9-51
L9-53
L9-61*
L9-62*
L9-63*
L9-64*
L9-65*
L9-66*
L9-67*
L9-68*
L9-69*

SOUTH AFRICA
South African Air Force/
Suid Afrikaanse Lugmag
Boeing 737-7ED
21 Sqn, Waterkloof
ZS-RSA

Dassault Falcon 900
21 Sqn, Waterkloof
ZS-NAN

Lockheed
C-130B/C-130BZ* Hercules
28 Sqn, Waterkloof
401

402*
403
404
405*
406*
407*

SPAIN
Ejército del Aire
Airbus A.310-304
Grupo 45, Torrejón
T.22-1 45-50
T.22-2 45-51

Airtech
CN.235M-10 (T.19A)/
CN.235M-100 (T.19B)/
CN.235M-100(MPA) (D.4)/
CN.235M VIGMA (T.19B)*
Grupo Esc, Matacán (74);
801 Esc, Palma/
 Son San Juan;
Guardia Civil (09)
D.4-01   (801 Esc)
D.4-02   (801 Esc)
D.4-03   (801 Esc)
D.4-04   (801 Esc)
D.4-05   (801 Esc)
D.4-06   (801 Esc)
TR.19A-01   403-01
TR.19A-02   403-02
T.19B-07   74-25
T.19B-11   74-29
T.19B-13   74-31
T.19B-14   74-14
T.19B-15   74-33
T.19B-16   74-34
T.19B-17   74-17
T.19B-18   74-36
T.19B-19   74-19
T.19B-20   74-38
T.19B-21*   09-501
T.19B-22*   09-502

Boeing 707
47 Grupo Mixto, Torrejón
TK.17-1   331B   47-01
T.17-2   331B   47-02
T.17-3   368C   47-03
TM.17-4   351C   47-04

CASA 101EB Aviojet
Grupo 54, Torrejón;
Grupo de Escuelas de
 Matacán (74);
AGA, San Javier (79);
Patrulla Aguila, San Javier*
E.25-01 79-01
E.25-06 79-06
E.25-08 79-08
E.25-11 79-11
E.25-12 79-12
E.25-13 79-13
E.25-14 79-14 [2]*
E.25-15 79-15
E.25-16 79-16
E.25-17 74-40
E.25-19 79-19
E.25-20 79-20
E.25-21 79-21
E.25-22 79-22 [1]*

E.25-23 79-23 [4]*
E.25-24 79-24
E.25-25 79-25 [7]*
E.25-26 79-26
E.25-27 79-27
E.25-28 79-28
E.25-29 74-45
E.25-31 79-31
E.25-34 74-44
E.25-35 54-20
E.25-37 79-37
E.25-38 79-38 [5]*
E.25-40 79-40 [3]*
E.25-41 74-41
E.25-43 74-43
E.25-44 79-44
E.25-45 79-45
E.25-46 79-46
E.25-47 79-47
E.25-48 79-48
E.25-49 79-49
E.25-50 79-33
E.25-51 74-07
E.25-52 79-34 [6]*
E.25-53 74-09
E.25-54 79-35
E.25-55 54-21
E.25-56 74-11
E.25-57 74-12
E.25-59 74-13
E.25-61 54-22
E.25-62 79-17
E.25-63 74-17
E.25-65 79-95
E.25-66 74-20
E.25-67 74-21
E.25-68 74-22
E.25-69 79-97 [8]*
E.25-71 74-25
E.25-72 74-26
E.25-73 79-98
E.25-74 74-28
E.25-75 74-29
E.25-76 74-30
E.25-78 79-02
E.25-79 79-39
E.25-80 79-03
E.25-81 74-34
E.25-83 74-35
E.25-84 79-04
E.25-86 79-32
E.25-87 79-29$
E.25-88 74-39

CASA 212 Aviocar
212A (T.12B)/
212S (D.3A)/
212S1 (D.3B)/
Ala 72, Alcantarilla;
801 Esc, Palma/
 Son San Juan;
803 Esc, Cuatro Vientos
D.3A-2   (803 Esc)
D.3B-3   (803 Esc)
D.3B-7   (801 Esc)
T.12B-13   72-01
T.12B-21   72-03
T.12B-37   72-05
T.12B-49   72-07
T.12B-55   72-08
T.12B-63   72-14

T.12B-65   72-11
T.12B-66   72-09
T.12B-67   72-12
T.12B-69   72-15
T.12B-70   72-17

CASA C-295M
Ala 35, Getafe
T.21-01   35-39
T.21-02   35-40
T.21-03   35-41
T.21-04   35-42
T.21-05   35-43
T.21-06   35-44
T.21-07   35-45
T.21-08   35-46
T.21-09   35-47
T.21-10   35-48
T.21-11   35-49
T.21-12   35-50
T.21-13   35-51

Cessna 560 Citation VI
403 Esc, Getafe
TR.20-01   403-11
TR.20-02   403-12
TR.20-03   403-21

Dassault Falcon 20D/E
47 Grupo Mixto, Torrejón
TM.11-1   20E   47-21
TM.11-2   20D   47-22
TM.11-3   20D   47-23
TM.11-4   20E   47-24

Dassault Falcon 900/900B*
Grupo 45, Torrejón
T.18-1   45-40
T.18-2   45-41
T.18-3*   45-42
T.18-4*   45-43
T.18-5*   45-44

Dassault
Mirage F.1BM*/F.1M
Ala 14, Albacete
C.14-13   14-07
C.14-15   14-09
C.14-17   14-11
C.14-22   14-15
CE.14-27* 14-70
CE.14-30* 14-76
C.14-36   14-18
C.14-37   14-19
C.14-38   14-20
C.14-41   14-22$
C.14-42   14-23$
C.14-43   14-24
C.14-45   14-26
C.14-56   14-31
C.14-57   14-32
C.14-60   14-34
C.14-63   14-36
C.14-64   14-37$
C.14-66   14-38
C.14-67   14-39
C.14-68   14-40
C.14-69   14-41
C.14-70   14-42
C.14-72   14-44
C.14-73   14-45
C.14-89   14-47

Eurofighter
EF.2000/EF.2000(T)* Tifón
Ala 11, Morón;
CASA, Getafe

CE.16-01*	11-70
CE.16-02*	11-71
CE.16-03*	11-72
CE.16-04*	11-73
CE.16-05*	11-74
CE.16-06*	11-75
CE.16-07*	11-76
CE.16-09*	11-78
CE.16-10*	11-79
CE.16-11*	11-80
CE.16-12*	11-81
CE.16-13*	
CE.16-14*	
CE.16-15*	
CE.16-16*	
CE.16-17*	
CE.16-18*	
CE.16-19*	
C.16-20	11-91
C.16-21	11-01
C.16-22	11-02
C.16-23	11-03
C.16-24	11-04
C.16-25	11-05
C.16-26	11-06
C.16-27	11-07
C.16-28	11-08
C.16-29	11-09
C.16-30	11-10
C.16-31	11-11
C.16-32	11-12
C.16-33	11-13
C.16-34	11-14
C.16-35	11-15
C.16-36	11-16
C.16-37	11-17
C.16-38	11-18
C.16-39	11-19
C.16-40	11-20
C.16-41	11-21
C.16-42	11-22$
C.16-43	11-23
C.16-44	11-24
C.16-45	11-25
C.16-46	11-26
C.16-47	11-27
C.16-48	11-28
C.16-49	
C.16-50	

Fokker
F.27M Friendship 400MPA
802 Esc, Gando, Las Palmas

D.2-01	
D.2-02	
D.2-03	

Lockheed
C-130H/C-130H-30/ KC-130H Hercules
311 Esc/312 Esc (Ala 31), Zaragoza

TL.10-01	C-130H-30	31-01
T.10-02	C-130H	31-02
T.10-03	C-130H	31-03
T.10-04	C-130H	31-04
TK.10-5	KC-130H	31-50
TK.10-6	KC-130H	31-51
TK.10-07	KC-130H	31-52
T.10-8	C-130H	31-05
T.10-9	C-130H	31-06
T.10-10	C-130H	31-07
TK.10-11	KC-130H	31-53
TK.10-12	KC-130H	31-54

Lockheed
P-3A/P-3M Orion
Grupo 22, Morón

P.3-01	P-3A	22-21
P.3B-08	P-3M	22-31
P.3B-09	P-3M	22-32
P.3B-10	P-3M	22-33
P.3B-11	P-3M	22-34
P.3B-12	P-3M	22-35

McDonnell Douglas
F-18 Hornet
Ala 12, Torrejón;
Ala 15, Zaragoza;
Esc 462, Gran Canaria
EF-18B+/EF-18BM Hornet

CE.15-1*	15-70$	
CE.15-2*	15-71	
CE.15-3	15-72	
CE.15-4*	15-73	
CE.15-5	15-74	
CE.15-6	15-75	
CE.15-7*	15-76	
CE.15-8*	12-71	
CE.15-9	15-77	
CE.15-10	12-73	
CE.15-11	12-74	
CE.15-12*	12-75	

EF-18A+/EF-18AM* Hornet

C.15-13*	12-01
C.15-14	15-01
C.15-15	15-02$
C.15-16*	15-03
C.15-18*	15-05
C.15-20	15-07
C.15-21	15-08
C.15-22*	15-09
C.15-23	15-10
C.15-24	15-11
C.15-25	15-12
C.15-26	15-13$
C.15-27	15-14
C.15-28	15-15
C.15-29	15-16
C.15-30	15-17
C.15-31	15-18
C.15-32	15-19
C.15-33	15-20
C.15-34*	12-50$
C.15-35	15-22
C.15-36	15-23
C.15-37	15-24
C.15-38	15-25
C.15-39	15-26
C.15-40	15-27
C.15-41	15-28$
C.15-43*	15-30
C.15-44*	12-02
C.15-45*	12-03
C.15-46*	12-04
C.15-47	15-31
C.15-48*	12-06
C.15-49*	12-07
C.15-50*	12-08
C.15-51*	12-09
C.15-52*	12-10
C.15-53*	12-11
C.15-54*	12-12
C.15-55	12-13
C.15-56	12-14
C.15-57*	12-15
C.15-59*	12-17
C.15-60	12-18
C.15-61	12-19
C.15-62	12-20
C.15-64	15-34
C.15-65*	12-23
C.15-66*	12-24
C.15-67	15-33
C.15-68*	12-26
C.15-69*	12-27
C.15-70*	12-28
C.15-72*	12-30

F/A-18A/EF-18AM* Hornet

C.15-73	46-01$
C.15-75	46-03
C.15-77	46-05
C.15-79	46-07
C.15-80	21-08
C.15-81	46-09
C.15-82	46-10
C.15-83	46-11
C.15-84	46-12
C.15-85	46-13
C.15-86*	46-14
C.15-87	46-15
C.15-88	46-16
C.15-89*	46-17
C.15-90	46-18
C.15-92	46-20
C.15-93*	46-21
C.15-94	46-22
C.15-95	46-23
C.15-96	46-24

Arma Aérea de l'Armada Española
BAe/McDonnell Douglas
EAV-8B/EAV-8B+/ TAV-8B Harrier II
Esc 009, Rota
EAV-8B

VA.1A-19	01-907
VA.1A-22	01-911

EAV-8B+

VA.1B-24	01-914
VA.1B-25	01-915
VA.1B-26	01-916
VA.1B-27	01-917
VA.1B-28	01-918
VA.1B-29	01-919
VA.1B-30	01-920
VA.1B-35	01-923
VA.1B-36	01-924
VA.1B-37	01-925
VA.1B-38	01-926
VA.1B-39	01-927

TAV-8B

VAE.1A-33	01-922

Cessna 550 Citation II
Esc 004, Rota

U.20-1	01-405
U.20-2	01-406
U.20-3	01-407

Cessna 650 Citation VII
Esc 004, Rota

U.21-01	01-408

SUDAN
Dassault Falcon 50
Sudanese Govt, Khartoum
ST-PSR

Dassault Falcon 900B
Sudanese Govt, Khartoum
ST-PSA

SWEDEN
Svenska Flygvapnet
Grumman
G.1159C Gulfstream 4
(Tp.102A/S.102B Korpen/
Tp.102C)
Flottiljer 17M,
  Stockholm/Bromma &
  Malmslätt
Tp.102A
102001 021
S.102B Korpen
102002 022
102003 023
Tp.102C
102004 024

Gulfstream Aerospace G.550
(Tp.102D)
Flottiljer 17M,
  Stockholm/Bromma &
  Malmslätt
102005 025

Lockheed
C-130H Hercules (Tp.84)
Flottiljer 7, Såtenäs
84001 841
84002 842
84003 843
84004 844
84005 845
84006 846
84007 847
84008 848

Rockwell
Sabreliner-40 (Tp.86)
FMV, Malmslätt
86001 861
SAAB JAS 39 Gripen
Flottiljer 4, Östersund/
  Frösön;
Flottiljer 7, Såtenäs [G];
Flottiljer 17, Ronneby/
  Kallinge;
Flottiljer 21, Luleå/
  Kallax
FMV, Malmslätt
JAS 39

39-5	55	FMV

JAS 39A

39131	131	F7
39132	132	F7
39133	133	FMV
39134	134	FMV
39135	135	F21
39136	136	F7
39138	138	F7
39143	143	F7
39144	44	SAAB
39146	146	F7
39150	150	F7
39151	151	F7
39154	154	F7
39159	159	F7
39167	167	F7
39168	168	F7
39170	170	F17
39171	171	F17
39172	172	F7
39174	174	F7
39176	176	F17
39179	179	F17
39180	180	F17
39181	181	F7
39182	182	F7
39183	183	F17
39185	185	F7
39188	188	F17
39189	189	F17
39190	190	F17
39191	191	F17
39192	192	F7
39193	193	F7
39194	194	F21
39195	195	F7
39196	196	F7
39198	198	F7
39199	199	F7
39200	200	F7
39201	201	F7
39202	202	F7
39203	203	F7
39204	204	F7
39205	205	F7
39206	206	F7

JAS 39B

39800	58	FMV
39801	801	F7
39802	802	SAAB
39804	804	F7
39805	805	F7
39806	806	F7
39807	807	F7
39808	808	F7
39809	809	F7
39810	810	F7
39811	811	F7
39812	812	F7
39813	813	F7
39814	814	F7

JAS 39C

39-6	6	SAAB
39208	208	F21
39209	209	F17
39210	210	F17
39211	211	F7
39212	212	F17
39213	213	F7
39214	214	F21
39215	215	F21
39216	216	F21
39217	217	F7
39218	218	F21
39219	219	F21
39220	220	F17
39221	221	F17
39222	222	F7
39223	223	F21
39224	224	F21
39225	225	F21
39226	226	F21
39227	227	F7
39228	228	F21
39229	229	F21
39230	230	F17
39231	231	F21
39232	232	F21
39233	233	F17
39246	246	F21
39247	247	F21
39248	248	F21
39249	249	F21
39250	250	F21
39251	251	FMV
39252	252	F21
39253	253	F21
39254	254	FMV
39255	255	F21
39256	256	F21
39257	257	F21
39258	258	F21
39260	260	F21
39261	261	F17
39262	262	F21
39263	263	F21
39264	264	FMV
39265	265	FMV
39266	266	F17
39267	267	F21
39268	268	F7
39269	269	F21
39270	270	F17
39271	271	F17
39272	272	F7
39273	273	F17
39274	274	F21
39275	275	F21
39276	276	F17
39277	277	F21
39278	278	F17
39279	279	F21
39280	280	F21
39281	281	F17
39282	282	F17
39283		
39284		
39285		
39286		
39287		
39288		
39289		
39290		
39291		
39292		
39293		
39294		

JAS 39D

39815	815	F21
39816	816	FMV
39817	817	F21
39818		
39821	821	F21
39822	822	SAAB
39823	823	F21
39824	824	F7
39825	825	F7
39826	826	F7
39827	827	F7
39829	829	FMV
39830		
39831		
39832		
39833		

39834
39835
39836
39837
39838
39839
39840
39841
39842
JAS 39NG
39-7   SAAB

SAAB
SF.340 (OS.100 & Tp.100C)/
SF.340AEW&C (S.100D)
Argus
Flottiljer 17, Ronneby/
  Kallinge;
Flottiljer 17M, Malmslätt;
TSFE, Malmslätt
OS.100
100001 001 F17M
Tp.100C
100008 008 F17
S.100D
100003 003 TSFE
100004 004 TSFE

Förvarsmaktens Helikopterflottilj
Aérospatiale
AS.332M-1 Super Puma
(Hkp.10/Hkp.10B[1]/Hkp.10D[2])
1.HkpSkv, Luleå/Kallax;
3.HkpSkv, Berga, Goteborg/Säve,
  & Ronneby/Kallinge
10401   91   3.HkpSkv
10402[2]   92   3.HkpSkv
10403[1]   93   1.HkpSkv
10405   95   3.HkpSkv
10406[1]   96   1.HkpSkv
10407[2]   97   3.HkpSkv
10408[1]   98   1.HkpSkv
10410[1]   90   3.HkpSkv
10411   88   3.HkpSkv
10412   89   3.HkpSkv

Agusta
A109LUH Power (Hkp.15)
2.HkpSkv, Linkoping/Malmen;
3.HkpSkv, Berga & Ronneby/Kallinge
Hkp.15A
15021   21   2.HkpSkv
15022   22   2.HkpSkv
15023   23   2.HkpSkv
15024   24   2.HkpSkv
15025   25   2.HkpSkv
15026   26   2.HkpSkv
15027   27   2.HkpSkv
15028   28   2.HkpSkv
15029   29   2.HkpSkv
15030   30   2.HkpSkv
15031   31   2.HkpSkv
15032   32   2.HkpSkv
15034   34   2.HkpSkv
Hkp.15B
15033   33   2.HkpSkv
15035   35   2.HkpSkv
15036   36   2.HkpSkv
15037   37   2.HkpSkv
15038   38   2.HkpSkv
15039   39   2.HkpSkv
15040   40   2.HkpSkv

MBB Bo.105CBS (Hkp.9A)
2.HkpSkv, Linkoping/Malmen;
3.HkpSkv, Berga, Ronneby/Kallinge
09201 01 2.HkpSkv
09202 02 2.HkpSkv
09203 03 2.HkpSkv
09208 08 3.HkpSkv
09211 11 2.HkpSkv
09212 12 2.HkpSkv
09215 15 2.HkpSkv
09216 16 3.HkpSkv
09217 17 2.HkpSkv
09218 18 2.HkpSkv
09219 19 2.HkpSkv
09220 20 2.HkpSkv

NH Industries
NH.90
1.HkpSkv, Luleå/Kallax;
2.HkpSkv, Linkoping/Malmen;
3.HkpSkv, Berga & Ronneby/Kallinge;
FMV, Malmslätt
NH.90-HCV (Hkp.14A)
141041 41
141042 42 2.HkpSkv
141043 43 2.HkpSkv
141044 44 2.HkpSkv
141045 45 2.HkpSkv
141046 46 FMV
141047 47 FMV
141048 48
141049 49
141050 50
141051 51
141052 52
141053 53
141054 54
NH.90-ASW (Hkp.14B)
142055 55 (on order)
142056 56 (on order)
142057 57 (on order)
142058 58 (on order)
142059 59 (on order)

Sikorsky UH-60M
Black Hawk (Hkp.16)
2.HkpSkv, Linkoping/Malmen;
FMV, Malmslatt
161325
161326 02 FMV
161327
161328
161329
161330
161331
161332
161333
161334
161335
161336
161337
161338
161339

Swedish Coast Guard
Bombardier DHC-8Q-311
Base: Nykoping
SE-MAA [501]
SE-MAB [502]
SE-MAC [503]

SWITZERLAND
Schweizerische Flugwaffe
(Most aircraft are pooled centrally.
Some carry unit badges but these
rarely indicate actual operators.)
Aérospatiale
AS.332M-1/AS.532UL
Super Puma
Lufttransport Staffel 3
  (LtSt 3), Dübendorf;
Lufttransport Staffel 5
  (LtSt 5), Payerne;
Lufttransport Staffel 6
  (LtSt 6), Alpnach;
Lufttransport Staffel 8
  (LtSt 8), Alpnach
Detachments at Emmen,
Meiringen & Sion
AS.332M-1
T-311
T-312
T-313
T-314
T-315
T-316
T-317
T-318
T-319
T-320
T-321
T-322
T-323
T-324
T-325
AS.532UL
T-331
T-332
T-333
T-334
T-335
T-336
T-337
T-338
T-339
T-340
T-342

Beech 1900D
Lufttransportdienst des
  Bundes, Dübendorf
T-729

Beech
King Air 350C
Lufttransportdienst des
  Bundes, Dübendorf
T-721

Cessna
560XL Citation Excel
Lufttransportdienst des
  Bundes, Dübendorf
T-784

Dassault Falcon 50
Lufttransportdienst des
  Bundes, Dübendorf
T-783

Eurocopter
EC.135P-2*/EC.635P-2
Lufttransportdienst des
  Bundes, Dübendorf (LTDB);
Lufttransport Geschwader 2
  (LTG 2), Alpnach;
Lufttransport Staffel 3

Switzerland

(LtSt 3), Dübendorf;
Lufttransport Staffel 5
(LtSt 5), Payerne;
Lufttransport Staffel 6
(LtSt 6), Alpnach;
Lufttransport Staffel 8
(LtSt 8), Alpnach
Detachments at Emmen,
Meiringen & Sion

T-351*	LTDB
T-352*	LTDB
T-353	LTG 2
T-354	LTG 2
T-355	LTG 2
T-356	LTG 2
T-357	LTG 2
T-358	LTG 2
T-359	LTG 2
T-360	LTG 2
T-361	LTG 2
T-362	LTG 2
T-363	LTG 2
T-364	LTG 2
T-365	LTG 2
T-366	LTG 2
T-367	LTG 2
T-368	LTG 2
T-369	LTG 2
T-370	LTG 2

McDonnell Douglas
F/A-18 Hornet
Flieger Staffel 11 (FlSt 11),
Meiringen;
Escadrille d'Aviation 17 (EdAv 17),
Payerne;
Flieger Staffel 18 (FlSt 18),
Payerne
F/A-18C
J-5001
J-5002
J-5003
J-5004
J-5005
J-5006
J-5007
J-5008
J-5009
J-5010
J-5011$
J-5012
J-5013
J-5014
J-5015
J-5016
J-5017$
J-5018$
J-5019
J-5020
J-5021
J-5022
J-5023
J-5024
J-5025
J-5026
F/A-18D
J-5232
J-5233
J-5234
J-5235
J-5236

J-5237
J-5238

Northrop F-5 Tiger II
Armasuisse, Emmen;
Escadrille d'Aviation 6 (EdAv 6),
Sion;
Flieger Staffel 8 (FlSt 8),
Meiringen;
Flieger Staffel 19 (FlSt 19),
Sion;
Patrouille Suisse, Emmen (*P. Suisse*)
F-5E
J-3004
J-3005
J-3014
J-3015
J-3030
J-3033
J-3036
J-3038
J-3041
J-3044
J-3052
J-3057
J-3062
J-3063
J-3065
J-3067
J-3068
J-3069
J-3070
J-3072
J-3073
J-3074
J-3076
J-3077
J-3079
J-3080 *P. Suisse*
J-3081 *P. Suisse*
J-3082 *P. Suisse*
J-3083 *P. Suisse*
J-3084 *P. Suisse*
J-3085 *P. Suisse*
J-3086 *P. Suisse*
J-3087 *P. Suisse*
J-3088 *P. Suisse*
J-3089 *P. Suisse*
J-3090 *P. Suisse*
J-3091 *P. Suisse*
J-3092
J-3093
J-3094
J-3095
J-3097
J-3098
F-5F
J-3201
J-3202
J-3203
J-3204
J-3205
J-3206
J-3207
J-3208
J-3209
J-3210
J-3211
J-3212

Pilatus
PC.6B/B2-H2 Turbo Porter
Lufttransport Staffel 7
(LtSt 7), Emmen
V-612
V-613
V-614
V-616
V-617
V-618
V-619
V-620
V-622$
V-623
V-631
V-632
V-633
V-634
V-635

Pilatus PC-7/NCPC-7*
Turbo Trainer
Instrumentation Flieger
Staffel 14 (InstruFlSt 14),
Dübendorf;
Pilotenschule, Emmen
A-904
A-909
A-912*
A-913*
A-914*
A-915*
A-916*
A-917*
A-918*
A-919*
A-922*
A-923*
A-924*
A-925*
A-926*
A-927*
A-928*
A-929*
A-930*
A-931*
A-932*
A-933*
A-934*
A-935*
A-936*
A-937*
A-938*
A-939*
A-940*
A-941*

Pilatus PC-9
Zielfliegerstaffel 12,
Sion
C-401
C-402
C-403
C-405
C-406
C-407
C-408
C-409
C-410
C-411
C-412

Pilatus PC-21
Pilotenschule, Emmen
A-101
A-102
A-103
A-104
A-105
A-106
A-107 (on order)
A-108 (on order)

Swiss Govt
Pilatus PC-12/45
Swiss Govt, Emmen
HB-FOG

SYRIA
Dassault Falcon 900
Govt of Syria, Damascus
YK-ASC

TANZANIA
Airbus A.340-542
Tanzanian Govt, Dar-es-Salaam
5H-... (on order)

Gulfstream Aerospace G.550
Tanzanian Govt, Dar-es-Salaam
5H-ONE

THAILAND
Airbus A.310-324
Royal Flight, Bangkok
L.13-1/34 (HS-TYQ) [60202]

Boeing 737-448/-4Z6/-8Z6
Royal Flight, Bangkok
HS-CMV   4Z6 [11-111, 90401]
HS-HRH   448 [99-999, 90409]
HS-TYS   8Z6 [55-555]

TUNISIA
Boeing 737-7HJ
Govt of Tunisia, Tunis
TC-CBK
TC-KOP

TURKEY
Türk Hava Kuvvetleri
Boeing 737-7FS AEW&C
131 Filo, Konya
06-001 (on order)
06-002 (on order)
06-003 (on order)
06-004 (on order)

Boeing
KC-135R Stratotanker
101 Filo, Incirlik
57-2609
58-0110
60-0325
60-0326
62-3539
62-3563
62-3567

Cessna 650 Citation VII
212 Filo, Ankara/Etimesgut
004
93-005

Grumman Aerospace G.550
211 Filo, Ankara/Etimesgut
91-003
TC-ATA
TC-GAP/001

Grumman
G.1159C Gulfstream IV
211 Filo, Ankara/Etimesgut
TC-CBK
TC-KOP

Lockheed
C-130E Hercules
222 Filo, Erkilet
63-3186
63-3187
63-3188
63-3189
65-451
67-455
68-1606
68-1608
68-1609
70-1610
70-1947
71-1468
73-0991 $

Transall C-160D
221 Filo, Erkilet
68-020
68-023
69-019
69-021
69-024
69-026
69-027
69-029
69-031
69-032
69-033 $
69-034
69-035
69-036
69-038
69-040 $

TUSAS-GD F-16C/F-16D*
Fighting Falcon
3 AJEÜ, Konya:
  132 Filo;
4 AJÜ, Akinci:
  141 Filo, 142 Filo
  & 143/Öncel Filo;
5 AJÜ, Merzifon:
  151 Filo & 152 Filo;
6 AJÜ, Bandirma:
  161 Filo & 162 Filo;
8 AJÜ, Diyarbakir:
  181 Filo & 182 Filo;
9 AJÜ, Balikesir:
  191 Filo & 192 Filo
07-1001   142 Filo
07-1002   (on order)
07-1003   (on order)
07-1004   (on order)
07-1005   (on order)
07-1006   (on order)
07-1007   (on order)
07-1008   (on order)

07-1009   (on order)
07-1010   (on order)
07-1011   (on order)
07-1012   (on order)
07-1013   (on order)
07-1014   (on order)
07-1015*   (on order)
07-1016*   (on order)
07-1017*   (on order)
07-1018*   (on order)
07-1019*   (on order)
07-1020*   (on order)
07-1021*   (on order)
07-1022*   (on order)
07-1023*   (on order)
07-1024*   (on order)
07-1025*   (on order)
07-1026*   (on order)
07-1027*   (on order)
07-1028*   (on order)
07-1029*   (on order)
07-1030*   (on order)
86-0066   Öncel Filo
86-0068   Öncel Filo
86-0069   Öncel Filo
86-0070   Öncel Filo$
86-0071   Öncel Filo
86-0072   Öncel Filo
86-0192*   Öncel Filo
86-0193*   Öncel Filo
86-0194*   Öncel Filo
86-0195*   Öncel Filo
86-0196*   Öncel Filo
87-0002*   Öncel Filo
87-0003*   Öncel Filo
87-0009   Öncel Filo
87-0010   Öncel Filo
87-0011   Öncel Filo
87-0013   Öncel Filo $
87-0014   Öncel Filo
87-0015   Öncel Filo
87-0016   Öncel Filo
87-0017   Öncel Filo
87-0018   Öncel Filo
87-0019   Öncel Filo
87-0020   Öncel Filo
87-0021   Öncel Filo
88-0013*   Öncel Filo
88-0014*   141 Filo
88-0015*   141 Filo
88-0019   Öncel Filo
88-0020   Öncel Filo
88-0021   142 Filo
88-0024   142 Filo
88-0025   142 Filo
88-0026   142 Filo
88-0027   142 Filo
88-0028   191 Filo
88-0029   142 Filo
88-0030   142 Filo
88-0031   142 Filo
88-0032   142 Filo
88-0033   141 Filo
88-0034   141 Filo
88-0035   141 Filo
88-0036   141 Filo
88-0037   141 Filo
89-0022   141 Filo
89-0023   141 Filo
89-0024   141 Filo
89-0025   141 Filo

89-0026	141 Filo	92-0016	182 Filo	94-0086	191 Filo
89-0027	141 Filo	92-0017	182 Filo	94-0088	142 Filo
89-0028	141 Filo	92-0018	182 Filo	94-0089	152 Filo
89-0030	141 Filo	92-0019	181 Filo	94-0090	152 Filo
89-0031	141 Filo	92-0020	181 Filo	94-0091	152 Filo
89-0034	162 Filo	92-0021	181 Filo	94-0092	152 Filo
89-0035	162 Filo	92-0022*	181 Filo	94-0093	152 Filo
89-0036	141 Filo	92-0023*	181 Filo	94-0094	152 Filo
89-0037	162 Filo	92-0024*	141 Filo	94-0095	152 Filo
89-0038	162 Filo	93-0001	181 Filo	94-0096	152 Filo
89-0040	162 Filo	93-0003	181 Filo	94-0105*	151 Filo
89-0041	162 Filo	93-0004	181 Filo	94-0106*	191 Filo
89-0042*	142 Filo	93-0005	181 Filo	94-0108*	151 Filo
89-0043*	162 Filo	93-0006	181 Filo	94-0109*	151 Filo
89-0044*	162 Filo	93-0007	181 Filo	94-0110*	152 Filo
89-0045*	182 Filo	93-0008	181 Filo	94-1557*	152 Filo
90-0004	162 Filo	93-0009	181 Filo	94-1558*	Öncel Filo
90-0005	162 Filo	93-0010	132 Filo	94-1559*	152 Filo
90-0006	162 Filo	93-0011	181 Filo	94-1560*	151 Filo
90-0007	162 Filo	93-0012	181 Filo	94-1561*	191 Filo
90-0008	162 Filo	93-0013	181 Filo	94-1562*	192 Filo
90-0009	162 Filo	93-0658	151 Filo	94-1563*	192 Filo
90-0010	162 Filo	93-0659	151 Filo	94-1564*	191 Filo
90-0011	162 Filo	93-0660	152 Filo		
90-0012	161 Filo	93-0661	151 Filo	**Turkish Govt**	
90-0013	161 Filo	93-0663	151 Filo	**Airbus A.319CJ-115X**	
90-0014	162 Filo	93-0664	151 Filo	Turkish Govt, Ankara	
90-0016	161 Filo	93-0665	152 Filo	TC-ANA	
90-0017	161 Filo	93-0667	151 Filo		
90-0018	161 Filo	93-0668	151 Filo	**Airbus A.330-243**	
90-0019	161 Filo	93-0669	151 Filo	Turkish Govt, Ankara	
90-0020	162 Filo	93-0670	151 Filo	TC-TUR (on order)	
90-0021	161 Filo	93-0671	151 Filo		
90-0022*	161 Filo	93-0672	152 Filo	**Gulfstream Aerospace G.550**	
90-0023*	161 Filo	93-0673	152 Filo	Turkish Govt, Ankara	
90-0024*	161 Filo	93-0674	152 Filo	TC-CBK	
91-0001	161 Filo	93-0675	152 Filo	TC-DAP	
91-0002	161 Filo	93-0676	192 Filo	TC-KOP	
91-0003	161 Filo	93-0677	192 Filo $		
91-0004	161 Filo	93-0678	192 Filo	**TURKMENISTAN**	
91-0005	161 Filo	93-0679	192 Filo	**BAe 1000B**	
91-0006	161 Filo	93-0680	192 Filo $	Govt of Turkmenistan,	
91-0007	161 Filo	93-0681	192 Filo	Ashkhabad	
91-0008	141 Filo	93-0682	192 Filo $	EZ-B021	
91-0010	141 Filo	93-0683	192 Filo		
91-0011	141 Filo $	93-0684	192 Filo	**Boeing 757-23A**	
91-0012	141 Filo	93-0685	192 Filo	Govt of Turkmenistan,	
91-0013	192 Filo	93-0687	192 Filo	Ashkhabad	
91-0014	141 Filo	93-0688	192 Filo	EZ-A010	
91-0015	182 Filo	93-0689	192 Filo		
91-0016	182 Filo	93-0690	192 Filo	**Boeing 777-22KLR**	
91-0017	182 Filo	93-0691*	151 Filo	Govt of Turkmenistan,	
91-0018	182 Filo	93-0692*	151 Filo $	Ashkhabad	
91-0020	182 Filo	93-0693*	152 Filo	EZ-A777	
91-0022*	141 Filo	93-0694*	192 Filo		
91-0024*	141 Filo	93-0695*	192 Filo	**UGANDA**	
92-0001	182 Filo	93-0696*	192 Filo $	**Gulfstream Aerospace G.550**	
92-0002	182 Filo	94-0071	192 Filo	Govt of Uganda,	
92-0003	162 Filo	94-0072	191 Filo	Entebbe	
92-0004	182 Filo	94-0073	191 Filo	5X-UGF	
92-0005	191 Filo	94-0074	191 Filo		
92-0006	182 Filo	94-0075	191 Filo	**UKRAINE**	
92-0007	182 Filo	94-0076	191 Filo	**Ukrainian Air Force**	
92-0008	191 Filo	94-0077	191 Filo	**Ilyushin Il-76MD**	
92-0009	191 Filo	94-0078	191 Filo	25 TABR, Melitopol	
92-0010	182 Filo	94-0079	191 Filo	& Zaporozhye	
92-0011	182 Filo	94-0080	191 Filo	76413	25 TABR
92-0012	182 Filo	94-0082	191 Filo	76423	25 TABR
92-0013	182 Filo	94-0083	191 Filo	76531	25 TABR
92-0014	182 Filo	94-0084	191 Filo	76557	25 TABR
92-0015	182 Filo	94-0085	191 Filo	76559	
				76564	25 TABR
				76566	

76580	25 TABR
76585	25 TABR
76596	25 TABR
76601	25 TABR
76621	25 TABR
76622	25 TABR
76633	25 TABR
76637	25 TABR
76645	25 TABR
76647	25 TABR
76660	25 TABR
76661	25 TABR
76683	25 TABR
76697	25 TABR
76698	25 TABR
76699	25 TABR
76700	25 TABR
76732	25 TABR
76777	25 TABR
78772	25 TABR
78820	25 TABR
86915	

Airbus A.319CJ-115X
Govt of Ukraine, Kiev
UR-ABA

Ilyushin Il-62M
Govt of Ukraine, Kiev
UR-86527
UR-86528

UNITED ARAB EMIRATES
United Arab Emirates Air Force
AgustaWestland AW.139
Dubai Air Wing
DU-139
DU-140
DU-141
DU-142
DU-143
Airbus A.330-243 MRTT
.... (on order)
.... (on order)

Boeing C-17A Globemaster III
1223 (10-0401)
1224 (10-0402)
1225 (10-0403)
1226 (10-0404)
1227 (on order)
1228 (on order)

Lockheed C-130H/L.100-30*
Hercules
Abu Dhabi
1211
1212
1213
1215*
1216*
1217*
Dubai
312*

UAE Govt
Airbus A.319CJ-113X
Dubai Air Wing
A6-ESH

Airbus A.320-232
Govt of Abu Dhabi;
Govt of Dubai
| A6-DLM | Abu Dhabi |
| A6-HMS | Dubai |

BAE RJ.85/RJ.100*
Govt of Abu Dhabi;
Govt of Dubai
| A6-AAB* | Abu Dhabi |
| A6-RJ1 | Dubai |

Boeing 737-7BC/7F0/8AJ/8EC/8EO/8EX
Govt of Abu Dhabi;
Govt of Dubai
A6-AUH	8EX	Dubai
A6-DFR	7BC	Abu Dhabi
A6-HEH	8AJ	Dubai
A6-HRS	7F0	Dubai
A6-MRM	8EC	Dubai
A6-MRS	8EO	Dubai

Boeing 747-412F/422/433/48E/4F6/8Z5
Dubai Air Wing;
Govt of Abu Dhabi
A6-COM	433	Dubai
A6-GGP	412F	Dubai
A6-HRM	422	Dubai
A6-MMM	422	Dubai
A6-PFA	8Z5	(on order)
A6-UAE	48E	Dubai
A6-YAS	4F6	Abu Dhabi

Boeing 747SP-31
Govt of Dubai
A6-SMR

Boeing 777-2ANER/-35RER*
Govt of Abu Dhabi
A6-ALN
A6-SIL*

Grumman G.1159C Gulfstream IV
Dubai Air Wing
A6-HHH

VENEZUELA
Fuerza Aérea Venezolana
Airbus A.319CJ-133X
Esc 41, Caracas
0001

YEMEN
Boeing 747SP-27
Govt of Yemen, Sana'a
7O-YMN

2012 will see a considerable reorganisation of the French Air Force's AS555 Fennec operations. This example, coded UY, wears its serial, 5387, in very small digits on the tail.

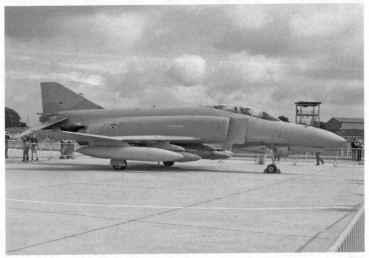

37+01 is one of the remaining F-4F Phantoms operated by the Luftwaffe's JG-71 at Wittmundhaven. It was the first F-4F for the Luftwaffe and still looks magnificent.

Coded 7, MB.339 MM54538 is operated by the flamboyant Italian Air Force 'Frecce Tricolori' team. The last three digits of its serial are carried on the inside of the nosewheel door

AH-64D Apache Q-17 of 301 Squadron wears special markings for the Dutch Air Force's Apache display team, which displayed it superbly.

This section lists the codes worn by some overseas air forces and, alongside, the serial of the aircraft currently wearing this code. This list will be updated occasionally and those with Internet access can download the latest version via the 'AirNet' Web Site, *www.aviation-links.co.uk* and via the MAM2009 Yahoo! Group.

FRANCE

D-BD Alpha Jet

Code	Serial
0 [PDF]	E134
1 [PDF]	E85
2 [PDF]	E163
3 [PDF]	E46
4 [PDF]	E130
5 [PDF]	E117
6 [PDF]	E44
7 [PDF]	E162
8 [PDF]	E158
9 [PDF]	E41
8-ME	E66
8-MI	E74
8-MO	E68
8-MP	E24
8-MQ	E143
102-AG	E109
102-AH	E99
102-FA	E140
102-FB	E86
102-FG	E14
102-FI	E32
102-FM	E105
102-FP	E168
102-LC	E87
102-LF	E9
102-LI	E53
102-LQ	E61
102-MB	E97
102-MM	E13
102-NA	E79
102-NB	E29
102-ND	E26
102-RJ	E76
102-RL	E91
102-UB	E11
118-FE	E119
118-LX	E89
118-UA	E103
120-AF	E108
120-AK	E144
120-AL	E154
120-FJ	E33
120-FN	E116
120-LM	E102
120-LT	E147
120-MA	E35
120-MN	E167
120-MR	E115
120-NE	E73
120-NF	E141
120-NL	E37
120-NP	E155
120-RE	E44
120-RN	E124
120-RP	E136
314-FL	E92
314-LK	E125
314-LL	E88
314-LM	E102
314-LN	E118
314-LO	E142
314-LR	E171
314-LV	E5
314-RR	E146
314-TI	E156
314-TL	E64
314-TT	E101
314-UC	E157
314-UF	E36
314-UG	E23
314-UH	E160
314-UK	E84
705-AA	E17
705-AB	E28
705-AC	E47
705-AD	E51
705-AE	E75
705-AH	E110
705-AK	E18
705-AO	E112
705-FC	E139
705-FD	E151
705-FK	E127
705-FO	E81
705-LA	E72
705-LB	E49
705-LE	E121
705-LG	E120
705-LH	E38
705-LI	E137
705-LP	E129
705-LS	E22
705-LU	E148
705-LW	E82
705-LY	E59
705-LZ	E132
705-MD	E30
705-MF	E98
705-MH	E48
705-MS	E20
705-RM	E123
705-RQ	E138
705-RS	E149
705-RT	E152
705-RU	E153
705-RW	E166
705-RX	E135
705-RY	E170
705-TA	E42
705-TB	E67
705-TC	E96
705-TD	E113
705-TF	E42
705-TG	E104
705-TH	E90
705-TJ	E25
705-TK	E58
705-TM	E128
705-TU	E7
705-TX	E93
705-TZ	E83
F-RCAI	E117
F-TERA	E41
F-TERB	E163
F-TERD	E121
F-TERE	E165
F-TERF	E158
F-TERH	E94
F-TERI	E117
F-TERJ	E162
F-TERK	E31
F-TERM	E134
F-TERN	E46
F-TERP	E130
F-TERQ	E95
F-TERR	E114
F-TEUD	E107
F-UHRE	E44
F-UHRF	E48

Dassault Mirage F.1

Code	Serial
33-CN	630
33-CQ	632
33-NJ	612
112-AA	631
112-AW	623
112-CB	647
112-CC	613
112-CF	604
112-CG	642
112-CH	645
112-CL	657
112-CP	637
112-CQ	632
112-CS	656
112-CT	620
112-CU	606
112-CV	653
112-CY	660
112-FA	622
112-NA	627
112-NC	654
112-ND	607
112-NF	662
112-NG	655
112-NI	641
112-NL	636
112-NM	611
112-NP	635
112-NQ	658
112-NR	614
112-NT	659
112-NU	603
112-NV	640
112-NW	646
112-NY	624
112-NZ	650
112-QA	242
112-QC	267
112-QF	273
112-QJ	274
112-QQ	271
112-QR	236
112-QS	226
112-QU	253
112-QW	229
112-SE	507
112-SG	278
112-SH	256
112-SI	516
112-SL	510
112-SR	518
118-CD	638

188

118-CE	643
118-CK	634
118-CR	649
118-MY	519
118-NC	654
118-NE	617
118-NK	661
118-NX	616
118-QD	280
118-QL	279
118-QX	223
118-SA	514
118-SC	517
118-SD	509
118-SW	502
330-AP	227

Dassault Mirage 2000

3-IF	609
3-IM	619
3-IW	684
3-JJ	639
3-XC	618
4-AB	333
4-AC	319
4-AG	369
4-AS	326
4-BH	329
4-BO	331
4-BP	317
4-CC	325
4-CJ	327
5-OF	11
12-KB	94
12-KR	102
102-AD	70
102-EA	49
102-ED	62
102-EI	38
102-EJ	43
102-EN	46
102-EP	47
102-ER	68
102-EW	48
102-EX	40
102-EY	42
102-EZ	54
102-FZ	41
102-ME	61
103-KC	120
103-KD	123
103-KE	101
103-KI	96
103-KL	106
103-KN	121
103-KQ	112
103-KR	102
103-KU	114
103-KV	88
103-LA	87
103-LB	81
103-LC	108
103-LI	80
103-LJ	105
103-LK	85
103-LL	86
103-YD	107
103-YE	122
103-YF	100
103-YH	109
103-YT	124
103-YU	98

104-MH	67
115-KA	89
115-KB	94
115-KF	111
115-KJ	523
115-KM	95
115-KS	528
115-LD	117
115-LE	79
115-OA	524
115-OB	20
115-OC	529
115-OD	506
115-OG	3
115-OH	12
115-OL	530
115-OQ	510
115-OR	527
115-OT	5
115-OX	16
115-OZ	17
115-YA	93
115-YB	99
115-YG	118
115-YK	97
115-YL	82
115-YM	115
115-YO	113
115-YP	526
115-YS	90
116-AD	339
116-AF	311
116-AH	343
116-AT	330
116-AU	306
116-AW	367
116-BB	364
116-BE	310
116-BF	337
116-BG	313
116-BI	336
116-BL	306
116-BN	332
116-BQ	358
116-BS	374
116-BT	341
116-BV	344
116-CA	304
116-CH	307
116-CP	322
116-CS	305
116-CX	324
116-EC	78
116-EE	71
116-EF	45
116-EL	58
116-EM	63
116-EO	66
116-ES	73
116-ET	57
116-EU	55
116-EV	59
116-MK	74
118-AM	525
118-AU	653
118-AW	92
118-AX	77
118-EB	76
118-EQ	44
118-IG	668
118-IQ	666
118-JK	612

118-MG	65
118-XH	616
125-AA	340
125-AE	355
125-AI	365
125-AJ	350
125-AK	359
125-AL	348
125-AM	353
125-AQ	351
125-AR	368
125-BA	342
125-BC	366
125-BD	371
125-BJ	354
125-BU	345
125-BX	356
125-CB	360
125-CD	320
125-CF	373
125-CG	338
125-CI	335
125-CK	361
125-CL	375
125-CM	372
125-CO	357
125-CQ	370
125-CU	362
133-AF	665
133-AG	681
133-AL	669
133-AS	635
133-IA	650
133-IC	626
133-ID	654
133-IE	642
133-IH	631
133-IJ	638
133-IL	622
133-IN	640
133-IO	647
133-IP	604
133-IR	674
133-IS	617
133-IV	683
133-IW	664
133-JB	678
133-JC	606
133-JD	643
133-JE	634
133-JF	660
133-JG	601
133-JH	686
133-JI	675
133-JL	628
133-JM	657
133-JN	658
133-JO	627
133-JP	611
133-JR	682
133-JT	677
133-JU	614
133-JV	636
133-JW	641
133-JX	679
133-JY	615
133-JZ	667
133-LF	605
133-LG	651
133-LH	655
133-MO	613
133-MP	623

Code	Value		Code	Value		Code	Value
133-MQ	646		113-IM	109		51-62	MM7182
133-XA	662		113-IN	110		51-63	MM7173
133-XE	632		113-IO	338		51-64	MM7179
133-XF	670		113-IP	111		51-65	MM7184
133-XG	625		113-IQ	112		51-66	MM7169
133-XI	661		113-IR	113		51-67	MM7185
133-XK	671		113-IS	114		RS-12	CSX7158
133-XL	603		113-IT	115		RS-14	MM7177
133-XM	680		113-IU	116		RS-18	MM55034
133-XN	652		113-IV	117			
133-XO	629		113-IW	118		**Aermacchi MB339**	
133-XQ	637		113-IY	120		0 [FT]	MM54539
133-XR	659		113-IZ	121		1 [FT]	MM54517
133-XT	648		118-EA	303		2 [FT]	MM54480
133-XV	672		118-EB	304		3 [FT]	MM54482
133-XX	610		118-EC	305		4 [FT]	MM54534
133-XY	649		118-GB	123		5 [FT]	MM54477
133-XZ	685		118-GH	129		6 [FT]	MM54510
188-EG	56		118-HT	323		7 [FT]	MM54538
188-EH	52		118-IR	113		8 [FT]	MM54485
188-IT	624		118-IX	119		9 [FT]	MM54505
188-IU	620		IF	331		10 [FT]	MM54479
188-KG	104		IG	332		11 [FT]	MM54551
188-XD	630					32-161	MM55089
188-XJ	602		**ITALY**			36-04	MM55076
188-YC	83		**Aeritalia-EMB AMX**			36-06	MM55074
188-YN	103		32-01	MM7147		61-01	MM54446
188-YR	91		32-02	MM7192		61-11	MM54457
330-AQ	64		32-05	MM7170		61-12	MM54458
330-AS	51		32-07	MM7196		61-15	MM55054
			32-13	MM7166		61-20	MM55055
Dassault Rafale			32-15	MM7129		61-21	MM54465
104-GC	124		32-16	MM7165		61-23	MM54467
104-GD	125		32-20	MM7180		61-24	MM54468
104-HD	311		32-21	MM7194		61-26	MM55059
104-HG	106		32-24	MM7149		61-32	MM54488
104-HP	314		32-25	MM7163		61-41	MM55058
113-EF	102		32-40	MM55031		61-42	MM54496
113-GA	122		32-41	MM55030		61-50	MM54443
113-GE	126		32-42	MM55051		61-55	MM54507
113-GF	127		32-47	MM55046		61-60	MM54510
113-GG	128		32-50	MM55029		61-61	MM54511
113-GI	130		32-51	MM55036		61-62	MM54512
113-HA	308		32-52	MM55040		61-64	MM54514
113-HB	309		32-53	MM55047		61-65	MM54515
113-HC	310		32-54	MM55039		61-66	MM54516
113-HE	105		32-55	MM55041		61-70	MM54518
113-HF	312		32-56	MM55042		61-72	MM54533
113-HH	104		32-57	MM55044		61-106	MM54548
113-HI	313		32-64	MM55037		61-107	MM54549
113-HJ	107		32-65	MM55043		61-126	MM55062
113-HK	315		32-66	MM55049		61-127	MM55063
113-HM	318		51-10	MM7159		61-130	MM55064
113-HN	319		51-11	MM7131		61-131	MM55065
113-HO	317		51-21	MM7143		61-132	MM55066
113-HQ	321		51-25	MM7146		61-133	MM55067
113-HR	103		51-37	MM7161		61-135	MM55069
113-HS	108		51-40	MM7164		61-136	MM55070
113-HU	322		51-41	MM7183		61-140	MM55072
113-HV	320		51-42	MM7177		61-141	MM55073
113-HX	325		51-43	MM7178		61-143	MM55075
113-HY	326		51-44	MM7198		61-145	MM55077
113-HZ	327		51-45	MM7191		61-146	MM55078
113-IA	307		51-46	MM7197		61-147	MM55079
113-IB	306		51-50	MM7186		61-150	MM55080
113-IC	328		51-51	MM7151		61-151	MM55081
113-IE	330		51-52	MM7171		61-152	MM55082
113-IH	333		51-54	MM7193		61-154	MM55084
113-II	334		51-55	MM7168		61-155	MM55085
113-IJ	335		51-57	MM7190		61-156	MM55086
113-IK	336		51-60	MM7174		61-157	MM55087
113-IL	337		51-61	MM7148		61-160	MM55088

Code	Serial
61-162	MM55090
RS-11	CSX54453
RS-30	CSX54544
RS-32	MM55091
RS-33	MM55068

Eurofighter Typhoon

Code	Serial
4-1	MM7270
4-2	MM7303
4-3	MM7287
4-4	MM7288
4-5	MM7289
4-6	MM7311
4-7	MM7290
4-10	MM7274
4-11	MM7291
4-12	MM7292
4-13	MM7294
4-14	MM7281
4-15	MM7307
4-16	MM7285
4-20	MM7299
4-21	MM7276
4-22	MM7301
4-23	MM55095
4-24	MM55097
4-25	MM55092
4-26	MM55128
4-27	MM55094
4-30	MM55096
4-31	MM55093
4-32	MM55129
4-33	MM55130
4-34	MM55131
36-02	MM7286
36-03	MM7271
36-04	MM7235
36-05	MM7278
36-10	MM7284
36-11	CSX7275
36-12	MM7300
36-14	MM7272
36-15	MM7282
36-20	MM7295
36-21	MM7304
36-22	MM7296
36-23	MM7297
36-24	MM7298
36-25	MM7302
36-26	MM7294
36-32	MM7310
36-33	MM7293
36-34	MM7312
36-35	MM7313
36-36	MM7308
36-37	MM7314
RMV-01	MMX603
RS-01	MMX602

Panavia Tornado

Code	Serial
6-01	MM7007
6-02	MM7039
6-04	MM7057
6-05	MM7025
6-06	MM7046
6-07	MM7075
6-10	MM7088
6-11	MM7058
6-12	MM7071
6-13	MM7011
6-14	MM7061
6-15	MM55006
6-20	MM7016
6-23	MM7022
6-25	MM7043
6-26	MM7063
6-27	MM7035
6-31	MM7006
6-32	MM7015
6-33	MM7080
6-34	MM7073
6-35	MM7026
6-36	MM7087
6-37	MM7038
6-42	MM55010
6-43	MM7003
6-44	MM55009
6-45	MM55008
6-51	MM55000
6-52	MM55001
6-53	MM7004
6-56	MM55007
6-57	MM7081
6-60	MM7086
6-61	MM7031
6-64	MM7049
6-66	MM7056
6-71	MM7067
6-72	MM7083
36-31	MM7023
36-41	MM7024
36-50	CSX7085
36-156	MM7013
50-01	MM7021
50-02	MM7052
50-03	MM7066
50-04	MM7030
50-05	MM7019
50-06	MM7070
50-07	MM7053
50-40	MM7054
50-41	MM7020
50-42	MM55055
50-44	MM7062
50-45	MM7051
50-46	MM7068
50-47	MM7059
50-52	MM7028
50-53	MM7033
50-54	MM7082
50-56	MM7065
50-57	MM7042
RS-05	CSX7047
RS-06	CSX7041

SPAIN

CASA 101EB Aviojet

Code	Serial
54-20	E.25-35
54-21	E.25-55
54-22	E.25-61
74-07	E.25-51
74-09	E.25-53
74-11	E.25-56
74-12	E.25-57
74-13	E.25-59
74-17	E.25-63
74-20	E.25-66
74-21	E.25-67
74-22	E.25-68
74-25	E.25-71
74-26	E.25-72
74-28	E.25-74
74-29	E.25-75
74-30	E.25-76
74-34	E.25-81
74-35	E.25-83
74-39	E.25-88
74-40	E.25-17
74-41	E.25-41
74-42	E.25-18
74-43	E.25-43
74-44	E.25-34
74-45	E.25-29
79-01	E.25-01
79-02	E.25-78
79-03	E.25-80
79-04	E.25-84
79-06	E.25-06
79-08	E.25-08
79-11	E.25-11
79-12	E.25-12
79-13	E.25-13
79-14	E.25-14
79-15	E.25-15
79-16	E.25-16
79-17	E.25-62
79-20	E.25-20
79-21	E.25-21
79-22	E.25-22
79-23	E.25-23
79-24	E.25-24
79-25	E.25-25
79-26	E.25-26
79-27	E.25-27
79-28	E.25-28
79-29	E.25-87
79-31	E.25-31
79-32	E.25-86
79-33	E.25-50
79-34	E.25-52
79-35	E.25-54
79-37	E.25-37
79-38	E.25-38
79-39	E.25-79
79-40	E.25-40
79-44	E.25-44
79-45	E.25-45
79-46	E.25-46
79-47	E.25-47
79-48	E.25-48
79-49	E.25-49
79-95	E.25-65
79-97	E.25-69
79-98	E.25-73

CASA 212 Aviocar

Code	Serial
72-01	T.12B-13
72-03	T.12B-21
72-05	T.12B-37
72-07	T.12B-49
72-08	T.12B-55
72-09	T.12B-66
72-11	T.12B-65
72-12	T.12B-67
72-14	T.12B-63
72-15	T.12B-69
72-17	T.12B-70

US Military Aircraft Markings

All USAF and US Army aircraft have been allocated a fiscal year (FY) number since 1921. Individual aircraft are given a serial according to the fiscal year in which they are ordered. The numbers commence at 0001 and are prefixed with the year of allocation. For example F-15C Eagle 84-001 (84-0001) was the first aircraft ordered in 1984. The fiscal year (FY) serial is carried on the technical data block which is usually stencilled on the left-hand side of the aircraft just below the cockpit. The number displayed on the fin is a corruption of the FY serial. Most tactical aircraft carry the fiscal year in small figures followed by the last three or four digits of the serial in large figures. Large transport and tanker aircraft such as C-130s and KC-135s sometimes display a five-figure number commencing with the last digit of the appropriate fiscal year and four figures of the production number. An example of this is KC-135R 58-0128 which displays 80128 on its fin.

US Army serials have been allocated in a similar way to USAF serials although in recent years an additional zero has been added so that all US Army serials now have the two-figure fiscal year part followed by five digits. This means that, for example C-20E 70140 is officially 87-00140 although as yet this has not led to any alterations to serials painted on aircraft.

USN and USMC serials follow a straightforward numerical sequence which commenced, for the present series, with the allocation of 00001 to an SB2C Helldiver by the Bureau of Aeronautics in 1940. Numbers in the 168000 series are presently being issued. They are usually carried in full on the rear fuselage of the aircraft.

US Coast Guard serials began with the allocation of the serial 1 to a Loening OL-5 in 1927.

UK-based USAF Aircraft

The following aircraft are normally based in the UK. They are listed in numerical order of type with individual aircraft in serial number order, as depicted on the aircraft. The number in brackets is either the alternative presentation of the five-figure number commencing with the last digit of the fiscal year, or the fiscal year where a five-figure serial is presented on the aircraft. Where it is possible to identify the allocation of aircraft to individual squadrons by means of colours carried on fin or cockpit edge, this is also provided.

Type	Notes	Type	Notes
McDonnell Douglas		86-0174 F-15C y	
F-15C Eagle/F-15D Eagle/		86-0175 F-15C y	
F-15E Strike Eagle		86-0176 F-15C y	
LN: 48th FW, RAF Lakenheath:		86-0178 F-15C y	
492nd FS blue/white		86-0182 F-15D y	
493rd FS black/yellow		91-0301 F-15E bl	
494th FS red/white		91-0302 F-15E bl	
00-3000 F-15E r		91-0303 F-15E bl	
00-3001 F-15E r		91-0306 F-15E r	
00-3002 F-15E r		91-0307 F-15E r	
00-3003 F-15E r		91-0308 F-15E bl	
00-3004 F-15E r		91-0309 F-15E bl	
01-2000 F-15E r		91-0310 F-15E r	
01-2001 F-15E m [48th OG]		91-0311 F-15E r	
01-2002 F-15E r [494th FS]		91-0312 F-15E bl	
01-2003 F-15E r		91-0313 F-15E r	
01-2004 F-15E m [48th FW]		91-0314 F-15E r	
83-0018 F-15C y		91-0315 F-15E r	
84-0001 F-15C y		91-0316 F-15E	
84-0010 F-15C y		91-0317 F-15E r	
84-0014 F-15C y		91-0318 F-15E r	
84-0015 F-15C y		91-0320 F-15E r	
84-0019 F-15C y		91-0321 F-15E bl	
84-0027 F-15C y [493rd FS]		91-0324 F-15E r	
84-0044 F-15D y		91-0326 F-15E r	
86-0147 F-15C y		91-0329 F-15E bl	
86-0154 F-15C y		91-0331 F-15E bl	
86-0156 F-15C y		91-0332 F-15E bl	
86-0159 F-15C y		91-0334 F-15E r	
86-0160 F-15C y		91-0335 F-15E r	
86-0163 F-15C y		91-0602 F-15E r	
86-0164 F-15C y		91-0603 F-15E r	
86-0165 F-15C y		91-0604 F-15E r	
86-0166 F-15C		91-0605 F-15E bl	
86-0167 F-15C y		92-0364 F-15E r	
86-0171 F-15C y		96-0201 F-15E bl	
86-0172 F-15C y		96-0202 F-15E bl	

Type		Notes	Type		Notes
96-0204	F-15E *bl*		50992 (FY65)	MC-130P	
96-0205	F-15E *bl*		60215 (FY66)	MC-130P	
97-0217	F-15E *bl*		60220 (FY66)	MC-130P	
97-0218	F-15E *bl*		70024 (FY87)	MC-130H*	
97-0219	F-15E *bl*		80195 (FY88)	MC-130H*	
97-0220	F-15E *bl*		81803 (FY88)	MC-130H*	
97-0221	F-15E *bl* [492nd FS]				
97-0222	F-15E *r*		**Boeing KC-135**		
98-0131	F-15E *bl*		**Stratotanker**		
98-0132	F-15E *bl*		351st ARS/100th ARW,		
98-0133	F-15E *bl*		RAF Mildenhall [D] *(r/w/bl)*		
98-0134	F-15E *bl*		00342 (FY60)	KC-135T	
98-0135	F-15E *bl*		00353 (FY60)	KC-135R	
			10304 (FY61)	KC-135R	
Sikorsky HH-60G			10306 (FY61)	KC-135R	
Pave Hawk			23499 (FY62)	KC-135R	
56th RQS/48th FW,			23540 (FY62)	KC-135R	
RAF Lakenheath [LN]			23565 (FY62)	KC-135R	
26109 (FY88)			37979 (FY63)	KC-135R	
26205 (FY89)			38006 (FY63)	KC-135R	
26206 (FY89)			38008 (FY63)	KC-135R	
26208 (FY89)			38019 (FY63)	KC-135R	
26212 (FY89)			70023 (FY87	MC-130H*	
			71488 (FY57)	KC-135R	
Lockheed MC-130 Hercules			71493 (FY57)	KC-135R	
352nd SOG, RAF Mildenhall:			80016 (FY58)	KC-135R	
7th SOS* & 67th SOS,			80094 (FY58)	KC-135R	
14854 (FY64)	MC-130P		80100 (FY58)	KC-135R	
50991 (FY65)	MC-130P		91492 (FY59)	KC-135R	

F-15C Eagle 86-0175 wears the black and yellow tail stripe of the USAF's 493rd Fighter Squadron, part of the 48th Fighter Wing, based at Lakenheath in Suffolk.

These aircraft are normally based in Western Europe with the USAFE. They are shown in numerical order of type designation, with individual aircraft in serial number order as carried on the aircraft. Fiscal year (FY) details are also provided if necessary. The unit allocation and operating bases are given for most aircraft.

Type		Notes
Fairchild		
A-10C Thunderbolt II		
SP: 52nd FW, Spangdahlem, Germany:		
81st FS yellow		
80-0275	y	
81-0945	y	
81-0948	y	
81-0952	y	[81st FS]
81-0956	y	
81-0960	y	
81-0962	y	
81-0963	y	
81-0965	y	
81-0966	y	
81-0976	y	
81-0978	y	
81-0980	y	
81-0981	y	
81-0985	y	
81-0988	y	
81-0991	y	
81-0992	y	
82-0646	y	
82-0647	y	
82-0649	y	
82-0650	y	
82-0654	y	
82-0656	y	
Beech		
C-12 Super King Air		
US Embassy Flight, Budapest, Hungary		
FY83		
30495 C-12D		
FY76		
60168 C-12C		
Lockheed (GD)		
F-16CM/F-16DM* Fighting Falcon		
AV: 31st FW, Aviano, Italy:		
510th FS purple/white		
555th FS green/yellow		
SP: 52nd FW, Spangdahlem,		
Germany:		
480th FS red		
87-0350	AV	gn
87-0351	AV	m [31st OSS]
87-0355	AV	pr
87-0359	AV	gn
88-0413	AV	pr
88-0425	AV	gn
88-0435	AV	gn
88-0443	AV	pr
88-0444	AV	pr
88-0446	AV	gn
88-0491	AV	pr
88-0510	AV	pr [510th FS]
88-0516	AV	pr
88-0525	AV	pr
88-0526	AV	gn
88-0532	AV	gn
88-0535	AV	gn
88-0541	AV	pr

Type			Notes
89-2001	AV	m [31st FW]	
89-2008	AV	pr	
89-2009	AV	pr	
89-2011	AV	pr	
89-2016	AV	pr	
89-2018	AV	gn	
89-2023	AV	gn	
89-2024	AV	gn	
89-2026	AV	pr	
89-2029	AV	pr	
89-2030	AV	pr	
89-2035	AV	gn [555th FS]	
89-2038	AV	gn	
89-2039	AV	gn	
89-2041	AV	gn	
89-2044	AV	gn	
89-2046	AV	pr	
89-2047	AV	pr	
89-2049	AV	pr [USAFE]	
89-2057	AV	pr	
89-2068	AV	gn	
89-2096	AV	pr	
89-2102	AV	pr	
89-2118	AV	pr	
89-2137	AV	pr [31st OG]	
89-2152	AV		
89-2178*	AV	gn	
90-0709	AV	pr	
90-0772	AV	gn	
90-0773	AV	gn	
90-0777*	AV	pr	
90-0795*	AV	gn	
90-0796*	AV	pr	
90-0800*	AV gn		
90-0813	SP	r	
90-0818	SP	r	
90-0827	SP	r	
90-0829	SP	r	
90-0833	SP	r	
91-0338	SP	r	
91-0340	SP	r	
91-0342	SP	r	
91-0343	SP	r	
91-0344	SP	r	
91-0351	SP	r	
91-0352	SP	m [52nd FW]	
91-0358	SP	r	
91-0360	SP	r	
91-0361	SP		
91-0366	SP	r [480 FS]	
91-0368	SP		
91-0402	SP		
91-0403	SP		
91-0407	SP	r	
91-0412	SP		
91-0416	SP		
91-0417	SP	r	
91-0472*	SP		
91-0481*	SP		
92-3918	SP	r	
96-0080	SP	r	
96-0083	SP	r	

194

Type	Notes	Type	Notes
Grumman		*FY01*	
C-20H Gulfstream IV		10076	
76th AS/86th AW, Ramstein,		*FY99*	
Germany		90402	
FY90			
00300		**Boeing C-40B**	
FY92		76th AS/86th AW, Ramstein,	
20375		Germany	
		FY02	
Gates C-21A		20042	
Learjet			
76th AS/86th AW, Ramstein,		**Lockheed C-130J**	
Germany		**Hercules II**	
FY84		37th AS/86th AW, Ramstein,	
40081		Germany [RS] (*bl/w*)	
40082		68610 (FY06)	
40083		68611 (FY06)	
40084		68612 (FY06)	
40085		78608 (FY07)	
40087		78609 (FY07)	
40109		78613 (FY07)	
40110		78614 (FY07)	
40111		88601 (FY08) [86th AW]	
		88602 (FY08) [86th OG]	
Gulfstream Aerospace		88603 (FY08) [37th AS]	
C-37A Gulfstream V		88604 (FY08)	
309th AS/86th AW, Chievres,		88605 (FY08)	
Belgium		88606 (FY08)	
		88607 (FY08)	

European-based US Navy Aircraft

Type	Notes	Type	Notes
Fairchild C-26D		900530 Sigonella	
NAF Naples, Italy;		900531 Naples	
NAF Sigonella, Italy		910502 Naples	
900528 Sigonella			

A-10C Thunderbolt II 82-0649 belongs to the USAF's 81st Fighter Squadron, part of the 52nd Fighter Wing, based at Spangdahlem in Germany.

Type	Notes	Type	Notes
Beech		08744	
C-12 Huron		08745	
'E' Co, 6th Btn, 52nd Avn Reg't,		08746	
Stuttgart;		08747	
'F' Co, 6th Btn, 52nd Avn Reg't,		08748	
Wiesbaden;		*FY07*	
'A' Co, 2nd Btn, 228th Avn Reg't,		08749	
Heidelberg;		08750	
1st Military Intelligence Btn,		08751	
Wiesbaden;		*FY09*	
SHAPE Flight Det, Chievres		08070	
FY92		08071	
13122 RC-12X 1st MIB		08072	
13123 RC-12X 1st MIB		08073	
13125 RC-12X 1st MIB			
FY93		**Sikorsky H-60 Black Hawk**	
00699 RC-12X 1st MIB		'A' Co, 3rd Btn, 158th Avn Reg't,	
00701 RC-12X 1st MIB		Ansbach;	
FY84		'B' Co, 3rd Btn, 158th Avn Reg't,	
40156 C-12U F/6-52nd Avn		Ansbach;	
40157 C-12U E/6-52nd Avn		'A' Co, 5th Btn, 158th Avn Reg't,	
40158 C-12U F/6-52nd Avn		Ansbach;	
40160 C-12U E/6-52nd Avn		'C' Co, 5th Btn, 158th Avn Reg't,	
40161 C-12U F/6-52nd Avn		Ansbach;	
40162 C-12U F/6-52nd Avn		SHAPE Flight Det, Chievres;	
40163 C-12U F/6-52nd Avn		'G' Co, 6th Btn, 52nd Avn Reg't,	
40165 C-12U F/6-52nd Avn		Coleman Barracks;	
40173 C-12U F/6-52nd Avn		'B' Co, 70th Transportation Reg't,	
40180 C-12U E/6-52nd Avn		Coleman Barracks;	
FY94		'A' Co, 1st Btn, 214th Avn Reg't,	
40315 C-12R A/2-228th Avn		Landstuhl;	
40316 C-12R A/2-228th Avn		'C' Co, 1st Btn, 214th Avn Reg't,	
40318 C-12R A/2-228th Avn		Landstuhl;	
40319 C-12R A/2-228th Avn		6th Avn Co, Vicenza, Italy	
FY85		*FY79*	
50147 RC-12K 1st MIB		23330 UH-60A C/1-214th Avn	
50148 RC-12K 1st MIB		*FY82*	
50150 RC-12K 1st MIB		23750 UH-60A C/1-214th Avn	
50152 RC-12K 1st MIB		23754 UH-60A C/1-214th Avn	
50153 RC-12K 1st MIB		23755 UH-60A C/1-214th Avn	
FY86		23756 UH-60A C/1-214th Avn	
60079 C-12J SHAPE Flt Det		23757 UH-60A C/1-214th Avn	
		FY83	
Grumman		23855 UH-60A C/1-214th Avn	
C-20E Gulfstream III		23869 UH-60A C/1-214th Avn	
HQ US Army Europe, Ramstein,		23888 UH-60A C/5-158th Avn	
Germany		*FY84*	
FY87		23936 UH-60A C/5-158th Avn	
70140		23951 UH-60A C/1-214th Avn	
		FY85	
Cessna UC-35A		24397 UH-60A C/5-158th Avn	
Citation V		24422 UH-60A C/1-214th Avn	
'F' Co, 6th Btn, 52nd Avn Reg't,		24437 UH-60A C/1-214th Avn	
Wiesbaden		*FY86*	
FY95		24531 UH-60A C/1-214th Avn	
50123		24532 UH-60A C/1-214th Avn	
50124		24551 UH-60A C/1-214th Avn	
FY97		*FY87*	
70101		24583 UH-60A SHAPE Flt Det	
70102		24584 UH-60A SHAPE Flt Det	
70105		24589 UH-60A G/6-52nd Avn	
		24614 UH-60A C/5-158th Avn	
Boeing-Vertol CH-47F		24642 UH-60A G/6-52nd Avn	
Chinook		24644 UH-60A C/1-214th Avn	
'B' Co, 5th Btn, 158th Avn Reg't,		24645 UH-60A C/1-214th Avn	
Ansbach		24656 UH-60A C/5-158th Avn	
FY07		26004 UH-60A C/5-158th Avn	

Type			Notes
26005	UH-60A	C/5-158th Avn	
FY88			
26019	UH-60A	C/1-214th Avn	
26023	UH-60A	C/1-214th Avn	
26027	UH-60A	G/6-52nd Avn	
26032	UH-60A	A/5-158th Avn	
26037	UH-60A	C/5-158th Avn	
26039	UH-60A	C/1-214th Avn	
26045	UH-60A	C/1-214th Avn	
26054	UH-60A	C/1-214th Avn	
26071	UH-60A	G/6-52nd Avn	
26075	UH-60A	C/5-158th Avn	
26080	UH-60A	C/1-214th Avn	
26082	UH-60A	C/5-158th Avn	
FY89			
26132	UH-60A	C/5-158th Avn	
26157	UH-60A	C/5-158th Avn	
26163	UH-60A	C/5-158th Avn	
FY92			
26452	UH-60L	A/5-158th Avn	
FY94			
26551	UH-60L	G/6-52nd Avn	
26570	UH-60L	A/5-158th Avn	
26572	UH-60L	A/5-158th Avn	
26573	UH-60L	A/5-158th Avn	
26577	UH-60L	A/5-158th Avn	
FY95			
26637	UH-60L	A/5-158th Avn	
26639	UH-60L	A/5-158th Avn	
26641	UH-60L	3-158th Avn	
26642	UH-60L	3-158th Avn	
26643	UH-60L	3-158th Avn	
26645	UH-60L	3-158th Avn	
26646	UH-60L	3-158th Avn	
26650	UH-60L	3-158th Avn	
26651	UH-60L	3-158th Avn	
26652	UH-60L	3-158th Avn	
26654	UH-60L	3-158th Avn	
26657	UH-60L	3-158th Avn	
FY96			
26674	UH-60L	3-158th Avn	
26675	UH-60L	3-158th Avn	
26676	UH-60L	3-158th Avn	
26677	UH-60L	3-158th Avn	
26678	UH-60L	3-158th Avn	
26679	UH-60L	3-158th Avn	
26680	UH-60L	3-158th Avn	
26682	UH-60L	3-158th Avn	
26683	UH-60L	3-158th Avn	
26684	UH-60L	3-158th Avn	
26685	UH-60L	3-158th Avn	
26687	UH-60L	3-158th Avn	
26688	UH-60L	3-158th Avn	
26689	UH-60L	3-158th Avn	
26690	UH-60L	3-158th Avn	
26691	UH-60L	3-158th Avn	
26692	UH-60L	3-158th Avn	
26696	UH-60L	3-158th Avn	
FY97			
26763	UH-60L	A/5-158th Avn	
26766	UH-60L	A/5-158th Avn	
26768	UH-60L	A/5-158th Avn	
FY05			
27062	UH-60L	3-158th Avn	
FY06			
27110	UH-60L	A/5-158th Avn	

Type		Notes
MDH AH-64D Apache		
2nd Btn, 159th Avn Reg't, Illesheim;		
3rd Btn, 159th Avn Reg't, Illesheim		
FY02		
05294	2-159th Avn	
05297	2-159th Avn	
05299	2-159th Avn	
FY03		
05357	2-159th Avn	
05372	2-159th Avn	
FY04		
05462	2-159th Avn	
05464	2-159th Avn	
05474	2-159th Avn	
05479	2-159th Avn	
FY05		
07005	2-159th Avn	
07007	2-159th Avn	
07008	2-159th Avn	
07009	2-159th Avn	
07011	2-159th Avn	
07012	2-159th Avn	
07013	2-159th Avn	
FY06		
07014	2-159th Avn	
07018	2-159th Avn	
07019	2-159th Avn	
07020	2-159th Avn	
07021	2-159th Avn	
FY07		
05502	2-159th Avn	
05503	2-159th Avn	
05504	2-159th Avn	
05505	2-159th Avn	
05506	2-159th Avn	
05507	2-159th Avn	
05516	2-159th Avn	
FY08		
05540	2-159th Avn	
05541	2-159th Avn	
05542	2-159th Avn	
05543	2-159th Avn	
05544	2-159th Avn	
05545	2-159th Avn	
05546	3-159th Avn	
05547	3-159th Avn	
05549	3-159th Avn	
05550	2-159th Avn	
05551	3-159th Avn	
05552	3-159th Avn	
05553	2-159th Avn	
05554	2-159th Avn	
05555	2-159th Avn	
05556	2-159th Avn	
05557	3-159th Avn	
Eurocopter UH-72A Lakota		
Joint Multinational Readiness		
Centre, Hohenfels		
FY07		
72029		
FY09		
72095		
72096		
72097		
72098		
72100		
72105		
72106		
72107		
72108		

US-based USAF Aircraft

The following aircraft are normally based in the USA but are likely to be seen visiting the UK from time to time. The presentation is in numerical order of the type, commencing with the B-1B and concluding with the C-135. The aircraft are listed in numerical progression by the serial actually carried externally. Fiscal year information is provided, together with details of mark variations and in some cases operating units. Where base-code letter information is carried on the aircrafts' tails, this is detailed with the squadron/base data; for example the 7th Wing's B-1B 60105 carries the letters DY on its tail, thus identifying the Wing's home base as Dyess AFB, Texas.

Type		Notes
Rockwell B-1B Lancer		
7th BW, Dyess AFB, Texas [DY]:		
9th BS (bk/w), 13th BS (r)		
& 28th BS (bl/w);		
28th BW, Ellsworth AFB,		
South Dakota [EL]:		
34th BS (bk/r) & 37th BS (bk/y);		
337th TES/53rd Wg, Dyess AFB,		
Texas [OT] bk/gy;		
77th WPS/57th Wg, Dyess AFB,		
Texas [WA] y/bk;		
419th FLTS/412th TW, Edwards AFB,		
California [ED]		
FY85		
50059	7th BW	bk/w$
50060	28th BW	bk/r
50061	7th BW	bl/w
50064	7th BW	bk/w
50065	7th BW	bl/w$
50066	28th BW	
50068	412th TW	
50069	7th BW	
50072	57th Wg	y/bk
50073	7th BW	bk/w$
50074	7th BW	bk/w
50075	412th TW	
50077	57th Wg	y/bk
50079	28th BW	bk/r
50080	7th BW	bk/w
50081	28th BW	bk/r
50084	28th BW	bk/r
50085	28th BW	bk/y
50088	7th BW	bk/w
50089	7th BW	bk/w
50090	7th BW	bl/w
50091	28th BW	bk/r
FY86		
60094	28th BW	bk/y$
60095	28th BW	bk/r
60097	7th BW	bl/w
60098	7th BW	bk/w
60099	28th BW	bk/y$
60100	7th BW	bl/w
60101	7th BW	bl/w
60102	28th BW	bk/y
60103	7th BW	bl/w
60104	28th BW	bk/y
60105	7th BW	bl/w
60107	7th BW	bl/w
60108	7th BW	bl/w
60109	7th BW	bk/w
60110	7th BW	bk/w
60111	28th BW	bk/r
60112	7th BW	bk/w
60113	28th BW	bk/y
60115	28th BW	bk/r
60117	7th BW	bk/w
60118	28th BW	bk/y
60119	7th BW	bl/w
60120	53rd Wg	bk/gy

Type		Notes
60121	28th BW	bk/y
60122	7th BW	r
60123	7th BW	bl/w
60124	7th BW	bl/w
60126	7th BW	bl/w
60129	28th BW	bk/r
60132	7th BW	bl/w
60133	7th BW	bk/w
60134	28th BW	bk/r
60135	7th BW	bl/w
60136	53rd Wg	bk/gy
60138	7th BW	y/bk
60139	28th BW	bl/y$
60140	7th BW	bk/w
Northrop B-2 Spirit		
419th FLTS/412th TW, Edwards AFB,		
California [ED];		
509th BW, Whiteman AFB,		
Missouri [WM]:		
13th BS, 393rd BS & 715th BS		
(Names are given where known.		
Each begins *Spirit of ...*)		
FY90		
00040	509th BW *Alaska*	
00041	509th BW *Hawaii*	
FY92		
20700	509th BW *Florida*	
FY82		
21066	509th BW *America*	
21067	509th BW *Arizona*	
21068	412th TW *New York*	
21069	509th BW *Indiana*	
21070	509th BW *Ohio*	
21071	509th BW *Mississippi*	
FY93		
31085	509th BW *Oklahoma*	
31086	509th BW *Kitty Hawk*	
31087	509th BW *Pennsylvania*	
31088	509th BW *Louisiana*	
FY88		
80328	509th BW *Texas*	
80329	509th BW *Missouri*	
80330	509th BW *California*	
80331	509th BW *South Carolina*	
80332	509th BW *Washington*	
FY89		
90128	509th BW *Nebraska*	
90129	509th BW *Georgia*	
Lockheed U-2		
9th RW, Beale AFB, California [BB]:		
1st RS, 5th RS		
& 99th RS (bk/r);		
Lockheed, Palmdale;		
Warner Robins		
Air Logistics Centre [WR]		
FY68		
68-10329	U-2S	9th RW
68-10331	U-2S	9th RW

Type			Notes
68-10336	U-2S	WR ALC	
68-10337	U-2S	9th RW	
FY80			
80-1064	TU-2S	9th RW	
80-1065	TU-2S	9th RW	
80-1066	U-2S	9th RW	
80-1067	U-2S	Lockheed	
80-1068	U-2S	9th RW	
80-1069	U-2S	9th RW	
80-1070	U-2S	9th RW	
80-1071	U-2S	9th RW	
80-1073	U-2S	9th RW	
80-1074	U-2S	9th RW	
80-1076	U-2S	9th RW	
80-1077	U-2S	9th RW	
80-1078	TU-2S	9th RW	
80-1079	U-2S	9th RW	
80-1080	U-2S	9th RW	
80-1081	U-2S	9th RW	
80-1083	U-2S	9th RW	
80-1084	U-2S	9th RW	
80-1085	U-2S	9th RW	
80-1086	U-2S	9th RW	
80-1087	U-2S	9th RW	
80-1089	U-2S	9th RW	
80-1090	U-2S	9th RW	
80-1091	TU-2S	9th RW	
80-1092	U-2S	9th RW	
80-1093	U-2S	9th RW	
80-1094	U-2S	9th RW	
80-1096	U-2S	9th RW	
80-1099	U-2S	9th RW	

Boeing E-3 Sentry
552nd ACW, Tinker AFB,
Oklahoma [OK] (*w*):
960th ACS, 963rd ACS,
964th ACS, 965th ACS
& 966th ACTS;
961st ACS/18th Wg, Kadena AB,
Japan [ZZ] (*or*);
962nd ACS/3rd Wg, Elmendorf AFB,
Alaska [AK] (*gn*)

FY80			
00137	E-3C	*w*	
00138	E-3C	*r*	
00139	E-3C	*gn*	
FY81			
10004	E-3C	*or*	
10005	E-3C	*or$*	
FY71			
11407	E-3B	*or$*	
11408	E-3B	*w*	
FY82			
20006	E-3C	*w*	
20007	E-3C	*r*	
FY83			
30008	E-3C	*w*	
30009	E-3C	*w*	
FY73			
31674	JE-3C	Boeing	
31675	E-3B	*w*	
FY75			
50556	E-3B	*w*	
50557	E-3B	*r*	
50558	E-3B	*gn*	
50559	E-3B	*r*	
50560	E-3B	*w*	
FY76			
61604	E-3B	*w*	

Type			Notes
61605	E-3B	*or*	
61606	E-3B	*or*	
61607	E-3B	*w*	
FY77			
70351	E-3B	*w*	
70352	E-3B	*w*	
70353	E-3B	*w*	
70355	E-3B	*gn*	
70356	E-3B	*w*	
FY78			
80576	E-3B	*r*	
80577	E-3B	*w*	
80578	E-3B	*w*	
FY79			
90001	E-3B	*w*	
90002	E-3B	*w*	
90003	E-3B	*m*	

Boeing E-4B
1st ACCS/55th Wg, Offutt AFB,
Nebraska [OF]

FY73	
31676	
31677	
FY74	
40787	
FY75	
50125	

Lockheed
C-5 Galaxy/C-5M Super Galaxy
60th AMW, Travis AFB, California:
21st AS (*bk/gd*) & 22nd AS (*bk/bl*);
137th AS/105th AW, Stewart AFB,
New York (*bl*);
155th AS/164th AW, Memphis,
Tennessee ANG (*r*);
167th AS/167th AW, Martinsburg,
West Virginia ANG [WV] (*r*);
68th AS/433rd AW AFRC, Kelly AFB,
Texas;
436th AW, Dover AFB, Delaware:
9th AS (*y/bl*);
337th AS/439th AW AFRC, Westover
ARB, Massachusetts (*bl/r*);
418th FLTS/412th TW, Edwards AFB,
California

FY70				
00445	C-5A	433rd AW		
00448	C-5A			
00449	C-5A	164th AW	*r*	
00451	C-5A			
00452	C-5A	167th AW	*r*	
00454	C-5A	164th AW	*r*	
00455	C-5A	167th AW	*r*	
00456	C-5A	433rd AW		
00457	C-5A			
00460	C-5A	105th AW	*bl*	
00461	C-5A			
00462	C-5A	167th AW	*r*	
00463	C-5A	167th AW	*r*	
00464	C-5A	105th AW	*bl*	
00465	C-5A	164th AW	*r*	
00467	C-5A	167th AW	*r*	
FY83				
31285	C-5M	436th AW		
FY84				
40060	C-5B	439th AW	*bl/r*	
40061	C-5M	436th AW	*y/bl*	
40062	C-5B	436th AW	*y/bl*	

C-5–KC-10

Type			Notes		Type			Notes
FY85					90009	C-5A	105th AW	*bl*
50001	C-5B	436th AW	*m*		90010	C-5A	164th AW	*r*
50002	C-5M	436th AW			90011	C-5A	167th AW	*r*
50003	C-5M	436th AW	*y/bl*		90012	C-5A	105th AW	*bl*
50004	C-5M	LMTAS			90013	C-5A	164th AW	*r*
50005	C-5M	LMTAS			90014	C-5A	433rd AW	
50006	C-5B	439th AW	*bl/r*		90015	C-5A	164th AW	*r*
50007	C-5M	436th AW	*y/bl*		90016	C-5A	433rd AW	
50008	C-5B	60th AMW	*bk/gd*		90018	C-5A	164th AW	*r*
50009	C-5B	439th AW	*bl/r*		90019	C-5A	164th AW	*pr*
50010	C-5B	60th AMW	*bk/gd*		90020	C-5A	433rd AW	
FY86					90021	C-5A	105th AW	*bl*
60011	C-5B	60th AMW	*bk/bl*		90022	C-5A	167th AW	*r*
60012	C-5B	439th AW	*bl/r*		90023	C-5A	105th AW	*bl*
60013	C-5M	436th AW	*y/bl*		90024	C-5M	436th AW	*y/bl*
60014	C-5B	439th AW	*bl/r*		90025	C-5A	164th AW	*r*
60015	C-5B	60th AMW	*w*		90026	C-5A	433rd AW	
60016	C-5B	60th AMW	*bk/bl*					
60017	C-5B	436th AW	*y/bl*		**Boeing E-8 J-STARS**			
60018	C-5B	439th AW	*bl/r*		116th ACW, Robins AFB,			
60019	C-5B	439th AW	*bl/r*		Georgia [WR]:			
60020	C-5B	436th AW	*y/bl*		12th ACCS (*gn*), 16th ACCS (*bk*),			
60021	C-5B	439th AW	*bl/r*		128th ACS/Georgia ANG (*r*)			
60022	C-5B	60th AMW	*bk/bl*		& 330th CTS (*y*);			
60023	C-5B	439th AW	*bl/r*		Grumman, Melbourne, Florida			
60024	C-5B	60th AMW	*bk/bl*		*FY00*			
60025	C-5M	436th AW	*y/bl*		02000	E-8C	116th ACW	
60026	C-5B	60th AMW	*bk/gd*		*FY90*			
FY87					00175	E-8A	Grumman	
70027	C-5B	436th AW	*y/bl*		*FY01*			
70028	C-5B	60th AMW	*w*		12005	E-8C	116th ACW	
70029	C-5B	436th AW	*y/bl*		*FY02*			
70030	C-5B	60th AMW	*bk/bl*		29111	E-8C	116th ACW	
70031	C-5B	439th AW	*bl/r*		*FY92*			
70032	C-5B	60th AMW	*bk/bl*		23289	E-8C	116th ACW	*m*
70033	C-5B	439th AW	*bl/r*		23290	E-8C	116th ACW	*bk*
70034	C-5B	60th AMW	*bk/bl*		*FY93*			
70035	C-5M	LMTAS			31097	E-8C	116th ACW	*r*
70036	C-5B	60th AMW	*w*		*FY94*			
70037	C-5B	439th AW	*bl/r*		40284	E-8C	116th ACW	*r*
70038	C-5B	439th AW	*bl/r*		40285	E-8C	116th ACW	*bk*
70039	C-5B	439th AW	*bl/r*		*FY95*			
70040	C-5B	60th AMW	*bk/gd*		50121	E-8C	116th ACW	*r*
70041	C-5B	439th AW	*bl/r*		50122	E-8C	116th ACW	*r*
70042	C-5B	60th AMW	*bk/bl*		*FY96*			
70043	C-5B	439th AW	*bl/r*		60042	E-8C	116th ACW	*bk*
70044	C-5B	60th AMW	*bk/bl*		60043	E-8C	116th ACW	*bl*
70045	C-5M	LMTAS			*FY97*			
FY68					70100	E-8C	116th ACW	*r*
80211	C-5A	167th AW	*r*		70200	E-8C	116th ACW	*bk*
80212	C-5A	105th AW	*bl*		70201	E-8C	116th ACW	*r*
80213	C-5C	60th AMW	*bk/gd*		*FY99*			
80214	C-5A	433rd AW			90006	E-8C	116th ACW	*gn*
80215	C-5A	433rd AW						
80216	C-5C	60th AMW	*bk/gd*		**McDonnell Douglas**			
80219	C-5A	433rd AW			**KC-10A Extender**			
80220	C-5A	433rd AW			60th AMW, Travis AFB, California:			
80221	C-5A	433rd AW			6th ARS & 9th ARS;			
80222	C-5A	167th AW	*r*		305th AMW, McGuire AFB,			
80223	C-5A	433rd AW			New Jersey:			
80224	C-5A	105th AW	*bl*		2nd ARS (*bl/r*) & 32nd ARS (*bl*)			
80226	C-5A	105th AW	*bl*		*FY82*			
FY69					20191		60th AMW	
90001	C-5A	167th AW	*r*		20192		60th AMW	
90002	C-5A	164th AW	*r*		20193		60th AMW	
90003	C-5A				*FY83*			
90005	C-5A	433rd AW			30075		60th AMW	
90006	C-5A	433rd AW			30076		60th AMW	
90007	C-5A	433rd AW			30077		60th AMW	
90008	C-5A	105th AW	*bl*		30078		60th AMW	

Type		Notes	Type	Notes
30079	305th AMW	bl/r	15th Wg, Hickam AFB,	
30080	60th AMW		Hawaii: 535th AS (r/y);	
30081	305th AMW	bl	60th AMW, Travis AFB,	
30082	305th AMW	bl	California:	
FY84			21st AS (bk/w);	
40185	60th AMW		62nd AW, McChord AFB,	
40186	305th AMW	bl/r	Washington (gn):	
40187	60th AMW		4th AS, 7th AS,8th AS	
40188	305th AMW	bl/r	& 10th AS;	
40189	60th AMW		58th AS/97th AMW, Altus AFB,	
40190	305th AMW	bl/r	Oklahoma (r/y);	
40191	60th AMW		137th AS/105th AW, Stewart AFB,	
40192	305th AMW	bl/y	New York (bl);	
FY85			172nd AW, Jackson Int'l	
50027	305th AMW	bl/r	Airport, Mississippi ANG:	
50028	305th AMW	bl/r	183rd AS (bl/gd);	
50029	60th AMW		305th AMW, McGuire AFB,	
50030	305th AMW	bl/r	New Jersey (bl):	
50031	305th AMW	bl/r	6th AS;	
50032	305th AMW	bl/y	418th FLTS/412th TW, Edwards AFB,	
50033	305th AMW	bl	California [ED];	
50034	305th AMW	bl/r	436th AW, Dover AFB, Delaware:	
FY86			3rd AS (y/r);	
60027	305th AMW	bl	437th AW, Charleston AFB,	
60028	305th AMW	bl/r	South Carolina (y/bl):	
60029	60th AMW		14th AS, 15th AS,	
60030	305th AMW	bl/r	16th AS & 17th AS;	
60031	60th AMW		445th AW AFRC, Wright-	
60032	305th AMW		Patterson AFB, Ohio (r/w):	
60033	60th AMW		89th AS;	
60034	60th AMW		452nd AMW AFRC, March ARB,	
60035	305th AMW	bl	California (or/y):	
60036	305th AMW	bl	729th AS	
60037	60th AMW		**FY00**	
60038	60th AMW		00171 C-17A 3rd Wg	w/bk
FY87			00172 C-17A 97th AMW	r/y
70117	60th AMW		00174 C-17A 3rd Wg	w/bk
70118	60th AMW		00175 C-17A 62nd AW	gn
70119	60th AMW		00176 C-17A 62nd AW	gn
70120	305th AMW	bl	00177 C-17A 97th AMW	r/y
70121	305th AMW	bl	00178 C-17A 97th AMW	r/y
70122	305th AMW	bl/r	00179 C-17A 62nd AW	gn
70123	60th AMW		00180 C-17A 62nd AW	gn
70124	305th AMW	bl/y	00181 C-17A 62nd AW	gn
FY79			00182 C-17A 62nd AW	gn
90433	305th AMW	bl	00183 C-17A 62nd AW	gn
90434	305th AMW	bl/r	00184 C-17A 62nd AW	gn
91710	305th AMW	bl/r	00185 C-17A 62nd AW	gn
91711	305th AMW	bl	**FY10**	
91712	305th AMW	bl/r	00213 C-17A 437th AW	y/bl
91713	305th AMW	bl	00214 C-17A 437th AW	y/bl
91946	60th AMW		00215 C-17A 437th AW	y/bl
91947	305th AMW	bl	00216 C-17A	
91948	60th AMW		00217 C-17A	
91949	305th AMW	bl/r	00218 C-17A	
91950	60th AMW		00219 C-17A	
91951	60th AMW		00220 C-17A	
			00221 C-17A	
Bombardier			00222 C-17A	
E-11A Global Express			**FY90**	
653rd ELSG, Hanscom Field			00532 C-17A 62nd AW	gn
FY11			00533 C-17A 15th Wg	r/y
19001			00534 C-17A 437th AW	y/bl
19355			00535 C-17A 445th AW	r/w
19358			**FY01**	
			10186 C-17A 62nd AW	gn
Boeing			10187 C-17A 62nd AW	gn
C-17 Globemaster III			10188 C-17A 437th AW	y/bl
3rd Wg, Elmendorf AFB,			10189 C-17A 437th AW	y/bl
Alaska: 517th AS (w/bk);			10190 C-17A 437th AW	y/bl

C-17

Type			Notes	Type			Notes
10191	C-17A	437th AW	y/bl	FY95			
10192	C-17A	97th AMW	r/y	50102	C-17A	97th AMW	r/y
10193	C-17A	437th AW	y/bl	50103	C-17A	105th AW	bl
10194	C-17A	97th AMW	r/y$	50104	C-17A	437th AW	y/bl
10195	C-17A	437th AW	y/bl	50105	C-17A	105th AW	bl
10196	C-17A	437th AW	y/bl	50106	C-17A	62nd AW	gn
10197	C-17A	437th AW	y/bl	50107	C-17A	437th AW	y/bl
FY02				FY05			
21098	C-17A	437th AW	y/bl	55139	C-17A	452nd AMW	or/y
21099	C-17A	437th AW	y/bl	55140	C-17A	452nd AMW	or/y
21100	C-17A	437th AW	y/bl	55141	C-17A	452nd AMW	or/y
21101	C-17A	437th AW	y/bl	55142	C-17A	452nd AMW	or/y
21102	C-17A	62nd AW	gn	55143	C-17A	452nd AMW	or/y
21103	C-17A	62nd AW	gn	55144	C-17A	452nd AMW	or/y
21104	C-17A	62nd AW	gn	55145	C-17A	452nd AMW	or/y
21105	C-17A	62nd AW	gn	55146	C-17A	15th Wg	r/y
21106	C-17A	62nd AW	gn	55147	C-17A	15th Wg	r/y
21107	C-17A	62nd AW	gn	55148	C-17A	15th Wg	r/y
21108	C-17A	62nd AW	gn	55149	C-17A	15th Wg	r/y
21109	C-17A	62nd AW	gn	55150	C-17A	15th Wg	r/y
21110	C-17A	62nd AW	gn	55151	C-17A	15th Wg	r/y
21111	C-17A	62nd AW	gn	55152	C-17A	15th Wg	r/y
21112	C-17A	172nd AW	bl/gd	55153	C-17A	15th Wg	r/y
FY92				FY96			
23291	C-17A	62nd AW	gn	60001	C-17A	62nd AW	gn
23292	C-17A	437th AW	y/bl	60002	C-17A	437th AW	y/bl
23293	C-17A	437th AW	y/bl	60003	C-17A	62nd AW	gn
23294	C-17A	62nd AW	gn	60004	C-17A	437th AW	y/bl
FY93				60005	C-17A	437th AW	y/bl
30599	C-17A	97th AMW	r/y	60006	C-17A	437th AW	y/bl
30600	C-17A	62nd AW	gn	60007	C-17A	172nd AW	bl/gd
30601	C-17A	62nd AW	gn	60008	C-17A	97th AMW	r/y
30602	C-17A	437th AW	y/bl	FY06			
30603	C-17A	445th AW	r/w	66154	C-17A	60th AMW	bk/w
30604	C-17A	445th AW	r/w	66155	C-17A	60th AMW	bk/w
FY03				66156	C-17A	60th AMW	bk/w
33113	C-17A	172nd AW	bl/gd	66157	C-17A	60th AMW	bk/w
33114	C-17A	172nd AW	bl/gd	66158	C-17A	60th AMW	bk/w
33115	C-17A	172nd AW	bl/gd	66159	C-17A	60th AMW	bk/w
33116	C-17A	172nd AW	bl/gd	66160	C-17A	60th AMW	bk/w
33117	C-17A	172nd AW	bl/gd	66161	C-17A	60th AMW	bk/w
33118	C-17A	172nd AW	bl/gd	66162	C-17A	60th AMW	bk/w
33119	C-17A	172nd AW	bl/gd	66163	C-17A	60th AMW	bk/w
33120	C-17A	62nd AW	gn	66164	C-17A	60th AMW	bk/w
33121	C-17A	412th TW		66165	C-17A	436th AW	y/r
33122	C-17A	437th AW	y/bl	66166	C-17A	436th AW	y/r
33123	C-17A	437th AW	y/bl	66167	C-17A	436th AW	y/r
33124	C-17A	437th AW	y/bl	66168	C-17A	436th AW	y/r
33125	C-17A	305th AMW	bl	FY97			
33126	C-17A	305th AMW	bl	70041	C-17A	437th AW	y/bl
33127	C-17A	305th AMW	bl	70042	C-17A	62nd AW	gn
FY94				70043	C-17A	452nd AMW	or/y
40065	C-17A	97th AMW	r/y	70044	C-17A	445th AW	r/w
40066	C-17A	62nd AW	gn	70045	C-17A	105th AW	bl
40067	C-17A	437th AW	y/bl	70046	C-17A	97th AMW	r/y $
40068	C-17A	445th AW	r/w	70047	C-17A	437th AW	y/bl
40069	C-17A	437th AW	y/bl	70048	C-17A	437th AW	y/bl
40070	C-17A	437th AW	y/bl	FY07			
FY04				77169	C-17A	436th AW	y/r
44128	C-17A	305th AMW	bl	77170	C-17A	436th AW	y/r
44129	C-17A	305th AMW	bl	77171	C-17A	436th AW	y/r
44130	C-17A	305th AMW	bl	77172	C-17A	60th AMW	bk/w
44131	C-17A	305th AMW	bl	77173	C-17A	436th AW	y/r
44132	C-17A	305th AMW	bl	77174	C-17A	436th AW	y/r
44133	C-17A	305th AMW	bl	77175	C-17A	436th AW	y/r
44134	C-17A	305th AMW	bl	77176	C-17A	436th AW	y/r
44135	C-17A	305th AMW	bl	77177	C-17A	436th AW	y/r
44136	C-17A	305th AMW	bl	77178	C-17A	436th AW	y/r
44137	C-17A	305th AMW	bl	77179	C-17A	60th AMW	bk/w
44138	C-17A	452nd AMW	or/y	77180	C-17A	437th AW	y/bl

Type			Notes
77181	C-17A	437th AW	y/bl
77182	C-17A	437th AW	y/bl
77183	C-17A	437th AW	y/bl
77184	C-17A	437th AW	y/bl
77185	C-17A	437th AW	y/bl
77186	C-17A	437th AW	y/bl
77187	C-17A	437th AW	y/bl
77188	C-17A	437th AW	y/bl
77189	C-17A	437th AW	y/bl
FY98			
80049	C-17A	97th AMW	r/y
80050	C-17A	62nd AW	gn
80051	C-17A	3rd Wg	w/bk
80052	C-17A	62nd AW	gn
80053	C-17A	62nd AW	gn
80054	C-17A	437th AW	y/bl
80055	C-17A	97th AMW	r/y
80056	C-17A	3rd Wg	w/bk
80057	C-17A	97th AMW	r/y
FY88			
80265	C-17A	62nd AW	gn
80266	C-17A	437th AW	y/bl
FY08			
88190	C-17A	437th AW	y/bl
88191	C-17A	437th AW	y/bl
88192	C-17A	62nd AW	gn
88193	C-17A	62nd AW	gn
88194	C-17A	62nd AW	gn
88195	C-17A	62nd AW	gn
88196	C-17A	62nd AW	gn
88197	C-17A	62nd AW	gn
88198	C-17A	305th AMW	bl
88199	C-17A	305th AMW	bl
88200	C-17A	305th AMW	bl
88201	C-17A	62nd AW	gn
88202	C-17A	305th AMW	bl
88203	C-17A	62nd AW	gn
88204	C-17A	437th AW	y/bl
FY99			
90058	C-17A	97th AMW	r/y $
90059	C-17A	62nd AW	gn
90060	C-17A	445th AW	r/w
90061	C-17A	97th AMW	r/y
90062	C-17A	97th AMW	r/y
90063	C-17A	97th AMW	r/y
90064	C-17A	97th AMW	r/y
90165	C-17A	62nd AW	gn
90166	C-17A	97th AMW	r/y
90167	C-17A	3rd Wg	w/bk
90168	C-17A	3rd Wg	w/bk
90169	C-17A	97th AMW	r/y
90170	C-17A	3rd Wg	w/bk
FY89			
91189	C-17A	437th AW	y/bl
91190	C-17A	62nd AW	gn
91191	C-17A	105th AW	bl
91192	C-17A	437th AW	y/bl
FY09			
99205	C-17A	437th AW	y/bl
99206	C-17A	437th AW	y/bl
99207	C-17A	437th AW	y/bl
99208	C-17A	437th AW	y/bl
99209	C-17A	62nd AW	gn
99210	C-17A	62nd AW	gn
99211	C-17A	62nd AW	gn
99212	C-17A	62nd AW	gn

Grumman
C-20 Gulfstream III/IV
89th AW, Andrews AFB, Maryland:
  99th AS;
OSAC/PAT, US Army, Andrews AFB,
  Maryland;
Pacific Flight Detachment,
  Hickam AFB, Hawaii
C-20B Gulfstream III
FY86
  60201 89th AW
  60202 89th AW
  60203 89th AW
  60204 89th AW
  60206 89th AW
C-20C Gulfstream III
FY85
  50049 89th AW
  50050 89th AW
FY86
  60403 89th AW
C-20E Gulfstream III
FY87
  70139 Pacific Flt Det
C-20F Gulfstream IV
FY91
  10108 OSAC/PAT

Boeing VC-25A
Presidential Airlift Sqn/
  89th AW, Andrews AFB,
  Maryland
FY82
  28000
FY92
  29000

Aeritalia
C-27J Spartan
135th AS/175th Wg,
  Maryland ANG,
  Baltimore;
164th AS/179th AW,
  Ohio ANG,
  Mansfield;
L3 CIS, Warner-Robins,
  Georgia
FY07
  27010 L3 CIS
  27011 179th AW
FY08
  27012 179th AW
  27013 179th AW
  27014 179th AW
  27015 179th AW
  27016 175th Wg
FY09
  27017 175th Wg
  27018 L3 CIS
  27019 L3 CIS
  27020 L3 CIS

Pilatus U-28
1st SOW, Hurlburt Field,
  Florida:
  34th SOS & 319th SOS;
318th SOS/27th SOW, Cannon AFB,
  New Mexico

Type	Notes	Type	Notes

U-28A

FY01
10415	318th SOS

FY05
50409	1st SOW
50419	1st SOW
50424	1st SOW
50447	1st SOW
50482	1st SOW
50556	1st SOW
50573	1st SOW
50597	318th SOS

FY07
70488	1st SOW

U-28B

FY04
40688	
60692	

FY06
60692	

FY07
70691	1st SOW
70711	
70712	1st SOW
70736	
70777	318th SOS
70790	1st SOW
70809	318th SOS
70821	
70829	1st SOW
70838	1st SOW
70840	

FY08
80790	1st SOW
80809	1st SOW
80822	
80835	

Boeing C-32

1st AS/89th AW, Andrews AFB, Maryland;
150th SOS/108th Wg, McGuire AFB,
New Jersey

FY00
09001	C-32B	150th SOS

FY02
24452	C-32B	150th SOS
25001	C-32B	150th SOS

FY98
80001	C-32A	89th AW
80002	C-32A	89th AW

FY99
90003	C-32A	89th AW
90004	C-32A	89th AW

FY09
90015	C-32A	89th AW
90016	C-32A	89th AW

FY99
96143	C-32B	150th SOS

**Gulfstream Aerospace
C-37 Gulfstream V**

6th AMW, MacDill AFB, Florida:
  310th AS;
15th Wg, Hickam AFB, Hawaii:
  65th AS;
89th AW, Andrews AFB, Maryland:
  99th AS;
OSAC/PAT, US Army, Andrews AFB,
  Maryland

C-37A Gulfstream V

FY01
10028	6th AMW
10029	6th AMW
10030	6th AMW
10065	15th Wg

FY02
21863	OSAC/PAT

FY04
41778	OSAC/PAT

FY97
71944	OSAC/PAT
70400	89th AW
70401	89th AW

FY99
90404	89th AW

C-37B Gulfstream V

FY06
60500	89th AW

FY09
90525	89th AW

FY11
10550	89th AW

IAI C-38A Astra

201st AS/113th FW, DC ANG,
  Andrews AFB, Maryland

FY94
41569	
41570	

Boeing C-40

15th Wg, Hickam AFB, Hawaii:
  65th AS;
86th AW, Ramstein,
  Germany:
  76th AS;
89th AW, Andrews AFB, Maryland:
  1st AS;
201st AS/113th FW, DC ANG,
  Andrews AFB, Maryland;
73rd AS/932nd AW AFRC, Scott AFB,
  Illinois

FY01
10015	C-40B	15th Wg
10040	C-40B	89th AW
10041	C-40B	89th AW

FY02
20042	C-40B	86th AW
20201	C-40C	201st AS
20202	C-40C	201st AS
20203	C-40C	201st AS
20204	C-40C	201st AS

FY05
50730	C-40C	932nd AW
50932	C-40C	932nd AW
54613	C-40C	932nd AW

FY09
90540	C-40C	932nd AW

Boeing B-52H Stratofortress

2nd BW, Barksdale AFB,
  Louisiana [LA]:
  11th BS (*gd*), 20th BS (*bl*)
  & 96th BS (*r*);
5th BW, Minot AFB,
  North Dakota [MT]:
  23rd BS (*r/y*) & 69th BS (*bk/y*);
49th TES/53rd TEG,
  Barksdale AFB,

Type		Notes	Type		Notes
Louisiana [OT];			10016	2nd BW	bl
93rd BS/307th BW AFRC,			10017	93rd BS	y/bl
Barksdale AFB,			10018	2nd BW	
Louisiana [BD] (y/bl);			10019	2nd BW	gd
419th FLTS/412th TW Edwards AFB,			10020	2nd BW	bl$
California [ED]			10021	93rd BS	y/bl
FY60			10028	2nd BW	bl
00001	2nd BW	r	10029	93rd BS	y/bl
00002	2nd BW	gd	10031	93rd BS	y/bl
00003	93rd BS	y/bl	10032	93rd BS	y/bl
00004	5th BW	r/y	10034	5th BW	r/y
00005	5th BW	r/y	10035	5th BW	r/y
00007	5th BW	r/y	10036	2nd BW	bl
00008	2nd BW	m $	10038	93rd BS	y/bl
00009	5th BW	bk/y	10039	5th BW	bk/y
00011	2nd BW	gd	10040	5th BW	r/y
00012	5th BW				
00013	2nd BW	bl	**Lockheed C-130 Hercules**		
00015	93rd BS	y/bl	1st SOS/353rd SOG, Kadena AB,		
00016	2nd BW	bl	Japan;		
00017	2nd BW	gd	4th SOS/1st SOW, Hurlburt Field,		
00018	5th BW	r/y	Florida;		
00021	2nd BW	r	6th SOS/1st SOW, Hurlburt Field,		
00022	2nd BW	r	Florida;		
00023	5th BW	r/y	7th SOS/352nd SOG,		
00024	2nd BW	bl	RAF Mildenhall, UK;		
00025	2nd BW	bl	8th SOS/1st SOW, Duke Field,		
00026	5th BW	r/y	Florida;		
00028	2nd BW	r	9th SOS/1st OG, Eglin AFB, Florida;		
00029	5th BW	r/y	15th SOS/1st SOW, Hurlburt Field,		
00031	53rd TEG		Florida;		
00032	2nd BW	r	16th SOS/27th SOW, Cannon AFB,		
00033	5th BW	r/y	New Mexico;		
00035	93rd BS	y/bl	17th SOS/353rd SOG, Kadena AB,		
00036	412th TW		Japan;		
00037	5th BW	r/y	19th AW Little Rock AFB,		
00038	2nd BW	r	Arkansas [LK]:		
00041	93rd BS	y/bl	41st AS (w), 50th AS (r),		
00042	93rd BS	y/bl	53rd AS (bk) & 61st AS (gn);		
00044	5th BW	bk/y	37th AS/86th AW, Ramstein AB,		
00045	93rd BS	y/bl	Germany [RS] (bl/w);		
00047	2nd BW		39th RQS/920th RQW AFRC,		
00048	2nd BW	bl	Patrick AFB, Florida [FL];		
00049	53rd TEG		40th FTS/46th TW, Eglin AFB, Florida;		
00050	412th TW		41st RQS/347th Wg, Moody AFB,		
00051	93rd BS	y/bl	Georgia [FT];		
00052	2nd BW	r	53rd WRS/403rd AW AFRC,		
00054	2nd BW	gd	Keesler AFB, Missouri;		
00055	5th BW	r/y	55th ECG, Davis-Monthan AFB,		
00056	5th BW	r/y	Arizona [DM]:		
00057	2nd BW	gd	41st ECS (bl) & 43rd ECS (r);		
00058	2nd BW	bl	58th SOW, Kirtland AFB,		
00059	2nd BW	r	New Mexico:		
00060	5th BW	bk/y	415th SOS & 550th SOS;		
00061	93rd BS	y/bl	67th SOS/352nd SOG,		
00062	2nd BW	bl	RAF Mildenhall, UK;		
FY61			71st RQS/347th Wg, Moody AFB,		
10001	5th BW	bk/y	Georgia [FT] (bl);		
10002	2nd BW	r $	73rd SOS/27th SOW, Cannon AFB,		
10003	2nd BW	bl	New Mexico;		
10004	2nd BW	bl	79th RQS/563rd RQG,		
10005	5th BW	r/y	Davis-Monthan AFB, Arizona [DM];		
10006	2nd BW	r	95th AS/440th AW AFRC,		
10008	93rd BS	y/bl	Pope AFB,		
10010	2nd BW	bl	North Carolina (w/r);		
10011	93rd BS	y/bl	96th AS/934th AW AFRC,		
10012	2nd BW	r	Minneapolis/St Paul,		
10013	2nd BW	bl	Minnesota (pr);		
10014	5th BW	bk/y	102nd RQS/106th RQW,		
10015	2nd BW	r	Suffolk Field, New York ANG [LI];		

Type	Notes
105th AS/118th AW, Nashville, Tennessee ANG (r);	
109th AS/133rd AW, Minneapolis/St Paul, Minnesota ANG [MN] (pr/bk);	
115th AS/146th AW, Channel Island ANGS, California ANG [CI] (gn);	
122nd FS/159th FW, NAS New Orleans, Louisiana ANG [JZ];	
130th AS/130th AW, Yeager Int'l Airport, Charleston West Virginia ANG [WV] (pr/y);	
130th RQS/129th RQW, Moffet Field, California ANG [CA] (bl);	
136th AS/107th AW, Niagara Falls, New York ANG;	
139th AS/109th AW, Schenectady, New York ANG [NY];	
142nd AS/166th AW, New Castle County Airport, Delaware ANG [DE] (bl);	
143rd AS/143rd AW, Quonset, Rhode Island ANG [RI] (r);	
144th AS/176th CW, Elmendorf AFB, Alaska ANG (bk/y);	
154th TS/189th AW, Little Rock, Arkansas ANG (r);	
156th AS/145th AW, Charlotte, North Carolina ANG [NC] (bl);	
157th FS/169th FW, McEntire ANGS, South Carolina ANG [SC];	
158th AS/165th AW, Savannah, Georgia ANG (r);	
159th FS/125th FW, Jacksonville, Florida ANG;	
164th AS/179th AW, Mansfield, Ohio ANG [OH] (bl);	
165th AS/123rd AW, Standiford Field, Kentucky ANG [KY];	
167th AS/167th AW, Martinsburg, West Virginia ANG [WV] (r);	
169th AS/182nd AW, Peoria, Illinois ANG [IL] (or);	
180th AS/139th AW, Rosencrans Memorial Airport, Missouri ANG [XP] (y);	
181st AS/136th AW, NAS Dallas, Texas ANG (bl/w);	
187th AS/153rd AW, Cheyenne, Wyoming ANG [WY] (y/bk);	
192nd AS/152nd AW, Reno, Nevada ANG [NV] (bl/y);	
193rd SOS/193rd SOW, Harrisburg, Pennsylvania ANG [PA];	
198th AS/156th AW, San Juan, Puerto Rico ANG;	
204th AS/15th Wg, Hickam AFB, Hawaii ANG [HH];	
210th RQS/176th CW, Elmendorf AFB, Alaska ANG [AK];	
314th AW, Little Rock AFB, Arkansas: 48th AS (y) & 62nd AS (bl);	
317th AG, Dyess AFB, Texas: 39th AS (r) & 40th AS (bl);	
327th AS/913th AW AFRC, NAS Willow Grove, Pennsylvania (bk);	
328th AS/914th AW AFRC,	

Type	Notes
Niagara Falls, New York [NF] (bl);	
357th AS/908th AW AFRC, Maxwell AFB, Alabama (bl);	
374th AW, Yokota AB, Japan [YJ]: 36th AS (r);	
412th TW Edwards AFB, California: 452nd FLTS [ED];	
522nd SOS/27th SOW, Cannon AFB, New Mexico;	
645th Materiel Sqn, Palmdale, California [D4];	
700th AS/94th AW AFRC, Dobbins ARB, Georgia [DB] (bl);	
711th SOS/919th SOW AFRC, Duke Field, Florida;	
731st AS/302nd AW AFRC, Peterson AFB, Colorado (pr/w);	
757th AS/910th AW AFRC, Youngstown ARS, Ohio [YO] (bl);	
758th AS/911th AW AFRC, Pittsburgh ARS, Pennsylvania (bk/y);	
773rd AS/910th AW AFRC, Youngstown ARS, Ohio [YO] (r);	
815th AS/403rd AW AFRC, Keesler AFB, Missouri [KT] (r);	
LMTAS, Marietta, Georgia	

Type			Notes
FY90			
00162	MC-130H	15th SOS	
00163	AC-130U	4th SOS	
00164	AC-130U	4th SOS	
00165	AC-130U	4th SOS	
00166	AC-130U	4th SOS	
00167	AC-130U	4th SOS	
FY80			
00320	C-130H	158th AS	r
00321	C-130H	158th AS	r
00322	C-130H	158th AS	r
00323	C-130H	158th AS	r
00324	C-130H	158th AS	r
00325	C-130H	158th AS	r
00326	C-130H	158th AS	r
00332	C-130H	158th AS	r
FY90			
01057	C-130H	142nd AS	bl
01058	MC-130W	73rd SOS	
FY90			
01791	C-130H	180th AS	y
01792	C-130H	180th AS	y
01793	C-130H	180th AS	y
01794	C-130H	180th AS	y
01795	C-130H	180th AS	y
01796	C-130H	180th AS	y
01797	C-130H	180th AS	y
01798	C-130H	180th AS	y
FY00			
01934	EC-130J	193rd SOS	
FY90			
02103	HC-130N	210th RQS	
09107	C-130H	757th AS	bl
09108	C-130H	757th AS	bl

Type			Notes	Type			Notes
FY81				21095	LC-130H	139th AS	
10626	C-130H	700th AS	bl	**FY02**			
10627	C-130H	700th AS	bl	21434	C-130J	143rd AS	r
10628	C-130H	700th AS	bl	**FY92**			
10629	C-130H	700th AS	bl	21451	C-130H	169th AS	or
10630	C-130H	700th AS	bl	21452	C-130H	169th AS	or
10631	C-130H	700th AS	bl	21453	C-130H	156th AS	bl
FY91				21454	C-130H	156th AS	bl
11231	C-130H	165th AS		**FY02**			
11232	C-130H	165th AS		21463	C-130J	115th AS	gn
11233	C-130H	165th AS		21464	C-130J	115th AS	gn
11234	C-130H	165th AS		**FY92**			
11235	C-130H	165th AS		21531	C-130H	187th AS	y/bk
11236	C-130H	165th AS		21532	C-130H	187th AS	y/bk
11237	C-130H	165th AS		21533	C-130H	187th AS	y/bk
11238	C-130H	165th AS		21534	C-130H	187th AS	y/bk
11239	C-130H	165th AS		21535	C-130H	187th AS	y/bk
FY01				21536	C-130H	187th AS	y/bk
11461	C-130J	115th AS	gn	21537	C-130H	187th AS	y/bk
11462	C-130J	115th AS	gn	21538	C-130H	187th AS	y/bk
FY91				**FY62**			
11651	C-130H	180th AS	y	21792	C-130E		
11652	C-130H	180th AS	y	21820	C-130E	198th AS	
11653	C-130H	187th AS	y/bk	21842	C-130E	198th AS	
FY01				21843	MC-130E	711th SOS	
11935	EC-130J	193rd SOS		21857	C-130E	6th SOS	
FY61				21858	C-130E	198th AS	
12358	C-130E			21863	HC-130P	71st RQS	bl
FY64				**FY92**			
14852	HC-130P	71st RQS	bl	23021	C-130H	773rd AS	r
14853	HC-130P	79th RQS		23022	C-130H	773rd AS	r
14854	MC-130P	67th SOS		23023	C-130H	773rd AS	r
14855	HC-130P	39th RQS		23024	C-130H	757th AS	bl
14858	MC-130P	58th SOW		23281	C-130H	96th AS	pr
14859	EC-130H	55th ECG		23282	C-130H	96th AS	pr
14860	HC-130P	79th RQS		23283	C-130H	96th AS	pr
14861	C-130H	105th AS r		23284	C-130H	96th AS	pr
14862	EC-130H	55th ECG		23286	C-130H	96th AS	pr
14863	HC-130P	71st RQS	bl	23287	C-130H	96th AS	pr
14864	HC-130P	39th RQS		23288	C-130H	96th AS	pr
14865	HC-130P	79th RQS		**FY02**			
14866	C-130H	159th FS		28155	C-130J	815th AS r	
FY91				**FY83**			
19141	C-130H	328th AS	bl	30486	C-130H	139th AS	
19142	C-130H	96th AS	pr	30487	C-130H	139th AS	
19143	C-130H	328th AS	bl	30488	C-130H	139th AS	
19144	C-130H	328th AS	bl	30489	C-130H	139th AS	
FY82				30490	LC-130H	139th AS	
20054	C-130H	144th AS	bk/y	30491	LC-130H	139th AS	
20055	C-130H	19th AW		30492	LC-130H	139th AS	
20056	C-130H	105th AS	r	30493	LC-130H	139th AS	
20057	C-130H	144th AS	bk/y	**FY93**			
20058	C-130H	144th AS	bk/y	31036	C-130H	19th AW	r
20059	C-130H	144th AS	bk/y	31037	C-130H	19th AW	r
20060	C-130H	144th AS	bk/y	31038	C-130H	19th AW	r
20061	C-130H	144th AS	bk/y	31039	C-130H	19th AW	r
FY92				31040	C-130H	19th AW	r
20253	AC-130U	4th SOS		31041	C-130H	19th AW	r
FY02				31096	LC-130H	139th AS	
20314	C-130J	314th AW	y $	**FY83**			
FY92				31212	MC-130H	1st SOS	
20547	C-130H	19th AW	r	**FY93**			
20548	C-130H	19th AW	r	31455	C-130H	156th AS	bl
20549	C-130H	19th AW	r	31456	C-130H	156th AS	bl
20550	C-130H	19th AW	r	31457	C-130H	156th AS	bl
20551	C-130H	19th AW	r	31458	C-130H	156th AS	bl
20552	C-130H	19th AW	r	31459	C-130H	156th AS	bl
20553	C-130H	19th AW	r	31561	C-130H	156th AS	bl
20554	C-130H	19th AW	r	31562	C-130H	156th AS	bl
21094	LC-130H	139th AS		31563	C-130H	156th AS	bl

C-130

Type			Notes		Type			Notes
FY73					41664	C-130H	19th AW	bk
31580	EC-130H	55th ECG	r		41665	C-130H	317th AG	bl
31581	EC-130H	55th ECG	$		41666	C-130H	317th AG	bl
31582	C-130H	317th AG	r		41667	C-130H	317th AG	r
31583	EC-130H	55th ECG	r		41668	C-130H	374th AW	r $
31584	EC-130H	55th ECG			41669	C-130H	317th AG	r
31585	EC-130H	55th ECG	bl		41670	C-130H	317th AG	
31586	EC-130H	55th ECG	bl		41671	C-130H	317th AG	bl
31587	EC-130H	55th ECG			41673	C-130H	317th AG	
31588	EC-130H	55th ECG			41674	C-130H	317th AG	
31590	EC-130H	55th ECG			41675	C-130H	317th AG	bl
31592	EC-130H	55th ECG	bl		41676	C-130H	317th AG	
31594	EC-130H	55th ECG	bl		41677	C-130H	317th AG	
31595	EC-130H	55th ECG			41679	C-130H	317th AG	bl
31597	C-130H	317th AG	r		41680	C-130H	19th AW	r
31598	C-130H	317th AG	r		41682	C-130H	317th AG	r
FY93					41684	C-130H	374th AW	r
32041	C-130H	169th AS	or		41685	C-130H	374th AW	r
32042	C-130H	169th AS	or		41687	C-130H	317th AW	r
32104	HC-130N	210th RQS			41688	C-130H	317th AG	bl
32105	HC-130N	210th RQS			41689	C-130H	19th AW	r
32106	HC-130N	210th RQS			41690	C-130H	374th AW	r
FY73					41691	C-130H	317th AG	
33300	LC-130H	139th AS			41692	C-130H	374th AW	r
FY93					42061	C-130H	317th AG	r
37311	C-130H	187th AS	y/bk		42062	C-130H	374th AW	r $
37312	C-130H	169th AS	or		42063	C-130H	317th AG	bl
37313	C-130H	187th AS	y/bk		42065	C-130H	374th AW	r
37314	C-130H	187th AS	y/bk		42066	C-130H		
FY63					42067	C-130H	374th AW	r
37786	C-130E	374th AW	bl		42069	C-130H	317th AG	bl
37815	C-130E	6th SOS			42070	C-130H	374th AW	r
37816	C-130E	6th SOS			42071	C-130H	374th AW	r
37828	EC-130E	193rd SOS			42072	C-130H	317th AG	bl
37831	C-130E				42130	C-130H	317th AG	r
37851	C-130E	198th AS			42131	C-130H	374th AW	r
FY03					42132	C-130H	317th AG	r
38154	C-130J	815th AS	r		42133	C-130H		
FY63					42134	C-130H	317th AG	r
39810	C-130E	71st RQS	bl		*FY04*			
39815	C-130E				43142	C-130J	314th AW	y
FY84					43143	C-130J	19th AW	w
40204	C-130H	700th AS	bl		43144	C-130J	314th AW	y
40205	C-130H	700th AS	bl		*FY94*			
40206	C-130H	142nd AS	bl		46701	C-130H	169th AS	or
40207	C-130H	142nd AS	bl		46702	C-130H	167th AS	r
40208	C-130H	142nd AS	bl		46703	C-130H	169th AS	or
40209	C-130H	142nd AS	bl		46704	C-130H		
40210	C-130H	142nd AS	bl		46705	C-130H	167th AS	r
40212	C-130H	142nd AS	bl		46706	C-130H	167th AS	r
40213	C-130H	142nd AS	bl		46707	C-130H	130th AS	pr/y
40476	MC-130H	1st SOS			46708	C-130H	130th AS	pr/y
FY64					47310	C-130H	731st AS	pr/w
40510	C-130E	198th AS			47315	C-130H	731st AS	pr/w
40515	C-130E	198th AS			47316	C-130H	731st AS	pr/w
40523	MC-130E	711th SOS			47317	C-130H	731st AS	pr/w
40544	C-130E	198th AS			47318	C-130H	731st AS	pr/w
40551	MC-130E	711th SOS			47319	C-130H	731st AS	pr/w
40561	MC-130E	711th SOS			47320	C-130H	731st AS	pr/w
40562	MC-130E	711th SOS			47321	C-130H	731st AS	pr/w
40565	MC-130E	711th SOS			*FY94*			
40566	MC-130E	711th SOS			48151	C-130J	19th AW	w
40568	MC-130E	711th SOS			48152	C-130J	19th AW	w
40571	MC-130E	711th SOS			*FY04*			
FY74					48153	C-130J	815th AS	r
41658	C-130H	374th AW	r		*FY85*			
41659	C-130H	374th AW	r		50011	MC-130H	15th SOS	
41660	C-130H	374th AW	r		50035	C-130H	357th AS	bl
41661	C-130H	317th AG			50036	C-130H	357th AS	bl
41663	C-130H	317th AG			50037	C-130H	357th AS	bl

Type			Notes	Type			Notes
50038	C-130H	357th AS	bl	60220	MC-130P	67th SOS	
50039	C-130H	357th AS	bl	60221	HC-130P	58th SOW	
50040	C-130H	357th AS	bl	60222	HC-130P	102nd RQS	
50041	C-130H	773rd AS	r	60223	MC-130P	9th SOS	
50042	C-130H	357th AS	bl	60225	MC-130P	9th SOS	
FY65				*FY86*			
50962	TC-130H	55th ECG		60410	C-130H	95th AS	w/r
50963	C-130H	105th AS	r	60411	C-130H	95th AS	w/r
50964	HC-130P	79th RQS		60413	C-130H	357th AS	bl
50966	C-130H	105th AS	r	60414	C-130H	95th AS	w/r
50967	HC-130P	122nd FS		60415	C-130H	95th AS	w/r
50968	C-130H	105th AS	r	60418	C-130H	95th AS	w/r
50970	HC-130P	39th RQS		60419	C-130H	95th AS	w/r
50971	MC-130P	58th SOW		*FY96*			
50973	HC-130P	71st RQS	bl	61003	C-130H	109th AS	pr/bk
50974	HC-130P	102nd RQS		61004	C-130H	109th AS	pr/bk
50975	MC-130P	58th SOW		61005	C-130H	109th AS	pr/bk
50976	HC-130P	39th RQS		61006	C-130H	109th AS	pr/bk
50977	HC-130H	39th RQS		61007	C-130H	109th AS	pr/bk
50978	HC-130P	102nd RQS		61008	C-130H	109th AS	pr/bk
50980	C-130H	105th AS	r	*FY86*			
50981	HC-130P	71st RQS	bl	61391	C-130H	154th TS	r
50982	HC-130P	71st RQS	bl	61392	C-130H	154th TS	r
50983	MC-130P	71st RQS	bl	61393	C-130H	154th TS	r
50984	C-130H	105th AS	r	61394	C-130H	154th TS	r
50985	C-130H	122nd FS		61395	C-130H	154th TS	r
50986	HC-130P	71st RQS	bl	61396	C-130H	154th TS	r
50987	HC-130P	71st RQS	bl	61397	C-130H	154th TS	r
50988	HC-130P	71st RQS	bl	61398	C-130H	154th TS	r
50989	EC-130H	55th ECG	r	*FY06*			
50991	MC-130P	67th SOS		61437	C-130J	143rd AS	r
50992	MC-130P	67th SOS		61438	C-130J	143rd AS	r
50993	MC-130P	9th SOS		61467	C-130J	115th AS	gn
50994	MC-130P	9th SOS		*FY86*			
FY95				61699	MC-130H	58th SOW	
51001	C-130H	109th AS	pr/bk	*FY06*			
51002	C-130H	109th AS	pr/bk	63171	C-130J	317th AG	
FY85				*FY76*			
51361	C-130H	181st AS	bl/w	63301	LC-130H	139th AS	
51362	C-130H	181st AS	bl/w	63302	LC-130H	139th AS	
51363	C-130H	181st AS	bl/w	*FY06*			
51364	C-130H	181st AS	bl/w	64631	C-130J	19th AW	w
51365	C-130H	181st AS	bl/w	64632	C-130J	19th AW	w
51366	C-130H	181st AS	bl/w	64633	C-130J	19th AW	w
51367	C-130H	181st AS	bl/w	64634	C-130J	19th AW	w
51368	C-130H	181st AS	bl/w	*FY96*			
FY05				65300	WC-130J	53rd WRS	
51435	C-130J	143rd AS	r	65301	WC-130J	53rd WRS	
51436	C-130J	143rd AS	r	65302	WC-130J	53rd WRS	
51465	C-130J	115th AS	gn	67322	C-130H	731st AS	pr/w
51466	C-130J	115th AS	gn	67323	C-130H	731st AS	pr/w
53145	C-130J	19th AW	w	67324	C-130H	731st AS	pr/w
53146	C-130J	314th AW	y	67325	C-130H	731st AS	pr/w
53147	C-130J	314th AW	y	68153	EC-130J	193rd SOS	
FY95				68154	EC-130J	193rd SOS	
56709	C-130H	156th AS	bl	*FY06*			
56710	C-130H	130th AS	pr/y	68159	C-130J	815th AS	r
56711	C-130H	156th AS	bl	68610	C-130J	37th AS	bl/w
56712	C-130H	156th AS	bl	68611	C-130J	37th AS	bl/w
FY05				68612	C-130J	37th AS	bl/w
58152	C-130J	815th AS	r	*FY87*			
58156	C-130J	815th AS	r	70023	MC-130H	7th SOS	
58157	C-130J	815th AS	r	70024	MC-130H	7th SOS	
58158	C-130J	815th AS	r	70125	MC-130H	15th SOS	
FY66				70126	MC-130H	1st SOS	
60212	HC-130P	130th RQS	bl	70128	AC-130U	4th SOS	
60215	MC-130P	67th SOS		*FY97*			
60216	HC-130P	130th RQS	bl	71351	C-130J	314th AW	y
60217	MC-130P	9th SOS		71352	C-130J	314th AW	y
60219	HC-130P	130th RQS	bl	71353	C-130J	314th AW	y

Type			Notes	Type			Notes
71354	C-130J	314th AW	y	82102	HC-130N	102nd RQS	
FY07				FY08			
71468	C-130J	115th AS	gn	83172	C-130J	317th AG	
FY97				83173	C-130J	317th AG	
71931	EC-130J	193rd SOS		83174	C-130J	317th AG	
FY07				83175	C-130J	317th AG	
73170	C-130J	317th AG		83176	C-130J	317th AG	
74635	C-130J	19th AW	w	83177	C-130J	317th AG	
74636	C-130J	19th AW	w	83178	C-130J	317th AG	
74637	C-130J	19th AW	w	83179	C-130J	317th AG	
74638	C-130J	19th AW	w	FY88			
74639	C-130J	19th AW	w	84401	C-130H	95th AS	w/r
FY97				84402	C-130H	95th AS	w/r
75303	WC-130J	53rd WRS		84403	C-130H	95th AS	w/r
75304	WC-130J	53rd WRS		84404	C-130H	95th AS	w/r
75305	WC-130J	53rd WRS		84405	C-130H	95th AS	w/r
75306	WC-130J	53rd WRS		84406	C-130H	95th AS	w/r
FY07				84407	C-130H	95th AS	w/r
76310	C-130J	19th AW		FY98			
76311	C-130J	19th AW	w	85307	WC-130J	53rd WRS	
76312	C-130J	19th AW	w	85308	WC-130J	53rd WRS	
78608	C-130J	37th AS	bl/w	FY08			
78609	C-130J	37th AS	bl/w	85675	C-130J	317th AG	
78613	C-130J	37th AS	bl/w	85679	C-130J	317th AG	
78614	C-130J	37th AS	bl/w	85683	C-130J	317th AG	
FY87				85684	C-130J	317th AG	
79281	C-130H	328th AS	bl	85685	C-130J	317th AG	
79282	C-130H	95th AS	w/r	85686	C-130J	317th AG	
79283	C-130H	96th AS	pr	86201	MC-130J		
79284	MC-130W	73rd SOS		86202	MC-130J		
79285	C-130H	328th AS	bl	86203	MC-130J		
79286	MC-130W	73rd SOS		88601	C-130J	37th AS	bl/w $
79287	C-130H	96th AS	pr	88602	C-130J	37th AS	bl/w $
79288	MC-130W	73rd SOS		88603	C-130J	37th AS	bl/w $
FY88				88604	C-130J	37th AS	bl/w
80191	MC-130H	1st SOS		88605	C-130J	37th AS	bl/w
80192	MC-130H	15th SOS		88606	C-130J	37th AS	bl/w
80193	MC-130H	16th SOS		88607	C-130J	37th AS	bl/w
80194	MC-130H	58th SOW		FY09			
80195	MC-130H	7th SOS		90108	HC-130J	79th RQS	
80264	MC-130H	1st SOS		90109	HC-130J	58th SOW	
FY78				FY89			
80806	C-130H	758th AS	bk/y	90280	MC-130J	1st SOS	
80807	C-130H	758th AS	bk/y	90281	MC-130H	15th SOS	
80808	C-130H	758th AS	bk/y	90282	MC-130H	58th SOW	
80809	C-130H	758th AS	bk/y	90283	MC-130H	15th SOS	
80810	C-130H	758th AS	bk/y	FY79			
80811	C-130H	758th AS	bk/y	90473	C-130H	192nd AS	bl/y
80812	C-130H	758th AS	bk/y	90474	C-130H	192nd AS	bl/y
80813	C-130H	758th AS	bk/y	90475	C-130H	192nd AS	bl/y
FY88				90476	C-130H	192nd AS	bl/y
81301	MC-130W	73rd SOS		90477	C-130H	192nd AS	bl/y
81302	MC-130W	73rd SOS		90478	C-130H	192nd AS	bl/y
81303	MC-130W	73rd SOS		90479	C-130H	192nd AS	bl/y
81304	MC-130W	73rd SOS		90480	C-130H	192nd AS	bl/y
81305	MC-130W	73rd SOS		FY89			
81306	MC-130W	73rd SOS		90509	AC-130U	4th SOS	
81307	MC-130W	73rd SOS		90510	AC-130U	4th SOS	
81308	MC-130W	73rd SOS		90511	AC-130U	4th SOS	
FY98				90512	AC-130U	4th SOS	
81355	C-130J	19th AW	w	90513	AC-130U	4th SOS	
81356	C-130J	19th AW	w	90514	AC-130U	4th SOS	
81357	C-130J			91051	MC-130W	73rd SOS	
81358	C-130J			91052	AC-130U	4th SOS	
FY88				91053	AC-130U	4th SOS	
81803	MC-130H	7th SOS		91054	AC-130U	4th SOS	
FY98				91055	C-130H	328th AS	bl
81932	EC-130J	193rd SOS		91056	AC-130U	4th SOS	
FY88				91181	C-130H	105th AS	r
82101	HC-130N	102nd RQS		91182	C-130H	105th AS	r

Type			Notes
91183	C-130H	105th AS	r
91184	C-130H	105th AS	r
91185	C-130H	105th AS	r
91186	C-130H	328th AS	bl
91187	C-130H	328th AS	bl
91188	C-130H	328th AS	bl
FY99			
91431	C-130J	143rd AS	r
91432	C-130J	143rd AS	r
91433	C-130J	143rd AS	r
91933	EC-130J	193rd SOS	
95309	WC-130J	53rd WRS	
FY69			
95819	MC-130P	9th SOS	
95820	MC-130P	9th SOS	
95821	MC-130P	58th SOW	
95822	MC-130P	58th SOW	
95823	MC-130P	9th SOS	
95824	HC-130N	39th RQS	
95825	MC-130P	17th SOS	
95826	MC-130P	17th SOS	
95827	MC-130P	9th SOS	
95828	MC-130P	17th SOS	
95829	HC-130N	58th SOW	
95830	HC-130N	39th RQS	
95831	MC-130P	17th SOS	
95832	MC-130P	17th SOS	
95833	HC-130N	58th SOW	
FY09			
96207	MC-130J	522nd SOS	
96208	MC-130J	522nd SOS	
96209	MC-130J	58th SOW	
96210	MC-130J	522nd SOS	
FY69			
96568	AC-130H	16th SOS	
96569	AC-130H	16th SOS	
96570	AC-130H	16th SOS	
96572	AC-130H	16th SOS	
96573	AC-130H	16th SOS	
96574	AC-130H	16th SOS	
96575	AC-130H	16th SOS	
96577	AC-130H	16th SOS	
FY89			
99101	C-130H	357th AS	bl
99102	C-130H	757th AS	bl
99103	C-130H	757th AS	bl
99104	C-130H	757th AS	bl
99105	C-130H	757th AS	bl
99106	C-130H	757th AS	bl

Boeing C-135
6th AMW, MacDill AFB, Florida:
 91st ARS (y/bl);
15th Wg, Hickam AFB, Hawaii:
 65th AS;
18th Wg, Kadena AB,
 Japan [ZZ]:
 909th ARS (or/bk);
22nd ARW, McConnell AFB, Kansas:
 344th ARS (y/bk), 349th ARS (y/bl)
 350th ARS (y/r) & 384th ARS (y/pr);
55th Wg, Offutt AFB, Nebraska [OF]:
 38th RS (gn), 45th RS (bk)
 & 343rd RS;
88th ABW, Wright-Patterson AFB, Ohio;
92nd ARW, Fairchild AFB,
 Washington:
 92nd ARS (bk), 93rd ARS (bl),
 & 97th ARS (y);

97th AMW, Altus AFB, Oklahoma:
 54th ARS (y/r);
100th ARW, RAF Mildenhall,
 UK [D]:
 351st ARS (r/w/bl);
106th ARS/117th ARW, Birmingham,
 Alabama ANG (w/r);
108th ARS/126th ARW,
 Scott AFB, Illinois ANG (w/bl);
117th ARS/190th ARW, Forbes Field,
 Kansas ANG (bl/y);
121st ARW, Rickenbacker ANGB,
 Ohio ANG:
 145th ARS & 166th ARS (bl);
126th ARS/128th ARW, Mitchell
 Field, Wisconsin ANG (w/bl);
132nd ARS/101st ARW, Bangor,
 Maine ANG (w/gn);
133rd ARS/157th ARW, Pease ANGB,
 New Hampshire ANG (bl);
141st ARS/108th Wg, McGuire AFB,
 New Jersey ANG (r);
151st ARS/134th ARW, Knoxville,
 Tennessee ANG (w/or);
168th ARS/168th ARW, Eielson AFB,
 Alaska ANG [AK] (bl/y);
171st ARS/127th Wg, Selfridge ANGB,
 Michigan ANG;
171st ARW, Greater Pittsburgh,
 Pennsylvania ANG:
 146th ARS (y/bk) &
 147th ARS (bk/y);
173rd ARS/155th ARW, Lincoln,
 Nebraska ANG (r/w);
174th ARS/185th ARW, Sioux City,
 Iowa ANG (y/bk);
191st ARS/151st ARW, Salt Lake City,
 Utah ANG (bl/bk);
196th ARS/163rd ARW, March ARB,
 California ANG (bl/w);
197th ARS/161st ARW, Phoenix,
 Arizona ANG;
203rd ARS/15th Wg, Hickam AFB,
 Hawaii ANG [HH] (y/bk);
366th Wg, Mountain Home AFB,
 Idaho [MO]:
 22nd ARS (y/gn);
412th TW, Edwards AFB,
 California [ED]:
 418th FLTS (or);
434th ARW AFRC, Grissom AFB,
 Indiana:
 72nd ARS (bl) & 74th ARS (r/w);
452nd AMW AFRC, March ARB,
 California:
 336th ARS (or/y);
459th ARW AFRC, Andrews AFB,
 Maryland:
 756th ARS (y/bk);
507th ARW AFRC,
 Tinker AFB, Oklahoma:
 465th ARS (bl/y);
645th Materiel Sqn, Greenville, Texas;
916th ARW AFRC,
 Seymour Johnson AFB,
 North Carolina:
 77th ARS (gn);
927th ARW AFRC, MacDill AFB, Florida:
 63rd ARS (pr/w);
L3 Systems, Greenville, Texas

Type			Notes	Type			Notes
FY60				10308	KC-135R	97th AMW	y/r
00313	KC-135R	18th Wg	or/bk	10309	KC-135R	126th ARS	w/bl
00314	KC-135R	434th ARW	r/w	10310	KC-135R	133rd ARS	bl
00315	KC-135R	126th ARS	w/bl	10311	KC-135R	22nd ARW	y
00316	KC-135R	174th ARS	y/bk	10312	KC-135R	97th AMW	y/r
00318	KC-135R	203rd ARS	y/bk	10313	KC-135R	916th ARW	gn
00319	KC-135R	22nd ARW		10314	KC-135R	22nd ARW	
00320	KC-135R	97th AMW	y/r	10315	KC-135R	97th AMW	y/r
00321	KC-135R	452nd AMW	or/y	10317	KC-135R	141st ARS	r
00322	KC-135R	434th ARW	bl	10318	KC-135R	141st ARS	r
00323	KC-135R	203rd ARS	y/bk	10320	KC-135R	412th TW	or
00324	KC-135R	22nd ARW		10321	KC-135R	97th AMW	y/r
00328	KC-135R	22nd ARW		10323	KC-135R	18th Wg	or/bk
00329	KC-135R	203rd ARS	y/bk	10324	KC-135R	452nd AMW	or/y
00331	KC-135R	92nd ARW		12662	RC-135S	55th Wg	bk
00332	KC-135R	168th ARS	bl/y	12663	RC-135S	55th Wg	bk
00333	KC-135R	92nd ARW	bk	12666	NC-135W	645th MS	
00334	KC-135R	168th ARS	bl/y	12667	WC-135W	55th Wg	bk
00335	KC-135T	22nd ARW		12670	OC-135B	55th Wg	
00336	KC-135T	22nd ARW		12672	OC-135B	55th Wg	
00337	KC-135R	92nd ARW	m	*FY64*			
00339	KC-135T	6th AMW	y/bl	14828	KC-135R	191st ARS	bl/bk
00341	KC-135T	121st ARW	bl	14829	KC-135R	117th ARS	bl/y
00342	KC-135T	100th ARW	r/w/bl	14830	KC-135R	6th AMW	y/bl
00343	KC-135T	22nd ARW		14831	KC-135R	197th ARS	
00344	KC-135T	6th AMW	y/bl	14832	KC-135R	203rd ARS	y/bk
00345	KC-135T	171st ARS		14833	KC-135R	L3 Systems	
00346	KC-135T	171st ARS		14834	KC-135R	434th ARW	r/w
00347	KC-135T	121st ARW	bl	14835	KC-135R	452nd AMW	or/y
00348	KC-135R	22nd ARW		14836	KC-135R	133rd ARS	bl
00349	KC-135R	916th ARW	gn	14837	KC-135R	22nd ARW	
00350	KC-135R	22nd ARW		14838	KC-135R	6th AMW	y/bl
00351	KC-135R	97th AMW	y/r	14839	KC-135R	108th ARS	w/bl
00353	KC-135R	100th ARW	r/w/bl	14840	KC-135R	121st ARW	bl
00355	KC-135R	22nd ARW		14841	RC-135V	55th Wg	bl
00356	KC-135R	22nd ARW		14842	RC-135V	55th Wg	gn
00357	KC-135R	22nd ARW		14843	RC-135V	55th Wg	gn
00358	KC-135R	108th ARS	w/bl	14844	RC-135V	55th Wg	gn
00359	KC-135R	434th ARW	r/w	14845	RC-135V	55th Wg	bl
00360	KC-135R	97th AMW	y/r	14846	RC-135V	55th Wg	gn
00362	KC-135R	22nd ARW		14847	RC-135U	55th Wg	bk
00363	KC-135R	434th ARW	bl	14848	RC-135V	55th Wg	gn
00364	KC-135R	434th ARW	r/w	14849	RC-135U	55th Wg	bk
00365	KC-135R	117th ARS	bl/y	*FY62*			
00366	KC-135R	141st ARS	r	23498	KC-135R	22nd ARW	
00367	KC-135R	121st ARW	bl	23499	KC-135R	100th ARW	r/w/bl
FY61				23500	KC-135R	126th ARS	w/bl
10264	KC-135R	121st ARW	bl	23502	KC-135R	18th Wg	or/bk
10266	KC-135R	117th ARS	bl/y	23503	KC-135R	507th ARW	bl/y
10267	KC-135R	22nd ARW		23504	KC-135R	191st ARS	bl/bk
10272	KC-135R	434th ARW	r/w	23505	KC-135R	97th AMW	y/r
10275	KC-135R	191st ARS	bl/bk	23506	KC-135R	133rd ARS	bl
10276	KC-135R	173rd ARS	r/w	23507	KC-135R	22nd ARW	
10277	KC-135R	117th ARS	bl/y	23508	KC-135R	141st ARS	r
10280	KC-135R	452nd AMW	or/y	23509	KC-135R	916th ARW	gn
10284	KC-135R	106th ARS	w/r	23510	KC-135R	434th ARW	r/w
10288	KC-135R	18th Wg	or/bk	23511	KC-135R	121st ARW	bl
10290	KC-135R	203rd ARS	y/bk	23512	KC-135R	126th ARS	w/bl
10292	KC-135R	18th Wg	or/bk	23513	KC-135R	132nd ARS	w/gn
10293	KC-135R	18th Wg	or/bk	23514	KC-135R	141st ARS	r
10294	KC-135R	916th ARW	gn	23515	KC-135R	133rd ARS	bl
10295	KC-135R	18th Wg	or/bk $	23516	KC-135R	197th ARS	
10298	KC-135R	126th ARS	w/bl	23517	KC-135R	6th AMW	y/bl
10299	KC-135R	97th AMW	y/r	23518	KC-135R	434th ARW	bl
10300	KC-135R	108th ARS	w/bl	23519	KC-135R		
10302	KC-135R	203rd ARS	y/bk	23520	KC-135R	133rd ARS	bl
10304	KC-135R	100th ARW	r/w/bl	23521	KC-135R	434th ARW	bl
10305	KC-135R	6th AMW	y/bl	23523	KC-135R	22nd ARW	
10306	KC-135R	100th ARW	r/w/bl	23524	KC-135R	106th ARS	w/r
10307	KC-135R	459th ARW	y/bk	23526	KC-135R	173rd ARS	r/w

Type			Notes	Type			Notes
23528	KC-135R	916th ARW	gn	37993	KC-135R	121st ARW	m
23529	KC-135R	6th AMW	y/bl	37995	KC-135R	22nd ARW	gy
23530	KC-135R	434th ARW	bl	37996	KC-135R	434th ARW	bl
23531	KC-135R	121st ARW	bl	37997	KC-135R	6th AMW	y/bl
23533	KC-135R	452nd AMW	or/y	37999	KC-135R	22nd ARW	
23534	KC-135R	22nd ARW		38000	KC-135R	6th AMW	y/bl
23537	KC-135R	916th ARW	gn	38002	KC-135R	22nd ARW	gy/si
23538	KC-135R	22nd ARW		38003	KC-135R	141st ARW	r
23540	KC-135R	100th ARW	r/w/bl	38004	KC-135R	117th ARS	bl/y
23541	KC-135R	22nd ARW		38006	KC-135R	100th ARW	r/w/bl
23542	KC-135R	916th ARW	gn	38007	KC-135R	106th ARS	w/r
23543	KC-135R	459th ARW	y/bk	38008	KC-135R	100th ARW	r/w/bl
23544	KC-135R	141st ARS	r	38011	KC-135R	6th AMW	y/bl
23545	KC-135R	22nd ARW		38012	KC-135R	22nd ARW	
23546	KC-135R	203rd ARS	y/bk	38013	KC-135R	121st ARW	bl
23547	KC-135R	133rd ARS	bl	38014	KC-135R	916th ARW	gn
23548	KC-135R	97th AMW	y/r	38015	KC-135R	168th ARS	bl/y
23549	KC-135R	6th AMW	y/bl	38017	KC-135R	18th Wg	or/bk $
23550	KC-135R	197th ARS		38018	KC-135R	173rd ARS	r/w
23551	KC-135R			38019	KC-135R	100th ARW	r/w/bl
23552	KC-135R	18th Wg	or/bk	38020	KC-135R	18th Wg	or/bk
23553	KC-135R	97th AMW	y/r	38021	KC-135R	6th AMW	y/bl
23554	KC-135R	22nd ARW		38022	KC-135R	22nd ARW	m
23556	KC-135R	459th ARW	y/bk	38023	KC-135R	197th ARS	
23557	KC-135R	916th ARW	gn	38024	KC-135R	452nd AMW	or/y
23558	KC-135R	452nd AMW	or/y	38025	KC-135R	22nd ARW	
23559	KC-135R	6th AMW	y/bl	38026	KC-135R	191st ARS	bl/bk
23561	KC-135R	97th AMW	y/r	38027	KC-135R	6th AMW	y/bl
23562	KC-135R	92nd ARW		38028	KC-135R	168th ARS	bl/y
23564	KC-135R	22nd ARW		38029	KC-135R	126th ARS	w/bl
23565	KC-135R	100th ARW	r/w/bl	38030	KC-135R	203rd ARS	y/bk
23566	KC-135R	174th ARS	y/bk	38031	KC-135R	97th AMW	y/r
23568	KC-135R	97th ARS	y/r	38032	KC-135R	434th ARW	bl
23569	KC-135R	22nd ARW		38033	KC-135R	22nd ARW	
23571	KC-135R	168th ARS	bl/y	38034	KC-135R	22nd ARW	
23572	KC-135R	117th ARS	bl/y	38035	KC-135R	106th ARS	w/r
23573	KC-135R	22nd ARW		38036	KC-135R	197th ARS	
23575	KC-135R	18th Wg	or/bk	38037	KC-135R	22nd ARW	
23576	KC-135R	133rd ARS	bl	38038	KC-135R	916th ARW	gn
23577	KC-135R	916th ARW	gn	38039	KC-135R	507th ARW	bl/y
23578	KC-135R	141st ARS	r	38040	KC-135R	141st ARS	r
23580	KC-135R	916th ARW	gn	38041	KC-135R	434th ARW	bl
23582	WC-135C	55th Wg	bk	38043	KC-135R	168th ARS	bl/y
24125	RC-135W	55th Wg	bk	38044	KC-135R	916th ARW	gn
24126	RC-135W	55th Wg	bl	38045	KC-135R	6th AMW	y/bl
24127	TC-135W	55th Wg		38871	KC-135R	22nd ARW	
24128	RC-135S	55th Wg		38872	KC-135R	132nd ARS	w/gn
24129	TC-135W	55th Wg	gn	38873	KC-135R	132nd ARS	w/gn
24130	RC-135W	55th Wg	gn	38874	KC-135R	97th AMW	y/r
24131	RC-135W	55th Wg	gn	38875	KC-135R	117th ARS	bl/y
24132	RC-135W	55th Wg	gn	38876	KC-135R	168th ARS	bl/y
24133	TC-135S	55th Wg	bk	38877	KC-135R	18th Wg	or/bk
24134	RC-135W	55th Wg	bl	38878	KC-135R	97th AMW	y/r
24135	RC-135W	55th Wg	bk	38879	KC-135R	92nd ARW	
24138	RC-135W	55th Wg	gn	38880	KC-135R	507th ARW	bl/y
24139	RC-135W	55th Wg	gn	38881	KC-135R	191st ARS	bl/bk
FY63				38883	KC-135R	97th AMW	y/r
37976	KC-135R	18th Wg	or/bk	38884	KC-135R	18th Wg	or/bk
37977	KC-135R	6th AMW	y/bl	38885	KC-135R	92nd ARW	
37978	KC-135R	18th Wg	or/bk	38887	KC-135R	6th AMW	y/bl
37979	KC-135R	100th ARW	r/w/bl	38888	KC-135R	6th AMW	y/bl
37980	KC-135R	412th TW	or	39792	RC-135V	55th Wg	gn $
37981	KC-135R	108th ARS	w/bl	**FY57**			
37982	KC-135R	92nd ARW	bk	71419	KC-135R	117th ARS	bl/y
37984	KC-135R	106th ARS	w/r	71427	KC-135R	117th ARS	bl/y
37985	KC-135R	507th ARW	bl/y	71428	KC-135R	151st ARS	w/or
37987	KC-135R	22nd ARW		71430	KC-135R	133rd ARS	bl
37988	KC-135R	173rd ARS	r/w	71432	KC-135R	106th ARS	w/r
37991	KC-135R	173rd ARS	r/w	71435	KC-135R	191st ARS	bl/bk
37992	KC-135R	121st ARW	bl	71436	KC-135R	151st ARS	w/or

C-135

Type			Notes	Type			Notes
71437	KC-135R	106th ARS	w/r	80063	KC-135R	507th ARW	bl/y
71438	KC-135R	97th AMW	y/r	80065	KC-135R	22nd ARW	
71439	KC-135R	18th Wg	or/bk	80066	KC-135R	507th ARW	bl/y
71440	KC-135R	92nd ARW	bl	80067	KC-135R	174th ARS	y/bk
71441	KC-135R	174th ARS	y/bk	80069	KC-135R	92nd ARW	
71451	KC-135R	151st ARS	w/or	80071	KC-135T	22nd ARW	
71453	KC-135R	106th ARS	w/r	80072	KC-135R	171st ARW	y/bk
71454	KC-135R	22nd ARW		80073	KC-135R	106th ARS	w/r
71456	KC-135R	916th ARW	gn	80074	KC-135R	171st ARW	y/bk
71459	KC-135R	452nd AMW	or/y	80075	KC-135R	459th ARW	y/bk
71461	KC-135R	173rd ARS	r/w	80076	KC-135R	434th ARW	r/w
71462	KC-135R	121st ARW	bl	80077	KC-135T	171st ARW	y/bk
71468	KC-135R	452nd AMW	or/y	80079	KC-135R	507th ARW	bl/y
71469	KC-135R	197th ARS		80083	KC-135R	121st ARW	bl
71472	KC-135R	434th ARW	bl	80084	KC-135T	171st ARW	y/bk
71473	KC-135R	117th AMW	bl/y	80085	KC-135R	452nd AMW	or/y
71474	KC-135R	97th AMW	y/r	80086	KC-135T	92nd ARW	
71483	KC-135R	92nd ARW		80088	KC-135T	171st ARS	
71486	KC-135R	197th ARS		80089	KC-135T	22nd ARW	
71487	KC-135R	459th ARW	y/bk	80092	KC-135R	92nd ARW	
71488	KC-135R	100th ARW	r/w/bl	80093	KC-135R		
71493	KC-135R	100th ARW	r/w/bl	80094	KC-135T	100th ARW	r/w/bl
71499	KC-135R	18th Wg	or/bk	80095	KC-135T	92nd ARW	
71502	KC-135R	92nd ARW		80098	KC-135T	133rd ARS	bl
71506	KC-135R	97th AMW	y/r	80099	KC-135T	171st ARW	y/bk
71508	KC-135R	203rd ARS	y/bk	80100	KC-135R	100th ARW	r/w/bl
71512	KC-135R	459th ARW	y/bk	80102	KC-135R	6th AMW	y/bl
71514	KC-135R	126th ARS	w/bl	80103	KC-135T	92nd ARW	bk
72593	KC-135R	121st ARW	bl	80104	KC-135R	108th ARS	w/bl
72597	KC-135R	151st ARS	w/or	80106	KC-135R	106th ARS	w/r
72598	KC-135R	452nd AMW	or/y	80107	KC-135R	132nd ARS	w/gn
72599	KC-135R	916th ARW	gn	80109	KC-135R	174th ARS	y/bk
72603	KC-135R	452nd AMW	or/y	80112	KC-135T	171st ARW	y/bk
72605	KC-135R	6th AMW	y/bl	80113	KC-135R	6th AMW	y/bl
72606	KC-135R	174th ARS	y/bk	80114	KC-135R	191st ARS	bl/bk
FY58				80117	KC-135T	171st ARW	
80001	KC-135R	92nd ARW	bk	80118	KC-135R	92nd ARW	bk
80004	KC-135R	106th ARS	w/r	80119	KC-135R	97th AMW	y/r
80008	KC-135R	133rd ARS	bl	80120	KC-135R	126th ARS	w/bl
80009	KC-135R	126th ARS	w/bl	80121	KC-135R	507th ARW	bl/y
80010	KC-135R	106th ARS		80122	KC-135R	117th ARS	bl/y
80011	KC-135R	22nd ARW		80123	KC-135R	22nd ARW	
80015	KC-135R	507th ARW	bl/y	80124	KC-135R	22nd ARW	
80016	KC-135R	100th ARW	r/w/bl	80125	KC-135T	92nd ARW	bl
80018	KC-135R	22nd ARW		80126	KC-135R	22nd ARW	y
80021	KC-135R	132nd ARS	w/gn	80128	KC-135R	97th AMW	y/r
80023	KC-135R	108th ARS	w/bl	80129	KC-135T	171st ARS	
80027	KC-135R	191st ARS	bl/bk	80130	KC-135R	126th ARS	w/bl
80030	KC-135R	132nd ARS	w/gn	**FY59**			
80034	KC-135R	22nd ARW		91444	KC-135R	121st ARW	bl
80035	KC-135R	22nd ARW	y	91446	KC-135R	132nd ARS	w/gn
80036	KC-135R			91448	KC-135R	151st ARS	w/or
80038	KC-135R	916th ARW	gn	91450	KC-135R	197th ARS	
80042	KC-135T	22nd ARW		91453	KC-135R	121st ARW	bl
80045	KC-135T	171st ARW	y/bk	91455	KC-135R		
80046	KC-135T	92nd ARW		91458	KC-135R	121st ARW	bl
80047	KC-135T	22nd ARW		91459	KC-135R	22nd ARW	
80049	KC-135T	171st ARS		91460	KC-135T	197th ARS	
80050	KC-135T	22nd ARW		91461	KC-135R	168th ARS	bl/y
80051	KC-135R	507th ARW	bl/y	91462	KC-135T	92nd ARW	
80052	KC-135R	452nd AMW	or/y	91463	KC-135R	173rd ARS	r/w
80054	KC-135T	171st ARW	y/bk	91464	KC-135T	92nd ARW	
80055	KC-135T	22nd ARW		91466	KC-135R	108th ARS	w/bl
80056	KC-135T	15th Wg		91467	KC-135R	171st ARW	bk/y
80057	KC-135R	174th ARS	y/bk	91468	KC-135T	171st ARW	
80058	KC-135R	507th ARW	bl/y	91469	KC-135R	459th ARW	y/bk
80059	KC-135R	126th ARS	w/bl	91470	KC-135T	92nd ARW	gn
80060	KC-135R	171st ARW	y/bk	91471	KC-135T	92nd ARW	bk
80061	KC-135T	22nd ARW		91472	KC-135R	203rd ARS	y/bk
80062	KC-135T	171st ARS		91474	KC-135T	97th AMW	y/r

Type			Notes	Type			Notes
91475	KC-135R	92nd ARW		91505	KC-135R	151st ARS	w/or
91476	KC-135R	92nd ARW		91506	KC-135R	132nd ARS	w/gn
91478	KC-135R			91507	KC-135R	117th ARS	bl/y
91480	KC-135T	92nd ARW	bk	91508	KC-135R	22nd ARW	
91482	KC-135R	452nd AMW	or/y	91509	KC-135R	141st ARS	r
91483	KC-135R	121st ARW	bl	91510	KC-135T	92nd ARW	
91486	KC-135R	22nd ARW		91511	KC-135R	22nd ARW	
91488	KC-135R	132nd ARS	w/gn	91512	KC-135T	452nd AMW	or/y
91490	KC-135T	171st ARW		91513	KC-135T	92nd ARW	bk
91492	KC-135R	100th ARW	r/w/bl	91515	KC-135R	92nd ARW	
91495	KC-135R	173rd ARS	r/w	91516	KC-135R	151st ARS	w/or
91498	KC-135R	132nd ARS	w/gn	91517	KC-135R	151st ARS	w/or
91499	KC-135R	151st ARS	w/or	91519	KC-135R	174th ARS	y/bk
91500	KC-135R	108th ARS	w/bl	91520	KC-135T	6th AMW	y/bl
91501	KC-135R	97th AMW	y/r	91521	KC-135R	168th ARS	bl/y
91502	KC-135R	97th AMW	y/r	91522	KC-135R	108th ARS	w/bl
91504	KC-135T	171st ARW	y/bk	91523	KC-135T	171st ARW	y/bk

US-based USN/USMC Aircraft

Type	Notes	Type			Notes
Lockheed P-3 Orion		156519	[519]	EP-3E	VQ-2
CinCLANT/VP-30, NAS Jacksonville,		156521	[LL-521]	P-3C	VP-30
Florida;		156528	[528]	EP-3E	VQ-1
CNO/VP-30, NAS Jacksonville, Florida;		156529	[529]	EP-3E	VQ-1
NASC-FS, Point Mugu, California;		157316	[316]	EP-3E	VQ-2
USNTPS, NAS Point Mugu, California;		157318	[PR-318]	EP-3E	VQ-1
VP-1, NAS Whidbey Island, Washington		157319	[LL-319]	P-3C	VP-30
[YB];		157325	[325]	EP-3E	VQ-2
VP-4, MCBH Kaneohe Bay, Hawaii [YD];		157326	[326]	EP-3E	VQ-2
VP-5, NAS Jacksonville, Florida [LA];		157329	[LL-329]	P-3C	VP-30
VP-8, NAS Jacksonville, Florida [LC];		157331	[PD-331]	P-3C	VP-9
VP-9, MCBH Kaneohe Bay, Hawaii [PD];		158204	[204]	NP-3C	VX-20
VP-10, NAS Jacksonville, Florida [LD];		158206	[JQ-21]$	P-3C	VQ-1
VP-16, NAS Jacksonville, Florida [LF];		158210	[210]	P-3C	VP-45
VP-26, NAS Jacksonville, Florida [LK];		158214	[LL-214]	P-3C	VP-30
VP-30, NAS Jacksonville, Florida [LL];		158215	[LF-215]	P-3C	VP-16
VP-40, NAS Whidbey Island, Washington		158222	[222]	P-3C	VP-4
[QE];		158224	[YD-224]	P-3C	VP-4
VP-45, NAS Jacksonville, Florida [LN];		158225	[225]	P-3C	VP-8
VP-46, NAS Whidbey Island, Washington		158227	[300]	NP-3D	VX-30
[RC];		158563	[YD-563]	P-3C	VP-4
VP-47, MCBH Kaneohe Bay, Hawaii [RD];		158564	[564]	P-3C	VP-26
VP-62, NAS Jacksonville, Florida [LT];		158567	[LF-567]	P-3C	VP-16
VP-69, NAS Whidbey Island, Washington		158570	[LL-570]	P-3C	VP-30
[PJ];		158571	[LL-571]	P-3C	VP-30
VPU-1, NAS Jacksonville, Florida;		158573	[RD-573]	P-3C	VP-47
VPU-2, MCBH Kaneohe Bay, Hawaii;		158574		P-3C	NASC-FS
VQ-1, NAS Whidbey Island, Washington		158912	[912]	P-3C	VX-20
[PR];		158914	[914]	P-3C	VP-16
VQ-2, NAS Whidbey Island, Washington;		158915	[915]	P-3C	VP-16
VX-1, NAS Patuxent River, Maryland;		158916	[916]	P-3C	VP-45
VX-20, Patuxent River, Maryland;		158917	[LA-917]	P-3C	VP-5
VX-30, NAS Point Mugu, California;		158918	[918]	P-3C	VP-40
VXS-1, Patuxent River, Maryland [RL]		158919	[RD-919]	P-3C	VP-9
150521	[341]	NP-3D	VX-30	158921	[LD-921]	P-3C	VP-10
150522	[340]	NP-3D	VX-30	158922	[LN-922]	P-3C	VP-45
153442	[RL-442]	NP-3D	VXS-1	158923	[YD-923]	P-3C	VP-4
153443	[302]	NP-3D	VX-30	158924	[RD-924]	P-3C	VP-47
154587	[RL-587]	NP-3D	VXS-1	158925	[925]	P-3C	VP-30
154589	[RL-589]	NP-3D	VXS-1	158926	[RC-926]	P-3C	VP-46
156507	[507]	EP-3E	VQ-1	158927	[LF-927]	P-3C	VP-16
156510	[LL-510]	P-3C	VP-30	158928		P-3C	VPU-2
156511	[511]	EP-3E	VQ-1	158929	[LA-929]	P-3C	VP-5
156514	[514]	EP-3E	VQ-1	158934	[LK-934]	P-3C	VP-26
156515	[LL-515]	P-3C	VP-30	158935	[LN-935]	P-3C	VP-45
156517	[517]	EP-3E	VQ-1	159318	[318]	P-3C	VP-8

Type			Notes	Type			Notes
159320 [320]	P-3C	VP-46		161764 [764]	P-3C	VP-46	
159322 [PD-322]	P-3C	VP-9		161765 [765]	P-3C	VP-1	
159323 [323]	P-3C	VP-8		161766 [YD-766]	P-3C	VP-4	
159326 [326]	P-3C	VP-4		161767 [PD-767]	P-3C	VP-49	
159329 [LN-329]	P-3C	VP-45		162314 [314]	P-3C	VP-30	
159503 [LF-503]	P-3C	VP-16		162315 [LD-315]	P-3C	VP-10	
159504	P-3C	VPU-2		162316 [LC-316]	P-3C	VP-8	
159507 [LN-507]	P-3C	VP-26		162317 [317]	P-3C	VP-9	
159512 [LF-512]	P-3C	VP-16		162318 [LD-318]	P-3C	VP-10	
159514 [LL-514]	P-3C	VP-30		162770 [770]	P-3C	VP-30	
159885 [885]	P-3C	VP-40		162771 [771]	P-3C	VP-45	
159887	EP-3E	VQ-2		162772 [772]	P-3C	VP-47	
159889 [YD-889]	P-3C	VP-4		162773 [773]	P-3C	VP-30	
159893 [26]	EP-3E	VQ-1		162774 [774]	P-3C	VX-20	
159894 [LD-894]	P-3C	VP-10		162775 [YD-775]	P-3C	VP-4	
160283 [283]	P-3C	VP-47		162776 [LD-776]	P-3C	VP-10	
160285	P-3C	VPU-1		162777 [777]	P-3C	VP-5	
160287 [LL-30]	P-3C	VP-30		162778 [PD-778]	P-3C	VP-9	
160290 [290]	P-3C	VX-20		162998 [998]	P-3C	VP-1	
160291 [291]	EP-3E	VQ-1		162999 [LF-999]	P-3C	VP-16	
160292 [292]	P-3C	VPU-2		163000 [000]	P-3C	VP-45	
160293	P-3C	NASC-FS		163001 [001]	P-3C	VP-16	
160610 [YD-610]	P-3C	VP-4		163002 [002]	P-3C	VP-46	
160761 [761]	P-3C	VP-16		163003 [LF-003]	P-3C	VP-16	
160762	P-3C	VPU-2		163004 [004]	P-3C	VP-69	
160764 [764]	EP-3E	VQ-1		163006 [006]	P-3C	VP-47	
160770 [PC]$	P-3C	VP-5		163289 [289]	P-3C	VP-40	
160999 [999]	P-3C	VP-9		163290 [290]	P-3C	VP-30	
161001 [PJ-001]	P-3C	VP-69		163291 [291]	P-3C	VP-45	
161005 [005]	P-3C	VP-30		163292 [292]	P-3C	VP-40	
161006 [QB-006]	P-3C	VPU-1		163293 [LK-293]	P-3C	VP-26	
161010 [LL-010]	P-3C	VP-30		163294 [LK-294]	P-3C	VP-26	
161011 [011]	P-3C	VP-46		163295 [295]	P-3C	VP-69	
161012 [LF-012]	P-3C	VP-16					
161121 [121]	P-3C	VQ-2		**Boeing E-6B Mercury**			
161122 [226]	P-3C	VPU-1		Boeing, McConnell AFB, Kansas;			
161124 [124]	P-3C	VX-20		VQ-3 & VQ-4, SCW-1,			
161126 [126]	P-3C	VP-46		Tinker AFB, Oklahoma			
161127 [LF-127]	P-3C	VP-16		162782 VQ-3			
161129 [LT-129]	P-3C	VP-62		162783 VQ-3			
161132 [132]	P-3C	VP-26		162784 VQ-4			
161329 [LT-329]	P-3C	VP-62		163918 VQ-3			
161332 [LN-332]	P-3C	VP-45		163919 VQ-3			
161333 [LF-333]	P-3C	VP-16		163920 VQ-3			
161337 [337]	P-3C	VP-47		164386 VQ-4			
161338 [QE-338]	P-3C	VP-40		164387 VQ-3			
161339 [339]	P-3C	VP-47		164388 VQ-4			
161404 [404]	P-3C	VP-1		164404 VQ-4			
161405 [405]	P-3C	VP-8		164405 VQ-4			
161406 [406]	P-3C	VP-30		164406 VQ-3			
161407 [407]	P-3C	VP-47		164407 VQ-4			
161408 [408]	P-3C	VP-69		164408 VQ-4			
161409 [LT-409]	P-3C	VP-62		164409 VQ-4			
161410	EP-3E	VQ-1		164410 VQ-4			
161411	P-3C	NASC-FS					
161412 [PJ-412]	P-3C	VP-69		**Boeing P-8A Poseidon**			
161413 [413]	P-3C	VX-20		Boeing, Seattle;			
161414 [414]	P-3C	VP-46		VX-1, NAS Patuxent River, Maryland;			
161415 [415]	P-3C	VP-8		VX-20, Patuxent River, Maryland			
161586 [QE-586]	P-3C	VP-40		167951 VX-20			
161587 [RL-587]	P-3C	VXS-1		167952 VX-1/VX-20			
161588 [588]	P-3C	VP-10		167953 VX-20			
161589 [589]	P-3C	VP-40		167954 VX-20			
161590 [590]	P-3C	VP-46		167955 Boeing			
161591 [44-P-4]$	P-3C	VP-5		167956 Boeing			
161593 [593]	P-3C	VP-8		168428 Boeing			
161594 [RD-594]	P-3C	VP-47					
161595 [LT-595]	P-3C	VP-62					
161596 [596]	P-3C	VP-1					
161763 [763]	P-3C	VP-47					

Type	Notes	Type	Notes

McDonnell Douglas
C-9B Skytrain II
VMR-1, Cherry Point MCAS,
North Carolina;
VR-46, Atlanta, Georgia [JS];
VR-52, Willow Grove NAS,
Pennsylvania [JT];
VR-61, Whidbey Island NAS,
Washington [RS];

159113	VR-61
159114	VR-61
159115	VR-61
159116	VR-61
159118	VR-61
160046	VMR-1
160047	VMR-1
160048	VR-52
160050	VR-52
160051	VR-52
161266	VR-46
161529	VR-46
161530	VR-46

Grumman C-20A/C-20D Gulfstream III/
C-20G Gulfstream IV*
VMR-Det, MCBH Kaneohe Bay, Hawaii;
VR-1, NAF Washington, Maryland;
VR-48, NAF Washington, Maryland [JR];
VR-51, MCBH Kaneohe Bay, Hawaii [RG]
C-20A

830500	VR-1

C-20D

163691	VR-1
163692	VR-1

C-20G

165093 [JR]	VR-48
165094	VR-51
165151	VR-48
165152	VR-51
165153	VMR-Det

Cessna C-35 Citation V
MAW-4, Miramar MCAS, California;
MWHS-1, Futenma MCAS, Japan;
MWHS-4, NAS New Orleans;
VMR-1, Cherry Point MCAS,
North Carolina;
VMR-2, NAF Washington, Maryland

165740 [EZ]	UC-35C	MWHS-4
165741 [EZ]	UC-35C	MWHS-4
165939	UC-35D	MWHS-1
166374	UC-35D	MWHS-1
166474	UC-35D	MAW-4
166500	UC-35D	MAW-4
166712	UC-35D	MWHS-1
166713	UC-35D	MWHS-1
166714	UC-35D	MAW-4
166715	UC-35D	VMR-1
166716	UC-35D	(on order)
166717	UC-35D	(on order)
166766	UC-35D	VMR-2
166767 [VM]	UC-35D	VMR-2

Gulfstream Aerospace
C-37B Gulfstream V
CFLSW Det, Hawaii;
VR-1, NAF Washington, Maryland

166375	CFLSW Det
166376	VR-1
166377	VR-1

166378	VR-1
166379	VR-1

Boeing C-40A Clipper
VR-56, NAS Oceana,
Virginia;
VR-57, NAS North Island,
California [RX];
VR-58, NAS Jacksonville,
Florida [JV];
VR-59, NAS Fort Worth JRB,
Texas [RY]

165829	VR-58
165830 [RY]	VR-59
165831	VR-59
165832	VR-58
165833	VR-59
165834	VR-58
165835	VR-57
165836	VR-57
166693	VR-57
166694	VR-59
166695	VR-58
166696	VR-56

Lockheed C-130 Hercules
VR-53, NAF Washington, Maryland
[AX];
VR-54, NAS New Orleans, Louisiana
[CW];
VR-55, NAS Point Mugu, California
[RU];
VR-62, NAS Jacksonville, Florida [JW];
VR-64, NAS Willow Grove,
Pennsylvania [BD];
VMGR-152, Futenma MCAS, Japan
[QD];
VMGR-234, NAS Fort Worth, Texas
[QH];
VMGR-252, Cherry Point MCAS,
North Carolina [BH];
VMGR-352, MCAS Miramar,
California [QB];
VMGR-452, Stewart Field,
New York [NY];
VX-20, Patuxent River, Maryland;
VX-30, NAS Point Mugu, California

148891 [403]	KC-130F	VX-30	
148893 [402]	KC-130F	VX-30	
148897 [400]	KC-130F	VX-30	
149807 [QD]	KC-130F	VMGR-152	
149808	KC-130F	VX-20	
160625	KC-130R	VX-20	
160626	KC-130R	VX-20	
160627	KC-130R	VX-20	
162308 [QH]	KC-130T	VMGR-234	
162309 [QH]	KC-130T	VMGR-234	
162310 [QH]	KC-130T	VMGR-234	
162311 [QH]	KC-130T	VMGR-234	
162785 [QH]	KC-130T	VMGR-234	
162786 [QH]	KC-130T	VMGR-234	
163022 [QH]	KC-130T	VMGR-234	
163023 [QH]	KC-130T	VMGR-234	
163310 [QH]	KC-130T	VMGR-234	
163311 [NY]	KC-130T	VMGR-452	
163591 [NY]	KC-130T	VMGR-452	
163592 [NY]	KC-130T	VMGR-452	
164105 [NY]	KC-130T	VMGR-452	
164106 [NY]	KC-130T	VMGR-452	
164180 [NY]	KC-130T	VMGR-452	

USN/USMC

Type			Notes	Type			Notes
164181 [NY]	KC-130T	VMGR-452		166380 [BH]	KC-130J	VMGR-252	
164441 [NY]	KC-130T	VMGR-452		166381 [BH]	KC-130J	VMGR-252	
164442 [NY]	KC-130T	VMGR-452		166382 [BH]	KC-130J	VMGR-252	
164597 [NY]	KC-130T-30	VMGR-452		166472 [BH]	KC-130J	VMGR-252	
164598 [QH]	KC-130T-30	VMGR-234		166473	KC-130J	VX-20	
164762 [CW]	C-130T	VR-54		166511 [BH]	KC-130J	VMGR-252	
164763	C-130T	Blue Angels		166512 [QB]	KC-130J	VMGR-352	
164993 [BD]	C-130T	VR-64		166513 [BH]	KC-130J	VMGR-252	
164994 [AX]	C-130T	VR-53		166514 [QD]	KC-130J	VMGR-152	
164995 [AX]	C-130T	VR-53		166762 [QB]	KC-130J	VMGR-352	
164996 [BD]	C-130T	VR-64		166763 [QD]	KC-130J	VMGR-152	
164997 [AX]	C-130T	VR-53		166764 [BH]	KC-130J	VMGR-252	
164998 [AX]	C-130T	VR-53		166765 [QB]	KC-130J	VMGR-352	
164999 [QH]	KC-130T	VMGR-234		167108 [QB]	KC-130J	VMGR-352	
165000 [QH]	KC-130T	VMGR-234		167109 [QB]	KC-130J	VMGR-352	
165158 [CW]	C-130T	VR-54		167110 [QB]	KC-130J	VMGR-352	
165159 [CW]	C-130T	VR-54		167111 [QB]	KC-130J	VMGR-352	
165160 [CW]	C-130T	VR-54		167112 [BH]	KC-130J	VMGR-252	
165161 [BD]	C-130T	VR-64		167923 [QD]	KC-130J	VMGR-152	
165162 [QH]	KC-130T	VMGR-234		167924 [QB]	KC-130J	VMGR-352	
165163 [QH]	KC-130T	VMGR-234		167925 [QD]	KC-130J	VMGR-152	
165313		VX-20		167926 [QD]	KC-130J	VMGR-152	
165314 [JW]	C-130T	VR-62		167927 [QD]	KC-130J	VMGR-152	
165315 [NY]	KC-130T	VMGR-452		167981 [QD]	KC-130J	VMGR-152	
165316 [NY]	KC-130T	VMGR-452		167982 [QD]	KC-130J	VMGR-152	
165348 [CW]	C-130T	VR-54		167983 [QD]	KC-130J	VMGR-152	
165349 [RU]	C-130T	VR-55		167984 [QB]	KC-130J	VMGR-352	
165350 [RU]	C-130T	VR-55		167985 [QB]	KC-130J	VMGR-352	
165351 [RU]	C-130T	VR-55		168065 [QD]	KC-130J	VMGR-152	
165352 [NY]	KC-130T	VMGR-452		168066 [QD]	KC-130J	VMGR-152	
165353 [NY]	KC-130T	VMGR-452		168067 [QB]	KC-130J	VMGR-352	
165378 [RU]	C-130T	VR-55		168068 [QB]	KC-130J	VMGR-352	
165379 [RU]	C-130T	VR-55		168069 [QB]	KC-130J	VMGR-352	
165735 [QB]	KC-130J	VMGR-352		168070 [BH]	KC-130J	VMGR-252	
165736 [QB]	KC-130J	VMGR-352		168071	KC-130J		
165737 [BH]	KC-130J	VMGR-252		168072 [QD]	KC-130J	VMGR-152	
165738 [BH]	KC-130J	VMGR-252		168073	KC-130J		
165739 [QB]	KC-130J	VMGR-352		168074 [QD]	KC-130J	VMGR-152	
165809 [BH]	KC-130J	VMGR-252		168075 [QD]	KC-130J	VMGR-152	
165810 [BH]	KC-130J	VMGR-252		168096 [BH]	KC-130J	VMGR-252	
165957 [QD]	KC-130J	VMGR-152					

00300 is a C-20H Gulfstream IV USAF VIP transport, based with the 86th Airlift Wing at Ramstein in Germany.

US-based US Coast Guard Aircraft

Type	Notes	Type			Notes
Gulfstream Aerospace		1707	HC-130H	Sacramento	
C-37A Gulfstream V		1708	HC-130H	Clearwater	
USCG, Washington DC		1709	HC-130H	Kodiak	
01		1711	HC-130H	Clearwater	
		1712	HC-130H	Sacramento	
Lockheed C-130 Hercules		1713	HC-130H	Sacramento	
USCGS Barbers Point, Hawaii;		1714	HC-130H	Sacramento	
USCGS Clearwater, Florida;		1715	HC-130H	Kodiak	
USCGS Elizabeth City, North Carolina;		1716	HC-130H	Clearwater	
USCGS Kodiak, Alaska;		1717	HC-130H	Barbers Point	
USCGS Sacramento, California		1718	HC-130H	Sacramento	
1500	HC-130H	Clearwater	1719	HC-130H	Clearwater
1502	HC-130H	Clearwater	1720	HC-130H	Clearwater
1503	HC-130H	Clearwater	1790	HC-130H	Kodiak
1504	HC-130H	Elizabeth City $	2001	HC-130J	Elizabeth City
1700	HC-130H	Clearwater	2002	HC-130J	Elizabeth City
1701	HC-130H	Barbers Point	2003	HC-130J	Elizabeth City
1702	HC-130H	Sacramento	2004	HC-130J	Elizabeth City
1703	HC-130H	Clearwater	2005	HC-130J	Elizabeth City
1704	HC-130H	Kodiak	2006	HC-130J	Elizabeth City
1706	HC-130H	Barbers Point			

Aircraft in US Government or Military Service with Civil Registrations

Type	Notes	Type	Notes
Canadair CL.601/CL.604*		N85	
Challenger		N86	
Federal Aviation Administration,		N87	
Oklahoma		N88*	

Military Aviation Sites on the Internet

The list below is not intended to be a complete list of military aviation sites on the Internet. The sites listed cover Museums, Locations, Air Forces, Companies and Organisations that are mentioned elsewhere in 'Military Aircraft Markings'. Sites listed are in English or contain sufficient English to be reasonably easily understood. Each site address was correct at the time of going to press. Additions are welcome, via the usual address found at the front of the book, or via e-mail to admin@aviation-links.co.uk. An up to date copy of this list is to be found at http://www.aviation-links.co.uk/.

Name of Site	Web address (All Prefixed 'Http://')
MILITARY SITES-UK	
No 2 Sqn	www.raf.mod.uk/organisation/2squadron.cfm
No 3 Sqn	www.raf.mod.uk/organisation/3squadron.cfm
No 4(R) Sqn	www.raf.mod.uk/organisation/4squadron.cfm
No 5 Sqn	www.raf.mod.uk/organisation/5squadron.cfm
No 6 Sqn	www.raf.mod.uk/organisation/6squadron.cfm
No 7 Sqn	www.raf.mod.uk/organisation/7squadron.cfm
No 8 Sqn	8squadron.co.uk/
No 9 Sqn	www.raf.mod.uk/organisation/9squadron.cfm
No 11 Sqn	www.raf.mod.uk/organisation/11squadron.cfm
No 12 Sqn	www.raf.mod.uk/organisation/12squadron.cfm
No 14 Sqn	www.raf.mod.uk/organisation/12squadron.cfm
No 15(R) Sqn	www.raf.mod.uk/organisation/14squadron.cfm
No 17(R) Sqn	www.raf.mod.uk/organisation/17squadron.cfm
No 18 Sqn	www.raf.mod.uk/organisation/18squadron.cfm
No 19(R) Sqn	www.raf.mod.uk/organisation/19squadron.cfm
No 22 Sqn	www.raf.mod.uk/organisation/22squadron.cfm
No 23 Sqn	www.raf.mod.uk/organisation/23squadron.cfm
No 24 Sqn	www.raf.mod.uk/organisation/24squadron.cfm
No 27 Sqn	www.raf.mod.uk/organisation/27squadron.cfm

Name of Site	Web address (All Prefixed 'Http://')
No 28 Sqn	www.raf.mod.uk/organisation/28squadron.cfm
No 29(R) Sqn	www.raf.mod.uk/organisation/29squadron.cfm
No 31 Sqn	www.raf.mod.uk/organisation/31squadron.cfm
No 32(The Royal) Sqn	www.raf.mod.uk/organisation/32squadron.cfm
No 33 Sqn	www.raf.mod.uk/organisation/33squadron.cfm
No 39 Sqn	www.raf.mod.uk/organisation/39squadron.cfm
No 41(R) Sqn	www.raf.mod.uk/organisation/41squadron.cfm
No 42(R) Sqn	www.raf.mod.uk/squadrons/h42.html
No 45(R) Sqn	www.raf.mod.uk/rafcranwell/aboutus/45sqn.cfm
No 51 Sqn	www.raf.mod.uk/organisation/51squadron.cfm
No 55(R) Sqn	www.raf.mod.uk/rafcranwell/aboutus/55sqn.cfm
No 60(R) Sqn	www.raf.mod.uk/organisation/60squadron.cfm
No 72(R) Sqn	www.raf.mod.uk/organisation/72squadron.cfm
No 76(R) Sqn	www.raf.mod.uk/raflintononouse/aboutus/76rsqn.cfm
No 78 Sqn	www.raf.mod.uk/organisation/78squadron.cfm
No 84 Sqn	www.raf.mod.uk/organisation/84squadron.cfm
No 99 Sqn	www.raf.mod.uk/organisation/99squadron.cfm
No 100 Sqn	www.raf.mod.uk/organisation/100squadron.cfm
No 101 Sqn	www.raf.mod.uk/organisation/101squadron.cfm
No 120 Sqn	www.raf.mod.uk/organisation/120squadron.cfm
No 201 Sqn	www.raf.mod.uk/organisation/201squadron.cfm
No 202 Sqn	www.raf.mod.uk/organisation/202squadron.cfm
No 207(R) Sqn	www.raf.mod.uk/organisation/207squadron.cfm
No 208(R) Sqn	www.raf.mod.uk/organisation/208squadron.cfm
No 216 Sqn	www.raf.mod.uk/organisation/216squadron.cfm
No 230 Sqn	www.raf.mod.uk/organisation/230squadron.cfm
No 617 Sqn	www.raf.mod.uk/organisation/617squadron.cfm
No 702 NAS	www.royalnavy.mod.uk/The-Fleet/Aircraft/Helicopters/Lynx-Mk8/702-Naval-Air-Squadron
No 703 NAS	www.royalnavy.mod.uk/The-Fleet/Shore-Establishments/Aircrew-Training/703-NAS-Elementary-Flying-Training
No 750 NAS	www.royalnavy.mod.uk/The-Fleet/Shore-Establishments/Aircrew-Training/703-NAS-Elementary-Flying-Training
No 771 NAS	www.royalnavy.mod.uk/The-Fleet/Aircraft/Helicopters/Sea-King-Mk5/771-Naval-Air-Squadron
No 814 NAS	www.royalnavy.mod.uk/The-Fleet/Aircraft/Helicopters/Merlin-MK1/814-Naval-Air-Squadron
No 815 NAS	/www.royalnavy.mod.uk/The-Fleet/Aircraft/Helicopters/Lynx-Mk8/815-Naval-Air-Squadron
No 820 NAS	www.royalnavy.mod.uk/The-Fleet/Aircraft/Helicopters/Merlin-MK1/820-Naval-Air-Squadron
No 824 NAS	www.royalnavy.mod.uk/The-Fleet/Aircraft/Helicopters/Merlin-MK1/824-Naval-Air-Squadron
No 829 NAS	www.royalnavy.mod.uk/The-Fleet/Aircraft/Helicopters/Merlin-MK1/829-Naval-Air-Squadron
No 845 NAS	www.royalnavy.mod.uk/The-Fleet/Aircraft/Helicopters/Sea-King-Mk4/845-Naval-Air-Squadron
No 846 NAS	www.royalnavy.mod.uk/The-Fleet/Aircraft/Helicopters/Sea-King-Mk4/846-Naval-Air-Squadron
No 847 NAS	www.royalnavy.mod.uk/The-Fleet/Aircraft/Helicopters/Lynx-Mk9/847-Naval-Air-Squadron
No 848 NAS	www.royalnavy.mod.uk/The-Fleet/Aircraft/Helicopters/Sea-King-Mk4/848-Naval-Air-Squadron
No 849 NAS	www.royalnavy.mod.uk/The-Fleet/Aircraft/Helicopters/Sea-King-ASaC/849-Naval-Air-Squadron
No 854 NAS	www.royalnavy.mod.uk/The-Fleet/Aircraft/Helicopters/Sea-King-ASaC/854-Naval-Air-Squadron
No 857 NAS	www.royalnavy.mod.uk/The-Fleet/Aircraft/Helicopters/Sea-King-ASaC/857-Naval-Air-Squadron
Aberdeen, Dundee and St Andrews UAS	dialspace.dial.pipex.com/town/way/gba87/adstauas/
The Army Air Corps	www.army.mod.uk/aviation/air.aspx
Cambridge University Air Squadron	www.raf.mod.uk/cambridgeuas/
East Midlands UAS	www.raf.mod.uk/eastmidlandsuas/
Fleet Air Arm	www.royalnavy.mod.uk/About-the-Royal-Navy/The-Navy-and-the-Environment/In-the-Air

Name of Site	Web address (All Prefixed 'Http://')
Liverpool University Air Squadron	www.raf.mod.uk/liverpooluas/
Manchester & Salford Universities Air Sqn	www.raf.mod.uk/manchesterandsalforduas/
Ministry of Defence	www.mod.uk/
Oxford University Air Sqn	www.raf.mod.uk/oxforduas/
QinetiQ	www.qinetiq.com/
RAF Benson	www.raf.mod.uk/rafbenson/
RAF Brize Norton	www.raf.mod.uk/rafbrizenorton/
RAF Church Fenton (unofficial)	www.rafchurchfenton.org.uk/
RAF College Cranwell	www.raf.mod.uk/rafcranwell/
RAF Coningsby	www.raf.mod.uk/rafconingsby/
RAF Cosford	www.raf.mod.uk/rafcosford/
RAF Cottesmore	www.raf.mod.uk/rafcottesmore/
RAF Leuchars	www.raf.mod.uk/rafleuchars/
RAF Linton-on-Ouse	www.raf.mod.uk/raflintononouse/
RAF Lossiemouth	www.raf.mod.uk/raflossiemouth/
RAF Lyneham	www.raf.mod.uk/raflyneham/
RAF Marham	www.raf.mod.uk/rafmarham/
RAF Northolt	www.raf.mod.uk/rafnortholt/
RAF Odiham	www.raf.mod.uk/rafodiham/
RAF Shawbury	www.raf.mod.uk/rafshawbury/
RAF Valley	www.raf.mod.uk/rafvalley/
RAF Waddington	www.raf.mod.uk/rafwaddington/
RAF Wittering	www.raf.mod.uk/rafwittering/
Red Arrows	www.raf.mod.uk/reds/
Royal Air Force	www.raf.mod.uk/
Royal Air Force Reserves	www.raf.mod.uk/rafreserves/
University of London Air Sqn	www.ulas.org.uk/
Yorkshire UAS	www.raf.mod.uk/yorkshireuas/

MILITARY SITES-US

Air Combat Command	www.acc.af.mil/
Air Force Reserve Command	www.afrc.af.mil/
Air National Guard	www.ang.af.mil/
Aviano Air Base	www.aviano.af.mil/
Liberty Wing Home Page (48th FW)	www.lakenheath.af.mil/
NASA	www.nasa.gov/
Mildenhall	www.mildenhall.af.mil/
Ramstein Air Base	www.ramstein.af.mil/
Spangdahlem Air Base	www.spangdahlem.af.mil/
USAF	www.af.mil/
USAF Europe	www.usafe.af.mil/
USAF World Wide Web Sites	www.af.mil/publicwebsites/index.asp
US Army	www.army.mil/
US Marine Corps	www.marines.mil/
US Navy	www.navy.mil/
US Navy Patrol Squadrons (unofficial)	www.vpnavy.com/

MILITARY SITES-ELSEWHERE

Armée de l'Air	www.defense.gouv.fr/air/
Aeronautica Militare	www.aeronautica.difesa.it
Austrian Armed Forces (in German)	www.bmlv.gv.at/
Belgian Air Component	www.mil.be/aircomp/index.asp?LAN=E
Finnish Defence Force	www.mil.fi/english/
Forca Aerea Portuguesa	www.emfa.pt/
Frecce Tricolori	users.iol.it/gromeo/
German Marine	www.deutschemarine.de/
Greek Air Force	www.haf.gr/en/
Irish Air Corps	www.military.ie/air-corps
Israeli Defence Force/Air Force	www.idf.il/english/
Luftforsvaret	www.mil.no/
Luftwaffe	www.luftwaffe.de/
NATO	www.nato.int/
Royal Australian Air Force	www.airforce.gov.au/
Royal Canadian Air Force	www.airforce.forces.gc.ca/v2/index-eng.asp
Royal Danish Air Force (in Danish)	forsvaret.dk/

INTERNET SITES

Name of Site	Web address (All Prefixed 'Http://')
Royal Netherlands AF	www.luchtmacht.nl/
Royal New Zealand AF	www.airforce.mil.nz/
Singapore Air Force	www.mindef.gov.sg/rsaf/
South African AF Site (unofficial)	www.saairforce.co.za/
Swedish Air Force	www.forsvarsmakten.se/sv/Forband-och-formagor/Flygvapnet/
Turkish Air Force	www.hvkk.tsk.tr/EN/Index.aspx

AIRCRAFT & AERO ENGINE MANUFACTURERS

AgustaWestland	www.agustawestland.com/
BAE Systems	www.baesystems.com/
Bell Helicopter Textron	www.bellhelicopter.textron.com/
Boeing	www.boeing.com/
Bombardier	www.bombardier.com/
Britten-Norman	www.britten-norman.com/
CFM International	www.cfm56.com/
Dassault	www.dassault-aviation.com/
EADS	www.eads.com/
Embraer	www.embraer.com/
General Electric	www.ge.com/
Gulfstream Aerospace	www.gulfstream.com/
Hawker Beechcraft	www.hawkerbeechcraft.com/
Kaman Aerospace	www.kaman.com/
Lockheed Martin	www.lockheedmartin.com/
Rolls-Royce	www.rolls-royce.com/
SAAB	www.saab.se/
Sikorsky	www.sikorsky.com/

UK AVIATION MUSEUMS

Aeroventure	www.aeroventure.org.uk/
Bournemouth Aviation Museum	www.aviation-museum.co.uk/
Brooklands Museum	www.brooklandsmuseum.com/
City of Norwich Aviation Museum	www.cnam.co.uk/
de Havilland Aircraft Heritage Centre	www.dehavillandmuseum.2ya.com/
Dumfries & Galloway Aviation Museum	www.dumfriesaviationmuseum.com/
Fleet Air Arm Museum	www.fleetairarm.com/
Gatwick Aviation Museum	www.gatwick-aviation-museum.co.uk/
Imperial War Museum, Duxford	www.iwm.org.uk/duxford/
Imperial War Museum, Duxford (unofficial)	dspace.dial.pipex.com/town/square/rcy85/
The Jet Age Museum	www.jetagemuseum.org/
Lincs Aviation Heritage Centre	www.lincsaviation.co.uk/
Midland Air Museum	www.midlandairmuseum.co.uk/
Museum of Army Flying	www.flying-museum.org.uk/
Museum of Berkshire Aviation	www.museumofberkshireaviation.co.uk/
Museum of Flight, East Fortune	www.nms.ac.uk/our_museums/museum_of_flight.aspx
Museum of Science & Industry, Manchester	mosi.org.uk/
Newark Air Museum	www.newarkairmuseum.org/
North East Aircraft Museum	www.neam.co.uk/
RAF Museum, Cosford & Hendon	www.rafmuseum.org.uk/
Science Museum, South Kensington	www.sciencemuseum.org.uk/
Yorkshire Air Museum, Elvington	www.yorkshireairmuseum.co.uk

AVIATION SOCIETIES

Air Britain	www.air-britain.com/
British Aircraft Preservation Council	www.bapc.org.uk/
Cleveland Aviation Society	homepage.ntlworld.com/phillip.charlton/cashome.html
East London Aviation Society	www.westrowops.co.uk/newsletter/elas.htm
LAAS International	www.laasdata.com/
Lowestoft Aviation Society	www.lowestoftaviationsociety.org/
Royal Aeronautical Society	www.raes.org.uk/
Scottish Air News	www.scottishairnews.co.uk/
Scramble (Dutch Aviation Society)	www.scramble.nl/
Solent Aviation Society	www.solent-aviation-society.co.uk/
Spitfire Society	www.spitfiresociety.com/

Name of Site	Web address (All Prefixed 'Http://')
The Aviation Society Manchester	www.tasmanchester.com/
Ulster Aviation Society	www.ulsteraviationsociety.org/
Wolverhampton Aviation Group	www.wolverhamptonaviationgroup.co.uk/

OPERATORS OF HISTORIC AIRCRAFT

The Aircraft Restoration Company	www.arc-duxford.co.uk/
Battle of Britain Memorial Flight	www.raf.mod.uk/bbmf/
The Catalina Society	www.catalina.org.uk/
De Havilland Aviation	www.dehavillandaviation.com/
Delta Jets	www.deltajets.com/
Hangar 11 Collection	www.hangar11.co.uk/
Hunter Flying	www.hunterflyingltd.co.uk/
Old Flying Machine Company	www.ofmc.co.uk/
Royal Navy Historic Flight	www.royalnavyhistoricflight.org.uk/
The Fighter Collection	www.fighter-collection.com/
The Real Aeroplane Company	www.realaero.com/
The Shuttleworth Collection	www.shuttleworth.org/
The Vulcan to the Sky Trust	www.tvoc.co.uk/

SITES RELATING TO SPECIFIC TYPES OF MILITARY AIRCRAFT

The 655 Maintenance & Preservation Society	www.xm655.com/
B-24 Liberator	www.b24bestweb.com/
EE Canberra	www.bywat.co.uk/
English Electric Lightning - Vertical Reality	www.aviation-picture-hangar.co.uk/Lightning.html
The Eurofighter site	www.eurofighter.com/
The ex FRADU Canberra Site	www.fradu-canberras.co.uk/
The ex FRADU Hunter Site	www.fradu-hunters.co.uk/
F-4 Phantom II Society	www.f4phantom.com/
F-15E.info: Strike Eagle	www.f-15e.info/
F-16: The Complete Reference	www.f-16.net/
F-86 Web Page	f-86.tripod.com/
The Gripen	www.gripen.com/
HerkyBirds.com	www.herkybirds.com/
Jet Provost Heaven	www.jetprovosts.com/
K5083 - Home Page (Hawker Hurricane)	www.k5083.mistral.co.uk/
Lockheed SR-71 Blackbird	www.wvi.com/~lelandh/sr-71~1.htm
The MiG-21 Page	www.topedge.com/panels/aircraft/sites/kraft/mig.htm
P-3 Orion Research Group	www.p3orion.nl/
Thunder & Lightnings (Postwar British Aircraft)	www.thunder-and-lightnings.co.uk/
UK Apache Resource Centre	www.ukapache.com/

MISCELLANEOUS

Aerodata	www.aerodata.org/
AeroResource	www.aeroresource.co.uk/
The AirNet Web Site	www.aviation-links.co.uk/
British Military Aviation Lists	www.bmal.org.uk
Delta Reflex	www.deltareflex.com/forum
Demobbed - Out of Service British Military Aircraft	demobbed.org.uk/
Euro Demobbed	www.eurodemobbed.org.uk/
Fighter Control	fightercontrol.co.uk/
Iconic Aircraft`	www.iconicaircraft.co.uk/
Joseph F. Baugher's US Military Serials Site	www.joebaugher.com/
Military Aviation	www.crakehal.demon.co.uk/aviation/aviation.htm
Military Aviation Review/MAP	www.mar.co.uk/
Pacific Aviation Database Organisation	www.gfiapac.org/
Plane Talk	forum.planetalk.net/
Scramble on the Web - Air Show Reports	www.scramble.nl/airshows.htm
Target Lock Military Aviation E-zine	www.targetlock.org.uk/
UK Airshow Review	www.airshows.co.uk/
UK Military Aircraft Serials Resource Centre	www.ukserials.com/
UK Military Spotting	www.thunder-and-lightnings.co.uk/spotting/

COMBAT AIRCRAFT MONTHLY

The World's Top Military Aviation Monthly

Renowned as the world's top military aviation magazine, *Combat Aircraft Monthly* is the magazine of choice for modern military aviation. Produced in US and Europe editions, the magazine covers military aviation subjects from around the world, from combat accounts from the cockpit over Afghanistan to air force overviews and emerging aerospace industry stories. *Combat Aircraft Monthly* delivers all the latest news, with added value from expert analysis, opinion and views from the front line of military aviation.

Combat Aircraft Monthly is the military aviation magazine that sets the pace, often with world exclusives, the best and most authoritative features every month, and all supported by imagery from the world's leading aviation photographers. With each issue packed with extensive news coverage and exciting features, *Combat Aircraft Monthly* delivers everything for the military aviation enthusiast in one magazine!